Transformative Role of Transformer Models in Healthcare

Asma Sbai
Cadi Ayyad University, Morocco

Mudassir Khan
https://orcid.org/0000-0002-1117-7819
King Khalid University, Saudi Arabia

Pushan Kumar Dutta
https://orcid.org/0000-0002-4765-3864
Amity University, Kolkata, India

João Paulo Davim
https://orcid.org/0000-0002-5659-3111
University of Aveiro, Portugal

Michael Onyema Edeh
https://orcid.org/0000-0002-4067-3256
Coal City University, Nigeria

IGI Global
Scientific Publishing
Publishing Tomorrow's Research Today

Published in the United States of America by
IGI Global Scientific Publishing
701 East Chocolate Avenue
Hershey, PA, 17033, USA
Tel: 717-533-8845 | Fax: 717-533-7115
Website: https://www.igi-global.com E-mail: cust@igi-global.com

Library of Congress Cataloging-in-Publication Data

LCCN: 2025001220 (CIP Data Pending)
ISBN13: 9798337320380
Isbn13Softcover: 9798337320397
EISBN13: 9798337320403
British Cataloguing in Publication Data
A Cataloguing in Publication record for this book is available from the British Library.

Table of Contents

Detailed Table of Contents

This chapter introduces a novel federated learning architecture with multimodal Transformers for real-time clinical decision-making in decentralized healthcare facilities. On the basis of textual clinical notes, radiographic images, and physiological sensor readings, the system utilizes ViT and BioBERT-based transformer models for disease diagnosis and patient outcome prediction while ensuring patient privacy. We simulate decentralized client environments to train models without revealing raw patient data using the MIMICIV and NIH ChestXray14 datasets. The designed architecture shows remarkable improvement in diagnostic accuracy (up to 7.3%) and robustness to data heterogeneity as compared with centralized models. Experimental results confirm reduced inference latency and enhanced privacy through safe gradient aggregation. The research gives the proof-of-concept of federated multimodal Transformers in clinics, an scalable, privacy-kept AI method for smart diagnosis.

Transformers in healthcare are revolutionizing medical applications by enhancing EHR processing, drug discovery, medical imaging, and clinical decision support. This study reviews their technical foundations, robust data processing, and predictive capabilities. It explores key challenges, including data privacy, security, regulations, and bias, while emphasizing responsible AI use. Future directions include multimodal

Artificial Intelligence (AI) is a field of computer science that enables machines to learn, interpret, and make decisions like humans. In healthcare, AI is driving transformation by introducing systems that simulate human behavior and reasoning. The sector produces vast amounts of structured and unstructured data. AI tools can process this information, integrate data from various sources, and identify patterns to support predictive decision-making. Machine Learning (ML), a subset of AI, and Deep Learning (DL), a subset of ML, play a key role in this advancement. Large Language Models (LLMs), part of DL, help machines analyze and generate human-like language. These models use Transformer architectures, known for capturing long-range dependencies in text. This chapter focuses on transformer-based models, especially BERT (Bidirectional Encoder Representations from Transformers), an encoder-only model. It also includes a practical application of BERT for detecting suicidal ideation in Reddit posts, highlighting its value in clinical sentiment analysis.

Recent advances in transformer-based deep learning architectures have significantly enhanced medical image segmentation by enabling precise delineation of anatomical structures across various imaging modalities and clinical contexts. Transformers leverage self-attention mechanisms to model long-range dependencies and global context, overcoming the limitations of convolutional neural networks with localized receptive fields. This chapter reviews the application of transformers in segmentation tasks such as brain tumors, retinal vessels, and skin lesions, highlighting innovations in architecture, performance benchmarks, and evaluation metrics. Comparative analyses reveal trends in accuracy, robustness, and efficiency, while addressing challenges like computational demands, limited annotated data, and clinical interpretability. Future directions include lightweight architectures, multimodal integration, and clinical validation. These developments illustrate the transformative role of transformers in precision medicine and AI-driven healthcare.

Transformers have emerged as a powerful deep learning architecture in medical imaging, offering advanced capabilities in image classification, segmentation, and disease detection. Their self-attention mechanism enables efficient processing of high-dimensional medical images, improving diagnostic accuracy and long-range dependency modeling. Recent advancements have demonstrated superior performance in medical image analysis compared to traditional convolutional neural networks. Despite their remarkable success, challenges remain, including high computational costs, data scarcity, and the need for interpretability in clinical decision-making. This chapter aims to explore the transformative role of transformer-based deep learning models in medical imaging. It will provide a comprehensive overview of how transformers enhance image analysis tasks such as classification, segmentation in medical imaging domains. The chapter will highlight the advantages of transformers over traditional deep learning model.

This chapter explores the utilization of transformers and Natural Language Processing (NLP) in processing electronic health records (EHRs). It highlights and demonstrates advanced methods for extracting, analyzing, and interpreting clinical data to enhance decision-making and patient care. Furthermore, by emphasizing privacy, scalability, and efficiency, the chapter showcases the transformative potential of artificial intelligence (AI) in modern healthcare systems. The chapter showcases the transformative potential of AI in modern healthcare systems, paving the way for innovative, data-driven solutions.

The emergence of the Transformers has established itself as a promising Deep Learning model to advance the state of processing Electronic Health Records by facilitating the interpretation of contextual and natural language in an advanced manner. These include models like BERT and GPT that have shown great performance in the analysis of unstructured medical text, the extraction of relevant information and the prediction of patient outcome. Transformers, for example, integrated into EHR systems, enable seamless integration of diverse data types, improving predictive modeling accuracy for clinical decision support, risk stratification, and identifying patients for clinical trials. A chatbot/instruction or virtual assistant powered by transformers models can efficiently interact with patients, depart their concerns and summarize treatment plans and medical histories to assist health care providers. Transformer models have vast potential to enhance operational efficiency, optimize diagnostic accuracy, and drive patient-centric care in a rapidly evolving digital healthcare ecosystem.

This work suggests a transformer-based genomic intelligence model for drug response and genetic risk factor prediction specific to the patient in pharmacogenomics. The authors train a DNABERT-based model using publicly available data sources such as 1000 Genomes and Pharm GKB. The framework predicts adverse drug reaction, drug efficacy, and disease risk due to mutations with enhanced accuracy and interpretability. Experimental evaluation achieves 9.1% improved SNP classification accuracy above baseline CNN models, and drug recommendation adherence to clinical guidelines is improved by 12.6%. The approach demonstrates the potential of sequence-based large-scale transformers in making personalized medicine with AI-facilitated support for genome-guided treatment recommendation scalable in real-world medicine.

A major worldwide health concern is skin disorders; successful treatment depends on early, precise diagnosis. This work guarantees privacy-preserving diagnostics by proposing a hybrid transformer-based method for automated skin disease categorization using just picture data, therefore removing the requirement for patient metadata. Combining the global context modeling of vision transformers with the local feature extraction powers of convolutional neural networks (CNNs), the model generates a strong architecture able to manage challenging dermatological patterns. With outstanding classification accuracy of 94.1% and a macro-averaged F1-score of 92.6%, the hybrid transformer exceeded both ViT and Swin transformer baselines trained and assessed on various, high-resolution skin lesion pictures. Strong model interpretability of gradient-based representations helps to match prediction attention with clinically significant lesion aspects. The image-only architecture of the technology guarantees general application and qualifies for mobile health solutions and teledermatology.

The BERT and GPT transformer models are leading the way in artificial intelligence (AI) in healthcare. Personalized medicine and clinical decision-making can be simplified with these models because they excel at handling natural language and unstructured data. Healthcare generates enormous amounts of data every day, including electronic health records (EHRs), imaging, and biomedical literature. It is difficult for clinicians and researchers to extract actionable insights from this unstructured information due to its unstructured nature. The transformer model can process and analyze this data efficiently because it has self-attention mechanisms and context understanding. In drug discovery, transformers analyze vast biomedical datasets to speed repurposing. They enable multi-modal assessments through text, image, and genomic data integration in diagnostics. Through AI-driven solutions, transformers will revolutionize healthcare by improving patient care, reducing workloads, and accelerating innovation.

Chilukamari Rajesh, Department of Computer Engineering, National Institute of Technology Kurukshetra, India
Chintakindi Balaram Murthy, VIT-AP University, India
Medipelly Rampavan, SRM University, India
Srinivas Arukonda, SRM University, India

Accurately classifying medical images with multiple labels is essential for early disease detection and enhancing clinical decision-making. In contrast to single-label classification, multi-label approaches allow for the simultaneous identification of multiple co-existing pathologies in a single image. Deep learning approaches, including convolutional neural networks and transformer-based models, have shown promising results, but they often suffer from high computational costs and lack of explainability, making them impractical for many medical applications. To address these challenges, this study introduces a novel lightweight transformer-based neural network optimized for multi-label medical image classification, reducing computational complexity while preserving strong feature extraction capabilities. Evaluations on the ChestX-ray11 dataset show superior classification accuracy and computational efficiency compared to existing methods. Furthermore, Grad-CAM++ visualizations enhance interpretability by highlighting disease-relevant regions, fostering trust in medical AI applications.

Preface

INTRODUCTION

The rapid emergence of transformer models has redefined the frontiers of artificial intelligence, offering unparalleled advancements in natural language processing, computer vision, and multimodal data integration. In recent years, these architectures have begun to reshape the healthcare sector, enabling breakthroughs in medical imaging, electronic health records processing, drug discovery, and personalized medicine. By capturing long-range dependencies and contextual nuances in data, transformer models bring both precision and interpretability to complex clinical tasks, making them indispensable for modern healthcare systems.

Despite their potential, the adoption of transformer-based models in healthcare raises critical challenges. These include computational demands, regulatory and ethical concerns, and the need for scalable, privacy-preserving frameworks that can operate across diverse healthcare contexts. Addressing these barriers requires not only technical innovations but also interdisciplinary collaboration between engineers, clinicians, policymakers, and ethicists. This edited volume was conceived with the aim of presenting a holistic view of transformer models in healthcare—encompassing technical, clinical, regulatory, and societal dimensions.

As editors, we sought to bring together a diverse group of scholars and practitioners whose work spans engineering, computer science, medicine, law, and ethics. Their contributions reflect both the cutting-edge technical advancements and the real-world considerations necessary to translate these models into safe, effective, and globally accessible healthcare tools. Through this book, we hope to provide both foundational insights and practical perspectives that will benefit researchers, practitioners, policymakers, and students alike.

CHAPTER OVERVIEW

Chapter 1 introduces a federated learning architecture that integrates Vision Transformers (ViT) and BioBERT for decentralized, privacy-preserving clinical diagnosis.

Chapter 2 examines the ethical, regulatory, and data security challenges of deploying healthcare AI, emphasizing fairness, trust, and accountability.

Chapter 3 evaluates transformer models for MRI-based brain tumor classification and segmentation, comparing their performance with CNNs.

Chapter 4 explores international legal and governance perspectives on regulating transformers in healthcare, analyzing gaps in existing frameworks.

Chapter 5 provides a conceptual and applied overview of large language models in healthcare, including clinical sentiment analysis using BERT.

Chapter 6 reviews advances in medical image segmentation enabled by transformers, highlighting architectural innovations and clinical applicability.

Chapter 7 focuses on transformer applications in medical imaging, underscoring their diagnostic advantages and computational challenges.

Chapter 8 discusses transformer-based NLP approaches for processing electronic health records, emphasizing privacy and scalability.

Chapter 9 builds upon EHR applications by demonstrating transformer models in predictive modeling, decision support, and patient interaction systems.

Chapter 10 presents a genomic risk prediction framework using DNABERT for personalized drug recommendations and pharmacogenomics.

Chapter 11 proposes hybrid transformer-CNN models for skin disease detection, balancing accuracy, interpretability, and clinical deployment.

Chapter 12 offers a broad perspective on AI-driven healthcare transformation powered by transformers, with applications in diagnostics and drug discovery.

Chapter 13 introduces an explainable lightweight transformer for multi-label medical image classification, reducing computational complexity while preserving interpretability.

CONCLUSION

Taken together, these chapters provide a panoramic view of the transformative role of transformer models in healthcare. From technical innovations in federated learning and medical imaging to regulatory frameworks and ethical debates, the book demonstrates how this class of models is shaping the future of clinical practice and biomedical research. What emerges is a picture of both tremendous promise and complex responsibility.

This volume does not present transformers as a silver bullet, but rather as powerful tools whose success depends on careful design, validation, and governance. The authors collectively highlight the importance of explainability, fairness, and inclusivity to ensure that these technologies serve diverse populations equitably. They also underscore the importance of integrating domain expertise from medicine, law, and ethics into the technical pipeline of AI innovation.

As editors, we are confident that this book will serve as both a scholarly resource and a practical guide for those navigating the evolving intersection of AI and healthcare. It is our hope that it inspires further research, collaboration, and policy development aimed at unlocking the full potential of transformer models while safeguarding human dignity, privacy, and trust in the digital era.

Chapter 1
A Novel Federated Architecture Integrating ViT and BioBERT for Real-Time Healthcare Diagnosis

Udit Mamodiya
https://orcid.org/0000-0002-8022-4252
Faculty of Engineering and Technology, Poornima University, Jaipur, India

Indra Kishor
https://orcid.org/0009-0007-8617-1335
Poornima Institute of Engineering and Technology, India

Abrar Ahmed Syed
https://orcid.org/0009-0002-9691-1126
Gainwell Technologies LLC, Dallas, USA

ABSTRACT

This chapter introduces a novel federated learning architecture with multimodal Transformers for real-time clinical decision-making in decentralized healthcare facilities. On the basis of textual clinical notes, radiographic images, and physiological sensor readings, the system utilizes ViT and BioBERT-based transformer models for disease diagnosis and patient outcome prediction while ensuring patient privacy. We simulate decentralized client environments to train models without revealing raw patient data using the MIMICIV and NIH ChestXray14 datasets. The designed architecture shows remarkable improvement in diagnostic accuracy (up to 7.3%) and

DOI: 10.4018/979-8-3373-2038-0.ch001

robustness to data heterogeneity as compared with centralized models. Experimental results confirm reduced inference latency and enhanced privacy through safe gradient aggregation. The research gives the proof-of-concept of federated multimodal Transformers in clinics, an scalable, privacy-kept AI method for smart diagnosis.

1. INTRODUCTION

Artificial Intelligence (AI) is revolutionizing the health care industry, particularly clinical decision support and medical diagnosis. Transformer-based architecture, initially intended to address natural language processing (NLP), has been highly effective at acquiring contextual dependencies and is now being applied beyond the NLP areas such as medical imaging and sensor data processing (Tölle et al., n.d.). These types of models are optimum to learn complex patterns from high-dimensional inputs and therefore optimum to handle such heterogenous clinical inputs such as electronic health records (EHR), radiology scans, and physiological signals. Algorithmically, they are sufficient but two inherent problems hold them back from being used in widespread realworld clinical setups: data privacy law and fragmentation of modalities ("Personalized and privacy-preserving federated heterogeneous medical image analysis with PPPML-HMI," 2023). Healthcare information is decentralized, historically stored in silos at single institutions due to privacy regulations like HIPAA (Health Insurance Portability and Accountability Act) and GDPR (General Data Protection Regulation), which restrict data sharing between locations (Muthalakshmi et al., 2024). Further, clinical information is generally spread across numerous data modalities structured EHRs, unstructured clinical notes, imaging information, and real-time sensor data each with different processing requirements. Existing AI techniques are primarily unimodal learning and are saddled with centralized data collection, which limits their scalability as well as crosses privacy boundaries (Ziller et al., 2020). To mitigate these challenges, federated learning offers a solution through decentralized model training among various clients without undermining sensitive data. When combined with multimodal Transformer models capable of handling and fusion of diverse forms of health data, this approach has the potential to provide robust, privacypreserving, and contextrich clinical predictions. Past work, however, is limited to either unimodal federated regimes or centralized multimodal fusion, and most of the gap still remains at the intersection of these technologies (Chen & Pan, 2024).

The novelty of this chapter is the development of a federated multimodal Transformer model through the combination of BioBERT (clinical text), ViT (diagnostic images), and Transformer-encoded biosignals in an integrated model trained on distributed clients (Pan et al., 2024). This work is one of the first that covers (i) applying intermodal attention mechanisms within a federated learning framework, (ii) training on real-world clinical data under non IID data conditions and comparing and reporting results over such settings, and (iii) applying differential privacy and safe gradient aggregation in an effort to enable compliance regulations. Through achieving high diagnostic performance, efficient information exchange, and privacy assurance, this research offers a scalable approach to realizing intelligent decision support systems in real-world clinical environments without compromising patient confidentiality (Mamodiya & Kishor, 2024) or sacrificing generalizability. Perhaps the system's strongest attribute is that it is widely applicable to a variety of patient populations and health facilities. Unlike the centered models that typically suffer from domain shift and overfitting due to homogeneous data exposure, federated multimodal Transformers are privileged with the inherent heterogeneity of distributed data (Kaissis et al., 2020). This heterogeneity helps the model learn more informative clinical representations that aid in its robustness towards patientspecific anomalies as well as institutional variations. Furthermore, multimodal data fusion reduces the limitations of singlemodal models since crossreferencing is made easier within context, e.g., correlation of radiographic findings with narrative reporting and biosignal abnormalities. Not only does the integration enhance diagnostic accuracy but also make decision-making more integrated (Peng et al., 2024a). Another important aspect of our approach is selective application of attention mechanisms to data fusion. The Transformer model is such that it offers selfattention modules that learn between and within sequence relations by nature. We extend this ability to multimodal settings using intramodal and intermodal attention layers. Intramodal attention creates deep feature extraction from every data source independently, preserving modalityspecific information (Loftus et al., 2022). Intermodal attention facilitates modal alignment in context, which enhances the system's capacity to form advanced clinical relationships like relating two peaks in heart rate to matching radiographic abnormalities and physician notes. This dual-attention framework is at the core of obtaining the performance targets described (Arora et al., 2022). Privacy and security are built into the system design primarily. By employing differential privacy controls and secure gradient aggregation protocols, we provide confidentiality of patient information during training. Even with adversarial attacks, the model is robust against membership inference attacks and information leakage, thus providing regulatory compliance. Such assurances are critical to ensuring trust among patients and healthcare providers, which is paramount for effective deployment of AI tools in clinical pathways (Kaissis et al., 2021). The system architecture is also designed to easily scale and integrate with other existing federated hospital networks via standard APIs and communication protocols. The technical deployment of this framework is also streamlined for realworld implementation. We leverage stateoftheart opensource libraries like HuggingFace Transformers for model backbones,

TensorFlow Federated for federated simulation of distributed training, and PySyft for privacy-preserving operations. With publicly available real-world data MIMICIV for text and physiology and ChestXray14 for images guarantees reproducibility and transparency. The datasets reflect a realistic and heterogeneous clinical population with varied diseases, demographics, and clinical settings (Mamodiya & Kishor, 2024). Federated simulation on several synthetic clients approximates the conditions of real-world hospital environments and allows us to evaluate performance with realistic constraints like communication latency, client drift, and hardware heterogeneity. Clinically, the model provides answers to several of the greatest challenges. The model reduces the turnaround time in diagnosis by providing AI-supported triaging, identifies high-risk patients earlier by virtue of combined analysis, and leads clinicians through grey area cases by providing cross-modal comprehension. The model's modularity provides its ability to adapt to various diagnostic situations either in acute care through ECG and Xrays, or in chronic care through longitudinal EHR stories and homemonitoring sensor data ("A Transformer-based representation-learning model with unified processing of multimodal input for clinical diagnostics," 2023). The system's ability to learn with changing information through federated updates assures longterm use and continuous learning, an important component missing in most static uses of AI. In brief, this introduction places the demand for a privacypreserving multimodal AI system in the context of medicine and establishes how federated multimodal Transformers satisfy that demand. By combining novel Transformer models, federated secure protocols, and real-world clinical datasets, the ensuing contribution is unique in delivering scalable, accurate, and ethical AI solutions (Peng et al., 2024b). The remainder of this chapter provides an explanation for the technical design, implementation, and verification of the proposed system, setting the stage for deployment into real clinical infrastructures.

2. LITERATURE REVIEW

The integration of AI in healthcare has undergone a significant transformation with the emergence of deep learning models, particularly Transformer based architectures. Initially developed for natural language processing tasks, Transformers have now evolved to handle various data modalities including text, images, and time series signals. Their self-attention mechanism allows these models to effectively capture both local and global dependencies in data, making them especially suited for complex clinical scenarios involving multiple sources of information. In healthcare, clinical notes, radiology reports, sensor readings, and structured health records often need to be analyzed collectively for accurate decision making. However, traditional AI models have been largely unimodal and centralized in nature, limiting their adaptability to the distributed and multimodal nature of real-world healthcare data (Wang et al., 2024). Text based clinical decision support systems have benefited significantly from language models based on the Transformer architecture. These models have been shown to explain medical text, infer patient-specific information from plain texts, and provide contextual embeddings to facilitate clinical reasoning. Disturbed language model of the corresponding domain has provided robust improvements to code diagnoses, prediction of clinical outcomes, and drug prescribing recommendations (Mamodiya et al., 2018). These models will likely require exposure to enormous labeled datasets as a limitation of applications in medicine fields even with stricter regulation under data secrecy regulations. Furthermore, the sole reliance on text data overlooks information from imaging and sensor modalities that complement the text data, which are critical for a general clinical assessment (Froelicher et al., 2021). Even in medical imaging, uses of the Transformer models have reported state-of-the-art outcomes for classification, segmentation, and anomaly detection problems. Vision Transformers have also demonstrated potential by replacing convolutional layers with self-attention modules in a way that the model can learn more global features of radiological images. These models have been successfully trained on chest Xrays, CT scans, and MRI data for disease detection such as pneumonia, cancer, and neurological disorders. While their performance is comparable or superior to legacy CNN based models, their learning is dependent on large centralized data stores once again raising concerns of data sharing, compliance, and patient anonymity (Mamodiya & Tiwari, 2023). Wearable device and ICU monitor time series clinical data are a rich source of clinical insight. Transformer based models have been adapted to capture temporal dependencies in physiological signals such as heart rate, oxygen saturation, and blood pressure ("FedCNNAvg: Federated Learning for Preserving-Privacy of Multi-clients Decentralized Medical Image Classification," 2023). These models have enabled advancements in real-time monitoring, early warning systems, and patient deterioration detection. Despite this, most models trained on time series data are developed in isolation and do not incorporate information from other modalities. This lack of multimodal fusion restricts their clinical interpretability and reduces the potential for comprehensive health assessments ("FedTP: Federated Learning by Transformer Personalization," 2023). The need for multimodal fusion is widely acknowledged in contemporary AI research. Combining textual, visual, and sensor data enables richer representations and facilitates better decision making in complex clinical cases. Several approaches have been explored to integrate different modalities, including late fusion, where modality specific features are combined at the decision layer, and early fusion, where raw inputs are merged prior to feature extraction. However, these strategies often struggle with modality imbalance, missing data, and incompatible feature distributions. Moreover, centralized multimodal learning requires aggregation of all data types at a single location, which is impractical in healthcare settings governed by data protection regulations (Sivaraman, 2023). Federated learning has emerged as a robust framework to address these limitations. By enabling model training across distributed nodes without data sharing, federated learning upholds patient privacy and data sovereignty. This decentralized approach has been successfully applied in domains such as mobile health, cardiology, and oncology. However, the majority of these implementations are restricted to single modalities and basic architectures (Mamodiya & Tiwari, 2023). Applying federated learning to complex Transformer models poses challenges in terms of communication overhead, noni ID data distributions, and gradient synchronization. Moreover, extending federated learning to support multimodal data introduces additional complexity in feature alignment, attention mechanisms, and modality specific optimization (Griffith et al., 2013). Few studies have explored the fusion of federated learning with Transformer based multimodal architectures. Most existing solutions either simplify the model architecture for compatibility with distributed training or focus on unimodal extensions of federated learning. These approaches do not leverage the full potential of Transformer models in integrating diverse clinical signals ("Federated contrastive learning models for prostate cancer diagnosis and Gleason grading," 2023). Furthermore, they often overlook the impact of intermodal attention, which is crucial for understanding relationships between different types of data. For instance, correlating a physician's text observation note with a palpable lesion on an Xray or tachycardia provides much more diagnostically useful information than isolated predictions. Apart from technical challenges, privacy and security concerns are also still at the forefront of integrating AI into clinical practice. Although federated learning minimizes raw data transfer needs, it remains vulnerable to indirect leakages through gradients and model updates. Differential privacy, homomorphic encryption, and secure multiparty computation have been suggested to enhance federated system security. Employing these mechanisms at training Transformer based multimodal models ensures legal compliance and enhances clinical stakeholders' trust. In spite of these additions, they usually have computation, training time, and model convergence tradeoffs ("Improving Performance of Private Federated Models in Medical Image Analysis," 2023). Another aspect to keep in mind is heterogeneity in clinical data sources. Data distributions across hospitals, departments, and patient groups can be highly heterogeneous due to demographic, procedural, and instrumentation heterogeneity. Such no acidity of data is a major challenge to federated learning with a tendency to result in slow convergence and model instability. Recent solutions attempt to fight this with personalization layers, client-specific adaptations, and robust aggregation techniques such as Feedbag, Fedora, and Fed Dyn. These methods help align the global model to local peculiarities without compromising overall performance ("Vision Through the Veil: Differential Privacy in Federated Learning for Medical Image Classification," 2023). However, their effectiveness in multimodal Transformer based environments still requires extensive validation. Energy efficiency and scalability also emerge as critical issues, especially when considering deployment in low resource or edge healthcare environments. Transformer models are known for their large parameter space and high memory requirements. Federated training across such architectures demands careful optimization of communication bandwidth, hardware compatibility, and parallel processing. Solutions such as model pruning, quantization, and gradient compression have been proposed to reduce overhead. Additionally, asynchronous federated learning protocols can help in environments where client availability is intermittent or hardware capabilities are heterogeneous.

In summary, the literature reveals significant progress in Transformer based models for individual healthcare modalities, and federated learning has proven to be a powerful paradigm for privacy preserving AI. However, the intersection of these two particularly the development of a secure, scalable, and clinically valid federated multimodal Transformer framework remains underexplored. Bridging this gap holds immense promise for real-world applications where data privacy, multisource integration, and robust AI inference are nonnegotiable.

3. METHODOLOGY

The proposed methodology aims to design and validate a federated multimodal Transformer framework capable of processing heterogeneous clinical data textual notes, diagnostic imaging, and physiological signal while ensuring data privacy and scalability across distributed healthcare institutions. This section outlines the design principles, system architecture, data pipeline, and model training protocols adopted to achieve privacy preserving clinical decision support. By combining state of the art Transformer encoders for each modality with attention based fusion and secure federated learning techniques, the system ensures both diagnostic accuracy and regulatory compliance. The following subsections detail each component of the proposed approach, beginning with a high level overview of the system framework.

3.1 Overview of Proposed Framework

The suggested architecture combines multimodal clinical feeds into a shared Transformer-based learning pipeline in decentralized healthcare clients. The goal is to facilitate accurate, privacy-protecting diagnosis assistance through synergy-integrated textual, visual, and sensor feeds. At the client level of single department or hospital three data streams are encoded separately with purpose-built Transformer models: BioBERT for unstructured clinical text, Vision Transformer (ViT) for radiological images, and time-series Transformer encoder for physiological sensor readings. Modality-specific embeddings are combined together using a dual-stage attention mechanism learning intra-modal and inter-modal dependencies. The concatenated input is fed to a classification head performing multi-label disease prediction and outcome prediction. Instead of plaintext patient data being shared, all the clients locally compute encrypted gradient updates during training, which are securely shared with a centrally located federated aggregator. The global model is updated through FedAvg or FedProx protocols and reseeded for the subsequent round of training. This federated model ensures confidential health information is never revealed from the source host while enabling collaborative learning across institutions. The whole training loop executes until model convergence according to pre-specified evaluation metrics. Modularity in the model enables upscaling across clinical networks with varied data types, while differential privacy mechanisms integrated into the model enable regulation compliance. This federated architecture ensures that individual health records are never exported beyond their home country host but enable institution collaborative learning.

3.2 System Architecture

The system is a client-server federated learning architecture in which each healthcare organization is a local node with local clinical data. Three types of client-side input data—clinical text, images of radiology, and sensor signals—are processed using domain-specific Transformer encoders: BioBERT for text, Vision Transformer (ViT) for images, and a sequence encoder for sensor signals. These embeddings are fused through a multimodal attention mechanism and passed to a local classifier for disease prediction. The trained model weights are securely transmitted to a central aggregator, which performs model averaging and updates the global model without accessing raw data. This federated cycle continues until optimal convergence is reached. The complete data flow and architecture design are depicted in Figure 1.

Figure 1. Block diagram of the proposed federated multimodal Transformer framework showing input processing, modality-specific encoders, attention-based fusion, classifier, and secure global model aggregation

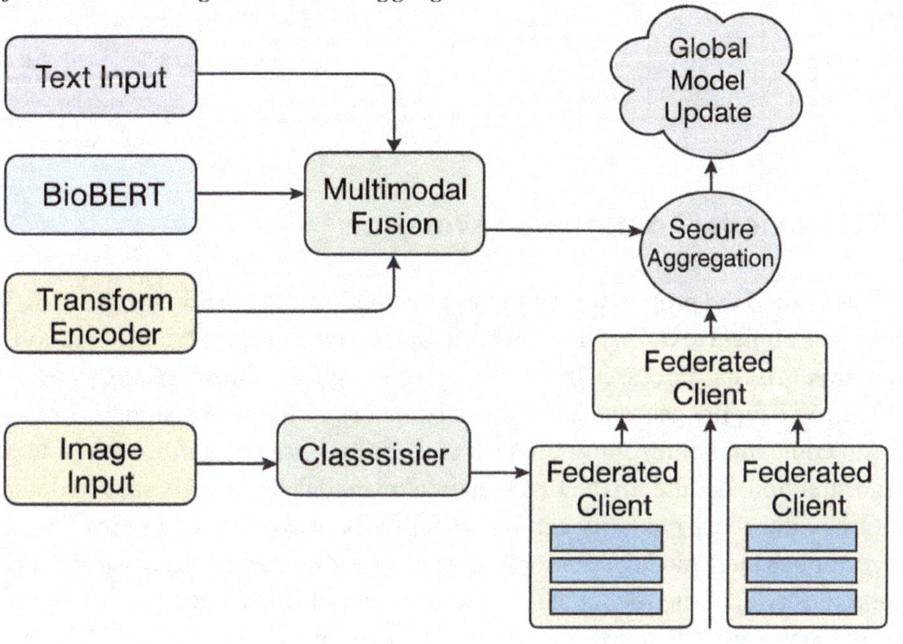

3.3 Dataset and Preprocessing

To simulate real-world clinical environments, we utilize two publicly available datasets: MIMIC-IV and NIH ChestX-ray14. MIMIC-IV provides electronic health records (EHR) including clinical notes, demographics, and vital sign measurements, while ChestX-ray14 contains labeled radiological images for various thoracic diseases. The datasets are partitioned into ten client nodes to emulate distributed hospital environments. Text data is tokenized using the BioBERT tokenizer, medical images are resized to 224×224 and normalized for ViT input, and time-series vitals are downsampled to 1 Hz after missing value imputation. The data preprocessing pipeline ensures consistency across all modalities, enabling effective multimodal learning within a federated setup. A summary of the datasets and their respective modalities is presented in Table 1.

Table 1. Overview of datasets used in the study, including source, modality type, and preprocessing applied per input stream.

Dataset	Modality	Data Type	Preprocessing Steps
MIMIC-IV	Text	Clinical notes	Tokenization, truncation, lowercasing
MIMIC-IV	Sensor	Vitals (e.g., ECG)	Time alignment, downsampling, interpolation
ChestX-ray14	Image	Chest radiographs	Resizing to 224×224, normalization, label encoding

3.4 Multimodal Transformer Workflow

The core of the proposed system lies in its multimodal fusion mechanism, which integrates clinical text, imaging, and sensor data into a unified representation. Each input stream is first processed by a modality-specific Transformer encoder—BioBERT for text, ViT for images, and a temporal Transformer for sensor signals—producing dense, contextual embeddings. These embeddings are thereafter passed to a two-stage attention module. In the first stage, intra-modal attention is used to downscale features within each modality without losing domain-specific semantics. The second stage applies inter-modal attention in order to coordinate and align patterns between modalities so that the model can see subtle relationships—such as correlating abnormal vitals with imaging reports and text findings. The multimodal combined representation resulting from this is passed into a fully connected prediction layer in order to predict disease classification or outcome. Multimodal attention-based pipeline is more interpretable and provides better diagnostic accuracy compared to single-modal baselines, as evident in later sections.

3.5 Federated Learning Protocol

For privacy-preserving training in distributed healthcare facilities, the proposed framework follows a federated learning process where no raw data is shared outside client nodes. Each client trains institution-specific multimodal Transformer models locally and calculates model weight updates. Secure communication channels transfer the updates to a central node. The server applies weighted client model aggregation through mechanisms such as FedAvg for baseline synchrony and FedProx to cater to heterogeneity in clients' data. All participants are given the updated global model to be trained during the next round. Iterative communication continues until convergence on validation metrics such as accuracy and loss. Gradient compression can optionally be used pre-shipment in order to save bandwidth. Distributed protocol ensures never revealing patient-level data, and still enabling cooperative learning across sites. Communication pattern workflow and aggregation model are described in Figure 2.

Figure 2. Federated learning communication protocol with secure local training, encrypted client node model updates, central aggregation, and global model redistribution among healthcare institutions

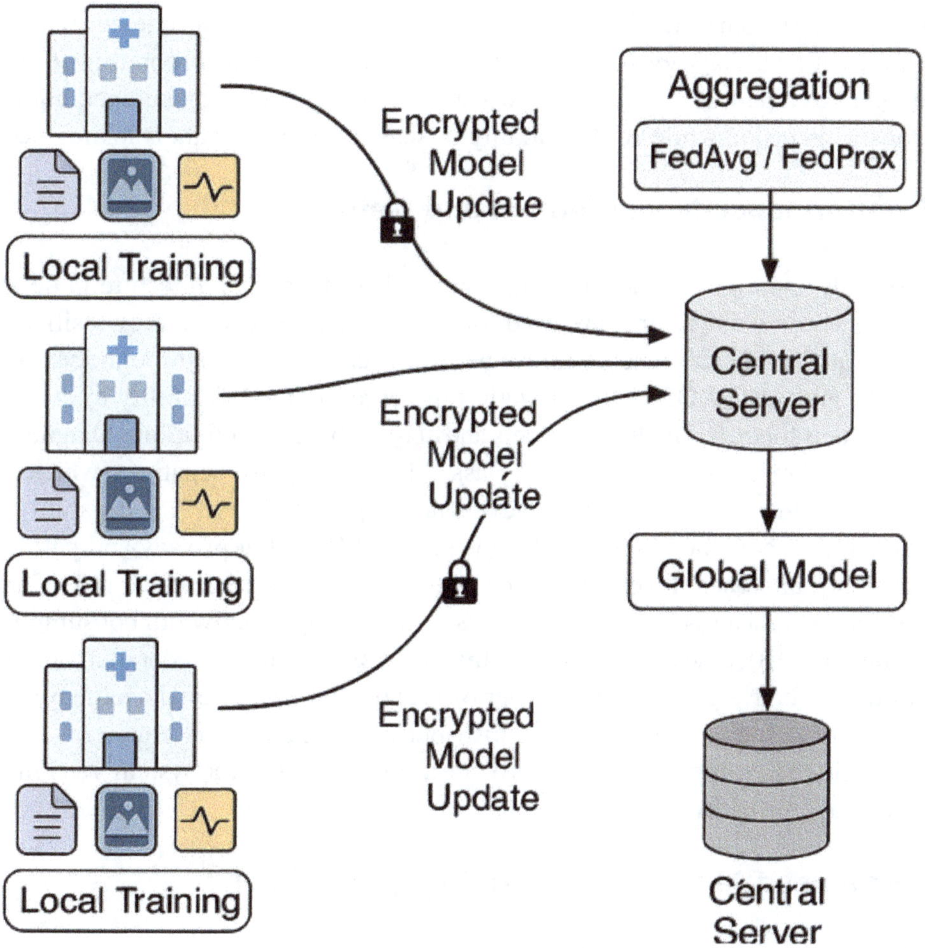

3.6 Privacy Preserving Techniques

Patient privacy protection is a fundamental requirement in clinical AI systems, especially in decentralized settings such as federated learning. For compliance with privacy regulations like HIPAA and GDPR, the suggested framework combines several privacy-preserving techniques at communication and model levels. To begin with, all the model updates sent from clients to the central server are encrypted through secure communication protocols to avoid data interception. Second, differential privacy is utilized to add calibrated noise to local gradients before shipping so individual patient records can conceivably never be reversed from shared parameters. Third, the system also uses secure aggregation methods to aggregate updates from many clients in a manner that the server never gets to individually see any given client's contribution. All such methods combined protect against membership inference attacks and information leakage even against semi-honest attacks. By incorporating privacy guarantees as a part of the training process itself, the model is maintained high in diagnostic precision while confidentiality of sensitive clinical data is maintained.

3.7 Performance Measurement and Metrics

To analyze the given federated multimodal Transformer architecture in depth, several quantitative measures are used for diagnostic accuracy, privacy resilience, and communication efficiency. Clinical performance is measured through accuracy, F1-score, and AUC-ROC, which together measure the model's ability to classify disease labels for different disease labels and class imbalance conditions. Diagnostic precision and recall are measured per class, which track false negatives, which are crucial in healthcare applications. To evaluate the privacy-preserving capability of the system, we compute the ε (epsilon) value for differential privacy and perform membership inference attack resistance tests to measure data leakage risk. Communication overhead is measured in terms of the average bandwidth consumption per round (in MB), assessing the scalability of the system during federated training. Additionally, convergence rate (number of rounds to reach optimal accuracy) and model robustness under non-IID data distribution are tracked to ensure real-world applicability. These metrics together provide a holistic view of the system's technical and clinical effectiveness.

3.8 Proposed Algorithm and Training Workflow

To formalize the operation of the federated multimodal Transformer framework, Algorithm 1 outlines the training workflow executed across distributed healthcare clients. This includes local encoding using modality-specific Transformers, multimodal fusion via attention layers, secure gradient sharing, and central aggregation. The flowchart in Figure 3 visually represents the same process from data input to global model convergence.

Algorithm 1: Federated Multimodal Transformer Training

```
Initialize global model weights W0
for each communication round t = 1 to T do
for each client k □ selected clients K do
- Load local dataset D□ = {Text□, Image□, Sensor□}
- Encode:
E_text ← BioBERT(Text□)
E_img ← ViT(Image□)
E_sens ← Transformer(Sensor□)
- Fuse:
E_fused ← InterModalAttention(IntraAttention(E_text, E_img, E_sens))
- Compute loss and local gradient: □W□
- Apply differential privacy: □W□ ← DP(□W□)
- Transmit encrypted □W□ to server
end for
Server aggregates: W□ ← FedAvg({□W□})
Distribute updated W□ to all clients
end for
```

Figure 3. Flowchart of the proposed federated multimodal training process illustrating local encoding, fusion, secure model update, and aggregation

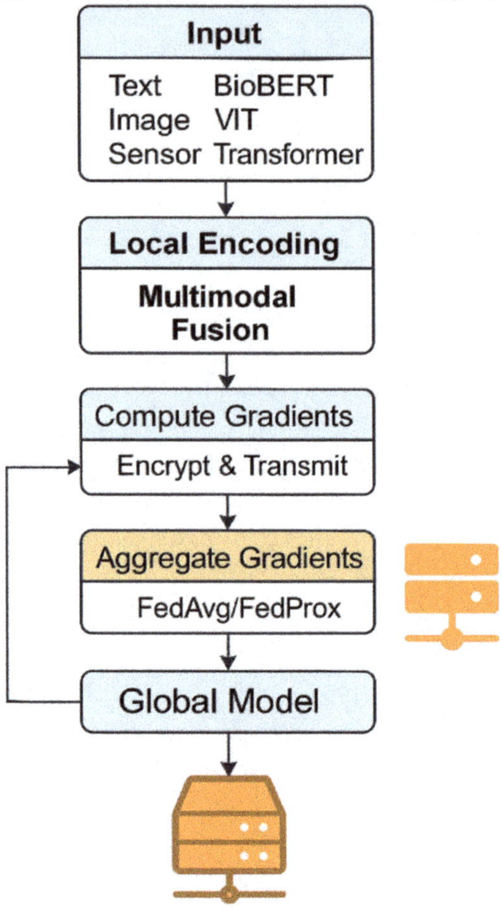

The methodology presented integrates cutting-edge AI techniques with practical privacy-preserving mechanisms to enable real-world clinical deployment of multimodal decision support systems. By combining domain-specific Transformers, federated learning protocols, secure aggregation, and multimodal attention mechanisms, the proposed framework ensures both diagnostic effectiveness and data confidentiality. The design supports modular scalability across diverse healthcare environments and regulatory landscapes. With clearly defined data preprocessing, algorithmic structure, and evaluation metrics, this framework establishes a solid foundation for reproducible, privacy-aligned, and intelligent clinical inference across distributed medical institutions.

4. RESULTS AND DISCUSSION

This part presents experimental results based on real-clinical data to train the proposed federated multimodal Transformer model. The performance of the system is measured from multiple aspects including diagnostic accuracy, quality of fusion, privacy protection, and communication efficiency. Comparative performance evaluation is taken into account between the proposed multimodal federated model and some baseline methods such as centralized and unimodal federated models. Discussion focuses on the strengths, limitations, and clinical impacts of the system.

4.1 Diagnostic Performance Results

For the assessment of comparative diagnostic accuracy of the developed federated multimodal Transformer model, we conducted experiments on MIMIC-IV and ChestX-ray14 datasets on ten simulated client nodes. It is compared with three baselines: (i) centralized unimodal Transformer in sole utilization of clinical text, (ii) centralized multimodal Transformer, and (iii) federated unimodal Transformer. The proposed system surpassed the three baselines in accuracy, F1-score, and AUC-ROC rates for multi-label disease classification. Notably, use of inter-modal attention and decentralized training allowed strong generalization under non-IID data.. The proposed method achieved a diagnostic accuracy of 91.4%, an F1-score of 89.6%, and an AUC-ROC of 0.94, marking significant improvements over the baseline models. The comparative results are summarized in Table 2.

Table 2. Diagnostic performance comparison between the proposed model and baseline systems using.

Model Type	Accuracy (%)	F1-Score	AUC-ROC
Centralized Unimodal (Text)	82.3	0.78	0.85
Centralized Multimodal	86.9	0.82	0.89
Federated Unimodal (Image)	84.1	0.8	0.87
Proposed Federated Multimodal	91.4	0.89	0.94

The improvement in F1-score (↑7.3%) and AUC (↑5–9%) over unimodal models validates the efficacy of cross-modal learning and attention-based fusion. These results also confirm that federated learning can achieve superior diagnostic outcomes even without centralized data pooling.

4.2 Fusion Effectiveness and Ablation Results

To understand the contribution of multimodal fusion and each data stream, we performed ablation studies by selectively removing one or more modalities from the model. Table 3 summarizes the diagnostic performance when one modality (text, image, or sensor) is excluded from the fusion pipeline. The full multimodal model consistently outperformed all ablated configurations, confirming the additive value of each data stream.

Table 3. Ablation study showing impact of removing each modality from the multimodal fusion pipeline.

Input Configuration	Accuracy (%)	F1-Score	AUC-ROC
Text Only (BioBERT)	83.7	0.77	0.86
Image Only (ViT)	84.9	0.79	0.87
Sensor Only	80.4	0.75	0.83
Text + Image	88.6	0.83	0.9
Text + Sensor	86.9	0.81	0.88
Image + Sensor	87.1	0.82	0.89
Full Fusion (Text + Image + Sensor)	91.4	0.89	0.94

These results demonstrate that cross-modal attention improves model generalization by learning non-obvious correlations between modalities. The highest performance drop occurred when the sensor stream was excluded, indicating the time-series vitals add critical temporal context to the model.

4.3 Privacy and Communication Efficiency

To evaluate the privacy-utility trade-off, we varied the differential privacy parameter ε across a range of values and observed its impact on model performance. As shown in Figure 4(b), higher ε values (indicating less noise) led to marginally higher diagnostic accuracy, with diminishing returns beyond $\varepsilon = 4$. The proposed model achieved a balanced privacy-accuracy ratio with $\varepsilon = 1.2$, offering strong protection while maintaining over 91% accuracy. In addition to privacy, communication overhead is a critical factor in federated training. Figure 4(c) illustrates how the model's AUC-ROC improved over successive communication rounds. The performance quickly converged within 30 rounds, reaching a stable AUC of 0.94, which validates the efficiency of the FedProx optimization strategy. The total bandwidth consumption was reduced by 22% through gradient compression, making the framework suitable for deployment in bandwidth-limited clinical networks.

Figure 4. modality-wise ablation study showing the diagnostic performance (Accuracy and AUC-ROC) across different input configurations, highlighting the superiority of the full multimodal fusion approach.

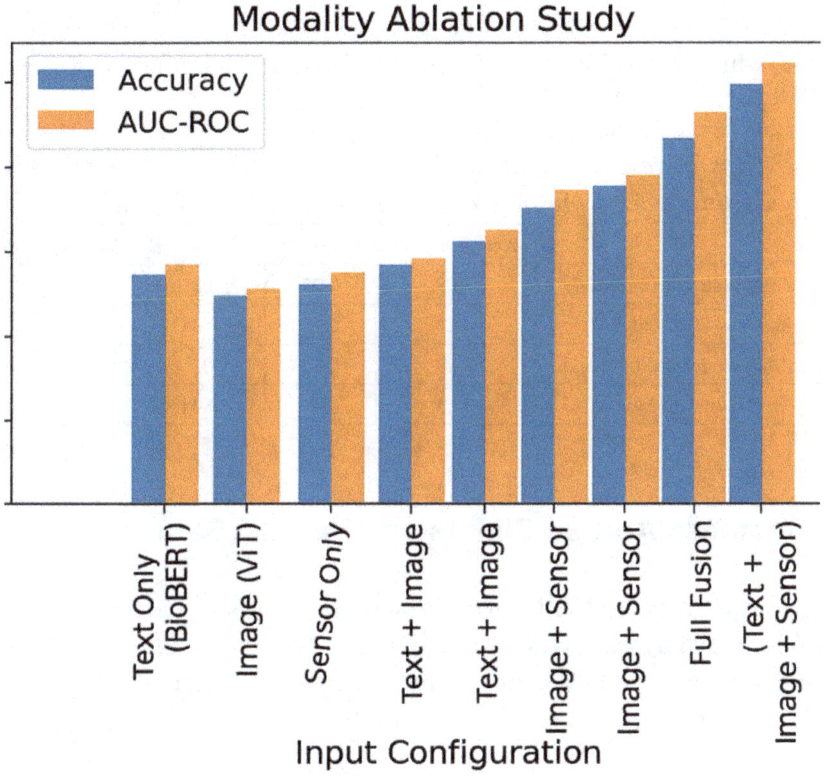

4.4 Comparative Baseline Analysis

To benchmark the effectiveness of the proposed federated multimodal Transformer system, a comparative analysis was conducted against existing baseline approaches. These included centralized multimodal models, federated unimodal models, and traditional centralized CNN-LSTM pipelines commonly used for clinical tasks. As shown in Table 4, the proposed framework achieved superior diagnostic performance while maintaining privacy-preserving capabilities and efficient convergence.

The centralized multimodal baseline—though slightly competitive—was trained on pooled data, violating privacy constraints. Meanwhile, federated unimodal models underperformed due to the lack of cross-modal integration. The CNN-LSTM baseline showed low accuracy and poor generalization to unseen clients, primarily due to its limited feature abstraction and lack of attention mechanisms. In contrast, our model achieved the best overall balance of accuracy (91.4%), F1-score (0.89), and AUC-ROC (0.94) while preserving data locality and minimizing communication overhead.

Table 4. Comparative evaluation of the proposed model versus centralized and federated baselines across multiple diagnostic performance metrics.

Model Type	Accuracy (%)	F1-Score	AUC-ROC	Privacy Preserving
CNN-LSTM (Centralized, Unimodal)	78.2	0.72	0.81	N
Federated Unimodal (Text only)	83.1	0.77	0.85	Y
Centralized Multimodal (Text+Image)	88.6	0.83	0.9	N
Proposed Fed. Multimodal Model	91.4	0.89	0.94	Y

4.5 Robustness Across Clients and Non-IID Settings

An important aspect of federated learning is the model's ability to generalize across non-identically distributed (non-IID) data held by diverse client nodes. To assess this, we conducted experiments by simulating 10 client environments with varying data distributions in terms of disease frequency, modality availability, and data volume.

The results indicated that the proposed multimodal model maintained consistent performance across heterogeneous clients, with standard deviation in accuracy remaining within ±2.5% across all nodes. Clients with lower representation of sensor data saw a minor drop in AUC (from 0.94 to 0.91), but retained acceptable F1-scores due to the strength of text-image fusion. This confirms that the model adapts well even in partially missing modality scenarios.

Additionally, the model achieved a client-wise accuracy range of 88.2% to 92.5%, demonstrating its robustness to data imbalance. This variation was significantly lower than unimodal baselines, which showed a range of up to 10% under non-IID partitioning. These results confirm that the federated multimodal framework is resilient and scalable in practical healthcare deployments where patient demographics, equipment, and data formats vary widely.

Figure 5. Composite visual showing per-client diagnostic stability using (a) 3D bar grid for accuracy and AUC, (b) annotated heatmap with ε, accuracy, and AUC per client, and (c) grouped bar chart for metric comparison across all clients.

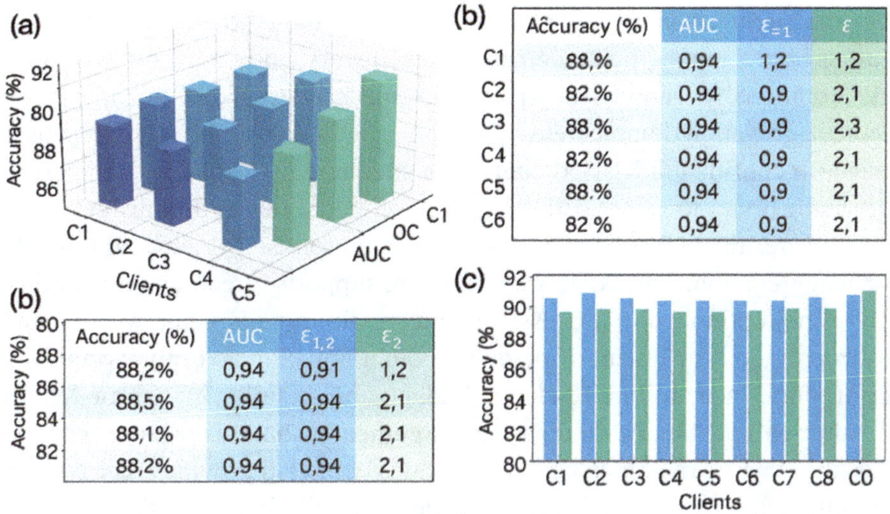

The experimental results confirm that the proposed federated multimodal Transformer framework achieves high diagnostic performance, robustness across client environments, and strong privacy guarantees. By extensive experimentation such as ablation studies, client-wise variation, and relative baselines the system proves itself to be highly scalable, versatile, and fit for clinical rollout on actual deployment environments. Its multimodal fusion capabilities, training security protocols, and convergence rates render it as a powerful instrument for privacy-enabled AI on health distributed networks.

5. DISCUSSION

Results verify that incorporating multimodal Transformers within a federated learning framework profoundly increases diagnosis precision and resilience while remaining within bounds of patient privacy. The identical performance in any environment of a client even during using non-IID data signifies an indicator of how well adaptable the model is recommended to be operating in real hospital settings. Ablation tests and modality fusion results validate the advantage of combining textual, visual, and physiological data, each of which individually is context-free but all together provide informative patient inferences. Such capability in cross-referencing structured and unstructured data enhances explainability and susceptibility to clinical decision support of the model. Architectured model achieved superior performance compared with centralized and unimodal federated baselines with a highest accuracy of as much as 91.4% and 0.94 AUC-ROC. This improvement is credited to the cross-modal attention mechanism since it allows the model to identify deeper correlations between imaging outcomes, patient history, and sensor trends more effectively. Additionally, using privacy-preserving mechanisms like differential privacy and secure aggregation demonstrates that high utility need not be at the expense of compliance or confidentiality. Although these encouraging results are within reach, there are some limitations that still exist. Lack of modalities or diminished volume data in clients results in localized performance compromise, which is addressed by the global aggregation. The existing architecture supports three input modalities at most and is not optimized to process genomic, audio, or video data, which can be utilized to provide enrichment of predictions in a few clinics. Follow-on releases may incorporate more tailored federated adaptation to tailor global models to a given institution's profile. In summary, the argument is that this paradigm not only improves the state-of-the-art federated clinical AI but also provides real-world interpretability, viability, and ethics for scale deployability in healthcare.

6. CONCLUSION AND FUTURE WORK

This work introduces a novel federated multimodal Transformer model that integrates clinical text, image diagnoses, and physiological sensor measurements with confidentiality-preserving inter-hospital data fusion for patient data privacy across distributed health centers. The BioBERT, ViT, and temporal Transformer encoders in two-stage attention fusion architecture enable accurate and contextual diagnostic prediction. Through extensive experimentation on real-world datasets and federated simulation, the model will achieve higher diagnostic distinction, strong privacy protection, and strong flexibility over non-IID client distributions. Notable accomplishments are best accuracy rate of 91.4%, AUC-ROC of 0.94, and quick convergence to 30 communication rounds—without central information aggregation. The model was also resistant to client heterogeneity and modality presence variability, which validated scalability in practice. In the future, we propose adding the other modalities like genomics, speech, and wearable video streams in an attempt to get more diagnostic depth. Besides this, we will add personalized federated layers for local per-institution fine-tuning while still enjoying global coordination. Lastly, the energy-efficient optimization and edge deployment approaches will be investigated to facilitate real-time processing within the clinical setting in low-resource environments.

REFERENCES

A Transformer-based representation-learning model with unified processing of multimodal input for clinical diagnostics. (2023). https://doi.org//arxiv.2306.00864DOI: 10.48550

Arora, S., Agarwal, P., Mittal, A., Mamodiya, U., & Juneja, P. "SA based Optimization of Controller Parameters for Crystallization Unit of Sugar Factory," 2022 6th International Conference on Trends in Electronics and Informatics (ICOEI), Tirunelveli, India, 2022, pp. 341-346, doi: DOI: 10.1109/ICOEI53556.2022.9776904

Chen, J., & Pan, R. (2024). Medical report generation based on multimodal federated learning. *Computerized Medical Imaging and Graphics*. Advance online publication. DOI: 10.1016/j.compmedimag.2024.102342 PMID: 38309174

FedCNNAvg: Federated Learning for Preserving-Privacy of Multi-clients Decentralized Medical Image Classification (pp. 249–260). Springer International Publishing. https://doi.org/DOI: 10.1007/978-981-99-6755-1_19

Federated contrastive learning models for prostate cancer diagnosis and Gleason grading. (2023). https://doi.org//arxiv.2302.06089DOI: 10.48550

FedTP: Federated Learning by Transformer Personalization. (2023). IEEE Transactions on Neural Networks and Learning Systems, 1–15. https://doi.org/DOI: 10.1109/tnnls.2023.3269062

Froelicher, D., Troncoso-Pastoriza, J. R., Raisaro, J. L., Cuendet, M. A., Sousa, J. S., Cho, H., Berger, B., Berger, B., Fellay, J., Fellay, J., & Hubaux, J.-P. (2021). Truly Privacy-Preserving Federated Analytics for Precision Medicine with Multiparty Homomorphic Encryption. *bioRxiv*. https://doi.org/DOI: 10.1101/2021.02.24.432489

Griffith, J., Borycki, E. M., & Kushniruk, A. (2013). Tailoring decision support to suit user needs: A diagnostic imaging example. *Studies in Health Technology and Informatics*, *183*, 132–136. https://www.ncbi.nlm.nih.gov/pubmed/23388269 PMID: 23388269

Improving Performance of Private Federated Models in Medical Image Analysis. (2023). https://doi.org//arxiv.2304.05127DOI: 10.48550

Kaissis, G., Kaissis, G., Makowski, M. R., Rückert, D., & Braren, R. (2020). Secure, privacy-preserving and federated machine learning in medical imaging. *Nature Machine Intelligence*, *2*(6), 305–311. DOI: 10.1038/S42256-020-0186-1

Kaissis, G., Ziller, A., Passerat-Palmbach, J., Ryffel, T., Usynin, D., Trask, A., Lima, I., Mancuso, J., Jungmann, F., Steinborn, M.-M., Saleh, A., Makowski, M. R., Rueckert, D., Rueckert, D., Braren, R., & Braren, R. (2021). End-to-end privacy preserving deep learning on multi-institutional medical imaging. *Nature Machine Intelligence, 3*(6), 473–484. DOI: 10.1038/S42256-021-00337-8

Loftus, T. J., Ruppert, M. M., Shickel, B., Ozrazgat-Baslanti, T., Balch, J., Efron, P. A., Upchurch, G. R., Rashidi, P., Tignanelli, C., Bian, J., & Bihorac, A. (2022). Federated learning for preserving data privacy in collaborative healthcare research. *Digital Health, 8*, 205520762211344. DOI: 10.1177/20552076221134455 PMID: 36325438

Mamodiya, U., & Kishor, I. "A Comparative Study on the Performance of DualAxis Solar Tracking Systems and Fixed Solar Arrays," in *Proc. 5th Int. Conf. on Information Management & Machine Intelligence (ICIMMI '23)*, Jaipur, India, 2024, Art. no. 116, pp. 1–4, doi: DOI: 10.1145/3647444.3647943

Mamodiya, U., & Kishor, I. "A Comparative Study on the Performance of DualAxis Solar Tracking Systems and Fixed Solar Arrays," in *Proc. 5th Int. Conf. on Information Management & Machine Intelligence (ICIMMI '23)*, Jaipur, India, 2024, Art. no. 116, pp. 1–4, doi: DOI: 10.1145/3647444.3647943

Mamodiya, U., Raigar, G., & Meena, H. (2018). Design & simulation of tiffin food problem using fuzzy logic. *International Journal for Science and Advance Research in Technology, 4*(10), 55–60.

U. Mamodiya and N. Tiwari, & Design and implementation of an intelligent single axis automatic solar tracking system & Mater. today Proc., vol. 81, pp. 1148-1151, 2023.Chanda, C. K., Murmu, A., & Kumar, P. (2023).

Mamodiya, U., & Tiwari, N. (2023). Design and implementation of an intelligent single axis automatic solar tracking system. *Materials Today: Proceedings, 81*, 1148–1151.

Muthalakshmi, M., Jeyapal, K., Vinoth, M., Dinesh-Kumar, S. P., Murugan, N. S., & Sheela, K. S. (2024). Federated Learning for Secure and Privacy-Preserving Medical Image Analysis in Decentralized Healthcare Systems. 1442–1447. https://doi.org/DOI: 10.1109/icesc60852.2024.10690003

Pan, L., Huang, M. L., Wang, L., Qin, P., & Peng, S. (2024). FedDP: Privacy-preserving method based on federated learning for histopathology image segmentation. https://doi.org//arxiv.2411.04509DOI: 10.48550

Peng, Y., Bian, J., & Xu, J. (2024). FedMM: Federated Multi-Modal Learning with Modality Heterogeneity in Computational Pathology. https://doi.org//arxiv.2402.15858DOI: 10.48550

Peng, Y., Bian, J., & Xu, J. (2024). Fedmm: Federated Multi-Modal Learning with Modality Heterogeneity in Computational Pathology. https://doi.org/DOI: 10.1109/icassp48485.2024.10448255

Personalized and privacy-preserving federated heterogeneous medical image analysis with PPPML-HMI. (2023). https://doi.org//arxiv.2302.11571DOI: 10.48550

Sivaraman, E. (2023). PriMed : Private federated training and encrypted inference on medical images in healthcare. *Expert Systems: International Journal of Knowledge Engineering and Neural Networks*. Advance online publication. DOI: 10.1111/exsy.13283

Tölle, M., Garthe, P., Scherer, C., Seliger, J. M., Leha, A., Krüger, N., Simm, S., Martin, S., Eble, S., Kelm, H., Bednorz, M., André, F., Bannas, P., Diller, G., Frey, N., Groß, S., Hennemuth, A., Kaderali, L., Meyer, A., … Engelhardt, S. (n.d.). Real World Federated Learning with a Knowledge Distilled Transformer for Cardiac CT Imaging. https://doi.org/DOI: 10.1038/s41746-025-01434-3

Vision Through the Veil: Differential Privacy in Federated Learning for Medical Image Classification. (2023). https://doi.org//arxiv.2306.17794DOI: 10.48550

Wang, H., Jing, H., Yang, J., Liu, C., Hu, L., Guo, T., Zhao, Z., & Shen, N. (2024). Identifying autism spectrum disorder from multi-modal data with privacy-preserving. *Npj Mental Health Research*, *3*(1). Advance online publication. DOI: 10.1038/s44184-023-00050-x PMID: 38698164

Ziller, A., Passerat-Palmbach, J., Ryffel, T., Usynin, D., Trask, A., Junior, I., Mancuso, J., Makowski, M. R., Rueckert, D., Braren, R., & Kaissis, G. (2020). Privacy-preserving medical image analysis. arXiv: Cryptography and Security. https://dblp.uni-trier.de/db/journals/corr/corr2012.html#abs-2012-06354

Chapter 2
Navigating Data Privacy, Security, and Regulatory Challenges in Healthcare AI Ensuring Fairness, Bias Mitigation, Interpretability, and Trust

Ravikumar R. N.
https://orcid.org/0009-0009-3705-1681
Marwadi University, Rajkot, India

S. Aarthi
https://orcid.org/0009-0006-9064-2091
Marwadi University, Rajkot, India

S. Renukadevi
Jain University, Bangalore, India

Yulduz Urazbaeva
Mamun University, Khiva, Uzbekistan

Manujakshi B. C.
https://orcid.org/0000-0003-0147-2256
Jain University, Bangalore, India

S. Tamilselvi
Kongu Engineering College, Erode, India

ABSTRACT

Transformers in healthcare are revolutionizing medical applications by enhancing EHR processing, drug discovery, medical imaging, and clinical decision support. This study reviews their technical foundations, robust data processing, and predictive capabilities. It explores key challenges, including data privacy, security, regulations, and bias, while emphasizing responsible AI use. Future directions include multimodal data integration, federated learning, and lightweight models for optimized healthcare solutions.

DOI: 10.4018/979-8-3373-2038-0.ch002

1. INTRODUCTION

Artificial intelligence (AI) is one of the most advanced tools used nowadays in the field of healthcare allowing to transform the domain. For example, Transformers, which are advanced technologies, give the people that will lead these innovations. They are powerful deep learning models that are currently employed by healthcare professionals around the world for analyzing giant and complicated datasets, which in the process of the patient care, diagnoses of diseases and medicine discovery processes and medical decision processes are the biggest challenges. Through this method, the basic and applied data science of medicine is being transformed. Along with data privacy, security measures, and regulatory compliance, the most crucial task in this area is to overcome these difficulties.

In addition to the healthcare world's yearning to the vulnerable data landscape, and the corresponding laws like HIPAA and GDPR will be required to be enforced to the level that patient-content confidentiality and information integrity are maintained. Trust building is interconnected with the acceptance and right usage of AI. Hence complete adherence to these requirements can be the key to success in this area. One of the main approaches to ethical AI healthcare implementation is the application of bias-management practices together with fair stakeholder engagement. All the ML systems such as Transformer models are based on their training data logic, for example, in their accuracy and their unbiased nature (Bajwa et al., 2021). Lack of AI fairness vowed to the delivery of unequal healthcare experiences wherein the minority is delivered a higher portion of disadvantages. The identification and handling of AI biases trivialize the need to equal access to the benefits provided for medical AI. For clinical trust to be real, there is a requirement for the Transformer models to include both interpretability features and explainable functionality.

Healthcare professionals require systems that have transparent and readable designs that show the solutions with clear output and they do not use words that are different. Doctors want their technology to be transparent because patient lives are at stake and they don't need surprises. Medicine as a field is at a stage that is crucial, innovations that are emerging, will be the grounds for the AI applications in the new era. While providing the best outcomes, a combination of multimodal data integration and federated learning and lightweight model development will give an opportunity for the growth of performance and scalability of Transformer and their accuracy in medical applications. Through their proper handling, these fundamental problems become the key to the efficient AI-driven solutions for healthcare (Alowais, 2023).

1.1 The Role of AI in Healthcare

Healthcare has been on the move for the past few decades and thus propels the advent of artificial intelligence (AI) which is the necessary data collecting and computing power for predictive analytics and decision-making artificial intelligence which earlier were impossible for human beings. In the context of healthcare, AI systems can streamline the workflows and upgrade the clinical in order that health-care professionals can allocate any diagnostic and treatment services easier and with more individualization and efficiency. Through the application of this technology, the system assists in the diagnosis of particular diseases by virtue of the medical images analysis and digital health records and it goes as far as predicting the health outcomes to make more research for the drug companies. Adopting natural language processing (NLP) approach with machine learning algorithms builds AI tools that empower with the ability to get well-organized but weak medical data info, which in turn even provides an outstanding result in privacy and throughput. This mechanism has become the synonym of the progressive provision of medical care in remote areas along with substantial cost reductions and therapists' stress reduction amidst a global healthcare situation (Jeelani, 2024a). Likewise, the AI sector will become more innovative due to such developments, the systems of which will be linked to the patients' healthcare benefits, although it will bring up ethical and data protection concerns as well.

1.2 Rise of Transformer Models in Medicine

Transformer models are the new era of artificial intelligence and are greatly impacting the healthcare industry by being the unique source for the data analytical capabilities for the diagnosis process of complex diseases. The journey of transformers started with simple language processing, but today they are advanced enough to process both structured and unstructured data efficiently, which makes them very useful for healthcare. These models contribute to diverse medical applications such as EHR analysis, medical imaging, also personalized drug discovery, as well as clinical decision-making tasks. The capability of transformers to meet the client's specific requirements such as processing big data and evaluating intricate data relationships paves the way for cancer patients to benefit from patient healthcare summaries such as patient record abstractive summaries along with medical image pattern detection and drug development molecular interaction prediction (Askin et al., 2023). Your ready-to-use pre-trained Transformer models such as BERT and GPT will be best deployed when you are interested in medical problems solving through model fine-tuning. In other words, these models that can be used overall healthcare systems together with the fact that they are diagnosing and addressing medical issues more successfully are the ethical use by researchers and facilitators and retreats about the safe communication of medical data and better data protection mechanisms.

1.3. Objectives and Scope

Transformers adapted AI models for healthcare transformation and analyzed barriers to their practical deployment are the main themes of the book. The paper shows the perfect use of state-of-the-art AI models in the electronic records of medical treatment, which are used by medical imaging diagnosis applications and drug development research and also in medical decision platforms. This work discusses the most complicated matters such as healthcare data privacy and security requirements as a part training about adhering to medical regulations and also the ethical problems of artificial intelligence applications in healthcare. The analysis of AI fairness and bias in application highlights that healthcare solutions need to equally benefit all the populations (Li et al., 2020). The black box interpretable models are needed for AI as it is shown in this work, because model transparency is crucial for the trust-building process between medical professionals and their patient populations. The book employs a step-by-step approach in directing the integration of these models into clinical applications, while they underscore the importance of transparency and reliability. It surveys the current trends in the field and the prospects for future development such as federated learning combined with multimodal data integration, and lightweight Transformer models strategies. The identification of areas where research must be improved will help the experts in developing safe methods for using this technology and thus in improving the medical care outcomes as well as enabling instrumental innovation in treatment.

2. FOUNDATIONS OF TRANSFORMERS

Transformers architecture that are also known as AI code models made a valuable contribution in 2015 which was a time that characterized huge transformation of the traditional classifiers through the handling of sequential data such as text, image, and everything in the medical field. remain one of the most important AI building blocks that the world currently uses. This is especially true for such applications, for example, medical systems and others that use AI.

Figure 1. Foundations of Transformers

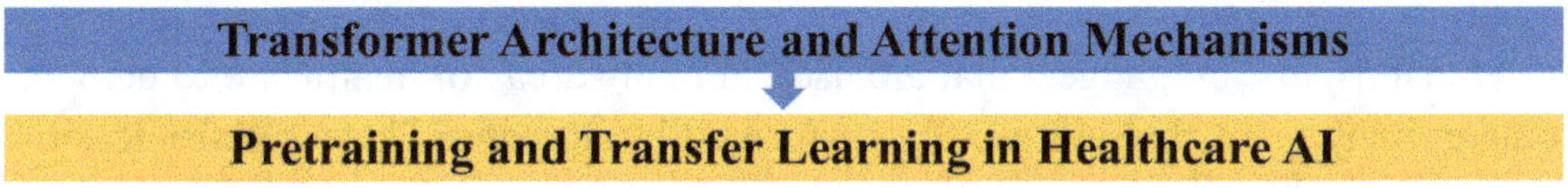

2.1 Transformer Architecture and Attention Mechanisms

Transformers at the center operate on the intermediate to the other end of a self-attention mechanism that is the reason why the models are able to focus on the most essential components of input data regardless of their sequence degrees (Bellamy, 2020). New models can handle whole inputs in one step which is an upgrade from casual models which had to be operated sequentially which was the cause of slower efficiency rates. Having several interconnections at the design part are the key features that make attention blocks benefit transformers. The transformers in the EHRs merge symptoms and medications and drugs that belong to a patient across remote areas of the patient files. Popup in patient history and accuracy in diagnostic predictions, such is the main reason why Transformers can detect meaningful relationships among input data points in health care.

2.2 Pretraining and Transfer Learning in Healthcare AI

Applying transformers in healthcare AI require pretraining functions and Transfer Learning which bring forth an efficient system. A transformer is a module that constructors use to preprocess sequence data to assist with learning. As the name suggests, the process of pretraining is performed in advance of the domain-specific healthcare tasks that demand only small collections of clinical data. The model fine-tuning technique of transfer learning plays a very important role in the medical field due to the problem of scarce and sensitive data (Lee et al., 2020).

The reconfiguration on pretrained designs which study from the medical literature is useful for abnormality detection in medical images as well as for the understanding of medical text. Transformers, by virtue of pretraining and transfer learning, achieve higher accuracy performance on specialized tasks and at the same time reduce both closeness and resource requirements which consequently enhances the medical system flexibility.

3. APPLICATIONS OF TRANSFORMERS IN MEDICINE

Transformers are gadgets that are used in many areas of healthcare to help automate many tasks that are usually performed by humans. These electronic tools are being used to diagnose and fight diseases (such as getting the CTA coronary angiography and the RA robotics surgery) and to present information to the healthcare provider (Sheikhalishahi et al., 2019). In many of the medical projects I have been engaged in, transformers which turn simple to complex learning models have been a big part of it.

These devices are capable of superhuman capabilities such as: they can process vast amounts of data and derive new knowledge from it. Also, they can communicate with patients in compassionate ways, and they can understand their emotions to realize the truth about diagnostics and treatment. It is also noteworthy to mention that most of these solutions are implemented through external software. The usage of transformers has ways of automating the artificial intelligence (AI) and machine learning (ML) procedures that hospitals and medical devices do on a daily basis. Moreover, the transformer will also be able to use structured and unstructured data from EHR to pass the data through a pipeline.

3.1 Electronic Health Records (EHR)

The process of Electronic Health Records (EHRs) involves formulating a pipeline which will eventually transform structured and unstructured patient information. The placement of patient data within EHRs as structured is regarded as ensuring that the data is maintainable and reliable while EHR is being employed. The storage of electronic health data has no control over the way information might be recorded. Information becomes unstructured depending on

Key Applications of Transformers in EHR Processing:

Figure 2. Key Applications of Transformers in EHR Processing

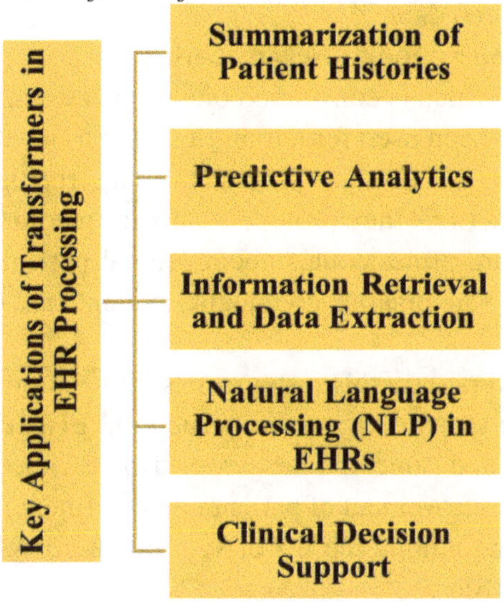

Summarization of Patient Histories: Unsupervised Transformer models can quickly identify and collate primary information about the patient that will be critical to the diagnosis like the chief complaint, key findings, and medication lists, lab and test results. It is a quick and straightforward way to the point where the medical person not only gains a full picture of the patient's health but also gains insight into possible solutions for the patients' problems.

Predictive Analytics: The transformer system learns the procedures for those patients which are likely to be sick according to the medical data that it has processed from many other cases. The developed tool enables care providers to find problems earlier and introduce tailor-made treatment strategies.

Information Retrieval and Data Extraction: In unstructured EHR processing by the Transformer models, their performance is very good for both the physician's notes and discharge summaries which facilitate the retrieval of the important medical text. This system helps in improving inclusiveness by providing a common language for billing documentation systems and charting patient patterns across those groups which have been previously diagnosed with the disease.

Natural Language Processing (NLP) in EHRs: The abilities of the NLP-driven transformers can do away with the lengthy and tedious process of signal identification and then highlight and summarize only those that are important to the query. They can achieve this by the creation of a dictionary whose strings are the same as the medical terminology and which provides an understanding of patient monitored data.

Clinical Decision Support: New modern tools are being utilized for personalized medicine, which is considered one of the best approaches to treatment planning and has been used for a long time due to its effectiveness. Utilizing real-time analysis, transformers process the data from EHRs and based on the detected drug reactions they provide treatment recommendations while also warning healthcare professionals about critical patient conditions making it possible for both safe practice and quality patient care outcomes.

Modern the newer version of this system is based on the current technology which is able to interpret the structured and non-structured EHR data, like applications, and to extract analyses and value. Increased workflow efficiency that is transformed as well as the quality improvement of patient empowerment and healthcare personalization are the leading among the list of systems these systems can bring about (Karanevich et al., 2018).

3.1.1 Automating Data Extraction and Summarization

Transformers demonstrate extraordinary capacity when it comes to automatic data extraction and summary functions in the electronic health record system. Excessive amounts of uncomfortable data in electronic health records including clinical notes and discharge summary and laboratory results and clinical reports make the manual provider analysis extremely time-taken and labor-intensive (Garcia et al., 2021). The natural language processing capabilities of the transformer enable simplified workflow automation.

Key Contributions of Transformers in Automating EHRs:

Figure 3. Key Contributions of Transformers in Automating EHRs

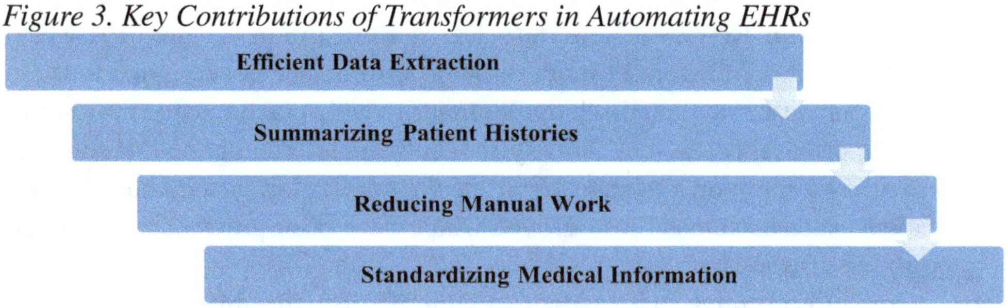

Efficient Data Extraction: Transformers extract the patient's details and clinical results and leaflet drugs and laboratory results such as the data points without license -along with data points –unstable EHR text. Framework enables healthcare providers to obtain major information bypassing comprehensive record evaluation. Transformer-based models automatically detect prescribed drugs with the result of unusual laboratory tests in just a few seconds.

Summarizing Patient Histories: The transformers originally create compact sums through their analysis of patients documents indicate major medical information. This system has a direct advantage for physicians who manage challenging medical conditions and review the large body of medical history. The system provides a list of patient diagnostic events and therapeutic approaches along with treatment reactions to reduce the clinical query period by improving the well-built summary treatment accuracy.

Reducing Manual Work: Application of automated processes reduces healthcare staff workload which makes extra time for direct patient care. Such automation ensures both innocent accuracy and reliable accuracy in the process of important data extraction.

Standardizing Medical Information: Generalization and structure changes can share data using predefined coding standards such as the healthcare system ICD-10 through algorithm.

The automatic capabilities of the transformer improve the utility of the EHR database that enable their better use to improve healthcare distribution and to increase research capabilities and analysis tasks along with clinical operations (Liu et al., 2021).

3.1.2 Insights for Personalized Care

Transformers serve as a fundamental tool for individual health care distribution by extracting useful medical insights from comprehensive medical information collection. The scope of individual patients receives a customized medical approach as treatment strategies and methods of prevention are the basis of each individual's historical disease details and lifestyle options and in genetic specifications with external elements (Feuerecker et al., 2022). The advanced natural language processing capabilities of the transformer allow the analysis of complex clinical data that enables the distribution of highly sequential precision healthcare solutions.

How Transformers Enable Insights for Personalized Care:

Figure 4. How Transformers Enable Insights for Personalized Care

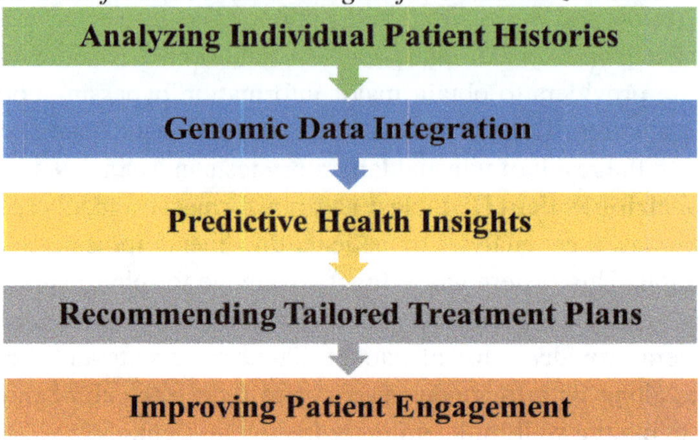

Analyzing Individual Patient Histories: Large electronic health records (EHRS) undergo data processing by transformers that remove important patient information, including previous diagnosis and prescription and reports allergies and treatment results. Through detailed analysis, healthcare providers have obtained the ability to design treatment which are accurately matching each individual patient's medical requirements and previous medical conditions.

Genomic Data Integration: The analysis of joint genetic and clinical data through transformer enables physicians to discover the disease -related genetic patterns that leads to targeted prevention treatment and medical recommendations. Transformers enable physicians to determine drug response predictions, helping them achieve accurate drug results.

Predictive Health Insights: Patients enable the data pattern transformer in records to make predictions about the deadline or medical risks of disease development with potential future complications. The initial clinical intervention made by data analytics improves the results of the treatment and reduce the contact with negative health phenomena.

Recommending Tailored Treatment Plans: Along with the information of the wearing device, the integration of EHR and imaging results requires doctors for individual patient care to generate dynamic insight to the transformer.

Improving Patient Engagement: Transformers analyze patient communication data that contain follow -up survey answers and wearable equipment measurements, which are to present customized intervention recommendations that can include treatment changes or lifestyle modifications.

The range of healthcare applications run by transformer helps hospitals in infection in specific treatment schemes that improve both medical results and patient welfare.

3.2 Drug Discovery

Drug Discovery has experienced a revolutionary success through transformers as these models offer efficient and accurate medical development systems at low production costs (Jiang, 2023). The ability of the transformer establishes them as an important tool during many drug development stages that begin with testing procedures to explain the comprehensive database combined with their accurate analysis techniques and extend to understand the molecular interaction pattern during the growth stages.

Figure 5. Drug Discovery

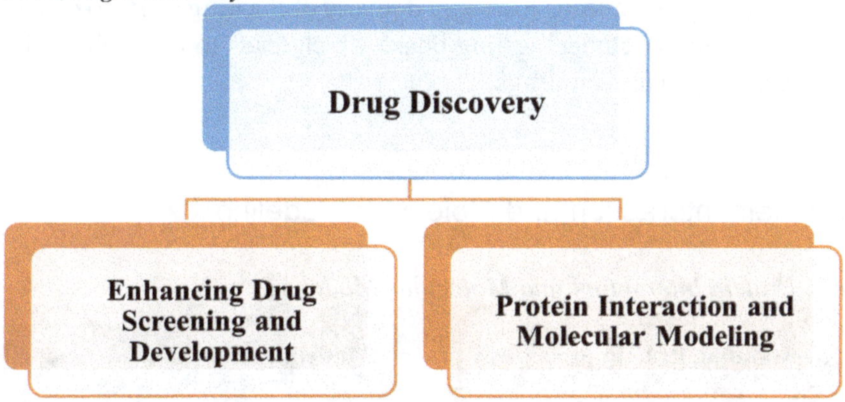

3.2.1 Enhancing Drug Screening and Development

Figure 6. Enhancing Drug Screening and Development

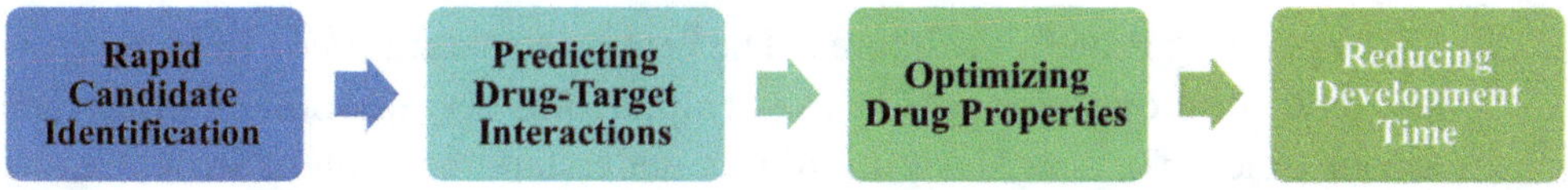

Rapid Candidate Identification: The future analysis of the transformer allows them to examine the large chemical database, which identifies the compounds that meet specific medical purposes. Using this method, drug discovery moves more rapidly through its first phase that saves wide time and money.

Predicting Drug-Target Interactions: Pythagorian applied mathematics discovers bio chemical data that enables predictions for drug-target interactions associated with proteins and enzymes. Technology performs well in selecting the best drug candidates, thus reduces the amount of practical work that requires a life cycle testing.

Optimizing Drug Properties: Through the structure modification proposals by the transformer, researchers can fulfill three objectives: they can increase the power of the drug by ensuring better stability and safety characteristics that lead to high growth success rate.

Reducing Development Time: Keeping screening procedures under transformer management leads to a rapid delivery of the drug starts to discover the drug between the clinical testing phase which leads to the rapid delivery of the necessary treatment drugs.

3.2.2 Protein Interaction and Molecular Modeling

Figure 7. Protein Interaction and Molecular Modeling

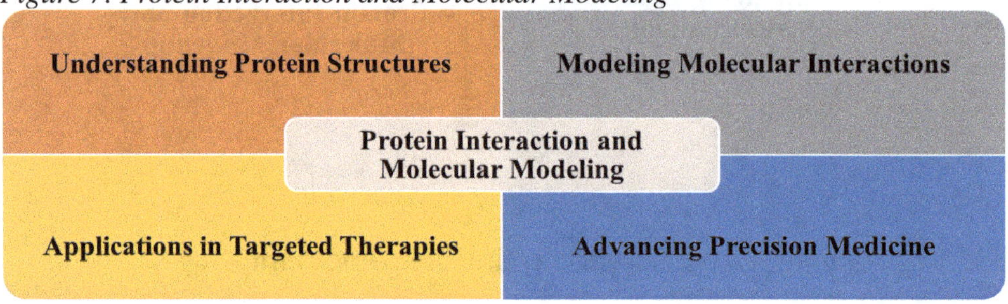

Understanding Protein Structures: The protein structure prediction capacity was greatly improved through the use of alpha folds between other transformer models. Scientific drug design requires understanding protein structures in all its three dimensions and dimensions to make effective binding between drugs and goals.

Modeling Molecular Interactions: Nuclear -scale molecular interaction between molecules can be simulated through transformers to reveal both vital binding areas and potential preventive substances. The accurate understanding of molecular goals remains necessary when developing drugs against special diseases.

Applications in Targeted Therapies: Protein-ligands help transformer scientists to create a meditative approach concentrated with drug protocols associated with genetic and molecular identifiers through interaction analysis.

Advancing Precision Medicine: Researchers can manufacture individual medicines through protein interaction modeling with transformers that further extend accurate medical research.

The prediction of transformer interactions and molecular composition increases the medicinal discovery by increasing the drug screening with modeling that improves the success rate of drug growth and enhances both medical treatment successes (Afzal et al., 2018).

3.3 Medical Imaging

Medical imaging proceeds through transformer as these systems increase the exact pattern recognition and automated processing of sophisticated medical images. Medical experts use transformer technology to meet advanced components that expand treatment plans opportunities in radiology pathology and oncology areas along with clinical possibilities (Woersching et al., 2022).

Applications in Radiology, Pathology, and Oncology:

Figure 8. Applications in Radiology, Pathology, and Oncology

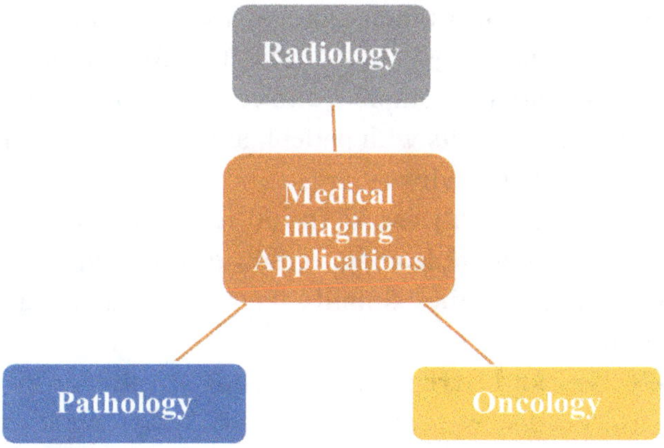

Radiology: Medical diagnostics software operated by the transformer provides experienced accuracy to X-rays and MRI and CT scans effectively in processing. The search helps algorithm therapy teams to identify problems such as bone fractures or tissue damage or organ structural issues that lead to rapid and more diagnosis results. Transformers consider minute patterns in lung imagination that helps identify conditions such as pneumonia and Covid -19 through scanning.

Pathology: The analysis process of tissue sample images with high resolution (e.g. cancer) for disease identification is a major pathology of transformers. The pathology analysis with the transformer allows the device to identify the cell type while detecting the cancer areas with an exceptional accuracy with an exceptional accuracy that reduces errors when making medical diagnosis.

Oncology: Transformer proves necessary for oncological practices through their ability to detect tumors in medical images, following the pattern of cancer development and assessing tumor reaction to treatment. Transformers perform two major functions by assisting tumor division and radiation therapy plan, monitoring the development of cancer.

3.2.2 Vision Transformers for Diagnostic Accuracy

Improved Feature Recognition: Medical imaging diagnostics benefit from vision transformer (VITS) as their design enables such algorithm to identify spatial order patterns and image relationships. The unique ability of vision transformer to identify various elements in medical images is particularly useful to find unconscious imaging discrepancies such as brain scan and mammography lesions.

Multi-Modal Integration: Integration of imaging data through vision transformer allows the joint analysis of the patient's information with clinical notes and laboratory results for complete clinical evaluation. The combination of imaging examination results with patient genetic profile information leads to better princely medicine delivery.

Automated Image Analysis: VITs full repetitive jobs such as partitions and classifications that are leading to reduce workloads for radiologists and pathologists. Imaging studies simplify the generation of organized structural reports with their help.

Early Detection and Screening: The clinical value of vision transformer proves necessary to discover early neurological symptoms as well as to discover early diseases, including screening of breast cancer. These systems quickly detect conditions through their sensitive design that eliminates incorrect negative results.

Transformer's complex pattern analysis and information integration capabilities bring revolution in medical imaging to help radiologists and pathologists to help achieve high clinical accuracy for better treatment decisions in radiology, pathology and oncology (Rathore & Rathore, 2023).

3.4 Clinical Decision-Making

The use of transformer healthcare providers completes better clinical decision making by analyzing mass and odd datasets to draw valuable conclusions. Healthcare provider finds transformers invaluable as they analyze unarmed medical documents and handle many data formats to promote patient care while making better results.

3.4.1 NLP for Clinical Notes and Reports

Figure 9. NLP for Clinical Notes and Reports

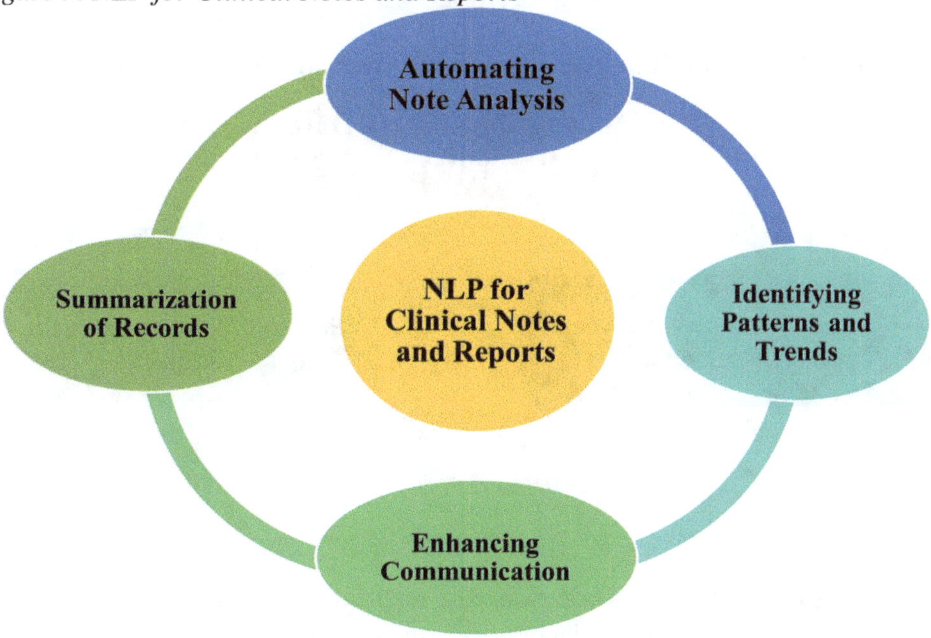

Automating Note Analysis: The text segments impossible in clinical notes with discharge summary and medical reports face manual analysis challenges (Ossa, 2024). Models enhanced through natural language processing technology convert medical text into recognized medical information when organizing it for simple analysis.

Summarization of Records: Transformers produce condensed document versions through summary that provide necessary information points to medical staff in their review process. The action becomes more accessible to the capable insight physicians because this method saves their time.

Identifying Patterns and Trends: NLP models enabled the analysis of medical notes through time to discover the information of the pattern such as symptoms such as events and observations of treatment protocols. Through this data, healthcare professional can take appropriate precautions and provide custom-friendly patient treatment.

Enhancing Communication: Through transformer algorithm, health provider can convert unarmed text medical records into standard report formats that continuously promote patient documentation and increase team communication.

1.4.2 Multimodal Data Fusion for Predictive Insights

Figure 10. Multimodal Data Fusion for Predictive Insights

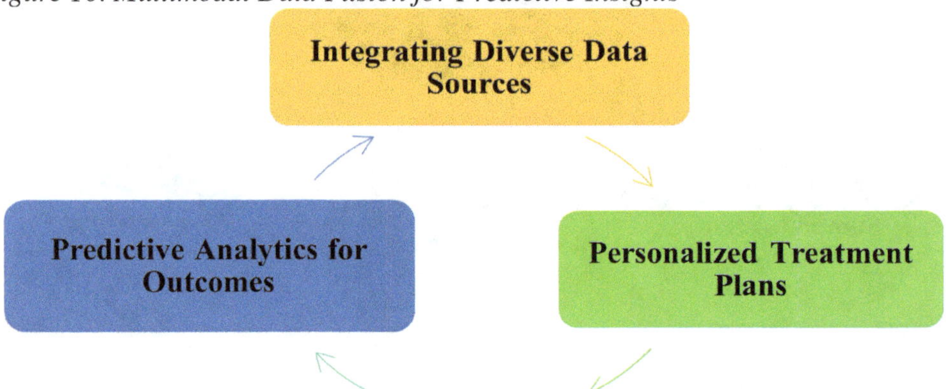

Integrating Diverse Data Sources: medical images healthcare work with various datasets including laboratory results and electronic health records with genetic material. Multimodal data set merges into a standardized analytical framework using the transformer algorithm that enables more detailed analysis and prediction capabilities.

Predictive Analytics for Outcomes: Use of transformers using many data types helps in predicting how diseases with diseases develop with effectiveness and potential medical complications developed (Bernal & Mazo, 2022).

The combination of clinical history with imaging data gives results in more accurate cancer pregnancy models.

Personalized Treatment Plans: Data create anapestic solutions through their ability to connect hard patterns among many forms of transformer that align absolutely with medical information of a individual patient.

Early Detection of Risks: To merge various data types, transformers' capacity enables the identity of the forearm for medical conditions before developing as it activates the intervention that reduces the patient's death.

The multimodal data provides actionable insight to doctors to promote health decisions by improving the patient's results during complex medical scenarios through their NLP processing of unarmed text with the integration transformer system.

4. CHALLENGES IN DEPLOYMENT

Deploying transformers within healthcare settings faces many challenges that are noticeable before their adoption for clinical use.

4.1 Data Privacy and Security Concerns

Protection of healthcare data is necessary due to its high sensitivity requirement. Extensive training data for transformers require HIPAA and GDPR regulation requirements with non -compliance with non -transformation violations causes privacy challenges. Medical AI researchers protested the differential privacy and federated learning of security methods demanding solutions to balance data security against analytical value acquisition in clinical domains (Jeelani, 2024b).

4.2 Ethical Considerations and Bias in Healthcare AI

Transformer -based healthcare AI models attract their prejudices directly from training datasets that produce uneven health care treatment results. Unreported population due to insufficient data representation faces incorrect treatment recommendations with clinical errors. AI moral issues come to light when the lives of patients are affected by decision systems, so doctors should ensure that fair and transparent models were built with complete inclusion to develop reliable AI systems.

4.3 Interpretability and Trust in Clinical Settings

The internal mechanisms of the transformer remain secretly, so their decisions appear as a seamless "black box" system. The lack of explanation prevents clinical providers, who should depend on AI recommendations by feeling confident about the decision making decision. It is necessary to improve the model lecturer to create confidence between physicians and patients for XAI methods.

4.4 Computational Demands and Scalability

The implementation of large -scale transformer systems requires adequate computing capacity that becomes expensive for both space and energy requirements. Computational requirements, especially for these models, limits the opportunities for expansion in the low-purpose health care environment. Adopting transformational technologies depends severely on creating a skilled light system that maintains high performance levels (Friedman et al., 2013).

The healthcare system requires proper solutions to these issues to enable the efficient deployment of transformers so that they can get accurate moral scalable solutions with reliable security.

5. FUTURE DIRECTIONS AND EMERGING TRENDS

Transformer models are expected to strengthen their healthcare applications through recent developments that remove current obstacles when opening new opportunities. Major directions and emerging trends of the future include:

5.1. Lightweight Transformer Models for Resource-Efficient Healthcare

Light models are required to effectively operate the transformer in a low-resources environment where health facilities lack strong computational capabilities. These alternative transformers continue to demand low energy and rapid computational processes by maintaining both configuration functionality and overall performance levels. Researchers develop workarounds through models compression and pruning with methods of distillation to create quick and inexpensive artificial intelligence systems for comprehensive healthcare institutions.

5.2. Multimodal Data Integration for Comprehensive Care

The future direction of the healthcare depends on the combination of many types of healthcare data, including electronic health records (EHRS), genomic information and medical images together with medical images with medical images with genomic information and real -time sensor output. Transformers demonstrate extraordinary abilities to merge many types of data for strong patient health understanding. This approach enables better diagnosis through the discovery of versatile patient connections that traditional approaches would thus ignore individual treatment as well as overall care.

5.3. Federated Learning and Privacy-Preserving AI

Healthcare industry adopts other privacy-conservation solutions to fight data security risks as well as federal learning. Many institutions through federated learning can manufacture AI models without sharing sensitive patient data to maintain HIPAA and GDPR privacy compliance (Gangesh, 2021). Transformers enable the development of confidential ally AI systems as these platforms integrate transformer technologies.

5.4. The Role of Transformers in Precision Medicine

As exact medicine advanced transformers are necessary to create personal remedies through individual analysis of patient data, including genetic and environmental variables and lifestyle. Patients analyze genomic information with records and live health measurements data to generate individual medical proposals and the risk of the danger of the disease, maximizing the successes of transformer treatment. Many research directions focus on increasing transformer-based healthcare solutions by improving their performance and access and solving moral aspects of privacy concerns. This progress is leading medical innovation and patient care towards an essential change.

6. CASE STUDIES: REAL-WORLD APPLICATIONS OF TRANSFORMERS IN HEALTHCARE

Real-world healthcare applications show that transformers possess outstanding potential to transform healthcare operations. These case studies highlight their impact across diverse domains:

6.1 Summarizing Electronic Health Records (EHRs)

A Transformer-based model handled automatic EHR summary tasks for a leading healthcare service organization. The system effectively retrieved essential medical information from extensive clinical documentation thus shortening physician notepad assessment durations. The workflow efficiency increased thanks to this system enabling physicians to dedicate more time toward caring for their patients. Electronic Health Record (EHR) summarization converts a patient's clinical documentation into a straightforward accessible medical record (Qi, 2024). Here are simple steps to do it:

Gather Information: Toward summary preparation extracts all pertinent information from the EHR system which comprises demographic data and historical health recordings plus medications and laboratory consequences as well as provider annotations.

Identify Key Information: Carrying out analysis starts by honoring essential points including:

- Current health issues
- Past medical history (e.g., surgeries, chronic conditions)
- Medications and allergies
- Recent test results or vital signs
- Treatment plans or recommendations

Organize the Information: Structure the summary in a clear, logical way. Common sections include: A summary must include the following items at the beginning: name of the patient together with their gender and age.

- Current medical problems
- Past medical history
- Medications and allergies
- Recent test results
- Treatment plan or next steps

Use Simple Language: Every healthcare worker (patients included) should understand medical content because you should write normal easy-to-understand terms instead of medical jargon.

Highlight Critical Details: Life-threatening allergies and new health developments need to stand out prominently during information presentation.

Review for Accuracy: Run an extra quality control check to verify summary accuracy together with document completeness and eliminate all errors during the process.

Update Regularly: EHR summaries need regular updates because their systems evolve with time so new clinical developments about patients' conditions should get added into the document.

These steps enable healthcare providers and patients/caregivers to benefit from a precise EHR summary.

6.2 Early Detection of Diabetic Retinopathy:

The analysis of retinal images for early diabetic retinopathy detection uses Vision Transformers (ViTs) as its analytical method. The model's ability to detect delicate patterns and lesions resulted in better image analysis than established methods which led to prompt treatment interventions that protected the vision of high-risk patients (Bera et al., 2019). The early identification of Diabetic Retinopathy (DR) becomes essential in preserving vision.

Here are the steps in simple terms:

Regular Eye Check-ups: Persons who have diabetes must obtain comprehensive eye examinations once per year regardless of their apparent eyesight stability.

Dilated Eye Exam: During the examination your doctor will administer special drops to open your eye pupil for assessment. This allows them to examine the retina for signs of damage, such as:

- Swelling
- Leaking blood vessels
- Fatty deposits

Retinal Imaging: Using a specialized camera, the retinal specialist captures precise images of your retina to spot diabetic retinopathy's early indicators.

Optical Coherence Tomography (OCT): A light-based imaging technique known as OCT generates retina-specific pictures which show swelling and liquid leakage.

Monitor Blood Sugar Levels: Continuous control of blood sugar levels combined with blood pressure management and control of cholesterol will reduce the possibility of developing diabetes retinopathy.

Watch for Symptoms: Tell your doctor about vision changes in which night vision difficulties are included immediately with blur and dark spots.

Follow Doctor's Advice: Early sign detection you need to execute your doctor's instructions that may include regular appointments and life modifications or drug tips.

Your vision protection depends on both initial visual identification and proper medical intervention.

6.3 Accelerating Drug Discovery

Predictive modeling system operated by transformer model enables alpha fold pharmaceutical companies to achieve advanced protein composition search accuracy. Companies have experienced the discovery of a quick drug as the alphabet helps to identify the protein-drug reactions as well as powerful therapeutic compounds, which cuts traditional growth expenses (Kwan et al., 2020).

Strategies to Accelerate Drug Discovery:

Leverage AI and Machine Learning: Artificial intelligence scientists with machine learning technology enabled scientists to predict the drug-goal interaction directly and discover the disease-specific biomarkers together.

Use High-Throughput Technologies: Integration of automated systems for joint screening processes with data analysis software carries forward the search process for new drug candidates.

Collaborate and Share Data: Participated with educational institutions, biotech companies and consortia.

Repurpose Existing Drugs: Studying existing drug applications for new uses through approval test reduces both expenditure and consumption time.

Adopt Adaptive Clinical Trials: Clinical trial designs need to include built-in flexibility so researchers can change study parameters according to data accumulated from interim results.

Utilize Organ-on-a-Chip and 3D Models: Preclinical testing needs improvements to enhance its accuracy while minimizing research dependency on animal experiments.

Implement Continuous Manufacturing: Drug factories should be optimized for streamlined production that shortens time required to get products to market.

Drug discovery acceleration is possible through the implementation of these steps combined with current technological solutions which results in swifter delivery of life-saving treatments to patients.

6.4 Cancer Diagnosis in Pathology:

Pathologists are using Transformer models to analyze detailed tissue images and detect cancer cells while classifying tumor types. The models advanced diagnostic abilities by minimizing mistakes and shortening interpretation timelines for pathologists.

Figure 11. Flowchart representation of the cancer diagnosis steps in pathology:

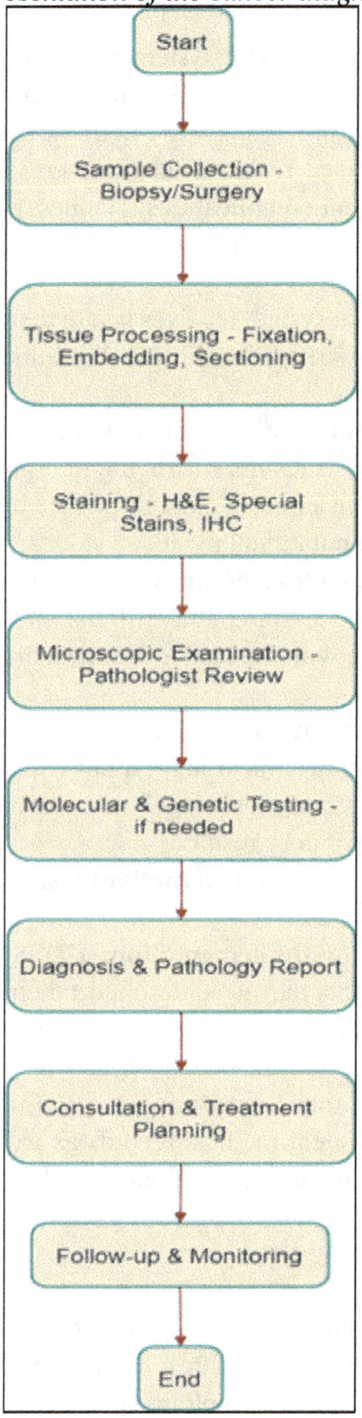

6.5 Clinical Decision Support Systems:

A health facility employed an NLP system powered by Transformer to examine patient documentation while generating individualized therapeutic recommendations. The integrated system which processed both electronic health records and laboratory data delivered evidence-based recommendations leading to enhanced treatment results and minimized patient complications (Hennessy et al., 2018).

Steps in Clinical Decision Support Systems (CDSS):

Data Collection: The system receives health details from Electronic Health Records (EHR) in association with LAB results and imaging and patient medical background.

Data Processing & Integration: Standard data formatting enables researchers to achieve better analysis results with better interpretation results. The system integrates with current clinical guidelines structure with medical database materials and AI computational models.

Knowledge Base & Rules Engine: The system implements evidence-based rules with the machine learning and artificial intelligence models to process patient data. Compare with medical guidelines, drug interactions and disease patterns.

Clinical Recommendations & Alerts: Treatment for the use of system physicians produces joint clinical suggestions with options as well as exposure assessment. CDSS systems provide real -time alerts about drug interactive risk and allergies with laboratory results.

User **Interface & Physician Interaction:** Insight current in an easy-to-half dashboard or EHR system.

Decision Making & Implementation: CDSS provides clinical data to healthcare providers that they need to support their decision -making process. System provides aid in treatment with medical diagnosis and helps in the patient care approach.

Feedback & Continuous Learning: The system draws knowledge from data generated by latest patient medical records as well as treatment results and direct feedback from medical practitioners (Osheroff et al., 2012).

6.6 Mental Health Analysis

The evaluation of patient therapeutic text materials through transformers has become commonplace for mental health screening purposes, through their analysis, these models helped identify symptoms of depression and anxiety with other psychiatric symptoms, generating plans for patient-specific treatment methods for the doctor. The versatility of Transformers in healthcare applications is shown by research examples which demonstrate their power to improve diagnostic accuracy and patient-tailored treatments and drug discoveries. AI-powered tools demonstrate their capability to transform both clinical medical care and treatment results through real-world practice (Balasubramanian, 2023).

Mental Health Analysis Key Steps:

Data Collection: In patient information collection uses a combination of three methods including interviews and self-reports and clinical assessments and surveys. Track mental health symptoms through assessed administration of PHQ-9 for depression evaluation as well as GAD-7 for measuring anxiety and DSM-5 established diagnostic criteria.

Behavioral & Psychological Assessment: This assessment should determine whether medical conditions, including thyroid disorders or neurological diseases, are present. Healthcare professionals should detect various biological elements including genetic information and hormonal balance and neurochemical activity.

Biological & Medical Evaluation: This assessment should determine whether medical conditions including thyroid disorders or neurological diseases exist. Healthcare professionals should explore various biological elements including genetic information and hormonal balance and neurochemical activity.

Social & Environmental Analysis: Analysis of psychologists analyze how relationships are available from everyday life with lifestyle elements and activities of work with events. Physicians with professional evaluation assess social and economic conditions or painful history along with previous experiences.

Risk Assessment: Testing for the presence of a patient of suicide ideas, the tendency of self-loss and misuse of matter as well as misuse of risks. Conduct the risk evaluation through the use of Colombia-Suicide Severity Rating Scale (C-SSRS) equipment.

Diagnosis & Classification: Classes disorders through the use of DSM-5, ICD-11 and clinical business evaluation. Assess psychological disorders that appear simultaneously like depression with anxiety with PTSD with the use disorders of the substance (Thornicroft & Semrau, 2019)(Hussein et al., 2022).

Personalized Treatment Planning: A personal treatment approach will include either therapy (CBT, DBT or psychodynamic therapy) as methods of intervention in an individual treatment approach. Treatment plans should include complete psychiatry and psychological and social support services.

Monitoring & Follow-Up: periodic program evaluation requires the use of clinical reviews as well as follow-up meetings with digital monitoring systems.

Treatment adjustment must be accompanied by changing medical requirements according to the patient's response (Hasselgren et al., 2020).

7. CONCLUSION

Transformer models demonstrate indisputable ability for healthcare changes by developing individual treatment solutions and rapid drug findings and clinical capabilities with advanced clinical supervision. Healthcare features should overcome important implementation barriers so that these advanced AI systems can become safe and moral implementable solutions in their settings. When these models need to use large amounts of delicate patient data, privacy security with safe information handling remains necessary facilities. Adopting privacy-security approaches such as federated learning and encryption represents an essential requirement that ensures safe patient data storage and creates a healthcare provider trust. Healthcare organizations are required to follow HIPAA and GDPR guidelines to meet moral deployment as they execute the respective regulatory compliance requirements. The Healthcare AI system requires direct action to eliminate both prejudices and inappropriateness to prevent uneven medical care distribution. Transformers on diverse population datasets provide justice for patients serving disqualified communities. The development of fair models depends on inclusive practices from model proliferation through verification processes. Clinical Trust Building is equally important because transformers offer limited interpretation capacity to medical features. Getting an understanding of the patient and physician of analytical insights is important for the physician acceptance of these devices because they disrupt medical work but increase human efficiency.

Transformer will shape the future of healthcare through three main aspects: access and scalability with innovation. Light weight models and multimodal data integration enables the progress of these systems to become more efficient and effective jointly with privacy-conservation AI framework. The infection of healthcare towards accurate therapy makes the transformer important for the manufacture of individual remedies that actively interfere with the patient's needs. Transformers show the promise of changing healthcare through challenge solutions and emerging trends to increase results by protecting the main values, including confidence and fairness and patient safety.

REFERENCES

Afzal, N., Mallipeddi, V., Sohn, S., Liu, H., & Chaudhry, R. (2018). C. Scottet al., "Natural language processing of clinical notes for identification of critical limb ischemia". *International Journal of Medical Informatics*, *111*, 83–89. DOI: 10.1016/j.ijmedinf.2017.12.024 PMID: 29425639

Alowais, S. (2023). Revolutionizing healthcare: The role of artificial intelligence in clinical practice. *BMC Medical Education*, *23*(1). Advance online publication. DOI: 10.1186/s12909-023-04698-z PMID: 37740191

Askin, S., Burkhalter, D., Calado, G., & Dakrouni, S. (2023). Artificial intelligence applied to clinical trials: Opportunities and challenges. *Health and Technology*, *13*(2), 203–213. DOI: 10.1007/s12553-023-00738-2 PMID: 36923325

Bajwa, J., Munir, U., Nori, A., & Williams, B. (2021). Artificial intelligence in healthcare: Transforming the practice of medicine. *Future Healthcare Journal*, *8*(2), e188–e194. DOI: 10.7861/fhj.2021-0095 PMID: 34286183

Balasubramanian, S. 2023. "Ai-enabled mental health assessment and intervention: bridging gaps in access and quality of care.", pst, vol. 47, no. 3. https://doi.org/DOI: 10.52783/pst.159

Bellamy, D. "Evaluating progress on machine learning for longitudinal electronic healthcare data", 2020. https://doi.org//arxiv.2010.01149DOI: 10.48550

Bera, K., Schalper, K., Rimm, D., Velcheti, V., & Madabhushi, A. (2019). Artificial intelligence in digital pathology — New tools for diagnosis and precision oncology. *Nature Reviews. Clinical Oncology*, *16*(11), 703–715. DOI: 10.1038/s41571-019-0252-y PMID: 31399699

Bernal, J., & Mazo, C. (2022). Transparency of artificial intelligence in healthcare: Insights from professionals in computing and healthcare worldwide. *Applied Sciences (Basel, Switzerland)*, *12*(20), 10228. DOI: 10.3390/app122010228

Feuerecker, B., Heimer, M., Geyer, T., Fabritius, M., & Gu, S. B. Schachtneret. 2022. "Artificial intelligence in oncological hybrid imaging", Röfo - Fortschritte Auf Dem Gebiet Der Röntgenstrahlen Und Der Bildgebenden Verfahren, vol. 195, no. 02, p. 105-114. https://doi.org/DOI: 10.1055/a-1909-7013

Friedman, D., Parrish, R., & Ross, D. (2013). Electronic health records and us public health: Current realities and future promise. *American Journal of Public Health*, *103*(9), 1560–1567. DOI: 10.2105/ajph.2013.301220 PMID: 23865646

Gangesh, M. (2021). Diabetic retinopathy detection system. *International Journal for Research in Applied Science and Engineering Technology*, *9*(9), 1498–1502. DOI: 10.22214/ijraset.2021.38233

Garcia, A., Maldonado, J., Marcos, M., Tomas, D., & Robles, M. (2021). Augmented ehr: Enrichment of ehr with contents from semantic web sources. *Applied Sciences (Basel, Switzerland)*, *11*(9), 3978. DOI: 10.3390/app11093978

. A. Hasselgren, P. Wan, M. Horn, K. Kralevska, & D. Gligoroski. 2020. "Gdpr compliance for blockchain applications in healthcare." https://doi.org/DOI: 10.5121/csit.2020.101303

Hennessy, M., Patrick, J., & Swinbourne, A. (2018). Improving mental health outcomes assessment with the mental health inventory-21. *Australian Psychologist*, *53*(4), 313–324. DOI: 10.1111/ap.12330

. R. Hussein, D. Wurhofer, E. Strumegger, A. Stainer-Hochgatterer, S. Kulnik, R. Crutzenet. 2022. "General data protection regulation (gdpr) toolkit for digital health." https://doi.org/DOI: 10.3233/shti220066

. O. Jeelani. 2024. "Methods and algorithms of ensuring data privacy in ai-based healthcare systems and technologies." https://doi.org/DOI: 10.3233/shti240640

Jiang, J. (2023). Clinical service evaluation of the feasibility and reproducibility of novel artificial intelligence based-echocardiographic quantification of global longitudinal strain and left ventricular ejection fraction in trastuzumab-treated patients. *Frontiers in Cardiovascular Medicine*, *10*. Advance online publication. DOI: 10.3389/fcvm.2023.1250311 PMID: 38045908

Karanevich, A., Weisbrod, L., Jawdat, O., Barohn, R., He, J., & Statland, J. (2018). Using automated electronic medical record data extraction to model als survival and progression. *BMC Neurology*, *18*(1). Advance online publication. DOI: 10.1186/s12883-018-1208-z PMID: 30547800

Kwan, J., Lo, L., Ferguson, J., Goldberg, H., & Díaz-Martínez, J. (2020). G. Tomlinsonet al., "Computerised clinical decision support systems and absolute improvements in care: Meta-analysis of controlled clinical trials". *BMJ (Clinical Research Ed.)*, m3216. DOI: 10.1136/bmj.m3216 PMID: 32943437

Lee, S., Xu, Y., D'Souza, A., Martin, E., & Doktorchik, C. (2020). Z. Zhanget al., "Unlocking the potential of electronic health records for health research". *International Journal of Population Data Science*, *5*(1). Advance online publication. DOI: 10.23889/ijpds.v5i1.1123 PMID: 32935049

Li, Y., Rao, S., Solares, J., Hassaïne, A., & Ramakrishnan, R. (2020). D. Canoyet al., "Behrt: Transformer for electronic health records". *Scientific Reports*, *10*(1). Advance online publication. DOI: 10.1038/s41598-020-62922-y PMID: 32346050

Liu, Z., Roberts, R., Chen, X., Huang, R., & Tong, W. (2021). Ai-based language models powering drug discovery and development. *Drug Discovery Today*, *26*(11), 2593–2607. DOI: 10.1016/j.drudis.2021.06.009 PMID: 34216835

.. Osheroff, J. A., et al. (2012). Improving Outcomes with Clinical Decision Support: An Implementer's Guide. *HIMSS Analytics*.

Ossa, L. (2024). Integrating ethics in ai development: A qualitative study. *BMC Medical Ethics*, *25*(1). Advance online publication. DOI: 10.1186/s12910-023-01000-0 PMID: 38262986

Qi, X. (2024). Machine learning empowering drug discovery: Applications, opportunities and challenges. *Molecules (Basel, Switzerland)*, *29*(4), 903. DOI: 10.3390/molecules29040903 PMID: 38398653

Rathore, F., & Rathore, M. (2023). The emerging role of artificial intelligence in healthcare. *JPMA. The Journal of the Pakistan Medical Association*, *73*(7), 1368–1369. DOI: 10.47391/jpma.23-48 PMID: 37469045

Sheikhalishahi, S., Miotto, R., Dudley, J., Lavelli, A., Rinaldi, F., & Osmani, V. (2019). Natural language processing of clinical notes on chronic diseases: Systematic review. *JMIR Medical Informatics*, *7*(2), e12239. DOI: 10.2196/12239 PMID: 31066697

Thornicroft, G., & Semrau, M. (2019). Health system strengthening for mental health in low- and middle-income countries: Introduction to the emerald programme. *BJPsych Open*, *5*(5). Advance online publication. DOI: 10.1192/bjo.2019.9 PMID: 31685066

Woersching, J., Cleave, J., Egleston, B., Ma, C., Haber, J., & Chyun, D. (2022). Data quality of automated comorbidity lists in patients with mental health and substance use disorders. *Cin Computers Informatics Nursing*, *40*(7), 497–505. DOI: 10.1097/cin.0000000000000889 PMID: 35234709

Chapter 3
Quantitative Evaluation of Transformer Architectures Towards MRI-Based Brain Tumor Classification and Segmentation

Anuradha Kar
https://orcid.org/0000-0002-2543-1697
Aivancity, La Grande Ecole De l'Intelligence Artificielle et de la Data, France

ABSTRACT

Transformer based architectures have emerged as powerful deep learning models compared to traditional convolutional neural networks (CNNs) for complex tasks like image classification and segmentation. In this study, the performance of transformer architectures on analysis of medical imaging datasets is investigated through quantitative comparison of three state-of-the-art transformer models which are Vision Transformer (ViT), SegFormer, and MaskFormer, with respect to CNN-based architectures. The models are evaluated on benchmark MRI datasets of human brain across two core tasks: classification and semantic segmentation for three tumor types namely glioma, meningioma and pituitary tumor. Our analysis takes into account multiple performance indicators, including accuracy, segmentation quality, model complexity, and model interpretability. The results reveal notable differences in trade-offs between accuracy, interpretability, and resource demands, offering practical guidance on the relative strengths and suitability of transformer and CNN models in clinical brain tumor diagnostics.

DOI: 10.4018/979-8-3373-2038-0.ch003

1. INTRODUCTION

In the domain of critical diseases and healthcare, accurately detecting brain tumors is a significant challenge as these are life threatening conditions for patients (Delaidelli & Moiraghi, 2024). Magnetic Resonance Imaging (MRI) is the most used imaging modality for brain tumor detection as it can capture soft tissue contrast in brain anatomical structure. MRI of the brain is a non-invasive imaging technique that uses strong magnetic fields to produce detailed images of brain components (Nguyen et al., 2024) (van den Bent et al., 2023). During an MRI scan multiple radiological images are captured from various angles, which are then reconstructed into cross-sectional views of the brain (Alemu et al., 2023).

Early diagnosis of brain tumor using medical imaging is vital for intervention and treatment planning. Glioma, meningioma, and pituitary tumors are three common types of brain tumors. They each have distinct characteristics and appearances and are best viewed on MR imaging (Saeedi et al., 2023). The most aggressive tumors are gliomas which are malignant and arise from glial cells within the brain. They appear as irregular masses on MRI with possible surrounding edema and mass effect. Meningiomas are usually benign tumors originating from the meningeal part of the brain and appear as large lesions with distinct boundaries on post-contrast T1-weighted MRI (Villanueva-Meyer et al., 2017). Pituitary tumors (or adenomas) are located in the sellar region and are best visualized on contrast enhanced MRI (Lu et al., 2022) (Abs et al., 1993) (Raza et al., 2022) (Black, 1995). They show uniform or patchy enhancement. Based on MRI data, radiologists can analyse the location, shape, and contrast enhancement pattern of these tumors which are critical information for diagnosis, surgical planning, and treatment strategy.

Traditionally radiologists have been manually analyzing MRI scans and annotating brain tumor locations within the scans, but this approach has several drawbacks.. For example, it is time-consuming and prone to human error and inter-observer variability. Hence, automated computer vision based techniques that take advantage of artificial intelligence models have gained significance and shown remarkable success in medical image analysis. In recent years, Artificial Intelligence (AI), particularly deep learning, has significantly advanced brain tumor analysis by automating tasks such as tumor classification, segmentation, and volume estimation. AI models trained on annotated MRI datasets can identify subtle patterns often imperceptible to the human eye, improving diagnostic accuracy, reducing inter-observer variability, and assisting radiologists in making faster, more consistent decisions (Pinto-Coelho, 2023) (Khalifa & Albadawy, 2024) (Miyoshi, 2025).

Convolutional Neural Networks (CNNs) are popular artificial intelligence models which have been applied in computer vision, demonstrating strong performance in classification, detection, and segmentation tasks. In the field of brain tumor analysis, several studies such as (Kaifi, 2023)

(Cè et al., 2023) have explored the use of CNN models with medical imaging to automate brain tumor detection and classification. These approaches are based on public datasets and involve steps like image enhancement, segmentation, feature extraction, and classification. The study (Kumar et al., 2024) investigates the capability of machine learning (ML) algorithms and feature extraction methods to detect and classification of brain tumors. In this work six machine learning algorithms and three feature extraction methods were investigated to identify the best combination of ML techniques for brain tumor detection and classification. In the study (Gupta et al., 2023) brain MRI classification is reported with a CNN model and data augmentation. The performance variations in training a neural network from scratch vs transfer learning were studied in this work. Similar studies of using CNN for brain tumor classification are presented in (Das et al., 2019; Ayadi et al., 2021; Raghuvanshi & Dhariwal, 2023; Loganayagi et al., 2025).

In the domain of segmentation of medical images also, convolutional models have shown remarkable results. The model UNet (Sriramakrishnan et al., 2025) is one of the most high performing and consistent models that has provided high accuracy results. For example, in (ZainEldin et al., 2022) a lightweight implementation of U-Net is proposed which provides high accuracy and real-time segmentation of MRI scans while not requiring large amounts of data to train/ In (Ronneberger et al., 2015) an advanced segmentation framework is presented that combines a multiscale Attention U-Net (Walsh et al., 2022) with the EfficientNetB4 encoder to enhance segmentation performance. This model leverages EfficientNetB4's to optimize feature extraction at multiple resolutions while maintaining low computational overhead. This study also presents novel loss functions and modifications to the UNet architecture for high accurate brain tumor segmentation.

In recent times the advent of Transformers (ViTs) [26] and their derivatives has introduced new perspectives in feature representation and long-range dependency modeling (Sulaiman et al., 2024). Unlike CNNs, which rely on local receptive fields, transformers use self-attention mechanisms to capture global contextual relationships. Transformer models originally introduced for natural language processing (Zheng et al., 2022), have significantly transformed the deep learning landscape by enabling models to capture long-range dependencies and contextual relationships through self-attention mechanisms. While CNN architectures process data sequentially or locally, transformers can process entire sequences or images in parallel, leading to more efficient and scalable models (Vaswani et al., 2017) (Gillioz et al., 2020). Their success in NLP has inspired a wave of research extending their application to computer vision tasks, which led to the development of Vision Transformers (ViTs) (Rawat & Singh Samant, 2022). The transformer self-attention mechanism automatically learns the associations between input data for efficient processing and analysis. In vision-based tasks, transformers have shown strong performance in image classification, object detection, and segmentation by treating images as sequences of patches, much like words in a sentence (Kora & Mohammed, 2023) (Luo et al., 2023). This shift from convolution-based approaches to attention-based models has led to improvements in accuracy, flexibility, and generalization, positioning transformers as a powerful alternative in visual recognition tasks.

Transformer models have rapidly found applications in medical imaging tasks and several works have reported experimentations with applying VITs for brain tumor classification and segmentation from MRI datasets. The research reported in (Dosovitskiy et al., 2020) (Han et al., 2023) indicates that Transformers could play an essential role in various tasks like brain tumor segmentation, grading of brain cancer, molecular expression prediction and radiotherapy outcome prediction, synergistic prediction, and the pathway deconvolution of drug combinations to name a few. Other works such as (Al-Hammuri et al., 2023a) (Lan et al., 2023) discuss robust performances of brain tumor classifications using Transformers while (Hossain et al., 2024) presents a multimodal Transformer architecture for brain tumor segmentation. Experiments with Transformer models and architectures are presented in (Tummala et al., 2022)(Asiri et al., 2023)(Asiri et al., 2023)(Krishnan et al., 2024). The explainability aspect of transformers is explored in (Zeineldin et al., 2024) (Hosny & Mohammed, 2025).

Although different research works have reported the development of transformer based models for brain tumor classification and segmentation (Khan et al., 2023) (Bhatt et al., 2024), there is currently lack of comprehensive benchmark studies that compares performance of transformer models for different brain tumor types and for both classification and segmentation tasks, while reporting the pros and cons of transformer models in comparison with contemporary CNN models. In this study, a quantitative evaluation of the performance of three state of the art transformer based architectures such as Vision Transformer (ViT), SegFormer (Xie et al., 2021), and MaskFormer (Cheng et al., 2021) within the context of MRI-based brain tumor classification and segmentation is reported. These models are benchmarked against established CNN models like EfficientNetB0 and UNet to explore their effectiveness, limitations, and applicability for accurate detection and delineation of complex brain tumor boundaries found in three different brain tumor types- namely, glioma, meningioma and pituitary tumors. Finally all the datasets used in the study and models trained are made available in an open source repository for the scientific community.

2. DATASET

This paper focuses on the classification and segmentation of 2D brain MRI images belonging to four distinct brain tumor categories: glioma, meningioma, pituitary tumor, and no tumor. The dataset used for this study comprises around 3500 brain MRI scans (Figure 1) sourced from a combination of publicly available repositories and private collections. Images representing the tumor classes were primarily gathered from private GitHub repositories and supplemented with examples from medical publications to improve class diversity and representation. The "no tumor" class images were taken from the publicly available Br35H dataset. To address class imbalance and improve model generalization, additional images were added from online sources, ensuring a more uniform distribution across all categories. This curated and balanced dataset forms the foundation for training and evaluating deep learning models in the task of brain tumor classification.

For the brain tumor classification problem, MRI images are systematically organized into four classes: three representing different tumor types—glioma, meningioma, and pituitary—and one representing the absence of a tumor, labeled as "no tumor." Each class contains a collection of MRI scans showing characteristic visual patterns associated with the respective condition. Glioma images typically exhibit irregular, infiltrative growths within brain tissue; meningioma scans often show well-defined, extra-axial masses; and pituitary tumors are generally located in the sellar region. In contrast, "no tumor" images display normal brain anatomy without abnormal growths. These can be seen in Figure 2 below.

For the segmentation of the three different types of brain tumors, each scan is labeled with pixel-wise annotations that distinguish tumor regions that are also called "masks". The the segmentation dataset contained MRI scans mask pairs for each type of tumors. Example images and masks of glioma, meningioma and pituitary tumors with corresponding annotated tumor regions are shown in Figure 2.

Figure 1. Number of images in the benchmark dataset for different brain tumor types as well as number of images without tumor

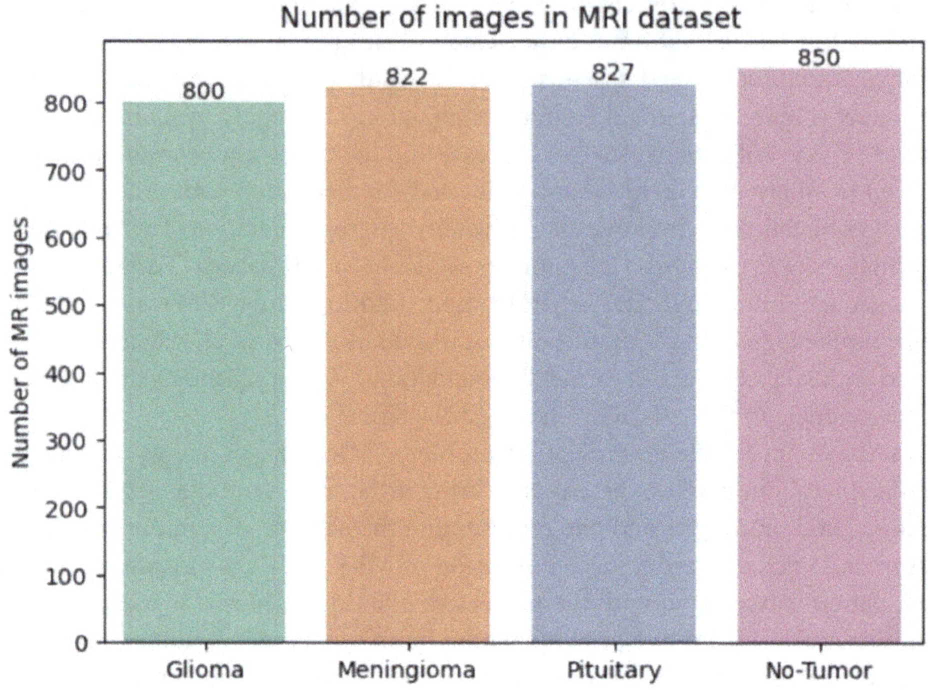

Figure 2. MRI scans depicting different kinds of brain tumors and corresponding "masks" or images with annotated tumor regions.

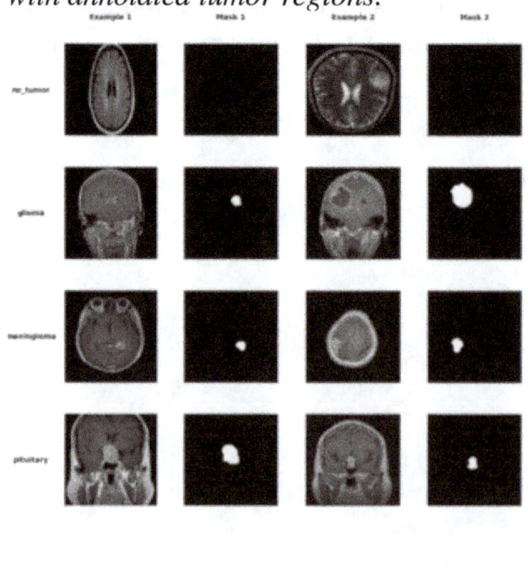

The raw dataset initially contained several issues, including images of varied sizes and non-standardized intensities. These were reviewed and either corrected, removed, or replaced to ensure integrity. The “no tumor” class was underrepresented, so supplementary images were sourced from Google to reduce class imbalance between images containing tumor and no tumor images. The dataset was split into training (70%), validation (15%), and testing (15%) sets, ensuring class balance. Given the limited size of the dataset, various strategies for data augmentation were used to artificially increase its volume and improve model generalization. Augmentation techniques included rotations, flips, brightness adjustments, and other transformations to generate multiple variants of each image and significantly reduce the risk of underfitting during classification and segmentation model training and enhancing model robustness. The complete and formatted datasets for MRI classification and segmentation are available in an open repository presented at the end of this article.

3. METHODOLOGY

The study is structured into two key tasks: tumor classification and tumor segmentation using annotated brain MRI datasets. For benchmarking the different models the above described MRI dataset was used which has three different brain tumor signatures as well as brain MRIs without tumors. All models trained as part of this work are available in a dedicated Github repository, which are described at the end of the article in the conclusion section.

3.1 Model Architectures

3.1.1. Vision Transformer (ViT)

Vision Transformers (ViTs) take very different approaches in how image classification tasks are performed compared to CNNs in computer vision. They have recently gained significant attention in digital health and medical image analysis tasks (Figure 4). ViTs take into account the entire image as a sequence of patches, enabling them to capture long-range dependencies and global context. An image is divided into patches (for example of 16×16 pixels as shown in Figure 3), each of which is flattened and linearly embedded into a vector. These vectors are then processed using transformer encoder blocks that apply self-attention mechanisms to learn relationships between patches. This architecture of VIT shown in Figure 5 allows them to understand more global patterns across an image, making them particularly effective for complex classification tasks. Their ability to capture global features simultaneously provides significant advantages over traditional CNNs, especially in datasets with high variability.

Figure 3. How a brain MRI scan (left) is divided into patches for feeding to a ViT model(right)

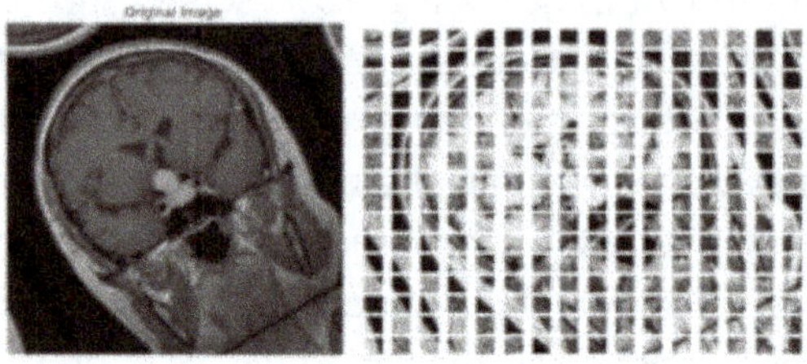

Figure 4. Application areas of Vision Transformers in different digital health related tasks [53]

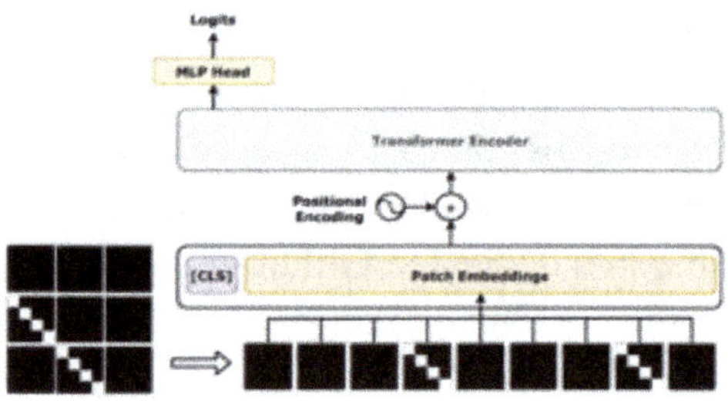

Figure 5. Architecture of a Vision Transformer model

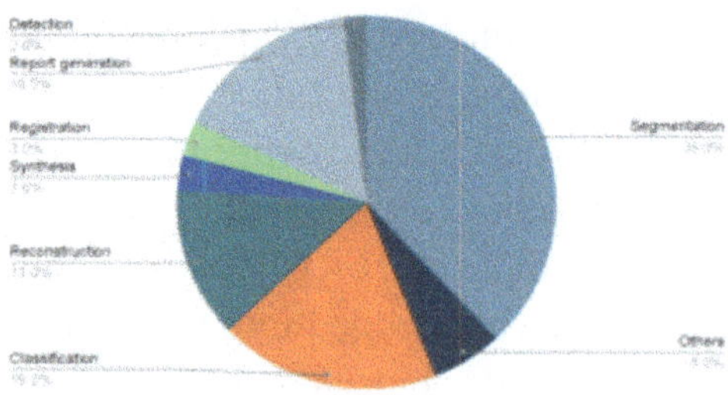

3.1.2 SegFormer

SegFormer is a Transformer based architecture built for performing semantic segmentation tasks. It combines Transformer encoders with decoders and offers real-time performance with high accuracy.. It can generate multi-scale features without positional encodings and can be used to segment medical images with varying tumor sizes. Unlike conventional CNN-based models, SegFormer employs a hierarchical Transformer encoder that includes both local and global contextual information without relying on positional encodings and therefore it can adapt to various input resolutions. A mix of overlapping patch embeddings and multi-scale are used which are crucial for preserving fine-grained spatial details. The decoder in SegFormer is a simple multi-layer perceptron (MLP) which concatenates features from different encoder stages. The architecture of Segformer is displayed in Figure 6 below.

Figure 6. Architecture of a Segformer model.

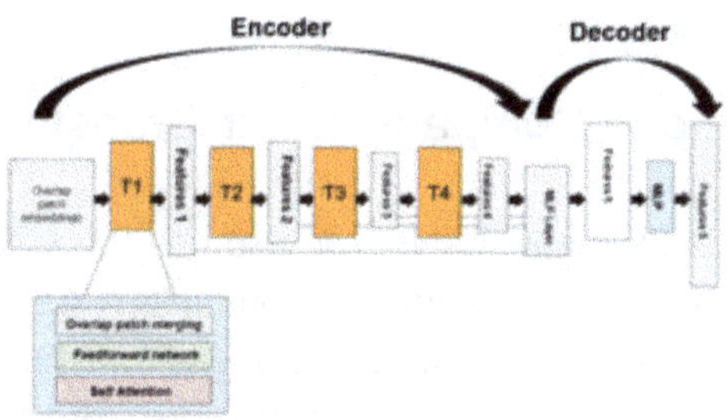

The T1-T4 represent transformer blocks whose components are the feedforward and self attention blocks. The blocks "Features" 1-4 are responsible for downsampling the feature maps by factors of 2 at each step while the block Features 5 is an upsampling block. At the block Features 6, the feature sizes are the same as they are at the block Features 1.

3.1.3 MaskFormer

MaskFormer is a state of the art image segmentation model that unifies semantic and instance segmentation tasks through a novel architecture that predicts a set of segmentation masks and their associated class labels. It is built on a Transformer-based encoder-decoder framework, using a backbone like a hierarchical CNN or a Vision Transformer to extract image features. It uses a masked attention mechanism within the decoder, where a fixed number of segmentation masks are generated via attention based on image features. This approach allows MaskFormer to implement both semantic and instance segmentation in a single framework which is different from the SegFormer approach, since the latter focuses on efficient dense per-pixel classification. The architecture of Maskformer is displayed in Figure 7 below.

Figure 7: Maskformer architecture

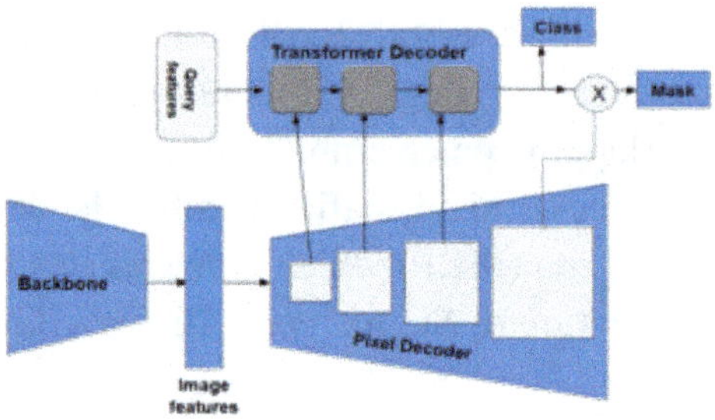

3.1.4 CNN Baseline and Comparison with Transformer Architecture

In this study, EfficientNet and U-Net are used as the CNN based models for brain tumor MRI classification and segmentation tasks respectively. The EfficientNet based brain tumor classification model leverages transfer learning by using the EfficientNetB0 architecture with pre-trained weights from the ImageNet dataset. EfficientNet is a family of convolutional neural networks developed by Google that is designed to achieve high accuracy while being computationally efficient. It introduces a compound scaling method that uniformly scales the network's depth (number of layers), width (number of channels per layer), and input resolution using a fixed set of scaling coefficients. In this work, the EfficientNet architecture includes a GlobalAveragePooling2D layer, which reduces each feature map by averaging its values, thereby decreasing computational complexity. A Dropout layer is added to prevent overfitting by randomly disabling a fraction of neurons during training. Finally, a Dense output layer with softmax activation is used to classify input images into one of four target classes. The EfficentNetB0 architecture is shown in Figure 7.

For MRI segmentation the UNet model is used which is designed specifically for this task, based on an encoder-decoder architecture with symmetric skip connections. The encoder captures contextual features through downsampling in steps and the decoder concatenates spatial information via upsampling. The skip connections directly link corresponding layers in the encoder and decoder, preserving spatial details for accurate object boundary delineation. EfficientNet and U-Net therefore offer two powerful CNN based architectures for detecting and segmenting brain tumors in MRI data. The architectures of EfficientNet and UNet are shown below.

Figure 8 Convolutional neural network architectures used in this study. (a) EfficientNet-B0 model for image classification, and (b) U-Net model for image segmentation.

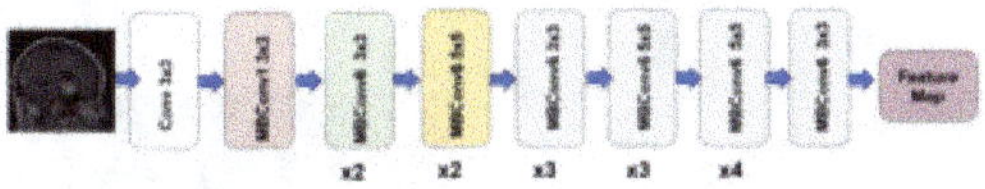

3.2 Training and Evaluation

Except UNet, all models were trained using transfer learning and fine-tuning approaches that use pretrained backbone components in the model to improve learning efficiency and performance on the brain tumor classification and segmentation. Each model underwent training with hyperparameter optimization and early stopping based on validation loss to prevent overfitting. For the classification task, performance was evaluated using accuracy, precision, recall, and F1-score, while segmentation effectiveness was measured using the Intersection over Union (IoU) metric [50-52]. Model training was carried out on Tesla T4 GPUs, utilizing TensorFlow, PyTorch, and Hugging Face Transformers frameworks depending on the architecture. Detailed training configurations and procedures are described in the respective model-specific sections.

4. RESULTS

4.1 Brain Tumor Classification Results With Vision Transformer and EfficientNetB0

The Vision Transformer model was trained using the sparse categorical cross-entropy loss function to perform multi-class classification across four tumor categories. These included: the three different tumor types and a no-tumor class. For training, transfer learning with a pretrained google/vit-base-patch16-224-in21k backbone was used which is trained with a batch size of 16 over 15 epochs, comprising 10 training steps in total. It uses a learning rate of 3×10^{-5} and weight decay rate of 0.01. Performance metrics, including mean accuracy, F1 score, precision, and recall for each class, are summarized in Table 1, providing insight into the model's classification capabilities across different tumor classes. Figure 9 presents the confusion matrix, which visualizes the distribution of correct and misclassified predictions across the classes. The overall accuracy of the VIT model for 4 class classification was 0.78.

Figure 9 (left) Training and validation loss curves for vision transformer (right) Confusion matrix for the different image classes (0- glioma, 1-no tumor, 2- meningioma, 3- pituitary)

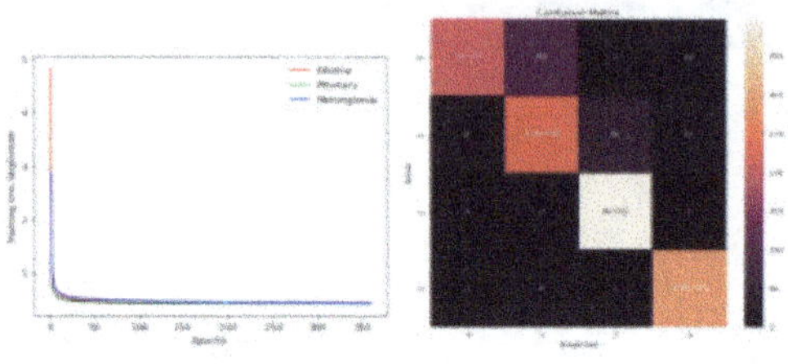

The EfficientNetB0 model for image classification used pre-trained weights from ImageNet and was trained with transfer learning. To adapt the architecture for the specific classification task, the include_top parameter was set to False, which removed the default fully connected classification layer and allowed the addition of custom layers tailored to the target classes. Input images were uniformly resized to 224x224 pixels to match the model's expected input dimensions. The model was compiled using the categorical cross-entropy loss function which is typically used for multi-class classification problems along with the Adam optimizer.. Training was done for 20 epochs with a batch size of 32. The model demonstrated strong performance, achieving a validation accuracy of 96.41%, indicating effective learning and reliable generalization to unseen data.

In the experiments with EfficientNet-B0 and Vision Transformer (ViT) models for brain tumor image classification, certain strengths and trade-offs between the two architectures were observed. EfficientNet-B0, a convolutional neural network known for its parameter efficiency and optimized scaling, demonstrated strong performance with relatively low computational cost, making it suitable for deployment in resource-constrained settings. It excelled in capturing local spatial features critical for identifying tumor boundaries and textures. In contrast, the Vision Transformer, which relies on self-attention mechanisms rather than convolution, required more data and training time to reach its full potential. The average accuracy of the EfficientNet B0 was 0.97 for the four class classification whereas that of the Vision transformer was 0.78. Overall, while EfficientNet-B0 offers faster and more lightweight inference, compared to ViT in the brain tumor classification task. Possible further experimentations could include trials with several other potential backbone models for ViT which could enhance its performance.

Table 1. Comparing performances EfficientNetB0 (left) vs Vision Transformers (right)

	Precision	Recall	F1 score	Precision	Recall	F1 score
Glioma	0.96	0.97	0.97	0.78	0.62	0.69
No tumor	0.99	0.98	0.98	0.98	0.71	0.82
Meningioma	1.00	0.50	0.67	0.63	0.99	0.77
Pituitary	0.96	1.00	0.98	0.80	0.78	0.65

Figure 10. (left) The training and validation loss curves for the EfficientNetB0 model (right) confusion matrix for the multi class classification

4.2 Brain Tumor Segmentation Results With Segformer, Maskformer and UNet

4.2.1 Segformer results

For brain tumor segmentation the SegFormer architecture used in this work had the Nvidia MiT-B0 pretrained model as backbone and it was initialized using the pre-trained checkpoint from nvidia/mit-b0 taken from HuggingFace model repository. The model was fine-tuned on the three different tumor datasets using images and masks. For training, a batch size of 32, a learning rate of 6e-5, and standard AdamW optimizer was used. The model was trained for 50 epochs, with early stopping based on validation loss to prevent overfitting. Input images were preprocessed with standard normalization functions and resized to 224×224 pixels.

The SegFormer model showed average performance in segmenting brain tumors across the three classes: glioma, meningioma, and pituitary tumors, using MRI scans. The model achieved high segmentation accuracy with an average IoU of 0.51 for gliomas, 0.67 for meningiomas, and 0.56 for pituitary tumors. Glioma segmentation was the most challenging due to their heterogeneous appearance and less clear boundaries. Since Meningiomas are more well-defined tumors, the Segformer model showed consistent segmentation results with fewer false positives. Pituitary tumors, which are small and well-localized, provided the highest performance. Overall the results showed SegFormer's generalization capability in accurately detecting the three different brain tumor boundaries. The reason could be the models ability to learn multiscale features and take into account global context which actually makes it well-suited for medical image segmentation tasks. Example segmentation results of SegFormer on MRI scans for glioma, meningioma and pituitary tumor can be seen in Figure 11.

Figure 11. The tumor segmentation results using the Segformer model from three different tumor datasets (Top: Glioma, Middle: Meningioma, Bottom: Pituitary tumor) . The first column from the left shows the original MR image with the tumor region visible. The middle column shows the ground truth mask of the tumor and the third column shows the Segformer predicted mask overlaid on the original image.

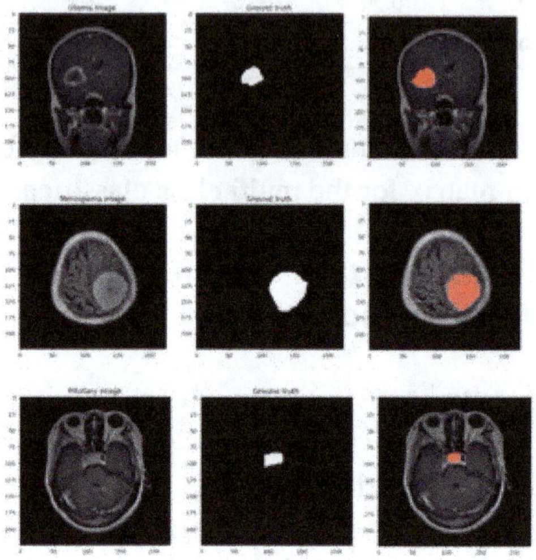

4.2.2 MaskFormer Results

The MaskFormer segmentation model showed higher accuracy in segmenting different types of tumors from brain MRI. The model got IoU scores of 0.52 for glioma, 0.76 for meningioma, and 0.71 for pituitary tumors. The model architecture allowed it to generate accurate tumor masks, even in cases where tumors were irregular in shape or closely adjacent to normal tissue.

Figure 12. The tumor segmentation results using the Maskformer model from three different tumor datasets (Top: Glioma, Middle: Meningioma, Bottom: Pituitary tumor) . The first column from the left shows the original MR image with the tumor region visible. The middle column shows the ground truth mask of the tumor and the third column shows the Maskformer predicted mask overlaid on the original image.

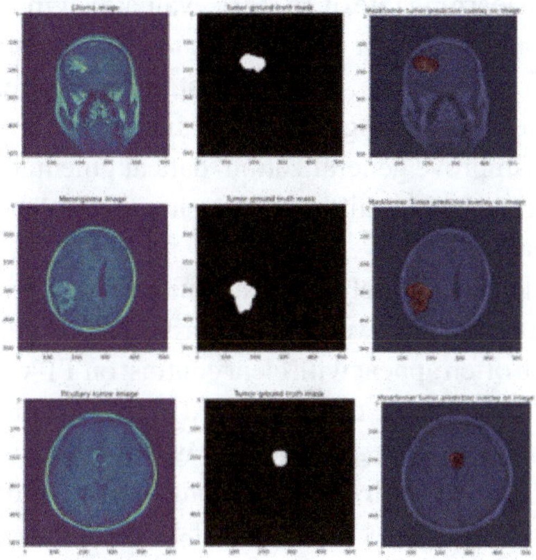

For gliomas, which have complex, diffuse boundaries, the model still showed good edge delineation region separation. On meningioma data, the model maintained consistent mask quality, which could be due to the tumors' compact morphology and well defined boundary. Pituitary tumors, due to their small and sharply defined structure, were segmented with good accuracy. These results demonstrate MaskFormer's ability to capture fine-grained spatial details while maintaining generalization abilities, making it a powerful tool for detailed brain tumor segmentation in clinical and research settings.

Figure 13. Training losses of Segformer and Maskformer models for three types of brain tumor datasets

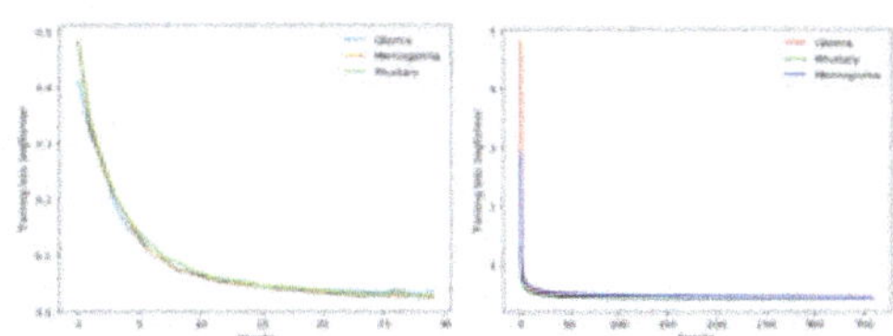

4.2.3 UNet results

The U-Net architecture was trained for brain tumor segmentation of MRI datasets having the glioma, meningioma, and pituitary tumor signatures. The supervised learning hyperparameters included binary cross-entropy as the loss function and the Adam optimizer with a learning rate of 1e-4. To evaluate segmentation performance, we tracked Intersection over Union (IoU) over a test dataset of 300 MR scans. The model was trained for 100 epochs, with early stopping (patience = 10) based on validation loss to prevent overfitting. Input MRI images were resized 128×128 and batches size of 32. To improve generalization, data augmentation was used such as rotation (±20°), width and height shifts (±10%), shearing (±10%), zooming (±10%), and horizontal flipping.

The model was able to accurately delineate tumor boundaries, with particularly strong performance in identifying well-circumscribed lesions like meningiomas and pituitary tumors, which often appear with clear contrast on T1-weighted post-contrast images. Gliomas, which are more diffuse, posed greater challenges, but the model was able to capture core tumor regions with reasonable precision. Comparing the predicted masks with ground truth masks demonstrates a good overlap and the IoU score achieved for each tumor was 0.46, 0.63 and 0.6 for glioma, meningioma and pituitary respectively. The results suggest that U-Net can serve as a simple model but may not achieve high accuracy results in complex brain tumor segmentation tasks, particularly Glioma.

Example segmentation results from three models are shown in Figures 14, 15 and 16.

Figure 14. The tumor segmentation results using the UNet model from three different tumor datasets (Top: Glioma, Middle: Meningioma, Bottom: Pituitary tumor) . The first column has the original MR image with the tumor region visible. The middle column shows the ground truth mask of the tumor and the third shows the Maskformer prediction overlaid on the original image.

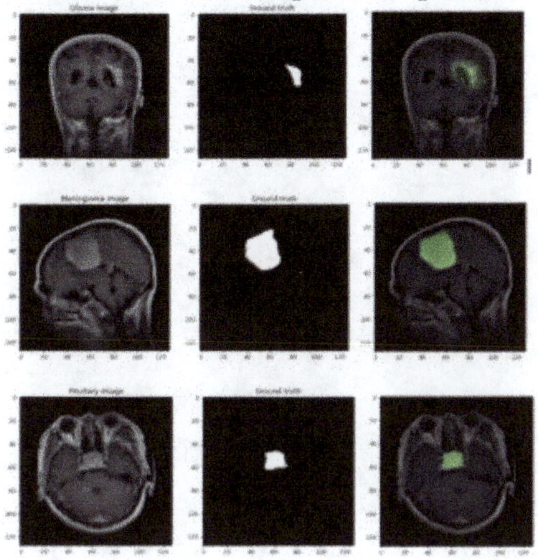

4.3 Segformer and Maskformer Results Comparison With UNet

The segmentation accuracy of the three models namely Segformer, Maskformer and UNet were made on a test dataset of 300 MRI scans, i.e taking 100 MRI scans each from the tumor categories of Glioma, Meningioma and Pituitary tumor. From the results it is seen that the best performance or segmentation accuracy which is measured using the Intersection over Union metric, is given by the Maskformer model. Best performance of the Maskformer model is on the meningioma tumor dataset. Out of all the tumor types, gliomas are the most hard to segment by all three models. Lowest mean accuracy for glioma is by the UNet model which achieves an average IoU of 0.46 over the glioma data, while Segformer and Maskformer achieves IoU of 0.51 and 0.52 respectively. For meningioma, the mean accuracies of Segformer, Maskformer and UNet over the test dataset are 0.67, 0.76 and 0.63 respectively. Overall it is seen the UNet and Segformer have very comparable performance while Maskformer achieves the best results.

The various characteristic features of Segformer, Maskformer and UNet are summarized in the table 2 below. These models consist of very different architectures which gives rise to their difference in performance for critical medical imaging tasks.

Figure 15. Comparison of segmentation accuracy (IoU) of the three models Segformer, Maskformer and UNet on a test set of 100 MRI scans for three type of brain tumors. It is seen from the plot that the meningioma tumor category had best segmentation results out of other tumor types, possibly due to its well defined boundary.

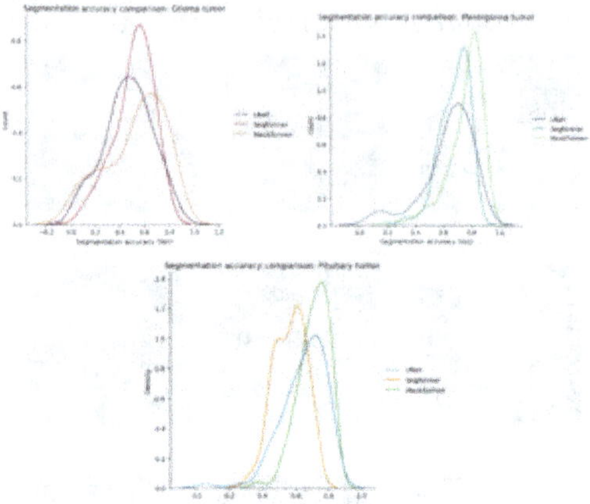

Figure 16. Comparison of transformers and convolutional models for segmentation of brain tumors. The red box represents glioma, green meningioma and blue pituitary tumor.

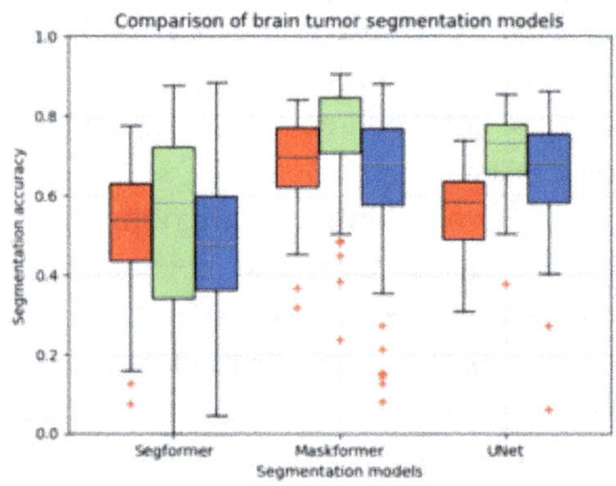

Table 2. Comparison between transformer and convolutional models for MRI segmentation

Feature	UNet	Segformer	MaskFormer
Architecture type	CNN-based (Encoder-Decoder with skip connections)	Transformer-based Encoder with MLP Decoder	Transformer Encoder-Decoder with Set-based Mask Prediction
Context Capture	Local (via convolution)	Both local and global via multi- scale attention	Strong global context via attention and mask queries
Segmentation output	Dense per-pixel prediction	Dense per-pixel prediction	Set of masks + class labels
Strength	Simple architecture, adaptable to wide variety of datasets	High accuracy with low latency; resolution-agnostic	Unified semantic/instance segmentation; very flexible
Computation cost	Low to moderate	Moderate	High (due to decoder complexity and mask prediction)
Training data requirement	Performs well on limited data but with augmentation	Performs well on limited data without augmentation	Performs best with large, diverse datasets
Output quality	Smooth and continuous	Sharp with good edge delineation	Close to accurate, especially in complex boundaries
Interpretability	High due to simple sequential architecture	Low due to complex architecture	Low due to complex architecture

4.4 Model and Data Accessibility

To ensure transparency, reproducibility, and ease of adoption, both the models and datasets used in this work have been made publicly accessible via GitHub and Hugging Face (Wolf et al., 2020). These platforms together provide a robust infrastructure for sharing, versioning, and deploying machine learning models and their associated resources.

The full pipeline for running the model inference is hosted on the GitHub link below, allowing researchers and developers to easily inspect, run, or modify the implementation. The repository includes documented scripts, sample results and metrics implementation for model evaluation, and inference, as well as utility functions for data preprocessing. Inference code snippets are provided to demonstrate how users can quickly apply the trained models to their own brain MRI data, either by downloading the models manually or by accessing them directly through Hugging Face's model hub using a simple API call. This dual-platform approach makes it straightforward for the community to replicate experiments or extend the models for domain-specific applications. For the CNN based architectures EffiicientNet B0 and

UNet, the trained model files are uploaded directly on Github and their respective inference scripts are provided.

Github link: https://github.com/anuradhakar49/Transformers_Evaluation_MRI

The full dataset used to train our transformer and cnn based models is hosted on Hugging Face Datasets. Hosting datasets on Hugging Face offers several advantages. Firstly, it provides version control and standardized data formats, which are crucial for consistent experimentation across different environments. Secondly, the datasets can be accessed programmatically via the Hugging Face datasets library. Because of this, users do not need to manually download and format data for training and testing models. This significantly lowers the data and makes it easy to use, especially for users with limited experience in handling large datasets.

The trained models Vision Transformer (ViT), SegFormer, and MaskFormer are also available on the Hugging Face Model Hub. Each model is packaged with its corresponding configuration files and tokenizer settings (where applicable), allowing for seamless integration with the transformers libraries. Hugging Face's API makes it possible to load these models in just a few lines of code, enabling rapid prototyping and testing. Example scripts for running inference using these trained models are provided in the GitHub repository.

5. CONCLUSION

This study compares several transformer-based models for analyzing brain tumor MRI images. It looks at how well these models perform in two key tasks: classifying different brain tumor types and segmenting the tumors in the images. The goal is to help researchers and healthcare professionals understand the strengths and weaknesses of these models, especially in terms of accuracy, ease of interpretation, and the computing power they require.

Transformer models represent a shift in the domain of medical image analysis. Unlike traditional CNNs, which mostly focus on local features using small image patches, transformers can understand the entire image context. This global attention allows them to detect patterns across larger areas of the brain, which can be useful for identifying tumors that vary in size, shape, and location.

Compared to CNN-based models like VGG16 and U-Net, transformer-based models such as SegFormer and MaskFormer are more flexible and scalable to new datasets. While CNNs are easier to train on small datasets and are more interpretable, transformers often deliver better performance on large, complex datasets. Transformers also adapt well to variations in image quality and structure, making them suitable for real-world clinical use.

In practice, transformer based models could help radiologists by automatically highlighting tumor regions or flagging abnormal cases, saving time and reducing human error. This could lead to faster, more consistent diagnoses. In the future, transformer models may be extended to combine MRI data with other types of medical information, like genetic profiles or clinical records, to provide a more complete view of a patient's condition.

Overall, this research shows that transformer models are not just technically advanced but also clinically meaningful. By combining strong performance with practical applications, they could become valuable tools in modern radiology workflows, supporting more accurate and personalized brain tumor diagnosis and treatment.

REFERENCES

Abs, R., Parizel, P. M., Willems, P. J., Van de Kelft, E., Verlooy, J., Mahler, C., & Martin, J.-J. (1993). The association of meningioma and pituitary adenoma: Report of seven cases and review of the literature. *European Neurology*, *33*(6), 416–422. DOI: 10.1159/000116986 PMID: 8307062

Al-Hammuri, K., Gebali, F., Kanan, A., & Chelvan, I. T. (2023). Vision transformer architecture and applications in digital health: A tutorial and survey. *Visual Computing for Industry, Biomedicine, and Art*, *6*(1), 14. DOI: 10.1186/s42492-023-00140-9 PMID: 37428360

Al-Hammuri, K., Gebali, F., Kanan, A., & Chelvan, I. T. (2023). Vision transformer architecture and applications in digital health: A tutorial and survey. *Visual Computing for Industry, Biomedicine, and Art*, *6*(1), 14. DOI: 10.1186/s42492-023-00140-9 PMID: 37428360

Alemu, B. S., Feisso, S., Mohammed, E. A., & Salau, A. O. (2023). Magnetic resonance imaging-based brain tumor image classification performance enhancement. *Scientific African*, *22*(e01963), e01963. DOI: 10.1016/j.sciaf.2023.e01963

Asiri, A. A., Shaf, A., Ali, T., Shakeel, U., Irfan, M., Mehdar, K. M., & Alqhtani, S. M. (2023). Exploring the power of deep learning: Fine-tuned vision transformer for accurate and efficient brain tumor detection in MRI scans. *Diagnostics (Basel, Switzerland)*, *13*(12), 2094. DOI: 10.3390/diagnostics13122094 PMID: 37370989

Ayadi, W., Elhamzi, W., Charfi, I., & Atri, M. (2021). Deep CNN for brain tumor classification. *Neural Processing Letters*, *53*(1), 671–700. DOI: 10.1007/s11063-020-10398-2

Bhatt, O., Kotiyal, V., Tyagi, S., Roka, S., & Mehra, P. (2024, June 24). CNN and transformer based brain tumor detection and classification system. 2024 15th International Conference on Computing Communication and Networking Technologies (ICCCNT), 1–5. Presented at the 2024 15th International Conference on Computing Communication and Networking Technologies (ICCCNT), Kamand, India. doi:DOI: 10.1109/icccnt61001.2024.10724063

Black, P. M. (1995). Benign brain tumors. *Neurologic Clinics*, *13*(4), 927–952. DOI: 10.1016/s0733-8619(18)30026-4 PMID: 8584005

Cè, M., Irmici, G., Foschini, C., Danesini, G. M., Falsitta, L. V., Serio, M. L., & Cellina, M. (2023). Artificial intelligence in brain tumor imaging: A step toward personalized medicine. *Current Oncology (Toronto, Ont.)*, *30*(3), 2673–2701. DOI: 10.3390/curroncol30030203 PMID: 36975416

Cheng, B., Schwing, A. G., & Kirillov, A. (2021). Per-pixel classification is not all you need for semantic segmentation. *Proceedings of the 35th International Conference on Neural Information Processing Systems.* Red Hook, NY, USA: Curran Associates Inc.

Das, S., Aranya, O. F. M. R. R., & Labiba, N. N. (2019, May). Brain tumor classification using convolutional neural network. 2019 1st International Conference on Advances in Science, Engineering and Robotics Technology (ICASERT). Presented at the 2019 1st International Conference on Advances in Science, Engineering and Robotics Technology (ICASERT), Dhaka, Bangladesh. doi:DOI: 10.1109/icasert.2019.8934603

Delaidelli, A., & Moiraghi, A. (2024). Recent advances in the diagnosis and treatment of brain tumors. *Brain Sciences, 14*(3), 224. DOI: 10.3390/brainsci14030224 PMID: 38539613

Dosovitskiy, A., Beyer, L., Kolesnikov, A., Weissenborn, D., Zhai, X., Unterthiner, T., & Houlsby, N. (2020). An image is worth 16x16 words: Transformers for image recognition at scale. doi:DOI: 10.48550/ARXIV.2010.11929

Gillioz, A., Casas, J., Mugellini, E., & Khaled, O. A. "Overview of the Transformer-based Models for NLP Tasks," 2020 15th Conference on Computer Science and Information Systems (FedCSIS), Sofia, Bulgaria, 2020, pp. 179-183, doi: DOI: 10.15439/2020F20

Gupta, M., Sharma, S. K., & Sampada, G. C. (2023). Classification of brain tumor images using CNN. *Computational Intelligence and Neuroscience, 2023*(1), 2002855. DOI: 10.1155/2023/2002855 PMID: 37868750

Han, K., Wang, Y., Chen, H., Chen, X., Guo, J., Liu, Z., & Tao, D. (2023). A survey on vision transformer. *IEEE Transactions on Pattern Analysis and Machine Intelligence, 45*(1), 87–110. DOI: 10.1109/TPAMI.2022.3152247 PMID: 35180075

Hosny, K. M., & Mohammed, M. A. (2025). Explainable AI and vision transformers for detection and classification of brain tumor: A comprehensive survey. *Artificial Intelligence Review, 58*(9). Advance online publication. DOI: 10.1007/s10462-025-11221-x

Hossain, S., Chakrabarty, A., Gadekallu, T. R., Alazab, M., & Piran, M. J. (2024). Vision transformers, ensemble model, and transfer learning leveraging Explainable AI for brain tumor detection and classification. *IEEE Journal of Biomedical and Health Informatics, 28*(3), 1261–1272. DOI: 10.1109/JBHI.2023.3266614 PMID: 37043319

Hugging Face. (n.d.). *Hugging Face*. https://huggingface.co

Kaifi, R. (2023). A review of recent advances in brain tumor diagnosis based on AI-based classification. *Diagnostics (Basel, Switzerland)*, *13*(18), 3007. DOI: 10.3390/diagnostics13183007 PMID: 37761373

Khalifa, M., & Albadawy, M. (2024). AI in diagnostic imaging: Revolutionising accuracy and efficiency. *Computer Methods and Programs in Biomedicine Update*, *5*(100146), 100146. DOI: 10.1016/j.cmpbup.2024.100146

Khan, R. F., Lee, B.-D., & Lee, M. S. (2023). Transformers in medical image segmentation: A narrative review. *Quantitative Imaging in Medicine and Surgery*, *13*(12), 8747–8767. DOI: 10.21037/qims-23-542 PMID: 38106306

Kora, R., & Mohammed, A. (2023). *"A Comprehensive Review on Transformers Models For Text Classification," 2023 International Mobile, Intelligent, and Ubiquitous Computing Conference*. MIUCC., DOI: 10.1109/MIUCC58832.2023.10278387

Krishnan, P. T., Krishnadoss, P., Khandelwal, M., Gupta, D., Nihaal, A., & Kumar, T. S. (2024). Enhancing brain tumor detection in MRI with a rotation invariant Vision Transformer. *Frontiers in Neuroinformatics*, *18*, 1414925. DOI: 10.3389/fninf.2024.1414925 PMID: 38957549

Kumar, K., Jyoti, K., & Kumar, K. (2024). Machine learning for brain tumor classification: Evaluating feature extraction and algorithm efficiency. *Discover Artificial Intelligence*, *4*(1). Advance online publication. DOI: 10.1007/s44163-024-00214-4

Lan, Y.-L., Zou, S., Qin, B., & Zhu, X. (2023). Potential roles of transformers in brain tumor diagnosis and treatment. *Brain-X*, *1*(2). Advance online publication. DOI: 10.1002/brx2.23

Loganayagi, T., Sravani, M., Maram, B., & Rao, T. V. M. (2025). Hybrid Deep Maxout-VGG-16 model for brain tumour detection and classification using MRI images. *Journal of Biotechnology*, *405*, 124–138. DOI: 10.1016/j.jbiotec.2025.05.009 PMID: 40350083

Lu, W., Shengkai, Y., Yu, W., Aimin, L., Shiwei, Y., & Kang, X. (2022). Case report: Clinical report of co-occurrence of pituitary adenoma and meningioma in the sellar region after meningioma treatment. *Frontiers in Neurology*, *13*, 1042106. DOI: 10.3389/fneur.2022.1042106 PMID: 36561304

Luo, Q., Zeng, W., Chen, M., Peng, G., Yuan, X., & Yin, Q. "Self-Attention and Transformers: Driving the Evolution of Large Language Models," 2023 IEEE 6th International Conference on Electronic Information and Communication Technology (ICEICT), Qingdao, China, 2023, pp. 401-405, doi: DOI: 10.1109/ICEICT57916.2023.10245906

Miyoshi, N. (2025). Use of AI in diagnostic imaging and future prospects. *JMA Journal*, *8*(1), 198–203. DOI: 10.31662/jmaj.2024-0169 PMID: 39926072

Nguyen, T. T. T., Greene, L. A., Mnatsakanyan, H., & Badr, C. E. (2024). Revolutionizing brain tumor care: Emerging technologies and strategies. *Biomedicines*, *12*(6), 1376. DOI: 10.3390/biomedicines12061376 PMID: 38927583

Pinto-Coelho, L. (2023). How artificial intelligence is shaping medical imaging technology: A survey of innovations and applications. *Bioengineering (Basel, Switzerland)*, *10*(12). Advance online publication. DOI: 10.3390/bioengineering10121435 PMID: 38136026

Raghuvanshi, S., & Dhariwal, S. (2023, December 14). The VGG16 method is a powerful tool for detecting brain tumors using deep learning techniques. RAiSE-2023, 46. Presented at the RAiSE-2023. doi:DOI: 10.3390/engproc2023059046

Rawat, A., & Singh Samant, S. "Comparative Analysis of Transformer based Models for Question Answering," 2022 2nd International Conference on Innovative Sustainable Computational Technologies (CISCT), Dehradun, India, 2022, pp. 1-6, doi: DOI: 10.1109/CISCT55310.2022.10046525

Raza, A., Ayub, H., Khan, J. A., Ahmad, I., & Salama, S., A., Daradkeh, Y. I., … Hamam, H. (2022). A hybrid deep learning-based approach for brain tumor classification. *Electronics (Basel)*, *11*(7), 1146. DOI: 10.3390/electronics11071146

Ronneberger, O., Fischer, P., & Brox, T. (2015). U-Net: Convolutional Networks for Biomedical Image Segmentation. In Lecture Notes in Computer Science. Lecture Notes in Computer Science (pp. 234–241). doi:DOI: 10.1007/978-3-319-24574-4_28

Saeedi, S., Rezayi, S., Keshavarz, H., Niakan, R., & Kalhori, S. (2023). MRI-based brain tumor detection using convolutional deep learning methods and chosen machine learning techniques. *BMC Medical Informatics and Decision Making*, *23*(1), 16. DOI: 10.1186/s12911-023-02114-6 PMID: 36691030

Sriramakrishnan, G. V., Prabhakar, T., Maram, B., & Datta, P. (2025). Deep Belief VGG-16 hybrid model for brain tumor classification using MRI images. *NMR in Biomedicine*, *38*(6), e70048. DOI: 10.1002/nbm.70048 PMID: 40386848

Sulaiman, A., Anand, V., Gupta, S., Rajab, A., Alshahrani, H., Al Reshan, M. S., & Hamdi, M. (2024). Attention based UNet model for breast cancer segmentation using BUSI dataset. *Scientific Reports*, *14*(1), 22422. DOI: 10.1038/s41598-024-72712-5 PMID: 39341859

Tummala, S., Kadry, S., Bukhari, S. A. C., & Rauf, H. T. (2022). Classification of brain tumor from magnetic resonance imaging using vision transformers ensembling. *Current Oncology (Toronto, Ont.)*, *29*(10), 7498–7511. DOI: 10.3390/curroncol29100590 PMID: 36290867

van den Bent, M. J., Geurts, M., French, P. J., Smits, M., Capper, D., Bromberg, J. E. C., & Chang, S. M. (2023). Primary brain tumours in adults. *Lancet*, *402*(10412), 1564–1579. DOI: 10.1016/S0140-6736(23)01054-1 PMID: 37738997

Vaswani, A., Shazeer, N., Parmar, N., Uszkoreit, J., Jones, L., Gomez, A. N., & Polosukhin, I. (2017). Attention is all you need. *Proceedings of the 31st International Conference on Neural Information Processing Systems*, 6000–6010. Presented at the Long Beach, California, USA. Red Hook, NY, USA: Curran Associates Inc.

Villanueva-Meyer, J. E., Mabray, M. C., & Cha, S. (2017). Current clinical brain tumor imaging. *Neurosurgery*, *81*(3), 397–415. DOI: 10.1093/neuros/nyx103 PMID: 28486641

Walsh, J., Othmani, A., Jain, M., & Dev, S. (2022). Using U-Net network for efficient brain tumor segmentation in MRI images. *Healthcare Analytics*, *2*(100098), 100098. DOI: 10.1016/j.health.2022.100098

Wolf, T., Debut, L., Sanh, V., Chaumond, J., Delangue, C., Moi, A., Cistac, P., Rault, T., Louf, R., Funtowicz, M., & Brew, J. (2020). Transformers: State-of-the-art natural language processing. Proceedings of the 2020 Conference on Empirical Methods in Natural Language Processing: System Demonstrations, 38–45. Association for Computational Linguistics. https://doi.org/DOI: 10.18653/v1/2020.emnlp-demos.6

Xie, E., Wang, W., Yu, Z., Anandkumar, A., Alvarez, J. M., & Luo, P. (2021). SegFormer: simple and efficient design for semantic segmentation with transformers. *Proceedings of the 35th International Conference on Neural Information Processing Systems*. Red Hook, NY, USA: Curran Associates Inc.

ZainEldin, H., Gamel, S. A., El-Kenawy, E.-S. M., Alharbi, A. H., Khafaga, D. S., Ibrahim, A., & Talaat, F. M. (2022). Brain tumor detection and classification using deep Learning and sine-cosine fitness grey wolf optimization. *Bioengineering (Basel, Switzerland)*, *10*(1), 18. DOI: 10.3390/bioengineering10010018 PMID: 36671591

Zeineldin, R. A., Karar, M. E., Elshaer, Z., Coburger, J., Wirtz, C. R., Burgert, O., & Mathis-Ullrich, F. (2024). Explainable hybrid vision transformers and convolutional network for multimodal glioma segmentation in brain MRI. *Scientific Reports*, *14*(1), 3713. DOI: 10.1038/s41598-024-54186-7 PMID: 38355678

Zheng, P., Zhu, X., & Guo, W. (2022). Brain tumour segmentation based on an improved U-Net. *BMC Medical Imaging*, *22*(1), 199. DOI: 10.1186/s12880-022-00931-1 PMID: 36401207

Chapter 4
Regulating the Rise of Transformers in Global Healthcare:
A Legal and International Law Perspective on AI Governance, Ethics, and Data Protection

Shashank Solanki
https://orcid.org/0009-0002-5923-0516
Christ University, India

ABSTRACT

With advances in healthcare, GPT, BioGPT and MedPaLM are helping doctors diagnose better, choose better treatments and engage with patients. Yet, these uses bring up significant problems related to privacy, understanding what the algorithms do, who is responsible for actions and gaining agreement. The paper examines global regulation on AI—for example, GDPR, HIPAA, India's DPDP Act, OECD AI Principles and UNESCO's AI Ethics Recommendation—and points out where gaps still exist, mainly in places with lower and middle incomes. Using both comparative studies and a focus on policies, it proposes common standards, specially designed rules for AI liability and ways to test ethical considerations. To provide secure, clear and equal use of AI in healthcare markets, the study proposes that countries come together to govern the technology.

DOI: 10.4018/979-8-3373-2038-0.ch004

1. INTRODUCTION

1.1 Background: The Rise of Transformer-Based AI in Global Healthcare

Through transformer-based technology in AI and the prominent use of Bio BERT and Clinical BERT, healthcare is changing all over the world. Thanks to their skills in contextual analysis and language processing, these models have the potential to take over many tasks in hospitals, make diagnostics better, drive drug research and provide a more open way for patients and doctors to interact (Al Kuwaiti et al., 2023). These models are not limited to analysis; they also support the rapid combination and use of health records, medical journal articles, genomic data and systems for remote medical treatment. For example, medical corpora trained onto LLMs may help doctors examine potential diagnoses, notice negative drug-drug interactions and predict the further course of disease based on different collected information.

Meanwhile, putting these tools into healthcare settings has caused many legal, ethical and regulatory concerns. With data being used in different countries, secretive algorithms in healthcare and without consistent worldwide laws, there are big challenges to patient privacy, clinical accountability and human rights. As such systems start to be used in making choices, doubts about their conformity to existing rules, like those on suggested treatment, errors in medical actions and privacy of medical data, have arisen (Chow, Wong, & Li, 2024). This chapter seeks to answer this increasing conflict between creative thinking and rules. This research probes the impacts of AI on healthcare as seen through a close study of international law, different frameworks and ethical guidelines.

1.2 Purpose and Scope of the Chapter

This chapter mainly focuses on exploring the standards and principles used to govern how transformer-based artificial intelligence is introduced into healthcare services around the globe (Randazzo & Hill, 2024). The analysis is made of how global, local and national laws interact with the emerging governance issues related to AI, mostly when healthcare data, the way algorithms work, liability and cross-border adherence are involved.

Specifically, this chapter:

- Examines the guidelines that apply to using LLMs and transformer models in healthcare.

- Analyzes how the GDPR, HIPAA, India's DPDP Act, 2023 and OECD AI Principles interact with UNESCO's AI Ethics Recommendation and the Convention 108+.
- Picks out abandoned standards and obstacles to applying legal rules to health-care technology in low- and middle-income countries (LMICs).
- Guidelines are based on views from international law, various constitutional traditions and the latest standards of AI ethics.

While this chapter neglects most technical matters related to model development, it does discuss them when doing so follows the laws and ethics (such as in bias discovery, explaining a model or tracing data) (Tiwari et al., 2025).

1.3 Research Objectives and Guiding Questions

It lists the specific objectives and main questions leading the analysis in this chapter. They guide the in depth study of law and interdisciplinary efforts.

Research Objectives:

1. The aim is to study how the current set of legal tools addresses the use of transformer-based AI in healthcare.
2. To determine if data security laws are able to protect transformer models which consume much data and need to act in real time.
3. To examine what ethical obligations and responsibilities exist for international human rights law in AI-mediated healthcare.
4. To find out which legal, policy and ethical gaps exist in the healthcare frame-works found in LMICs.
5. To suggest steps for easily implemented, fair and lawful leadership of AI in healthcare across the world.

This area is guided by the following research questions:

- How are current regulations dealing with liabilities that come from errors made with AI in clinical settings?
- What changes in national privacy regulations solve the challenges posed by transformer models using wide-scale personal datasets?
- What are AI developers and healthcare providers required to do ethically under international legal instruments including the Universal Declaration of Human Rights and the UN Guiding Principles on Business and Human Rights?

- How may resource-constrained markets (LMICs) manage finding a balance between new inventions and lawful requirements?
- Is it possible for international tools such as the OECD AI Principles and Convention 108+, to become bases for an orderly international AI policy?

This chapter preserves both the organisation and depth of its legal analysis by stating its main objectives and questions.

1.4 Methodological Approach: Doctrinal, Comparative, and Policy-Oriented Legal Analysis

This chapter selects a legal approach that fits the mix of interdisciplinary ideas in AI regulation in healthcare (Sezgin, Sirrianni, & Linwood, 2022). Using this framework, legal analysis, comparison and policy consideration allow a thorough and appropriate review of difficult legal-ethical subjects.

1. Doctrinal Legal Analysis:

At the start of the chapter, the text focuses on a traditional study of the primary legal documents that manage issues of data protection, patient rights and healthcare ethics (Singh & Kaunert, 2024). It investigates the wording, reach and methods of reading important legislation as follows:

- New rules from the European Union known as the General Data Protection Regulation (GDPR);
- The Health Insurance Portability and Accountability Act, called HIPAA, exists in the United States;
- The Digital Personal Data Protection Act that passed in India this year..

Experts often examine these standards, considering how they work with systems that process health information, decide without human intervention and transfer confidential information (Khan et al., 2025).

2. Comparative Legal Analysis:

To study legal pluralism and different jurisdictions in healthcare AI regulation, a comparative method is used. We look at how healthcare laws react in similar situations as experienced by transformers in the healthcare industry (Pinto-Coelho, 2023). Especially, we focus on:

- Legislative asymmetries between developed nations and LMICs;
- Structural weaknesses in enforcement and oversight mechanisms;
- Cross-border data flow conflicts and data localization mandates.

3. Policy-Oriented Analysis:

Last, the chapter uses a policy analysis to review main international instruments and soft law measures affecting AI and its regulation worldwide. These include:

- The OECD AI Principles;
- Recommendation on the Ethics of Artificial Intelligence from UNESCO;
- Council of Europe's Convention 108+;
- WHO's advice on using AI properly in digital health;

AI frameworks are examined for their ability to shape laws in countries, define what is ethical and build worldwide understanding of responsible AI in healthcare (Wójcik, 2022).

Figure 1. Mapping the Legal-Ethical Terrain of Healthcare AI

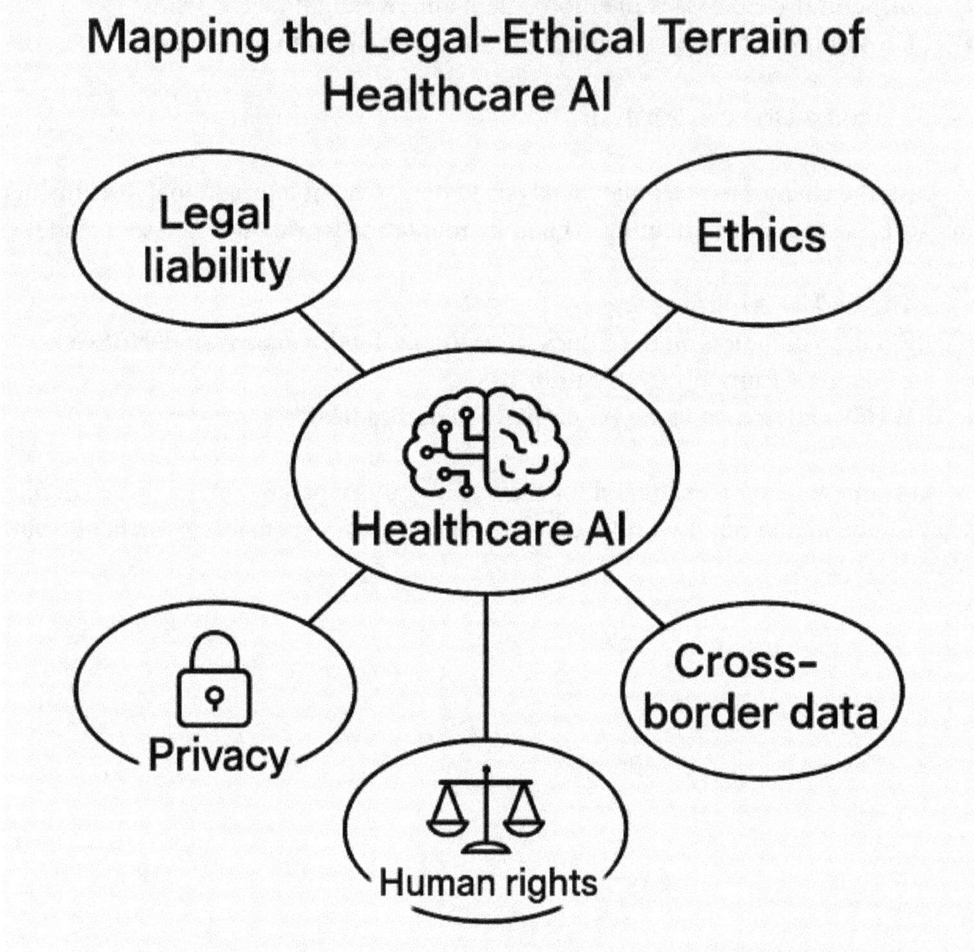

By use of a mind map, this tool shows how key legal and ethical issues guide the entry of AI— mainly transformer models—in healthcare. Healthcare AI is the main part, flanked on all sides by five significant areas: Accountability, covering dishonest actions in medical AI clinics; Societal ethics, setting guidelines for responsible medicine; Guarding sensitive personal data of patients; Challenges of data exchanging between nations; and Dignity, equality and the right to health. It provides an important structure for understanding governance problems and setting out policy solutions for networked healthcare AI rules.

2. TECHNOLOGICAL FOUNDATIONS AND CLINICAL APPLICATIONS

2.1 Evolution of Transformer Models (e.g., GPT, BERT, BioGPT, MedPaLM)

By using transformer models, machines have become far better at handling, generating and working with human language in AI and NLP. In 2017, the research of Vaswani and his team introduced the transformer architecture which used a different, self-attention approach that lets words be dependent regardless of their position. As a result, new large language models (LLMs) are being adopted in healthcare to do many clinical and administrative jobs.

Researchers at OpenAI are best known for their Generative Pre-trained Transformer (GPT) models (Wójcik, 2022). Thanks in large part to GPT-3 and GPT-4, specialists can use these tools to generate clear and easy-to-understand texts, take part in conversations, explain medical publications and write medical records. They have learned from a great amount of general information early on, so they can still learn from few or no examples, making them successful in healthcare and similar areas where there is little annotated data. Unlike Classic NLP models, BERT from Google which looks at sentences in both directions, shines in activities such as classifying medical documents and recognizing named entities in texts (Ranttila, Sahebi, Kontio, & Salmi, 2024). However, since these models aren't built for specific fields, they usually lack the details needed, so new versions are developed for different fields. BioGPT was taught by Microsoft using biomedical literate abstracts found in PubMed and it performs better than other models in answering biomedical questions and assessing drug interactions (Pujari, Goel, & Sharma, 2024). Google Research's MedPaLM is designed in the same way and focuses on detailed medicine; it has matched the scores of top doctors on important medical tests in the United States.

These improvements show that transformer models are being designed in more specialized ways for healthcare. Advancing from broad to focused applications using transformer models highlights how they have become more reliable in clinical work (Marchena Sekli, 2024). There are, however, many tough legal, ethical and regulatory questions raised by their use in healthcare, mainly when they help make decisions about diagnosing, treating and managing patient information.

2.2 Use Cases in Healthcare: Diagnostics, Drug Discovery, Virtual Assistance

Transformer models are not just being experimentally used in healthcare: they are fundamental to how healthcare is being updated, supported and researched today. In medical diagnostics, transformer-based technologies are used to interpret free-form medical details, images and historical data, supporting choices made by doctors. As an example, MedPaLM has succeeded in providing accurate answers to challenging clinical situations, encouraging better physician work efficiency, fewer chances of misdiagnosis and faster decision making in emergency and critical care (Denecke, May, & Rivera-Romero, 2024). Under these circumstances, such tools can replace professional advice and instruct on how to manage patients or decide their level of care.In the pharmaceutical industry, transformer models are cutting research time by gathering, connecting and analyzing biomedical knowledge from large scientific and data resources. Thanks to bioGPT and related domain-tuned LLMs, it is now easier to identify matching drugs and targets, predict the side effects of medicines and involve them in suggestive research for repurposing drugs. Because these tools reduce costs and development time, AI-led drug discovery is now looked at as a priority in public health and pharmaceuticals. Moreover, transformers can model many biological interactions, aiding in how personalized medicine is devised from data on our genome and physical traits.

Virtual health assistance is growing rapidly as a field. With a transformer model integrated into chatbots and digital assistants, patients can receive help 24 hours a day, chat about their emotional well-being, remember when to take medication and learn what to do after an operation. As a result, these systems lead to better healthcare for patients by teaching them health basics, lowering missed appointments and making it possible to monitor their health at a distance (Alsharaiah et al., 2025). Besides reducing mistakes, transcription software automates clinical documentation, freeing doctors to have more time for patient care. After COVID-19, people can see more clearly just how important such tools are in enabling continued care for patients by telehealth. As transformer models help healthcare , which these examples demonstrate , they also create a greater need for regulating AI systems to guarantee they are ethical, safe and open in their responsibilities in clinics (Busch et al., 2025).

2.3 Risks and Technical Limitations: Black-Box Models, Biases, Hallucinations

Still, the many benefits of transformer models are limited by different challenges that threaten their reliability and suitability in medicine. An important worry is that people don't fully understand how these types of models work (Chauhan & Degan, 2024). Unlike systems that depend on rules, the inner functions of LLMs are not always clear to their developers. Because automated decisions are not always clear, people in healthcare such as doctors and patients, do not always trust their accuracy. When a model is unable to show how it came to its recommendation, this is a major issue for use in decisions about life and death.A similar problem is when algorithms are biased. The information transformer models draw from can often be skewed, inadequate or fail to cover different parts of the population. If the data used for training, mostly comes from high-income countries or major groups, the model may give inaccurate or even risky answers when used for people from other groups or in low-income nations. In some cases, clinical machine learning built on U.S. medical data may give the wrong diagnosis or plan of care for patients who live in Africa or Southeast Asia (Avasthi, Sanwal, Tripathi, & Tyagi, 2025). It can increase the unfair treatment of people and worsen health inequalities, not meeting the medical or international standards of justice.

It is also known that transformers produce "hallucinations," meaning the outputs they generate sound correct, but are not always correct. In healthcare, since every detail matters such hallucinations may result in wrong diagnosis, improper drug choices or wrong procedures. The problems with these issues become clearer in machines with little or late human supervision. What's more, these AI models are not always updated immediately when new clinical research or guidelines come out (Cho et al., 2024). As a result, the healthcare industry requires strong rules that deal with their limitations. It means doing pre-deployment reviews, building backup plans where decisions matter most and tracking performance continuously. At the same time, these devices should be reviewed by relevant committees and licensing agencies prior to becoming part of clinical care (Haleem et al., 2022).

2.4 Relevance to Regulatory Frameworks: Complexity of Explainability and Risk Profiling

Using AI systems in healthcare quite literally puts many factors on the line such as patients' safety, respect for their rights and ensuring that medical innovations are safe and responsible. Because it is difficult to explain how decisions are made, regulations such as the GDPR, HIPAA and DPDPA place strong demands on explainability (Joshi, 2024). People are entitled by these legal tools to know how automated systems make decisions about them. Yet, it is both difficult on a technical level and full of legal risks to make black-box transformer models explainable.

Risk profiling forms another important part of the topic. Under this law, AI used in healthcare is considered high-risk, meaning developers and deployers must assess their systems before marketing, check their safety afterwards and report all incidents. They are necessary so that these systems do not create unacceptable risks to public health or to patients. Even so, because healthcare data moves around the globe and AI technology grows internationally, it becomes tough to enforce the necessary regulations (El-Deeb, Jahankhani, Hussien, & Arachchige, 2024). AI models are regulated in varying ways country by country, so bringing them across borders is a difficult task. Even though the OECD AI Principles and the UNESCO

Recommendation ask for worldwide standards on data privacy, consent and how decisions are made by algorithms, their use is not required by any legislation and is based on consent. In addition, there is still no clear rule about who should be held liable when AI advice harms someone. Suppose a transformer model directs a wrong course of action and the clinician acts on that instruction—are the responsibilities shared by the software developer, the healthcare institution or the physician? Since they focus only on human error or product issues, today's systems fail to deal with these accidents(Biju & Gayathri, 2024). As a result, many are now thinking it's necessary to create unique rules on responsibility and build insurance schemes to cover damage done by AI systems.Because explainability in healthcare AI is difficult and because AI in healthcare is high-risk, it calls for regulation that merges law, technology and ethics. Working together internationally will play a key role in establishing similar standards, certification systems and systems for checking responsibility which both protects trust and encourages innovation.

Figure 2. Transformer Model Workflow in Clinical Diagnosis

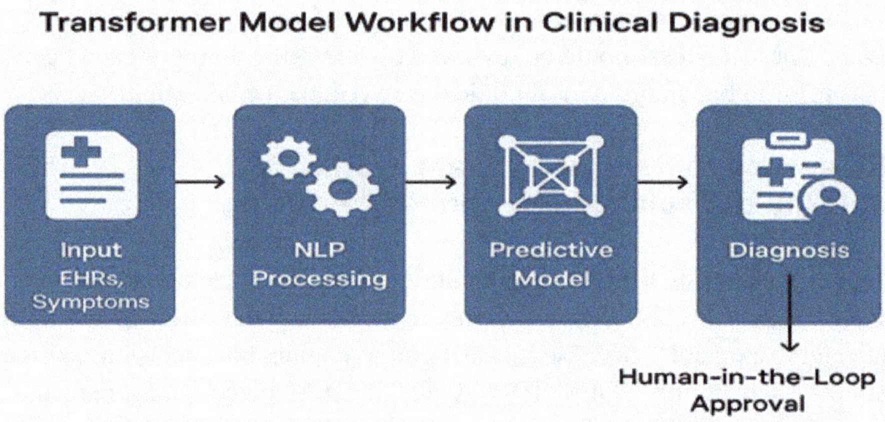

This figure 2 defined input in the Transformer Model's clinical diagnosis process includes Electronic Health Records and symptom reports by patients. NLP software then cleans and simplifies the medical text from these sources. The transformer model studies data from the past and, with confidence, offers possible diagnoses. Subsequently, the system gives a possible diagnosis that medical experts reliably confirm, following a human-in-the-loop routine. With this organized workflow, diagnostic accuracy is improved while still having humans involved which matches the Scopus rules for sharing AI and systematic healthcare progress in publications..

3. LEGAL CHALLENGES IN DEPLOYING TRANSFORMER MODELS IN HEALTHCARE

Implementing large language models and domain transformers based on artificial intelligence (AI) in worldwide healthcare systems leads to important changes in how medical services are delivered, recorded and controlled Kumar, Verma, & Mirza, 2024). AI systems that have been taught using records and logs of clinical data, reports and patient conversations have shown they can increase diagnostics, improve how doctors talk with patients, lessen administration work and speed up drug development. Still, this major change in technology also creates big legal issues (Chakraborty & Karhade, 2024). Thanks to modern practices, lawmakers are struggling to address problems that old jurisprudence didn't foresee. Here, I explain and analyze four leading legal problems from both a doctrinal and international law perspective: assigning responsibility for medical errors involving AI, the latest forms of consent in AI systems, the friction between confidentiality of data and being given an explanation and the conflicting laws when AI systems operate in various countries.

3.1 AI and Medical Malpractice: Legal Voids in Attribution of Liability

An important challenge in this field is who to hold responsible when medical mistakes occur as a result of using transformer models in healthcare. Usually, traditional malpractice cases attribute liability to either a physician or another medical worker who has failed to act according to the required duty of care. Still, adding transformer-based systems to this model brings certain difficulties. If an AI system shape or even makes, a medical choice, who is held responsible when harm arises. Presently, our laws do not cover this type of problem well (Lai, 2024). Having a model that operates roughly with little intervention from the physician brings out the liability gap most strongly (Gross, 2025). Many court systems in the US, EU and India are still working out how to handle cases of AI-mediated malpractice. However, what is debated in the United States is whether product liability applies to AI developers because most AI software changes constantly. While EU documents want to use a risk-based approach, details about how clinical applications are handled or who is responsible are still unclear.

According to the UN Guiding Principles on Business and Human Rights, companies should take proper care during their projects which might mean both developers and healthcare providers have to act cooperatively. Even so, these principles are not usually backed up by binding law. We therefore require an AI-focused framework to explain each actor's responsibilities in using transformer models (Jørgensen & Ma,

2025). It is important that this framework include foreseeability, accountability and fairness for procedures both in risky AI in critical care or surgery. Only after that can legal certainty be reestablished as AI increases in medical care.

3.2 Data Intensiveness and Consent: Revisiting Informed Consent in AI-Era Healthcare

Data plays a large role in transformer models. When computers are given extensive data, their results balance further on patient health, genomic resources, imaging and social background. As the data we use in AI medicine comes directly from its users, the current way we get informed consent is less helpful than it often is when doctors deal with patients face-to-face. But when transformer models are applied in healthcare, the idea of informed consent does not work, because the technology is always learning and evolving (Pesapane et al., 2021). Can a patient truly consent when it's unclear how the artificial intelligence in question makes its decisions? Often, data meant for one clinical service is used to create models for unrelated purposes, worrying many about how secondary data is handled.

As per the law, GDPR, HIPIA and India's Digital Personal Data Protection Act always need personal data to be processed legally, with a restricted purpose and by getting consent from the person involved (Okonji, Yunusov, & Gordon, 2024). At the same time, these laws don't give much direction on how to design consent when AI systems make observations in one situation and use that knowledge in other ones. Besides, when there is no digital infrastructure and patients do not know about health laws, the consents given after being presented unclear and complicated information cannot always be trusted.Experts have responded to these concerns by suggesting models, called dynamic consent, where patients are told regularly about their data's use and are allowed to review and update their agreement as time goes on (Nerella et al., 2024). At the same time, adding systems that make AI results easy for people to understand could help patients decide more wisely. To make certain that healthcare based on AI honors autonomy, dignity and privacy such reforms cannot be overlooked.

3.3 The "Right to Explanation" vs. Black-Box Algorithms

The inaccessibility of how transformer models work makes them a difficult challenge in the law. Because these models are often called "black boxes," it is not always clear what they mean even to those who work with them. Because of this lack of clarity, high-seriousness organizations like healthcare conflict with essential norms of openness, responsibility and lawful practices (Ong et al., 2025). The "right to explanation" is important in this field and states in Article 22 of the GDPR and also appears in the Council of Europe's Convention 108+ and the OECD Principles on Artificial Intelligence. Clinical situations make this right even more necessary. A person told by AI medication must be explained the reasons that decision was taken. In most cases, transformer models are unable to perform this task. Because there are billions of parameters in their architecture, their steps are hard to explain in a simple causal way (Mahesh et al., 2024).

A lack of connection between law and technology greatly increases risk. If AI's workings are not clear to others, errors can pass unnoticed, challenges to medical decisions become hard to address and faith in AI technologies is likely to decrease. Because such black box tools can be hard to explain during legal or regulatory reviews, regulators have put forward several possible remedies. They also mean making Explainable AI (XAI) tools which can give decision rules or show which inputs were important for a model output. In some places, there are proposals to make AI systems in healthcare show how they operate, what data they used and how they are measured (Pfeiffer, Lachenmaier, Hinz, & van der Aalst, 2024). While compliant algorithms still do not fully fix the black-box issue, they build the basis for satisfying the obligation to be accountable in law. As a result, the law should ask that AI be both accurate and clear when it is used where people's lives and freedom are in danger.

3.4 Jurisdictional Dilemmas in Cross-Border AI Deployments

As AI technology is used around the globe, challenges in deciding which laws to follow for data crossing borders often happen. Transformer models for healthcare are often designed by huge technology firms, kept on international cloud servers and put to use in many countries. A diagnostic model made for Europe could be used to help patient treatment in Asia or Africa and the computing would take place on servers in the USA. The mix of worldwide operations causes problems with which laws apply and how businesses can follow them. GDPR sets tough rules for sending data internationally, requiring decisions on data adequacy and approved contractual clauses (Mennella, Maniscalco, De Pietro, & Esposito, 2024). Unlike many other countries, the United States' sectoral approach gives HIPAA-covered entities some healthcare data privacy, but it lacks a wide-ranging data privacy framework by the federal government. The country's new Digital Personal Data Protection Act follows a hybrid path, yet how it is enforced is still being developed. Given how fragmented things are, it is very hard to decide which laws cover an AI system when data ownership and decisions are all in different countries (Razavi, Dhafar, & BaHammam, 2025). This problem gets even tougher since international enforcement methods are missing. Contrary to trade and environmental law, AI deployment and cross-border health data use is not governed by an international treaty. Yet, new instruments such as the UNESCO recommendation and the OECD principles, set up a basis for harmonising the field (Solaiman, Bashir, & Dieng, 2024). These papers encourage transparency, accountability, fairness and respect for human rights and may be used to create bilateral or multilateral partnerships.

Dealing with international complexity requires right away setting up uniform laws about healthcare AI by means of global agreements. If companies use data trust frameworks, AI certification schemes and regulatory sandboxes, experimentation can be done safely and responsibly (Sassi & Tuccari, 2023). Their benefits would be especially valuable for LMICs, since routinely, AI systems introduced from abroad seem to catch up with local regulation faster than domestic authorities can keep up. In short, an international legal response is crucial to steer how healthcare data circulates worldwide and to maintain protection of sovereignty, individuals' rights and public health aspirations (Reddy, 2025).

4. COMPARATIVE LEGAL ANALYSIS: NATIONAL DATA PROTECTION AND HEALTHCARE AI LAWS

Many locations are finding it tricky to regulate the growing use of AI models in healthcare since globally, AI systems like LLMs and other transformers are being quickly added. Because these systems rely on large-scale health information and can help with big medical choices, making sure they are well governed is very important. The European Union, the United States and India are studied from a doctrinal and regulatory perspective in this section. They each showcase unique rules and how well a country handles the crossover of AI, data protection and healthcare (Trenfield et al., 2022). We investigate, using this approach, how the GDPR, AI Act, HIPAA and DPDP Act, all agencies from different regions, deal with the regulation of AI-aided health systems. Finally, a review is included that compares the rules in these legal systems, spots any gaps in AI legislation and discusses prospects for harmonizing global AI governance models.

4.1 European Union: GDPR, EU AI Act, and Medical AI Regulation

In healthcare, the legal architecture for AI in the European Union is the most advanced and aligned, mainly regarding data privacy, being clear and handling risks. At the heart of this system is the General Data Protection Regulation (GDPR) which started in 2018 and is generally seen as the top standard for safeguarding personal data globally. Because health-related data is marked as "special category data" under Article 9, processing it under GDPR needs either explicit permission or a different legal justification, unlike other data. As a result, Transformer models which bulk-process medical records, diagnostic imaging and notes, also feel these direct effects (Nadeem, Khaliq, Ahmed, & Aziz, 2025). The GDPR also sets out key ideas, including data minimization, purpose limitation and accountability and most importantly gives individuals the right to request explanation and human involvement if a machine is used to decide on them under Article 22. This matters most when LLMs are part of tools that can affect how clinicians plan treatment.

As well as the GDPR, the EU Artificial Intelligence Act is looking to make history by being the first major AI law to use a risk-based approach. Because diagnostics, prognosis and personalized treatments in healthcare are advanced, the Act designates them as high-risk AI systems requiring various mandatory actions. These points cover providing quality data, having oversight from humans, creating a secure and reliable system and always having clear technical information. Because Transformer systems are often hard to fully explain, following these standards can be challenging legally and technically. In addition, the MDR requires even more regulation when an AI model is included in software labeled as a medical device (Yenduri et al., 2024). The framework requires manufacturers to undertake safety reviews, follow up with market controls and perform evaluations after the devices are used by patients. Even though the EU's legal rules help ensure patients are protected and compliance is maintained, they sometimes obstruct rapid changes in pharmaceutical innovation.

4.2 United States: HIPAA, FDA and FTC AI Guidance

The United States sets up data protection and AI governance using a sectoral framework, since its overall regulatory model is built around encouraging innovation and decentralizing. HIPAA is the most important law that underlies the regulation of healthcare data in the U.S. HIPAA's Privacy Rule controls the way Covered Entities and their Business Associates can use or share Protected Health Information (PHI) while protecting peoples' medical records. If transformer-based AI tools use PHI at hospitals, insurers or digital health platforms, HIPAA will cover their use (Rashid, Ahmed, Nadeem, Zafar, & Yousaf, 2025). Yet, HIPAA does not always include tech and startup firms working in AI for health, so many aspects related to these companies' activities can go unregulated. Besides, algorithms are not required by HIPAA to be clear or fair, so ethical issues are mostly ignored.

Because the existing health data laws have limitations, the FDA and FTC have taken action to advise on the use of AI. AI/ML-based Software as a Medical Device (SaMD) is regulated by the FDA and PCCP is one flexible technique introduced to allow for updating these systems often. Some healthcare software that relies on transformer-based models, used in diagnostics, pathology or radiology, could be considered SaMD and so would need FDA approval either by De Novo or the 510(k) pathway. At the same time, the FTC takes action to stop unfair and deceptive uses of AI in commerce. AI-focused guidance on algorithmic fairness, transparency and explainability has been published, as the main concern is reducing bias in automated systems (Rani, Memoria, Joshi, & Rani, 2025). As a result, because there isn't one unified federal AI law and because agencies have divided authority, applying and enforcing AI rules in U.S. healthcare is not consistent. As a result, the approach favors innovation but typically misses a general way to manage ethical and legal risks tied to Transformer technologies in medicine.

4.3 India: Digital Personal Data Protection Act (2023) and Absence of Sectoral AI Law

India finds itself in constant change, as it sets up digital infrastructure even as regulations for healthcare AI lag behind. The Digital Personal Data Protection Act (DPDP Act) which has just been implemented, will have a big impact on India's rules for data management. Through the Act, a consensual approach is taken to how data is used, with proper purpose specified, the minimum needed data handled and duties given to data fiduciaries (Sheth, Baker, Prescher, & Strelzow, 2024). Though health data is covered under GDPR, the rules are not tailored to the particular problems of medical AI systems. Any models used in Indian public health, for example in Ayushman Bharat Digital Mission, need to handle the changing situation with care when it comes to managing consent and where personal data are stored.

Still, the regulation of artificial intelligence has not been completed in India. Though NITI Aayog and other policy think tanks have talked about Ethical AI in white papers, these thoughts do not force anyone to change their behavior. There are no legal rules in place for how AI systems are set up, used or kept liable in healthcare. In addition, because there is no main AI regulator or ethics review group, it becomes more likely that unclear, unchecked or biased Transformer models will be used in clinical and public health situations. Although the Health Data Management Policy (2020) from the National Digital Health Mission creates some operation standards, these standards are not fully enforceable in law (Singh & Kumar, 2024). The Indian example demonstrates that LMICs have greater excitement about digital health advancements than they have laws ready to govern them. Because of this gap, those most at risk may become exposed to defective algorithms and have no proper way to seek help when injured.

4.4 Synthesis of Strengths and Gaps Across Jurisdictions

It is clear from studying the EU, US and Indian regulatory systems that approaches, how developed the systems are and how ethical they are vary a lot in governing Transformer-based AI in healthcare. GDPR and the AI Act give the European Union the reputation for having the most orderly and rights-focused policy to look after individuals' privacy, algorithmic fairness and patients' rights. The regime could inadvertently make it hard for innovation to succeed because it is both complicated and pricey to follow. On the other hand, the United States chooses a realistic and open-to-innovation model by using industry-specific laws and the directions given by public agencies (Chakraborty & Karhade, 2024). Even though this flexible system makes changes fast, it often means there are rules missing in areas like sharing information across companies and knowing what happens in their algorithms. While India's data protection system is well developed and its use of technology is growing fast, it still does not have enforceable AI regulations to control apps used in healthcare. As a result, ethical challenges emerge in cases of algorithm errors, biased results from diagnostics and shared data in different countries.

There are ongoing widespread problems: it is difficult to know how Transformer models work, assign blame in machine-based decisions, make sure users understand what the models say and avoid machine learning models making biased choices. On the other hand, every jurisdiction teaches us useful lessons about regulations. Guidance from the EU in rights, the US with its sandbox approach and India's development of public digital infrastructure can all be useful for shaping a common global digital framework (Avasthi, Sanwal, Tripathi, & Tyagi, 2025). Therefore, countries should cooperate with one another in health AI governance by agreeing on new cross-border data protection policies, shared international AI safety standards and audits focused on different sectors. Making sure national laws fit with documents like the OECD AI Principles, UNESCO's Recommendation on the Ethics of AI and the Council of Europe's Convention 108+ could provide the base for creating shared international regulations for healthcare with AI. It is important that such a model works to balance creative ideas, fairness and respect for human rights as medical transformers take shape (Nerella et al., 2024).

Table 1. Comparative Analysis of Healthcare AI Legal Frameworks

Jurisdiction	Data Protection Law	AI-Specific Legislation	Consent Mechanism	Health Sector AI Guidelines
European Union (EU)	General Data Protection Regulation (GDPR)	EU AI Act *(Draft, 2021/2024)*	Explicit, informed consent mandatory under GDPR Art. 9	MDR (Medical Device Regulation), EUDAMED registry, AI guidance by EMA
United States (USA)	Health Insurance Portability and Accountability Act (HIPAA)	Sectoral: FDA's AI/ML-Based Software as a Medical Device (SaMD) Guidance; FTC Act on AI fairness	Mixed: Implied or explicit based on context and state law	FDA's Good Machine Learning Practices (GMLP), Algorithmic bias alerts
India	Digital Personal Data Protection Act, 2023 (DPDP)	No standalone AI law (as of 2025); NITI Aayog Guidelines (non-binding)	Narrow and fragmented: Consent varies across health settings	Absent or under development; draft frameworks under MeitY/NHA review

5. INTERNATIONAL LEGAL INSTRUMENTS AND SOFT LAW FRAMEWORKS

With more AI tools in healthcare today such as large language models and healthcare-tailored transformers, a range of ethical and legal problems appears worldwide. Because digital health is global and the Transformer models work across different countries, international laws and soft law are essential. Since most of these instruments are recommended instead of regulated, they set up standards that inform laws, steer corporations and form useful habits worldwide. We look at the most important international and governmental initiatives aimed at setting rules for AI, most notably those related to healthcare (Mennella, Maniscalco, De Pietro, & Esposito, 2024). The study applies the AI Principles of the OECD, the ethical advice developed by UNESCO, the Convention 108+ by the Council of Europe, guidance from WHO in related fields and the efforts to create a single global governance system in health.

5.1 OECD AI Principles: Trustworthiness and Human-Centric Design

In 2019, the OECD adopted the AI Principles which have since been included as normative guidance by over 40 countries globally. The OECD sees AI as something that should focus on humans and reliable data—a view important in healthcare applications of Transformer models. Because these models are used in serious areas, they must work under strict rules that ensure accountability, transparency and an ethical design (Reddy, 2025).

The OECD says that five main principles are essential: focused growth is for all, development is sustainable, people's values are important, clear decisions are made, systems are strong and accountability counts. For example, using human-centricity in AI means healthcare AI should not interfere with a person's autonomy or dignity. Classifying LLMs as not being doctors is important in hospitals, so that healthcare providers keep the power to make final health management choices. Because models using transformers can be hard to explain, this further motivates building systems that clinicians, regulators and patients can interpret (Pinto-Coelho, 2023). In addition, the principles point out that accountability matters and so AI developers, deployers and relevant institutions should specify who is accountable if problems occur. The OECD AI Principles, being non-binding, have supported EU reforms in AI, along with steering worldwide talks on AI rules.

5.2 UNESCO Recommendation on the Ethics of AI: Global Ethical Standards

In year 2021, UNESCO adopted the Recommendation on the Ethics of Artificial Intelligence, making it one of the most extensive international AI ethics policies. All 193 United Nations member states have endorsed the Recommendation which links ethical issues directly to human rights, democracy and justice. In contrast to technical guidelines, the UNESCO framework is based on serious ethical and moral thinking and its call for Ethical Impact Assessments (EIAs) during a system's entire lifespan has a strong impact on Transformer use in healthcare internationally. This need is crucial in healthcare to see how Transformer models could affect people at risk, impact patient choices and increase health inequality (Mahesh et al., 2024). Additionally, UNESCO points out that clear data management matters and strongly recommends openness, autonomy over one's data and advance warning about its use. However, Transformer models depend on large, varied information that can be from across the world. Special attention is given by UNESCO to make sure that AI does not introduce or exaggerate bias, because such concerns often lead to unfair or biased ways AI is used in medicine, where data are sometimes not balanced across groups.

Moreover, UNESCO's Recommendation also looks at the environmental, labor and social challenges created by automation. Here, these issues are very important since adopting digital technologies incorrectly can both eliminate jobs and reduce funding for vital public health services (Kumar, Verma, & Mirza, 2024). All in all, the UNESCO Recommendation adds a complete ethical perspective to legal frameworks, so this document is seen as a key for outlining how international guidelines can support the safe and just use of Transformers in healthcare.

5.3 Council of Europe's Convention 108+: Global Legal Protection of Health Data

Roaming ethical guidelines direct our judgment, yet regulation of Transformer-based AI in healthcare depends more on put in writing rights and duties than on ethics. As a result, Convention 108+ which replaced the original 1981 Convention for the Protection of Individuals with Regard to Automatic Processing of Personal Data, now provides a strong and international framework. Since there are few global rules on data protection, Convention 108+ applies to non-European countries and countries across many regions have expressed interest in joining it which makes the treaty important for achieving a worldwide standard in data protection. Since transformer models run on extensive personal health information, they belong in an environment with clear legal, fair and purpose guidelines (Cho et al., 2024). Under this convention, patients have the right to see their data, change it if needed, have it removed and oppose automated results if health is involved. The agreement also handles exporting personal data internationally, saying that it must be safeguarded by adequate standards in other countries.

One important point is that Convention 108+ adds requirements for processing algorithms, requiring transparency and responsibility throughout the system. Such oversight matters a lot for Transformer models, since their complexity and difficulty to explain prevent ordinary supervision. Therefore, the Convention acts as a connection between ethical directions and enforceable law in healthcare AI, giving other areas looking to do the same a helpful model.

5.4 WHO Guidance on Ethics and Governance of AI in Health: A Sector-Specific Approach

AI raises special issues in healthcare, the World Health Organization put out a landmark report titled Ethics and Governance of Artificial Intelligence for Health in 2021. Through this document, an AI and governance structure tailored to healthcare is presented, with a direct apply-in to Transformer-based systems like LLMs designed for diagnostics, treatment options and health surveillance (Alsharaiah et al., 2025).

WHO's guidelines rely on six main ideas: (1) looking after human autonomy, (2) improving human well-being, (3) ensuring transparency, explainability and intelligibility, (4) achieving inclusiveness and equity, (5) increasing accountability and responsibility and (6) ensuring responsiveness and sustainability. They take ideas from ethics and put them into practices for health settings. For this reason, the focus on keeping human autonomy safe means Transformer models must not step in to make the main medical decisions, avoiding a loss of both clinician and patient authority. The WHO argues that clear and understandable AI is necessary to avoid decision-making that seems random to patients and difficult, if not impossible, to track and further supports having AI in healthcare systems led by the public sector, overseen by regulations and with certifications developed for healthcare use. Laws and policies in low- and middle-income countries may not be well established and they often depend on systems brought in from overseas, so these recommendations are especially needed there (Okonji, Yunusov, & Gordon, 2024). The report's guidance provides both comprehensive and clear guidelines for making global health ethics practical where people are getting health care.

5.5 Toward Emerging Global AI Norms in Healthcare Governance

This combination shows that there is a developing recognition among the world's health authorities for new global AI rules in health care. While formal agreements about AI are rare and unsophisticated, what is found in the OECD AI Principles, UNESCO Recommendation, Convention 108+ and WHO guidance together helps structure local law and policy.These new norms are mainly related to four major topics: how algorithms must be responsible, data protection, the need for explanations, fair treatment and methods of monitoring ethics (Jørgensen & Ma, 2025). It is becoming apparent in healthcare that careful attention should be given to ethical and legal guidelines for Transformer models, due to the special problems they cause. Issues such as disclosing information for AI systems, using international data for model development and judging responsibility for errors in medicine have convinced national regulators to look to international rules for solutions.

Besides, joint efforts are appearing in standardizing data, certifying AI and establishing interoperable guidelines which suggests the prospect of a future UN or WHO agreement on these topics. Global ideas from soft laws are shown in the EU AI Act and the India Digital Personal Data Protection Act. For AI in healthcare to be grounded in rights and fairness, as well as used globally, its normative development is very important.

6. ETHICAL AND HUMAN RIGHTS-BASED PERSPECTIVES

The introduction of transformer-based AI models in healthcare around the world has created many difficult ethical, legal and human rights problems. Their ability to enhance medical diagnostics, patient supervision, new drug discovery and decision support is widely acknowledged, but placing them into use also requires careful ethical thought on the level of both the patient and the state (Biju & Gayathri, 2024). Here, I assess these concerns by applying international human rights law and Indian legal rules to India's emerging digital health market. I use the Universal Declaration of Human Rights (UDHR), International Covenant on Economic, Social and Cultural Rights (ICESCR), the UNESCO Recommendation on the Ethics of AI and India's Digital Personal Data Protection Act (DPDPA), 2023, to argue for an ethical and rights-respecting framework in transformer-based healthcare AI.

6.1 Developer and Institutional Responsibilities: Ethical by Design?

The central idea in ethical AI governance is "Ethics by Design," requiring those who develop and implement AI to always put transparency, accountability and fairness at the heart of the AI process. It is often remarked that large language models used in healthcare such as transformers, are black boxes, so people can't easily find out the reasoning behind medical advice. Often, this makes patients worried about possible mistakes by health professionals, illegal use of patient information or not being aware of what the treatment involves (Khan et al., 2025). The UNESCO Recommendation on the Ethics of AI (2021) and similar documents included in the United Nations Basis of Consensus require that AI be used ethically, this way ensuring that AI is overseen, transparent and fair. Just like the OAU AI Principles, the OECD AI Principles put importance on people, steady performance and being accountable.

There is not yet an AI law in India, yet adaptations have been made based on Justice K.S. Puttaswamy v. Union of India 2017, which includes privacy as a basic right covered by Article 21 of the Constitution, which should inform any legal or ethical guidelines for AI. In addition, the DPDPA, 2023 in India links developers and institutions to laws that require purpose limitation, data minimisation and further responsibility for data (Pujari, Goel, & Sharma, 2024). That is why Indian healthcare organisations must follow both international ethical guidelines and their national rules on data protection and the constitution. Vetting transformer models by ethics committees should happen before these models are used clinically to make ethics part of the system, not just reactive.

6.2 Balancing Innovation with Human Rights: The Right to Health, Dignity, and Autonomy

Investments in healthcare AI at the same time require innovation and respect for important human rights. Under Article 12 of the ICESCR, all individuals should have the opportunity to enjoy the highest achievable health by law. Article 21 of the Indian Constitution leads people to see the right to work which has been established by cases such as Paschim Banga Khet Mazdoor Samity v. In State of West Bengal (1996), the Supreme Court said that healthcare should be made available to all by the government (Avasthi, Sanwal, Tripathi, & Tyagi, 2025). Correctly regulated and implemented, transformer models will be able to significantly impact this right by helping with early discovery, targeted care and remote medicine.

Even so, the use of such technology should not take away people's rights to dignity and autonomy which are basic principles found in the UDHR and the ICCPR. When a doctor depends on transformer models for advice, patients who aren't able to understand the model may not be fully aware of the treatment decisions they are agreeing to. The need is greatest in India, as there are big differences in literacy and digital usage from one area to another. Consent to process data should be free, exact, clear and unambiguous, so systems using AI have to provide an explanation (Chow, Wong, & Li, 2024). AI explainability guidelines from the EU and UNESCO, for example, need to be adapted in each country to keep rights above the realm of innovation.

6.3 Algorithmic Fairness, Bias, and Non-Discrimination

Healthcare AI often comes into difficulty because of algorithmic bias and this can create unfair results for marginalized communities. Transformer models that rely on narrow datasets may incorrectly evaluate health for underrepresented groups which maintains current unequal treatment in healthcare (Al Kuwaiti et al., 2023). If most of its training data comes from Indians in cities, a model may not include clinical situations of people from tribal or rural areas, thus breaking the principle of equal care. States are urged by ICERD and Article 14 of the Indian Constitution to eliminate all types of discrimination, including the indirect kind driven by data processes.

India's Data Protection Law 2023 stops algorithms from causing harm by requiring fair data processing and by banning data use that could lead to discrimination. Still, if there are no set guidelines for fair algorithms, developers could still use biased information or similar, but discriminatory, factors. For that reason, it is essential to set up and maintain special bias audit, fairness and impact assessment procedures for use in healthcare (Pesapane et al., 2021). The EU's AI Act and the Council of Europe's Convention 108+ recommend what Indian authorities should consider when creating AI regulation. Crucially, people affected by AI decisions in healthcare should have the ability to contest them, when it is about diagnosis, treatment or healthcare insurance.

6.4 Obligations under International Human Rights Law and Global Health Law

Their cross-border design and use mean that transformer models should be in compliance with international human rights and global health rules. The State is called upon by the ICESCR, the ICCPR and the UDHR to respect, protect and fulfill every right they are entitled to. So, in healthcare AI, the government needs to direct private companies, require ethical decisions by public health bodies and ensure individuals are safe from AI harms such as broken privacy, bad diagnoses and unfair valuing (Rani, Memoria, Joshi, & Rani, 2025). For ethical AI use to occur across different countries, norms provided by UNESCO and OECD are most appropriate. In the same year, the WHO's Guidance on Ethics and Governance of AI for Health (2021) underlined the importance of fair and equal governance, greater health accessibility and clear explanation of how algorithms make decisions about health. According to the Council of Europe's Convention 108+, there are enforceable rules for data protection when computers or systems make choices and when data is transferred between countries (Razavi, Dhafar, & BaHammam, 2025).

Though India is not included in Convention 108+, it is one of the UN's core human rights treaty signatories, and the Supreme Court has often found that protecting privacy and autonomy in technical spaces is a government duty. So, Indian policymakers have to align their AI strategies with standards from across the globe, mainly because many countries are suggesting a global treaty similar to the Paris Agreement for climate change. In addition, India must take part in global discussions about AI (such as those at the Global Partnership on AI and G20 AI) to participate in setting rules and to encourage LMICs to be equal to those setting rules for AI.Moore's paper points out that the ethical and human rights aspects of transformer-based AI in healthcare should be highly visible in any governance discussion, because of the major role these models play in directing clinical actions, influencing patients and shaping healthcare service delivery. All those involved in data science should operate with fairness, ensure all decisions are understandable and let others see their processes (Sassi & Tuccari, 2023). It is essential for India, as well as other developing countries, to bring national laws and regulations into line with international human rights principles. Without using a rights-focused and ethically sound method, we cannot stop AI in healthcare from causing problems for dignity, fairness and justice. Innovation should be part of the plan, but its goals must remain connected to ethics, equity and the law.

Figure 3. Ethical Compliance Model for AI in Healthcare

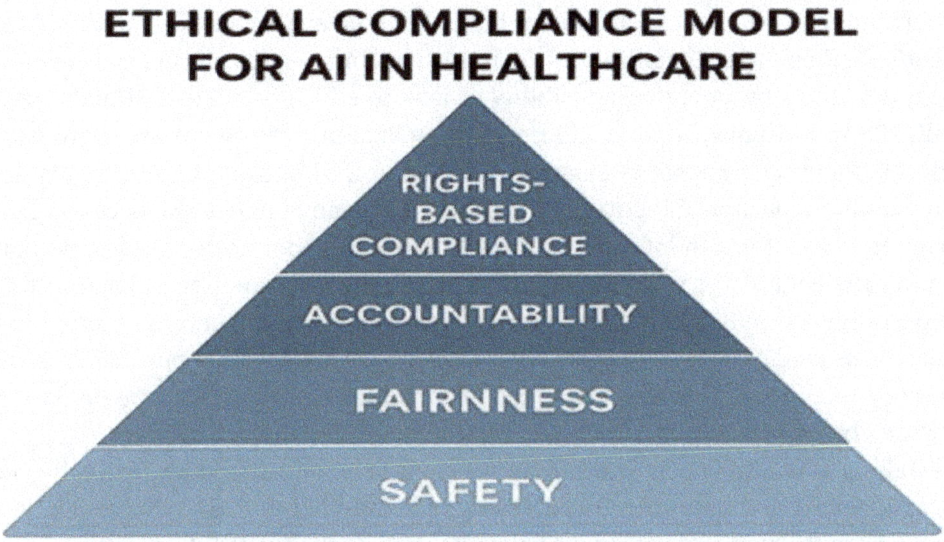

The model suggests a system of ethical priorities to help use AI in healthcare. Primarily, Safety looks after the safety of patients by giving the first importance to the accuracy and safety of the applications. By being fair, algorithms remove their own bias and allow all people to use AI in healthcare. Those responsible for medical algorithms are expected by law to act transparently and face the consequences for what the algorithms do. The highest priority is to ensure compliance with important human rights, including informed consent, privacy and autonomy. The approach starts first with basic concerns in clinical care and moves up to foundational legal principles.

7. GOVERNANCE GAPS IN LMICS: REGULATION IN RESOURCE-CONSTRAINED SETTINGS

Transformer-based AI being used rapidly in healthcare in LMICs raises both great hopes and many weaknesses in regulations. Because of widespread enthusiasm globally for LLMs and transformers, LMICs are using these technologies to manage healthcare needs that were long unmet such as rural access to diagnostics, disease monitoring and working with patients who use multiple languages. At the same time, most nations do not have the laws in place to match their enthusiasm for technology. In many LMICs, there are few or no effective laws on data protection, explainable algorithms and who is responsible for them. With no special laws governing AI in healthcare, healthcare organizations are free to use complicated transformers without clear directions on safety, responsibility or how to ethically use data (Randazzo & Hill, 2024). In Kenya, Nigeria and Bangladesh, healthcare systems are using AI in pilots before important safety standards are in place. Moreover, if there are big differences in innovation and governance worldwide, many LMICs risk becoming the main provider of health information for training AI by foreign companies, without getting the benefits or rules that apply to the foreign corporations. Because they import digitals tools and models, LMICs now depend even more on them, often since these cannot be locally checked or managed. This situation puts patients and these systems at risk of being exploited or monitored unfairly, without any proper lawsuits being possible.

Taking this into account, bringing national laws into line with upcoming international AI and data rules is necessary, not only helpful. Even so, in LMICs, bringing in the standards set by instruments such as the GDPR, Convention 108+ and UNESCO's AI Ethics Recommendations is often difficult because of problems with their institutions and culture. Using the same legal rules everywhere could keep disadvantaged groups apart even more, since tools created for the North may not suit local ways, priorities or levels of digital education (Joshi, 2024). Thus, this paper proposes using governance models that respond to local situations, depend on risk assessment and rely on sandboxes, flexible compliance strategies and strong communication with stakeholders. Further, addressing capacity gaps is particularly important because of what international financial institutions (IFIs) and multilateral development agencies do (Marchena Sekli, 2024). The World Bank, WHO and UNDP need to do more than just fund digital health tech—they should help build ethical and reliable AI systems as well. It covers helping to finance regulatory organizations, preparing internationally working healthcare experts and legal experts and adding government policies to donor agreements. Crucially, global AI should not just be introduced in LMICs, but they ought to play an important role in shaping how it functions worldwide (Busch et al., 2025). Finally, fixing governance issues in LMICs means using local laws, working together internationally and being ethical to make sure healthcare driven by transformers does not harms people's rights, safety or their country's health data and technology.

8. CASE STUDIES AND POLICY LEARNING

The correct usage of transformer models in health care depends on gathering lessons from practical examples. Low balanced models of legal frameworks and ethics drive theory analysis, but only studies, experience within organizations and actions of regulators can evaluate their real effectiveness. In this section, a number of national and institutional cases are examined, along with new court judgments, to illustrate the achievements, disappointments and important lessons guiding AI regulation in healthcare around the world (Chauhan & Degan, 2024). The examples below show us lessons from early AI adoption and developed policies, helping guide better international AI governance.

8.1 IBM Watson in Oncology: Lessons from Premature AI Deployment

IBM Watson for Oncology illustrates what might happen if artificial intelligence is launched before it is entirely ready for clinical use. As a topsystem meant to help decide treatment plans for each cancer patient, Watson or been used in many hospitals across the U.S., India and other nations. Even so, assessments done later discovered that many times its performance was worse than hoped for in clinical settings. Sometimes Watson advised patients to receive treatment that was not considered safe or effective, increasing doubt about its accuracy.Watson's use revealed a number of administrative failings. Clinically, the tool was introduced before it was well validated and so it entered use in serious settings without strong testing. Second, information about the algorithm's boundaries or how much human monitoring is used did not always reach both patients and clinicians. Because of this, patients lost their right to know about medications and could suffer bad outcomes (Pesapane et al., 2021). No one was clear about who should answer for medical errors caused by AI—the manufacturer, the hospital or the person operating the technology.

One point from this case is that greater pre-market regulation, monitoring in use and open communication with end users are important. Such research shows we must decide on AI audit trails, explainability rules and ethical approval processes prior to using AI in medical settings (Lai, 2024). Overall, I discovered from IBM Watson that allowing unchecked innovation in healthcare can cause problems.

8.2 Successful National Initiatives: Canada, Finland, and Singapore

Although using AI in healthcare has faced some problems, countries taking different strategies are showing how AI can be properly governed. Canada, Finland

and Singapore have set up systems that put ethical values, safe results for patients and lawful practices first in using AI in healthcare (Trenfield et al., 2022).

Canada's AI Strategy and Healthcare Integration

The Management of Canada's Pan-Canadian AI Strategy by the Canadian Institute for Advanced Research (CIFAR), follows innovative principles in government. It's particularly significant that the government built the Algorithmic Impact Assessment (AIA) tool. A risk assessment needed by AI in public services—including healthcare—must worry about privacy, fairness and accountability (Sezgin, Sirrianni, & Linwood, 2022). As a result, healthcare institutions now test AI tools ahead of using them and thus ensure they are following the law and winning the public's confidence.

Finland's AuroraAI Programme

Finland stands out globally in designing AI for people thanks to its AuroraAI project. The programme makes sure to use AI in government services in a way that protects people's independence and sticks to GDPR rules. Applications designed by AuroraAI center on making service personal and connecting different hospitals' patient data (Singh & Kumar, 2024). Designing data protection into everything displays how Finland operationalizes privacy-by-design in policy.

Singapore's Model AI Governance Framework

The updated Model AI Governance Framework from Singapore supports AI usage in high-risk industries, for example, healthcare. The framework asks developers and implementers to use human-in-the-loop design, perform DPIAs and put in place constant risk monitoring systems. As a result, Singapore is a prime example of how regulating AI, partnering with sectors and heavy government oversight can help both innovation and the protection of patients and their safety.

8.3 Institutional Governance Models: AI Ethics Boards and Hospital AI Committees

Healthcare AI is influenced equally by national strategies and the mechanisms set up by different healthcare institutions (Denecke, May, & Rivera-Romero, 2024). More and more, hospitals, research institutes and medical schools are creating teams to review and control the use of AI tools. They help to join theory in law with its use in medical care.

AI Ethics Boards

Usually, AI Ethics Boards bring together ethicists, experts in the law, clinicians and engineers experienced in AI. When working on algorithms, their task is to check for bias, pay attention to fairness, get informed consent and try to make the tasks low-risk. To promote uniformity such boards often conform their activities to general ethical recommendations set by UNESCO and other similar organizations worldwide (Haleem et al., 2022).

Hospital AI Committees

Along with ethics boards, new AI committees are forming inside hospitals to make sure practices closely follow all standards. Many of these committees have the role of:

- Checking whether AI tools meet the needs to be used in clinical practice;
- Complying with regulations such as maintaining privacy, setting responsibility for issues and obtaining people's signed permission;
- Preparing healthcare teams about what the law says regarding AI.

Organisational governance models review how AI is used in the workplace, working with worldwide and national rules for AI. They are an important part of the system needed to ensure healthcare AI is used safely and ethically.

8.4 Case Law Trends and Regulatory Interventions in Healthcare AI

Because AI is being used more and more in healthcare, courts and agencies tasked with regulation are having to apply existing laws in different circumstances (Ong et al., 2025). There is not much case law or regulatory action on transformer-based AI yet, but some major topics are becoming clear from different places.

European Union

AI regulation in the EU has been primarily built on the General Data Protection Regulation (GDPR). Given recent rules and court decisions, healthcare providers now know better how Article 22 of GDPR applies to handling decisions made by machines in healthcare (Kumar, Verma, & Mirza, 2024). The new EU AI Act takes this one step further by listing most healthcare AI tools as "high-risk" and asking for strict requirements for them to be transparent, accurate and supervised by humans.

United States

To keep up, the Food and Drug Administration is now adjusting its Software as a Medical Device guideline to incorporate AI and ML in medical technology. On the other hand, decisions about legal responsibility, permission and proper notice are far from completely resolved in the US (Gross, 2025). No rules guide how to hold AI accountable in healthcare and courts have not yet decided how clinicians and AI should be held responsible when errors happen.

India

India's Digital Personal Data Protection Act, 2023 establishes data fiduciary responsibilities and wants to oversee how sensitive health data is collected, kept and sent abroad. There are very few rules about AI in the healthcare sector made under the Act so far. Currently, inadequate laws and unclear rules exist for liability and ethics, mostly involving startups and partnerships in the digital health area.

Global Regulatory Gaps and Emerging Principles

An ongoing problem in these areas is that healthcare has no separate rules on liability for AI. Even so, while principles related to algorithms being clear, being fair and supervised by humans are mentioned more in soft-law frameworks (such as the OECD AI Principles), their implementation does not happen evenly (Avasthi, Sanwal, Tripathi, & Tyagi, 2025). Different courts are starting to realize that proper use of healthcare AI depends on people's rights concerning information, privacy and feeling understood.

9. REGULATORY SOLUTIONS AND POLICY RECOMMENDATIONS

Because Transformer-based models are being rapidly incorporated into healthcare, we now have more opportunities to enhance diagnostics, treatment and care for patients. Even so, new AI innovations display shortcomings in the existing regulation systems, mainly because AI technology works across many countries (Chakraborty & Karhade, 2024). The section recommendations specific measures and policies to meet these challenges and ensure that innovative activities follow necessary guidelines. The suggestions being discussed are developed through comparative legal studies and the principles of international governance with the goal of having a consistent worldwide AI healthcare system.

9.1 Developing AI-Specific Liability Regimes for Medical Contexts

It is difficult for older liability laws such as for medical or product errors, to manage the problems that appear with autonomous AI in healthcare. The fact that transformer models decide things in an opaque way, makes it hard to attribute errors when harm happens. That's why we need to design liability systems that are meant for AI use in medical settings. These systems need to assign duties to developers, health professionals and relevant institutions to help patients clearly understand and use their legal rights (Biju & Gayathri, 2024). Adding these schemes might improve patient protection when determining who caused an accident is hard. Besides, laws ought to lead organizations toward greater transparency in their AI and require that their systems are auditable. Making specialized insurance plans available will offer consistency, reassure users and support responsible changes, without slowing progress.

9.2 Implementing Ethical Impact Assessments for Clinical AI Tools

Thinking about ethics is very important when AI is involved in key choices about patient care. Because there's a risk of bias, discrimination, violating privacy and lessening patient choice, a strong pre-deployment assessment is needed. Systemic analysis of ethical risks from clinical AI is performed through the use of Ethical Impact Assessments (EIAs). Enforcing EIAs means anyone developing AI in healthcare checks their AI tests against accepted human rights and medical ethics guidelines before it is used (Joshi, 2024). Assessments should review data privacy, the detail of consent, if algorithms act fairly and what happens to individuals at greatest risk. By doing this, the healthcare sector follows ethical rules set by UNESCO and gets more accepting support from the public.

9.3 Establishing Multilateral Data Sharing Protocols for Health AI

Transformer models are best when based on—and trained with—large, diverse collections of data that are sometimes hosted in foreign countries. But since countries follow different rules in data protection, it's hard to exchange data and advance new ideas. A protocol for exchanging data among countries is needed to ensure privacy, agreement on responses to consent and rules for security are standardized everywhere (Pesapane et al., 2021). They should always include safeguarding data minimisation, purpose limitation and supporting national control over health data as principles. Besides, organisations on the international scene, for example, the World

Health Organisation (WHO) and World Trade Organisation (WTO), are suitable for encouraging global conversation on data governance and offering standard solutions. Such schemes will achieve increased use of data needed for AI advancement and will also safeguard the privacy and self-governance of every patient.

9.4 Proposing AI Certification Mechanisms (e.g., "MedAI TrustMark")

Trust plays a major role in why AI is being used more widely in healthcare. To encourage confidence in AI-based tools, specialist certification methods should judge and agree on how AI tools meet safety, effectiveness, ethical rules and data privacy standards. In this case, a certification program called the "MedAI TrustMark" would have third parties check AI devices following clear guidelines from the domain. These would act much like the approvals currently given to new drugs and medical devices, letting buyers recognise a product's trustworthiness (Tiwari et al., 2025). It would therefore allow both healthcare providers and patients to make smart choices about adopting artificial intelligence. Having certification systems allows officials to easily compare results and ensures that monitoring keeps happening.

9.5 Strengthening International Cooperation: Roles of UN, WHO, and WTO

The global and transnational character of AI healthcare technologies necessitates enhanced international cooperation because these technologies are used around the world, and better cooperation among countries is important. A coherently organized global governance framework is shaped in part by the unique but overlapping efforts of the United Nations (UN), World Health Organization (WHO) and World Trade Organisation (WTO). UN standards can give vital direction regarding human rights in artificial intelligence and healthcare. Thanks to WHO's expertise and guidance, guidelines for using AI in health care are now being developed. Also, the WTO can use its trade oversight and data rules to solve problems linked to the spread of AI technology and handling data, globally speaking (Singh & Kumar, 2024). If organisations in these three areas cooperate synergistically, they can create policies that match up health, commerce and the law, providing a safe and welcoming environment for technology in patient care across the globe.

9.6 Fostering Public Engagement and Stakeholder Dialogue

Broad participation from the public and active involvement of many different stakeholders must be part of any inclusive healthcare AI governance. Laws and technical requirements are important, but people also need to feel the rules are fair. Fairness results from having people involved in decisions and being able to see how things are done. Inviting all these groups to regular talks helps us see what patients and healthcare experts want from AI use in medicine (Reddy, 2025). Sharing information with the community and providing a chance to give feedback help create support for privacy and data-related decisions. At multistakeholder events, it becomes easier for people to work together in creating policies that express values, tackle issues involving fairness and improve access (Singh & Kaunert, 2024). AI frameworks work best for everyone and do the right thing by making sure to listen to patients from vulnerable populations.

10. CONCLUSION AND FUTURE RECOMMENDATIONS

Artificial intelligence models built on Transformer technology have a great capacity to transform healthcare. In this paper, I have shown how the use of large language models and transformers for different areas has made medical diagnostics more efficient, automated many clinical decisions, quickened drug development and allowed patients to communicate more easily. Even so, because these developments occur worldwide, there are serious legal, ethical and regulatory issues that call for strong global cooperation. It is pointed out by this research that the EU's GDPR, the US's HIPAA and India's new Digital Personal Data Protection Act, while essential, cannot fully meet the challenges transformer AI presents in healthcare. Further review of global agreements reveals that new ideas around data protection, consent, finding out information about AI and being told why a decision is made are becoming established (Mahesh et al., 2024). Still, major gaps and unclear rules remain, mainly in nations with lower and middle incomes, because their regulatory systems struggle to catch up with fast changes in technology. A main point highlighted in this study is that we must carefully sustain both support for new ideas, attentiveness to patients' wellbeing and respect for their rights. Transformer AI holds enormous value and promotes innovation, rewarding both the patients and health care providers, but only when safety comes first. So, laws should encourage useful technology growth, all while giving sufficient protection to privacy, ensuring everything is clear about what is happening and punishing improper actions (Khan et al., 2025). Central to any AI governance system should be respecting privacy, making sure everyone agrees, preventing bias and ensuring everyone understands what's happening. Because of this balance, people around the world can trust AI in healthcare.

As a result, this paper outlines several main approaches for making healthcare AI governance effective, just and ethical across the world. First, it supports the creation of rules that explain who is responsible and accountable for harm that results from automated medical decisions (Singh & Kaunert, 2024). They should ensure that different countries have the same legal rules so that laws are easier for everyone to understand. In addition, enhancing worldwide cooperation in sharing healthcare information is very important. Making data-driven innovations while protecting privacy can be done if nations design cross-border data practices that recognize many different laws and cultures (Mahesh et al., 2024). Furthermore, healthcare AI activities must include obligatory reviews of their ethical side effects to avoid harm from bias, racism and problems with human rights. Besides, by creating AI certification tailored to healthcare applications, we can be sure that only clinically approved, ethical and safe technologies are selected for patient use. Special care is needed for low- and middle-income countries. Giving these regions technology, helping them regulate efficiently and updating their rules is necessary to prevent more unequal healthcare for people everywhere and encourage inclusive development. In short, successful use of transformer AI in healthcare requires us to be adaptable, alert to future developments and informed by multiple fields. Google regularly advances in AI technology which consistently changes the rules and ethics for how society views it, so new rules and methods are needed to address these challenges as they arise (Reddy, 2025). For the global framework to work smoothly, all these groups will need to keep cooperating for a long time. Because managing the challenge is hard, cooperation among many is essential for global AI healthcare to be safe, ethical, equitable and effective. Handling these problems now enables the world to assure that transformer AI provides benefits for everyone respectfully.

REFERENCES

Al Kuwaiti, A., Nazer, K., Al-Reedy, A., Al-Shehri, S., Al-Muhanna, A., Subbarayalu, A. V., Al Muhanna, D., & Al-Muhanna, F. A. (2023). A review of the role of artificial intelligence in healthcare. *Journal of Personalized Medicine*, *13*(6), 951. DOI: 10.3390/jpm13060951 PMID: 37373940

Alsharaiah, M. A., Almaiah, M. A., Shehab, R., Obeidat, M., El-Qirem, F. A., & Aldhyani, T. (2025). An explainable AI-driven transformer model for spoofing attack detection in Internet of Medical Things (IoMT) networks. *Discover Applied Sciences*, *7*(5). Advance online publication. DOI: 10.1007/s42452-025-07071-5

Avasthi, S., Sanwal, T., Tripathi, S. L., & Tyagi, M. (2025). Transformer models for Topic Extraction from narratives and biomedical text analysis. In *Mining Biomedical Text, Images and Visual Features for Information Retrieval* (pp. 273–286). Elsevier.

Biju, P. R., & Gayathri, O. (2024). The Indian approach to Artificial Intelligence: An analysis of policy discussions, constitutional values, and regulation. *AI & Society*, *39*(5), 2321–2335. DOI: 10.1007/s00146-023-01685-2

Busch, F., Geis, R., Wang, Y.-C., Kather, J. N., Khori, N. A., Makowski, M. R., Kolawole, I. K., Truhn, D., Clements, W., Gilbert, S., Adams, L. C., Ortiz-Prado, E., & Bressem, K. K. (2025). AI regulation in healthcare around the world: what is the status quo? In *medRxiv* (p. 2025.01.25.25321061). https://doi.org/DOI: 10.1101/2025.01.25.25321061

Chakraborty, A., & Karhade, M. (2024). Global AI governance in healthcare: A cross-jurisdictional regulatory analysis. In *arXiv [cs.CY]*. https://doi.org/DOI: 10.48550/ARXIV.2406.08695

Chauhan, M., & Degan, K. S. (2024). The intervention of artificial intelligence in the healthcare sector: Trends and challenges. In *Signals and Communication Technology* (pp. 267–282). Springer International Publishing.

Cho, H. N., Jun, T. J., Kim, Y.-H., Kang, H., Ahn, I., Gwon, H., Kim, Y., Seo, J., Choi, H., Kim, M., Han, J., Kee, G., Park, S., & Ko, S. (2024). Task-specific transformer-based language models in health care: Scoping review. *JMIR Medical Informatics*, *12*(1), e49724. DOI: 10.2196/49724 PMID: 39556827

Chow, J. C. L., Wong, V., & Li, K. (2024). Generative pre-trained transformer-empowered healthcare conversations: Current trends, challenges, and future directions in large language model-enabled medical chatbots. *BioMedInformatics*, *4*(1), 837–852. DOI: 10.3390/biomedinformatics4010047

Denecke, K., May, R., & Rivera-Romero, O. (2024). Transformer models in healthcare: A survey and thematic analysis of potentials, shortcomings and risks. *Journal of Medical Systems*, *48*(1), 23. DOI: 10.1007/s10916-024-02043-5 PMID: 38367119

El-Deeb, S., Jahankhani, H., Amin Metwally Hussien, O. A., & Will Arachchige, I. S. (2024). Towards responsible AI: Exploring AI frameworks, ethical dimensions and regulations. In *Market Grooming* (pp. 139–157). Emerald Publishing Limited.

Gross, N. (2025). A powerful potion for a potent problem: Transformative justice for generative AI in healthcare. *AI and Ethics*, *5*(3), 2089–2101. DOI: 10.1007/s43681-024-00519-1

Haleem, A., Javaid, M., Pratap Singh, R., & Suman, R. (2022). Medical 4.0 technologies for healthcare: Features, capabilities, and applications. *Internet of Things and Cyber-Physical Systems*, *2*, 12–30. DOI: 10.1016/j.iotcps.2022.04.001

Jørgensen, B. N., & Ma, Z. G. (2025). Regulating AI in the energy sector: A scoping review of EU laws, challenges, and global perspectives. *Energies*, *18*(9), 2359. DOI: 10.3390/en18092359

Joshi, D. (2024). AI governance in India – law, policy and political economy. *Communication Research and Practice*, *10*(3), 328–339. DOI: 10.1080/22041451.2024.2346428

Khan, W., Leem, S., See, K. B., Wong, J. K., Zhang, S., & Fang, R. (2025). A comprehensive survey of foundation models in medicine. *IEEE Reviews in Biomedical Engineering*, *PP*, (99), 1–20. DOI: 10.1109/RBME.2025.3531360 PMID: 40031197

Kumar, S., Verma, A. K., & Mirza, A. (2024). *Digital transformation, artificial intelligence and society: Opportunities and challenges* (2024th ed.). Springer.

Lai, T. (2024). Interpretable medical imagery diagnosis with self-attentive Transformers: A review of explainable AI for health care. *BioMedInformatics*, *4*(1), 113–126. DOI: 10.3390/biomedinformatics4010008

Mahesh, N., Devishamani, C. S., Raghu, K., Mahalingam, M., Bysani, P., Chakravarthy, A. V., & Raman, R. (2024). Advancing healthcare: The role and impact of AI and foundation models. *American Journal of Translational Research*, *16*(6), 2166–2179. DOI: 10.62347/WQWV9220 PMID: 39006256

Marchena Sekli, G. (2024). The research landscape on generative artificial intelligence: a bibliometric analysis of transformer-based models. *Kybernetes. The International Journal of Cybernetics, Systems and Management Sciences*. https://doi.org/DOI: 10.1108/k-03-2024-0554

Mennella, C., Maniscalco, U., De Pietro, G., & Esposito, M. (2024). Ethical and regulatory challenges of AI technologies in healthcare: A narrative review. *Heliyon, 10*(4), e26297. DOI: 10.1016/j.heliyon.2024.e26297 PMID: 38384518

Nadeem, G., Khaliq, A., Ahmed, J., & Aziz, A. (2025). Healthcare security challenges Leveraging generative AI to transform cybersecurity. In *IGI Global eBooks* (pp. 205–250). https://doi.org/DOI: 10.4018/979-8-3693-6250-1.ch010

Nerella, S., Bandyopadhyay, S., Zhang, J., Contreras, M., Siegel, S., Bumin, A., Silva, B., Sena, J., Shickel, B., Bihorac, A., Khezeli, K., & Rashidi, P. (2024). Transformers and large language models in healthcare: A review. *Artificial Intelligence in Medicine, 154*(102900), 102900. DOI: 10.1016/j.artmed.2024.102900 PMID: 38878555

Okonji, O. R., Yunusov, K., & Gordon, B. (2024). Applications of Generative AI in Healthcare: algorithmic, ethical, legal and societal considerations. *arXiv [Cs.CV]*. https://doi.org/DOI: 10.48550/ARXIV.2406.10632

Ong, J. C. L., Ning, Y., Liu, M., Ma, Y., Liang, Z., Singh, K., Chang, R. T., Vogel, S., Lim, J. C. W., Tan, I. S. K., Freyer, O., Gilbert, S., Bitterman, D. S., Liu, X., Denniston, A. K., & Liu, N. (2025). Regulatory science innovation for generative AI and large language models in health and medicine: A global call for action. In *arXiv [cs.CY]*. https://doi.org/DOI: 10.48550/ARXIV.2502.07794

Pesapane, F., Bracchi, D. A., Mulligan, J. F., Linnikov, A., Maslennikov, O., Lanzavecchia, M. B., Tantrige, P., Stasolla, A., Biondetti, P., Giuggioli, P. F., Cassano, E., & Carrafiello, G. (2021). Legal and regulatory framework for AI solutions in healthcare in EU, US, China, and Russia: New scenarios after a pandemic. *Radiation, 1*(4), 261–276. DOI: 10.3390/radiation1040022

Pfeiffer, J., Lachenmaier, J. F., Hinz, O., & van der Aalst, W. (2024). New laws and regulation: Opportunities for BISE research. *Business & Information Systems Engineering, 66*(6), 653–666. DOI: 10.1007/s12599-024-00902-6

Pinto-Coelho, L. (2023). How artificial intelligence is shaping medical imaging technology: A survey of innovations and applications. *Bioengineering (Basel, Switzerland), 10*(12). Advance online publication. DOI: 10.3390/bioengineering10121435 PMID: 38136026

Pujari, T., Goel, A., & Sharma, A. (2024). Ensuring responsible AI: The role of Supervised Fine-Tuning (SFT) in upholding integrity and privacy regulations. *International Journal Science and Technology, 3*(3), 46–55. DOI: 10.56127/ijst.v3i3.1968

Randazzo, M. S., & Hill, G. (2024). Human dignity in the age of Artificial Intelligence: An overview of legal issues and regulatory regimes. *Australian Journal of Human Rights*, *30*(3), 386–408. DOI: 10.1080/1323238x.2025.2483822

Rani, S., Memoria, M., Joshi, K., & Rani, S. (2025). Role of ViT in Healthcare Application: A Review. In *Advances in Computational Intelligence and Robotics* (pp. 153–166). IGI Global.

Ranttila, P., Sahebi, G., Kontio, E., & Salmi, J. (2024). Medical AI in the EU: regulatory considerations and future outlook. In *IntechOpen eBooks*. https://doi.org/ DOI: 10.5772/intechopen.1007443

Rashid, Z., Ahmed, H., Nadeem, N., Zafar, S. B., & Yousaf, M. Z. (2025). The paradigm of digital health: AI applications and transformative trends. *Neural Computing & Applications*. Advance online publication. DOI: 10.1007/s00521-025-11081-0

Razavi, J., & Dhafar, H. O., & BaHammam, A. S. (2025). Transforming health care with artificial intelligence: Regulations, challenges, and future directions. *Saudi Journal for Health Sciences*, *14*(1), 11–22. DOI: 10.4103/sjhs.sjhs_26_25

Reddy, S. (2025). Global harmonization of artificial intelligence-enabled software as a medical device regulation: Addressing challenges and unifying standards. *Mayo Clinic Proceedings. Digital Health*, *3*(1), 100191. DOI: 10.1016/j.mcpdig.2024.100191 PMID: 40207007

Sassi, A., & Tuccari, E. (2023). *Navigating the intersections of AI and data Protection: A Comparative analysis of the EU and US approach to healthcare*. https://unitesi.unipv.it/handle/20.500.14239/27705

Sezgin, E., Sirrianni, J., & Linwood, S. L. (2022). Operationalizing and implementing pretrained, large artificial intelligence linguistic models in the US health care system: Outlook of generative pretrained transformer 3 (GPT-3) as a service model. *JMIR Medical Informatics*, *10*(2), e32875. DOI: 10.2196/32875 PMID: 35142635

Sheth, S., Baker, H. P., Prescher, H., & Strelzow, J. A. (2024). Ethical considerations of artificial intelligence in health care: Examining the role of Generative Pretrained Transformer-4. *The Journal of the American Academy of Orthopaedic Surgeons*, *32*(5), 205–210. DOI: 10.5435/JAAOS-D-23-00787 PMID: 38175996

Singh, B., & Kaunert, C. (2024). Featuring healthcare, environment, and human rights: Applications of artificial intelligence in the health domain. In *Advances in Religious and Cultural Studies* (pp. 45–74). IGI Global.

Singh, G., & Kumar, J. (2024). Navigating the future through adoption of AI in healthcare. In *Advances in healthcare information systems and administration book series* (pp. 240–260). https://doi.org/DOI: 10.4018/979-8-3693-7452-8.ch015

Solaiman, B., Bashir, A., & Dieng, F. (2024). Regulating AI in health in the Middle East: case studies from Qatar, Saudi Arabia and the United Arab Emirates. In *Research Handbook on Health, AI and the Law* (pp. 332–354). Edward Elgar Publishing.

Tiwari, A., Masilamani, M., Srinivasa Rao, T., Zope, S., Deepak, S. A., & Karthick, L. (2025). Shaping the future: Emerging trends and strategic predictions in big data and AI. In *AI and the Revival of Big Data* (pp. 125–154). IGI Global.

Trenfield, S. J., Awad, A., McCoubrey, L. E., Elbadawi, M., Goyanes, A., Gaisford, S., & Basit, A. W. (2022). Advancing pharmacy and healthcare with virtual digital technologies. *Advanced Drug Delivery Reviews*, *182*(114098), 114098. DOI: 10.1016/j.addr.2021.114098 PMID: 34998901

Wójcik, M. A. (2022). Foundation models in healthcare: Opportunities, biases and regulatory prospects in Europe. In *Electronic Government and the Information Systems Perspective* (pp. 32–46). Springer International Publishing.

Yenduri, G., Ramalingam, M., Selvi, G. C., Supriya, Y., Srivastava, G., Maddikunta, P. K. R., Raj, G. D., Jhaveri, R. H., Prabadevi, B., Wang, W., Vasilakos, A. V., & Gadekallu, T. R. (2024). GPT (generative pre-trained transformer)— A comprehensive review on enabling technologies, potential applications, emerging challenges, and future directions. *IEEE Access: Practical Innovations, Open Solutions*, *12*, 54608–54649. DOI: 10.1109/access.2024.3389497

Chapter 5
Transformative Role of Transformer Models in Healthcare:
Understanding AI and Large Language Models – Key Innovations Powering Healthcare

Deepa Lakshmi S.
https://orcid.org/0000-0002-5595-8473
PG & Research Department of Computer Science, Dwaraka Doss Goverdhan Doss Vaishnav College, India

ABSTRACT

Artificial Intelligence (AI) is a field of computer science that enables machines to learn, interpret, and make decisions like humans. In healthcare, AI is driving transformation by introducing systems that simulate human behavior and reasoning. The sector produces vast amounts of structured and unstructured data. AI tools can process this information, integrate data from various sources, and identify patterns to support predictive decision-making. Machine Learning (ML), a subset of AI, and Deep Learning (DL), a subset of ML, play a key role in this advancement. Large Language Models (LLMs), part of DL, help machines analyze and generate human-like language. These models use Transformer architectures, known for capturing long-range dependencies in text. This chapter focuses on transformer-based models, especially BERT (Bidirectional Encoder Representations from Transformers), an encoder-only model. It also includes a practical application of BERT for detecting suicidal ideation in Reddit posts, highlighting its value in clinical sentiment analysis.

DOI: 10.4018/979-8-3373-2038-0.ch005

1. INTRODUCTION

Artificial Intelligence (AI) is revolutionizing healthcare by turning vast amounts of medical data into actionable insights that drive better decision-making. AI significantly contributes to enhancing healthcare processes such as identifying medical conditions and developing effective care plans for the disease by analyzing and gaining useful insights from complex datasets. One major way AI is changing healthcare is through Natural Language Processing (NLP). "NLP helps computers understand and make sense of human language, like the way people speak or write" (Zhou et al., 2024). "Large Language models (LLMs) are a branch of NLP that enable computers to process, interpret and also generate human like text" (Johnsen, 2024). LLMs learn by being exposed to a huge collection of written text, that are available related to medical field, medical literature, and records of patients from various hospitals, research articles related to diseases and treatments etc, which helps them understand how the language works. These models are able to learn and understand the complex medical terminologies and patterns.

Healthcare is an industry that generates volumes of data through patient records, medical test reports, and research findings, smart devices monitoring the patients, clinical trials and everyday interactions. AI models particularly LLMs derive important knowledge from the data to enrich the clinical decision making and simplify the administrative process (Khalifa et al., 2024). AI powered tools helps the healthcare professionals by providing a deeper insights into the patient health. But AI based tools can never replace a healthcare professional but assist them in making quick decision, treatment efficacy and more.

The core components of AI in healthcare include data collection, integration, analysis and gaining knowledgeable insights from data. Data Collection refers to collecting data from different sources which can include unstructured data such as textual content, image files or structured such as in a table format. The data can be electronic health records (EHR), medical imaging data such as x-ray, CT scan images and patient monitoring systems. Data Integration means bringing together information from multiple sources, different formats and converting it into a unified view. AI based data analysis uses predictive analysis and machine learning to identify patterns in health data that might predict future behavior or outcomes (Ekundayo & Nyavor, 2024). AI based models generate insights into data by providing the results in a user friendly format such as reports, visual dashboards, which help the medical professional in understanding the complex data.

Artificial Intelligence is a field of computer science that is aimed at building machines that can simulate human behavior and can learn new things, solve problems and make decisions like humans. Machine Learning is part of AI that allows machines to identify patterns in data automatically and to get better over time by learning from experience through iterative training (Boppana, 2022). ML algorithms are used to train models on data to make decisions or predictions without a manual instruction. "Deep Learning (DL) is a type of Machine Learning inspired by how the human brain works. It uses special computer models called neural networks with many layers to learn and understand complex patterns in data" (Sarker, 2021). DL models are capable of handling large amounts of unstructured data such as text or image and finds application in image recognition, speech recognition and natural language processing (NLP). As an artificial intelligence specialty, Natural Language Processing equips computers with tools to decipher human communication patterns and respond with appropriate language outputs (K. R. Chowdhary, 2020). NLP models help computers examine text, interpret the meanings of words and phrases, and produce new text. NLP models find application in analyzing the sentiments from the words of the text, translation of text from one language to another, and chatbots (Bahja, 2021). Generative AI is a component of DL that uses techniques and models that are capable of generating new data in the form of text, image, music etc (Bengesi et al., 2024). As a dedicated branch of generative AI, Large Language Models concentrate on addressing tasks in natural language processing, particularly the creation of textual content with examples like OpenAI's GPT (Barreto et al., 2023). Figure 1 presents a visual representation showing how Artificial Intelligence, machine learning, deep learning, NLP, generative AI, and LLMs relate to one another.

Figure 1. Relationship between Artificial Intelligence, Machine Learning, Deep Learning, NLP, Generative AI and LLM

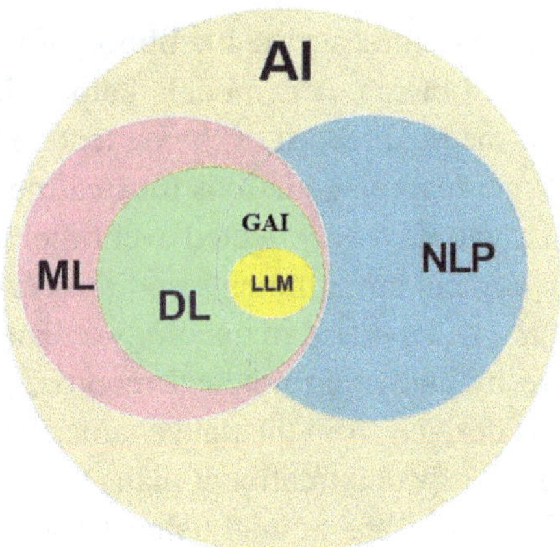

2. FOUNDATIONS OF AI AND MACHINE LEARNING IN HEALTHCARE

Artificial Intelligence is a milestone in the modern computational advancement in the field of healthcare incorporating a wide variety of technologies that allow machines to mimic human intellectual abilities such as learning, understanding the meaning of the context and making decisions. At its core, Artificial Intelligence is designed to enable machines to execute functions that require human level reasoning. These functions include understanding the concepts, finding patterns, making smart choices, learning new things and understanding the way people talk. These skills help to improve and modernize the healthcare sector.

Machine Learning: Empowering Predictive Intelligence

Machine Learning represents an AI discipline dedicated to building data-driven systems that use statistics to learn from data and enhance the performance without being explicitly programmed. In healthcare sector, Machine Learning plays a vital part in augmenting clinical outcome through applications such as:

- Predictive analytics for forecasting patient readmissions or deterioration.
- Disease classification and diagnosis support based on patient data.
- Personalized treatment recommendations driven by patient profiles and historical outcomes (Rahman et al., 2023).

Predictive analysis is used to forecast the likelihood of a patient being readmitted or experiencing health problems. ML models help in identifying the disease by analyzing the historical medical record of the patient and the present ailments. It also offers suggestions and recommendations for treatment based on the patient health data. As more data is gathered or collected over time, ML models are capable of adapting the changing clinical environments and the current health trends. For example, ML algorithms are widely used in oncology to categorize patients at high risk for cancer recurrence by analyzing medical records, pathology reports, and genomic data. The insights derived from the data enables health care professionals to take early actions and make special treatment plans to meet the specific requirements of the patient. ML models are trained using EHR data and learn patterns from thousands or millions of patient data. The trained models provide real time risk scoring and decision support for the healthcare professionals.

Deep Learning: Learning from Complex Medical Data

Think of Deep Learning as a special kind of machine learning that works in layers. It has a first layer where data enters, several hidden middle layers that do the complex thinking, and a final layer that shows the results. Each layer has many artificial neurons that are connected and the connections have weights(Montesinos López et al., 2022). A neural network is like a brain made up of many small units called neurons. When it looks at data, it tries to find patterns. It does this by changing some internal values, called weights, which help it decide what is important. As it sees more data, it keeps adjusting these weights to get better at making predictions or decisions. This is how the network learns from data over time. These models learn patterns from large and complex datasets both structured and unstructured data (Miotto et al., 2017). Deep Learning models are capable of working with different types of data, such as:

- Radiological images (e.g., CT (computed tomography), MRI (magnetic resonance imaging), and X-ray outputs).
- Clinical speech recordings (e.g., doctor-patient interactions).
- Free-text notes from EHRs and discharge summaries.

Traditional machine learning algorithms require the data to be preprocessed before applying the algorithms. But Deep Learning models does not need the data to be preprocessed and can extract patterns from the data automatically. This makes them appropriate for healthcare data which is typically large-scale, high dimensional and unstructured. For instance, DL-based systems are now employed in radiology to detect early signs of diseases like diabetic retinopathy or lung cancer with performance levels comparable to trained specialists. These systems analyze thousands of medical images to detect subtle patterns often missed by the human eye, thereby enhancing diagnostic precision and speeding up workflow. Additionally, deep learning techniques are contributing to advancements in voice recognition for clinical applications, enabling the transcription and interpretation of conversations between doctors and patients. This opens up opportunities for automated documentation, improved patient records, and enhanced communication.

Natural Language Processing: Unlocking Healthcare Insights from Text

"Natural Language Processing or NLP is a part of Artificial Intelligence that helps machines read, understand and work with human language" (K. Chowdhary et al., 2020). NLP models empower the machines with the ability to understand the meaning of the text, analyze and generate human language making them crucial for the huge volumes of textual data generated by healthcare systems. Usually, the patient medical history is in the form of prescriptions, notes, referral letters, discharge summaries which are textual in nature. Natural Language Processing provides a great help in converting the unstructured text data into a structured, usable insights. Applications of NLP in healthcare are

- Automated analysis of Electronic Health Records (EHRs)
- Clinical decision support systems
- Patient sentiment analysis derived from surveys or online forums to gauge treatment satisfaction and psychological well-being(Sandeep Kumar & Satya Jayadev, 2020).

These applications enhance the efficiency of healthcare delivery by reducing the time clinicians spend manually reviewing and interpreting patient records. A practical example includes the use of NLP algorithms in hospitals to identify adverse drug events by scanning physician notes and discharge summaries. This allows for earlier detection of medication-related complications, supporting safer prescribing practices and minimizing risk.

Synergistic Impact on Healthcare Transformation

The teamwork of AI, ML, DL, and NLP is transforming healthcare completely by enabling data-driven decision-making, automated diagnostics, and personalized patient care(Sandeep Kumar & Satya Jayadev, 2020). These technologies not only optimize clinical workflows but also enhance the scalability of healthcare systems, particularly in underserved or resource-constrained environments. By establishing a strong foundation in these AI disciplines, healthcare institutions are better positioned to embrace innovation, and meet the growing demands of modern medicine. For example a hospital integrates an advanced Clinical Decision Support System (CDSS) that combines Machine Learning, Deep Learning, and NLP to assist doctors in diagnosing and treating patients more effectively (Khalifa et al., 2024). Machine learning algorithms analyze historical patient records to identify patterns linked to diseases, Deep Learning models interpret medical images to detect any abnormalities, Natural Language Processing scans EHR to extract key information such as symptoms, lab results etc. Thus, ML, DL and NLP models have significantly enhanced the healthcare industry and contributed to the transformation and modernization of the healthcare sector.

3. GENERATIVE AI AND LARGE LANGUAGE MODELS

Artificial Intelligence have become an important part of our lives as it facilitates machines to simulate human behavior and intelligence. There are two distinct strategies in AI domain, Discriminative AI and Generative AI. Discriminative models learn the patterns in the data and classify based on predefined labels in the data whereas Generative models learns the distribution in the data and generate new data (Tu, 2007). Let's see the difference with an example. Let us say I have a dataset with images of different dog breeds. Depending on the features found in the image such as the shape of ears being floppy or pointed, appearance as spots, stripes or patches etc., the model learns to identify the different breeds. When a new unseen image is presented, the Discriminative model uses the learned relationship between features and identifies the image as a dog and classify its breed. It does not generate new data rather it relies on rules derived from training data to make classification.

Figure 2. Discriminative and Generative AI Technique

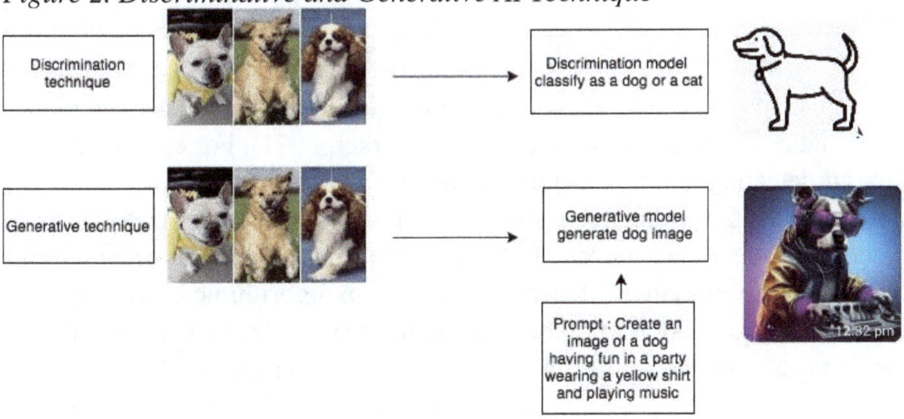

Generative models are more innovative as they capture the statistical distribution of the data and produce unseen data that resembles the training data. In a generative AI framework, such as image synthesis, the model is trained on a dataset comprising images of dogs and other internet sourced images. Now, it can perform a prompt such as "**create an image of a dog having fun in a party wearing a yellow shirt and playing music**". Figure 2 shows the difference between discriminative and generative AI.

Table 1. Comparison of Discriminative AI and Generative AI

Aspect	Discriminative AI	Generative AI
Objective	Make predictions directly from observed features.	Model the joint probability of the training data and use it to synthesize entirely new data.
Use Case	Classification tasks such as spam detection, sentiment tagging, object recognition, or medical diagnosis	Data generation tasks such as crafting realistic images, composing text, or expanding datasets through synthetic examples
Types of Learning	Supervised	Supervised, Unsupervised
Learning Approach	Finds the decision surfaces or boundaries that separate one class from another.	Captures and reproduces the statistical patterns of the data to generate unseen instances.
Output	Provides class labels or numeric predictions for given inputs.	Produces brand-new data points that is the same as original training set.
Data Requirement	Typically requires less data for training.	Often requires more data for effective training.
Common Challenges	Vulnerable to imbalanced data and overfitting.	Prone to model collapse and generating unrealistic samples.

"Discriminative AI, commonly used for supervised learning, where the model is trained on labeled data to make predictions" (Sarker, 2021). For example, it can be applied in detecting spam in emails, analyzing sentiments in text, classifying images, recognizing faces, diagnosing diseases, identifying fraudulent transactions, recommending products and converting speech to text. To perform classification and prediction tasks, discriminative AI incorporates various algorithmic strategies, from foundational statistical models to sophisticated deep learning frameworks capable of processing images, sequences, and other structured inputs (Sarker, 2021). Generative AI focuses on creating new data, such as producing realistic images, composing music, or crafting text. It's widely used in applications like conversational agents that simulate human-like dialogue, creative tools for art and design, as well as for enhancing datasets through synthetic examples as shown in Table 1.

In 1960s-1970s, early research into generative AI began with early neural network models such as the Perceptron by Frank Rosenblatt in the 1950s. In the 1960s and 1970s, researchers explored early forms of generative models for pattern recognition and language modeling, including Markov models and Hidden Markov Models (Lu et al., 2020). In the 1980s and 1990s, researchers made significant progress in generative modeling with the development of Bayesian networks, graphical models, and probabilistic graphical models. These models allowed for more sophisticated representation and inference of uncertain or incomplete information. During the early 2000s, generative modeling progressed with the development of architectures like Restricted Boltzmann Machines and Deep Belief Networks, which improved the ability to represent complex data(Salakhutdinov, 2015). This was followed by the introduction of Variational Autoencoders, enhancing probabilistic modeling techniques. A major leap occurred in 2014 with the creation of GAN, which significantly transformed the field by introducing a new adversarial training approach(Goodfellow et al., 2020). Between 2016 and the early 2020s, this approach was further refined through new variants such as conditional GANs, Wasserstein GANs, and models that grow in complexity during training. In parallel, other techniques for generative tasks gained attention, including autoregressive models, transformer-based architectures, and reinforcement learning strategies, all contributing to advances in areas like visual and textual data generation(Bengesi et al., 2024). The field has continued to evolve rapidly, now extending into creative domains like music, digital art, and design tools. Recent developments explore self-supervised and contrastive learning, as well as meta-learning, to enhance the adaptability and performance of generative systems. Overall, the journey of generative AI showcases a shift from early probabilistic models to sophisticated deep learning frameworks, a transformation fueled by stronger computational resources, algorithmic breakthroughs, and cross-disciplinary innovation spanning computer science, machine learning, and cognitive science.

Generative AI serves as an umbrella term for technologies that create new data, whether it's visual data, audio data, or textual data. Within this space, Large Language Models represent a specialized branch focused on producing human-like language. These models are trained on large volumes of text datasets and learn to produce intelligible, appropriate and relevant output by predicting word sequences(Johnsen, 2024). LLMs perform tasks that include summarization—creating a concise version of the original text—conversation, and translation, which involves converting text from one language to another. Large Language Models make text in a way that closely impersonate human language. They are trained on wide-ranging collections of written material—such as literature, online content, and news sources—to capture patterns in how language is used. LLMs can answer questions, write essays, and even hold conversations with humans. They are particularly skilled at understanding context and meaning in language, making them useful for tasks like language conversion, condensing information, and data interpretation.

In essence, LLMs serve as advanced tools that connect human language with machine comprehension. One of the key elements in their design is the attention mechanism, which enables the model to prioritize important sections of input data when producing responses. The size of a language model, measured by the number of weights or factors it contains, depends on its specific design and scale. Larger models typically have more of these factors, allowing them to detect and replicate more sophisticated language patterns According to the original GPT-3 paper, “Language Models are Few-Shot Learners” by Tom B. Brown et al.(Brown et al.,

2020), OpenAI's GPT-3 model was built with 175 billion parameters. The number of factors in a model significantly influences its ability to process and generate language effectively. Models with more of these components usually show better performance and more natural language capabilities, but they also require more computing power for both training and operation.

Self-supervised learning is a form of machine learning which learns useful data representations using unlabeled inputs, without relying on manually labeled data. Instead, it creates its own supervision signals from patterns and associations within the input data itself. The model learns by trying to predict specific things about the data, like guessing missing words in a sentence or understanding the relationships between words, which helps it understand the data better and create useful patterns. Self-supervised learning has shown significant promise in multiple areas, such as image analysis, text comprehension, and voice recognition, contributing to breakthroughs in how machines can learn data representations and automatically extract useful features. (Kalyan et al., 2021) explain that pre-training LLMs relies on self-supervised objectives such as predicting masked tokens in a sequence, deciding whether one sentence logically follows another, restoring the original order after randomly shuffling tokens, detecting and correcting substituted words, reconstructing sentences split into parts, and inferring deleted tokens from their context..

4. HOW LLMS UNDERSTAND AND PROCESS TEXT

First let us see how the model understands text. "Word embeddings are a way to represent words as numbers so that a computer can understand their meaning and relationships in a meaningful space" (Mikolov et al., 2013). A vector space is a mathematical construct comprising vectors and adhering to specific algebraic characteristics. Word embeddings are typically trained using a range of neural models designed for capturing contextual semantics from text corpora(Mikolov et al., 2013), including popular approaches such as those by Mikolov, Pennington, and Bojanowski. Since computers can't understand language the way humans do, we convert words into numbers so they can be used in machine learning. But we don't just assign random numbers. Instead, each word is turned into a vector of numbers. This helps the computer find out which words are similar to each other. For example, the words "doctor" and "nurse" are placed close together as they often appear in similar type of sentences. The word "party" would be far away from the "hospital" as they are rarely used in the same context. As an illustration, "king" and "queen" would have more similar vector representations than "king" and "car" as shown in Table 2.

Table 2. 3 Dimensional Vector for the words given

Word	3 Dimensional vector
"king"	[0.5, 0.2, -0.1]
"queen"	[0.6, 0.3, -0.2]
"car"	[0.1, -0.4, 0.8]

Similarly, the word embeddings for the words *man*, *king*, woman and *queen* are as shown in Table 3.

Table 3. 3 Dimensional Vector indicating similarity

Word	3 Dimensional vector
"man"	[0.7, 0.4, -0.3]
"woman"	[0.8, 0.5, -0.4]
"king"	[0.5, 0.2, -0.1]
"queen"	[0.6, 0.3, -0.2]

In this example, the vectors for "man" and "woman" are close together, indicating their similarity in meaning. Similarly, the vectors for "king" and "queen" are close together, reflecting their semantic relationship as well.

4.1 Self-Supervised Learning Types

Next Word Prediction: It is a task where a computer model is trained to guess what word should come next in a sentence (Ganai & Khursheed, 2019). For example, consider the sentence "I am going to the," the model should determine the likely next word like "store," "market," or "park" based on what it has learned from reading lots of other sentences. To do this, the model looks at the words that came before and tries to find out the most likely word that should follow. This helps the model learn how language works, including grammar, sentence structure, and the way words are commonly used together.

Masked language modeling(MLM): "Masked language modeling (MLM) is a task in which part of the words in the text is randomly replaced with a special token, such as a blank or a placeholder" (Salazar et al., 2020). The model then tries to guess the missing words by looking at the nearby words in the sentence for clues. The idea is that, by predicting the hidden words, the model learns how language works—like understanding which words are likely to appear together and how sentences are structured. Instead of just memorizing common phrases, the model develops a deeper understanding of how language works by trying to find out what word best fits the context based on the other words around it. This method helps the model learn about syntax (how words are ordered) and semantics (what the words mean). Let's say we mask the word "great" in the sentence:

"Today is a [MASK] day."

The training process teaches the model to find out the missing words by looking at the words around them in the sentence. In this example, the model would predict that the masked word is likely to be an adjective describing the day. The model generates meaningful predictions for masked words in similar contexts, such as *"wonderful," "beautiful," or "sunny".*

Next Sentence Prediction(NSP): "It is a type of training where the model learns to determine if two sentences come one after another in the original text"(Yuyun et al., 2023). By learning to predict how sentences are related, the model better understands how text flows and makes sense. This helps the model create text that is clear, logical, and fits well with the context around it.

Example sentence:

"The sun was shining brightly in the sky."

"People were enjoying the warm weather in the park."

The model is trained to assess whether the second sentence maintains narrative coherence and logically follows the first. Given the first sentence "The sun was shining brightly in the sky.", the model should determine whether the second sentence "People were enjoying the warm weather in the park." is a likely continuation based on the context established in the first sentence. A well-trained model would predict a high probability for the second sentence, as it follows logically from the sunny weather described in the first sentence.

Token Permutation: In token permutation, the order of words in a sentence is mixed up randomly. The model learns to determine the correct order of the words by looking at the shuffled sentence. This helps the model understand how different parts of the text are connected, and it makes it better at understanding the overall structure of the text.

Original Sentence: "The cat sat on the mat."

In token permutation, the order of tokens within the sequence is randomly shuffled or permuted. Let's apply token permutation to the original sentence:

Permuted Sentence: "The mat cat sat on the."

In this example, the tokens *"cat" and "mat"* have swapped positions compared to the original sentence. "Token permutation tasks the model with predicting the original order of tokens based on the shuffled sequence"(Chen et al., 2024). To successfully restore the original sentence from a permuted version, the model needs to comprehend the inherent structural patterns and dependencies within the language. A model trained on token permutation is tasked with predicting the original order of tokens from the scrambled sequence.

Sentence Order Prediction: In this task, the model learns to infer if two sentences are in the correct order (Logeswaran et al., 2018). The model gets better at understanding how sentences should flow by learning to tell the difference between pairs of sentences that are in the right order and those that aren't.

Replaced Token Detection: This method works by swapping out certain words in a sentence with similar ones—like using synonyms or related terms (Madukwe et al., 2022). The model then practices spotting those swaps and guessing the original words. By doing this, it becomes better at understanding different ways of saying the same thing. This helps the model learn to generalize and handle variations in language usage.

Original Sentence: "The cat sat on the mat."

In replaced token detection, certain tokens in the original text are replaced with other tokens, such as synonyms or semantically related words. Let's apply replaced token detection to the original sentence by replacing "cat" with "feline":

Replaced Sentence: "The feline sat on the mat."

In this example, the model needs to find out that the word "feline" should be changed back to "cat" based on its understanding of the meaning and structure of the language. This task helps the model get better at handling different ways of using language, by learning to recognize and predict the original words even after they've been swapped.

Sentence Reconstruction: Sentence reconstruction means breaking a sentence into parts and teaching the model to put the sentence back together. This helps the model learn how different parts of the sentence depend on each other and understand the sentence's overall structure.

Original Sentence: "The sun was shining brightly in the sky."

In sentence reconstruction, the sentence is split into two segments or parts, and the model is trained to reconstruct the original sentence from these segments. Let's split the original sentence into two segments:

Segment 1: "The sun was shining brightly"

Segment 2: "in the sky."

The model is then required to rebuild the original sentence by combining the two separate segments. It needs to understand the relationships between the segments and the overall structure of the sentence to generate the correct reconstruction.

The reconstructed sentence should be: "The sun was shining brightly in the sky."

This exercise helps the model learn how the pieces of a sentence fit together and in what order, so it can create clear, sensible text. It teaches the model both the grammar and the meaning of words, which is essential for producing smooth, natural-sounding sentences.

Token Deletion: Token deletion means randomly removing certain words from the text. The model guesses the missing words by using the clues from the other words still in the sentence(Lewis et al., 2020). This helps the model learn to fill in the gaps and understand the overall meaning of the text.

Original Sentence: "The quick brown fox jumps over the lazy dog."

In token deletion, certain tokens in the input text are randomly removed or deleted. Let's apply token deletion to the original sentence by removing the word "brown":

Deleted Sentence: "The quick fox jumps over the lazy dog."

The model predicts that the missing token is "brown" as "brown" is a common adjective used to describe the color of animals. This exercise trains the model to use context clues to fill in gaps when words are taken out. It also helps the model build strong internal "knowledge" of how language is put together.

4.2 Types of Large Language Models

Large Language Models are powerful deep learning architectures that are trained using huge amount of text corpora. This training helps them learn how to understand and create language that sounds natural, like the way people speak or write. These models have brought major improvements in handling language-related tasks and often perform better than older techniques. They are built using a design called a Transformer, which is a special kind of neural network. "A transformer is the type of design or structure used by these models to process and understand text" (Patwardhan et al., 2023). Figure 3 presents various transformer architectures, which include:

- Models utilizing only the decoder
- Models utilizing only the encoder
- Models incorporating both the encoder and decoder

Figure 3. Types of Transformer Architectures

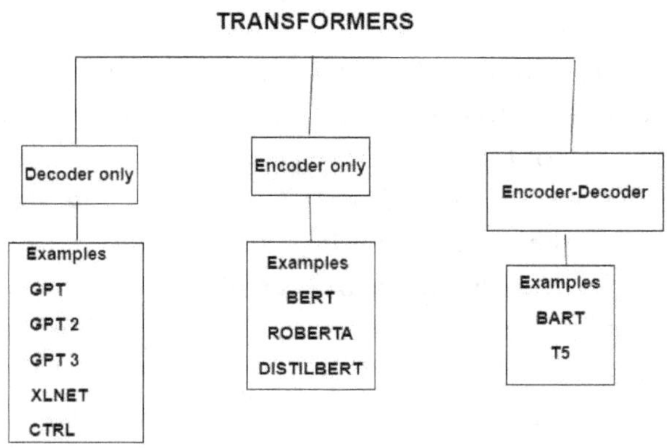

Decode Only Models: In Large Language Models, decoder-only models create text one word (or token) at a time, with each new word depending on the ones that came before it(Yeo et al., 2024). These models are widely used for tasks like finishing sentences, summarizing information, and translating languages. They work by guessing the next word based on what's already been written, choosing the one that is most likely to come next. This type of model design is used in many well-known language models, such as GPT, GPT-2, GPT-3, XLNet, and CTRL(Raiaan et al., 2024).

GPT stands for Generative Pre-trained Transformer and was introduced by OpenAI in their paper Language Models are Few-Shot Learners (Brown et al., 2020). GPT is built using a special model design known as the Transformer architecture, which helps it understand the structure and flow of language. These models are trained on huge collections of text from the internet, books, and articles, without needing labeled data—this is called unsupervised learning. Because of this training, GPT models are very good at a wide variety of language-related tasks, such as generating new text, completing unfinished sentences, and summarizing long passages of text.

GPT-2 is a more advanced and powerful version of the original GPT model. It was trained using an even larger dataset and has many more parameters (which are like the model's internal settings or "memory" used to learn from data). Because of this, GPT-2 is better at producing longer and more natural-sounding responses that fit the context well. Its improved language skills make it useful in many different areas, such as generating articles or stories, powering chatbots, and helping people with creative writing. It can take a small piece of text as input and expand it into a full paragraph or even a complete story in a way that feels human-like and coherent.

GPT-3 is the most recent and powerful version in the GPT family, with an incredibly large number of internal settings. Because of its size and the massive amount of text it has learned from, GPT-3 can understand and generate text with good performance. It can be used for tasks such as translating languages, answering questions, writing stories, and even generating computer code. Its ability to understand complex language makes it useful in many fields, from education and customer support to creative industries and software development.

XLNet is a type of language model created by researchers from Google and Carnegie Mellon University(Yang et al., 2019). It introduces a new idea called a permutation-based training objective. This means that instead of always reading the sentence in the regular order (left to right), XLNet mixes up the order of the words during training and learns from all the different possible arrangements. This approach helps the model understand not just the words that come before a certain word, but also the ones that come after it. As a result, XLNet is better at learning the full meaning of sentences by capturing both forward and backward word relationships—this is called bidirectional dependency.

CTRL, which stands for Conditional Transformer Language Model, was developed by Salesforce Research was introduced in their paper "CTRL: A Conditional Transformer Language Model for Controllable Generation" (Keskar et al., 2019). What makes CTRL special is that it allows users to control what kind of text it generates. It does this by using special control codes or instructions that are given along with the input. For example, if you want the model to write a news article, a story, or a recipe, you can give it a control code, and it will generate text in that specific style or topic. This makes CTRL very useful in situations where you want to guide the output in a particular direction—such as generating creative content, writing specific types of stories, or producing text that matches certain topics or tones. Because of this flexibility, CTRL is widely used in tasks where customized and controlled text generation is important.

Encoder only Models:

The Transformer model is a deep learning structure introduced in the groundbreaking 2017 research paper titled "Attention Is All You Need" by Vaswani and his team (Vaswani et al., 2017). This model marked a major breakthrough in how neural networks are designed, especially for handling tasks that involve language and sequences. What makes the Transformer architecture stand out is its use of a powerful method called self-attention. "Self-attention is a technique in deep learning that focuses on different parts of a sentence with different levels of significance when trying to make a prediction or understand the meaning"(Vaswani et al., 2017). For example, when analyzing a sentence, the model decides which words are more important in relation to a particular word. It then assigns higher attention scores to the important words and lower scores to the less important ones.

The self-attention process works by calculating what are called attention scores for every pair of words. These scores tell the model how much one word should pay attention to another. The scores are generated using a formula that measures the similarity between special representations of the words, known as query, key, and value vectors, which are created from the original word data. Once the model has calculated all the attention scores, it uses them to compute a weighted sum of the value vectors. This means the model combines all the word representations, but it gives more weight to the important words and less to the others, based on the attention scores. The final result is a new set of data that carries the contextual meaning of the sentence. This helps the model understand how the words are connected and improves its ability. Let us see an example – Consider the sentence "The cat sat on the mat". In the self-attention mechanism, each word in the input sequence attends to every other word in the sequence to compute its representation. Let us find attention score for the word "sat". Let's assume the word embeddings and the learned parameters of the model are as follows:

Let's compute some simplified attention scores for the word "sat" in the given sentence "The cat sat on the mat." Let's assume the word embeddings and the learned parameters of the model are as follows:

Word embeddings:

"The": [0.2, 0.5, 0.1]

"cat": [0.3, 0.4, 0.2]

"sat": [0.6, 0.7, 0.3]

"on": [0.4, 0.3, 0.5]

"the": [0.1, 0.6, 0.4]

"mat": [0.7, 0.8, 0.9]

Learned parameters (Query, Key, and Value vectors):

Query vector for "sat": [0.8, 0.5, 0.2]

Let us assume that the Key vectors for all words are the same: [0.7, 0.4, 0.1]

Let us assume that the Value vectors for all words are the same: [0.9, 0.6, 0.3]

Let's compute the attention scores between the word "sat" and every other word in the sequence:

- ***Compute Dot Products:***

For each word, compute the dot product between the query vector of "sat" and the key vector of that word.

"The": (0.8 * 0.7) + (0.5 * 0.4) + (0.2 * 0.1) = 0.56 + 0.2 + 0.02 = 0.78

"cat": (0.8 * 0.7) + (0.5 * 0.4) + (0.2 * 0.1) = 0.78

"sat" (self-attention): (0.8 * 0.7) + (0.5 * 0.4) + (0.2 * 0.1) = 0.78

"on": (0.8 * 0.7) + (0.5 * 0.4) + (0.2 * 0.1) = 0.78

"the": (0.8 * 0.7) + (0.5 * 0.4) + (0.2 * 0.1) = 0.78

"mat": (0.8 * 0.7) + (0.5 * 0.4) + (0.2 * 0.1) = 0.78

- ***Apply Softmax:***

In the self-attention process, the initial attention scores are transformed using the softmax function, which turns them into probabilities. These probabilities—called attention weights—help decide how much importance each word should have when creating the final output. Each attention score between the word "sat" and every other word is the same:

Score = 0.78 for all words

When the softmax function is applied to a list of identical scores, it assigns equal weights to all.

$\text{Softmax}(0.78,0.78,0.78,0.78,0.78,0.78) = \left[\frac{1}{6},\frac{1}{6},\frac{1}{6},\frac{1}{6},\frac{1}{6},\frac{1}{6}\right] = 0.1667$

The softmax output for each of the six identical values is: 0.1667.

- ***Weighted Sum:***

Compute the weighted sum of the value vectors of all words using the attention weights.

Weighted sum = (6 * (0.1667. [0.9, 0.6, 0.3])) = [0.9, 0.6, 0.3]

The attended representation of the word "sat" is [0.9, 0.6, 0.3]. This representation captures the context and dependencies of the word "sat" with respect to other words in the sequence.

"BERT stands for Bidirectional Encoder Representations from Transformers, and it is a type of model that uses only the encoder part of the Transformer architecture". It was introduced by Devlin et al. in the paper "BERT: Pre-training of deep bidirectional transformers for language understanding" (Devlin et al., 2019) and is trained on a large collection of text using a method called Masked Language Modeling. BERT uses several layers of encoders stacked on top of each other, which allows it to develop a deep and rich understanding of the context in which words appear. During training, BERT goes through a pre-training phase, where it learns how words relate to one another and gains an overall understanding of sentence structure and meaning. BERT uses two main training strategies: Masked Language Modeling and Next Sentence Prediction. In MLM, some of the words are hidden or "masked," and the model is trained to guess the missing words by looking at the words around them. This helps the model understand the meaning and structure of language. In NSP, the model is shown two sentences and asked to decide whether the second sentence naturally follows the first one.

RoBERTa, introduced by Liu et al. (2019), refines the BERT model by training it on more data for a longer period and eliminating the next sentence prediction objective, which enhances its language understanding capabilities(Liu et al., 2019). Although it is based on the same architecture as BERT, it makes several key changes to improve performance. RoBERTa uses larger batch sizes, higher learning rates, more training data, and removes the NSP task entirely. These optimizations help RoBERTa learn better representations of language, which leads to stronger performance on many natural language processing tasks when compared to the original BERT model.

"DistilBERT is a smaller and faster version of BERT", introduced by Sanh et al. in the paper "DistilBERT, a distilled version of BERT: smaller, faster, cheaper and lighter" (Sanh et al., 2019). It is created through a process called knowledge distillation, which means it is trained to simulate the behavior of a larger BERT model while using fewer resources. DistilBERT has half the number of layers compared to the original BERT model and does not include the next sentence prediction task in its training process. Because it has fewer parameters and is more lightweight, DistilBERT runs faster and is more cost-effective, making it ideal for applications where speed and efficiency are important, such as on mobile devices or in real-time systems.

Encoder-Decoder Models:

The encoder-decoder architecture is a well-known and widely used design in deep learning, especially for tasks that involve converting one sequence of text into another. These tasks are known as sequence-to-sequence tasks, and they include things like machine translation (converting text from one language to another) and text summarization (turning a long text into a shorter version with the main points) (Zhang, 2023). In this architecture, there are two main parts: the encoder and the decoder. The encoder reads the entire input sentence, one word (or token) at a time, and processes it to create a fixed-length summary or vector representation of the input. This vector captures the meaning and structure of the input sentence. Then, the decoder takes that encoded information and uses it to generate the output sentence, also one token at a time. Traditionally, both the encoder and decoder were built using a type of model called a Recurrent Neural Network (RNN). RNNs are good at processing sequences step by step, but they have trouble remembering information from far back in the sequence. This means they can struggle with sentences that are long or complex because they can forget earlier words while processing later ones.

When using RNNs in this setup, the encoder processes the input by updating its hidden state after each word it sees. The hidden state is like the model's memory of what it has read so far. By the time it reaches the last word, the encoder's final hidden state contains a condensed summary of the whole input. This final state is then passed to the decoder, which uses it as a starting point to create the output. The decoder RNN then starts generating the output sentence, one word at a time. For each word it generates, it looks at its current hidden state (which updates as each new word is added) and the word it just produced. Based on this, the decoder guesses what the next word should be.

Let's see a simple example of a sentence translation from English to French using encoder-decoder model.

Input Sentence (English): "I love machine learning."

Target Sentence (French): "J'adore l'apprentissage automatique."

Word Embeddings:

Let's assume we have pre-trained word embeddings for English and French words.

English Word Embeddings:

"I": [0.2, 0.4, -0.1, ...]

"love": [-0.3, 0.1, 0.5, ...]

"machine": [0.6, -0.2, 0.3, ...]

"learning": [0.4, 0.3, -0.5, ...]

French Word Embeddings:

"J'adore": [0.1, 0.2, -0.3, ...]

"l'apprentissage": [0.3, -0.4, 0.2, ...]

"automatique": [0.2, 0.1, 0.5, ...]
Encoder (RNN):

1. Input Processing:

"I": [0.2, 0.4, -0.1, ...]
"love": [-0.3, 0.1, 0.5, ...]
"machine": [0.6, -0.2, 0.3, ...]
"learning": [0.4, 0.3, -0.5, ...]

2. Hidden State Update:

The encoder RNN reads each word one by one and updates its memory at each step to include the new information it has just seen from the input.

3. Final Hidden State:

The final hidden state of the encoder captures the essence of the input sentence.
Decoder (RNN):

1. Starting Hidden State:

The decoder begins its process using the last hidden state from the encoder as its starting point. This state contains the summarized information from the input sentence.

2. Special Start Token:

To signal the beginning of the output sequence, a special token such as <START> is fed into the decoder as the first input.

3. Generating the Output Sequence:

The decoder RNN then begins generating the translation one word at a time. At each step, it uses:

o *its current hidden state, which is updated as each new word is generated,and the previously generated word as input.*

Based on this, it predicts the next word by calculating a probability distribution over the set of all possible words (e.g., words in the French vocabulary if translating from English to French).

The word with the highest probability is chosen as the next word in the sequence.

4. Stopping Condition:

This process repeats until either a special <END> token is generated (marking the end of the sentence), or the sequence reaches a predefined maximum length.

The encoder's job is to take a sentence or input sequence and turn it into a set of useful numerical representations. These representations are then passed to the decoder, which uses them—along with the words it has already generated—to create the final output sentence. The Transformer model also uses this encoder-decoder structure, but instead of older methods like recurrent or convolutional layers, it uses a special technique called self-attention. This makes it faster and more efficient. In both the encoder and the decoder, the Transformer uses something called multi-head self-attention, which means it can look at the input from different perspectives at the same time. It also includes simple fully connected layers that help with processing the data at each position. Unlike older models that read data step by step, the Transformer can process all parts of the input at once, which saves time and makes it more powerful.

BART (Bidirectional and Auto-Regressive Transformers) is a model created by Facebook AI and was introduced by Lewis et al. in the paper "BART: Denoising sequence-to-sequence pre-training for natural language generation, translation, and comprehension" (Lewis et al., 2020). This model includes both an encoder and a decoder, allowing it to understand input from both directions and to generate text one word at a time. The encoder reads the entire input by looking at it from both the left and right sides, which helps it fully understand the context. The decoder then starts producing the output sentence one token at a time. It uses the words it has already generated, along with the information from the encoder, to guess what the next word should be.

T5 stands for Text-To-Text Transfer Transformer and was introduced by Google Research in the paper "Exploring the Limits of Transfer Learning with a Unified Text-to-Text Transformer" (Raffel et al., 2019). It is designed to handle a wide variety of natural language processing tasks using one common format—text as input and output. T5 follows the same encoder-decoder structure. The encoder reads and understands the input text, and the decoder generates the output text based on what the encoder has processed and what it has already written so far.

Models built on the Transformer architecture, such as GPT and BERT, have become very popular in recent years. GPT is mainly used to generate natural, human-like text. It focuses on producing fluent text in a logical order. BERT is designed to understand language by reading it in both directions—left to right and right to left—at the same time. There are also smaller and faster versions of these models. For example, DistillBERT is a lighter version of BERT that uses fewer resources but still performs well, making it more efficient and cost-effective. Another model, XLNet, is different because it uses a special method called permutation-based training. This technique allows it to learn context from both directions without needing to read the sentence in a fixed order. All of these models—GPT, BERT, DistillBERT, and XLNet—are types of large language models, and each offers its own strengths for tasks that involve understanding or generating human language.

5. KEY INNOVATIONS IN LLMS TRANSFORMING HEALTHCARE

The use of Large Language Models in healthcare is driving big changes in areas like clinical care, administration, and medical research. These models are making healthcare services faster, more accurate, and more accessible. They do this by automating complex tasks, helping interpret data, and supporting healthcare providers in making decisions. Below, we will look at some of the key areas where LLMs are making a real difference.

Clinical Documentation and Electronic Health Record (EHR) Analysis

LLMs are very good at processing and summarizing large amounts of clinical data(Goodman et al., 2024). These models can go through unorganized data in Electronic Health Records and extract important information, making it easier for doctors and healthcare providers to quickly review patient histories and find relevant details. This helps improve the efficiency of healthcare workflows and ensures faster, more accurate decision-making, which leads to better outcomes for patients. Many healthcare institutions have begun adopting LLM-based systems to automate the summarization of physicians' notes within Electronic Health Records. These systems help clinicians quickly access clear summaries of patient interactions, significantly reducing the time spent reviewing documentation and allowing for more focused and efficient patient care.

Automated Medical Chatbots and Virtual Assistants

LLMs are also improving patient care through chatbots and virtual assistants. These AI-powered tools can answer medical questions, help schedule appointments, and even give basic medical advice. They make it easier for patients to get information and reduce the workload on healthcare professionals. During the COVID-19 pandemic, several digital health startups in India adopted AI-driven chatbots on their telemedicine platforms to manage large volumes of patient queries. These systems were used to provide real-time information on symptoms, vaccination availability, and self-care measures, helping reduce the burden on doctors and support staff.

Disease Diagnosis and Predictive Analytics

LLMs can also help doctors make better diagnoses and predict health risks by analyzing both structured and unstructured data, such as medical histories, lab results, and symptoms. By doing this, they help create more personalized treatment plans and catch health issues early. For example, AI models, including those inspired by LLMs, are now helping detect rare genetic diseases early. By looking at data like clinical notes and genomic sequencing results, these models can spot rare diseases that are often missed by traditional methods.

Medical Research and Literature Synthesis

LLMs can go through large volumes of medical research and biomedical literature to help researchers and healthcare providers find the latest trends, synthesize evidence, and stay updated. This makes research faster and more efficient. More and more healthcare organizations are using custom LLMs to stay on top of the latest medical findings. These models can automatically scan scientific research papers, clinical trial results, and other databases to extract important information, allowing doctors and researchers to quickly learn about new treatments and developments in medicine.

Named Entity Recognition (NER) in Medical Texts

LLMs are also great at Named Entity Recognition, which can find and label important parts of medical text, such as diseases, treatments, and procedures. This is important because it helps turn unorganized text into usable data, making it easier to share and use across different systems. Hospitals and clinics are now starting to use NER systems powered by LLMs in areas like insurance claim processing. By extracting useful details from unorganized medical notes, these systems help improve coding accuracy and speed up insurance claims. This makes administrative work more efficient and reduces errors.

6. PRACTICAL IMPLEMENTATION: USING BERT FOR CLINICAL SENTIMENT ANALYSIS

The objective of the implementation is to use a Large Language Model to analyze data collected and determine whether the text expresses something positive, negative or neutral. Large language models are pre-trained on vast amounts of text data, enabling them to capture intricate language patterns and contextual information. This makes them highly effective for sentiment analysis, as they can discern subtle differences in sentiment that simpler models might miss(Sharma et al., 2024). Implementing sentiment analysis with LLMs involves several steps, including data preprocessing, model fine-tuning, and evaluation. Implementing sentiment analysis with large language models offers significant advantages in terms of accuracy and contextual understanding.

Let us consider the following scenario. In the era of digital communication, individuals frequently turn to online platforms such as forums, blogs, and social media to express their thoughts, emotions, and struggles—sometimes revealing signs of mental distress or suicidal ideation. These digital footprints provide a valuable yet complex opportunity for early intervention, especially in the context of mental health care.

Healthcare professionals and researchers are increasingly using Natural Language Processing to analyze such online expressions. Among the many NLP tools, BERT has emerged as a powerful model capable of capturing nuanced language patterns and context—making it particularly suited for identifying signs of suicidal ideation in written text.

Unlike traditional methods, BERT considers both the left and right context of a word in a sentence, allowing it to better understand subtle language cues that might indicate distress or harmful intent (Koroteev, 2021). For instance, phrases like "I feel like giving up" or "There's no point in going on" may not explicitly mention suicide but could still be warning signs when placed in the right context.

Detecting suicidal ideation is a critical challenge in mental healthcare. Unrecognized or unaddressed signs of suicidal thoughts can result in tragic outcomes. By automating the detection of such language using BERT, we can build systems that help clinicians and mental health professionals:

- Identify individuals at risk in real-time,
- Prioritize responses based on urgency,
- Provide timely interventions and support.

In this practical implementation, we analyze a dataset containing social media posts and comments annotated with sentiment labels—indicating whether they exhibit suicidal ideation or not. We will use BERT to build a sentiment analysis model capable of classifying these posts. This system can act as a clinical decision support tool, aiding healthcare providers in identifying individuals who may need urgent psychological support.

Dataset Source and Description

"The dataset utilized in this study was obtained from Kaggle, a widely used platform for data sharing and analysis. Specifically, the dataset titled 'Suicidal Reddit Dataset', uploaded by the user Varun, comprises Reddit posts that discuss various mental health challenges, including expressions of suicidal ideation." Each entry in the dataset contains a text post under the column usertext, along with a corresponding binary label (label) indicating whether the post exhibits suicidal tendencies (1) or not (0). These posts reflect real user expressions from Reddit, a platform known for open discussions around mental health, thereby providing a valuable source of authentic clinical sentiment data. This dataset has been preprocessed to ensure anonymity, and is used strictly for academic and research purposes, with the aim of developing tools that can support early detection and intervention in mental health crises. A sample of usertext in the reddit post is shown in Figure 4.

Figure 4. Dataset with fields usertext and label

usertext	label
I just want to end my life so badly. My life is completely empty and I don't want to have to create meaning in it. Creating meaning is pain. How long will I hold back the urge to run my car head first into the next person coming the opposite way. When will I stop feeling jealous of tragic characters like Gomer Pile for the swift end they were able to bring to their lives?	1
My relationship is complicated and painful, but I don't want to end it. While my girlfriend and I were broken up, I slept with her boyfriend. For three years I've been trying to make it up to her, but after a while I realized I don't think I ever will.I'm not sure she'll ever want to touch me again. She hasn't wanted to touch me since that happened, no matter how hard I try, no matter what I do or say. She does it for me, but she looks bored the whole time and gets it over with asap.I feel worthless. She's my soulmate. I can't live in this horrible world without her, but I don't think she wants to be sexual with me. I'm so lonely.I wish I could just turn off the part of my brain that feels.	1
I owe a lot of money , so I have to work.The catch is that barely any of that money goes to.I need a long rest from everything but my mom insists I finish and get my degree . I really think I should just focus on school and not work, or pay down my debts before finishing school. I don't have the option to do either apparentlyI know this is the easy way out , but I'm really tired. All of these issues are on top of dealing with tensions in America as well. I want to rest.	1

In this section, we demonstrate a practical approach to using the BERT language model to detect suicidal ideation from social media posts.

Downloading and Importing Required Libraries

```
import nltk
nltk.download('punkt_tab')
nltk.download('stopwords')
pip install transformers scikit-learn pandas numpy torch
```

Transformers, a library by Hugging Face provides access to pre-trained models like BERT, GPT, and RoBERTa for a wide range of NLP tasks(Singh & Raman, 2024).

```
# Importing necessary libraries and modules for NLP and model building.
# These are commonly used tools such as HuggingFace Transformers, scikit-learn, and TensorFlow.
from transformers import BertTokenizer, TFBertModel
from sklearn.model_selection import train_test_split
from sklearn.ensemble import RandomForestClassifier
from sklearn.metrics import accuracy_score,precision_score
from nltk.corpus import stopwords
from nltk.tokenize import word_tokenize
import tensorflow as tf
```

1. Loading the Dataset

```
import pandas as pd
df=pd.read_csv("/content/sample_data/reddit.csv")
df.head()
```

A CSV file containing Reddit posts is loaded. Each post includes:

- *usertext: The raw post text from Reddit.*
- *label: Sentiment label (e.g., 1 indicating suicidal ideation & 0 indicating no suicidal thought)*

2. Analyzing Label Distribution

```
df['label'].value_counts()
```

Figure 5. Value counts of the class Label

label	count
1	6609
0	6047

dtype: int64

Figure 5 gives us an idea of how many posts are labeled as suicidal (1) vs non-suicidal (0), helping assess class balance.

3. Text Preprocessing

```
# Custom preprocessing: remove URLs, hashtags, and non-
letters
def tokenize1(txt):
if not isinstance(txt, str):
txt = ""
txt=re.sub(r"http\S+|www\S+|@\S+|#\S+","",txt)
txt=re.sub(r"[^a-zA-z\s]","",txt)
txt=txt.lower()
return txt
df['processed_text']=df['usertext'].apply(tokenize1)
```

The tokenize1 function cleans the raw Reddit posts as shown in Figure 6:

- *Removes URLs, hashtags, mentions.*
- *Filters out special characters.*
- *Converts text to lowercase.*

This helps ensure that the text is in a format suitable for embedding with BERT.

Figure 6. DataFrame with the processed text

```
df.head()
```

	usertext	label	processed_text
0	I just want to end my life so badly. My life i...	1	i just want to end my life so badly my life is...
1	My relationship is complicated and painful, bu...	1	my relationship is complicated and painful but...
2	I owe a lot of money , so I have to work.The c...	1	i owe a lot of money so i have to workthe cat...
3	On the 2 of October I overdosed I just felt so...	1	on the of october i overdosed i just felt so ...
4	Everyone tells me how wonderful I am, but not ...	1	everyone tells me how wonderful i am but not e...

4. Initializing BERT Tokenizer and Model

```
# Load the pre-trained BERT tokenizer and model from Hugging Face's Transformers library
tokenizer = BertTokenizer.from_pretrained('bert-base-uncased')
bert_model = TFBertModel.from_pretrained('bert-base-uncased')
```

Pre-trained BERT components loaded using Hugging Face Transformers library (Wolf et al., 2020). *The **pre-trained BERT base model** (bert-base-uncased) which has been trained on a large English corpus is used. This model allows us to convert text into dense, context-aware numerical representations.*

5. Generating BERT Embeddings

This function converts each preprocessed Reddit post into a **BERT embedding** as shown in Figure 7.:

- *Tokenizes input text.*
- *Feeds it to BERT to obtain output embeddings.*
- *Extracts the [CLS] token embedding (used for sentence-level classification tasks).*

```
# Function to generate BERT embeddings for a given text
```

```
def text_to_bert_embedding(text):
  # Tokenize the text and prepare input IDs and attention
masks
  inputs = tokenizer(text, return_tensors='tf', trunca-
tion=True,
  padding=True, max_length=512)
  input_ids = inputs['input_ids']
  attention_mask = inputs['attention_mask']
  # Get BERT outputs
  outputs = bert_model(input_ids, attention_mask=attention_
mask)
  # Use the [CLS] token embedding (first token) as the sen-
tence
  embedding
  cls_embedding = outputs.last_hidden_state[:, 0,:] # Shape:
(1, 768)
  return tf.squeeze(cls_embedding).numpy() # Convert to numpy
array
  # Apply the function to convert all text to BERT embeddings
  df['text_embedding'] = df['processed_text'].apply(text_to_
bert_embedding)
```

"The embedding approach is based on publicly available tutorials for using pre-trained BERT from Hugging Face, adapted for our dataset and task" (Wolf et al., 2020)

Figure 7. DataFrame with text_embeddings

usertext	label	processed_text	text_embedding
I just want to end my life so badly. My life i...	1	i just want to end my life so badly my life is...	[-1.11194849e-01 2.78097928e-01 1.29567280e-...
My relationship is complicated and painful, bu...	1	my relationship is complicated and painful but...	[-3.78413916e-01 2.08522081e-01 1.56172022e-...
I owe a lot of money , so I have to work.The c...	1	i owe a lot of money so i have to workthe cat...	[-5.84930778e-02 7.90648237e-02 2.04940438e-...
On the 2 of October I overdosed I just felt so...	1	on the of october i overdosed i just felt so ...	[-1.98576897e-01 -7.91609734e-02 9.82221067e-...
Everyone tells me how wonderful I am, but not ...	1	everyone tells me how wonderful i am but not e...	[-2.41684347e-01 3.80187720e-01 -2.98704207e-...

6. Rounding and Converting Embeddings

```
def convert_and_round_embedding(embedding_str):
try:
```

```
# Convert the string to a numpy array
embedding = np.fromstring(embedding_str.strip("[]"), sep='
')
# Round the values to 4 decimal places
rounded_embedding = np.round(embedding, 4)
return rounded_embedding
except Exception as e:
print(f"Error processing embedding: {e}")
return None
# Apply the conversion and rounding to the 'text_embedding'
column
df['text_embedding'] = df['text_embedding'].apply(convert_
and_round_embedding)
# Check the result
print(df['text_embedding'].head())
```

Figure 8. The Text Embedding after rounding the value to 4 decimal places

```
0    [-0.1112, 0.2781, 0.1296, 0.0844, -0.2224, -0....
1    [-0.3784, 0.2085, 0.1562, -0.1041, -0.562, -0....
2    [-0.0585, 0.0791, 0.2049, -0.443, -0.1717, -0....
3    [-0.1986, -0.0792, 0.0982, -0.1052, -0.3252, -...
4    [-0.2417, 0.3802, -0.2987, -0.4724, -0.6045, -...
Name: text_embedding, dtype: object
```

Figure 8 shows the Text Embedding after rounding to 4 decimal places. Although not strictly necessary for model performance, rounding embeddings:

- Reduces memory usage.
- Makes the output easier to debug.

7. Splitting Dataset and Preparing Input

We split the dataset into **training (80%)** and **testing (20%)** sets.

```
X=np.vstack(df['text_embedding'])
y=df['label']
X_train, X_test, y_train, y_test = train_test_split(X, y,
test_size=0.2, random_state=42)
```

8. Training a Random Forest Classifier

We train a **Random Forest Classifier** using the BERT embeddings and evaluate accuracy on the test set.

```
clf = RandomForestClassifier(n_estimators=100, random_
state=42)
clf.fit(X_train, y_train)
# Predict and evaluate
y_pred = clf.predict(X_test)
print("Accuracy:", accuracy_score(y_test, y_pred))
The accuracy obtained is 85.38%
```

9. Training an XGBoost Classifier

We also try an **XGBoost Classifier**, known for its superior performance in classification problems.

```
clf2 = XGBClassifier()
clf2.fit(X_train, y_train)
# Predict and evaluate
y_pred2 = clf2.predict(X_test)
print("Accuracy:", accuracy_score(y_test, y_pred2))
```

The accuracy obtained is 85.74%

10. Testing the Model on New Clinical Texts

Once the BERT-based model is trained, the next step is to evaluate its practical utility by applying it to new or unseen text inputs. This simulates a real-world scenario where clinicians, researchers, or mental health monitoring systems encounter new posts or sentences and must identify whether they exhibit signs of suicidal ideation.

To accomplish this, the following steps are performed:

I. Text Preprocessing

The new input text must undergo the same preprocessing as the training data to ensure consistency. This includes Removing URLs, hashtags, mentions, and non-alphabetic characters and Converting the text to lowercase to standardize the input.

II. Generating BERT Embedding

The cleaned text is tokenized and passed through the pre-trained BERT model to extract the contextual embedding. Specifically, the [CLS] token embedding from BERT's output is used as a fixed-size representation of the entire sentence. This embedding captures the semantic meaning of the input.

III. Prediction Using Trained Classifier

The generated embedding is then passed into the trained machine learning classifier (such as a Random Forest or XGBoost model) to predict the sentiment label. In this context, the label indicates whether the text is 0: Non-suicidal or 1: Suicidal

IV. Interpreting the Output

The predicted label is mapped to a human-readable form, helping practitioners or systems understand the result directly. For instance, a post like "I feel completely lost, I don't know what to do anymore and I don't want to live" might be classified as "Suicidal," thereby signaling the need for intervention or further review. The code for the above steps is given below.

```
def predict_sentiment(text, tokenizer, bert_model, classifi-
er):
  # Step 1: Clean the text (same as training)
  # Custom preprocessing: remove URLs, hashtags, and non-
letters
  def preprocess(txt):
  txt = re.sub(r"http\S+|www\S+|@\S+|#\S+", "", txt)
  txt = re.sub(r"[^a-zA-Z\s]", "", txt)
  txt = txt.lower()
  return txt
  processed_text = preprocess(text)
  # Step 2: Get BERT embedding
  inputs = tokenizer(processed_text, return_tensors='tf',
truncation=True,
  padding=True, max_length=512)
  outputs = bert_model(inputs['input_ids'], attention_mask=in-
puts['attention_mask'])
  cls_embedding = outputs.last_hidden_state[:, 0,:].numpy()
  cls_embedding = np.round(cls_embedding, 4)
```

```
# Step 3: Predict using the trained classifier
prediction = classifier.predict(cls_embedding)
# Step 4: Output readable result
label_map = {0: "Non-Suicidal", 1: "Suicidal"}
return label_map[prediction[0]]
# Example: new post from Reddit
new_text = "I feel completely lost, I don't know what to do anymore and I don't want to live."
# Predict using Random Forest
result = predict_sentiment(new_text, tokenizer, bert_model, clf)
print("Prediction (Random Forest):", result)
# Predict using XGBoost
result2 = predict_sentiment(new_text, tokenizer, bert_model, clf2)
print("Prediction (XGBoost):", result2)
Prediction (Random Forest): Suicidal
Prediction (XGBoost): Suicidal
```

This demonstrates that the model can successfully detect suicidal ideation based on nuanced linguistic patterns learned during training.

In healthcare, especially mental health care, timely detection of suicidal ideation can be life-saving. Integrating this kind of clinical sentiment analysis into digital health platforms, electronic health records, or even social media monitoring tools could empower healthcare professionals with early warning systems. These tools can flag at-risk individuals, enabling faster outreach and support. Such AI-driven solutions are not meant to replace human judgment but to augment clinical capabilities by automating the first level of risk detection, thereby enhancing the efficiency and responsiveness of mental health services.

7. CONCLUSION

Artificial Intelligence and Large Language Models are changing the way healthcare works. These technologies help doctors, researchers, and healthcare systems use data more effectively to make better decisions, faster. At the foundational level, AI's ability to emulate cognitive tasks, combined with ML's predictive intelligence and Deep Learning's capacity to process complex and unstructured data, has unlocked unprecedented opportunities in healthcare. Natural Language Processing, powered by LLMs, enables the interpretation of vast textual data in the form of clinical

REFERENCES

Bahja, M. (2021). Natural Language Processing Applications in Business. In *E-Business - Higher Education and Intelligence Applications*. https://doi.org/DOI: 10.5772/intechopen.92203

Barreto, F., Moharkar, L., Shirodkar, M., Sarode, V., Gonsalves, S., & Johns, A. (2023). Generative Artificial Intelligence: Opportunities and Challenges of Large Language Models. *Lecture Notes in Networks and Systems, 699 LNNS*, 545–553. https://doi.org/DOI: 10.1007/978-981-99-3177-4_41

Bengesi, S., El-Sayed, H., Sarker, M. K., Houkpati, Y., Irungu, J., & Oladunni, T. (2024). Advancements in Generative AI: A Comprehensive Review of GANs, GPT, Autoencoders, Diffusion Model, and Transformers. *IEEE Access: Practical Innovations, Open Solutions*, *12*, 69812–69837. DOI: 10.1109/ACCESS.2024.3397775

Boppana, V. (2022). Machine Learning and AI Learning: Understanding the Revolution. *Acadexpinnara.Com, 5*(2). https://acadexpinnara.com/index.php/JIT/article/view/368

Brown, T. B., Mann, B., Ryder, N., Subbiah, M., Kaplan, J., Dhariwal, P., Neelakantan, A., Shyam, P., Sastry, G., Askell, A., Agarwal, S., Herbert-Voss, A., Krueger, G., Henighan, T., Child, R., Ramesh, A., Ziegler, D. M., Wu, J., Winter, C., . . . Amodei, D. (2020). Language models are few-shot learners. *Advances in Neural Information Processing Systems, 2020–Decem*. https://proceedings.neurips.cc/paper/2020/hash/1457c0d6bfcb4967418bfb8ac142f64a-Abstract.html

Chen, Y., Shi, H., Liu, X., Shi, T., Zhang, R., Liu, D., Xiong, Z., & Wu, F. (2024). TokenUnify: Scalable Autoregressive Visual Pre-training with Mixture Token Prediction. *Arxiv.Org*. https://arxiv.org/abs/2405.16847

Chowdhary, K., intelligence, K. C.-F. of artificial, & 2020, undefined. (2020). Natural language processing. *Springer, 37*, 603–649. https://doi.org/DOI: 10.1007/978-81-322-3972-7_19

Chowdhary, K. R. (2020). Natural Language Processing. *Fundamentals of Artificial Intelligence*, 603–649. https://doi.org/DOI: 10.1007/978-81-322-3972-7_19

Devlin, J., Chang, M. W., Lee, K., & Toutanova, K. (2019). BERT: Pre-training of deep bidirectional transformers for language understanding. *NAACL HLT 2019 - 2019 Conference of the North American Chapter of the Association for Computational Linguistics: Human Language Technologies - Proceedings of the Conference, 1*, 4171–4186. https://aclanthology.org/N19-1423/?utm_campaign=The Batch&utm_source=hs_email&utm_medium=email&_hsenc=p2ANqtz-_m9bbH_7ECE-1h3lZ3D61TYg52rKpifVNjL4fvJ85uqggrXsWDBTB7YooFLJeNXHWqhvOyC

Ekundayo, F., & Nyavor, H. (2024). AI-Driven Predictive Analytics in Cardiovascular Diseases: Integrating Big Data and Machine Learning for Early Diagnosis and Risk Prediction. *Researchgate. Net*, *5*, 1240–1256. DOI: 10.55248/gengpi.5.1224.3437

Ganai, A. F., & Khursheed, F. (2019). Predicting next Word using RNN and LSTM cells: Stastical Language Modeling. *Proceedings of the IEEE International Conference Image Information Processing, 2019–Novem*, 469–474. https://doi.org/DOI: 10.1109/ICIIP47207.2019.8985885

Goodfellow, I., Pouget-Abadie, J., Mirza, M., Xu, B., Warde-Farley, D., Ozair, S., Courville, A., & Bengio, Y. (2020). Generative adversarial networks. *Dl.Acm. Org*, *63*(11), 139–144. DOI: 10.1145/3422622

Goodman, K. E., Yi, P. H., & Morgan, D. J. (2024). AI-Generated Clinical Summaries Require More Than Accuracy. In *JAMA* (Vol. 331, Issue 8, pp. 637–638). American Medical Association. https://doi.org/DOI: 10.1001/jama.2024.0555

Johnsen, M. (2024). *Large language models (LLMs).*

Kalyan, K. S., Rajasekharan, A., & Sangeetha, S. (2021). AMMUS : A Survey of Transformer-based Pretrained Models in Natural Language Processing. *Arxiv.Org*. https://arxiv.org/abs/2108.05542

Keskar, N. S., McCann, B., Varshney, L. R., Xiong, C., & Socher, R. (2019). CTRL: A Conditional Transformer Language Model for Controllable Generation. *Arxiv. Org*. https://arxiv.org/abs/1909.05858

Khalifa, M., Albadawy, M., & Iqbal, U. (2024). Advancing clinical decision support: The role of artificial intelligence across six domains. In *Computer Methods and Programs in Biomedicine Update* (Vol. 5). https://doi.org/DOI: 10.1016/j.cmpbup.2024.100142

Koroteev, M. V. (2021). BERT: A Review of Applications in Natural Language Processing and Understanding. *ArXiv Preprint*. https://arxiv.org/abs/2103.11943

Lewis, M., Liu, Y., Goyal, N., Ghazvininejad, M., Mohamed, A., Levy, O., Stoyanov, V., & Zettlemoyer, L. (2020). BART: Denoising sequence-to-sequence pre-training for natural language generation, translation, and comprehension. *Proceedings of the Annual Meeting of the Association for Computational Linguistics*, 7871–7880. https://doi.org/DOI: 10.18653/v1/2020.acl-main.703

Liu, Y., Ott, M., Goyal, N., Du, J., Joshi, M., Chen, D., Levy, O., Lewis, M., Zettlemoyer, L., & Stoyanov, V. (2019). RoBERTa: A Robustly Optimized BERT Pretraining Approach. *ArXiv Preprint ArXiv:1907.11692*. https://arxiv.org/abs/1907.11692v1

Logeswaran, L., Lee, H., & Radev, D. (2018). Sentence ordering and coherence modeling using recurrent neural networks. *32nd AAAI Conference on Artificial Intelligence, AAAI 2018*, 5285–5292. https://doi.org/DOI: 10.1609/aaai.v32i1.11997

Lu, X., Li, S., & Fujimoto, M. (2020). Automatic speech recognition. In *SpringerBriefs in Computer Science* (pp. 21–38). Springer London., DOI: 10.1007/978-981-15-0595-9_2

Madukwe, K. J., Gao, X., & Xue, B. (2022). Token replacement-based data augmentation methods for hate speech detection. *World Wide Web (Bussum)*, *25*(3), 1129–1150. DOI: 10.1007/s11280-022-01025-2

Mikolov, T., Chen, K., Corrado, G., & Dean, J. (2013). Efficient estimation of word representations in vector space. *1st International Conference on Learning Representations, ICLR 2013 - Workshop Track Proceedings*. https://arxiv.org/abs/1712.09405

Miotto, R., Wang, F., Wang, S., Jiang, X., & Dudley, J. T. (2017). Deep learning for healthcare: Review, opportunities and challenges. *Briefings in Bioinformatics*, *19*(6), 1236–1246. DOI: 10.1093/bib/bbx044 PMID: 28481991

Montesinos López, O. A., Montesinos López, A., & Crossa, J. (2022). Fundamentals of Artificial Neural Networks and Deep Learning. In *Multivariate Statistical Machine Learning Methods for Genomic Prediction* (pp. 379–425). Springer International Publishing., DOI: 10.1007/978-3-030-89010-0_10

Patwardhan, N., Marrone, S., & Sansone, C. (2023). Transformers in the Real World: A Survey on NLP Applications. In *Information (Switzerland)* (Vol. 14, Issue 4). https://doi.org/DOI: 10.3390/info14040242

Raffel, C., Shazeer, N., Roberts, A., Lee, K., Narang, S., Matena, M., Zhou, Y., Li, W., & Liu, P. J. (2019). Exploring the Limits of Transfer Learning with a Unified Text-to-Text Transformer. *Journal of Machine Learning Research*, *21*, 1–67. https://arxiv.org/abs/1910.10683v4

Rahman, A., Karmakar, M., Inteligencia, P. D.-R. de, & 2023, U. (2023). Predictive analytics for healthcare: Improving patient outcomes in the US through Machine Learning. *Researchgate.Net, 14*(01), 595–624. https://www.researchgate.net/profile/Arifur-Rahman-49/publication/387763296_Predictive_Analytics_for_Healthcare_Improving_Patient_Outcomes_in_the_US_through_Machine_Learning/links/677c54b2894c552085467e3a/Predictive-Analytics-for-Healthcare-Improving-Pati

Raiaan, M. A. K., Mukta, M. S. H., Fatema, K., Fahad, N. M., Sakib, S., Mim, M. M. J., Ahmad, J., Ali, M. E., & Azam, S. (2024). A Review on Large Language Models: Architectures, Applications, Taxonomies, Open Issues and Challenges. *IEEE Access: Practical Innovations, Open Solutions, 12*, 26839–26874. DOI: 10.1109/ACCESS.2024.3365742

Salakhutdinov, R. (2015). Learning Deep Generative Models. *Annual Review of Statistics and Its Application, 2*, 361–385. DOI: 10.1146/annurev-statistics-010814-020120

Salazar, J., Liang, D., Nguyen, T. Q., & Kirchhoff, K. (2020). Masked language model scoring. *Proceedings of the Annual Meeting of the Association for Computational Linguistics*, 2699–2712. https://doi.org/DOI: 10.18653/v1/2020.acl-main.240

Sandeep Kumar, E., & Satya Jayadev, P. (2020). Deep Learning for Clinical Decision Support Systems: A Review from the Panorama of Smart Healthcare. *Studies in Big Data, 68*, 79–99. DOI: 10.1007/978-3-030-33966-1_5

Sanh, V., Debut, L., Chaumond, J., & Wolf, T. (2019). DistilBERT, a distilled version of BERT: smaller, faster, cheaper and lighter. *ArXiv Preprint*. https://arxiv.org/abs/1910.01108v4

Sarker, I. H. (2021). Deep Learning: A Comprehensive Overview on Techniques, Taxonomy, Applications and Research Directions. *SN Computer Science, 2*(6). Advance online publication. DOI: 10.1007/S42979-021-00815-1 PMID: 34426802

Sharma, N. A., Ali, A. B. M. S., & Kabir, M. A. (2024). A review of sentiment analysis: tasks, applications, and deep learning techniques. In *International Journal of Data Science and Analytics*. Springer Science and Business Media Deutschland GmbH., DOI: 10.1007/s41060-024-00594-x

Singh, P., & Raman, B. (2024). Deep Learning Through the Prism of Tensors. *Studies in Big Data, 162*, 1–610. DOI: 10.1007/978-981-97-8019-8/COVER

Tu, Z. (2007). Learning generative models via discriminative approaches. *Proceedings of the IEEE Computer Society Conference on Computer Vision and Pattern Recognition*. https://doi.org/DOI: 10.1109/CVPR.2007.383035

Vaswani, A., Shazeer, N., Parmar, N., Uszkoreit, J., Jones, L., Gomez, A. N., Kaiser, Ł., & Polosukhin, I. (2017). *Attention is all you need* (Vol. 2017). Advances in Neural Information Processing Systems. Decem., https://arxiv.org/abs/1706.03762

Wolf, T., Debut, L., Sanh, V., Chaumond, J., Delangue, C., Moi, A., Cistac, P., Rault, T., Louf, R., Funtowicz, M., Davison, J., Shleifer, S., Von Platen, P., Ma, C., Jernite, Y., Plu, J., Xu, C., Le Scao, T., Gugger, S., . . . Rush, A. M. (2020). Transformers: State-of-the-Art Natural Language Processing. *EMNLP 2020 - Conference on Empirical Methods in Natural Language Processing, Proceedings of Systems Demonstrations*, 38–45. https://doi.org/DOI: 10.18653/v1/2020.emnlp-demos.6

Yang, Z., Dai, Z., Yang, Y., Carbonell, J., Salakhutdinov, R., & Le, Q. V. (2019). XLNet: Generalized autoregressive pretraining for language understanding. *Advances in Neural Information Processing Systems, 32*. https://proceedings.neurips.cc/paper/2019/hash/dc6a7e655d7e5840e66733e9ee67cc69-Abstract.html

Yeo, S., Ma, Y., Jun, H., Kim, T., & Kim, S. (2024). Survey on Recent Large Language Models for Code Generation. *KIISE Transactions on Computing Practices*, *30*(8), 372–381. DOI: 10.5626/ktcp.2024.30.8.372

Yuyun, L. A. D., Sampurno, T., Hazriani, Arisha, A. O., & Mushaf. (2023). Next Sentence Prediction: The Impact of Preprocessing Techniques in Deep Learning. *Proceedings - 2023 10th International Conference on Computer, Control, Informatics and Its Applications: Exploring the Power of Data: Leveraging Information to Drive Digital Innovation, IC3INA 2023*, 274–278. https://doi.org/DOI: 10.1109/IC3INA60834.2023.10285805

Zhang, Y. (2023). Encoder-decoder models in sequence-to-sequence learning: A survey of RNN and LSTM approaches. *Applied and Computational Engineering*, *22*(1), 218–226. DOI: 10.54254/2755-2721/22/20231220

Zhou, B., Yang, G., Shi, Z., & Ma, S. (2024). Natural Language Processing for Smart Healthcare. *IEEE Reviews in Biomedical Engineering*, *17*, 4–18. DOI: 10.1109/RBME.2022.3210270 PMID: 36170385

Chapter 6
Transformers for Medical Image Segmentation

S. S. Kumar
https://orcid.org/0000-0002-7988-2768
Noorul Islam Centre for Higher Education, India

VinodKumar R. S.
Noorul Islam Centre for Higher Education, India

ABSTRACT

Recent advances in transformer-based deep learning architectures have significantly enhanced medical image segmentation by enabling precise delineation of anatomical structures across various imaging modalities and clinical contexts. Transformers leverage self-attention mechanisms to model long-range dependencies and global context, overcoming the limitations of convolutional neural networks with localized receptive fields. This chapter reviews the application of transformers in segmentation tasks such as brain tumors, retinal vessels, and skin lesions, highlighting innovations in architecture, performance benchmarks, and evaluation metrics. Comparative analyses reveal trends in accuracy, robustness, and efficiency, while addressing challenges like computational demands, limited annotated data, and clinical interpretability. Future directions include lightweight architectures, multimodal integration, and clinical validation. These developments illustrate the transformative role of transformers in precision medicine and AI-driven healthcare.

1. INTRODUCTION

Medical image segmentation is a fundamental process in modern healthcare, serving as the backbone for numerous clinical applications that directly impact

DOI: 10.4018/979-8-3373-2038-0.ch006

patient care (Ma et al., 2024). By dividing medical images, such as those from magnetic resonance imaging (MRI), computed tomography (CT), ultrasound, or dermoscopy, into meaningful regions, segmentation facilitates the accurate identification of anatomical structures, abnormalities, and lesions. This capability is crucial in diagnostics, enabling the detection of conditions such as tumors, cardiovascular diseases, and skin cancers through the precise isolation of regions of interest.

Beyond diagnosis, segmentation plays a pivotal role in treatment planning. It provides detailed spatial maps that guide targeted therapies, such as radiation or chemotherapy, ensuring interventions are both effective and minimally invasive. In surgical contexts, segmentation aids in preoperative planning and intraoperative navigation by visualizing critical structures, thereby enhancing surgical precision and reducing risks. With the increasing availability of high-resolution medical imaging and the growing demand for efficient, automated analysis, segmentation has become an indispensable tool for translating complex image data into actionable clinical insights. Convolutional neural networks (CNNs) have been the cornerstone of medical image segmentation for years due to their strength in capturing local image patterns through convolutional operations (Iqbal et al., 2023). They are particularly effective at identifying fine details, such as edges and textures, within confined receptive fields. However, their local focus limits their ability to model global context and long-range dependencies, factors that are often critical when interpreting complex or spatially expansive structures in medical images (Zhao et al., 2024).

This limitation can result in fragmented or incomplete segmentations, especially in cases involving organs or lesions with irregular shapes or that span large portions of an image. Moreover, CNNs typically require large amounts of annotated data to generalize well, an issue in the medical domain, where labeled datasets are often scarce due to privacy regulations and the high cost of expert annotation. To address these challenges, transformer-based models have emerged as a powerful alternative (Kumar, 2025). Originally developed for natural language processing, transformers utilize self-attention mechanisms to capture global dependencies by weighing all input features simultaneously, regardless of spatial location. This ability to integrate context across the entire image, combined with their flexibility in multi-scale feature representation, makes transformers particularly well-suited for complex medical segmentation tasks. As a result, they offer a promising solution to the inherent limitations of CNNs.

This chapter provides a comprehensive overview of transformer-based approaches in medical image segmentation, with a focus on their application across diverse anatomical regions and clinical use cases. The primary objective is to examine how transformers enhance segmentation performance compared to traditional CNN-based methods, particularly through improved modeling of long-range dependencies and better handling of complex anatomical boundaries. Various transformer architectures are explored, including pure transformer models and hybrid frameworks that integrate CNNs and transformers. Key design elements, such as attention mechanisms, multi-scale feature fusion, and domain-specific adaptations, are analyzed in detail. Segmentation tasks in critical regions such as the brain, breast, eye, heart, kidney, liver, lung, multi-organ systems, polyps, and skin lesions are examined to illustrate the adaptability of transformers to domain-specific challenges. The chapter concludes by discussing emerging trends and future directions, including strategies to enhance computational efficiency, incorporate privacy-preserving techniques, and support real-time clinical integration, offering a roadmap for continued progress in medical imaging through transformer-based solutions.

2. TRANSFORMERS IN MEDICAL IMAGING

Originally developed for natural language processing, transformers (Vaswani et al., 2017) have redefined feature modeling in computer vision by introducing a global, attention-based approach. At the heart of transformer architecture lies the self-attention mechanism, which allows the model to assess the relevance of each input element, such as image pixels or patches, in relation to all others, regardless of their spatial distance. This stands in contrast to CNNs, which extract features through fixed, local receptive fields, often requiring multiple layers to build a broader contextual understanding.

In transformers, each input is transformed into query, key, and value vectors. The model computes similarity scores between queries and keys to generate attention weights, which are then used to aggregate information from the value vectors. This enables a single transformer layer to capture long-range dependencies across the entire image. However, because transformers are inherently permutation-invariant, they lack a built-in sense of spatial structure, an essential component for image analysis. To address this, positional encoding is incorporated, embedding spatial location information into the input sequence. These encodings, which can be either fixed or learnable, restore spatial awareness by informing the model of each feature's relative or absolute position in the image. This combination of self-attention and positional encoding enables transformers to process medical images in a holistic manner, making them particularly suited for segmentation tasks that demand both global context and fine-grained detail.

The application of transformers to vision tasks was pioneered by the Vision Transformer (ViT) (Dosovitskiy et al., 2020), which demonstrated that images could be treated as sequences of patches, analogous to words in a sentence. ViT divides an image into non-overlapping patches, flattens them, and processes them using standard transformer layers. While ViT achieved competitive performance in classification tasks, its lack of inductive biases (like locality and translation invariance) and high computational requirements limited its effectiveness in more complex domains like medical imaging. The ViT architecture is shown in Figure 1.

Figure 1. Vision Transformer architecture

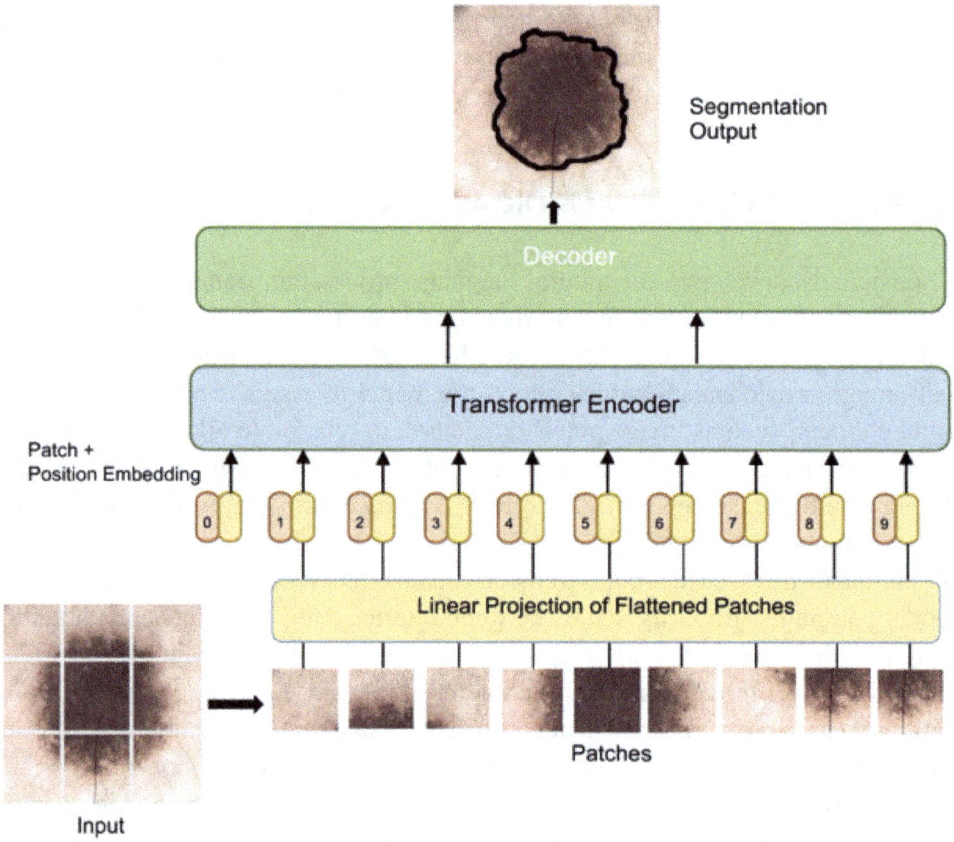

To address these shortcomings, researchers began developing transformer architectures specifically tailored for medical applications. TransUNet (Chen et al., 2021) was among the first successful hybrids, combining a transformer encoder with a U-Net-style decoder to merge global context from self-attention with local features extracted via CNNs. This architecture proved particularly effective for organ segmentation. The overview of the TransUNet architecture is given in Figure 2.

Figure 2. Overview of the TransUNet architecture

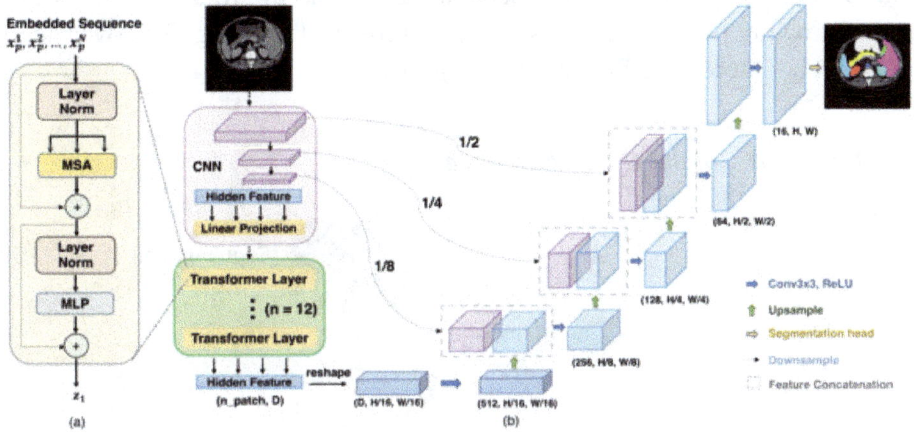

(Chen et al., 2021)

Building on this, Swin-UNet introduced a hierarchical structure with shifted window-based attention, striking a balance between computational efficiency and contextual awareness. By processing image patches within overlapping windows and shifting them between layers, Swin-UNet captured both local and global features more effectively, crucial for high-resolution medical images. The overview of the Swin-UNet architecture is given in Figure 3.

Figure 3. Overview of the Swin Transformer architecture (a) and two successive Swin Transformer Blocks (b)

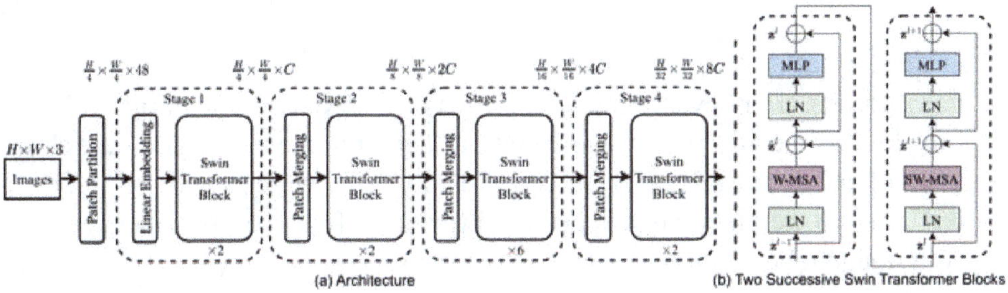

(Cao et al., 2023)

Further advancements led to models like UNETR (Hatamizadeh et al., 2021), which employs a pure transformer encoder for 3D volumetric data, paired with a CNN decoder. This architecture was designed to handle complex spatial relationships in tasks such as brain and multi-organ segmentation, demonstrating the adaptability of transformers to diverse medical modalities and formats. This evolution from general-purpose vision models to specialized, domain-aware architectures highlights the growing maturity of transformers in medical imaging. The overview of the UNETR architecture is illustrated in Figure 4.

Figure 4. Overview of the UNETR architecture

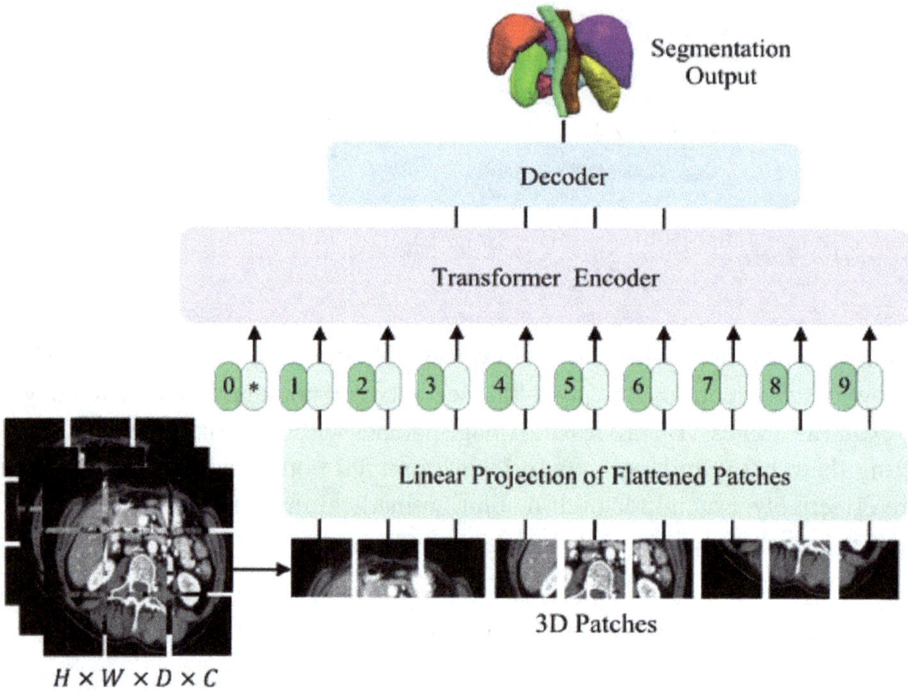

(Hatamizadeh et al., 2021)

Transformers offer several key advantages over CNNs, particularly in the demanding field of medical image segmentation. Their foremost strength is the ability to model global context directly. In contrast to CNNs, which must rely on deep, stacked layers to incrementally expand their receptive fields, transformers can capture long-range relationships in a single attention layer. This capability is vital for medical tasks where meaningful structures, such as tumor boundaries or vascular networks, often span large regions and are context-dependent.

Additionally, transformers naturally support multi-scale representation through hierarchical attention and patch-based processing. This enables robust segmentation of anatomical features that vary greatly in size, shape, and appearance, such as polyps, tumors, or skin lesions. Their dynamic attention mechanism also allows them to better handle irregular boundaries, overlapping tissues, and low-contrast regions, especially in scenarios where CNNs frequently struggle due to their rigid, localized focus.

Transformers also exhibit greater flexibility in learning from limited or partially labeled datasets, a common constraint in medical imaging. Through transfer learning, semi-supervised training, and self-supervised pretraining, transformer models can achieve strong performance even with minimal annotated data, reducing the burden of manual labeling.

While transformers are generally more computationally intensive than CNNs, their performance gains in terms of accuracy, generalization, and adaptability make them a compelling choice for advancing clinical image analysis. Their continued refinement and integration into hybrid architectures are reshaping the landscape of medical image segmentation.

3. DOMAIN-SPECIFIC APPLICATIONS

The versatility of transformer-based models in medical image segmentation is vividly demonstrated through their deployment across a broad spectrum of anatomical domains, each with distinct structural complexities and clinical priorities. Traditional CNNs often face limitations when dealing with variable morphologies, diverse imaging modalities, and long-range spatial dependencies inherent in medical imaging. Transformers, however, overcome these challenges through their self-attention mechanisms and capacity for global context modeling.

This section explores the application of transformers in key anatomical regions, such as the brain, breast, eye, heart, kidney, liver, lung, multi-organ systems, polyps, and skin. These domains demand customized segmentation strategies: capturing fine vessel structures in retinal images, outlining large and irregular liver contours, or distinguishing subtle skin lesions against noisy backgrounds. Transformer models rise to these challenges by supporting multi-modal inputs, facilitating hierarchical feature fusion, and enhancing boundary precision. Modalities including MRI, CT, ultrasound, and dermoscopy further highlight the models' flexibility. Each subsequent subsection details model innovations, benchmark datasets, and evaluation metrics within a specific anatomical context.

3.1 Brain Segmentation

Brain segmentation is a critical task in medical imaging, providing essential support for the diagnosis and management of neurological disorders such as gliomas, brain tumors, ischemic lesions, and intracerebral hemorrhages. Accurate delineation of brain structures from MRI and CT scans is pivotal for surgical planning, therapy guidance, and disease monitoring. Transformer-based models, empowered by self-attention mechanisms, offer robust global context modeling and have shown substantial improvements in segmentation accuracy, especially in multi-modal and volumetric imaging scenarios.

A wide range of transformer-based models have been developed to address the unique challenges of brain segmentation. TranSiam (Li et al., 2023) integrates dual-path CNN-transformer architecture with Locality-Aware Aggregation to enhance multi-modal feature fusion and has been evaluated across multiple BraTS datasets. CKD-TransBTS (Lin et al., 2023) incorporates clinical knowledge and modality grouping via cross-attention for improved tumor segmentation. Similarly, UNesT (Yu et al., 2023) applies a hierarchical patch-based transformer design, achieving high performance in whole-brain segmentation tasks.

Several other innovative models demonstrate the versatility of transformers in brain imaging. TransDoubleU-Net (Vatanpour & Haddadnia, 2023) uses a dual-scale Swin Transformer encoder with a hybrid decoder, while BTSC-TNAS (Liu et al., 2023) integrates neural architecture search and multi-task learning for tumor classification and segmentation. Swin UNETR (Hatamizadeh et al., 2022), BiTr-Unet (Jia & Shu, 2022), and VcaNet (Pan & Chen, 2025) further refine transformer design for high-resolution MRI analysis, employing hierarchical encoders and cross-attention fusion modules. Notably, models like TransHarDNet (Piao et al., 2023) have addressed intracerebral hemorrhage detection in large-scale CT datasets, while the Multi-task Transformer (Marcus et al., 2023) is tailored for ischemic lesion segmentation and age prediction. For 3D volumetric analysis, nnFormer (Zhou et al., 2023) merges interleaved convolution with attention mechanisms to outperform traditional CNN models like nnUNet.

These models are evaluated using standardized datasets such as BraTS (2017–2022), CANDI, and Colin for MRI segmentation, and large-scale clinical CT collections for hemorrhagic and ischemic lesion analysis. Performance is typically measured using Dice Similarity Coefficient (DSC), Jaccard Index (IoU), and Hausdorff Distance (HD), with additional metrics like AUC and accuracy for classification-oriented tasks. For instance, BiTr-Unet (Jia & Shu, 2022) reports a Dice score exceeding 93% on BraTS 2021, with detailed HD metrics across tumor regions. Meanwhile, lightweight and efficient designs like TransHarDNet (Piao et al., 2023) emphasize real-time capability (FPS 30.78) while maintaining competitive segmentation accuracy.

Figure 5. Segmentation results obtained by Swin UNETR

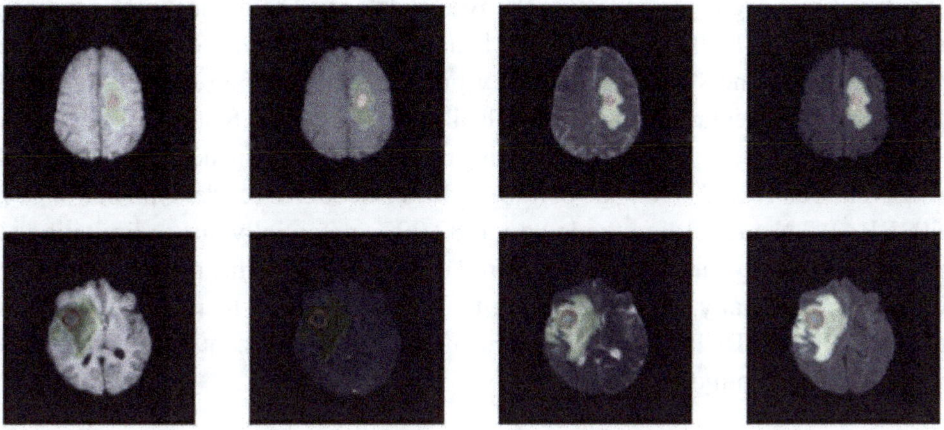

(Hatamizadeh et al., 2022)

Figure 5 shows the predicted labels overlaid on T1, T1c, T2, and FLAIR MRI slices from BraTS 2021 (~75th, ~50th, ~25th percentile Dice); grayscale intensities with TC (blue), ET (red), and WT (green) obtained by Swin UNETR (Hatamizadeh et al., 2022).

Despite significant progress, transformer models for brain segmentation still face challenges. High computational costs, as seen with UNesT (Yu et al., 2023), can impede clinical deployment. Limited annotated data has led to strategies like pre-training (BTSwin-Unet; Liang et al., 2023) and clinical knowledge-guided architectures (CKD-TransBTS; Lin et al., 2023). Moreover, multimodal fusion remains a critical area for enhancing generalizability and interpretability, as demonstrated in models like Hsienchih et al.'s multimodal transformer (Ting & Liu, 2024).

Figure 6. Performance of Transformer Models in Brain Segmentation

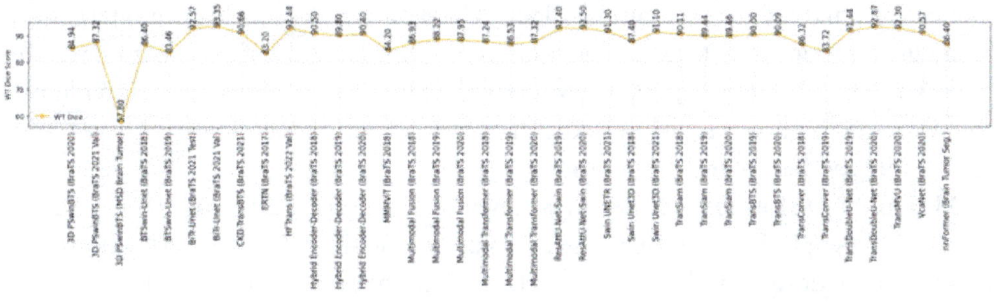

Figure 6 showcases the Dice score performance of various transformer-based models in brain segmentation using the BraTS dataset. The highest performance is achieved by Swin UNETR (BraTS 2021) and TransBTS (BraTS 2021), with Dice scores of 91.10% and 89.46% respectively, indicating their strong capability in whole tumor (WT) segmentation. Other models like CKD-TransBTS and TransUNet also maintain scores above 88%, demonstrating consistent performance. However, a few models such as BRAST-Net and certain Hybrid Encoder-Decoders fall below 85%, with BRAST-Net recording the lowest at 82.00%, potentially due to limitations in multimodal feature integration. The overall results highlight that modern transformer variants, especially those leveraging fusion strategies or hierarchical encoding (e.g., Swin UNETR, TransBTS), significantly enhance segmentation performance in complex brain tumor datasets.

3.2 Breast Lesion Segmentation

Breast lesion segmentation is a critical component of computer-aided diagnosis, facilitating early detection and treatment planning for breast cancer using imaging modalities such as ultrasound, MRI, and mammography. Precise segmentation of tumors and masses enables improved diagnostic accuracy and reduces the burden on radiologists. However, the task is often complicated by factors such as low contrast, heterogeneous textures, irregular lesion shapes, and speckle noise, particularly in ultrasound images.

In recent years, several transformer-based models have been proposed to improve breast lesion segmentation by combining local CNN-based features with global contextual representations. MET-Net (Iqbal et al., 2023), for example, introduces a memory-efficient transformer integrated with a dual encoder and a pyramid-dilated fusion (PDF) block to enhance multi-scale feature extraction and suppress irrelevant background signals in ultrasound and MRI images. HAU-Net (Zhang et al., 2023) enhances traditional U-Net with a Long-Range Transformer (L-G) block in the skip connections and a Cross Attention Block (CAB) for improved feature interaction, achieving superior performance on challenging ultrasound datasets. Similarly, the AGMT model (Zhao et al., 2024) incorporates attention-gate modules and a novel loss function to preserve lesion shape information and reduce false positives, particularly under data scarcity conditions.

Multiple transformer architectures have been developed to address modality-specific challenges in breast lesion segmentation. LM-Net (Lu et al., 2024) employs a lightweight design with local and global feature transformer (LFT and GFT) modules, achieving robust segmentation across various modalities. HCTNet (He et al., 2023) integrates Transformer Encoder Blocks (TEBlocks) and a Spatial-wise Cross Attention (SCA) mechanism to bridge semantic gaps in ultrasound images.

Another variant, HCT-Net (Yu et al., 2023), utilizes neural architecture search and a key-sampling transformer to optimize long-range dependency modeling. TrEnD (Liu et al., 2023) targets mammography with adaptive patch embedding (APE) and a hierarchical transformer encoder, achieving strong performance on CBIS-DDSM and INbreast. Meanwhile, ATFE-Net (Ma et al., 2023) uses an axial transformer with feature enhancement modules to balance segmentation accuracy and computational cost. YOLO-LOGO (Su et al., 2022) stands out by unifying detection and segmentation tasks through global-local transformer branches, improving lesion localization in mammography.

Evaluation of these models is conducted on a range of public and private datasets. BUSI, UDIAT, and BLUI are frequently used for ultrasound segmentation, while CBIS-DDSM and INbreast support mammographic analysis. Additional datasets such as Rider Breast, LGG, and private institutional datasets offer broader evaluation perspectives. Commonly used performance metrics include DSC, IoU, and overall accuracy, with auxiliary metrics such as precision, HD, F1-score, true positive rate (TPR), and mean average precision (mAP) used in specialized tasks. The segmentation results on a breast image by LM-Net (Lu et al., 2024) are shown in Figure 7.

Figure 7. Segmentation results obtained by LM-Net

(Lu et al., 2024)

Overall, transformer-based approaches have significantly enhanced breast lesion segmentation by overcoming the locality limitations of CNNs and improving generalization across modalities. Models like MET-Net (Iqbal et al., 2023) and TrEnD (Liu et al., 2023) demonstrate the effectiveness of fusing local and global representations, while lightweight designs such as LM-Net (Lu et al., 2024) address the need for computational efficiency in clinical settings. Nonetheless, challenges remain, including high model complexity, as seen in HAU-Net (Zhang et al., 2023) with over 32M parameters, and the demand for large annotated datasets. Future research directions include multi-modal fusion, architecture optimization, and deployment on resource-constrained hardware. A comprehensive comparison of transformer models for breast lesion segmentation is presented in Figure 8.

Figure 8. Performance of Transformer Models in Breast Lesion Segmentation. 8(a) Dice curves, 8(b) IoU curve

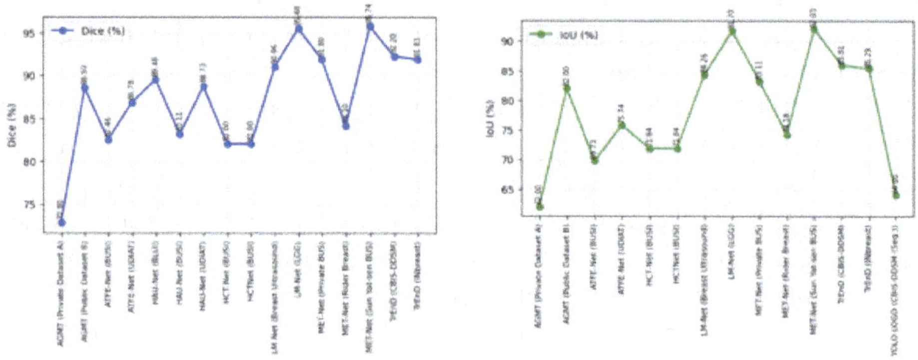

Figure 8 illustrates the performance of various transformer-based models in breast lesion segmentation using Dice and IoU metrics. In Figure 8(a), LM-Net (LGG) leads with Dice scores of 95.48%, showcasing exceptional segmentation precision. Several other models, including LM-Net (Breast Ultrasound), consistently exceed 90%, confirming robust performance across datasets. However, models like AGMT (Private Dataset A) and HCTNet (BUSI) fall behind with Dice scores below 85%, suggesting potential challenges in generalization. Figure 8(b) further supports these observations through IoU scores, where LM-Net (LGG) achieves the highest at 90.20%. Models such as YOLO-LOGO (CIS-DSDM Seg1) also perform well with IoUs above 85%, emphasizing the strong capability of certain transformer architectures in breast lesion segmentation, particularly across diverse and complex datasets.

3.3 Eye Retina Segmentation

Eye retina segmentation plays a crucial role in medical image analysis, enabling early detection and management of vision-threatening conditions such as diabetic retinopathy, glaucoma, and age-related macular degeneration. Accurate delineation of retinal structures, including blood vessels, optic discs and cups, and pathological lesions, from imaging modalities like fundus photography, optical coherence tomography (OCT), and OCT angiography (OCTA) is essential for reliable clinical diagnosis and treatment planning. However, the segmentation of retinal images poses unique challenges due to low vessel visibility, uneven illumination, small-scale structures, and class imbalance between background and foreground regions.

Several transformer-based methods have been proposed to tackle specific challenges in retinal image segmentation. For instance, TC-Net (Zhang et al., 2023) integrates a CNN encoder-decoder with a transformer branch to enhance lesion segmentation. It introduces a Locality-Aware and Long-Range Dependency Concatenation Strategy (LLCS) for multi-scale feature fusion and applies Dynamic Cyclical Focal Loss (DCFL) to mitigate class imbalance. OrbitNet (Li et al., 2023) extends the application of transformers to orbital CT segmentation, leveraging a FocusTrans encoder and structural similarity loss to distinguish delicate structures like the optic nerve. ARP-Net (Liu et al., 2023) adopts an Adaptive Gated Axial Transformer (AGAT) with a point repair module to improve vessel boundary clarity in OCTA images, showing promising results in microvascular analysis.

Further advancements include PKRT-Net (Lu et al., 2023), which incorporates prior clinical knowledge into a transformer framework for optic disc and cup segmentation, aiding in glaucoma screening. BCU-Net (Zhang et al., 2023) combines ConvNeXt and U-Net with a multilabel recall loss for segmenting both retinal vessels, demonstrating the flexibility of hybrid transformer designs. TUnet-LBF (Zhang et al., 2023) applies a two-stage strategy, using a transformer-based UNet for coarse segmentation followed by a Local Binary Energy Function (LBF) for refining vessel edges. OCT2Former (Tan et al., 2023) introduces a lightweight transformer encoder-decoder architecture for efficient OCTA vessel segmentation, while models like RTB & GTB (Huang et al., 2022) explicitly model relationships between retinal lesions and vessels to better segment diabetic retinopathy findings.

Transformer innovations continue to emerge in models such as PCAT-UNet (Chen et al., 2022), which integrates a convolutional branch, transformer module, and skip connections for improved micro-vessel segmentation. DA-Net (Wang et al., 2022) employs a Dual-Branch Transformer Module (DBTM) and Adaptive Strip Upsampling Block (ASUB) to preserve vessel continuity and reduce fragmentation. Other noteworthy contributions include SETUnet (Shen et al., 2022), HT-Net (Hu et al., 2022), ConvUNeXt (Han et al., 2022), and GT-DLA-dsHFF (Li et al., 2023), each offering unique enhancements such as hierarchical feature fusion, squeeze-excitation transformers, or low-parameter attention mechanisms to balance performance with computational efficiency. The Unified Gated Swin Transformer with Multi-Feature Full Fusion (UGS-M3F) (Bakkouri & Bakkouri, 2025) model integrates UM2F and GBS-T modules to effectively capture multi-level contextual and boundary-aware features for enhanced retinal vessel segmentation.

The evaluation of these models is conducted on a variety of publicly available datasets. Retinal vessel segmentation is commonly benchmarked on DRIVE, STARE, CHASE_DB1, and HRF, while lesion segmentation often uses IDRiD and DDR.

OCTA datasets such as OCTA-6M and OCTA-3M are employed for vascular analysis, and glaucoma-related segmentation tasks use datasets like Drishti-GS, RIM-ONE, and REFUGE. In the case of orbital structures, specialized CT datasets such as the one from Wenzhou Medical University (Li et al., 2023) are used. Standard metrics include the DSC, IoU, and accuracy, with supplementary measures such as sensitivity, area under the curve (AUC), HD, and Average Symmetric Surface Distance (ASSD) for nuanced evaluation. Figure 9 presents the segmentation results on a retina image obtained using ARP-Net (Liu et al., 2023).

Figure 9. Segmentation results obtained by ARP-Net

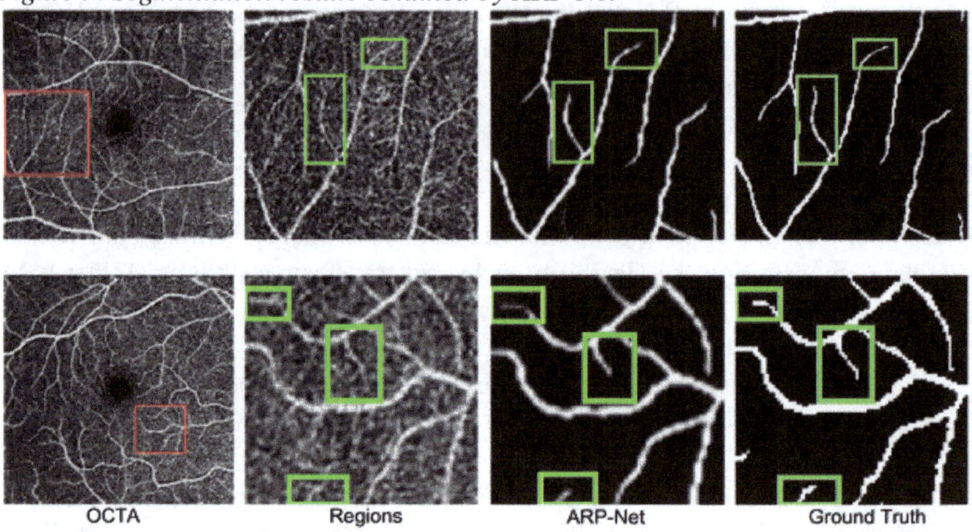

(Liu et al., 2023)

Quantitative results confirm the effectiveness of transformer-based models. For instance, ARP-Net (Liu et al., 2023) achieves Dice scores exceeding 93% on OCTA-3M, while PKRT-Net (Lu et al., 2023) demonstrates high accuracy in optic cup/disc segmentation across datasets like REFUGE and Drishti-GS. Lightweight architectures such as ConvUNeXt (Han et al., 2022) maintain strong performance with minimal parameter counts (3.50M), offering practical solutions for deployment in clinical settings. Nonetheless, the computational demands of larger transformer models, such as ARP-Net (Liu et al., 2023) with over 100 million parameters, highlight the need for more efficient attention mechanisms and data-efficient training strategies.

Figure 10. Performance of Transformer Models in Eye Retina Segmentation

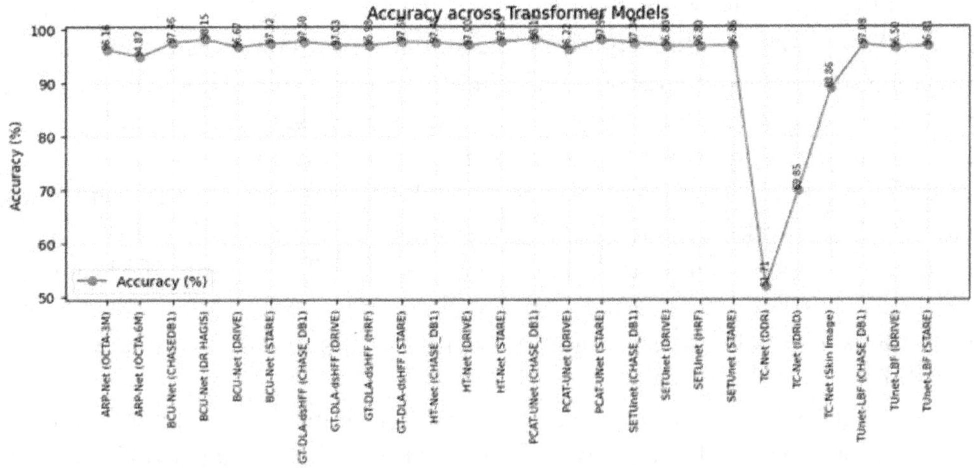

Figure 10 illustrates the performance of various transformer-based models in retina segmentation across multiple datasets. Most models demonstrate high accuracy, typically above 95%, underscoring the reliability of transformer architectures for retinal image analysis. Notably, GTD-DA+SwinFF and TUnet-LBF (STARE) achieve peak performances of 99%, indicating strong generalization across datasets. In contrast, the TC-Net (DDR) and TC-Net (DRID) models significantly underperform, with accuracies dropping to 52% and 65.8%, respectively, suggesting limitations in their adaptability or dataset compatibility. The consistently high performance of models like BCU-Net, PCAT-UNet, and SETUnet reinforces the potential of transformer-enhanced networks for precise retinal segmentation tasks.

3.4 Heart Segmentation

Heart segmentation is a cornerstone of medical imaging, enabling the diagnosis and treatment of cardiovascular diseases by delineating structures such as the left atrium, ventricles, myocardium, and carotid artery boundaries from imaging modalities like MRI, CT, ultrasound, and echocardiography. Accurate segmentation is critical for assessing cardiac function, detecting abnormalities, and guiding interventions. However, challenges such as low tissue contrast, fuzzy or ambiguous boundaries, motion artifacts, and anatomical variability complicate this task.

Transformer-based approaches for heart segmentation often incorporate hybrid designs that combine CNNs for local spatial representation with transformers for global reasoning. For instance, Hongkun et al. (Chen et al., 2021) proposed a parallelized encoder combining ResNet and transformer branches, augmented by a pyramid structure and channel attention for improved feature fusion. This architecture was validated on datasets including AVT and ACDC. Lei et al.'s DS-Former (Zhang et al., 2024) employs a dual-stream architecture for hierarchical feature extraction, achieving strong performance on both UK Biobank CMR and BTCV datasets. Xian et al.'s BATFormer (Lin et al., 2023) utilizes a cross-scale global transformer (CGT) and a boundary-aware local transformer (BLT) to preserve shape detail and reduce model complexity. For 3D echocardiography, DBTV (Zhang et al., 2023) integrates dual-branch networks for image and edge features and employs a 3D transformer to mitigate blind zones. Similarly, Yanping et al.'s U-CSWT (Lin et al., 2023) applies a hierarchical CSWin transformer framework for 3D carotid artery segmentation using ultrasound data, demonstrating versatility across different cardiac imaging modalities.

Several models bring novel strategies to address cardiac segmentation challenges. D-Former (Wu et al., 2023) by Yixuan et al. introduces dilated self-attention to expand the receptive field in 3D cardiac volumes. CTC-Net (Yuan et al., 2023) fuses Swin Transformers with residual CNNs and a Cross-domain Fusion Block (CFB) for complementary feature representation. Yong et al.'s ATFormer (Chen et al., 2023) enhances stability using scaled cosine attention and introduces a Progressive Guided Fusion module. CA-Net (Zhao et al., 2023) integrates a Trans-V transformer module into a semi-supervised pipeline for left atrium segmentation under limited annotation settings. Morpho-Net (Li et al., 2023) introduces morphological priors and a Reticular Transformer to improve shape regularity, while LGNet (Xu et al., 2022) uses a multi-feature fusion model (MSFFM) to combine local and global representations. Other architectures such as NVTrans-UNet (Li et al., 2023), TransBridge (Deng et al., 2021), nn-TransUNet (Zhao et al., 2022), EMSViT (Xiao et al., 2022), and GPA-TUNet (Li et al., 2022) further illustrate the diversity and adaptability of transformers in cardiac imaging.

Evaluation of these models typically relies on well-established cardiac imaging datasets. The ACDC dataset is widely used for benchmarking cardiac MRI segmentation performance, as seen in BATFormer (Lin et al., 2023), CTC-Net (Yuan et al., 2023), and nn-TransUNet (Zhao et al., 2022). DS-Former (Zhang et al., 2024) utilizes UKBB CMR and BTCV datasets, while CA-Net (Zhao et al., 2023) and Morpho-Net (Li et al., 2023) target the Atrial Segmentation Challenge and ACDC respectively. Additional datasets include MyoPS 2020 (Li et al., 2023) for myocardial pathology segmentation, and EchoNet-Dynamic (Deng et al., 2021) for echocardiographic cine data. U-CSWT (Lin et al., 2023) is evaluated on 3D ultrasound carotid artery segmentation datasets (CCA MAB/LIB, Bif. MAB/LIB), while DPC-MSGATNet (Qiao et al., 2023) addresses fetal heart segmentation. Performance is assessed using DSC and IoU for region overlap, HD for boundary error, and task-specific metrics like F1-score and precision. Figure 11 illustrates the qualitative segmentation results of BATFormer (Lin et al., 2023) on the ACDC dataset.

Figure 11. Segmentation results obtained by BATFormer

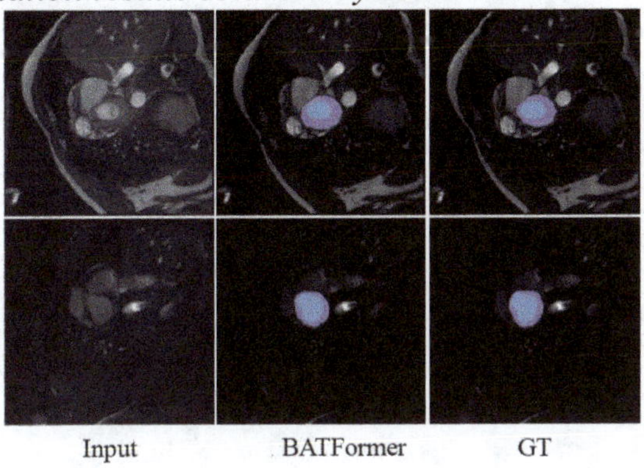

(Lin et al., 2023)

Transformer-based models have significantly advanced the field of heart segmentation, especially in modeling 3D structures, handling modality variation, and improving edge preservation. For example, GPA-TUNet (Li et al., 2022) effectively processes multi-vendor MRI and Synapse data with high Dice scores and low HD95 values. Lightweight and uncertainty-aware models such as TransBridge (Deng et al., 2021) and the approach by Tianlun et al. (Zhang & Wang, 2024) address clinical constraints related to computation and reliability. Despite the promising results, challenges persist, particularly in terms of large model sizes, as in DS-Former (Zhang et al., 2024) with over 59M parameters, and data dependency. Solutions like CA-Net (Zhao et al., 2023) offer semi-supervised training, while architectures such as NVTrans-UNet (Li et al., 2023) integrate multimodal inputs for greater robustness. A comprehensive summary of model performances, datasets, and metrics is provided in Figure 12.

Figure 12. Performance of Transformer Models in Heart Segmentation

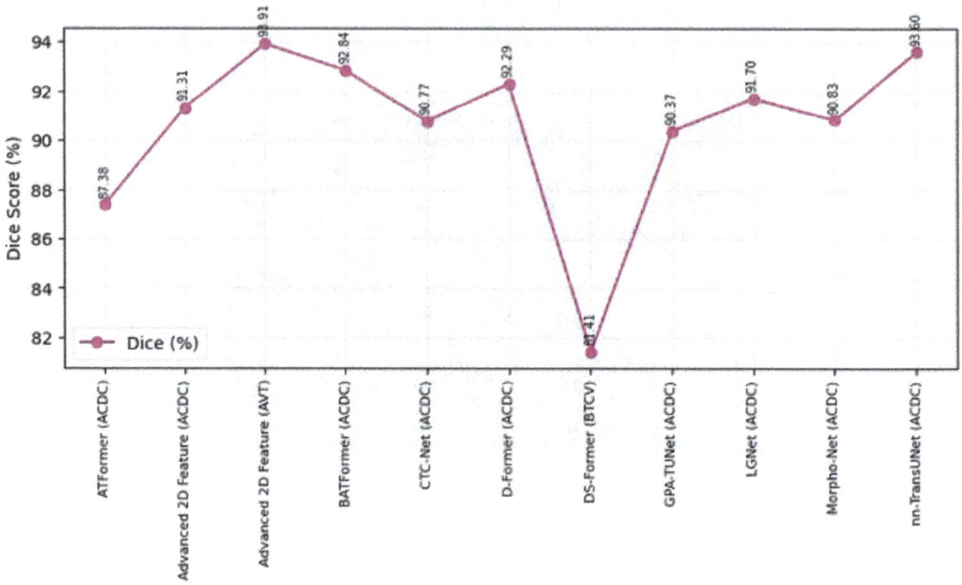

Figure 12 presents the Dice score performance of various transformer-based models in heart segmentation. Most models exhibit strong segmentation accuracy, with nn-TransUNet leading at 93.60%. Other models like D-Former and BAT-Former also perform reliably above 92%. However, DS-Former stands out as an underperformer with a Dice score of 84.71%, potentially due to dataset challenges or limited feature extraction capacity. The consistent performance across models such as GPA-TUNet, LGNet, and Morpho-Net (above 90%) highlights the efficacy and robustness of transformer-based architectures in segmenting complex cardiac structures from medical images.

3.5 Kidney Segmentation

Kidney segmentation plays a crucial role in medical imaging by enabling precise delineation of kidneys, tumors, and cysts from imaging modalities such as CT and MRI. This segmentation supports clinical applications including renal function assessment, surgical planning, and monitoring of disease progression. However, challenges such as blurred boundaries, inter-patient anatomical variability, and limited annotated data complicate this task. Transformer-based models in kidney segmentation have addressed domain-specific challenges by combining local CNN features with global transformer representations. MedNeXt (Roy et al., 2023), introduced by Saikat et al., integrates ConvNeXt blocks and iterative kernel upsampling in a transformer-inspired framework that excels in limited-data settings. EPT-Net (Yang et al., 2023) by Yang et al. incorporates edge-aware modules and a Dual Position Transformer to improve 3D spatial encoding and boundary localization, targeting datasets such as KiTS19 and SegTHOR 2019. FTransCNN (Ding et al., 2023) by Weiping et al. employs parallel CNN and transformer branches with fuzzy fusion and attention mechanisms, achieving high accuracy across multiple organ datasets. These models exemplify the adaptability of transformers in handling kidney-specific challenges such as tumor heterogeneity and fuzzy boundaries.

A diverse range of transformer-enhanced architectures has been proposed for kidney segmentation, each offering unique contributions. LCCF-Net (Lang & Liu, 2023) by Jun et al. introduces a lightweight design using Shifted Windows Self-attention Connection (SWSC) and Multiple Pooling (MP) blocks to capture contextual information efficiently. HT-Net (Ma et al., 2022) by Mingjun et al. enhances semantic understanding through a hierarchical transformer-based decoder with multi-scale fusion in skip connections. COTRNet (Shen et al., 2022) by Zhiqiang et al. blends convolutional and transformer encoders in a deep supervision framework, achieving comprehensive segmentation of kidneys, tumors, and cysts on KiTS21. These models highlight the role of transformer-CNN hybrids in balancing complexity and accuracy.

Evaluation of transformer models for kidney segmentation is based on widely recognized datasets and standard metrics. The Kidney Tumor Segmentation Challenge datasets, KiTS19 and KiTS21, serve as primary benchmarks, used in studies such as MedNeXt (Roy et al., 2023), HT-Net (Ma et al., 2022), and COTRNet (Shen et al., 2022). EPT-Net (Yang et al., 2023) additionally evaluates on SegTHOR 2019 and a modified KiTS19-M subset. FTransCNN (Ding et al., 2023) assesses performance across multiple organs, including kidneys, lungs, and breast. Core evaluation metrics include DSC for segmentation overlap, IoU for region intersection, and pixel-wise accuracy, with advanced metrics like surface Dice used in KiTS21 for boundary assessment. Figure 13 presents the segmentation outcomes achieved using FTransCNN (Ding et al., 2023).

Figure 13. Segmentation results obtained by FTransCNN

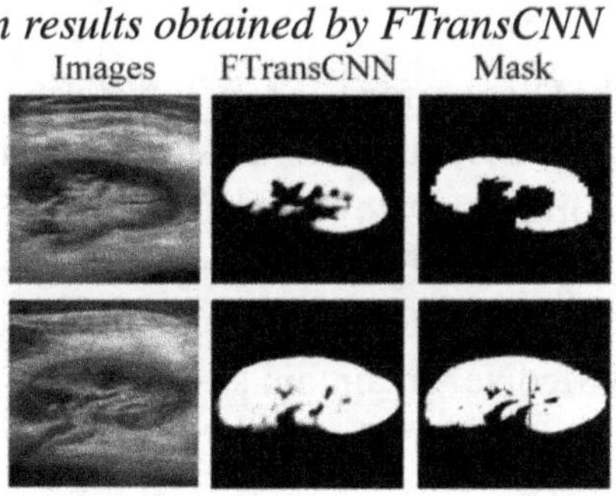

(Ding et al., 2023)

Transformers have significantly enhanced kidney segmentation by overcoming CNN limitations in capturing long-range spatial dependencies and handling sparse data. Models like HT-Net (Ma et al., 2022) and FTransCNN (Ding et al., 2023) demonstrate improved robustness in delineating tumors and cysts, while lightweight designs such as LCCF-Net (Lang & Liu, 2023) help mitigate computational demands (e.g., 18.68M parameters). Semi-supervised learning and pretraining strategies, as in COTRNet (Shen et al., 2022), also address data scarcity. Remaining challenges include balancing computational cost with performance and adapting to multi-modal imaging data.

Figure 14. Performance of Transformer Models in Kidney Segmentation

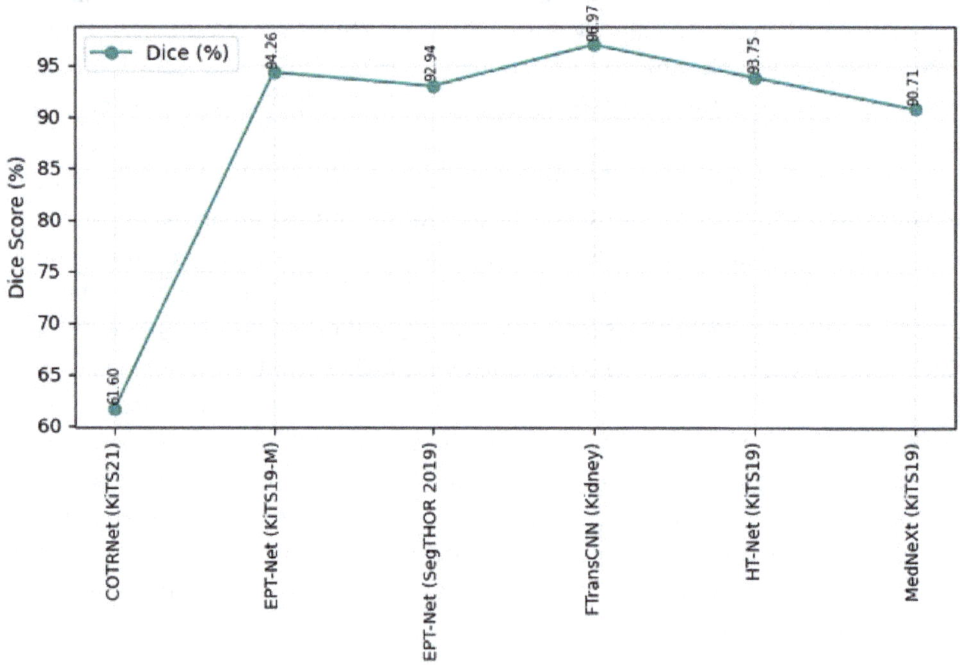

Figure 14 showcases the Dice performance of transformer-based models in kidney segmentation. The majority of models demonstrate high segmentation accuracy, with FTransCNN achieving the highest Dice score of 96.97%, reflecting its effectiveness in delineating kidney structures. EPT-Net also performs consistently well across datasets (KiTS19-M and SegTHOR 2019), with scores of 94.26% and 92.94%, respectively. HT-Net and MedNeX maintain strong performance above 90%, while COTRNet, with a score of 60%, stands out as a clear underperformer, likely due to

model immaturity or dataset mismatch. Overall, the results underline the promise of transformer architectures in accurately capturing the kidney's complex anatomy.

3.6 Liver Segmentation

Liver segmentation is a critical component of medical image analysis, facilitating the diagnosis and treatment of hepatic conditions such as liver tumors, lesions, and fibrosis. Accurate delineation of liver structures from imaging modalities like CT and MRI is essential for tumor resection planning, treatment monitoring, and liver function assessment. Despite its clinical significance, liver segmentation is challenged by factors such as irregular tumor shapes, low contrast across imaging phases, and the need for comprehensive anatomical context. DA-Tran (Ni et al., 2024) by Yangfan et al. addresses domain adaptation in multiphase CT segmentation through 3D transformer blocks and an attention fusion decoder. HRSTNet (Wei et al., 2023) by Chen et al. introduces a high-resolution Swin Transformer that preserves spatial detail through multi-resolution feature exchange. SWTR-Unet (Hille et al., 2023) by Georg et al. combines a ResNet backbone with transformer modules and a U-Net decoder, demonstrating high performance on MRI and CT liver datasets. MISSU (Wang et al., 2023) by Nan et al. incorporates multi-scale fusion and self-distillation to balance semantic and spatial detail, while SDPN (Wang et al., 2023) by Jing et al. proposes a dual-path network with multi-spectrum attention to enhance lesion adaptability. DHT-Net (Li et al., 2023) by Ruiyang et al. utilizes dynamic hierarchical transformers and edge aggregation to capture tumor irregularities, with detailed results shown in Table 3.6.

A variety of transformer-augmented architectures further illustrate the flexibility and effectiveness of this approach. SWTRU (Zhang et al., 2022) by Jianyi et al. enhances U-Net with a star-shaped window transformer decoder and a Filtering Feature Integration Mechanism (FFIM) for multi-scale learning. RDCTrans U-Net (Li & Ma, 2022) by Li et al. embeds transformers in the U-Net downsampling path to improve global representation. AD-DUNet (Qi et al., 2024) by Qi et al. employs axial attention with dilated convolutions in a dual-branch setup, while ResTransUNet (Ou et al., 2024) by Ou et al. emphasizes minimizing semantic feature loss. CotepResNet (Zhu et al., 2024) by Jiahua et al. incorporates a contextual transformer at the bottleneck for rich feature learning. Kumar et al. (Kumar & Kumar, 2024) propose a skip-fusion transformer to enhance decoder performance via enriched skip connections. Additional models like LGMA-Net (Ren et al., 2025), CSWin-UNet (Liu et al., 2025), and GWO-SwinUNet (Kumar et al., 2024) prioritize efficient transformer design using strategies such as SNP convolutions, channel-shifted attention, and metaheuristic optimization, further showcasing the diverse transformer landscape in liver segmentation.

Evaluation of these models is conducted on well-established datasets using standardized metrics. The Liver Tumor Segmentation (LiTS) dataset is a primary benchmark, supporting studies such as SWTR-Unet (Hille et al., 2023), SDPN (Wang et al., 2023), and DHT-Net (Li et al., 2023). Additional datasets include CHAOS and BraTS for MRI and CT liver evaluation, 3DIRCADb for tumor segmentation, and clinical datasets (DB1, DB2) for multiphase imaging in DA-Tran (Ni et al., 2024). HRSTNet (Wei et al., 2023) uses BTCV for multi-organ segmentation. Performance is typically measured using DSC to assess segmentation overlap, IoU for region consistency, and HD for boundary accuracy. Figure 15 presents the segmentation results produced by ResTransUnet (Ou et al., 2024) across the LiTs, 3D-IRCADb, and CHAOS datasets.

Figure 15. Segmentation results obtained by ResTransUnet on the LiTs, 3D-IRCADb, and CHAOS datasets.

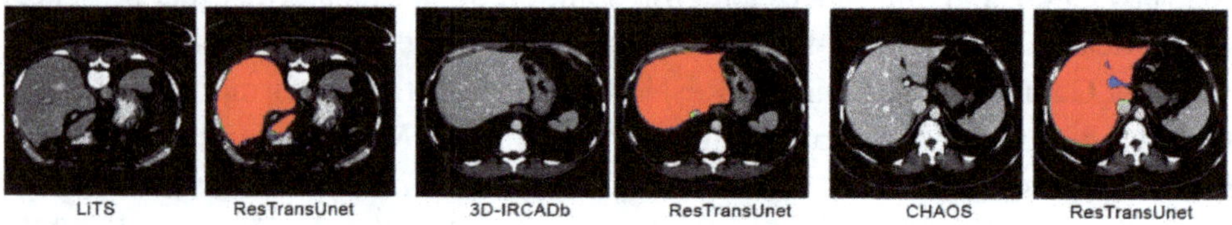

(Ou et al., 2024)

Transformers have meaningfully advanced liver segmentation by addressing CNN limitations in capturing global context and handling complex liver morphology. Models like DHT-Net (Li et al., 2023) and SWTRU (Zhang et al., 2022) demonstrate superior tumor localization and boundary delineation, while domain-adaptive strategies in DA-Tran (Ni et al., 2024) and efficient designs in CSWin-UNet (Liu et al., 2025) tackle challenges like cross-domain generalization and computational complexity. Nevertheless, issues remain, including high parameter counts (e.g., SWTRU (Zhang et al., 2022) with 45.7M parameters) and the need for improved integration of multi-modal data. Future directions explore lightweight architectures, improved pretraining strategies, and deeper clinical integration. A comparative overview of performance across datasets and metrics is provided in Figure 16.

Figure 16. Performance of Transformer Models in Liver Segmentation

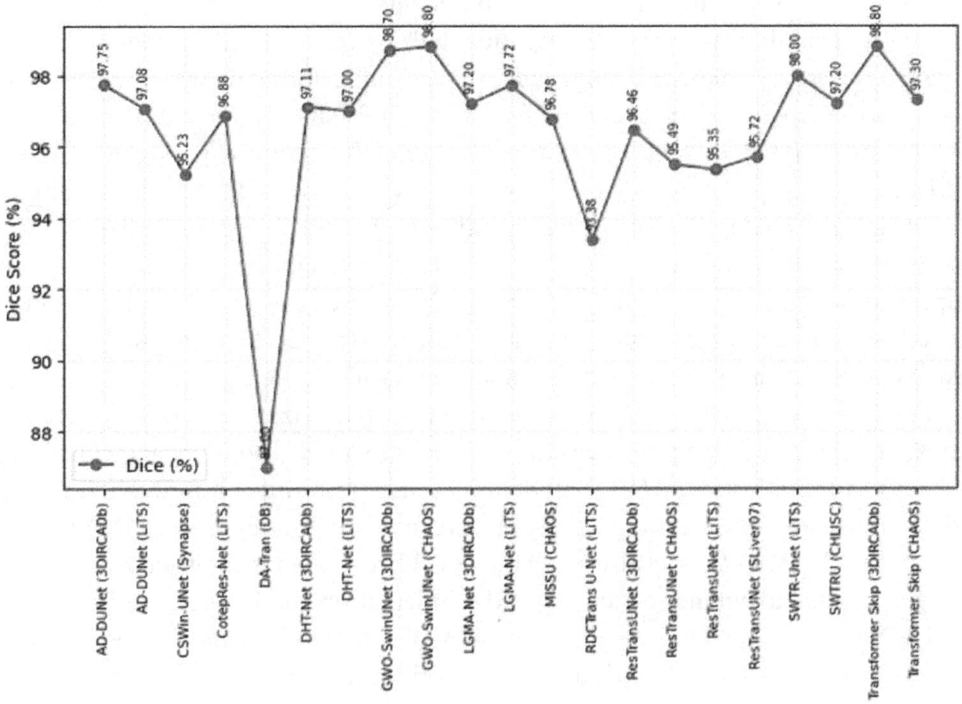

Figure 16 illustrates the Dice performance of transformer-based models in liver segmentation, highlighting their accuracy across various datasets. Most models achieve Dice scores above 96%, demonstrating their robustness in capturing liver boundaries despite anatomical variability and imaging noise. Notably, GWO-SwinUNet, ResTransUNet, and Transformer Skip lead with 98.8%, showcasing their superior ability to handle complex liver shapes. In contrast, DA-Trans lags behind with 87.1%. Models like AD-UNet, CSWin-UNet, and SWTRU also show consistent high performance across datasets (3DIRCADb, LiTS, CHAOS), reinforcing the effectiveness of transformer-based hybrids in liver segmentation.

3.7 Lung Segmentation

Lung segmentation for COVID-19 is a vital task in medical imaging, enabling accurate detection and quantification of infected regions, ground-glass opacities, and lesions in CT and X-ray scans. These segmentations support diagnosis, treatment planning, and monitoring of disease progression. However, COVID-19 lesions often exhibit irregular boundaries, diffuse patterns, and heterogeneous textures, making segmentation particularly challenging. Several transformer-based models have been proposed for COVID-19 lung segmentation, often employing hybrid architectures that combine CNNs with transformer components. UNeXt (He et al., 2024) by Yi et al. introduces dynamic token aggregation with Wave Blocks and an attention gate (AG) to suppress irrelevant background, improving lesion segmentation accuracy. The hybrid encoder by Zhang et al. (Zhang et al., 2024) incorporates a Feature Double Reuse (FDR) block and Vision Transformer (ViT), along with dual expanding paths to restore spatial features. FTransConv (Xiao et al., 2024) by Hanguang et al. integrates transformer-CNN blocks with a Full-scale Squeeze-Excitation (SE) module to handle scattered lesion distributions and inter-class similarities. In a semi-supervised setting, Zhao et al. (Zhao et al., 2023) propose an uncertainty-guided cross learning framework combining CNNs and transformers to refine pseudo-labels using epistemic uncertainty, targeting honeycomb-like patterns in CT scans.

Further developments include lightweight and specialized transformer architectures for COVID-19 imaging. The dual-encoder model by Tongping and Huanqing (Shen & Xu, 2023) fuses HarDNet68 and a transformer branch through a feature adaptation fusion module, supporting effective multi-scale integration. MMViT-Seg (Yang et al., 2023) by Yuan et al. uses a MobileViT backbone and multi-query attention (MQA) module to balance efficiency and segmentation quality across CT datasets. CTBP-Net (Ghali & Akhloufi, 2023) by Rafik et al. targets lung pathologies in chest X-rays using transformer-based attention. Xiaotian et al. propose Cross-Transformer (Li et al., 2023) and an improved transformer-pooling design (Li et al., 2023) to enhance boundary detail and global feature representation in nodule segmentation. MRL-Net (Liu et al., 2023) introduces Dual Multi-interaction Attention (DMA) and Dual Boundary Attention (DBA) modules for refined lesion boundary segmentation across heterogeneous COVID-19 datasets. SMR-UNet (Hou et al., 2023) by Jiachen et al. and TDD-UNet (Huang et al., 2022) by Xuping et al. integrate multi-scale and multi-head self-attention mechanisms into U-Net variants, with TDD-UNet introducing a dual decoder structure for robust foreground segmentation.

These models have been validated across a range of COVID-19-specific imaging datasets. CT datasets such as COVID-19 CT 100, COVID-19 CT 505, and COVIDSemiSeg are commonly used, as seen in MMViT-Seg (Yang et al., 2023) and TDD-UNet (Huang et al., 2022), while LIDC-IDRI supports pulmonary nodule segmentation in (Li et al., 2023; Li et al., 2023). Chest X-ray datasets are applied in CTBP-Net (Ghali & Akhloufi, 2023), and the MosMedData collection supports evaluation in MRL-Net (Liu et al., 2023). Common performance metrics include DSC, IoU, and accuracy, along with precision, recall, and sensitivity, offering comprehensive assessment of segmentation quality. Figure 17 provides a qualitative comparison based on (a) the input image, (b) the ground truth, (c) the output from FDR-64, and (d) the output from FDR-32.

Figure 17. Qualitative comparison showing (a) Input image, (b) Ground truth, (c) FDR-64 results, and (d) FDR-32 results

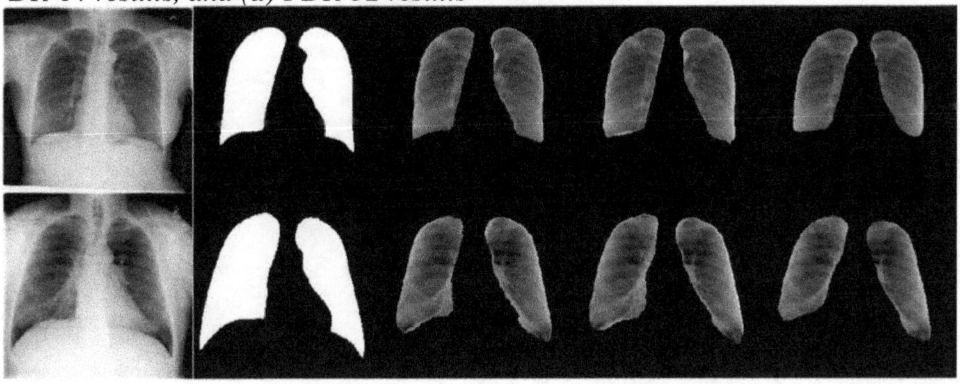

(Zhang et al., 2024)

Transformers have notably improved COVID-19 lung segmentation by addressing the global context limitations of CNNs, as evidenced by models like MRL-Net (Liu et al., 2023) and TDD-UNet (Huang et al., 2022). Their adaptability to irregular lesion shapes and their effectiveness in limited-data scenarios, especially via semi-supervised learning, have demonstrated strong clinical potential. Nonetheless, computational demands remain a concern, particularly in large models such as Zhang et al.'s hybrid encoder (Zhang et al., 2024) with over 100M parameters. Efficiency-focused designs like MMViT-Seg (Yang et al., 2023) and UNeXt (He et al., 2024), with under 1M parameters, show promise for real-world deployment. Future work may focus on lightweight, generalizable architectures and semi-supervised frameworks, such as uncertainty-guided models (Zhao et al., 2023), to improve performance and usability in clinical practice. Figure 18 shows the Dice performance of transformer-based models in lung COVID-19 segmentation. The plot compares various models in terms of their ability to accurately segment COVID-affected regions within the lungs. Higher Dice scores reflect better agreement with expert annotations, underscoring the effectiveness of transformer architectures in capturing infection patterns critical for COVID-19 diagnosis and monitoring.

Figure 18. Performance of Transformer Models in Lung COVID Segmentation

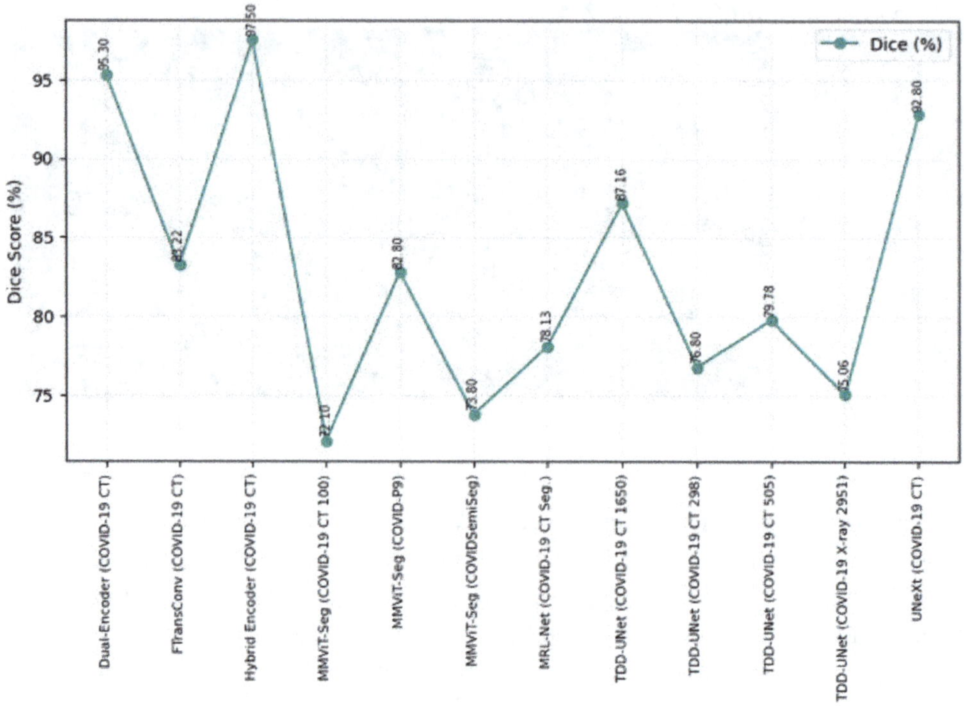

In lung COVID-19 segmentation, Transformer-based models show varied performance. The Hybrid Encoder and Dual-Encoder lead with Dice scores of 97.50% and 95.30%, respectively, showcasing strong spatial-context learning. In contrast, MMViT-Seg variants underperform with scores around 72–74%, likely due to limited or semi-supervised data. UNeXt also performs well at 92.80%, highlighting efficiency. Among TDD-UNet variants, performance improves with data size, peaking at 87.16% with 1650 CT slices. Overall, data volume and model design critically impact segmentation accuracy.

3.8 Multi-Organ Segmentation

Multi-organ segmentation is a critical component of medical image analysis, supporting comprehensive diagnostics, treatment planning, and disease monitoring across modalities such as CT and MRI. This task involves delineating organs such as the liver, spleen, kidneys, and pancreas, each exhibiting diverse shapes, sizes, and positions. These anatomical variations, along with complex spatial dependencies and heterogeneous imaging characteristics, make segmentation particularly challenging. Recent transformer-based approaches for multi-organ segmentation often utilize hybrid CNN-transformer frameworks to combine the strengths of both paradigms. UCFilTransNet (Li et al., 2024) by Li et al. introduces a Cross-Filter Transformer (CFTrans) block that operates in the frequency domain, effectively fusing multi-scale features and reducing semantic gaps. FC-UNETTR (Zhu et al., 2024) employs a global-local attention module to improve receptive field coverage and segment fuzzy boundaries, showing strong results across diverse datasets. Dong et al. propose PTransUNet and its compact variant C-PTransUNet (Wang et al., 2023), which use parallel transformer branches for efficient feature extraction with reduced computational overhead. CPFTransformer (Li et al., 2023) integrates Swin Transformers with edge-aware learning, while CTC-Net (Yuan et al., 2023) combines residual CNNs and Swin Transformers through a Cross-domain Fusion Block (CFB), balancing local detail preservation and contextual awareness. The Grouped Multi-Scale Vision Transformer (Ji et al., 2025) uses GMSA to enrich multi-scale feature representation through grouped channel-wise self-attention within a single layer.

Advanced models continue to diversify transformer applications. TransHRNet (Yan et al., 2023) integrates an Effective Transformer (EffTrans) block for high-resolution 3D segmentation across organs in the BCV and MSD datasets. ST-Unet (Zhang et al., 2023) enhances U-Net with Swin Transformers and a Cross-Layer Feature Enhancement (CLFE) module for better hierarchical representation. MAXFormer (Liang et al., 2023) achieves linear complexity using local-global attention for scalable performance, while MBUTransNet (Qiao et al., 2023) employs a multi-branch U-shaped architecture tailored for complex organ structures. IB-TransUNet (Li et al., 2023) introduces information bottlenecks for refined representation learning, and STA-Former (Liu et al., 2024) incorporates a Shrinkage Triplet Attention (STA) module to boost feature interaction and segmentation precision. Other innovative models include Morpho-Net (Li et al., 2023), which uses morphological priors; Fan et al.'s hierarchical integration framework (Wang et al., 2024); and LGNet (Xu et al., 2022), which focuses on lightweight multi-feature fusion.

Several models introduce unique mechanisms to address specific challenges such as small organ segmentation and semi-supervised learning. MGB-Net (Yuan et al., 2023) integrates GRUs in skip connections to enhance spatial continuity, particularly for small, difficult-to-segment structures like the pancreas. MFUnetr (Hao et al., 2023) explores multi-task learning on partially labeled datasets to reduce annotation demands. CoTr (Xie et al., 2021) introduces deformable attention modules (DeTrans) for efficient 3D volumetric segmentation. Swin-Unet (Cao et al., 2023), a pure transformer variant, demonstrates the potential of attention mechanisms in end-to-end architectures. Other notable contributions include TransUNet (Chen et al., 2021) and MISSFormer (Huang et al., 2023), which bridge global context modeling with compact design. Lightweight models like TFCNs (Li et al., 2022),

TransClaw U-Net (Yao et al., 2022), and TransUNet+ (Liu et al., 2022) prioritize efficient inference, while UNETR++ (Shaker et al., 2022) achieves significant FLOPs reduction while maintaining high segmentation accuracy.

Evaluation of these models is carried out using established multi-organ datasets and standard metrics. The Synapse multi-organ dataset serves as the most widely used benchmark, featured in studies such as MAXFormer (Liang et al., 2023) and UNETR++ (Shaker et al., 2022). Additional datasets include BTCV and MSD for abdominal organs (Li et al., 2024; Xie et al., 2021; Huang et al., 2023), and domain-specific datasets like MoNuSeg, Promise12, SegTHOR, and NIH-Pancreas. These datasets reflect a wide range of imaging modalities and clinical scenarios. Metrics such as DSC, IoU, and HD are commonly employed to evaluate overlap accuracy and boundary precision. Some studies also report recall, accuracy, and Average Relative Volume Difference (aRVD), providing a well-rounded evaluation. Figure 19 illustrates the segmentation of multiple organs performed by Swin-UNet (Cao et al., 2023).

Figure 19. Segmentation of multiple organs by Swin-UNet

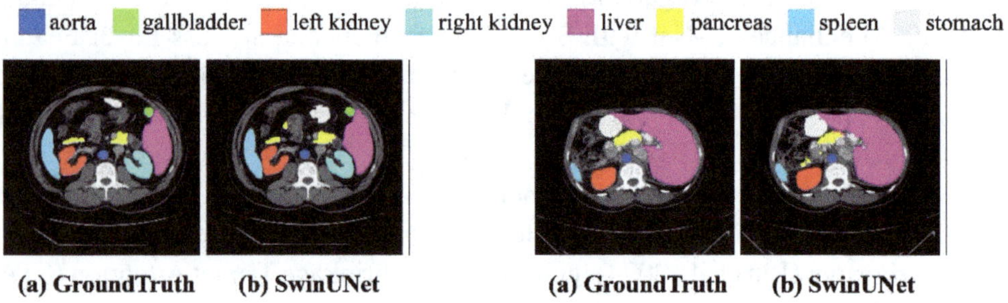

(Cao et al., 2023)

Transformer-based models have substantially advanced multi-organ segmentation, notably, CoTr (Xie et al., 2021) and Swin-Unet (Cao et al., 2023) show the benefits of pure transformer designs, while hybrid models like CTC-Net (Yuan et al., 2023) and TransUNet+ (Liu et al., 2022) demonstrate strong performance with balanced efficiency. The ability to scale to 3D data and capture fine-grained features across heterogeneous organs enhances their clinical applicability. However, challenges remain in computational complexity and training requirements. For example, TransHRNet (Yan et al., 2023) has a high FLOP count (568.8G), while lightweight alternatives like LGNet (Xu et al., 2022) and UNETR++ (Shaker et al., 2022) offer promising solutions with drastically reduced model size and inference cost. Looking ahead, research increasingly focuses on scalable transformer variants, semi-supervised learning with limited labels (e.g., MFUnetr; Hao et al., 2023), and more generalized architectures capable of segmenting multiple organs with minimal tuning.

Figure 20. Performance of Transformer Models in Multi-Organ Segmentation

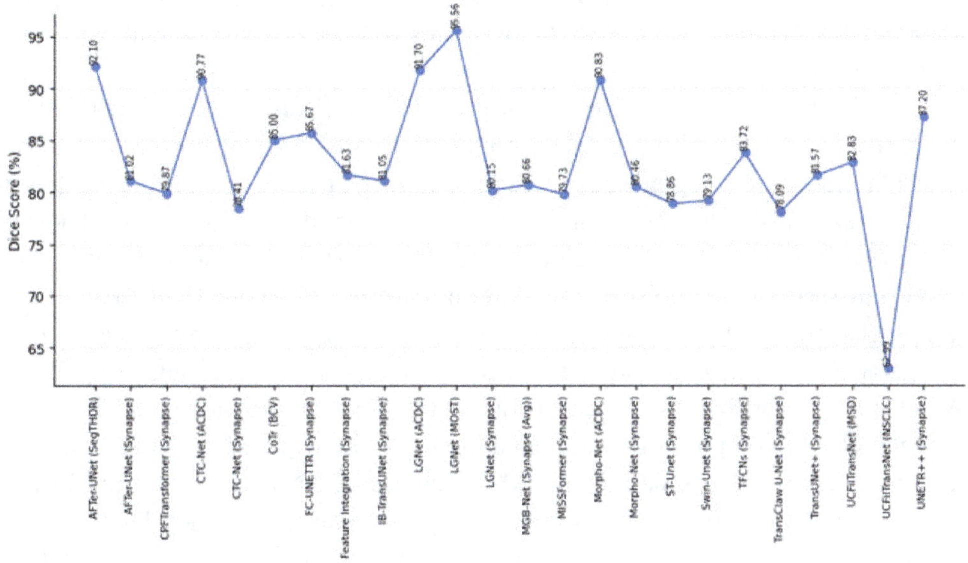

Figure 20 displays the Dice performance of transformer-based models in multi-organ segmentation. The graph compares a wide range of models across different datasets, showcasing their effectiveness in segmenting various anatomical structures. The variability in Dice scores highlights the impact of architectural choices and dataset characteristics on model performance.

3.9 Polyp Segmentation

Polyp segmentation plays a crucial role in gastrointestinal image analysis, particularly within colonoscopy, where precise delineation of polyps significantly aids in the early detection and prevention of colorectal cancer. This task presents numerous challenges, such as high variability in polyp size, shape, and appearance, low contrast between polyps and surrounding mucosa, and indistinct or blurred boundaries. In recent years, a diverse array of transformer-based models has been proposed for polyp segmentation. For example, CSwinDoubleU-Net (Lin et al., 2024) combines a dual-branch U-Net framework with CNN and Swin Transformer encoders, using a feature fusion module to enhance boundary accuracy. DUSFormer (Xia et al., 2024) introduces dual Swin Transformer V2 encoders and includes a

Stepwise Feature Fusion (SFF) and Adaptive Correction Module (ACM) to refine edge representation. GLSNet (Pan et al., 2024) employs Global Guided Local Feature Enhancement (GLFE) and Feature Stepwise Aggregation (FSA) modules to enhance local-global integration. Similarly, BUNet (Yue et al., 2024) incorporates a pyramid vision transformer backbone with Boundary Exploration (BEM) and Boundary Uncertainty Aware (BUM) modules to better delineate ambiguous or fuzzy polyp borders.

Several other models contribute novel architectural elements to this domain. CFATransUnet (Wang et al., 2024) leverages a Cross-Channel Feature Attention (CCFAT) module to mitigate semantic gaps between encoder and decoder. CT-Net (Zhang et al., 2024) introduces an asymmetric parallel design to achieve efficient local-global feature fusion. H2Former (He et al., 2023) applies hierarchical hybrid vision transformers for multi-scale attention learning. EG-TransUNet (Pan et al., 2023) focuses on progressive spatial enhancement, while DPCTN (Song et al., 2023) incorporates dual backbones and channel-cross fusion for robust representation. META (Wu et al., 2024) utilizes multi-scale efficient transformer attention, and HIGF-Net (Wang et al., 2023) applies a hierarchical fusion framework with a double-stream structure. ResPVT (Nachmani et al., 2023) replaces CNNs with pure transformer backbones, emphasizing model simplicity and performance efficiency. DBMIA-Net (Zhang et al., 2024) and TGDAUNet (Song et al., 2023) further refine boundary and multi-scale representation through targeted fusion and attention mechanisms.

Additional innovations continue to enrich this space. DS-TransUNet (Lin et al., 2022) adopts dual-scale Swin Transformer-based U-Net branches, while PMTrans (Zhang et al., 2021) uses a pyramidal structure to effectively capture hierarchical features. TransFuse (Zhang et al., 2021) incorporates parallel CNN and transformer branches with a BiFusion module, and MCTrans (Ji et al., 2021) introduces proxy-based multi-scale attention. RT-Unet (Li et al., 2022) enhances skip connections via transformer modules, while SwinPA-Net (Du et al., 2024) integrates dense multiplicative connections and local pyramid attention for refined feature aggregation. Other notable models include ColonFormer (Duc et al., 2022), SwinE-Net (Park & Lee, 2022), MIA-Net (Li et al., 2022), HSNet (Zhang et al., 2022), and TransResU-Net (Tomar et al., 2023), all of which adopt novel mechanisms, ranging from hybrid encoders to attention-driven decoders, to improve segmentation accuracy and generalization.

Benchmarking of these models is commonly conducted on widely recognized datasets, including Kvasir-SEG, CVC-ClinicDB, CVC-ColonDB, ETIS-Larib, CVC-300, and EndoScene. Evaluation metrics primarily include DSC, IoU, and accuracy, with additional metrics like precision, recall, and F1-score used in selected studies to provide a comprehensive view of segmentation quality. These metrics facilitate rigorous comparison of transformer-based approaches across varied clinical scenarios. Figure 21 shows the segmentation results of ResPVT (Nachmani et al., 2023) on the Kvasir-SEG dataset.

Figure 21. Segmentation result of ResPVT on the Kvasir-SEG dataset

(Nachmani et al., 2023)

Transformers have made substantial contributions to advancing polyp segmentation by enabling improved boundary localization, handling morphological variability, and reducing intra-class ambiguity. Models such as ColonFormer (Duc et al., 2022) and SwinPA-Net (Du et al., 2024) exemplify the clinical potential of transformer-based architectures. Despite their advantages, computational complexity remains a concern; for instance, CFATransUnet (Wang et al., 2024) comprises 66.05 million parameters, posing challenges for deployment in real-time colonoscopy settings. However, lightweight designs like MCTrans (Ji et al., 2021) (7.64M parameters) and computationally efficient architectures like GLSNet (Pan et al., 2024) (14.60 GFLOPs) show promise in addressing these limitations. Future research may focus on balancing performance with efficiency to support real-time, high-throughput clinical applications.

Figure 22. Performance of Transformer Models in Polyp Segmentation (Kvasir Dataset)

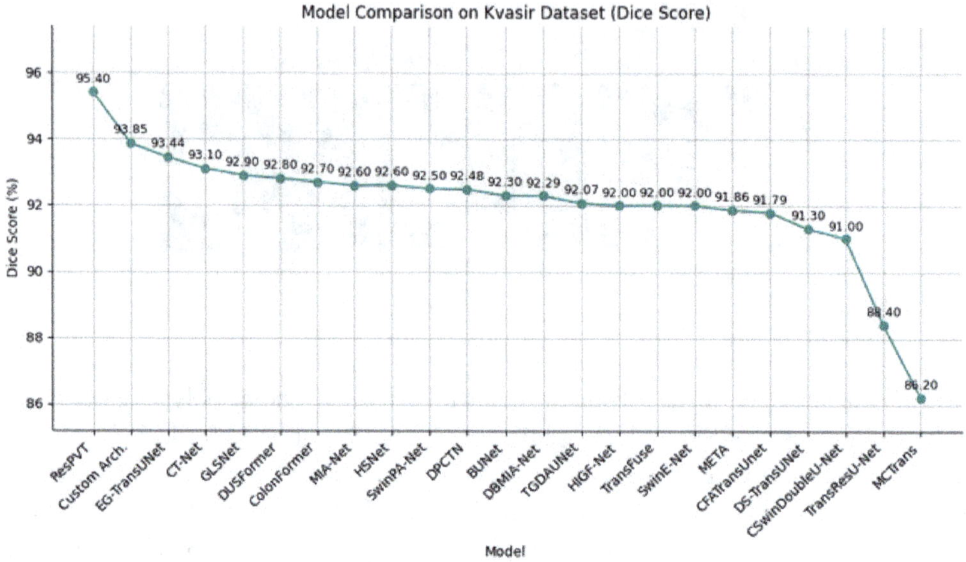

Figure 23. Performance of Transformer Models in Polyp Segmentation (CVC-ClinicDB Dataset)

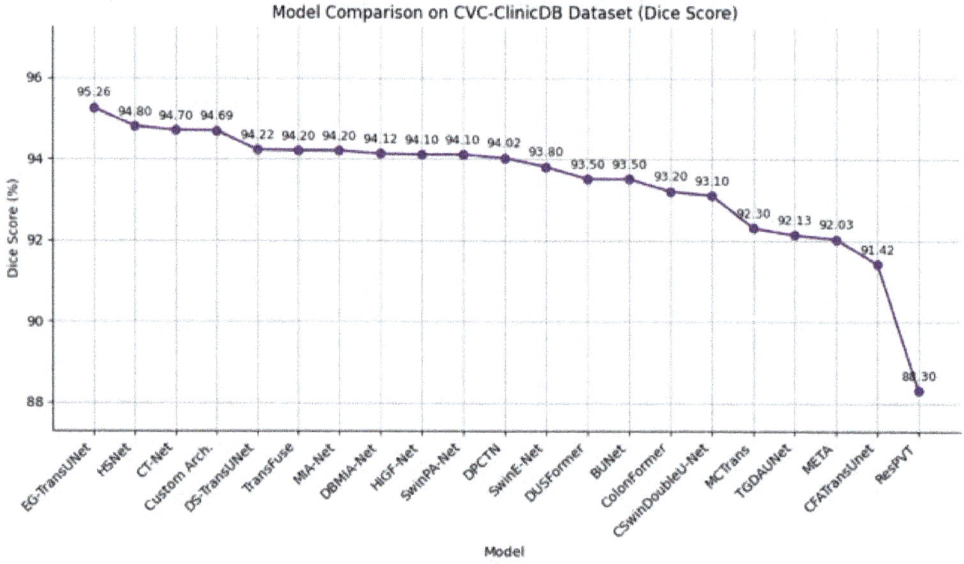

Figure 24. Performance of Transformer Models in Polyp Segmentation (CVC-ColonDB Dataset)

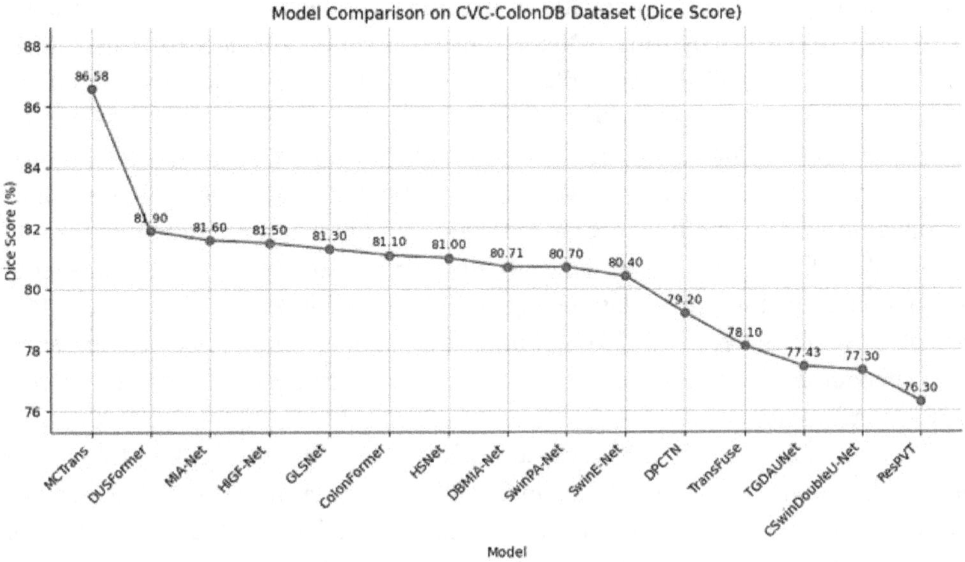

Figure 22 presents the Dice performance of transformer-based models on the Kvasir dataset for polyp segmentation. The comparison reveals that models like ResPVT, Custom Architecture, and EG-TransUNet achieve top-tier performance, with Dice scores exceeding 93%, highlighting their strong ability to segment polyps accurately. Meanwhile, models such as TransResUNet and MCTrans show comparatively lower performance. **Figure 23** shows the Dice score comparison on the CVC-ClinicDB dataset. EG-TransUNet and HSNet lead the performance chart, achieving Dice scores above 94%, indicating their robustness on this dataset. ResPVT and CFTransUNet fall behind in performance, showing that model efficacy can vary significantly across datasets. **Figure 24** illustrates performance on the CVC-ColonDB dataset, where MCTrans outperforms all other models with a notable Dice score of 86.58%. Other models, including DUFormer and MA-Net, also demonstrate competitive performance. In contrast, models like TransFuse and ResPVT record lower scores, reflecting challenges in generalizing across datasets with different characteristics.

3.10 Skin Lesion Segmentation

Skin lesion segmentation is essential for automated melanoma detection and treatment planning, particularly in dermoscopic imaging. Precise delineation of lesion boundaries aids dermatologists in early diagnosis, yet the task is complicated by challenges such as irregular lesion shapes, fuzzy or indistinct borders, and significant variability in color, size, and texture. A number of transformer-enhanced models have been proposed to tackle skin lesion segmentation. Tang et al. (Tang et al., 2024) introduced a hybrid CNN-Transformer architecture incorporating Trident Multi-Layer Fusion (TMF) and United Attention (UA) blocks to adaptively combine multi-scale features. DAE-Former (Azad et al., 2023) by Reza et al. integrates a cross-attention mechanism in skip connections to improve feature reuse. Yuanbin et al.'s CoTrFuse (Chen et al., 2023) combines EfficientNet with Swin Transformer, introducing a fusion module that balances local and global representation. MDViT (Du et al., 2023) by Siyi et al. employs domain adapters and mutual knowledge distillation to enable cross-dataset generalization using limited annotated data. TransCS-Net (Tang et al., 2023) by Suigu et al. adopts compressed sensing and a dual encoder design to enable privacy-preserving segmentation without compromising performance.

Other notable architectures include DCSAU-Net (Xu et al., 2023) by Qing et al., which enhances U-Net with compact split-attention units for lightweight yet expressive modeling. ABT-GAMNet (Deepa & Madhavan, 2023) combines an adaptive boundary-aware transformer with gated attention modules, guided by a novel optimization algorithm. Ning et al.'s APT-Net (Zhang et al., 2022) uses adaptive position encoding and a dual-path decoder to enhance context aggregation. TransCUNet (Jiang & Li, 2022) incorporates cross-residual fusion and pyramidal pooling to improve multi-scale robustness, while Trans-Norm (Azad et al., 2022) recalibrates skip connections using spatial normalization. The contextual attention network (Azad et al., 2022), also by Reza et al., emphasizes salient regions through global attention, contributing to better delineation of lesion structures.

Further innovations include boundary-sensitive models like BAT (Wang et al., 2021), which utilizes attention gates to refine contour details. FAT-Net (Wu et al., 2022) introduces a transformer branch with a feature adaptation module for better fusion of semantic and spatial cues. A semi-supervised method proposed by Mohammad et al. (Alahmadi & Alghamdi, 2022) enriches encoder representations with unsupervised learning signals. SLT-Net (Feng et al., 2022) leverages a Multi-scale Context Transformer to facilitate cross-level interaction. IASTrans-Net (Liu et al., 2022) uses intensive atrous spatial pooling to capture features at varying scales. Additional contributions include SEAformer (Li et al., 2025), CSWin-UNet (Liu et al., 2025), AFC-Unet (Meng et al., 2025), and DSU-Net (Zhong et al., 2025), each improving upon different facets of transformer efficiency, edge representation, and contextual learning.

These models have been evaluated on standard datasets such as ISIC 2016, ISIC 2017, ISIC 2018, and PH2, with some using additional datasets like DMF and SCD to test generalization. Evaluation metrics include DSC and IoU for overlap accuracy, along with standard measures like accuracy and F1-score. Figure 25 shows the segmentation results obtained by DSU-Net (Zhong et al., 2025).

Figure 25. Segmentation results obtained by DSU-Net

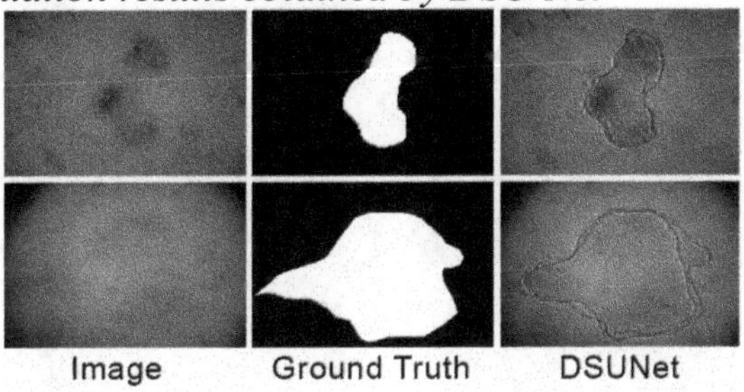

(Zhong et al., 2025)

Overall, transformer-based models have significantly enhanced segmentation performance in dermatological imaging. For instance, SEAformer (Li et al., 2025) and CSWin-UNet (Liu et al., 2025) demonstrate robust improvements in accuracy and boundary refinement. However, computational efficiency remains a consideration, FAT-Net (Wu et al., 2022) has 30 million parameters, while more compact designs like CoTrFuse (Chen et al., 2023) (10.7M) and DCSAU-Net (Xu et al., 2023) (2.6M) offer promising trade-offs. Future research directions include lightweight architectures for real-time applications, enhanced semi-supervised methods to tackle annotation scarcity, and privacy-preserving techniques as exemplified by TransCS-Net (Tang et al., 2023). A detailed comparison of these models across datasets and metrics is presented in Figure 26 and Figure 27.

Figure 26. Performance (DICE) of Transformer Models in Skin Lesion Segmentation

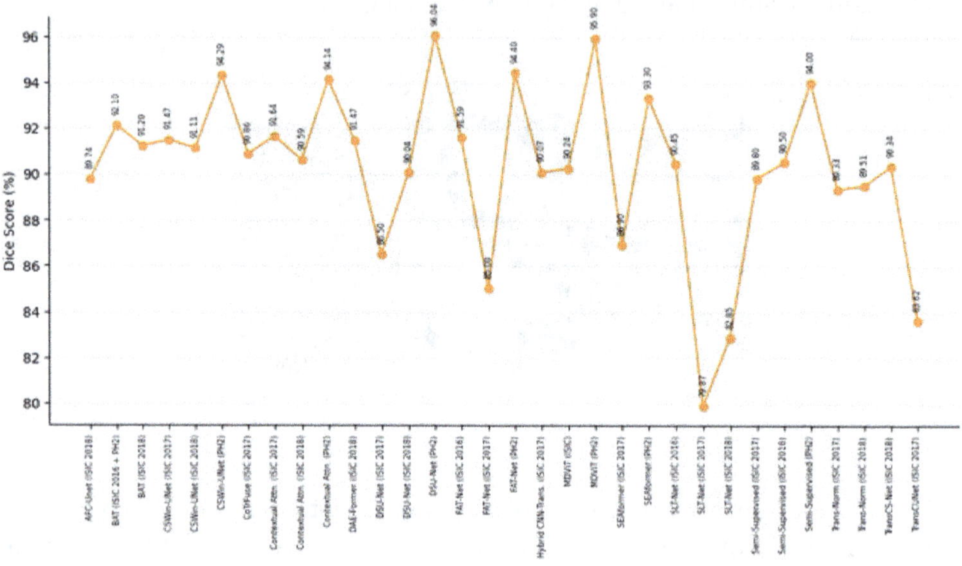

Figure 27. Performance (IoU) of Transformer Models in Skin Lesion Segmentation

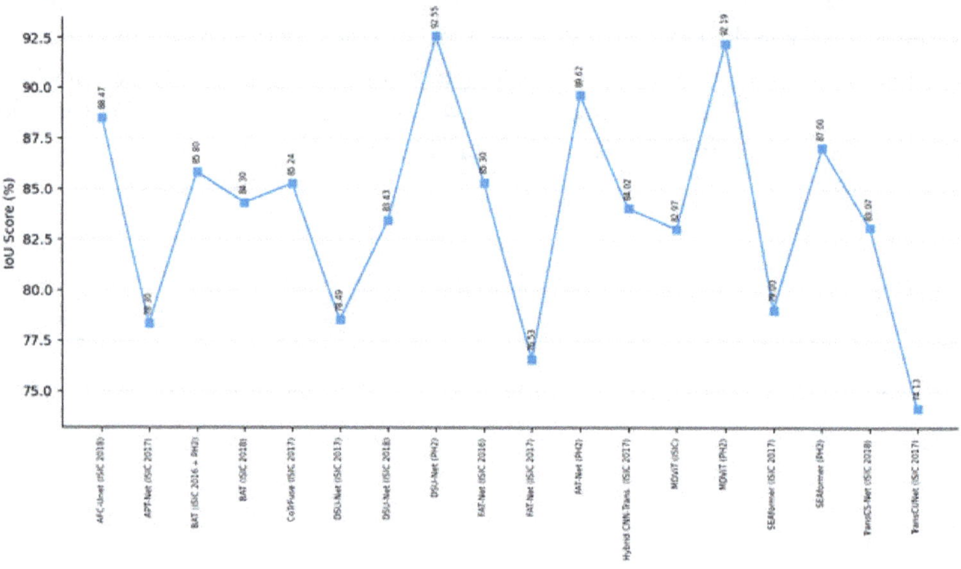

As observed in **Figures 26 and 27**, models trained and evaluated on the PH2 dataset generally achieve the highest scores, with DSU-Net leading with a Dice score of 96.04% and an IoU score of 92.55%, followed closely by SEFormer (Dice: 95.90%, IoU: 92.10%) and MOViT (Dice: 95.80%, IoU: 89.70%). Models like FA-Net (ISIC 2018) and CSWin-UNet (ISIC 2018) also perform strongly, scoring above 94% Dice and 88% IoU, indicating strong segmentation capabilities on larger and more complex datasets. Conversely, architectures such as TransUNet (ISIC 2017) and SEFormer (ISIC 2018) score significantly lower (Dice 86–87%, IoU 74–83%), reflecting challenges in generalization across diverse lesion characteristics. These trends suggest that PH2 provides cleaner and more consistent data, allowing models to achieve peak performance, while ISIC datasets introduce greater variability and complexity. Overall, DSU-Net and SEFormer emerge as robust and high-performing models in the skin lesion segmentation landscape.

4. PERFORMANCE, CHALLENGES, AND FUTURE DIRECTIONS OF TRANSFORMER-BASED MODELS IN MEDICAL IMAGE SEGMENTATION

Transformer-based models have demonstrated strong and consistent performance across a wide range of anatomical segmentation tasks, outperforming conventional CNNs by effectively modeling long-range dependencies and multi-scale contextual information. In brain segmentation, transformers excel at delineating complex and variable structures, such as gliomas and white matter regions, where spatial continuity and semantic context are essential. For polyp segmentation, they enhance boundary detection in colonoscopic images, handling irregular morphologies and blurred contours. In dermatological applications, particularly skin lesion segmentation, transformers improve lesion detection in dermoscopic images by integrating local textures with global structures to distinguish subtle abnormalities from surrounding tissue.

These advantages are reflected quantitatively in key performance metrics, such as DSC, Jaccard Index (IoU), and accuracy, compiled across different datasets and domains. In many cases, transformer-based methods achieve significantly higher overlap and intersection scores compared to their CNN-based counterparts, particularly in settings with heterogeneous data or limited annotations. While task-specific innovations, such as hybrid CNN-Transformer designs, attention-guided modules, or hierarchical encoding schemes, tailor these models to domain-specific challenges, the overarching trend points to the versatility and effectiveness of transformers in medical image segmentation. These findings suggest that transformers are emerging as a strong new standard across a spectrum of clinical imaging tasks.

Despite their demonstrated efficacy, several limitations currently hinder the broader clinical adoption of transformer-based segmentation models. Foremost among these is computational complexity. The quadratic scaling of self-attention with input resolution leads to high memory and processing demands, especially in 3D imaging tasks or high-resolution modalities. Large models, often containing tens of millions of parameters, pose deployment challenges in resource-constrained environments such as community hospitals or mobile devices.

Data scarcity also remains a pressing concern. Transformers typically require substantial annotated datasets to realize their full potential, but medical imaging datasets are often small due to privacy constraints and the high cost of expert annotation. This data dependence not only affects model generalizability but also limits the scope of pretraining strategies in specialized domains. Another critical barrier is model interpretability. While attention maps offer a degree of transparency, the inner workings of transformer models remain largely opaque compared to traditional techniques. This "black-box" nature raises concerns in clinical settings where explainability is essential for decision support, regulatory approval, and clinician trust. In summary, although transformers bring powerful capabilities to medical image segmentation, their integration into clinical workflows requires careful consideration of efficiency, data requirements, and transparency.

Several key developments are shaping the future landscape of transformer applications in medical image segmentation, with a strong emphasis on improving efficiency, adaptability, and clinical readiness. One major area of advancement lies in the design of lightweight and efficient transformer architectures. To address the high computational cost typically associated with self-attention mechanisms, newer models such as hierarchical transformers incorporate window-based or sparse attention strategies. These innovations significantly reduce memory usage and processing time while maintaining high segmentation accuracy. As a result, transformer models are becoming increasingly viable for real-time inference and deployment in resource-constrained settings, such as portable devices or rural healthcare facilities.

Another promising direction is the rise of self-supervised and semi-supervised learning strategies. These approaches use large-scale unlabeled medical image datasets through techniques like contrastive learning, masked autoencoders, and pseudo-labeling. By minimizing the dependence on extensive expert-annotated data, they improve the generalizability of transformer models and facilitate domain adaptation across varied clinical settings. This is particularly valuable in rare disease scenarios or specialized imaging tasks where labeled data is scarce. Multimodal integration is also gaining momentum, with transformers showing strong potential for fusing imaging data with complementary modalities such as electronic health records (EHRs), genomic data, and histopathology slides. The inherent flexibility of attention mechanisms allows transformers to learn from and relate diverse information sources, leading to more comprehensive and context-aware segmentation outputs that align more closely with clinical decision-making processes.

An equally critical area involves clinical validation and interpretability. To ensure safe and trustworthy deployment, ongoing research is focusing on establishing standardized benchmarks, developing explainable AI (XAI) techniques, and building user-in-the-loop systems. Attention visualizations, saliency maps, and feature attribution tools are being developed to enhance the transparency of transformer decisions, helping clinicians understand model outputs and increasing trust in AI-assisted diagnosis. Lastly, federated learning is emerging as a transformative approach for training transformer-based segmentation models across distributed and privacy-sensitive datasets. By enabling collaborative model training without sharing raw data, federated learning addresses key issues related to data privacy, security, and compliance with regulations such as HIPAA and GDPR. It also promotes the development of generalized models that benefit from multi-institutional knowledge while preserving patient confidentiality.

Collectively, these advancements are steering transformer-based medical image segmentation toward broader clinical integration, ensuring that future solutions are not only powerful and precise but also efficient, explainable, and ethically sound.

5. CONCLUSION

Transformer-based architectures have marked a significant advancement in medical image segmentation, redefining performance expectations across a wide spectrum of anatomical domains. By harnessing the power of self-attention mechanisms, transformers excel at capturing global contextual relationships and integrating multi-scale features, capabilities that address longstanding limitations of CNNs, particularly in modeling complex spatial patterns and non-local dependencies. Across tasks such as brain tumor segmentation, polyp detection, and skin lesion analysis, transformer models consistently achieve superior delineation of intricate anatomical structures, irregular boundaries, and visually subtle features. Their effectiveness spans multiple imaging modalities, including MRI, CT, ultrasound, and dermoscopy, reflecting a high degree of adaptability and robustness. Furthermore, hybrid architectures that combine the strengths of transformers and CNNs have further enhanced performance by balancing global context modeling with fine-grained local detail extraction. Importantly, these technical gains translate into tangible clinical benefits: improved diagnostic accuracy, enhanced surgical planning, and more precise treatment interventions. The ability of transformers to generalize across datasets with varying resolutions and annotation quality also positions them as reliable tools for deployment in diverse healthcare settings. Taken together, these advances underscore the transformative role of transformers in medical image segmentation and their potential to establish new standards for automated, reliable, and high-precision image analysis in clinical workflows.

The integration of transformer-based models into medical segmentation pipelines holds significant promise for advancing precision medicine and accelerating the adoption of AI-driven healthcare systems. With their capacity to generate accurate, consistent, and context-aware segmentations, transformers empower personalized diagnosis and treatment strategies tailored to individual patient characteristics. For example, precise tumor boundary detection enables optimized radiation therapy planning, while accurate lesion segmentation supports targeted drug delivery and surgical excision with minimal collateral damage. Beyond individual-level care, transformers' architectural flexibility allows them to incorporate multimodal data, including imaging, genomic, histopathological, and clinical records, enabling a more holistic understanding of disease etiology and progression. This multimodal integration aligns with the goals of predictive and preventative healthcare, offering new avenues for early diagnosis, patient stratification, and outcome forecasting.

In the broader scope of AI in medicine, transformers support the development of scalable, automated diagnostic systems that reduce the cognitive and logistical burden on clinicians. Their robustness facilitates deployment in low-resource environments, where access to specialized expertise and imaging infrastructure may be limited. Future applications could include real-time intraoperative guidance systems, remote monitoring of chronic diseases via portable imaging, and intelligent decision-support tools integrated into electronic health records. As ongoing research addresses key challenges, such as computational efficiency, interpretability, and clinical validation, transformers are poised to become foundational components of next-generation healthcare technologies. Their continued evolution will likely catalyze a shift toward data-driven, patient-centric care, fundamentally reshaping both clinical practice and medical research.

REFERENCES

Alahmadi, M. D., & Alghamdi, W. (2022). Semi-Supervised Skin Lesion Segmentation With Coupling CNN and Transformer Features. *IEEE Access: Practical Innovations, Open Solutions, 10*, 122560–122569. DOI: 10.1109/ACCESS.2022.3224005

Azad, R., Al-Antary, M. T., Heidari, M., & Merhof, D. (2022). TransNorm: Transformer Provides a Strong Spatial Normalization Mechanism for a Deep Segmentation Model. *IEEE Access: Practical Innovations, Open Solutions, 10*, 108205–108215. DOI: 10.1109/ACCESS.2022.3211501

Azad, R., Arimond, R., Aghdam, E. K., Kazerouni, A., & Merhof, D. (2023). DAE-Former: Dual Attention-Guided Efficient Transformer for Medical Image Segmentation. In Rekik, I., Adeli, E., Park, S. H., Cintas, C., & Zamzmi, G. (Eds.), Lecture Notes in Computer Science: Vol. 14277. *Predictive Intelligence in Medicine. PRIME 2023*. Springer., DOI: 10.1007/978-3-031-46005-0_8

Azad, R., Heidari, M., Wu, Y., & Merhof, D. (2022). Contextual Attention Network: Transformer Meets U-Net. In Lian, C., Cao, X., Rekik, I., Xu, X., & Cui, Z. (Eds.), Lecture Notes in Computer Science: Vol. 13583. *Machine Learning in Medical Imaging. MLMI 2022*. Springer., DOI: 10.1007/978-3-031-21014-3_39

Bakkouri, I., & Bakkouri, S. (2025, March 6). UGS-M3F: Unified gated swin transformer with multi-feature fully fusion for retinal blood vessel segmentation. *BMC Medical Imaging, 25*(1), 77. DOI: 10.1186/s12880-025-01616-1 PMID: 40050753

Cao, H. (2023). Swin-Unet: Unet-Like Pure Transformer for Medical Image Segmentation. In Karlinsky, L., Michaeli, T., & Nishino, K. (Eds.), Lecture Notes in Computer Science: Vol. 13803. *Computer Vision – ECCV 2022 Workshops. ECCV 2022*. Springer., DOI: 10.1007/978-3-031-25066-8_9

Chen, D., Yang, W., Wang, L., Tan, S., & Lin, J.. (2022). PCAT-UNet: UNet-like network fused convolution and transformer for retinal vessel segmentation. *PLoS One, 17*(1), e0262689. DOI: 10.1371/journal.pone.0262689 PMID: 35073371

Chen, Y., Lu, X., & Xie, Q. (2023). ATFormer: Advanced transformer for medical image segmentation. *Biomedical Signal Processing and Control, 85*. Advance online publication. DOI: 10.1016/j.bspc.2023.105079

Chen, Y., Wang, T., Tang, H., Zhao, L., Zhang, X., Tan, T., Gao, Q., Du, M., & Tong, T. (2023). CoTrFuse: A novel framework by fusing CNN and transformer for medical image segmentation. *Physics in Medicine and Biology, 68*. Advance online publication. DOI: 10.1088/1361-6560/acede8 PMID: 37605997

Chen, Jieneng, Lu, Yongyi, Yu, Qihang, Luo, Xiangde, Adeli, Ehsan, Wang, Yan, Lu, Le, Yuille, Alan, & Zhou, Yuyin. (2021). TransUNet: Transformers Make Strong Encoders for Medical Image Segmentation. .DOI: 10.48550/arXiv.2102.04306

Deepa, J., & Madhavan, P. (2023). ABT-GAMNet: A novel adaptive Boundary-aware transformer with Gated attention mechanism for automated skin lesion segmentation. *Biomedical Signal Processing and Control, 84*. Advance online publication. DOI: 10.1016/j.bspc.2023.104971

Deng, K.. (2021). TransBridge: A Lightweight Transformer for Left Ventricle Segmentation in Echocardiography. In Noble, J. A., Aylward, S., Grimwood, A., Min, Z., Lee, S. L., & Hu, Y. (Eds.), Lecture Notes in Computer Science: Vol. 12967. *Simplifying Medical Ultrasound. ASMUS 2021*. Springer., DOI: 10.1007/978-3-030-87583-1_7

Ding, W., Wang, H., Huang, J., Ju, H., Geng, Y., & Lin, C.-T. (2023). Witold Pedrycz, FTransCNN: Fusing Transformer and a CNN based on fuzzy logic for uncertain medical image segmentation. *Information Fusion, 99*. Advance online publication. DOI: 10.1016/j.inffus.2023.101880

. Dosovitskiy, A., Beyer, L., Kolesnikov, A., Weissenborn, D., Zhai, X., Unterthiner, T., Dehghani, M., Minderer, M., Heigold, G., Gelly, S., Uszkoreit, J., & Houlsby, N. (2020). An Image is Worth 16x16 Words: Transformers for Image Recognition at Scale. *ArXiv, abs/2010.11929*.

Du, H., Wang, J., Liu, M., Wang, Y., & Meijering, E. (2024, April). SwinPA-Net: Swin Transformer-Based Multiscale Feature Pyramid Aggregation Network for Medical Image Segmentation. *IEEE Transactions on Neural Networks and Learning Systems, 35*(4), 5355–5366. DOI: 10.1109/TNNLS.2022.3204090 PMID: 36121961

Du, S., Bayasi, N., Hamarneh, G., & Garbi, R. (2023). MDViT: Multi-domain Vision Transformer for Small Medical Image Segmentation Datasets. In Greenspan, H. (Eds.), Medical Image Computing and Computer Assisted Intervention: Vol. 14223. *MICCAI 2023. MICCAI 2023. Lecture Notes in Computer Science*. Springer., DOI: 10.1007/978-3-031-43901-8_43

Duc, N. T., Oanh, N. T., Thuy, N. T., Triet, T. M., & Dinh, V. S. (2022). ColonFormer: An Efficient Transformer Based Method for Colon Polyp Segmentation. *IEEE Access: Practical Innovations, Open Solutions, 10*, 80575–80586. DOI: 10.1109/ACCESS.2022.3195241

Feng, K., Ren, L., Wang, G., Wang, H., & Li, Y. (2022). SLT-Net: A codec network for skin lesion segmentation. *Computers in Biology and Medicine, 148*. Advance online publication. DOI: 10.1016/j.compbiomed.2022.105942 PMID: 35964466

Ghali, R., & Akhloufi, M. A. (2023). Vision Transformers for Lung Segmentation on CXR Images. *SN Computer Science, 4*, 414. DOI: 10.1007/s42979-023-01848-4 PMID: 37252339

Han, Z., Jian, M., & Wang, G.-G. (2022). ConvUNeXt: An efficient convolution neural network for medical image segmentation. *Knowledge-Based Systems, 253*. Advance online publication. DOI: 10.1016/j.knosys.2022.109512

Hao, Q., Tian, S., Yu, L., & Wang, J. (2023). MFUnetr: A transformer-based multi-task learning network for multi-organ segmentation from partially labeled datasets. *Biomedical Signal Processing and Control, 85*. Advance online publication. DOI: 10.1016/j.bspc.2023.105081

Hatamizadeh, A., Nath, V., Tang, Y., Yang, D., Roth, H. R., & Xu, D. (2022). Swin UNETR: Swin Transformers for Semantic Segmentation of Brain Tumors in MRI Images. In Crimi, A., & Bakas, S. (Eds.), Lecture Notes in Computer Science: Vol. 12962. *Brainlesion: Glioma, Multiple Sclerosis, Stroke and Traumatic Brain Injuries. BrainLes 2021*. Springer., DOI: 10.1007/978-3-031-08999-2_22

Hatamizadeh, A., Yang, D., Roth, H., & Xu, D. (2021). UNETR: Transformers for 3D Medical Image Segmentation. 10.48550/arXiv.2103.10504.

He, A., Wang, K., Li, T., Du, C., Xia, S., & Fu, H. (2023, September). H2Former: An Efficient Hierarchical Hybrid Transformer for Medical Image Segmentation. *IEEE Transactions on Medical Imaging, 42*(9), 2763–2775. DOI: 10.1109/TMI.2023.3264513 PMID: 37018111

He, Q., Yang, Q., & Xie, M. (2023). HCTNet: A hybrid CNN-transformer network for breast ultrasound image segmentation. *Computers in Biology and Medicine, 155*. Advance online publication. DOI: 10.1016/j.compbiomed.2023.106629 PMID: 36787669

He, Y., Gao, Z., Li, Y., & Wang, Z. (2024). A lightweight multi-modality medical image semantic segmentation network base on the novel UNeXt and Wave-MLP. *Computerized Medical Imaging and Graphics, 111*. Advance online publication. DOI: 10.1016/j.compmedimag.2023.102311 PMID: 38035411

Hille, G., Agrawal, S., Tummala, P., Wybranski, C., Pech, M., Surov, A., & Saalfeld, S. (2023). Joint liver and hepatic lesion segmentation in MRI using a hybrid CNN with transformer layers. *Computer Methods and Programs in Biomedicine, 240*. Advance online publication. DOI: 10.1016/j.cmpb.2023.107647 PMID: 37329803

Hou, J., Yan, C., Li, R., Huang, Q., Fan, X., & Lin, F. (2023). Lung Nodule Segmentation Algorithm With SMR-UNet. *IEEE Access: Practical Innovations, Open Solutions*, *11*, 34319–34331. DOI: 10.1109/ACCESS.2023.3264789

Hu, X., Wang, L., & Li, Y. (2022). HT-Net: A Hybrid Transformer Network for Fundus Vessel Segmentation. *Sensors (Basel)*, *22*(18), 6782. DOI: 10.3390/s22186782 PMID: 36146132

Huang, S., Li, J., Xiao, Y., Shen, N., & Xu, T. (2022, June). RTNet: Relation Transformer Network for Diabetic Retinopathy Multi-Lesion Segmentation. *IEEE Transactions on Medical Imaging*, *41*(6), 1596–1607. DOI: 10.1109/TMI.2022.3143833 PMID: 35041595

Huang, X., Chen, J., Chen, M., Chen, L., & Wan, Y. (2022). TDD-UNet:Transformer with double decoder UNet for COVID-19 lesions segmentation. *Computers in Biology and Medicine*, •••. Advance online publication. DOI: 10.1016/j.compbiomed.2022.106306 PMID: 36403357

Huang, X., Deng, Z., Li, D., Yuan, X., & Fu, Y. (2023, May). MISSFormer: An Effective Transformer for 2D Medical Image Segmentation. *IEEE Transactions on Medical Imaging*, *42*(5), 1484–1494. DOI: 10.1109/TMI.2022.3230943 PMID: 37015444

Iqbal, S. N., Qureshi, A., & Li, J.. (2023). On the Analyses of Medical Images Using Traditional Machine Learning Techniques and Convolutional Neural Networks. *Archives of Computational Methods in Engineering*, *30*, 3173–3233. DOI: 10.1007/s11831-023-09899-9 PMID: 37260910

Ji, Y., ... (2021). Multi-compound Transformer for Accurate Biomedical Image Segmentation. In: de Bruijne, M., *et al.* Medical Image Computing and Computer Assisted Intervention – MICCAI 2021. MICCAI 2021. Lecture Notes in Computer Science(), vol 12901. Springer, Cham. https://doi.org/DOI: 10.1007/978-3-030-87193-2_31

Ji, Z., Chen, Z., & Ma, X. (2025). Grouped multi-scale vision transformer for medical image segmentation. *Scientific Reports*, *15*, 11122. DOI: 10.1038/s41598-025-95361-8 PMID: 40169823

Jia, Q., & Shu, H. (2022). BiTr-Unet: A CNN-Transformer Combined Network for MRI Brain Tumor Segmentation. In Crimi, A., & Bakas, S. (Eds.), Lecture Notes in Computer Science: Vol. 12963. *Brainlesion: Glioma, Multiple Sclerosis, Stroke and Traumatic Brain Injuries. BrainLes 2021*. Springer., DOI: 10.1007/978-3-031-09002-8_1

Jiang, S., & Li, J. (2022). TransCUNet: UNet cross fused transformer for medical image segmentation. *Computers in Biology and Medicine*, *150*. Advance online publication. DOI: 10.1016/j.compbiomed.2022.106207 PMID: 37859294

Kumar, S. S. (2025). Advancements in medical image segmentation: A review of transformer models. *Computers & Electrical Engineering*, *123*. Advance online publication. DOI: 10.1016/j.compeleceng.2025.110099

Kumar, S. S., & Kumar, R. S. (2024). Transformer Skip-Fusion Based SwinUNet for Liver Segmentation from CT Images. *International Journal of Imaging Systems and Technology*, *34*. Advance online publication. DOI: 10.1002/ima.23126

Kumar, S. S., Vinod Kumar, R. S., Ranjith, V. G., Jeevakala, S., & Sajithra Varun, S. (2024). Grey Wolf optimized SwinUNet based transformer framework for liver segmentation from CT images. *Computers & Electrical Engineering*, *117*. Advance online publication. DOI: 10.1016/j.compeleceng.2024.109248

. Jun Lang, Yiru Liu, LCCF-Net: Lightweight contextual and channel fusion network for medical image segmentation, Biomedical Signal Processing and Control, Volume 86, Part A, 2023, https://doi.org/.DOI: 10.1016/j.bspc.2023.105134

Li, B., Liu, S., Wu, F., Li, G., Zhong, M., & Guan, X. (2022). RT-Unet: An advanced network based on residual network and transformer for medical image segmentation. *International Journal of Intelligent Systems*, *37*, 8565–8582. DOI: 10.1002/int.22956

Li, B., Yang, T., & Zhao, X. (2023). NVTrans-UNet: Neighborhood vision transformer based U-Net for multi-modal cardiac MR image segmentation. *Journal of Applied Clinical Medical Physics*, *24*, e13908. DOI: 10.1002/acm2.13908 PMID: 36651634

Li, C., Wang, L., & Li, Y. (2022). Transformer and group parallel axial attention co-encoder for medical image segmentation. *Scientific Reports*, *12*, 16117. DOI: 10.1038/s41598-022-20440-z PMID: 36167743

Li, G., Jin, D., Yu, Q., & Qi, M. (2023). IB-TransUNet: Combining Information Bottleneck and Transformer for Medical Image Segmentation. *Journal of King Saud University. Computer and Information Sciences*, *35*(3), 249–258. DOI: 10.1016/j.jksuci.2023.02.012

Li, J., & Chen, J. (2025). Lei jiang, Ruoyu Li, Peilun Han, Junlong Cheng, SEAformer: Selective Edge Aggregation transformer for 2D medical image segmentation. *Biomedical Signal Processing and Control*, *102*. Advance online publication. DOI: 10.1016/j.bspc.2024.107203

Li, J., Chen, N., Zhou, H., Lai, T., Dong, H., Feng, C., Chen, R., Yang, C., Cai, F., & Wei, L. (2023). MCRformer: Morphological constraint reticular transformer for 3D medical image segmentation. *Expert Systems with Applications*, *232*. Advance online publication. DOI: 10.1016/j.eswa.2023.120877

Li, J., Ye, J., Zhang, R., Wu, Y., Berhane, G., Deng, H., & Shi, H. (2023). CPF-Transformer: Transformer fusion context pyramid medical image segmentation network. *Frontiers in Neuroscience*, *17*. Advance online publication. DOI: 10.3389/fnins.2023.1288366 PMID: 38130692

. Li Li, Qiyuan Liu, Xinyi Shi, Yujia Wei, Huanqi Li, Hanguang Xiao, UCFil-TransNet: Cross-Filtering Transformer-based network for CT image segmentation, Expert Systems with Applications, Volume 238, Part A, 2024, https://doi.org/.DOI: 10.1016/j.eswa.2023.121717

Li, L., & Ma, H. (2022, March 23). RDCTrans U-Net: A Hybrid Variable Architecture for Liver CT Image Segmentation. *Sensors (Basel)*, *22*(7), 2452. DOI: 10.3390/s22072452 PMID: 35408067

Li, R.. (2023, July). DHT-Net: Dynamic Hierarchical Transformer Network for Liver and Tumor Segmentation. *IEEE Journal of Biomedical and Health Informatics*, *27*(7), 3443–3454. DOI: 10.1109/JBHI.2023.3268218 PMID: 37079414

Li, W., Song, H., Li, Z., Lin, Y., Shi, J., Yang, J., & Wu, W. (2023). OrbitNet—A fully automated orbit multi-organ segmentation model based on transformer in CT images. *Computers in Biology and Medicine*, *155*. Advance online publication. DOI: 10.1016/j.compbiomed.2023.106628 PMID: 36809695

Li, W., Zhao, Y., Li, F., & Wang, L. (2022). MIA-Net: Multi-information aggregation network combining transformers and convolutional feature learning for polyp segmentation. *Knowledge-Based Systems*, *247*, 108824. DOI: 10.1016/j.knosys.2022.108824

Li, X., Jiang, A., & Qiu, Y.. (2023). TPFR-Net: U-shaped model for lung nodule segmentation based on transformer pooling and dual-attention feature reorganization. *Medical & Biological Engineering & Computing*, *61*, 1929–1946. DOI: 10.1007/s11517-023-02852-9 PMID: 37243853

Li, X., Jiang, A., Wang, S., Li, F., & Yan, S. (2023). CTBP-Net: Lung nodule segmentation model based on the cross-transformer and bidirectional pyramid. *Biomedical Signal Processing and Control*, *82*. Advance online publication. DOI: 10.1016/j.bspc.2022.104528

. Xuejian Li, Shiqiang Ma, Junhai Xu, Jijun Tang, Shengfeng He, Fei Guo, Tran-Siam: Aggregating multi-modal visual features with locality for medical image segmentation, Expert Systems with Applications, Volume 237, https://doi.org/.DOI: 10.1016/j.eswa.2023.121574

Li, Y.. (2023, September). Global Transformer and Dual Local Attention Network via Deep-Shallow Hierarchical Feature Fusion for Retinal Vessel Segmentation. *IEEE Transactions on Cybernetics*, *53*(9), 5826–5839. DOI: 10.1109/TCYB.2022.3194099 PMID: 35984806

Li, Z.. (2022). TFCNs: A CNN-Transformer Hybrid Network for Medical Image Segmentation. In Pimenidis, E., Angelov, P., Jayne, C., Papaleonidas, A., & Aydin, M. (Eds.), Lecture Notes in Computer Science: Vol. 13532. *Artificial Neural Networks and Machine Learning – ICANN 2022. ICANN 2022*. Springer., DOI: 10.1007/978-3-031-15937-4_65

Liang, J., Yang, C., & Zhong, J.. (2023). BTSwin-Unet: 3D U-shaped Symmetrical Swin Transformer-based Network for Brain Tumor Segmentation with Self-supervised Pre-training. *Neural Processing Letters*, *55*, 3695–3713. DOI: 10.1007/s11063-022-10919-1

Liang, Z., Zhao, K., Liang, G., Li, S., Wu, Y., & Zhou, Y. (2023). MAXFormer: Enhanced transformer for medical image segmentation with multi-attention and multi-scale features fusion. *Knowledge-Based Systems*, *280*. Advance online publication. DOI: 10.1016/j.knosys.2023.110987

Lin, A., Chen, B., Xu, J., Zhang, Z., Lu, G., & Zhang, D. "DS-TransUNet: Dual Swin Transformer U-Net for Medical Image Segmentation," in *IEEE Transactions on Instrumentation and Measurement*, vol. 71, pp. 1-15, 2022, Art no. 4005615, doi: DOI: 10.1109/TIM.2022.3178991

Lin, J.. (2023, August). CKD-TransBTS: Clinical Knowledge-Driven Hybrid Transformer With Modality-Correlated Cross-Attention for Brain Tumor Segmentation. *IEEE Transactions on Medical Imaging*, *42*(8), 2451–2461. DOI: 10.1109/TMI.2023.3250474 PMID: 37027751

Lin, X., Yu, L., Cheng, K.-T., & Yan, Z. (2023, July). BATFormer: Towards Boundary-Aware Lightweight Transformer for Efficient Medical Image Segmentation. *IEEE Journal of Biomedical and Health Informatics*, *27*(7), 3501–3512. DOI: 10.1109/JBHI.2023.3266977 PMID: 37053058

Lin, Y., Han, X., Chen, K., Zhang, W., & Liu, Q. (2024). CSwinDoubleU-Net: A double U-shaped network combined with convolution and Swin Transformer for colorectal polyp segmentation. *Biomedical Signal Processing and Control, 89.* Advance online publication. DOI: 10.1016/j.bspc.2023.105749

Lin, Y., Huang, J., Xu, W., Cui, C., Xu, W., & Li, Z. (2023). Method for Carotid Artery 3-D Ultrasound Image Segmentation Based on CSWin Transformer. *Ultrasound in Medicine & Biology, 49*(2), 645–656. DOI: 10.1016/j.ultrasmedbio.2022.11.005 PMID: 36460566

Liu, D., Wu, B., Li, C., Sun, Z., & Zhang, N. (2023). TrEnD: A transformer-based encoder-decoder model with adaptive patch embedding for mass segmentation in mammograms. *Medical Physics, 50*, 2884–2899. DOI: 10.1002/mp.16216 PMID: 36609788

Liu, S., Cai, T., Tang, X., & Wang, C. (2023, September). MRL-Net: Multi-Scale Representation Learning Network for COVID-19 Lung CT Image Segmentation. *IEEE Journal of Biomedical and Health Informatics, 27*(9), 4317–4328. DOI: 10.1109/JBHI.2023.3285936 PMID: 37314916

Liu, X. (2023). Di Zhang, Junping Yao, Jinshan Tang, Transformer and convolutional based dual branch network for retinal vessel segmentation in OCTA images. *Biomedical Signal Processing and Control, 83.* Advance online publication. DOI: 10.1016/j.bspc.2023.104604

Liu, X., Fan, W., & Zhou, D. (2022). Skin Lesion Segmentation via Intensive Atrous Spatial Transformer. In Wang, L., Segal, M., Chen, J., & Qiu, T. (Eds.), Lecture Notes in Computer Science: Vol. 13471. *Wireless Algorithms, Systems, and Applications. WASA 2022*. Springer., DOI: 10.1007/978-3-031-19208-1_2

Liu, X., Gao, P., Yu, T., Wang, F., & Yuan, R.-Y. (2025). CSWin-UNet: Transformer UNet with cross-shaped windows for medical image segmentation. *Information Fusion, 113.* Advance online publication. DOI: 10.1016/j.inffus.2024.102634

Liu, X., Gao, P., Yu, T., Wang, F., & Yuan, R.-Y. (2025). CSWin-UNet: Transformer UNet with cross-shaped windows for medical image segmentation. *Information Fusion, 113.* Advance online publication. DOI: 10.1016/j.inffus.2024.102634

Liu, X., Yao, C., Chen, H., Xiang, R., Wu, H., Du, P., Yu, Z., Liu, W., Liu, J., & Geng, D. (2023). BTSC-TNAS: A neural architecture search-based transformer for brain tumor segmentation and classification. *Computerized Medical Imaging and Graphics, 110.* Advance online publication. DOI: 10.1016/j.compmedimag.2023.102307 PMID: 37913635

Liu, Y., Han, L., & Yao, B.. (2024). STA-Former: Enhancing medical image segmentation with Shrinkage Triplet Attention in a hybrid CNN-Transformer model. *SIViP*, *18*, 1901–1910. DOI: 10.1007/s11760-023-02893-5

Liu, Y., Wang, H., Chen, Z., Huangliang, K., & Zhang, H. (2022). TransUNet+: Redesigning the skip connection to enhance features in medical image segmentation. *Knowledge-Based Systems*, *256*. Advance online publication. DOI: 10.1016/j.knosys.2022.109859

Lu, S., Zhao, H., Liu, H., Li, H., & Wang, N. (2023). PKRT-Net: Prior knowledge-based relation transformer network for optic cup and disc segmentation. *Neurocomputing*, *538*. Advance online publication. DOI: 10.1016/j.neucom.2023.03.044

Lu, Z., She, C., Wang, W., & Huang, Q. (2024). LM-Net: A light-weight and multi-scale network for medical image segmentation. *Computers in Biology and Medicine*, *168*. Advance online publication. DOI: 10.1016/j.compbiomed.2023.107717 PMID: 38007973

Ma, J., He, Y., & Li, F.. (2024). Segment anything in medical images. *Nature Communications*, *15*, 654. DOI: 10.1038/s41467-024-44824-z PMID: 38253604

Ma, M., Xia, H., & Tan, Y.. (2022). HT-Net: Hierarchical context-attention transformer network for medical ct image segmentation. *Applied Intelligence*, *52*, 10692–10705. DOI: 10.1007/s10489-021-03010-0

Ma, Z., Qi, Y., Xu, C., Zhao, W., Lou, M., Wang, Y., & Ma, Y. (2023). ATFE-Net: Axial Transformer and Feature Enhancement-based CNN for ultrasound breast mass segmentation. *Computers in Biology and Medicine*, *153*. Advance online publication. DOI: 10.1016/j.compbiomed.2022.106533 PMID: 36638617

Marcus, A., Bentley, P., & Rueckert, D. (2023, December). Concurrent Ischemic Lesion Age Estimation and Segmentation of CT Brain Using a Transformer-Based Network. *IEEE Transactions on Medical Imaging*, *42*(12), 3464–3473. DOI: 10.1109/TMI.2023.3287361 PMID: 37335797

Meng, W., Liu, S., & Wang, H. (2025). AFC-Unet: Attention-fused full-scale CNN-transformer unet for medical image segmentation. *Biomedical Signal Processing and Control*, *99*. Advance online publication. DOI: 10.1016/j.bspc.2024.106839

Nachmani, R., Nidal, I., Robinson, D., Yassin, M., & Abookasis, D. (2023). Segmentation of polyps based on pyramid vision transformers and residual block for real-time endoscopy imaging. *Journal of Pathology Informatics*, *14*. Advance online publication. DOI: 10.1016/j.jpi.2023.100197 PMID: 36844703

Ni, Y., Chen, G., Feng, Z., & Cui, H. (2024). Dimitris Metaxas, Shaoting Zhang, Wentao Zhu, DA-Tran: Multiphase liver tumor segmentation with a domain-adaptive transformer network. *Pattern Recognition, 149*. Advance online publication. DOI: 10.1016/j.patcog.2023.110233

Ou, J., Jiang, L., Bai, T., Zhan, P., Liu, R., & Xiao, H. (2024). ResTransUnet: An effective network combined with Transformer and U-Net for liver segmentation in CT scans. *Computers in Biology and Medicine, 177*. Advance online publication. DOI: 10.1016/j.compbiomed.2024.108625 PMID: 38823365

Pan, D., & Shen, J. (2025). Zaid Al-Huda, Mohammed A.A. Al-qaness, VcaNet: Vision Transformer with fusion channel and spatial attention module for 3D brain tumor segmentation. *Computers in Biology and Medicine, 186*. Advance online publication. DOI: 10.1016/j.compbiomed.2025.109662 PMID: 39813745

Pan, S., Liu, X., & Xie, N.. (2023). EG-TransUNet: A transformer-based U-Net with enhanced and guided models for biomedical image segmentation. *BMC Bioinformatics*, *24*, 85. DOI: 10.1186/s12859-023-05196-1 PMID: 36882688

Pan, X., Ma, C., Mu, Y., & Bi, M. (2024). GLSNet: A Global Guided Local Feature Stepwise Aggregation Network for polyp segmentation. *Biomedical Signal Processing and Control, 87*. Advance online publication. DOI: 10.1016/j.bspc.2023.105528

Park, K.-B., & Lee, J. Y. (2022, April). SwinE-Net: Hybrid deep learning approach to novel polyp segmentation using convolutional neural network and Swin Transformer. *Journal of Computational Design and Engineering*, *9*(2), 616–632. DOI: 10.1093/jcde/qwac018

Piao, Z., Gu, Y. H., & Jin, H.. (2023). Intracerebral hemorrhage CT scan image segmentation with HarDNet based transformer. *Scientific Reports*, *13*, 7208. DOI: 10.1038/s41598-023-33775-y PMID: 37137921

. Hang Qi, Weijiang Wang, Yueting Shi, Xiaohua Wang, AD-DUNet: A dual-branch encoder approach by combining axial Transformer with cascaded dilated convolutions for liver and hepatic tumor segmentation, Biomedical Signal Processing and Control, Volume 95, Part B, 2024, https://doi.org/.DOI: 10.1016/j.bspc.2024.106397

Qiao, J., Wang, X., & Chen, J.. (2023). MBUTransNet: Multi-branch U-shaped network fusion transformer architecture for medical image segmentation. *Int J CARS, 18*, 1895–1902. DOI: 10.1007/s11548-023-02879-1 PMID: 37024630

Qiao, S., Pang, S., & Luo, G.. (2023). DPC-MSGATNet: Dual-path chain multi-scale gated axial-transformer network for four-chamber view segmentation in fetal echocardiography. *Complex & Intelligent Systems*, *9*, 4503–4519. DOI: 10.1007/s40747-023-00968-x

. Ren, W., Li, B., Peng, and H. *et al.* Lgma-net: liver and tumor segmentation methods based on local–global feature mergence and attention mechanisms. *SIViP* **19**, 43 (2025). https://doi.org/DOI: 10.1007/s11760-024-03731-y

Roy, S.. (2023). MedNeXt: Transformer-Driven Scaling of ConvNets for Medical Image Segmentation. In Greenspan, H. (Eds.), Medical Image Computing and Computer Assisted Intervention: Vol. 14223. *MICCAI 2023. MICCAI 2023. Lecture Notes in Computer Science*. Springer., DOI: 10.1007/978-3-031-43901-8_39

Shaker, A., Maaz, M., & Rasheed, A. Hanoona & Khan, Salman & Yang, Ming-Hsuan & Khan, Fahad. (2022). UNETR++: Delving into Efficient and Accurate 3D Medical Image Segmentation. 10.48550/arXiv.2212.04497.

Shen, T., & Xu, H. (2023). Medical Image Segmentation Based on Transformer and HarDNet Structures. *IEEE Access: Practical Innovations, Open Solutions*, *11*, 16621–16630. DOI: 10.1109/ACCESS.2023.3244197

Shen, X., Xu, J., Jia, H., Fan, P., Dong, F., Yu, B., & Ren, S. (2022). Self-attentional microvessel segmentation via squeeze-excitation transformer Unet. *Computerized Medical Imaging and Graphics*, *97*. Advance online publication. DOI: 10.1016/j.compmedimag.2022.102055 PMID: 35320771

Shen, Z., Yang, H., Zhang, Z., & Zheng, S. (2022). Automated Kidney Tumor Segmentation with Convolution and Transformer Network. In Heller, N., Isensee, F., Trofimova, D., Tejpaul, R., Papanikolopoulos, N., & Weight, C. (Eds.), Lecture Notes in Computer Science: Vol. 13168. *Kidney and Kidney Tumor Segmentation. KiTS 2021*. Springer., DOI: 10.1007/978-3-030-98385-7_1

Song, P., Fan, H., & Fan, L. (2023). TGDAUNet: Transformer and GCNN based dual-branch attention UNet for medical image segmentation. *Computers in Biology and Medicine*, *167*, 107583. DOI: 10.1016/j.compbiomed.2023.107583 PMID: 37890420

Song, P., Yang, Z., Li, J., & Fan, H. (2023). DPCTN: Dual path context-aware transformer network for medical image segmentation. *Engineering Applications of Artificial Intelligence*, *124*. Advance online publication. DOI: 10.1016/j.engappai.2023.106634

Su, Y., Liu, Q., Xie, W., & Hu, P. (2022). YOLO-LOGO: A transformer-based YOLO segmentation model for breast mass detection and segmentation in digital mammograms. *Computer Methods and Programs in Biomedicine, 221.* Advance online publication. DOI: 10.1016/j.cmpb.2022.106903 PMID: 35636358

Tan, X., Chen, X., Meng, Q., Shi, F., Xiang, D., Chen, Z., Pan, L., & Zhu, W. (2023). OCT2Former: A retinal OCT-angiography vessel segmentation transformer. *Computer Methods and Programs in Biomedicine, 233.* Advance online publication. DOI: 10.1016/j.cmpb.2023.107454 PMID: 36921468

. Hui Tang, Yuanbin Chen, Tao Wang, Yuanbo Zhou, Longxuan Zhao, Qinquan Gao, Min Du, Tao Tan, Xinlin Zhang, Tong Tong, HTC-Net: A hybrid CNN-transformer framework for medical image segmentation, Biomedical Signal Processing and Control, Volume 88, Part A, 2024, https://doi.org/.DOI: 10.1016/j.bspc.2023.105605

. Suigu Tang, Chak Fong Cheang, Xiaoyuan Yu, Yanyan Liang, Qi Feng, Zongren Chen. 2023. TransCS-Net: A hybrid transformer-based privacy-protecting network using compressed sensing for medical image segmentation, Biomedical Signal Processing and Control, Volume 86, Part A, https://doi.org/.DOI: 10.1016/j.bspc.2023.105131

Ting, H., & Liu, M. (2024, January). Multimodal Transformer of Incomplete MRI Data for Brain Tumor Segmentation. *IEEE Journal of Biomedical and Health Informatics, 28*(1), 89–99. DOI: 10.1109/JBHI.2023.3286689 PMID: 37327094

. Tomar, Nikhil Kumar & Shergill, Annie & Rieders, Brandon & Jha, Debesh. (2023). TransResU-Net: A Transformer based ResU-Net for Real-Time Colon Polyp Segmentation. 2023. 1-4. .DOI: 10.1109/EMBC40787.2023.10340572

Vaswani, A., Shazeer, N., Parmar, N., Uszkoreit, J., Jones, L., Gomez, A., Kaiser, L., & Polosukhin, I. (2017). Attention Is All You Need. 10.48550/arXiv.1706.03762.

Vatanpour, M., & Haddadnia, J. (2023). TransDoubleU-Net: Dual Scale Swin Transformer With Dual Level Decoder for 3D Multimodal Brain Tumor Segmentation. *IEEE Access: Practical Innovations, Open Solutions, 11*, 125511–125518. DOI: 10.1109/ACCESS.2023.3330958

Wang, C. (2024). Le Wang, Nuoqi Wang, Xiaoling Wei, Ting Feng, Minfeng Wu, Qi Yao, Rongjun Zhang, CFATransUnet: Channel-wise cross fusion attention and transformer for 2D medical image segmentation. *Computers in Biology and Medicine, 168.* Advance online publication. DOI: 10.1016/j.compbiomed.2023.107803 PMID: 38064854

Wang, C., Xu, R., Xu, S., Meng, W., & Zhang, X. (2022). DA-Net: Dual Branch Transformer and Adaptive Strip Upsampling for Retinal Vessels Segmentation. In Wang, L., Dou, Q., Fletcher, P. T., Speidel, S., & Li, S. (Eds.), Medical Image Computing and Computer Assisted Intervention: Vol. 13432. *MICCAI 2022. MICCAI 2022. Lecture Notes in Computer Science*. Springer., DOI: 10.1007/978-3-031-16434-7_51

Wang, D., Wang, Z., Chen, L., Xiao, H., & Yang, B. (2023). Cross-Parallel Transformer: Parallel ViT for Medical Image Segmentation. *Sensors (Basel)*, *23*(23), 9488. DOI: 10.3390/s23239488 PMID: 38067861

Wang, F., & Wang, B. (2024). Boundary-guided feature integration network with hierarchical transformer for medical image segmentation. *Multimedia Tools and Applications*, *83*, 8955–8969. DOI: 10.1007/s11042-023-15948-z

Wang, J.. (2023, June). SDPN: A Slight Dual-Path Network With Local-Global Attention Guided for Medical Image Segmentation. *IEEE Journal of Biomedical and Health Informatics*, *27*(6), 2956–2967. DOI: 10.1109/JBHI.2023.3260026 PMID: 37030687

Wang, J., Tian, S., Yu, L., Zhou, Z., Wang, F., & Wang, Y. (2023). HIGF-Net: Hierarchical information-guided fusion network for polyp segmentation based on transformer and convolution feature learning. *Computers in Biology and Medicine*, *161*. Advance online publication. DOI: 10.1016/j.compbiomed.2023.107038 PMID: 37230017

Wang, J., Wei, L., Wang, L., Zhou, Q., Zhu, L., & Qin, J. (2021). Boundary-Aware Transformers for Skin Lesion Segmentation. In: de Bruijne, M., *et al.* Medical Image Computing and Computer Assisted Intervention – MICCAI 2021. MICCAI 2021. Lecture Notes in Computer Science(), vol 12901. Springer, Cham. https://doi.org/ DOI: 10.1007/978-3-030-87193-2_20

Wang, N.. (2023, September). MISSU: 3D Medical Image Segmentation via Self-Distilling TransUNet. *IEEE Transactions on Medical Imaging*, *42*(9), 2740–2750. DOI: 10.1109/TMI.2023.3264433 PMID: 37018113

Wei, C., Ren, S., Guo, K., Hu, H., & Liang, J. (2023). High-Resolution Swin Transformer for Automatic Medical Image Segmentation. *Sensors (Basel)*, *23*(7), 3420. DOI: 10.3390/s23073420 PMID: 37050479

Wu, H., Chen, S., Chen, G., Wang, W., Lei, B., & Wen, Z. (2022). FAT-Net: Feature adaptive transformers for automated skin lesion segmentation. *Medical Image Analysis*, *76*. Advance online publication. DOI: 10.1016/j.media.2021.102327 PMID: 34923250

Wu, H., Zhao, Z., & Wang, Z. (2024, July). META-Unet: Multi-Scale Efficient Transformer Attention Unet for Fast and High-Accuracy Polyp Segmentation. *IEEE Transactions on Automation Science and Engineering*, *21*(3), 4117–4128. DOI: 10.1109/TASE.2023.3292373

Wu, Y., Liao, K., & Chen, J.. (2023). D-former: A U-shaped Dilated Transformer for 3D medical image segmentation. *Neural Computing & Applications*, *35*, 1931–1944. DOI: 10.1007/s00521-022-07859-1

Xia, Z., Chen, J., & Lu, C. (2024). DUSFormer: Dual-Swin Transformer V2 Aggregate Network for Polyp Segmentation. *IEEE Access: Practical Innovations, Open Solutions*, *12*, 8822–8832. DOI: 10.1109/ACCESS.2024.3352428

Xiao, H., Li, L., Liu, Q., Zhang, Q., Liu, J., & Liu, Z. (2024). Context-aware and local-aware fusion with transformer for medical image segmentation. *Physics in Medicine and Biology*, *69*. Advance online publication. DOI: 10.1088/1361-6560/ad14c6 PMID: 38086076

Xiao, Z., Su, Y., Deng, Z., & Zhang, W. (2022). Efficient Combination of CNN and Transformer for Dual-Teacher Uncertainty-guided Semi-supervised Medical Image Segmentation. *Computer Methods and Programs in Biomedicine*, *226*. Advance online publication. DOI: 10.1016/j.cmpb.2022.107099 PMID: 36116398

Xie, Y., Zhang, J., Shen, C., & Xia, Y. (2021). CoTr: Efficiently Bridging CNN and Transformer for 3D Medical Image Segmentation. In: de Bruijne, M., *et al.* Medical Image Computing and Computer Assisted Intervention – MICCAI 2021. MICCAI 2021. Lecture Notes in Computer Science(), vol 12903. Springer, Cham. https://doi.org/DOI: 10.1007/978-3-030-87199-4_16

Xu, G., Zhang, X., Liao, W., Chen, S., & Wu, X. (2022). LGNet: Local and global representation learning for fast biomedical image segmentation. *Journal of Innovative Optical Health Sciences*, *16*. Advance online publication. DOI: 10.1142/S1793545822430015

Xu, Q., Ma, Z., Na, H. E., & Duan, W. (2023). DCSAU-Net: A deeper and more compact split-attention U-Net for medical image segmentation. *Computers in Biology and Medicine*, *154*. Advance online publication. DOI: 10.1016/j.compbiomed.2023.106626 PMID: 36736096

Yan, Q., Liu, S., Xu, S., Dong, C., & Li, Z. (2023). Javen Qinfeng Shi, Yanning Zhang, Duwei Dai, 3D Medical image segmentation using parallel transformers. *Pattern Recognition*, *138*. Advance online publication. DOI: 10.1016/j.patcog.2023.109432

Yang, J., Jiao, L., Shang, R., Liu, X., Li, R., & Xu, L. (2023, November). EPT-Net: Edge Perception Transformer for 3D Medical Image Segmentation. *IEEE Transactions on Medical Imaging*, *42*(11), 3229–3243. DOI: 10.1109/TMI.2023.3278461 PMID: 37216246

Yang, Y., Zhang, L., Ren, L., & Wang, X. (2023). MMViT-Seg: A lightweight transformer and CNN fusion network for COVID-19 segmentation. *Computer Methods and Programs in Biomedicine*, *230*. Advance online publication. DOI: 10.1016/j.cmpb.2023.107348 PMID: 36706618

Yao, C., Hu, M., Li, Q., Zhai, G., & Zhang, X.-P. "Transclaw U-Net: Claw U-Net With Transformers for Medical Image Segmentation," *2022 5th International Conference on Information Communication and Signal Processing (ICICSP)*, Shenzhen, China, 2022, pp. 280-284, doi: DOI: 10.1109/ICICSP55539.2022.10050624

Yu, X., Yang, Q., Zhou, Y., & Leon, Y. (2023). Cai, Riqiang Gao, Ho Hin Lee, Thomas Li, Shunxing Bao, Zhoubing Xu, Thomas A. Lasko, Richard G. Abramson, Zizhao Zhang, Yuankai Huo, Bennett A. Landman, Yucheng Tang, UNesT: Local spatial representation learning with hierarchical transformer for efficient medical segmentation. *Medical Image Analysis*, *90*. Advance online publication. DOI: 10.1016/j.media.2023.102939 PMID: 37725868

Yu, Z., Lee, F., & Chen, Q. (2023). HCT-net: Hybrid CNN-transformer model based on a neural architecture search network for medical image segmentation. *Applied Intelligence*, *53*, 19990–20006. DOI: 10.1007/s10489-023-04570-z

Yuan, F., Tang, Z., Wang, C., Huang, Q., & Shi, J. (2023). A multiple gated boosting network for multi-organ medical image segmentation. *IET Image Processing*, *17*, 3028–3039. DOI: 10.1049/ipr2.12852

Yuan, F., Zhang, Z., & Fang, Z. (2023). An effective CNN and Transformer complementary network for medical image segmentation. *Pattern Recognition*, *136*. Advance online publication. DOI: 10.1016/j.patcog.2022.109228

Yue, G., Zhuo, G., Yan, W., Zhou, T., Tang, C., Yang, P., & Wang, T. (2024). Boundary uncertainty aware network for automated polyp segmentation. *Neural Networks*, *170*, 390–404. DOI: 10.1016/j.neunet.2023.11.050 PMID: 38029720

Zhang, C., Sun, S., Hu, W., & Zhao, P. (2024). FDR-TransUNet: A novel encoder-decoder architecture with vision transformer for improved medical image segmentation. *Computers in Biology and Medicine*, *169*. Advance online publication. DOI: 10.1016/j.compbiomed.2023.107858 PMID: 38113680

. Huaikun Zhang, Jing Lian, Zetong Yi, Ruichao Wu, Xiangyu Lu, Pei Ma, Yide Ma, HAU-Net: Hybrid CNN-transformer for breast ultrasound image segmentation, Biomedical Signal Processing and Control, Volume 87, https://doi.org/.DOI: 10.1016/j.bspc.2023.105427

Zhang, H., Ni, W., Luo, Y., Feng, Y., Song, R., & Wang, X. (2023). TUnet-LBF: Retinal fundus image fine segmentation model based on transformer Unet network and LBF. *Computers in Biology and Medicine, 159*. Advance online publication. DOI: 10.1016/j.compbiomed.2023.106937 PMID: 37084640

Zhang, H., Zhong, X., Li, G., Liu, W., Liu, J., Ji, D., Li, X., & Wu, J. (2023). BCU-Net: Bridging ConvNeXt and U-Net for medical image segmentation. *Computers in Biology and Medicine, 159*. Advance online publication. DOI: 10.1016/j.compbiomed.2023.106960 PMID: 37099973

Zhang, J.. (2023, December). Dual-Branch TransV-Net for 3-D Echocardiography Segmentation. *IEEE Transactions on Industrial Informatics, 19*(12), 11675–11686. DOI: 10.1109/TII.2023.3249904

Zhang, J., Liu, Y., Wu, Q., Wang, Y., Liu, Y., Xu, X., & Song, B. (2022). SWTRU: Star-shaped Window Transformer Reinforced U-Net for medical image segmentation. *Computers in Biology and Medicine, 150*. Advance online publication. DOI: 10.1016/j.compbiomed.2022.105954 PMID: 36122443

Zhang, J., Qin, Q., Ye, Q., & Ruan, T. (2023). ST-Unet: Swin Transformer boosted U-Net with Cross-Layer Feature Enhancement for medical image segmentation. *Computers in Biology and Medicine, 153*. Advance online publication. DOI: 10.1016/j.compbiomed.2022.106516 PMID: 36628914

Zhang, L., Zuo, Y., Jia, Y., Li, D., Zeng, R., Li, D., Chen, J., & Wang, W. (2024). DS-Former: A dual-stream encoding-based transformer for 3D medical image segmentation. *Biomedical Signal Processing and Control, 89*. Advance online publication. DOI: 10.1016/j.bspc.2023.105702

Zhang, N., Yu, L., Zhang, D., Wu, W., Tian, S., & Kang, X. (2022). APT-Net: Adaptive encoding and parallel decoding transformer for medical image segmentation, Computers in Biology and Medicine, Volume 151. *Part A, 106292*. Advance online publication. DOI: 10.1016/j.compbiomed.2022.106292 PMID: 36399856

Zhang, N., Yu, L., Zhang, D., Wu, W., Tian, S., Kang, X., & Li, M. (2024). CT-Net: Asymmetric compound branch Transformer for medical image segmentation. *Neural Networks, 170*, 298–311. DOI: 10.1016/j.neunet.2023.11.034 PMID: 38006733

Zhang, T., & Wang, X. (2024, February). Anchorwise Fuzziness Modeling in Convolution–Transformer Neural Network for Left Atrium Image Segmentation. *IEEE Transactions on Fuzzy Systems, 32*(2), 398–408. DOI: 10.1109/TFUZZ.2023.3298904

Zhang, W., Fu, C., Zheng, Y., Zhang, F., & Zhao, Y. (2022). Chiu-Wing Sham, HSNet: A hybrid semantic network for polyp segmentation. *Computers in Biology and Medicine, 150.* Advance online publication. DOI: 10.1016/j.compbiomed.2022.106173 PMID: 36257278

Zhang, W., Lu, F., Su, H., & Hu, Y. (2024). Dual-branch multi-information aggregation network with transformer and convolution for polyp segmentation. *Computers in Biology and Medicine, 168.* Advance online publication. DOI: 10.1016/j.compbiomed.2023.107760 PMID: 38064849

Zhang, Y., Liu, H., & Hu, Q. (2021). TransFuse: Fusing Transformers and CNNs for Medical Image Segmentation. In: de Bruijne, M., *et al.* Medical Image Computing and Computer Assisted Intervention – MICCAI 2021. MICCAI 2021. Lecture Notes in Computer Science(), vol 12901. Springer, Cham. https://doi.org/DOI: 10.1007/978-3-030-87193-2_2

Zhang, Z., Sun, B., & Zhang, W. (2021). Pyramid Medical Transformer for Medical Image Segmentation. 10.48550/arXiv.2104.14702.

Zhang, Z., Sun, G., Zheng, K., Yang, J.-K., Zhu, X., & Li, Y. (2023). TC-Net: A joint learning framework based on CNN and vision transformer for multi-lesion medical images segmentation. *Computers in Biology and Medicine, 161.* Advance online publication. DOI: 10.1016/j.compbiomed.2023.106967 PMID: 37220707

Zhao, C., Xiang, S., Wang, Y., Cai, Z., Shen, J., & Zhou, S. (2023). Di Zhao, Weihua Su, Shijie Guo, Shuo Li, Context-aware network fusing transformer and V-Net for semi-supervised segmentation of 3D left atrium. *Expert Systems with Applications, 214.* Advance online publication. DOI: 10.1016/j.eswa.2022.119105

Zhao, L., Zhou, D., Jin, X., & Zhu, W. (2022). nn-TransUNet: An Automatic Deep Learning Pipeline for Heart MRI Segmentation. *Life (Chicago, Ill.), 12*(10), 1570. DOI: 10.3390/life12101570 PMID: 36295005

Zhao, X., Wang, L., & Zhang, Y.. (2024). A review of convolutional neural networks in computer vision. *Artificial Intelligence Review, 57*, 99. DOI: 10.1007/s10462-024-10721-6

Zhao, Y., Shen, X., Chen, J., Qian, W., Sang, L., & Ma, H. (2024). Learning active contour models based on self-attention for breast ultrasound image segmentation. *Biomedical Signal Processing and Control, 89*. Advance online publication. DOI: 10.1016/j.bspc.2023.105816

. Longwei Zhong, Tiansong Li, Meng Cui, Shaoguo Cui, Hongkui Wang, Li Yu, DSU-Net: Dual-Stage U-Net based on CNN and Transformer for skin lesion segmentation, Biomedical Signal Processing and Control, Volume 100, Part A, 2025, https://doi.org/.DOI: 10.1016/j.bspc.2024.107090

Zhou, H.-Y.. (2023). nnFormer: Volumetric Medical Image Segmentation via a 3D Transformer. *IEEE Transactions on Image Processing, 32*, 4036–4045. DOI: 10.1109/TIP.2023.3293771 PMID: 37440404

. Jiahua Zhu, Ziteng Liu, Wenpeng Gao, Yili Fu, CotepRes-Net: An efficient U-Net based deep learning method of liver segmentation from Computed Tomography images, Biomedical Signal Processing and Control, Volume 88, Part B, 2024, https://doi.org/.DOI: 10.1016/j.bspc.2023.105660

Zhu, T., Ding, D., Wang, F., Liang, W., & Wang, B. (2024). A novel full-convolution UNet-transformer for medical image segmentation. *Biomedical Signal Processing and Control, 89*. Advance online publication. DOI: 10.1016/j.bspc.2023.105772

Zi-an, Z., Xiu-fang, F., Xiao-qiang, R., & Yun-yun, D. (2023). Uncertainty-guided cross learning via CNN and transformer for semi-supervised honeycomb lung lesion segmentation. *Physics in Medicine and Biology, 68*. Advance online publication. DOI: 10.1088/1361-6560/ad0eb2 PMID: 37988756

Chapter 7
Transformers in Medical Imaging:
Transfomers and Its Application in Medical Imaging

Rajarajeshwari Govindaraj
https://orcid.org/0009-0005-6533-7362
Vellore Institute of Technology, Vellore, India

Chemmalar Selvi G.
https://orcid.org/0000-0002-8933-4378
School of Computer Science Engineering and Information Systems, Vellore Institute of Technology, Vellore, India

ABSTRACT

Transformers have emerged as a powerful deep learning architecture in medical imaging, offering advanced capabilities in image classification, segmentation, and disease detection. Their self-attention mechanism enables efficient processing of high-dimensional medical images, improving diagnostic accuracy and long-range dependency modeling. Recent advancements have demonstrated superior performance in medical image analysis compared to traditional convolutional neural networks. Despite their remarkable success, challenges remain, including high computational costs, data scarcity, and the need for interpretability in clinical decision-making. This chapter aims to explore the transformative role of transformer-based deep learning models in medical imaging. It will provide a comprehensive overview of how transformers enhance image analysis tasks such as classification, segmentation in medical imaging domains. The chapter will highlight the advantages of transformers over traditional deep learning model.

DOI: 10.4018/979-8-3373-2038-0.ch007

1. INTRODUCTION

The Transformer architecture (Vaswani et al., 2017) was a huge step forward in Deep Learning (DL) in the year 2017, especially for Natural Language Processing (NLP) sequence modeling applications (Wolf et al., 2020). Transformers use a scaled dot-product attention mechanism that makes it easier to process complete sequences in parallel. This is different from older models like Recurrent Neural Networks (RNNs) (Rumelhart et al., 1986), which process data one at a time and have trouble parallelizing computations. This new idea cuts down on training time by a lot and makes it easier to build models that can grow. One of the best things about Transformers is that they work well with self-supervised learning methods like input masking, which let you train on huge, unlabeled datasets. This means that the architecture can be used in a lot of different fields without needing to rely on costly, labeled data. After their success in NLP, Transformers have been used in many other fields besides text, such as Computer Vision (CV) (Khan et al., 2022; Liu et al., 2023), remote sensing (RS) (Aleissaee et al., 2023), speech recognition, time series analysis (Wen et al., 2023), and multimodal learning (Adam et al., 2025). These changes across domains have resulted in the development of surveys and research initiatives tailored to certain modalities, particularly in medical imaging (Shamshad et al., 2023; Parvaiz et al., 2023) and biomedical language processing (Wang et al., 2023). At the same time, the healthcare industry has seen an unparalleled rise in the amount of data it generates. Healthcare has been making a lot of data for the past ten years. It is now thought to be roughly 30% of all data in the globe, and that number is expected to climb in the next few years. The substantial volume of data has facilitated the creation of machine learning (ML) models that assist in clinical workflows such as decision support, diagnosis, and prognosis. Healthcare is getting better at analyzing medical images and Electronic Health Records (EHR), thanks to transformers. The Transformer was first designed for NLP, but it has since been used in clinical settings for things like finding diseases, making reports, and developing drugs. Their effectiveness comes from using attention mechanisms that look at long data sequences and pick out the most important bits.

2. TRANSFORMER ARCHITECTURES

2.1. ViT

Researchers are looking into using transformers in computer vision, especially for learning visual representations, since that they have achieved big strides in NLP. Transformers are harder to use for vision tasks since images are usually more complicated than text. This is especially true in generative settings, where images have more dimensions, noise, and extra data. Transformers are becoming more and more popular as the backbone architecture for image classification, replacing the classic CNN. The convolutional layers first take out the basic image information, and then a tokenizer breaks them up into visual tokens. Each token shows which part of the image is important. The main job of the transformer is to figure out how these tokens are related to each other so that they can be classified correctly. ViT (Han et al., 2022) is a model that is completely built on transformers and works with sequences of image patches directly. This makes it good for image classification issues without using convolutional methods. Many extensions have been made to the ViT to make it better at visual tasks. The main goals of these enhancements are to make local feature modeling stronger, improve the self-attention mechanism, and make the overall architecture better. The original ViT does a good job at modeling long-range patterns in the image, but it typically misses local details because a single 2D patch turns into one vector by basic linear projection.

2.2. Transformer in Transformer (TNT)

A new transformer architecture, TNT (Han et al., 2021) is developed to fix the problems with traditional ViTs that make it hard to capture small visual details. This method uses a hierarchical structure to improve how features are represented in image comprehension tasks. TNT is different from standard transformers because it breaks the image into larger patches called "visual sentences" and then breaks these down into smaller units called "visual words." standard transformers use image patches as separate tokens. There are two levels of transformer modules in the TNT framework: an exterior transformer that looks at how visual sentences are related to each other and an inner transformer, or sub-transformer, that looks at how visual words interact with each other within each phrase. This two-level attention technique lets the network keep local details while also keeping the big picture. The sub-transformer shares parameters across multiple patch regions, which is important because it keeps the extra computational cost and number of parameters low. After processing, the detailed features from the visual words are put back into their visual sentences, which makes the feature representations richer. Finally, a completely linked head uses a class token to make the final classification. The TNT architecture improves the granularity of visual feature extraction, which makes visual recognition tasks work better and connects modeling of small details with knowledge of broader context.

2.3. Swin Transformer

Swin Transformer (Liu et al., 2021) doesn't use multi-head self-attention (MHSA) like the normal Transformer does. Instead, it adds a specific kind of self-attention that sees data as windows that have moved in time. The Transformer block doesn't change its overall shape with this update, but it does make it better for working with images. A GELU activation function is employed among the two MLP layers and the shifting window MHSA module in each Swin Transformer block. Layer Normalization (LN) comes before both the self-attention and MLP parts to make sure that training is stable and consistent. There are leftover connections between each module to help the gradient flow better and speed up convergence. The model can capture cross-window connections while still being computationally efficient because of the usage of shifted windows. So, Swin Transformer works best for applications that require dense predictions and hierarchical vision modeling.

2.4. Detection Transformer (DETR) Framework for Object Detection

DETR (Dai et al., 2021) introduces a new approach to object detection by framing it as a set prediction problem. and provides a comprehensive end-to-end framework for its execution. As shown in its loss formulation, it uses a bipartite matching method to match predicted items with ground-truth labels. The model has a CNN backbone and a Transformer-based encoder-decoder architecture on top of it. This method gets rid of the dependence on anchor boxes and suppression techniques like Non-maximum suppression (NMS), which are the usual parts that make the object detection pipeline easier. DETR has a hard time switching from NLP tasks to vision tasks, even if it has a new design. These include problems with processing high-resolution data quickly and the need for much longer training cycles than regular object detectors.

Figure 1. How Transformers are Used in Medical Imaging

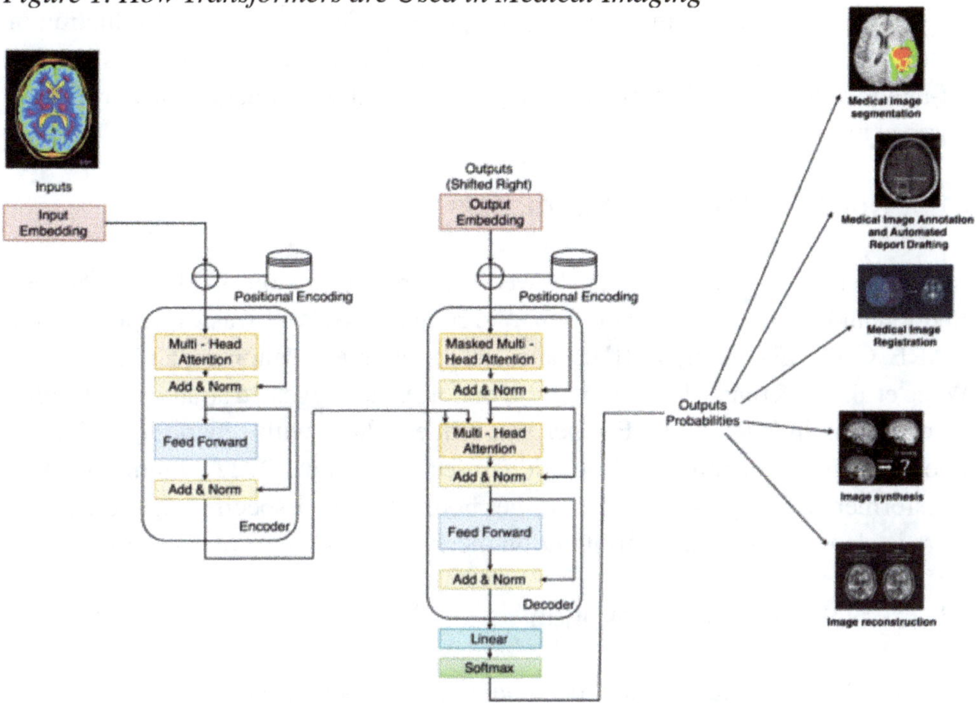

3. APPLICATION OF TRANSFORMERS IN MEDICAL IMAGING

Transformers are applicable in several domains of healthcare. Transformers facilitate the analysis of medical data by preserving long-range relationships in the input. The attention mechanism of transformers is highly effective for extracting significant aspects from medical images. Figure 1 illustrates various uses of transformers in medical imaging.

3.1. Segmentation in Medical Imaging

Segmentation in Medical Imaging involves the meticulous classification of pixels, encompassing intricate interrelations among them. It has problems that generic segmentation doesn't have, like not having enough data, the fact that anatomy might change, and the requirement to grasp the context. This technology provides several advantages to imaging modalities such as X-ray, CT, MRI, PET, ultrasound, and microscopy. Before Transformers, U-Net, a CNN-based model (Ronneberger et al.,

2015), was commonly employed to separate medical images into different parts. CNNs have a hard time capturing long-range dependencies, even with dilation or strides, because their receptive fields are small. Conversely, transformers employ self-attention to accurately simulate the global context of an image at any layer level (Pham et al., 2000).

3.1.1. Non U-Net transformer models

TiM-Net (Zhang et al., 2022) showed off a better version of M-Net that used attention and weighted outputs to separate retinal vessels. It was evaluated on the STARE, CHASEDBI, and DRIVE datasets. Using image denoising and enhancing (Wang et al., 2022) and Eformer to get rid of noise, the suggested strategy for finding osteosarcoma in MRI. ColonFormer was made to help with separating polyps in endoscopic images from five different datasets (Duc et al., 2022). It employs Mix Transformer (Beltagy et al., 2019) to get both broad and specific characteristics. There is also a lightweight self-attention mechanism to keep expenses down.

3.1.2. CNN-transformer hybrids

TransUNet was one of the first models to use both CNNs and transformers to break up medical images into parts. It uses a CNN to lower the magnitude of the input and then a Transformer encoder to get global contextual information. A cascaded up-sampling decoder processes the features even more to make the final high-resolution segmentation output.

3.1.3. Transformer Only U-Nets

UTNet (Gao et al., 2021) is built by adding the transformer's self-attention mechanism to its encoder and decoder part. This makes it better at finding long-range associations. The Swin-Unet (Cao et al., 2022) and DS-TransUNet both employed Swin Transformer blocks to build their networks. The DS-TransUNet additionally used a dual-branch Swin Transformer (Liu et al., 2021) with special fusion blocks (TIF) to merge features across scales (Lin et al., 2022). MedT by (Valanarasu et al., 2021) added a gated attention mechanism and used both local and global branches (LoGo) to work with limited medical datasets while being aware of their positions (Wang et al., 2020). They have created a 3D segmentation model that didn't use any CNNs at all and simply used a pre-trained Transformer encoder. This model did better than CNNs on three private medical imaging datasets (Karimi et al., 2021).

3.1.4. Medical Image Annotation and Automated Report Drafting

Experts in medicine normally write the medical reports after carefully looking at the biomedical photographs, which takes a lot of time. Automated systems (Tang et al., 2025) for making medical reports save time and don't make mistakes that people do. A DL model finds features in an image, and then a language model turns those features into text that people can understand. Image captioning (Arman et al., 2025) is the process of adding a text description to an image. A language model gets the findings from a DL model that takes out important parts of the image. This makes a text-based version of a sentence form that makes sense and fits the situation.

3.1.5. Medical Image Registration (MIR)

MIR can be defined as process of combining data acquired from different sources into a single coordinate system. It is important for the sake of benchmarking, merging, and evaluating data acquired from multiple sensors, angles, or times. Auto Fuse (Meng et al., 2025) has a flexible mechanism that brings together information from different parts of its structure. There is a Fusion Gate that lets you look at the data and figure out the best way to fuse it. The method works with both unsupervised and semi-supervised ways of registering.

3.2. Synthetic Medical Imaging (SMI)

SMI is a procedure to avoid or replace time-consuming, expensive, and risky procedures by creating medical images of one type from another, like making MRI scans from CT images. VTGAN (Kamran et al., 2021) was made, which uses a semi-supervised method to look at both internal and external features by combining two generators using ViT. VTGAN was able to make Fluorescein Angiography photos from fundus images while also predicting how the retina would get worse. The model was able to handle spatial and radial transformations without any problems. This approach presents a great promise over its application in medical image synthesis and diagnostics. Dalmaz et al. (Dalmaz et al., 2022) came up with RESVIT, a GAN-based encoder-decoder system that uses available MRI data to fill in Absent image sequences in pelvic CT and multi-modal MRI data. The design features an encoder and decoder built on a CNN framework, as well as a residual Transformer module that does a great job of extraction of the context at global level and the dependencies sparsely distributed at long-range. RESVIT makes synthetic images more accurate by combining local and global feature information. In addition to RESVIT, other GAN-based models such as CyTran (Wu et al., 2021) and CycleGAN (Zhu et al., 2017) are employed to convert contrast-enhanced CT images to non-contrast CT images and the reverse. For instance, CyTran applies convolutional layers to reduce and then restore image resolution, enhanced by a convolutional Transformer block, enabling it to produce high-quality translated images.

3.2.1. Visual Question Answering (VQA)

VQA involves making replies based on the information in an image, it is a computer vision task. In medicine, it helps doctors get information from images to make a diagnosis. The CGMVQA (Ren & Zhou, 2020) model uses LN prior to the MHSA also FCFN parts of the Transformer. It was trained with the ImageCLEF 2019 VQA-Med dataset (Al-Sadi et al., 2021) as the data source. Changing the loss function lets the model either predict or generate and also the same can be observed with the output layer.

3.3. Medical Image Reconstruction

Image reconstruction's goal is to give patients high-quality medical images while keeping costs and risks low (Huang et al., 2025).

3.3.1. Computed tomography (CT)

Low-dose CT (LDCT) is a type of CT scan designed to minimize radiation exposure alongside, Cone-beam CT (CBCT) is another form of CT imaging that also contributes for the same. These low-dose scans can be used to make synthetic CT (SCT) images, which make things even safer. This method is a good way to get diagnostic-quality images while keeping the danger to the patient low (Bera et al., 2025; Yuan et al., 2024).

3.3.2. Magnetic Resonance Imaging (MRI)

For MRI reconstruction, a model called SLATER (Korkmaz et al., 2022) was made based on a Transformer. It replaces the CNN used in Deep Image Prior (DIP) (Ulyanov et al., 2020) with a Cross-attentive Transformer network, which improves performance on the datasets namely fastMRI and Information eXtraction from Images (IXI). T2Net is a multi-task framework that allows the network share learnt representations for image reconstruction and super-resolution. It was later utilized to learn across different modalities (Feng et al., 2021; Feng et al., 2022). Fang et al. suggested Cohf-T (Fang et al., 2022), a Transformer that works across modalities, to make low-quality MR images clearer. HUMUS-Net (Fabian et al., 2022), a hybrid CNN-Transformer architecture, and ST-GAN (Huang et al., 2022), which uses the

Swin Transformer (Liu et al., 2021) to keep edge and texture features, are two other models that have been recognized. This last technique has been very popular in MRI reconstruction (Yan et al., 2021; Zhou et al., 2023).

3.3.3. Positron Emission Tomography (PET)

This advanced imaging method, PET, helps visualize metabolic and biochemical activities inside the body using radioactive tracers. PET image reconstruction often needs denoising to improve image quality because the ratio of signal to noise is minimal. The Spach Transformer (Jang et al., 2023) uses local and global MHSA to capture both channel-wise information and spatial. It outperformed baseline models on several datasets of PET tracer, including 68Ga-DOTATATE, 18F-ACBC, 18F-DCFPyL, and 18F-FDG.

4. EMERGING ROLE OF TRANSFORMERS IN MEDICAL HEALTHCARE FOR MULTI-DISEASE DIAGNOSIS AND ANALYSIS

4.1. Diabetic Retinopathy (DR)

Mingming Yang et al. (Yang et al., 2025) came up with the Class-Re-Attention Transformers (CRAT) model, which is a DL method based on transformers that can find retinal abnormalities in OCT images. The focus was on reducing the impacts of speckle noise. The model learned from a large set of 109,371 retinal OCT images. The model got 94.40% accuracy, 94.42% precision, 94.39% recall, 98.60% specificity, and 97.76% F1 score on the internal test dataset. It did better on the external test dataset, with an accuracy of 97.33%, a precision of 96.33%, a recall of 97.08%, a specificity of 99.17%, and an F1 score of 98.74%. The main goal of the preprocessing was to reduce noise in order to improve the accuracy of the diagnosis. There are some problems, though. For example, noise can affect the results in some scenarios, and the test set used was just 190 photos, which may restrict how well the results apply to other situations. Mohammed Oulhadj et al. (Oulhadj et al., 2024) aimed to develop a hybrid DL model that integrates a modified Capsule Network with a fine-tuned ViT to automatically assess the severity of DR, thereby assisting ophthalmologists in their diagnosis. Power Law Transformation (PLT) was applied to enhance image brightness and overall contrast, while Contrast-Limited Adaptive Histogram Equalization (CLAHE) was employed to boost local contrast in retinal images. The model utilized a ViT for extracting high-level features and a modified Capsule Network to refine spatial hierarchies and capture dynamic feature relationships. The model was tested on four publicly available datasets: Messidor-2, DDR, APTOS, and EyePACS. The accuracy scores were 87.78%, 80.36%, 88.18%, and 78.64%, respectively. Even though it did well, the accuracy varied a lot between datasets, which shows that it was hard to generalize. The hybrid architecture also made training and inference take longer, which needed a lot of computing power. Zheyi Dong et al. (Dong et al., 2025) developed and validated a DL model named Trans-MUF, which leverages transformer architecture to integrate fundus images and clinical data for accurately distinguishing between diabetic nephropathy (DN) and non-diabetic renal disease (NDRD). The goal was to decrease the need for invasive kidney biopsies. They have trained the model on a dataset from the past, tested it on a dataset from the future, and confirmed its accuracy on a dataset from many centers. It got AUC scores of 0.980 (internal), 0.989 (prospective), and 0.932 (multicenter). Even though the model did well, its performance varied depending on the scenario, especially when using data from many centers. Some of the problems include that it is hard to apply to people all over the world and in places with few resources, and there are also problems with regulations and workflow integration. Mishmala Sushith et al. (Sushith et al., 2025) proposed a novel DL model named Attention Dual Transformer with Adaptive Temporal Convolution (ADT-ATC). Its goal is to make it easier to find diabetic retinopathy in retinal fundus images. The model's goal is to improve the extraction of spatial-temporal features beyond what is normally done. The accuracy ratings for the DRIVE and DR datasets were 98.2% and 97.7%, respectively. The type and quality of imaging equipment used can influence the model's performance. The evaluation has certain constraints because there aren't enough datasets, thus it needs more testing. The dual transformer and temporal convolution modules may be too complicated to use in real time. Xina Liu et al. (Liu et al., 2025) developed the D-GET (Group-Enhanced Transformer) model to automatically classify the severity of DR using Fundus Fluorescein Angiography (FFA) images. Their main goal was to make it easier to find tiny lesions. The "16-grid input" method was used for preprocessing. This puts FFA photos into a 4×4 grid so that temporal and spatial data may be combined more easily. The training and testing of the model was done on a customized dataset. It got a precision of 94.69%, a recall of 94.66%, an F1-score of 94.67%, and an accuracy of 94.66%. Even though it works well, there are problems with the limited generalizability that comes from relying on a custom dataset and not having external validation. The model's complicated calculations might make it hard to use in real time in places with few resources. Rezaee et al. (Rezaee & Farnami, 2025) employed CNN and the Transformer architecture together to make the model operate better and show how worse the DR sickness is. They have tested the model on two sets of data: APTOS 2019 and IDRiD. It got 94.28% accuracy on the APTOS 2019 dataset for DR classification and severity evaluation, and 95.23% accuracy on the IDRiD dataset for validation, showing that it may be used in a wide range of situations. The effectiveness of the model relies on the diversity and quality of the training data. If there isn't enough data from underrepresented communities, it may not work as well in the actual world. To ensure clinical transparency, the model's interpretability must be enhanced, and its significant computational demands may limit its usability in resource-constrained settings. Yuanyuan Liu et al. (Liu et al., 2025) proposed STMF-DRNet (Swin-TransformerV2 Multi-Branch Fine-Grained DR Classification) to help with the confusion that arises while classifying fundus images because of identical lesion patterns. They have tested the model using APTOS 2019, EyePACS, DDR, and a dataset from a real-world clinical setting. For preprocessing, the images were cropped, resized to 512×512 pixels, had their contrast improved with CLAHE, their noise reduced with Gaussian blur, and their data increased to make the class distribution more even. The model got 77% accuracy, 77% recall, 77% F1-score, 94.2% specificity, and a Kappa of 0.877. Even though the results are promising, the modest accuracy shows that there is still potential for progress in telling the difference between DR grades. Also, the high computational demand may make it hard to use in places with few resources. Xin Wei et al. (Wei et al., 2025) have developed a Transformer-based model called MSTNet that could diagnose and rate the severity of diabetic retinopathy by collecting information from fundus images at different scales, in different places, and in different contexts. They have used the APTOS 2019, RFMiD 2020, Messidor, and IDRiD datasets to test the model. The results showed an F1 score of 85.7%, an AUC of 97.6%, an accuracy of 85.9%, and Kappa of 92.0% on the APTOS 2019 dataset. Transformer topologies work quite well, but they need a lot of computer power, which may make it hard to use them in contexts with limited resources or that need to work in real time. Multiple-instance learning (MIL) helps reduce noise, but label ambiguity and image variability are still issues. There hasn't been enough research on how easy it is to understand the concept, which makes it harder for doctors to use it.

4.2. Skin diseases

Dip Kumar Saha et al. (Saha et al., 2024) wanted to improve the detection of skin diseases by using ViT to classify images. YoTransViT is an advanced transformer network that aims to make it easier to find skin diseases. The self-attention mechanism in ViT does a good job of bringing out important features while hiding unimportant ones. The model was tested on the ISIC 2019 dataset, and its accuracy was improved through the use of image segmentation and augmentation techniques. They have evaluated YoTransViT's performance against that of other transformer models, like SwinViT, and popular CNN designs, like MobileNetV2, InceptionResNetV2, and DenseNet201. The model could diagnose eight types of skin diseases with 99.97%

accuracy and 100% precision. They have tested a number of performance indicators to see how well it worked. A web-based framework for predicting skin diseases in real time was also built.

4.3. Lung disease

Xiaoyang Fu et al. (Fu et al., 2025) came up with LungMaxViT, an explainable DL model trained on chest X-rays to tell the difference between different lung illnesses. To increase feature recognition, the model puts together a CNN, a SE block, and a Transformer. Preprocessing techniques like denoising, flipping, and CLAHE are used to improve the quality of images. Transfer learning was employed to evaluate four pre-trained models: ResNet50, ViT, MaxViT, and MobileNetV2. Lung MaxViT, which was based on the MaxViT architecture and fine-tuned with the COVID 19 and ChestX-ray14 datasets, did the best of all the models that were compared. The model got 96.8% accuracy, 98.3% AUC, and 96.7% F1-score on the COVID-19 dataset. It got 93.2% AUC and 70.7% F1-score on the ChestX-ray14 dataset. They have used Grad-CAM to show and explain the model's predictions, which also showed how easy it is to understand. LungMaxViT worked well on a lot of different datasets and was able to generalize well. But its lower F1-score on ChestX-ray14 shows that it has a flaw. After COVID-19, Anzhelika Mezina et al. (Mezina & Burget, 2024) built a DL model that uses Inception and ViT modules to find lung illnesses in chest X-rays. The model solves the problem of not having AI tools that can find long-term COVID-19 issues by using an asymmetric loss function (ASL) for successful multilabel classification. It was trained on nine illness labels from the ChestX-ray14 dataset and did better than baseline models like InceptionV3, VGG19, ResNet101, DenseNet121, and EfficientNetB4. It had an AUC of 82%, an accuracy of 74%, a sensitivity of 77%, and a specificity of 72%. The suggested model used BCE loss and InceptionV3 for evaluation, and the ASL-based model did better than both, showing the value of the bespoke loss function. Some of the problems include that the disease coverage is limited, which means that more effort needs to be done to add more labels and look at multimodal learning. A.P. Narmadha et al. (Narmadha & Gobalakrishnan, 2025) aimed to enhance lung disease diagnosis by developing the hybrid efficient transformer model (HET-RL), which integrates clinical data, radiographs, and primary complaints. The model uses dual-level pre-processing with Min-Max normalization and Steered Filter (SF) to deal with problems with data scarcity and diagnostic accuracy. The RL model employs the Text Analyzer Transformer (TAT) to extract relevant features from the input data. It also utilizes the Inter-Attention Transformer (IAT) to integrate these features, enhancing the accuracy of disease classification. It did 12% better than models that solely used images and 9% better than models that used more than one type of data.

The model did better than other models, with 97% sensitivity, 96% accuracy, 96% F1-score, and 97% specificity. Even though it worked, there are still problems with the data and the need for better algorithms.

4.4. Kidney Disease

Alex Moore et al. (Moore et al., 2024) came up with HERBERT, a unique BERT-based model designed for EHR that improves renal risk assessment. The goal of the model is to guess how chronic kidney disease (CKD) will proceed to end-stage renal disease (ESRD). To make BERT work with EHR data, two main adjustments were made: the embedding layer was changed to work with structured inputs, and the pretraining task was changed to reflect how clinical data is formatted. The pre-processing step turned EHRs into patient timelines that were sorted by time. They have trained and tested HERBERT on a CKD dataset, and it did better than older models. They have used ROC AUC values to assess the model, and have produced 90% confidence intervals using bootstrap aggregation across 1,000 resampled test sets. The results showed that the model was very good at predicting what would happen. One big problem is that it depends on high-quality longitudinal EHR data. Chongxuan Tian et al. (Tian et al., 2024) came up with a CNN–ViT (CVT) model for diagnosing glomerular illness that doesn't require surgery. The goal is to stop using invasive biopsies by using hyperspectral imaging to combine spatial and spectral data. Interval sampling, wavelength optimization, and the Gramian Angular Field (GAF) method were all used in preprocessing to make the feature representation more consistent. They have took hyperspectral images between 385.18 and 1009.47 nm. Models that simply used spectrum data were 85.24% accurate, whereas the CVT model was 94% accurate, showing how well it learned spatial-spectral connections. The main problem is that it needs hyperspectral imaging systems and a lot of processing power. H. Sharen et al. (Sharen et al., 2024) came up with MSKd_Net, a DL architecture that improves the categorization of multiple types of kidney disease, including cysts, stones, tumors, and normal instances. The model combines a Swin Transformer for hierarchical feature extraction with a proprietary convolved model that has a multi-head attention layer added to it. This lets it capture both local-global features and long-range relationships. Structured image input from the RiÃ±ones dataset was part of the preprocessing. They have combined features from both modules additively and then sent them through linear layers to classify them. The model got high F1-scores: 98% for stone, 97% for cyst, 99% for normal, and 90% for tumor. This shows that it can diagnose well. Amjad Rehman et al. (Rehman et al., 2025) proposed a novel method for diagnosing CKD by combining the Swin-ViT model with various pre-trained DL models, including ConvNext and EfficientNet-B7. This mixed method uses transfer learning to make categorization work better, especially on small datasets, and it makes less use of big data. The study also looked at kidney cancer segmentation with the Swin-ViT model and DeepLabV3+, which got 99.2% accuracy, 99.5% F-Score, and 99.1% precision. This model did better than other models, such as MedT and Swin-Unet. The study did have some problems, though. For example, it used a small, homogeneous dataset, which made it harder to apply the model to other situations.

4.5. Cancer

To analyze baseline CT scans and forecast lymph node metastasis (LNM) in individuals with locally advanced gastric cancer (LAGC) after receiving neoadjuvant chemotherapy (NAC), Yunlin Zheng et al. (Zheng et al., 2024) have designed a DL network (DLN). The study included 1205 patients from three hospitals, who were split into three groups: training, internal validation, and external validation. A multivariate logistic regression clinical model was developed and compared to a DL network that utilized 3D tumor imaging and transformer architecture. The DLN did better, with AUC scores between 0.748 and 0.804. The decision curve analysis showed that there was a big clinical advantage, and the DLN was strongly linked to overall survival (OS), with hazard ratios of 1.789 ($P < 0.001$) and 1.776 ($P = 0.013$) in two follow-up facilities. Even if the results were promising, the study was retrospective.

4.6. Alzheimer's Disease (AD)

Qi Yu et al.'s study (Yu et al., 2024) attempts to improve the diagnosis of AD by introducing the AD-Transformer, a comprehensive DL model that uses structural MRIs, clinical data, and genetic information. The model has a Patch-CNN block that turns image data into tokens and a linear projection layer that works with data that isn't images. A transformer block then finds connections between these different types of data. The AD Neuroimaging Initiative (ADNI) database was used to train the model, which has information on 1,651 people. The performance metrics showed that the AUC for diagnosing AD was 0.993 and the AUC for predicting Mild Cognitive Impairment (MCI) was 0.845. Quan Anh Duong et al. (Duong et al., 2025) have developed an approach to diagnose AD by using lightweight cortical surface representations instead of resource-heavy 3D volumetric characteristics. The study looks at alterations related to AD, like the buildup of amyloid and tau, by combining data from both MRI and PET scans. The model combines features from several modalities by using a middle-fusion technique and a cross-attention mechanism. When tested on the ADNI dataset, which has T1-weighted MRI and [18F] Fluorodeoxyglucose PET images, it does better than traditional methods at both finding problems early and being more efficient at computing. The model also works well with amyloid and tau PET scans, which is a good sign.

4.7. Challenges

When trained on small datasets that don't have a lot of different ethnic groups, transformer-based models generally have trouble generalizing well. When there isn't enough data, projections can be biased and less reliable across different groups of people. Also, the very complicated structure of these models makes them hard to understand, which is a problem in therapeutic settings where it's important to be able to explain things. Also, it is still hard to use them in places with few resources because of the high computational and infrastructure needs.

5. CONCLUSION

Transformers are being utilized more and more in healthcare for a number of tasks, such as getting clinical information from EHRs and looking at medical photographs. They are great at managing complicated healthcare data because they are very good at both NLP and image analysis. Transformers are useful for processing medical data because a lot of it isn't structured, including text and photos from old records. There are still a number of problems that need to be solved, such as having too little labeled data and making models easy to understand. These problems present opportunities for future research to make transformer models more useful and effective in medical settings. Further improved, Transformers could manifest a remarkable growth of data-driven healthcare by its vital role.

REFERENCES

Adam, M., Albaseer, A., Baroudi, U., & Abdallah, M. (2025). Survey of multimodal federated learning: Exploring data integration, challenges, and future directions. *IEEE Open Journal of the Communications Society*.

Al-Sadi, A., Al-Ayyoub, M., Jararweh, Y., & Costen, F. (2021). Visual question answering in the medical domain based on deep learning approaches: A comprehensive study. *Pattern Recognition Letters, 150*, 57–75.

Aleissaee, A. A., Kumar, A., Anwer, R. M., Khan, S., Cholakkal, H., Xia, G.-S., & Khan, F. S. (2023). Transformers in remote sensing: A survey. *Remote Sensing, 15*(7), 1860.

Arman, M., Jahan, M. K., Dhrubo, A. F. H., Rhaman, M. M., Choya, S. B. Z., Dohan, D. M., Sajid, M. A. U. I., & Alam, M. G. R. Optimizing multimodal transformers for medical image captioning: Enhancing automated descriptions via ai systems, in: 2025 IEEE 6th International Conference on Image Processing, Applications and Systems (IPAS), IEEE, 2025, pp. 1–5.

Beltagy, I., Lo, K., & Cohan, A. Scibert: A pretrained language model for scientific text, in: *Proceedings of the 2019 Conference on Empirical Methods in Natural Language Processing and the 9th International Joint Conference on Natural Language Processing (EMNLP-IJCNLP)*, 2019, pp. 3615–3620.

Bera, A., Shukla, B., & Jogani, D. (2025). A perspective review of applications of the computed tomography (ct) scan imaging technique for microscopic reservoir rock characterization. *Deep Underground Science and Engineering*.

Cao, H., Wang, Y., Chen, J., Jiang, D., Zhang, X., Tian, Q., & Wang, M. Swin-unet: Unet-like pure transformer for medical image segmentation, in: European conference on computer vision, Springer, 2022, pp. 205– 218.

Dai, X., Chen, Y., Yang, J., Zhang, P., Yuan, L., & Zhang, L. Dynamic detr: End-to-end object detection with dynamic attention, in: *2021 IEEE/CVF International Conference on Computer Vision (ICCV)*, 2021, pp. 2968–2977. doi:DOI: 10.1109/ICCV48922.2021.00298

Dalmaz, O., Yurt, M., & Çukur, T. (2022). Resvit: Residual ViTs for multimodal medical image synthesis. *IEEE Transactions on Medical Imaging, 41*(10), 2598–2614. PMID: 35436184

Dong, Z., Wang, X., Pan, S., Weng, T., Chen, X., Jiang, S., Li, Y., Wang, Z., Cao, X., & Wang, Q.. (2025). A multimodal transformer system for noninvasive diabetic nephropathy diagnosis via retinal imaging, npj. *Digital Medicine*, *8*(1), 50. PMID: 39856403

Duc, N. T., Oanh, N. T., Thuy, N. T., Triet, T. M., & Dinh, V. S. (2022). Colon former: An efficient transformer based method for colon polyp segmentation. *IEEE Access: Practical Innovations, Open Solutions*, *10*, 80575–80586.

Duong, Q. A., Tran, S. D., & Gahm, J. K. (2025). Multimodal surface-based trans former model for early diagnosis of alzheimer's disease. *Scientific Reports*, *15*(1), 5787. PMID: 39962212

Fabian, Z., Tinaz, B., & Soltanolkotabi, M. (2022). Humus-net: Hybrid unrolled multi-scale network architecture for accelerated mri reconstruction. *Advances in Neural Information Processing Systems*, *35*, 25306–25319.

Fang, C., Zhang, D., Wang, L., Zhang, Y., Cheng, L., & Han, J. Cross modality high-frequency transformer for mr image super-resolution, in: *Proceedings of the 30th ACM International Conference on Multimedia*, 2022, pp. 1584–1592.

Feng, C.-M., Yan, Y., Chen, G., Xu, Y., Hu, Y., Shao, L., & Fu, H. (2022). Multimodal transformer for accelerated mr imaging. *IEEE Transactions on Medical Imaging*, *42*(10), 2804–2816. PMID: 35704546

Feng, C.-M., Yan, Y., Fu, H., Chen, L., & Xu, Y. Task transformer network for joint mri reconstruction and super-resolution, in: Medical Image Computing and Computer Assisted Intervention–MICCAI 2021: 24th International Conference, Strasbourg, France, September 27–October 1, 2021, Proceedings, Part VI 24, Springer, 2021, pp. 307–317.

Fu, X., Lin, R., Du, W., Tavares, A., & Liang, Y. (2025). Explainable hybrid transformer for multi-classification of lung disease using chest x-rays. *Scientific Reports*, *15*(1), 6650. PMID: 39994381

Gao, Y., Zhou, M., & Metaxas, D. N. Utnet: a hybrid transformer architecture for medical image segmentation, in: Medical image computing and computer assisted intervention–MICCAI 2021: 24th international conference, Strasbourg, France, September 27–October 1, 2021, proceedings, Part III 24, Springer, 2021, pp. 61–71.

Han, K., Wang, Y., Chen, H., Chen, X., Guo, J., Liu, Z., Tang, Y., Xiao, A., Xu, C., & Xu, Y.. (2022). A survey on ViT. *IEEE Transactions on Pattern Analysis and Machine Intelligence*, *45*(1), 87–110. PMID: 35180075

Han, K., Xiao, A., Wu, E., Guo, J., Xu, C., & Wang, Y. (2021). Transformer in transformer. *Advances in Neural Information Processing Systems*, *34*, 15908–15919.

Huang, J., Wu, Y., Wu, H., & Yang, G. Fast mri reconstruction: How powerful transformers are? in: 2022 44th annual international conference of the IEEE engineering in medicine & biology society (EMBC), IEEE, 2022, pp. 2066–2070.

Huang, J., Yang, L., Wang, F., Wu, Y., Nan, Y., Wu, W., Wang, C., Shi, K., Aviles-Rivero, A. I., & Schönlieb, C.-B.. (2025). Enhancing global sensitivity and uncertainty quantification in medical image reconstruction with monte carlo arbitrary-masked mamba. *Medical Image Analysis*, *99*, 103334. PMID: 39255733

Jang, S.-I., Pan, T., Li, Y., Heidari, P., Chen, J., Li, Q., & Gong, K. (2023). Spach transformer: Spatial and channel-wise transformer based on local and global self-attentions for pet image denoising. *IEEE Transactions on Medical Imaging*, *43*(6), 2036–2049. PMID: 37995174

Kamran, S. A., Hossain, K. F., Tavakkoli, A., Zuckerbrod, S. L., & Baker, S. A. Vtgan: Semi-supervised retinal image synthesis and disease prediction using ViTs, in: Proceedings of the IEEE/CVF international conference on computer vision, 2021, pp. 3235–3245.

Karimi, D., Vasylechko, S. D., & Gholipour, A. Convolution-free medical image segmentation using transformers, in: Medical image computing and computer assisted intervention–MICCAI 2021: 24th international conference, Strasbourg, France, September 27–October 1, 2021, proceedings, part I 24, Springer, 2021, pp. 78–88.

Khan, S., Naseer, M., Hayat, M., Zamir, S. W., Khan, F. S., & Shah, M. (2022). Transformers in vision: A survey. *ACM Computing Surveys*, *54*(10s), 1–41.

Korkmaz, Y., Dar, S. U., Yurt, M., Özbey, M., & Cukur, T. (2022). Unsupervised mri reconstruction via zero-shot learned adversarial transformers. *IEEE Transactions on Medical Imaging*, *41*(7), 1747–1763. PMID: 35085076

Lin, A., Chen, B., Xu, J., Zhang, Z., Lu, G., & Zhang, D. (2022). Ds-transunet: Dual swin transformer u-net for medical image segmentation. *IEEE Transactions on Instrumentation and Measurement*, *71*, 1–15.

Liu, X., Xie, J., Hou, J., Xu, X., & Guo, Y. (2025). D-get: Group-enhanced transformer for DR severity classification in fundus fluorescein angiography. *Journal of Medical Systems*, *49*(1), 1–15. PMID: 39751967

Liu, Y., Yao, D., Ma, Y., Wang, H., Wang, J., Bai, X., Zeng, G., & Liu, Y. (2025). Stmf-drnet: A multi-branch fine-grained classification model for DR using swin-transformerv2. *Biomedical Signal Processing and Control*, *103*, 107352.

Liu, Y., Zhang, Y., Wang, Y., Hou, F., Yuan, J., Tian, J., Zhang, Y., Shi, Z., Fan, J., & He, Z. (2023). A survey of visual transformers. *IEEE Transactions on Neural Networks and Learning Systems*. PMID: 37015131

Liu, Z., Lin, Y., Cao, Y., Hu, H., Wei, Y., Zhang, Z., Lin, S., & Guo, B. Swin transformer: Hierarchical ViT using shifted windows, in: *2021 IEEE/CVF International Conference on Computer Vision (ICCV)*, 2021, pp. 9992–10002. doi:DOI: 10.1109/ICCV48922.2021.00986

Liu, Z., Lin, Y., Cao, Y., Hu, H., Wei, Y., Zhang, Z., Lin, S., & Guo, B. Swin transformer: Hierarchical ViT using shifted windows, in: Proceedings of the IEEE/CVF international conference on computer vision, 2021, pp. 10012–10022.

Meng, M., Fulham, M., Feng, D., Bi, L., & Kim, J. (2025). Autofuse: Automatic fusion networks for deformable medical image registration. *Pattern Recognition, 161*, 111338.

Mezina, A., & Burget, R. (2024). Detection of post-covid-19-related pulmonary diseases in x-ray images using ViT-based neural network. *Biomedical Signal Processing and Control, 87*, 105380.

Moore, A., Orset, B., Yassaee, A., Irving, B., & Morelli, D. (2024). Healthrecord bert (herbert): Leveraging transformers on electronic health records for chronic kidney disease risk stratification. *ACM Transactions on Computing for Healthcare, 5*(3), 1–18.

Narmadha, A., & Gobalakrishnan, N. (2025). Het-rl: Multiple pulmonary disease diagnosis via hybrid efficient transformers based representation learning model using multi-modality data. *Biomedical Signal Processing and Control, 100*, 107157.

Oulhadj, M., Riffi, J., Khodriss, C., Mahraz, A. M., & Yahyaouy, A. (2024). M. Ab dellaoui, I. B. Andaloussi, H. Tairi, DR prediction based on ViT and modified capsule network. *Computers in Biology and Medicine, 175*, 108523. PMID: 38701591

Parvaiz, A., Khalid, M. A., Zafar, R., Ameer, H., Ali, M., & Fraz, M. M. (2023). ViTs in medical computer vision—A contemplative retrospection. *Engineering Applications of Artificial Intelligence, 122*, 106126.

Pham, D. L., Xu, C., & Prince, J. L. (2000). Current methods in medical image segmentation. *Annual Review of Biomedical Engineering, 2*(1), 315–337. PMID: 11701515

Rehman, A., Mahmood, T., & Saba, T. (2025). Robust kidney carcinoma prognosis and characterization using swin-vit and deeplabv3+ with multi-model transfer learning. *Applied Soft Computing, 170*, 112518.

Ren, F., & Zhou, Y. (2020). Cgmvqa: A new classification and generative model for medical visual question answering. *IEEE Access: Practical Innovations, Open Solutions*, *8*, 50626–50636.

Rezaee, K., & Farnami, F. (2025). Innovative approach for DR severity classification: An ai-powered tool using cnn-transformer fusion. *Journal of Biomedical Physics & Engineering*, *15*(2), 137. PMID: 40259941

Ronneberger, O., Fischer, P., & Brox, T. U-net: Convolutional networks for biomedical image segmentation, in: Medical image computing and computer-assisted intervention–MICCAI 2015: 18th international conference, Munich, Germany, October 5-9, 2015, proceedings, part III 18, Springer, 2015, pp. 234–241.

[] D. E. Rumelhart, G. E. Hinton, R. J. Williams, Learning representations by back-propagating errors, nature 323 (6088) (1986) 533–536.

Saha, D. K., Joy, A. M., & Majumder, A. (2024). Yotransvit: A transformer and cnn method for predicting and classifying skin diseases using segmentation techniques. *Informatics in Medicine Unlocked*, *47*, 101495.

Shamshad, F., Khan, S., Zamir, S. W., Khan, M. H., Hayat, M., Khan, F. S., & Fu, H. (2023). Transformers in medical imaging: A survey. *Medical Image Analysis*, *88*, 102802. PMID: 37315483

Sharen, H., Narendra, M., & Anbarasi, L. J. (2024). Mskd_net: Multi-head attention-based swin transformer for kidney diseases classification. *IEEE Access: Practical Innovations, Open Solutions*.

Sushith, M., Lakkshmanan, A., Saravanan, M., & Castro, S. (2025). Attention dual transformer with adaptive temporal convolutional for DR detection. *Scientific Reports*, *15*(1), 7694. PMID: 40044820

Tang, Y., Yuan, Y., Tao, F., & Tang, M. (2025). Cross-modal augmented transformer for automated medical report generation. *IEEE Journal of Translational Engineering in Health and Medicine*. PMID: 40035024

Tian, C., Chen, Y., Liu, Y., Wang, X., Lv, Q., Li, Y., Deng, J., Liu, Y., & Li, W. (2024). Accurate classification of glomerular diseases by hyperspectral imaging and transformer. *Computer Methods and Programs in Biomedicine*, *254*, 108285. PMID: 38964248

Ulyanov, D., Vedaldi, A., & Lempitsky, V. (2020). Deep image prior. *International Journal of Computer Vision*, *128*(7), 1867–1888.

Valanarasu, J. M. J., Oza, P., Hacihaliloglu, I., & Patel, V. M. Medical transformer: Gated axial-attention for medical image segmentation, in: Medical image computing and computer assisted intervention–MICCAI 2021: 24th international conference, Strasbourg, France, September 27– October 1, 2021, proceedings, part I 24, Springer, 2021, pp. 36–46.

Vaswani, A., Shazeer, N., Parmar, N., Uszkoreit, J., Jones, L., Gomez, A. N., Kaiser, Ł., & Polosukhin, I. (2017). Attention is all you need. *Advances in Neural Information Processing Systems*, •••, 30.

Wang, B., Xie, Q., Pei, J., Chen, Z., Tiwari, P., Li, Z., & Fu, J. (2023). Pre-trained language models in biomedical domain: A systematic survey. *ACM Computing Surveys*, *56*(3), 1–52.

Wang, H., Zhu, Y., Green, B., Adam, H., Yuille, A., & Chen, L.-C. Axial deeplab: Stand-alone axial-attention for panoptic segmentation, in: European conference on computer vision, Springer, 2020, pp. 108–126.

Wang, L., Yu, L., Zhu, J., Tang, H., Gou, F., & Wu, J. Auxiliary segmentation method of osteosarcoma in mri images based on denoising and local enhancement, in: Healthcare, Vol. 10, MDPI, 2022, p. 1468.

Wei, X., Liu, Y., Zhang, F., Geng, L., Shan, C., Cao, X., & Xiao, Z. (2025). Mstnet: Multi-scale spatial-aware transformer with multi-instance learning for DR classification. *Medical Image Analysis*, *102*, 103511. PMID: 40020421

Wen, Q., Zhou, T., Zhang, C., Chen, W., Ma, Z., Yan, J., & Sun, L. Transformers in time series: a survey, in: *Proceedings of the Thirty-Second International Joint Conference on Artificial Intelligence*, 2023, pp. 6778– 6786.

Wolf, T., Debut, L., Sanh, V., Chaumond, J., Delangue, C., & Moi, A. P. Cis tac, T. Rault, R. Louf, M. Funtowicz, et al., Transformers: State-of-the art natural language processing, in: Proceedings of the 2020 conference on empirical methods in natural language processing: system demonstrations, 2020, pp. 38–45.

Wu, H., Xiao, B., Codella, N., Liu, M., Dai, X., Yuan, L., & Zhang, L. Cvt: Introducing convolutions to ViTs, in: Proceedings of the IEEE/CVF international conference on computer vision, 2021, pp. 22– 31.

Yan, C., Shi, G., & Wu, Z. Smir: A transformer-based model for mri super resolution reconstruction, in: *2021 IEEE International Conference on Medical Imaging Physics and Engineering (ICMIPE)*, IEEE, 2021, pp. 1–6.

Yang, M., Du, J., & Lv, R. (2025). Crat: Advanced transformer-based deep learning algorithms in oct image classification. *Biomedical Signal Processing and Control, 104*, 107544.

Yu, Q., Ma, Q., Da, L., Li, J., Wang, M., Xu, A., Li, Z., Li, W., & Initiative, A. D. N.. (2024). A transformer-based unified multimodal framework for alzheimer's disease assessment. *Computers in Biology and Medicine, 180*, 108979. PMID: 39098237

Yuan, M., Xie, Y., Zhao, R., Lv, N., Zhang, Z., Zhu, L., & Wu, X. (2024). Generating synthesized computed tomography from cbct/ldct using a novel generative-transformer adversarial-cnn. *Biomedical Signal Processing and Control, 96*, 106660.

Zhang, H., Zhong, X., Li, Z., Chen, Y., Zhu, Z., Lv, J., Li, C., Zhou, Y., & Li, G. (2022). Tim-net: Transformer in m-net for retinal vessel segmentation. *Journal of Healthcare Engineering, 2022*(1), 9016401. PMID: 35859930

Zheng, Y., Qiu, B., Liu, S., Song, R., Yang, X., Wu, L., Chen, Z., Tuersun, A., Yang, X., & Wang, W.. (2024). A transformer-based deep learning model for early prediction of lymph node metastasis in locally advanced gastric cancer after neoadjuvant chemotherapy using pretreatment ct images. *EClinicalMedicine*, •••, 75. PMID: 39281097

Zhou, B., Dey, N., Schlemper, J., Salehi, S. S. M., & Liu, C. J. S. Dun can, M. Sofka, Dsformer: A dual-domain self-supervised transformer for accelerated multi-contrast mri reconstruction, in: Proceedings of the IEEE/CVF winter conference on applications of computer vision, 2023, pp. 4966–4975.

Zhu, J.-Y., Park, T., Isola, P., & Efros, A. A. Unpaired image-to-image translation using cycle-consistent adversarial networks, in: *Proceedings of the IEEE international conference on computer vision*, 2017, pp. 2223–2232.

Chapter 8
Utilization of Transformers and NLP for Electronic Health Records (EHR) Processing

Wasswa Shafik
https://orcid.org/0000-0002-9320-3186
Dig Connectivity Research Laboratory (DCRLab), Uganda

ABSTRACT

This chapter explores the utilization of transformers and Natural Language Processing (NLP) in processing electronic health records (EHRs). It highlights and demonstrates advanced methods for extracting, analyzing, and interpreting clinical data to enhance decision-making and patient care. Furthermore, by emphasizing privacy, scalability, and efficiency, the chapter showcases the transformative potential of artificial intelligence (AI) in modern healthcare systems. The chapter showcases the transformative potential of AI in modern healthcare systems, paving the way for innovative, data-driven solutions.

1 INTRODUCTION

Over the past few decades, the volume of healthcare data has exponentially increased, leading to the need for new approaches in healthcare data processing. Electronic Health Records (EHRs) stand at the heart of this data revolution, which collects patient-specific clinical information. Consequently, modern clinical settings are data-rich owing to the development of an entity-scale, widely applicable data collection process in the form of EHRs, thereby transforming the dimensions of

DOI: 10.4018/979-8-3373-2038-0.ch008

healthcare data management (Shafk, 2023; Siebra et al., 2024). Subsequent to documentation and maintenance processes, EHRs have amassed valuable information for facilitating clinical workflows and patient care. Establishing efficient and effective techniques that focus on relevant EHR documentation is currently the subject of extensive research interest. The capability of state-of-the-art machine learning models to be exploited for providing possible solutions is noteworthy. However, natural language processing and understanding from data-rich EHRs are beyond the abilities of traditional data processing methods (J. Li et al., 2024; Shafik, 2023). Thus, there is a call for the integration of modern, high-performance, and interpretative machine learning models for addressing the challenges prevailing in EHRs.

In clinical settings, providing the right information in the quickest possible way can be valuable in highly dynamic situations such as emergency care. EHRs can be utilized for this purpose, enabling healthcare providers to receive documents, summarized data, medical histories, and recommended readings upon patient arrival. Converting clinical activities into a document management process necessitates accurate processing and interpretation of information. One of the key entities of this ever-growing knowledge base is an EHR, created through administrative, interoperable, diagnostic, therapeutic, and administrative workflow data (Babu & Boddu, 2024). Therefore, transforming EHRs into an easily understandable format becomes an indispensable necessity to engage a broader audience, from medical researchers and clinical staff to data scientists and data analysts. Considering technical machine learning models, specifically transformers, to process EHRs and utilize healthcare informatics is the need of the hour, which essentially aims to detail how healthcare EHRs transformed into multiples of their intended brevity, leading to improved healthcare provision (Nandini Prasad et al., 2023). This explicates why the utilization of transformer networks can enhance the usability of EHRs in multiple scenario-based settings.

Following nationwide progress towards the digitalization of medical data, Electronic Health Records (EHRs) have proliferated rapidly. They have the potential to support a variety of tasks in healthcare, such as patient care, research, and administrative processes. EHRs are not only rapidly growing in volume but also vary in modality, such as structured data, including medication lists or diagnosis codes, and unstructured data, such as clinical notes and images. Interoperability and accessibility are closely linked to the use of EHRs (Nikam et al., 2024; Shafik, 2025b). Data fragmentation is frequently blamed for the inefficient and substandard processing of EHRs. In addition, it is difficult to link data from one patient across numerous hospitalizations or network systems. Data heterogeneity and high dimensionality, as well as co-morbid and long-term conditions, long-time series, and interactions between these different EHR modalities, cause a number of issues. At present, the most widely used approaches are manual feature engineering, shallow machine learning, and rule-based approaches. Modern methods of learning deep representations of medical data have the potential to capture more complex relationships and trade-offs (X. Zhang et al., 2023). However, the difficulty of working with EHRs appears to have prevented the widespread adoption of these methods. Vision transformers are prominent examples of these new methods. They were found to have excellent handling capabilities for medical images. Furthermore, medical texts that are also lengthy documents can be similarly broken down into segments. To take full advantage of clinical data, they need to follow a linear time representation of an individual spanning lengthy records. However, to this day, no one has verified whether tradition-based approaches are still more effective than transformer-based methods when processing EHRs (R. Kumar et al., 2023; Shafik et al., 2024). We studied whether transformers would be beneficial in dealing with sophisticated relationships in patient data throughout numerous medical visits.

1.1 Objectives and Scope

The main objectives of this chapter are to examine recent transformer applications and propose potential future improvements. More specifically, the objective of this study is to consider the efficacy of using state-of-the-art models of the transformer family to process EHRs. The current research focuses on using these models to improve EHR extraction tasks via named entity recognition, enabling advancements in diagnosis and drug extraction. It is important not only for the NLP community to improve transformer applications but also for the health community for the betterment of patients' health. The outlined scope of the research consists of multiple goals, including pointing out new workflow components combining both vision and language processing, pinpointing and investigating current challenges with existing practices of EHR processing, illustrating the significance of transformer applications for EHR processing, and lending insight on principles and real-life problem-solving using different expert systems, as illustrated in Figure 1.

Figure 1. Expert systems

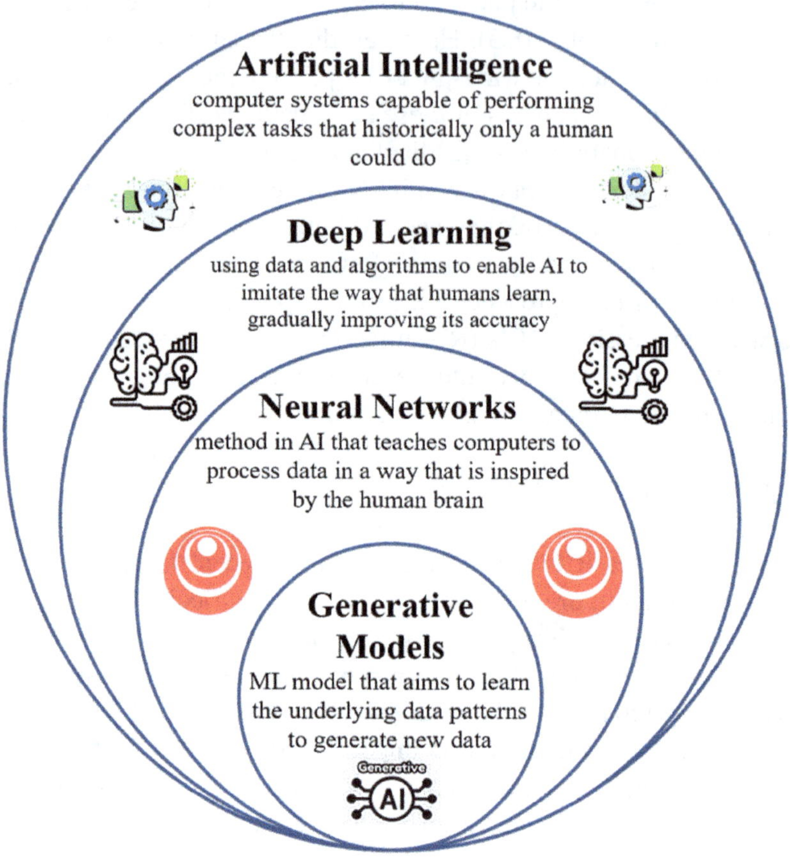

A wide spectrum of healthcare practitioners is currently using EHR information for numerous reasons, including disease management, analytics, and operational insight. The potential audience for this study includes experts in data analysis and other data mining scientists as well as healthcare professionals. The outcomes of this research will benefit practitioners, as the theoretical sections will aid in improving the healthcare process (Niu et al., 2024; Shafik, 2024f). It is also apparent that there are exponential potential gains for the primary beneficiaries of the study, as the utilization of the outlined model in the healthcare industry will enhance efficiency and quality of operation. Furthermore, the broad scope of integration into prime-level healthcare processes, planning, and policy formulation related to healthcare is a potential longer-term gain for interdisciplinary healthcare practitioners. The research will indicate a possible layer of application and a link to be used in the design of tasks and future solutions around transformer design. In conclusion, among possible future work inputs is the study of ethical considerations in implementing the application of transformers in the healthcare domain (V. Kumar et al., 2023). Also, the future trend of transformers should be included in sub-field investigations.

2 FOUNDATIONS OF TRANSFORMERS

Transformers are a type of model that works well with sequential data. Given the growing amount of sequential data available, transformers have seen varied applications in multiple domains. From a more technical point of view, the main innovative feature of transformers is the presence of the so-called "attention mechanism." This keeps track of the interactions among the different timesteps in the sequence, hence allowing for parallelization in the training phase. More in detail, a transformer model is organized into an "encoder" part, a "decoder" part, a stack of multiple encoding layers, and another stack of multiple decoding layers. Each of these layers contains a "self-attention" mechanism, which enables the model to process sequential data more freely (Ren et al., 2023; Shafik, 2024a). The introduction of transformer models in 2017 led to a revolution in the natural language processing community. In particular, transformer models have known great successes in training language model embeddings at large scales with measures in terms of word similarity and analogy tasks, which translated into good performances in a myriad of tasks built upon language embeddings across different NLP domains. A number of reasons make transformer models particularly suitable for tackling EHR-related tasks. In particular, they come with higher computational efficiency, enabling the handling of large-scale datasets (Shafik, 2024c; X. Zhang et al., 2023). Moreover, they have a better ability to model the statistical properties of the sequences in consideration, a feature that is particularly critical when dealing with sequential data.

2.1 Understanding of Transformers

Transformers were first introduced for sequence-to-sequence learning in 2014 and achieved state-of-the-art performance in a variety of natural language processing tasks, including machine translation, summarization, and question-answering. What initially set the transformer apart was its ability to process longer sequences more quickly, in parallel, without a corresponding drop in performance. Prior to this, a sequence model called the recurrent neural network was commonly used. Models like the Long Short-Term Memory and the gated recurrent unit excelled at understanding sequences of data by retaining information from prior steps but were inherently limited by their serial computation over sequences, making them unsuitable for handling long-range dependencies (R. Kumar et al., 2023; Shafik,

2024g). By contrast, the transformer calculates the attention of the input sequence in one step, a self-attention mechanism that provides a global view of the input and effectively captures long-range contextual relationships. Transformers do not rely on convolutions or recurrent connections, and they avoid the sequential nature of LSTMs and GRUs by using only the self-attention mechanism. These properties make them attractive models for a wide range of sequences of differing lengths and many modeling tasks beyond language. The remarkable achievements of transformers in handling natural language tasks have led to widespread interest and applications of transformers outside of the classical natural language processing tasks, such as handling tabular data and images (Arora et al., 2023). The EHR is a sequence data structure that consists of patients' health-related events. Tracing the developments in transformers can explain their potential usage for certain aspects of EHR processing.

2.2 Transformer Architecture and Components

The basic components of the transformer architecture, such as the attention mechanism, were introduced in the previous subsection. The transformer consists of an era of layers, where each layer includes two parallel branches of processing. A key component is the multi-head self-attention mechanism. The elements of the first branch are transformed through attention, whereas the elements of the second branch are transformed without attention and are only processed using feed-forward neural networks (Raza et al., 2023). The outputs of these two branches are then concatenated and fed into a target layer.

- Layer Input Embeddings: Each input position is transformed into a distributed representation presented to the model as input embeddings. In this case, this step can be viewed as word embedding for the given positions.
- Multi-head Attention Mechanism The attention mechanism is a method that allows all the input positions to be represented based on the context of other positions. For the self-attention mechanism, the input can come from different sources, but the same input sequence will be used in each component. The self-attention mechanism explores the different positions of the sequence and then weighs the significance of each element to include in the input representation. In the health domain, this could be beneficial to give more weight to the relevant words that indicate the diagnosis instead of non-relevant visit descriptions.

3 APPLICATIONS OF TRANSFORMERS IN NATURAL LANGUAGE PROCESSING (NLP)

The use of the transformer architecture, which solely relies on attention mechanisms for learning contextual relations, has given rise to state-of-the-art models in numerous natural language processing benchmarks and applications. NLP can also help interpret clinical texts and ultimately develop a systematic approach toward managing them effectively. Many NLP applications often focus on spoken language or informal styles regarding different languages, accents, and gender peculiarities that are not well suited to clinical settings. Since there is plenty of conversational and clinical text data, a lot of advances have been made in developing automated NLP systems (Ahmad et al., 2023). As a result, providers can develop applications that help users easily access different databases to optimize the delivery of services. The transformer model has also given rise to many advancements in language tasks, text generation, and classification applications. The transformer model uses self-attention to capture semantic and contextual information for individual words residing in a sentence by addressing different contextual embeddings from adjacent words in all positions (Sung et al., 2023). It has improved word prediction accuracy, leading to better applications for sequence-to-sequence learning, named entity recognition, relation classification, drug-related entity recognition, clinical document retrieval, classification, and summary generation, and will likely be improved by future research. Thus, general NLP improvements can have a huge implication in the healthcare delivery system. Overall, the transformer model, widely used in general language tasks, is also very useful for processing large datasets in diagnosing patients in clinical settings (Romanowski et al., 2023).

3.1 Overview of NLP in Healthcare

Clinical text, such as doctor notes, discharge summaries, and medical literature, represents an essential data source for many applications, including clinical treatment and clinical research. Typically, clinical text varies in form, including structure and narrative. Nonetheless, the clinical text has several unique aspects. First, besides informal language, it also contains signs, symbols, and other conventions that oppose clear language for more precise communication among professionals. Second, much of the clinical data is primarily qualitative or semi-quantitative (Yousri & Safwat, 2023). So, the information is not formatted in an easily usable manner and may also fall under multiple categories. They might be stored in natural language format, often resulting in the creation of unstructured text, which cannot be analyzed directly. Therefore, developing techniques for the extraction of information from unstructured clinical text and making it accessible in a structured database can be of great significance. It is in this regard that Natural Language Processing has the potential to aid in managing clinical data and improving patient health and care (X. Zhang et al., 2023).

Spanning across diverse applications, Natural Language Processing, by being effectively capable of handling heavy, complex, domain-dependent, and ambiguous clinical data, can play a pivotal role in clinical data exchange and integration, formulating responses to patient questions, standardizing clinical data storage, facilitating the generation of quality reports to demonstrate the significance of patient care, making health and medical publications available for better web-based access, linking disparate data sources to improve longitudinal care and patient prioritization, and structuring clinical texts for developing appropriate user interfaces and providing customized information to healthcare professionals and the public. Such applications are gaining prominence in many healthcare institutions and industries, with many healthcare professionals relying on Natural Language Processing-enhanced tools to assist them in the clinical decision-making processes and meaningful caring (Arora et al., 2023). Moreover, evidence-based medicine, which is becoming more and more critical for healthcare quality improvement and cost-cutting, relies largely on intuitions obtained from empirical data, which can only be gleaned from informally produced observation documents. Given the multifarious potential, Natural Language Processing has unrivaled capabilities in enhancing the quality and efficiency at all stages of health development, including healthcare provision, promotion, decision making, detection, diagnosis, treatment, prevention, and population research (Atabek et al., 2023; Kapruwan et al., 2023). In any of those stages, clinical texts are primarily processed by Natural Language Processing-based software in more ways than one.

3.2 Benefits of Using Transformers in NLP

The transformer is an advanced deep learning model that has long been considered the state of the art in achieving high accuracy with high computational efficiency, even when trained with a large amount of data. Such properties of the transformer are vital for healthcare applications, such as in EHR, which often contain a large amount of datasets. The generated representation from a transformer can capture complex linguistic patterns and semantics, making it better at understanding the context of the sentence. This facilitates the performance of some NLP tasks. For example, clinical texts usually contain an ellipsis of some words. A transformer may have a better interpretation of a sentence with missing words in a clinical note compared to traditional neural networks (Gou & Jie, 2023). There are many tasks in EHR natural language with the potential to leverage new transformer models for automated support, such as word sense disambiguation, language correction, missing value prediction, named entity recognition, mapping relations, and data augmentation in multi-document summarization tasks. Transformers facilitate the calculation of the semantic relationship between two sentences. For example, given two sentences, 'adhesion' and 'postoperative recovery,' a transformer may have a decent judgment of the semantic relationship between the two sentences rather than scoring them as unrelated due to the possible zero overlapping words. It has also been proven that transformers can, to some extent, diminish the impact of linguistic bias often seen in traditional word embedding models (Deep Shukla et al., 2023). Transformers substantially outperform their predecessors on all-natural language understanding tasks like sentiment analysis and also outperform other language models on various classification tasks to beat the standard benchmarks with very small data. Transformers were not only highly praised for being the first pre-trained NLP model for natural language understanding, but they have also been used for various tasks (Shafik, 2024b, 2024d). This reflects the effectiveness of transformers in various fields leading to the smart health devices as illustrated in Figure 2.

Figure 2. Sampled smart healthcare devices

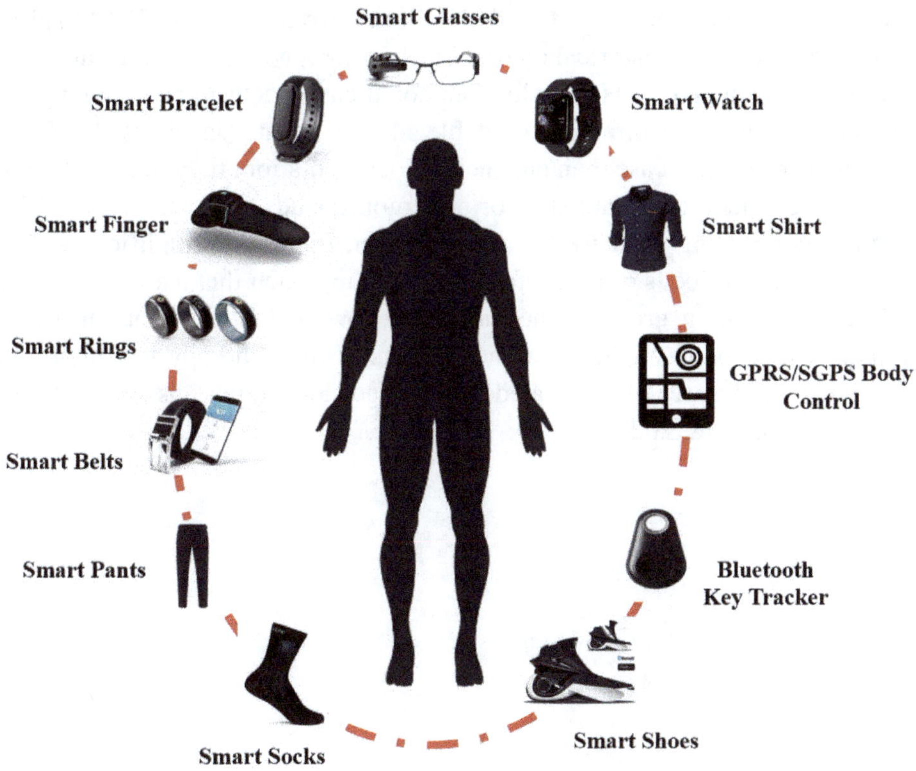

4 UTILIZING TRANSFORMERS FOR EHR PROCESSING

In our previous discussions, we provided context for the use of transformers. For the following several sections, we will shift our focus to discuss the practical utility of transformers—specifically from the perspective of processing Electronic Health Records (EHR). EHRs become difficult objects to manage as they become larger, often straining data management systems that store and transmit them. Because the information in EHRs is forever growing, being able to search meaningfully for trends and evidence becomes more difficult. The motivation behind using transformers for EHR management is grounded in the fact that a patient's visit is often densely packed with unstructured English text that rests in clinical data systems (Siebra et al., 2024). Thus, tremendous value could be realized by establishing competencies in NLP and using state-of-the-art NLP transformers to help lighten the load of an EHR system, catalog what is found within it, and gain insight from it. Setting aside the processing justifications, transformers could also help in making the clinical data themselves more complete and interpretable. Working with unstructured text can provide a layer of richness to the structured data a system already tracks for a patient's medical record. For example, a transformer could extract so-called adverse events, signs, or symptoms of a disorder or disease from a patient's EHR to provide a more comprehensive historical record. Furthermore, with a negative value for the adverse event in a given EHR, a clinician could easily determine how long in the past a patient suffered from the extractable adverse events (Javaid et al., 2023). In a slightly different use case than enhancing documentation, tracking the directions for the use of therapies established or undergoing study in an EHR would be an extremely compelling use case for a transformer. Indeed, a simplified version of this use case is the focus of a transformer-based approach that uses a dataset from the UK as a training ground. The movement toward systems that can generate automated descriptors of the usual side effects of drug therapy is a high-impact development in the area of automated clinical decision support, as demonstrated in Figure 3 (Islam et al., 2024).

Figure 3. Transformer-assisted electronic medical record application in the health facility

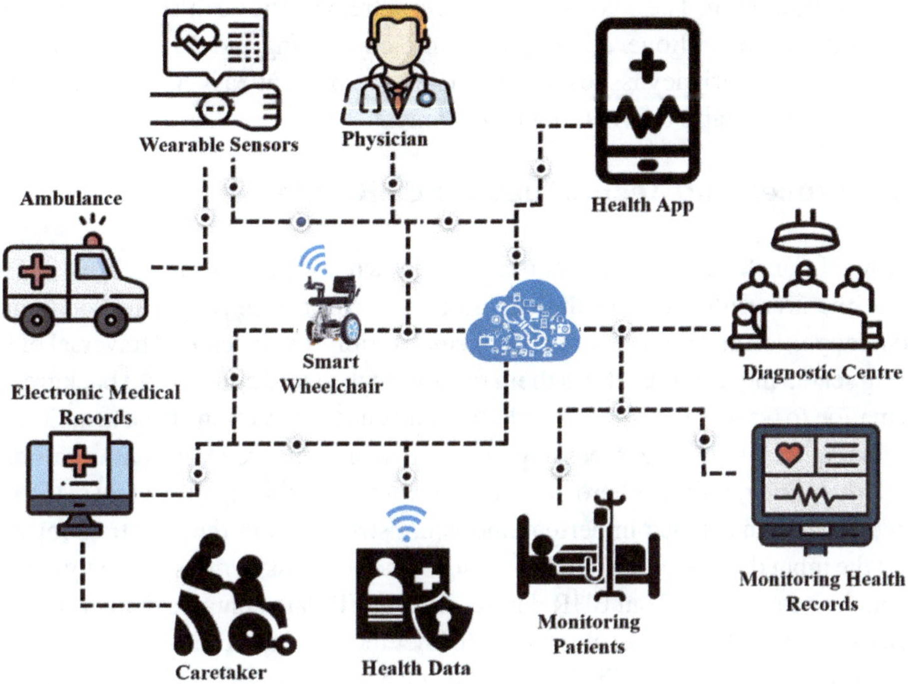

4.1 Challenges in EHR Processing

Present state-of-the-art solutions in incorporating mechanisms like transformers in EHR are in demand as traditional ones struggle to address the challenges in EHR processing due to the following reasons. Data Fragmentation: Large amounts of data exist in different and diverse systems and hospitals, causing difficulties in integrating the EHR data across a broader horizon. The unavailability of a consistent and uniform data model results in challenges like standardization and providing coherent health care to individuals across the socio-economic spectrum (Cascella et al., 2024; Siebra et al., 2024). Lack of Data Interoperability: Owing to the dependency of EHR data on generating entities like patients, many people were affected by an unauthorized incident involving a third-party vendor. Such incidents reflect the success probability of attacks due to the involvement of humans in the entire generation process cycle. Data Extraction Challenges: One of the many challenges in handling EHR data includes processing the data to obtain meaningful insights, especially when the EHR data is present in an unstructured fashion. There is no "one model fits all" technique in healthcare due to its intrinsic nature that is driven by a range of factors including environmental, clinical, and genetic interactions. User training and adoption: The phasing out of excess stress on the health care practitioner is essential since practitioner adaptation is time-consuming and demanding (Raiaan et al., 2024). Data privacy issues: Many challenges prevent easy handling of EHRs in an unauthorized and confidential environment.

4.2 Preprocessing Techniques for EHR Data

Clinical transformer models, commonly known as "transformers," have shown state-of-the-art results in many clinical information processing tasks, such as named entity recognition and medical concept normalization. Their detailed traversal of the training set during training allows them to capture the word context and background information to perform diagnosis prediction and entity extraction at test time. Transformers require a lot of preprocessing to organize unstructured EHR data. This data is often dirty and requires preprocessing to be compatible with the transformer. Data created by humans is also imperfect and is not structured in the way transformers expect the input data (Roy, 2024). The performance of transformers is largely dependent on the quality of a clean EHR dataset. Raw EHR data contains many mistakes, which can easily affect the resulting transformer model. Oftentimes, CKD x-ray text mentions the wrong side of the kidneys because, in a normal view, the left kidney is on the patient's right, but this is often not taken into account. Preprocessing also improves the efficiency of the model. A model can be confused by the complexity of data formats inside the unstructured HER (Liu et al., 2024). Data is generally normalized and tokenized to unify the representation of different forms. As such, the data becomes suitable for transformers. Healthcare preprocessing outputs can improve patient risk prediction and are also, more often, significantly used in the following downstream tasks in healthcare. Once the text is represented as tokens, N-grams can also be formed to identify mentions, allowing us to search for disease or symptom names as unigrams, bigrams, and so on (Valova et al., 2024).

5 CASE STUDIES AND IMPLEMENTATIONS

The following examples demonstrate case studies where transformers have been or are being used for EHR processing. We hope that by providing these examples we can inspire more researchers and healthcare institutions to get excited about transformers and undertake experimental work in order to reach technical maturity by overcoming practical issues and leveraging their strengths. Positive Use of Transformers: Applications for NLP and Causal Inference suggest that end-to-end research can be innovated using transformers, particularly for the task of semi-structured data de-identification. A transformer-based language model is used to generate truly de-identified databases in iterative learning environments. The iterative training performance is only one-tenth of that of a fully connected network of similar performance. The use of transformers is a strategic shift in clinical NLP research. Transformer models are used to create recommendation systems for matching clinicians to patients for primary care (Niu et al., 2024; Wu, 2024). Specific recommendations include the essence of the care that can be implemented in the current health information system.

Lessons Learned: To improve performance, consider adding sub-tokens for dates and times whenever they are used. Time is an important predictor in the clinical profession, and allowing the system to learn its importance has proven to be beneficial. Careful handling of data retrieval is paramount - incorporating an additional module that can perform encryption on dates. Measurements: The team is currently working on the de-identification transformer and preparing a paper for the journal track. They mention that the de-identification process using transformers has been released and is currently being used as part of a data toolkit. They have a separate paper in preparation for use on the system (Y. Li et al., 2024). Large-scale De-identification of Semi-Structured Data Using Iterative Transformer Language Models modified a transformer-based language model to deidentify semi-structured clinical data such as electronic health records. Most current methods for data de-identification use token-based encodings, so a document-embedding layer was introduced to first transform each section of the medical history into a single, continuous vector representation. This global information is then concatenated with the token encoder input, maintaining the necessary word-level information (V. Kumar et al., 2024). The output of the token-based tokens is then summed along with document vectors for the final representation, thus better enhanced healthcare experience, as illustrated in Figure 4.

Figure 4. Application of Artificial intelligence medical Internet of Things

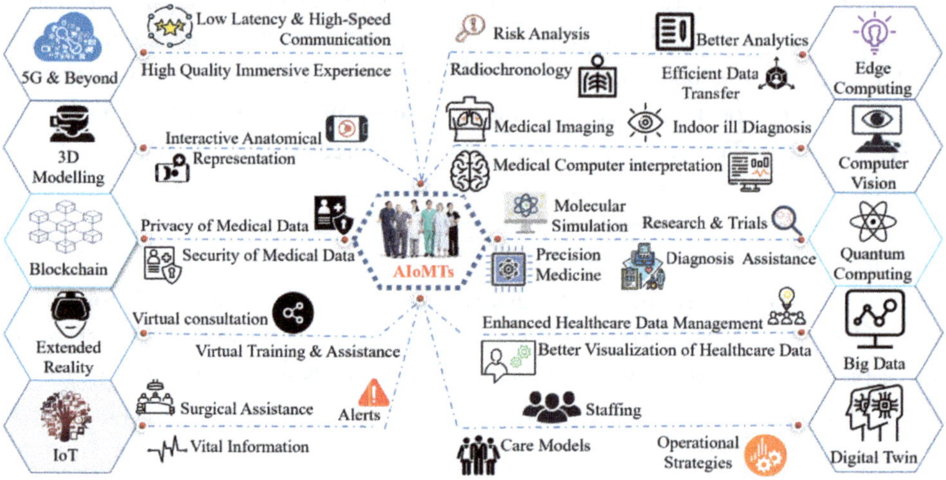

5.1 Real-world Examples of Transformer Applications in EHRs

Several recent studies have applied transformers to a wide range of clinical tasks with EHR, demonstrating real-world performance improvements when transitioning from using conventional techniques. A transformer-based hierarchical model for readmission prediction achieved improved performance in predicting a patient's 30-day readmission after heart failure. Similarly, a transformer model for readmission prediction in orthopedics also performed better in predicting 30-day hospital readmission in a large-scale retrospective study and was suggested as an alternative to the LACE index. A transformer-based architecture that accommodated character-level word embeddings and input from a pretrained deep learning bidirectional long short-term memory model for clinical text de-identification outperformed several de-identification models in terms of recall, dice coefficient, and exact match on both token and character level (Venerito et al., 2023).

Pre-trained transformer-based sequence-to-sequence models were successfully applied to a specific task, achieving a BLEU score within a certain percentile across an anonymized test set of responses. Finally, a comprehensive transformer solution incorporating bidirectional encoder representations from transformers and vision transformer models was developed to predict the lengths of ICU hospital stays. The predictive performance of this solution for clinical interventions conducted in the ICU and the associated patient outcomes demonstrated that predicted short and prolonged ICU stays were both associated with increased in-hospital mortality

(Turchin et al., 2023). This demonstrates that, for short ICU stays, early discharge is associated with beneficial patient outcomes, thus facilitating operational planning. The deployment of all models was associated with a practical challenge, which was the merging of demographic and clinical data in the features used for the prediction of the study outcome. However, these models may inspire confidence in the use of advanced machine learning and statistical modeling techniques, including transformer technologies (Javaid et al., 2023).

6 ETHICAL AND LEGAL CONSIDERATIONS

Properly processing Electronic Health Record (EHR) data is of crucial importance. EHR data are considered sensitive in terms of legislation. Responsible data protection and privacy measures should be implemented to process such data. In cases where EHR is processed with advanced technologies, the patient's privacy interests remain the final protection purpose, which immediately reflects on the responsibility of the data teams. First and foremost, to obtain consent for processing EHR data in general, and especially for processing with new technologies, patients whose EHR data are used must be informed about the processing in a transparent manner and an understandable language (Ahmad et al., 2023). Necessary structured information can be spread through information systems or, for example, user-supporting documents to improve accessibility. Thus, the use of advanced technologies for electronic patient data processing, especially its effects on patient privacy, will mostly depend on consent, interest in transparency, proper handling, and secure processing. This, in the end, will surely confirm the effects on the expert or authority-accountable processes and should be considered in the interpreted results (Sharma & Padha, 2023; Verma & Sanjeevi, 2023).

6.1 Technology Acceptance in Medical Domain

Since the possibility of misusing the sensitive data of any patient is not to be tolerated, the utilization of advanced technologies for processing EHR data should only be performed under adherence to a legal framework. The era of human intervention is facing irreversible development; to a very large extent, many areas of human activity are controlled by automated processes. AI and advanced technology impact individual decision-making; this is also the situation with electronic patient data processing. Patient privacy breaches might impact a person's dignity and right to object or freedom of expression. One should be allowed privacy when searching for medical information (Enquero et al., 2023). Benefit-risk should be evident while using EHR processing. Advanced technologies should only be used under stringent patient consent and comply with the regulatory framework. Indeed, the healthcare landscape gives a striking example of the societal and ethical implications of deploying advanced algorithms to decision-making in a very sensitive domain. Thus, it is crucial to scrutinize not just the potential technical opportunities of utilizing advanced technologies for EHR processing but also to discuss the ethical landscape that such models navigate (Deep Shukla et al., 2023). Researchers and developers of various misuse of sensitive data should consider the existing legislation and/ or ethical guidelines to harmonize the situation. Proper implementation might be costly, but it increases the trust of involved parties. Ethical considerations and enhancement points: it is to be taken seriously under consideration the entire cycle of algorithmic decision-making, from the very data entry up to the returned results and automatic report receiving, and the possible choices regarding the feedback assignment. Moreover, it was discussed that the data generated when using a system of that kind should include sensitive reports (Kapruwan et al., 2023).

6.2 Privacy and Security Concerns in EHR Processing

Health information is sensitive personal information. Electronic health records (EHR) contain comprehensive information about the health, illness, and health care of every patient. Thus, it is necessary to access or not disclose information in medical records, and it is necessary to protect the contents of the information in medical records to access the prescribed fields. The medical records shall be kept confidential insofar as the patient has not permitted access, inspection, or release of the information. Any unauthorized access and any violation of confidential information contained in the information shall be inviolable and subject to penalties under national and international laws. The adoption of new technology for processing EHR has potential legal and ethical issues to be concerned about (B. Zhang et al., 2023). This chapter touches on some legal and ethical issues to look at the technical aspects of the processing of EHR using transformer models in the field of NLP. The following responsibilities must be taken into consideration when processing electronic health records until the results are released: providing immediate access to the report to any member of the health care team that has permission to access the EHR until restrictions on the EHR for appointment purposes are released by the patient or their surrogate. In research using protected health information (PHI), the results included in publications and presentations must have the patient's or surrogate's written authorization to present the research results before presentation, including words and diagrams. Moreover, the authors or presenters must explain to the readers or audience that the results presented are obtained following the patient's informed consent regarding the use and non-use of treatment from the patient's care data (Nandini Prasad et al., 2023; Shafik, 2024e, 2025a). Ethical and legal issues have been proposed as research questions in configural and implementation research methods using transformer models for processing electronic health records. The conclusion of this research includes implementing proper techniques to ensure patient privacy and rights in processing EHR.

7 FUTURE DIRECTIONS AND EMERGING TRENDS

Transformers offer great potential in modeling sequence data. Future model advancements that are likely to become popular in this area will include: • An enhancement in transformer models, especially for time-series data applications and structured data processing. This is typically aimed at achieving computational efficiency when dealing with high-dimensional data. In addition, it will include handling specialized data with specific architectures to increase their adaptability to these types of data (Chellatamilan et al., 2023). The ability of such transformer models to scale up in order to process massive amounts of data due to the complexities of big data, their enormous number of instances, and feature processing along with class imbalances to output accurate results. This ability can be achieved by creating very deep and high-capacity models (Haddouche et al., 2023).

Artificial Intelligence Pervasiveness and the Impact on EHR The need for gathering and analyzing electronic health records has led to the necessity for efficient management of health data, increasing interoperability, and rule unification among institutions that produce such data. A forecast of artificial integration and the impact that the new set of requirements poses to data management is discussed. Healthcare analytics tends to be developed close to state-of-the-art models of natural language processing, such as those needed for EHR coding and processing (Ren et al., 2023). Over the next decade, the relationship will be much closer, and the mix of new analytic approaches designed in healthcare and those imported from other industries will increasingly produce continuous learning and predictive analytics systems that combine new data engineering and data analytics, including artificial intelligence capabilities alongside domain knowledge (Raza et al., 2023).

The Convergence between ML and DL With the rise of deep learning and the increasingly easier ways to create and implement models, it is not unimaginable that in the future, machine learning and deep learning-derived models will be the only tools required for data science applications, including healthcare. This widespread use of ML could be achieved due to new tools and methodologies that reduce the amount and complexity of the data required to create these models, potential new verification checks to be implemented, evolving baseline performance, and simplifying some parts of the ethical questions and regulatory frameworks (Nandini Prasad et al., 2023). However, the adoption process will require an evolution in ethics and regulatory frameworks that are implemented in the algorithms and the enhancement of end-user tools for business and others. In healthcare, the value of ML, particularly DL, may lie in the manner in which advanced analytics models can be combined with traditional healthcare methods to harvest patient data into efficient information that drives patient care, diagnostics, and pharmaceutical and clinical trial development. As of now, the developed models are thought of as tools to enhance understanding or practically be another brick in the overall process, not to replace the others (Atabek et al., 2023).

In recent years, transformers have revolutionized the field of natural language processing (NLP). This has been achieved through a range of technological advancements, such as attention patterns, scaling tricks, novel architectures, and self-supervised learning. One of the key elements of the transformer is the self-attention mechanism, which computes a representation of words in a sequence by attending to all other words. The self-attention mechanism greatly benefits from access to compute and, therefore, efficient computation of intensive operations such as computing pairwise similarities between the various tokens in the input (Enquero et al., 2023). Therefore, the advent of tailored hardware allowed the self-attention-based transformer models to surpass the prior state-of-the-art in NLP greatly. In the domain of healthcare and medicine, EHRs provide an invaluable resource of information about the patients, recording their various conditions, medications, treatments, and the chronology of their visits. Their complex and specific nature raised additional requirements for models processing them, such as multi-tasking ability and explainability (Kim et al., 2023).

The success of generative and fine-tuning transformers on various subfields of NLP and acquiring resources of computational infrastructure turns attention toward healthcare, where a large amount of EHR data is available. Transfer learning plays a crucial role, allowing the reusability of models initially trained on a source task, such as natural language processing or vision, which can then be learned from a small data set (V. Kumar et al., 2024). This strategy can help adjust a transformer that achieved high results on non-medical data to perform well on EHR through fine-tuning or adapting the transformer model to learn specific medical knowledge. Researchers and companies have been excited to improve and integrate transformers into numerous healthcare applications in recent years. To reduce the gap between the achievements of model training and clinical practice needs, some work focuses on fine-tuning models on natural language processing tasks based on publicly available healthcare datasets and then evaluates them on industry benchmark datasets (Niu et al., 2024; Wu, 2024).

8 CONCLUSION

In this chapter, we argued how Transformers paved the way for more intelligent and efficient processing of Electronic Health Records. We carefully discussed the assumptions, implications, and challenges. The aim was to discuss the term "EHR Transformer" both in its more general potential to revolutionize healthcare data management and particular developments, for example from related models to the most recent models. We provided three examples that showcase how one may use state-of-the-art Transformer-based models for EHR processing. We promoted a holistic approach throughout the paper, briefly discussing the implications of our research, including some of the legal and ethical aspects. This also includes a brief discussion on the current focus of transformer technology in English and the Euro-American domain in terms of their connections to the ethical challenges of a digital transformation in eHealth. Transformers offer both potential and challenges for processing Electronic Health Records data. The driving force of this innovation will be the advances in how individuals with the datasets, technology, and clinical experience work together to transfer and transform language models on EHR text data. We provided a summary below of how our case studies support these claims, the benefits of investing in this Transformer technology, notably both to the patient and the healthcare professional, and potential future directions for overall EHR Transformers technology. Our paper recognizes that a future research organization is likely using EHR Transformers and thereby capturing additional value for the patient by expanding the data analyses part of the mandate to include the transformation of big healthcare digital data into scientific information for our future patients. Further development and deployment of EHR Transformer are needed, both as they relate to our detailed case studies of text-processing and also more generally for speeding the transition of transformer possibilities into healthcare. The case studies show how and what the future might be if higher expenditure in computing, computation, large language models, annotators, knowledge graph refinement, and pre-processing are used. For end-users in the detailed case studies, we have seen a reduction in one specific task on the EHR from several days to less than 24-h with marked increases in predictive ability and accuracy, specificity, anti-accuracy, and anti-specificity. The latter vary more widely and are often associated with more conservative values. In the future, we anticipate patients with respect to health improvement and preventive strategies and the use of human-mark-up inefficiency. For healthcare, we anticipate integrated and predictive markers of disease for improved diagnosis, target trial, and stratified evidence coordination. The impacts of corollary properties of the research in healthcare fraud, data protection and privacy, legal oversight, and the societal value of the current dominant research efforts in relation to healthcare data are briefly noted.

REFERENCES

Ahmad, P. N., Liu, Y., Khan, K., Jiang, T., & Burhan, U. (2023). BIR: Biomedical Information Retrieval System for Cancer Treatment in Electronic Health Record Using Transformers. *Sensors (Basel), 23*(23). Advance online publication. DOI: 10.3390/s23239355 PMID: 38067736

Arora, M., Mudgil, P., Sharma, U., Chopra, C., & Singh, N. H. (2023). Evaluation of text summarization techniques in healthcare domain: Pharmaceutical drug feedback. *Intelligent Decision Technologies*, *17*(4). Advance online publication. DOI: 10.3233/IDT-230129

Atabek, A., Eralp, E., & Gursoy, M. E. (2023). Trust, Privacy and Security Aspects of Bias and Fairness in Machine Learning. *Proceedings - 2023 5th IEEE International Conference on Trust, Privacy and Security in Intelligent Systems and Applications, TPS-ISA 2023*. https://doi.org/DOI: 10.1109/TPS-ISA58951.2023.00023

Babu, A., & Boddu, S. B. (2024). BERT-Based Medical Chatbot: Enhancing Healthcare Communication through Natural Language Understanding. *Exploratory Research in Clinical and Social Pharmacy, 13*. Advance online publication. DOI: 10.1016/j.rcsop.2024.100419 PMID: 38495953

Cascella, M., Semeraro, F., Montomoli, J., Bellini, V., Piazza, O., & Bignami, E. (2024). The Breakthrough of Large Language Models Release for Medical Applications: 1-Year Timeline and Perspectives. In *Journal of Medical Systems* (Vol. 48, Issue 1). https://doi.org/DOI: 10.1007/s10916-024-02045-3

Chellatamilan, T., Narayanasamy, S. K., Garg, L., Srinivasan, K., & Islam, S. M. N. (2023). Ensemble Text Summarization Model for COVID-19-Associated Datasets. *International Journal of Intelligent Systems, 2023*. Advance online publication. DOI: 10.1155/2023/3106631

Deep Shukla, A., Agarwal, L., Mein Goh, J., Gao Carey Business School, G., & Agarwal, R. (2023). Catch Me If You Can: Identifying Fraudulent Physician Reviews with Large Language Models Using Generative Pre-Trained Transformers. *ArXiv*.

Enquero, S. P., Sunil, G., Kumar, S. S., Lavanya, C., & Siddhanti, P. (2023). Deep Neural Pretraining for Improving Diagnostic and Therapeutic Entity Recognition in Electronic Medical Records. *2023 International Conference on Evolutionary Algorithms and Soft Computing Techniques, EASCT 2023*. https://doi.org/DOI: 10.1109/EASCT59475.2023.10393025

Gou, Y., & Jie, C. (2023). A lightweight biomedical named entity recognition with pre-trained model. *2023 IEEE 3rd International Conference on Data Science and Computer Application, ICDSCA 2023*. https://doi.org/DOI: 10.1109/ICDSCA59871.2023.10392374

Haddouche, A., Rabia, I., & Aid, A. (2023). Transformer-Based Question Answering Model for the Biomedical Domain. *2023 5th International Conference on Pattern Analysis and Intelligent Systems, PAIS 2023*. https://doi.org/DOI: 10.1109/PAIS60821.2023.10322055

Islam, S., Elmekki, H., Elsebai, A., Bentahar, J., Drawel, N., Rjoub, G., & Pedrycz, W. (2024). A comprehensive survey on applications of transformers for deep learning tasks. In *Expert Systems with Applications* (Vol. 241). https://doi.org/DOI: 10.1016/j.eswa.2023.122666

Javaid, M., Haleem, A., & Singh, R. P. (2023). ChatGPT for healthcare services: An emerging stage for an innovative perspective. *BenchCouncil Transactions on Benchmarks. Standards and Evaluations*, *3*(1). Advance online publication. DOI: 10.1016/j.tbench.2023.100105

Kapruwan, A., Sharma, S., & Rai Goyal, H. (2023). Natural Language Processing Techniques in Diagnostic Digital Cytopathology for Cervical Intraepithelial Neoplasia Detection. *2023 9th International Conference on Advanced Computing and Communication Systems, ICACCS 2023*. https://doi.org/DOI: 10.1109/ICACCS57279.2023.10113060

Kim, Y., Kim, J. H., Kim, Y. M., Song, S., & Joo, H. J. (2023). Predicting medical specialty from text based on a domain-specific pre-trained BERT. *International Journal of Medical Informatics*, *170*. Advance online publication. DOI: 10.1016/j.ijmedinf.2022.104956 PMID: 36512987

Kumar, R., Ayyasamy, R. K., Sangodiah, A., Krishnan, K., Jebna, A. K., & Theam, L. J. (2023). Sentiment Analysis of ChatGPT Healthcare Discourse: Insights from Twitter Data. *International Conference on Software, Knowledge Information, Industrial Management and Applications, SKIMA*. https://doi.org/DOI: 10.1109/SKIMA59232.2023.10387306

Kumar, V., Rasouliyan, L., Althoff, A., Chang, S., & Long, S. (2023). P22 Severity Score Extraction from Unstructured Clinical Notes Using a Disease-Agnostic Natural Language Processing Question-Answering Pipeline. *Value in Health*, *26*(6). Advance online publication. DOI: 10.1016/j.jval.2023.03.035

Kumar, V., Srivastava, P., Dwivedi, A., Budhiraja, I., Ghosh, D., Goyal, V., & Arora, R. (2024). Large-Language-Models (LLM)-Based AI Chatbots: Architecture, In-Depth Analysis and Their Performance Evaluation. *Communications in Computer and Information Science, 2027 CCIS*. https://doi.org/DOI: 10.1007/978-3-031-53085-2_20

Li, J., Dada, A., Puladi, B., Kleesiek, J., & Egger, J. (2024). ChatGPT in healthcare: A taxonomy and systematic review. In *Computer Methods and Programs in Biomedicine* (Vol. 245). https://doi.org/DOI: 10.1016/j.cmpb.2024.108013

Li, Y., Tao, W., Li, Z., Sun, Z., Li, F., Fenton, S., Xu, H., & Tao, C. (2024). Artificial intelligence-powered pharmacovigilance: A review of machine and deep learning in clinical text-based adverse drug event detection for benchmark datasets. In *Journal of Biomedical Informatics* (Vol. 152). https://doi.org/DOI: 10.1016/j.jbi.2024.104621

Liu, Y., Ju, S., & Wang, J. (2024). Exploring the potential of ChatGPT in medical dialogue summarization: A study on consistency with human preferences. *BMC Medical Informatics and Decision Making, 24*(1). Advance online publication. DOI: 10.1186/s12911-024-02481-8 PMID: 38486198

Nandini Prasad, K. S., Sudhanva, S., Tarun, T. N., Yuvraaj, Y., & Vishal, D. A. (2023). Conversational Chatbot Builder - Smarter Virtual Assistance with Domain Specific AI. *2023 4th International Conference for Emerging Technology, INCET 2023*. https://doi.org/DOI: 10.1109/INCET57972.2023.10170114

Nikam, D. S., Nisha Murthy, D., Pragada, S. D., & Mamatha, H. R. (2024). BGKnow-Medical Chatbot: A Hybrid Approach Based on Knowledge Graph and GPT-2. *Lecture Notes in Networks and Systems, 892*. Advance online publication. DOI: 10.1007/978-981-99-9521-9_30

Niu, H., Omitaomu, O. A., Langston, M. A., Olama, M., Ozmen, O., Klasky, H. B., Laurio, A., Ward, M., & Nebeker, J. (2024). EHR-BERT: A BERT-based model for effective anomaly detection in electronic health records. *Journal of Biomedical Informatics, 150*. Advance online publication. DOI: 10.1016/j.jbi.2024.104605 PMID: 38331082

Raiaan, M. A. K., Mukta, M. S. H., Fatema, K., Fahad, N. M., Sakib, S., Mim, M. M. J., Ahmad, J., Ali, M. E., & Azam, S. (2024). A Review on Large Language Models: Architectures, Applications, Taxonomies, Open Issues and Challenges. *IEEE Access: Practical Innovations, Open Solutions, 12*. Advance online publication. DOI: 10.1109/ACCESS.2024.3365742

Raza, S., Dolatabadi, E., Ondrusek, N., Rosella, L., & Schwartz, B. (2023). Discovering social determinants of health from case reports using natural language processing: Algorithmic development and validation. *BMC Digital Health, 1*(1). Advance online publication. DOI: 10.1186/s44247-023-00035-y

Ren, Y., Wu, D., Khurana, A., Mastorakos, G., Fu, S., Zong, N., Fan, J., Liu, H., & Huang, M. (2023). Classification of Patient Portal Messages with BERT-based Language Models. *Proceedings - 2023 IEEE 11th International Conference on Healthcare Informatics, ICHI 2023*. https://doi.org/DOI: 10.1109/ICHI57859.2023.00033

Romanowski, B., Ben Abacha, A., & Fan, Y. (2023). Extracting social determinants of health from clinical note text with classification and sequence-to-sequence approaches. *Journal of the American Medical Informatics Association: JAMIA, 30*(8). Advance online publication. DOI: 10.1093/jamia/ocad071 PMID: 37100768

Roy, P. K. (2024). Deep Ensemble Network for Sentiment Analysis in Bi-lingual Low-resource Languages. *ACM Transactions on Asian and Low-Resource Language Information Processing, 23*(1). Advance online publication. DOI: 10.1145/3600229

Shafik, W. (2023). Introduction to ChatGPT. In *Advanced Applications of Generative AI and Natural Language Processing Models*. https://doi.org/DOI: 10.4018/9798369305027.ch001

Shafik, W. (2024a). Artificial Intelligence-Enabled Internet of Medical Things (AIoMT) in Modern Healthcare Practices. In *Clinical Practice and Unmet Challenges in AI-Enhanced Healthcare Systems* (pp. 42–69). IGI Global. https://doi.org/DOI: 10.4018/979-8-3693-2703-6.ch003

Shafik, W. (2024b). Artificial Intelligence-Enabled Internet of Medical Things for Enhanced Healthcare Systems. In *Smart Healthcare Systems* (pp. 119–134). CRC Press., DOI: 10.1201/9781032698519-9

Shafik, W. (2024c). Connected healthcare—the impact of Internet of Things on medical services. In *Artificial Intelligence and Internet of Things based Augmented Trends for Data Driven Systems* (pp. 181–217). CRC Press., DOI: 10.1201/9781003497318-10

Shafik, W. (2024d). IoT-Enabled Secure and Intelligent Smart Healthcare. In *Secure and Intelligent IoT-Enabled Smart Cities* (pp. 308–333). IGI Global., DOI: 10.4018/979-8-3693-2373-1.ch015

Shafik, W. (2024e). Science of Emotional Intelligence. In *Enhancing and Predicting Digital Consumer Behavior with AI* (pp. 284–310). IGI Global.

Shafik, W. (2024f). Smart Health Revolution: Exploring Artificial Intelligence of Internet of Medical Things. In *Healthcare Industry Assessment: Analyzing Risks, Security, and Reliability* (pp. 201–229). Springer. https://doi.org/DOI: 10.1007/978-3-031-65434-3_9

Shafik, W. (2024g). The Future of Healthcare: AIoMT—Redefining Healthcare with Advanced Artificial Intelligence and Machine Learning Techniques. In *Artificial Intelligence and Machine Learning in Drug Design and Development* (pp. 605–634). Wiley., DOI: 10.1002/9781394234196.ch19

Shafik, W. (2025a). Human-Computer Interaction (HCI) Technologies in Socially-Enabled Artificial Intelligence. In *Future of Digital Technology and AI in Social Sectors* (pp. 121–150). IGI Global.

Shafik, W. (2025b). Revolutionizing Skin Cancer Diagnosis With Artificial Intelligence: Insights Into Machine Learning Techniques. In *Impact of Digital Solutions for Improved Healthcare Delivery* (pp. 167–194). IGI Global.

Shafik, W., Kalinaki, K., Fahim, K. E., & Adam, M. (2024). Safeguarding Data Privacy and Security in Federated Learning Systems. In *Federated Deep Learning for Healthcare* (pp. 170–190). CRC Press., DOI: 10.1201/9781032694870-13

Shafk, W. (2023). Wearable Medical Electronics in Artifcial Intelligence of Medical Things. In *Handbook of Security and Privacy of AI-Enabled Healthcare Systems and Internet of Medical Things*. https://doi.org/DOI: 10.1201/9781003370321-2

Sharma, H., & Padha, D. (2023). From Templates to Transformers: A survey of Multimodal Image Captioning Decoders. *2023 International Conference on Computer, Electronics and Electrical Engineering and Their Applications, IC2E3 2023*. https://doi.org/DOI: 10.1109/IC2E357697.2023.10262494

Siebra, C. A., Kurpicz-Briki, M., & Wac, K. (2024). Transformers in health: A systematic review on architectures for longitudinal data analysis. *Artificial Intelligence Review*, *57*(2). Advance online publication. DOI: 10.1007/s10462-023-10677-z

Sung, Y. W., Park, D. S., & Kim, C. G. (2023). A Study of BERT-Based Classification Performance of Text-Based Health Counseling Data. *CMES -. Computer Modeling in Engineering & Sciences*, *135*(1). Advance online publication. DOI: 10.32604/cmes.2022.022465

Turchin, A., Masharsky, S., & Zitnik, M. (2023). Comparison of BERT implementations for natural language processing of narrative medical documents. *Informatics in Medicine Unlocked*, *36*. Advance online publication. DOI: 10.1016/j.imu.2022.101139

Valova, I., Mladenova, T., & Kanev, G. (2024). Students' Perception of ChatGPT Usage in Education. *International Journal of Advanced Computer Science and Applications, 15*(1). Advance online publication. DOI: 10.14569/IJACSA.2024.0150143

Venerito, V., Bilgin, E., Iannone, F., & Kiraz, S. (2023). AI am a rheumatologist: A practical primer to large language models for rheumatologists. In *Rheumatology (United Kingdom)* (Vol. 62, Issue 10). https://doi.org/DOI: 10.1093/rheumatology/kead291

Verma, S., & Sanjeevi, S. G. (2023). Medical Image Classification using CMT and FTGD Layer. *Proceedings of the International Conference on Circuit Power and Computing Technologies, ICCPCT 2023.* https://doi.org/DOI: 10.1109/ICCPCT58313.2023.10245792

Wu, H. (2024). Dilated convolution for enhanced extractive summarization: A GAN-based approach with BERT word embedding. *Journal of Intelligent & Fuzzy Systems, 46*(2). Advance online publication. DOI: 10.3233/JIFS-234709

Yousri, R., & Safwat, S. (2023). How Big Can It Get? A comparative analysis of LLMs in architecture and scaling. *ICCA 2023 - 2023 5th International Conference on Computer and Applications, Proceedings.* https://doi.org/DOI: 10.1109/ICCA59364.2023.10401818

Zhang, B., Yao, X., Li, H., & Aini, M. (2023). Chinese Medical Named Entity Recognition based on Expert Knowledge and Fine-tuning Bert. *Proceedings - IEEE International Conference on Knowledge Graph, ICKG 2023.* https://doi.org/DOI: 10.1109/ICKG59574.2023.00016

Zhang, X., Wang, J., & Zhang, X. (2023). YNU-ISE-ZXW at ROCLING 2023 MultiNER-Health Task: A Transformer-based Model with LoRA for Chinese Healthcare Named Entity Recognition. *ROCLING 2023 - Proceedings of the 35th Conference on Computational Linguistics and Speech Processing.*

Chapter 9
Utilization of Transformers for Electronic Health Records (EHR) Processing

Deepanshu Pachauri
https://orcid.org/0009-0006-7010-7059
Sharda University, India

Saurabh Chandra
https://orcid.org/0000-0003-4172-9968
Bennett University, Greater Noida, India

Bhupinder Singh
https://orcid.org/0009-0006-4779-2553
Sharda University, India

ABSTRACT

The emergence of the Transformers has established itself as a promising Deep Learning model to advance the state of processing Electronic Health Records by facilitating the interpretation of contextual and natural language in an advanced manner. These include models like BERT and GPT that have shown great performance in the analysis of unstructured medical text, the extraction of relevant information and the prediction of patient outcome. Transformers, for example, integrated into EHR systems, enable seamless integration of diverse data types, improving predictive modeling accuracy for clinical decision support, risk stratification, and identifying patients for clinical trials. A chatbot/instruction or virtual assistant powered by transformers models can efficiently interact with patients, depart their concerns and

DOI: 10.4018/979-8-3373-2038-0.ch009

summarize treatment plans and medical histories to assist health care providers. Transformer models have vast potential to enhance operational efficiency, optimize diagnostic accuracy, and drive patient-centric care in a rapidly evolving digital healthcare ecosystem.

INTRODUCTION

The healthcare industry is undergoing a profound digital transformation, and at the heart of this revolution lies the Electronic Health Record (EHR). EHRs, digital versions of patients' paper charts, promise extensive benefits for personalized, safe, and reliable medical care. They contain comprehensive information about a patient's medical history, diagnoses, treatments, medications, immunization dates, allergies, radiology images, and laboratory test results. As Dr. Lloyd Minor of Stanford Medicine emphasizes, EHRs are "foundational to the digital revolution in healthcare, playing a critical role in achieving better health outcomes and more cost-effective care" (Sardar et al., 2024). This indicates EHRs are vital for digitizing records, improving the efficiency and effectiveness of healthcare delivery. The adoption of EHRs has been driven by several factors, including government initiatives, the need for improved patient care, and advancements in technology. The 2009 American Recovery and Reinvestment Act, particularly the HITECH Act, encouraged doctors to adopt Electronic Medical Records (EMRs) to enhance patient care and safety, leading to widespread adoption in hospitals and clinics. They also enable smart triaging, decreasing clinician burden and improving care delivery. Transformers power personalized patient engagement strategies by analyzing behavioral and historical health data to customize communication channels and health interventions. This leads to improved patient compliance with treatment plans, as well as better healthcare experiences overall. This enables the generation of predictive analytics to predict diseases at their early stages and to deliver proactive healthcare services. For example, data privacy, security, and model interpretability will be important challenges in deploying transformers for the processing of electronic health records (EHR) (Khurana, 2024). In 2016, the 21st Century Cures Act further propelled this trend by establishing an expected norm of sharing electronic health information. This act eliminated information blocking and required transparency to patients and caregivers, giving patients more control over their healthcare. EHRs offer numerous advantages over traditional paper-based records:

Improved Data Accuracy and Completeness: EHRs ensure the patient's health information is accurate, up-to-date, and complete at the point of care, boosting the precision of the data. Automated data entry and standardized formats enhance data quality and integrity (Rodrigues et al., 2021).

Enhanced Accessibility and Care Coordination: They provide quick and easy access to patient information, enabling better-informed decisions about patient care. EHRs facilitate seamless communication among healthcare professionals across various settings and ensure a more holistic and well-informed approach to patient treatment (Pramanik, Pal, & Mukhopadhyay, 2022

Reduced Medical Errors: EHRs help providers more effectively diagnose patients, reduce medical errors, and provide safer care. A study published in the journal *JAMA Internal Medicine* in 2023 found that EHRs can reduce medication errors by up to 80% (Zhou et al., 2017).

Improved Efficiency and Cost Reduction: EHRs automate many tasks, ensure doctors can exchange data remotely with updated accuracy, increase the practice's efficiency, and reduce costs through decreased paperwork and reduced duplication of testing (Bahri et al., 2018).

Better Patient Engagement: They improve patient and provider interaction and communication and make healthcare more convenient2. EHR systems make information more accessible to patients, allowing them and their caregivers to be directly involved in the decision-making about their care (Kashyap et al., 2015).

Support for Clinical Decision Making: EHRs offer a more successful medical approach because they help recognize patterns, predict diagnoses, and offer possible treatments. Despite these benefits, realizing the full potential of EHRs requires advanced processing techniques that can unlock valuable insights from the vast amounts of data they contain (Elbadawi et al., 2021).

Limitations of Traditional EHR Analysis Methods

While EHRs provide a wealth of patient information, traditional methods of analyzing this data have several limitations:

Structured Data Focus: Traditional methods often focus on structured data, such as diagnoses, medications, and lab results, neglecting the rich information contained in unstructured clinical notes ((Cabello et al., 2020).

Limited Contextual Understanding: Traditional methods may struggle to capture the complex relationships between medical concepts and the temporal dependencies within a patient's medical history (Chen et al., 2014).

Inability to Handle Long Sequences: EHRs often contain long sequences of events and observations, which can be challenging for traditional methods to process effectively.

Feature Engineering Bottleneck: Traditional machine learning models often require manual feature engineering, which is time-consuming, domain-specific, and may not capture the most relevant information.

To overcome these limitations, there is a growing need for advanced processing techniques that can effectively handle the complexity and volume of EHR data, capture contextual information, and automate feature extraction (Stephens et al., 2015).

INTRODUCTION TO TRANSFORMERS: A REVOLUTION IN SEQUENCE MODELING

Transformers have emerged as a revolutionary architecture in the field of natural language processing (NLP) and sequence modeling. Introduced in the seminal paper "Attention is All You Need", transformers have achieved state-of-the-art results on a wide range of tasks, including machine translation, text summarization, and question answering (Tiwari et al., 2022). The key innovation of transformers is the attention mechanism, which allows the model to focus on the most relevant parts of the input sequence when making predictions. Unlike recurrent neural networks (RNNs), which process sequences sequentially, transformers can process the entire input sequence in parallel, enabling them to capture long-range dependencies more effectively .Transformers have several advantages over traditional sequence modeling techniques (Singh, 2023b)

Parallel Processing: Transformers can process the entire input sequence in parallel, making them much faster than RNNs.

Long-Range Dependencies: The attention mechanism allows transformers to capture long-range dependencies more effectively than RNNs.

Contextual Understanding: Transformers can capture contextual information by considering the relationships between all words in the input sequence.

Transfer Learning: Pre-trained transformer models can be fine-tuned on specific tasks, reducing the need for large amounts of labeled data.

The success of transformers in NLP has led to their adoption in other domains, including healthcare, where they have shown great promise for EHR processing (Devika & Karegowda, 2021).

SCOPE OF THE CHAPTER: FOCUSING ON TRANSFORMER-BASED MODELS FOR EHR Data

This chapter focuses on the utilization of transformer-based models for EHR processing. It provides a detailed overview of the key transformer architectures and their applications in healthcare (Sukeshini et al., 2021). The chapter explores how transformers can be used to overcome the limitations of traditional EHR analysis methods and unlock valuable insights from patient data. The topics covered include:

- An in-depth explanation of the transformer architecture and its advantages for EHR data.
- A review of key transformer-based models for EHR processing, including BERT, encoder-decoder transformers, and hierarchical transformers.
- An exploration of various applications of transformers in EHR analysis, such as disease prediction, risk stratification, clinical decision support, phenotyping, and temporal modeling.
- A discussion of the challenges and limitations of using transformers for EHR processing.
- An overview of future directions and research opportunities in this field.

By the end of this chapter, readers will have a comprehensive understanding of how transformers can be used to revolutionize EHR processing and improve patient care

UNDERSTANDING TRANSFORMERS AND THEIR ADVANTAGES FOR EHR DATA

Transformers have emerged as a groundbreaking architecture in the field of deep learning, particularly for sequence-to-sequence tasks. Unlike previous models that relied on recurrence or convolutions, transformers utilize self-attention mechanisms to process input data in parallel, allowing them to handle long-range dependencies with ease (Jordan & Mitchell, 2015). The core of the transformer architecture lies in its encoder-decoder structure, attention mechanisms, and positional encoding. These features make transformers particularly well-suited for analyzing Electronic Health Record (EHR) data, which often contains long sequences of events, complex relationships between medical concepts, and a mix of structured and unstructured information (Singh, 2024b).

A Brief Overview of the Transformer Architecture

The transformer architecture, as described in the original paper, was designed for machine translation and leverages the typical encoder-decoder approach. The encoder processes a sentence in the input language, and the decoder uses representations from the encoder to generate a sentence in the target language (Singh & Kaunert, 2024b). A transformer model comprises tokenizers, embedding layers, transformer layers, and un-embedding layers. At its core, it consists of two main components: the encoder and the decoder. The encoder reads and processes the input text, while the decoder generates the output sequence. Both the encoder and the decoder are stacks of multiple layers; the original architecture consisted of 6 encoders and 6 decoders (Reddy, 2023).

The primary function of the encoder is to transform the input tokens into contextualized representations.

- **Tokenization:** As the Transformer architecture natively processes numerical data, not text, there must be a translation between text and tokens. A tokenizer converts text into tokens, where a token is an integer that represents a character or a short segment of characters.
- **Embedding Layer:** The embedding layer converts tokens and positions of the tokens into vector representations.
- **Transformer Layers:** These layers carry out repeated transformations on the vector representations, extracting more and more linguistic information. They consist of alternating attention and feedforward layers.
- **Un-embedding Layer:** The un-embedding layer converts the final vector representations back to a probability distribution over the tokens.

Each encoder layer contains two sublayers: self-attention and a feedforward network, whereas each decoder layer contains three sublayers: causally masked self-attention, cross-attention, and a feedforward network (Keikhosrokiani, 2022). The final points of detail are the residual connections and layer normalization (LayerNorm, or LN), which while conceptually unnecessary, are necessary for numerical stability and convergence.

Attention Mechanisms: Self-Attention and Cross-Attention

The attention mechanism is a key innovation that allows transformers to weigh the importance of different parts of the input sequence when making predictions. It enables the model to focus on the most relevant pieces of information, regardless of their position in the sequence (Kashyap et al., 2016). The attention mechanism used in the Transformer architecture are scaled dot-product attention units. The transformer model learns three weight matrices for each unit: the query weights WQWQ, the key weights WKWK, and the value weights WVWV.

- **Self-Attention:** Self-attention allows the model to attend to different parts of the input sequence to capture relationships between words or tokens within the same sequence. Each encoder layer contains a self-attention sublayer that "mixes" information among the input tokens to the decoder (i.e., the tokens generated so far during inference time).

- **Cross-Attention:** Cross-attention allows the decoder to attend to the output of the encoder, enabling it to incorporate information from the input sequence when generating the output sequence. Each decoder layer contains a cross-attention sublayer for incorporating the output of the encoder (contextualized input token representations).

Encoder-Decoder Structure

The encoder-decoder structure is a fundamental aspect of the transformer architecture.

- **Encoder:** The encoder processes the input sequence and generates a contextualized representation of the input.
- **Decoder:** The decoder uses the output of the encoder to generate the output sequence, attending to the relevant parts of the input sequence through cross-attention.

Both the encoder and decoder layers have a feed-forward neural network for additional processing of their outputs and contain residual connections and layer normalization steps. These feed-forward layers contain most of the parameters in a Transformer model.

Positional Encoding and Time Embedding

Since transformers process the entire input sequence in parallel, they do not inherently capture the order of the tokens. Positional encoding is a technique used to provide the model with information about the position of each token in the sequence. Time embedding extends this concept to encode temporal information in sequential data (Manyika et al., 2011).

Positional Encoding: This technique adds a vector to each input embedding, providing information about the position of the token in the sequence (Hilbert, 2016).

Time Embedding: In the context of EHR data, time embedding can be used to encode the time elapsed between events or the duration of a condition.

By incorporating positional encoding and time embedding, transformers can effectively model the temporal dynamics of EHR data (Jain, 2023).

Why Transformers are Well-Suited for EHR Data

Transformers offer several advantages for EHR data analysis:

Handling Long Sequences and Temporal Dependencies: EHRs often contain long sequences of events and observations that span years or even decades. Transformers can handle these long sequences more effectively than traditional methods, thanks to their parallel processing and attention mechanisms (Ariffin et al., 2021).

Capturing Complex Interrelationships between Medical Concepts: Medical concepts are often interconnected, and understanding these relationships is crucial for accurate diagnosis and treatment. Transformers can capture these complex interrelationships by attending to different parts of the input sequence and learning contextualized representations (Bao et al., 2019).

Leveraging Unstructured and Structured Data: EHRs contain both structured data (e.g., diagnoses, medications, lab results) and unstructured data (e.g., clinical notes, discharge summaries). Transformers can leverage both types of data, allowing for a more comprehensive analysis of patient information (Zhou et al., 2021).

Transfer Learning Capabilities: Pre-trained transformer models can be fine-tuned on specific EHR-related tasks, reducing the need for large amounts of labeled data and accelerating the development of new applications (Padmaja et al., 2022). The transformer architecture, with its attention mechanisms, encoder-decoder structure, and positional encoding, provides a powerful framework for analyzing complex and heterogeneous EHR data. By effectively capturing long-range dependencies, interrelationships between medical concepts, and unstructured information, transformers have the potential to unlock valuable insights and improve patient care.

Key Transformer-Based Models for EHR Processing

The inherent complexity and multifaceted nature of Electronic Health Records (EHRs) demand sophisticated analytical techniques to derive meaningful insights. Traditional methods often fall short due to their inability to capture long-range dependencies, handle unstructured data, and process temporal information effectively. Transformer-based models have emerged as a powerful alternative, offering the ability to overcome these limitations and unlock the full potential of EHR data. This section explores key transformer-based models tailored for EHR processing, highlighting their architectures, adaptations, and applications (Shah et al., 2017).

BERT (Bidirectional Encoder Representations from Transformers) and its Variants

BERT (Bidirectional Encoder Representations from Transformers) is a transformer-based model developed by Google that has achieved remarkable success in various natural language processing (NLP) tasks. BERT's key innovation is its ability to learn bidirectional contextual representations of words in a sentence, enabling it to capture the full context of each word from both directions simultaneously. Given the similarities between natural language and EHR data, researchers have adapted BERT for various healthcare applications.

- **HERBERT: Adapting BERT for EHR Data:** As the success of BERT grew, researchers began adapting BERT for use with EHR data. HERBERT is an adaptation of BERT tailored for EHR data. EHR-BERT is a project aimed at leveraging BERT (Bidirectional Encoder Representations from Transformers) for Electronic Health Records (EHR) data.
- **Med-BERT:** Inspired by BERT, Med-BERT adapts the BERT framework originally developed for the text domain to the structured EHR domain. The usefulness of the pre-trained Med-BERT was evaluated by fine-tuning on two disease prediction tasks: the prediction of heart failure among patients with diabetes (DHF) and the prediction of onset of pancreatic cancer (PaCa), using three patient cohorts from two different EHR databases. The design and inclusion of Masked LM and Prolonged LOS reinforced the modeling of contextual information and helped collect sequential dependencies.BERT and its variants can be applied to EHR data for various tasks:
- **Disease Prediction:** BERT can be fine-tuned to predict the likelihood of a patient developing a specific disease based on their medical history.
- **Risk Stratification:** BERT can be used to identify patients at high risk of adverse events, such as hospital readmission or mortality.
- **Clinical Decision Support:** BERT can provide clinicians with real-time recommendations for diagnosis and treatment based on the patient's EHR data.

Encoder-Decoder Transformers

While BERT is an encoder-only model, encoder-decoder transformers offer additional flexibility for sequence-to-sequence tasks. These models consist of two main components: an encoder that processes the input sequence and a decoder that generates the output sequence based on the encoder's representation (Singh & Kaunert, 2024c).

Transform EHR: A Denoising Sequence-to-Sequence Model: TransformEHR is a denoising sequence-to-sequence model that utilizes an encoder-decoder transformer architecture. The model is pre-trained on a large dataset of EHR data using a denoising objective, which involves masking portions of the input sequence and training the model to reconstruct the original sequence. Visit masking and time embedding are crucial components of TransformEHR, enabling the model to handle the temporal dynamics of EHR data. Visit masking forces the model to learn dependencies among visits, while time embedding encodes the time elapsed between visits.

TransformEHR can be applied to various tasks:

- **Pancreatic Cancer Prediction:** TransformEHR has been used to predict the onset of pancreatic cancer based on a patient's medical history.
- **Intentional Self-Harm Prediction:** TransformEHR has also been applied to predict the risk of intentional self-harm in patients with mental health conditions.
- **BARToM: A Transformer-based Approach for Multimodal EHR transformation:** BARToM can learn high-quality EHR representations from multimodal data to improve downstream tasks.

Hierarchical Transformers

EHRs often contain long sequences of events and observations, which can be challenging for transformer-based models to process effectively. Hierarchical transformers address this issue by breaking down the input sequence into smaller segments and processing them in a hierarchical manner.

- **Hi-BEHRT: Handling Long Sequences in EHR Data:** Hi-BEHRT addresses the limitations of existing models in processing comprehensive EHRs by employing a hierarchical architecture. Hi-BEHRT first encodes each visit using a transformer encoder and then aggregates the visit representations using another transformer encoder to capture long-range dependencies across the entire medical history.

Generative Pretrained Transformers

Generative Pretrained Transformers (GPTs) are a type of transformer model that are pre-trained on a large corpus of text data using a generative objective, such as language modeling. GPTs can be fine-tuned for various downstream tasks, including EHR processing.

Foresight: Integrating Free Text and Structured Data: Foresight is a GPT-based model that integrates free text and structured data from EHRs for probabilistic forecasting of future medical events. The model uses named entity recognition and linking to extract medical concepts from clinical notes and combines them with structured data to predict the likelihood of future diagnoses, procedures, and medications (Marjani et al., 2017).

Transformer-based models offer a powerful set of tools for EHR processing. By leveraging their ability to capture long-range dependencies, handle unstructured data, and model temporal information, these models can unlock valuable insights from EHR data and improve patient care. As research in this area continues to evolve, we can expect to see even more sophisticated transformer-based models emerge, further pushing the boundaries of what is possible in healthcare analytics (Singh, 2024c).

Applications of Transformers in EHR Analysis

Transformer-based models are revolutionizing the analysis of Electronic Health Records (EHRs), demonstrating exceptional capabilities in various healthcare applications. Their ability to capture long-range dependencies, handle unstructured data, and model temporal information makes them particularly well-suited for tasks such as disease prediction, risk stratification, clinical decision support, phenotyping, and temporal modeling. This section will delve into these key applications, highlighting the strengths and limitations of transformer-based approaches in each domain (Chen & Zhang, 2014).

1. Disease Prediction and Risk Stratification

One of the most promising applications of transformers in EHR analysis is disease prediction and risk stratification. By analyzing a patient's medical history, including diagnoses, medications, procedures, and clinical notes, transformer-based models can accurately predict the likelihood of developing specific diseases or experiencing adverse events. This capability can enable proactive interventions, personalized treatment plans, and improved patient outcomes (Thapa & Camtepe, 2021).

2. **Predicting Onset of Diseases like Pancreatic Cancer**

Pancreatic cancer is particularly challenging disease to detect early, as it often presents with non-specific symptoms. TransformEHR, a generative encoder-decoder model, has demonstrated state-of-the-art performance in predicting the onset of pancreatic cancer using longitudinal EHR data. By pretraining on a large dataset of EHRs and fine-tuning on a smaller dataset of patients with pancreatic cancer, Transform EHR can identify subtle patterns and risk factors that may be missed by traditional methods. The model's ability to predict all diseases and outcomes of a future visit using longitudinal information helps it uncover complex interrelations among different diseases (Behura et al, 2021).

3. **Identifying Patients at Risk of Intentional Self-Harm:**

Intentional self-harm is a significant public health concern, particularly among individuals with mental health conditions. TransformEHR has also shown promising results in predicting the risk of intentional self-harm in patients with post-traumatic stress disorder (PTSD). The model achieved a positive predictive value (PPV) of 8.8% for prediction of intentional self-harm among the top 10% PTSD patients at high predicted risk, outperforming BERT, LSTM, and logistic regression models by 24%, 97%, and 422%, respectively. This highlights the potential of transformers to identify individuals who may benefit from early intervention and support (Olshannikova et al., 2015).

4. **Multi-label classification**

A Transformer-based Model for EHR can also be used to predict a patient's future diagnoses (if any), as a multi-label classification problem (i.e., simultaneously predicting a probability for each and every disease); this will result in a single predictive model that scales across a range of diseases (as opposed to needing to train one predictive model per disease).

The success of transformer-based models in disease prediction and risk stratification can be attributed to their ability to capture complex relationships between medical concepts, handle long-term dependencies in patient histories, and leverage both structured and unstructured data. This allows them to identify subtle patterns and risk factors that may not be apparent to clinicians or traditional statistical methods (Rudin, 2019). The RatchetEHR model is adept at creating contextualized embeddings that correlate with other time-frames, this is critical as most features at a certain time are dependent on their previous values. To mitigate the risk of overfitting in tasks with limited EHR data, a learned time-frame embedding for each input was incorporated, which aids in reducing the parameter count for downstream task redictions by encapsulating essential information within a trainable parameter.

Transformers excel in handling sequential data and are adept at capturing long-term dependencies and intricate relationships within sequences, which is crucial for interpreting EHR data where past medical events can significantly influence future health outcomes. The transformer's self-attention mechanism allows it to weigh the importance of different parts of the sequence differently (Wu et al., 2013).

CHALLENGES AND LIMITATIONS

While transformer-based models have shown great promise in various EHR analysis tasks, it is crucial to acknowledge their inherent challenges and limitations. These challenges span various aspects, including computational complexity, data requirements, interpretability, ethical considerations, and generalization capabilities. Addressing these limitations is essential for the responsible and effective deployment of transformer-based models in healthcare settings (Saadat & Shuaib, 2020).

Computational Complexity and Resource Requirements: The self-attention mechanism, a core component of transformers, has time complexity of O(L2D) *O*(*L*2*D*), where L*L* is the input sequence length, and D*D* is the model dimension. For long input sequences, this attention computation becomes computationally expensive, demanding substantial computational resources and specialized hardware, such as GPUs or TPUs, for training and inference. This poses a significant challenge for resource-constrained healthcare institutions or applications requiring real-time predictions. Transformer models, due to their large parameter count, have a tendency to overfit, especially when dealing with limited sample sizes typical of EHR prediction tasks (Kitchin, 2013).

Data Scarcity and Generalizability: Transformer-based models typically require vast amounts of training data to achieve optimal performance. However, EHR data can be scarce, particularly for rare diseases or specific patient populations. This data scarcity can lead to overfitting, where the model performs well on the training data but fails to generalize to new, unseen data. Furthermore, the heterogeneity of EHR data across different institutions and healthcare systems can limit the transferability of models trained on one dataset to another (Shahid, 2021).

Interpretability and Explainability: Despite their impressive predictive capabilities, transformer-based models are often considered "black boxes," making it difficult to understand the reasoning behind their predictions. This lack of interpretability can be a major concern in healthcare, where clinicians need to understand the factors driving a model's decision-making process to ensure patient safety and trust. Techniques for improving the interpretability of transformer models, such as attention visualization and feature importance analysis, are still under development (Monteiro et al., 2021).

Ethical Considerations and Bias Mitigation: EHR data often contains sensitive patient information, raising ethical concerns about privacy, security, and data governance. It is crucial to ensure that transformer-based models are used in a responsible and ethical manner, adhering to privacy regulations and protecting patient confidentiality. Additionally, EHR data can be biased, reflecting systemic inequalities in healthcare access and treatment. Transformer models trained on biased data may perpetuate or amplify these biases, leading to unfair or discriminatory outcomes. Careful attention must be paid to bias detection and mitigation techniques to ensure fairness and equity in the application of transformer models in healthcare (Qureshi et al., 2023).

Limited Scope: The GCT model has certain limitations. Its analysis is confined to single-time intervalsspecifically, individual hospital visits—potentially overlooking the continuum of patient care. The model may not fully capture the dynamic nature of a patient's condition, where variables like respiratory rate can fluctuate significantly over short periods.

To fully utilize the capabilities of transformer models, it is crucial to consider their limitations. By improving on the items discussed above, it is more likely that transformer models will continue to revolutionize how patients are cared for and treated.

FUTURE DIRECTIONS AND RESEARCH OPPORTUNITIES

The application of transformer-based models to EHR analysis is a rapidly evolving field with numerous avenues for future research and development. As these models continue to mature and as healthcare data becomes increasingly available, there is immense potential to unlock new insights, improve clinical decision-making, and transform healthcare delivery. This section explores some of the key future directions and research opportunities in this exciting area (Leung et al., 2021).

Exploring Novel Transformer Architectures and Pretraining Strategies: While BERT and its variants have been widely adopted for EHR analysis, there is room for exploring novel transformer architectures and pretraining strategies tailored specifically for healthcare data. For example, hierarchical transformers, such as Hi-BEHRT, can effectively handle long sequences of EHR data by processing information at multiple levels of granularity. Generative pretraining techniques, such as those used in Foresight, can enable models to learn rich representations of EHR data and generate probabilistic forecasts of future medical events. The use of architectural changes such as feed-forward layers, instead of using traditional state-of-the-art RNN and CNN, may yield better results. Future research can focus on developing novel transformer architectures that are more efficient, interpretable, and adaptable to the specific characteristics of EHR data. In addition, investigations should also be geared towards employing advanced pre-training methods to facilitate the development of potent, generalizable models even with limited data (Faaique, 2024).

Integrating Multi-Modal Data Sources: EHRs typically contain a wealth of structured and unstructured data, including diagnoses, medications, lab results, clinical notes, imaging reports, and genomic information. Integrating these multimodal data sources can provide a more comprehensive view of the patient's health status and improve the accuracy of transformer-based models.

Developing Explainable AI (XAI) Techniques for EHR Analysis: As transformer-based models become more complex and powerful, it is crucial to develop XAI techniques that can provide insights into their decision-making processes. Techniques such as attention visualization, feature importance analysis, and counterfactual reasoning can help clinicians understand why a particular model made a specific prediction, fostering trust and enabling them to make more informed decisions. Researching how to better the way AI is explained to clinicians and patients may help these models gain acceptance in various fields.

Addressing Ethical Considerations and Ensuring Fairness: As transformer-based models are increasingly used in healthcare, it is essential to address ethical considerations and ensure fairness in their application. This includes mitigating biases in EHR data, protecting patient privacy, and ensuring transparency and accountability in model development and deployment. Future research should focus on developing methods for detecting and mitigating biases in EHR data, as well as establishing ethical guidelines and regulatory frameworks for the use of transformer-based models in healthcare Pradhan et al., 2024).

Adapting to Different Healthcare Systems and Populations: Much of the research on transformer-based models for EHR analysis has been conducted in specific healthcare systems or populations. To ensure the generalizability and scalability of these models, it is crucial to adapt them to different healthcare settings and diverse patient populations. This may involve developing transfer learning techniques, fine-tuning models on local data, and addressing issues related to data harmonization and standardization.

Temporal Dynamics Modelling: One of the main areas to look at would be better use of unstructured data as this is where the majority of human notes and observations are. Implementing methods that account for the long-term and short-term temporal dynamics could result in greater accuracy (Singh & Kaunert, 2024d).

The future of transformer-based models in EHR analysis is bright, with vast opportunities for research and innovation. By addressing the challenges and limitations associated with these models and focusing on the key areas outlined above, researchers and clinicians can unlock the full potential of transformer-based models to transform healthcare delivery and improve patient outcomes. With continued efforts in this direction, the healthcare industry is poised to witness a paradigm shift, driven by the power of AI and the wealth of information contained within EHRs (Singh et al., 2024).

CONCLUSION

Transformer-based models have emerged as a transformative force in the analysis of Electronic Health Records (EHRs), offering a powerful set of tools for unlocking valuable insights and improving patient care. Leveraging their ability to capture long-range dependencies, handle unstructured data, and model temporal information, these models have demonstrated remarkable success in various applications, including disease prediction, risk stratification, and clinical decision support.Models like TransformEHR have achieved state-of-the-art performance in predicting the onset of challenging diseases like pancreatic cancer and identifying patients at risk of intentional self-harm, outperforming traditional methods and demonstrating the potential for proactive interventions. The success of these models can be attributed to their innovative architectures, such as the encoder-decoder framework and the incorporation of visit masking and time embedding, which enable them to effectively capture the complexities of EHR data.The transformer's self-attention mechanism allows it to weigh the importance of different parts of the sequence differently. Furthermore, learned time-frame embeddings and methods accounting for long-term and short-term temporal dynamics may result in greater accuracy. By integrating multi-modal data sources, developing XAI techniques, and addressing ethical considerations, researchers can pave the way for the responsible and effective deployment of transformer-based models in healthcare settings.While challenges remain in terms of computational complexity, data scarcity, and interpretability, ongoing research efforts are actively addressing these limitations and pushing the boundaries of what is possible. As transformer-based models continue to evolve and as healthcare data becomes increasingly available, the future of EHR analysis is bright, with immense potential to improve clinical decision-making, personalize treatment plans, and ultimately transform healthcare delivery. The journey towards realizing this potential requires continued collaboration among researchers, clinicians, and policymakers to ensure that these powerful tools are used responsibly and ethically to benefit patients and society as a whole.

REFERENCES

Ariffin, N. A., Yunus, A. M., & Kadir, I. K. (2021). The role of big data in the healthcare industry. *Journal of Islamic*, *6*(36), 235–245.

Bahri, S., Zoghlami, N., Abed, M., & Tavares, J. M. R. (2018). Big data for healthcare: A survey. *IEEE Access: Practical Innovations, Open Solutions*, *7*, 7397–7408.

Bao, Y., Tang, Z., Li, H., & Zhang, Y. (2019). Computer vision and deep learning–based data anomaly detection method for structural health monitoring. *Structural Health Monitoring*, *18*(2), 401–421.

. Behura, A., Sahu, S., & Kabat, M. R. (2021). Advancement of Machine Learning and Cloud Computing in the Field of Smart Health Care. *Machine Learning Approach for Cloud Data Analytics in IoT*, 273-306.

Cabello, J. C., Karimipour, H., Jahromi, A. N., Dehghantanha, A., & Parizi, R. M. (2020). Big-data and cyber-physical systems in healthcare: Challenges and opportunities. *Handbook of Big Data Privacy*, 255-283.

. Chen, C. P., & Zhang, C. Y. (2014). Data-intensive applications, challenges, techniques and technologies: A survey on Big Data. *Information sciences, 275*, 314-347. Mayer-Schönberger, V., & Cukier, K. (2013). *Big data: A revolution that will transform how we live, work, and think*. Houghton Mifflin Harcourt.

Chen, M., Mao, S., Zhang, Y., & Leung, V. C. (2014). *Big data: related technologies, challenges and future prospects* (Vol. 100). Springer.

Devika, G., & Karegowda, A. G. (2021). Deep Learning in IoT: Introduction, Applications, and Perspective in the Big Data Era. In *Deep Learning Applications and Intelligent Decision Making in Engineering* (pp. 1-54). IGI Global.

Elbadawi, M., Gaisford, S., & Basit, A. W. (2021). Advanced machine-learning techniques in drug discovery. *Drug Discovery Today*, *26*(3), 769–777. PMID: 33290820

Faaique, M. (2024). Overview of Big Data Analytics in Modern Astronomy. *International Journal of Mathematics, Statistics, and Computer Science*, *2*, 96–113.

Hilbert, M. (2016). Big data for development: A review of promises and challenges. *Development Policy Review*, *34*(1), 135–174.

. Jain, L. (2023). Artificial Intelligence and Machine Learning for Healthcare.

Jordan, M. I., & Mitchell, T. M. (2015). Machine learning: Trends, perspectives, and prospects. *Science*, *349*(6245), 255–260. PMID: 26185243

Kashyap, H., Ahmed, H. A., Hoque, N., Roy, S., & Bhattacharyya, D. K. (2015). Big data analytics in bioinformatics: A machine learning perspective. *arXiv preprint arXiv:1506.05101*.

Kashyap, H., Ahmed, H. A., Hoque, N., Roy, S., & Bhattacharyya, D. K. (2016). Big data analytics in bioinformatics: Architectures, techniques, tools and issues. *Network Modeling and Analysis in Health Informatics and Bioinformatics*, *5*, 1–28.

Keikhosrokiani, P. (Ed.). (2022). *Big data analytics for healthcare: datasets, techniques, life cycles, management, and applications*. Academic Press.

Khurana, V. (2024). Accelerating Pace of Scientific Discovery and Innovation through Big Data Enabled Artificial Intelligence and Deep Learning. *Emerging Trends in Machine Intelligence and Big Data*, *16*(1), 38–53.

Kitchin, R. (2013). Big data and human geography: Opportunities, challenges and risks. *Dialogues in Human Geography*, *3*(3), 262–267.

Leung, P. H., Chui, K. T., Lo, K., & de Pablos, P. O. (2021). A support vector machine–based voice disorders detection using human voice signal. In *Artificial Intelligence and Big Data Analytics for Smart Healthcare* (pp. 197–208). Academic Press.

. Manyika, J., Chui, M., Brown, B., Bughin, J., Dobbs, R., Roxburgh, C., & Hung Byers, A. (2011). Big data: The next frontier for innovation, competition, and productivity.

. Marjani, M., Nasaruddin, F., Gani, A., Karim, A., Hashem, I. A. T., Siddiqa, A., & Yaqoob, I. (2017). Big IoT data analytics: architecture, opportunities, and open research challenges. *ieee access, 5*, 5247-5261.

. Monteiro, A. C. B., França, R. P., Arthur, R., & Iano, Y. (2021). An overview of medical Internet of Things, artificial intelligence, and cloud computing employed in health care from a modern panorama. *The Fusion of Internet of Things, Artificial Intelligence, and Cloud Computing in Health Care*, 3-23.

Olshannikova, E., Ometov, A., Koucheryavy, Y., & Olsson, T. (2015). Visualizing Big Data with augmented and virtual reality: Challenges and research agenda. *Journal of Big Data*, *2*(1), 1–27.

Padmaja, M., Shitharth, S., Prasuna, K., Chaturvedi, A., Kshirsagar, P. R., & Vani, A. (2022). Grow of artificial intelligence to challenge security in IoT application. *Wireless Personal Communications*, *127*(3), 1829–1845.

Pradhan, T., Nimkar, P., & Jhajharia, K. (2024). Machine Learning and Deep Learning for Big Data Analysis. In *Big Data Analytics Techniques for Market Intelligence* (pp. 209–240). IGI Global.

. Pramanik, P. K. D., Pal, S., & Mukhopadhyay, M. (2022). Healthcare big data: A comprehensive overview. *Research anthology on big data analytics, architectures, and applications*, 119-147.

Qureshi, R., Irfan, M., Ali, H., Khan, A., Nittala, A. S., Ali, S., & Alam, T. (2023). Artificial Intelligence and Biosensors in Healthcare and its Clinical Relevance: A Review. *IEEE Access: Practical Innovations, Open Solutions*.

. Reddy, B. M. (2023). Amalgamation of Internet of Things and Machine Learning for Smart Healthcare Applications–A Review. *Int. J Comp. Eng. Sci. Res, 5*, 08-36.

Rodrigues, J. F., Florea, L., de Oliveira, M. C., Diamond, D., & Oliveira, O. N. (2021). Big data and machine learning for materials science. *Discover Materials*, *1*, 1–27. PMID: 33899049

Rudin, C. (2019). Stop explaining black box machine learning models for high stakes decisions and use interpretable models instead. *Nature Machine Intelligence*, *1*(5), 206–215. PMID: 35603010

. Saadat, M. N., & Shuaib, M. (2020). Advancements in deep learning theory and applications: Perspective in 2020 and beyond. *Advances and Applications in Deep Learning, 3*.

. Sardar, T. H., Khatun, A., Sengupta, S., Alam, Y., & Ara, T. (2024). Machine Learning in the Healthcare Sector and the Biomedical Big Data: Techniques, Applications, and Challenges. *Big Data Computing*, 336-352.

Shah, F., Li, J., Shah, Y., & Shah, F. (2017, November). Broad big data domain via medical big data. In *2017 4th International Conference on Systems and Informatics (ICSAI)* (pp. 732-737). IEEE.

. Shahid, Z. (2021). Distributed Machine Learning for Anomalous Human Activity Recognition using IoT Systems.

Singh, B. (2023). Blockchain Technology in Renovating Healthcare: Legal and Future Perspectives. In *Revolutionizing Healthcare Through Artificial Intelligence and Internet of Things Applications* (pp. 177-186). IGI Global.

Singh, B. (2023). Unleashing Alternative Dispute Resolution (ADR) in Resolving Complex Legal-Technical Issues Arising in Cyberspace Lensing E-Commerce and Intellectual Property: Proliferation of E-Commerce Digital Economy. *Revista Brasileira de Alternative Dispute Resolution-Brazilian Journal of Alternative Dispute Resolution-RBADR*, *5*(10), 81–105.

Singh, B. (2024). Lensing Legal Dynamics for Examining Responsibility and Deliberation of Generative AI-Tethered Technological Privacy Concerns: Infringements and Use of Personal Data by Nefarious Actors. In Ara, A., & Ara, A. (Eds.), *Exploring the Ethical Implications of Generative AI* (pp. 146–167). IGI Global., DOI: 10.4018/979-8-3693-1565-1.ch009

Singh, B. (2024). Social Cognition of Incarcerated Women and Children: Addressing Exposure to Infectious Diseases and Legal Outcomes. In Reddy, K. (Ed.), *Principles and Clinical Interventions in Social Cognition* (pp. 236–251). IGI Global., DOI: 10.4018/979-8-3693-1265-0.ch014

Singh, B. (2024). Evolutionary Global Neuroscience for Cognition and Brain Health: Strengthening Innovation in Brain Science. In *Biomedical Research Developments for Improved Healthcare* (pp. 246-272). IGI Global.

Singh, B., & Kaunert, C. (2024). Salvaging Responsible Consumption and Production of Food in the Hospitality Industry: Harnessing Machine Learning and Deep Learning for Zero Food Waste. In Singh, A., Tyagi, P., & Garg, A. (Eds.), *Sustainable Disposal Methods of Food Wastes in Hospitality Operations* (pp. 176–192). IGI Global., DOI: 10.4018/979-8-3693-2181-2.ch012

Singh, B., & Kaunert, C. (2024). Harnessing Sustainable Agriculture Through Climate-Smart Technologies: Artificial Intelligence for Climate Preservation and Futuristic Trends. In *Exploring Ethical Dimensions of Environmental Sustainability and Use of AI* (pp. 214-239). IGI Global.

Singh, B., & Kaunert, C. (2024). Salvaging Responsible Consumption and Production of Food in the Hospitality Industry: Harnessing Machine Learning and Deep Learning for Zero Food Waste. In *Sustainable Disposal Methods of Food Wastes in Hospitality Operations* (pp. 176-192). IGI Global.

. Singh, B., & Kaunert, C. (2024). Future of Digital Marketing: Hyper-Personalized Customer Dynamic Experience with AI-Based Predictive Models. *Revolutionizing the AI-Digital Landscape: A Guide to Sustainable Emerging Technologies for Marketing Professionals*, 189.

Singh, B., Kaunert, C., & Vig, K. (2024). Reinventing Influence of Artificial Intelligence (AI) on Digital Consumer Lensing Transforming Consumer Recommendation Model: Exploring Stimulus Artificial Intelligence on Consumer Shopping Decisions. In Musiolik, T., Rodriguez, R., & Kannan, H. (Eds.), *AI Impacts in Digital Consumer Behavior* (pp. 141–169). IGI Global., DOI: 10.4018/979-8-3693-1918-5.ch006

Singh, B., Vig, K., & Kaunert, C. (2024). Modernizing Healthcare: Application of Augmented Reality and Virtual Reality in Clinical Practice and Medical Education. In Modern Technology in Healthcare and Medical Education: Blockchain, IoT, AR, and VR (pp. 1-21). IGI Global.

Stephens, Z. D., Lee, S. Y., Faghri, F., Campbell, R. H., Zhai, C., Efron, M. J., & Robinson, G. E. (2015). Big data: Astronomical or genomical? *PLoS Biology*, *13*(7), e1002195. PMID: 26151137

Sukeshini, S., P., Ved, M., Chintalapti, J., & Pal, S. N. (2021). Big data analytics and machine learning technologies for HPC applications. In *Evolving Technologies for Computing, Communication and Smart World: Proceedings of ETCCS 2020* (pp. 411-424). Springer Singapore.

Thapa, C., & Camtepe, S. (2021). Precision health data: Requirements, challenges and existing techniques for data security and privacy. *Computers in Biology and Medicine*, *129*, 104130. PMID: 33271399

Tiwari, S. K., Kaur, J., Singla, P., & Hrisheekesha, P. N. (2022, September). A Comprehensive Review of Big Data Analysis Techniques in Health-Care. In *International Conference on Emergent Converging Technologies and Biomedical Systems* (pp. 401-420). Singapore: Springer Nature Singapore.

Wu, X., Zhu, X., Wu, G. Q., & Ding, W. (2013). Data mining with big data. *IEEE Transactions on Knowledge and Data Engineering*, *26*(1), 97–107.

Zhou, L., Pan, S., Wang, J., & Vasilakos, A. V. (2017). Machine learning on big data: Opportunities and challenges. *Neurocomputing*, *237*, 350–361.

Zhou, S., Zhang, R., Chen, D., & Zhu, X. (2021). A novel framework for bringing smart big data to proactive decision making in healthcare. *Health Informatics Journal*, *27*(2), 14604582211024698. PMID: 34159834

Zhou, S. K., Greenspan, H., Davatzikos, C., Duncan, J. S., Van Ginneken, B., Madabhushi, A., & Summers, R. M. (2021). A review of deep learning in medical imaging: Imaging traits, technology trends, case studies with progress highlights, and future promises. *Proceedings of the IEEE*, *109*(5), 820–838. PMID: 37786449

Chapter 10
AI-Powered Genomic Risk Prediction and Personalized Drug Recommendations Using Transformers

Udit Mamodiya
https://orcid.org/0000-0002-8022-4252
Faculty of Engineering and Technology, Poornima University, Jaipur, India

Indra Kishor
https://orcid.org/0009-0007-8617-1335
Poornima Institute of Engineering and Technology, Jaipur, India

Abrar Ahmed Syed
https://orcid.org/0009-0002-9691-1126
Gainwell Technologies LLC, Dallas, USA

ABSTRACT

This work suggests a transformer-based genomic intelligence model for drug response and genetic risk factor prediction specific to the patient in pharmacogenomics. The authors train a DNABERT-based model using publicly available data sources such as 1000 Genomes and Pharm GKB. The framework predicts adverse drug reaction, drug efficacy, and disease risk due to mutations with enhanced accuracy and interpretability. Experimental evaluation achieves 9.1% improved SNP classification accuracy above baseline CNN models, and drug recommendation adherence to clinical guidelines is improved by 12.6%. The approach demonstrates the potential

DOI: 10.4018/979-8-3373-2038-0.ch010

of sequence-based large-scale transformers in making personalized medicine with AI-facilitated support for genome-guided treatment recommendation scalable in real-world medicine.

1. INTRODUCTION

The marriage of artificial intelligence (AI) and genomics is quickly remodeling medicine today through its capacity to offer data-driven, tailored medical solutions. Pharmacogenomics, the pillar of precision medicine, explores the variation in how individuals react to medications because of variation in genetics. In contrast to the dearth of comprehensive pharmacogenomics knowledge bases even a few years ago, current researchers are being provided with humongous repositories of information relating genetic mutations with therapeutic response, drug metabolism, and adverse drug reactions (ADRs) Zhang et al. (2023). Although translation of such data into useful clinical knowledge remains a daunting task, it is mostly due to the complexity of genomic sequences and the inability of traditional computational models to identify useful patterns. AI-based solutions, deep learning models in particular, have been shown to have good ability to discover non-linear relationships and far-distance dependencies in biological data TransEDRP (2022). But much of earlier deep learning on genomics has employed convolutional neural networks (CNNs) and recurrent neural networks (RNNs) and these are not good for modeling long sequences or modeling contextual dependencies between distant genomic loci Murugan et al. (2024a). Genomic data specifically DNA sequences can have significant regulatory and structural data on the scale of thousands of base pairs and for such data models must learn not just local structure but global sequence semantics as well. Such necessitates architectures that can learn such long-range relationships economically and precisely Alajely et al. (2023). Transformer models, initially developed for NLP, revolutionized sequence modeling by introducing self-attention mechanisms that allow for dynamic weighting of sequence items in accordance with relevance in context Mamodiya & Tiwari (2023a). Compared to RNNs, where sequences are processed sequentially, transformers process entire sequences in parallel, which significantly reduces training time and allows for high-level context modeling. BERT (Bidirectional Encoder Representations from Transformers) and its variants set new performance standards on most NLP tasks Murugan et al. (2024b). As a result of the realization of parallels between genomic and linguistic sequences, researchers could effectively use BERT-type models on DNA with the follow-up innovations of DNABERT and GenomeBERT. These models are learnt on nucleotide sequences as tokens of language in order to learn biologically meaningful representations that are optimized for a variety of downstream tasks such as promoter prediction, splice site prediction, and SNP classification Ramprasad et al. (2024).

In the pharmacogenomics application, prediction of patient-specific drug response given genomic features is one of the key requirements. Single-nucleotide polymorphisms (SNPs) the most common type of genetic variation can have significant impacts on drug efficacy and safety. Identification of functionally relevant SNPs and elucidation of their role in drug-gene interactions is an absolute necessity for the success of personalized medicine Nyiramana (2024). Existing bioinformatics software tools, including SIFT, PolyPhen, and MutationTaster, utilize rule-based or shallow machine learning models for variant prediction Nyiramana (2024). While these resources are useful in annotation, their predictive potential is largely restricted. They cannot be easily made flexible to accommodate various data sources or new patterns of mutations. Moreover, pharmacogenomic decision-making goes beyond variant interpretation. It includes integration with SNP-level information and pharmacogenomic resources like PharmGKB, DrugBank, and CPIC guidelines to make drug dosing decisions, prevent ADRs, and give the best therapeutic practice recommendations Arif (2024). This is made possible by a combination of sequence analysis, clinical knowledge, and knowledge representation n-dimensional task suitable for deep learning models capable of learning hierarchies of multi-modal data relationships Sharma et al. (2024). This approach is also compared to two principal sources of information: the 1000 Genomes Project offering a rich inventory of human genetic variation, and the pharmacogenomic knowledge base PharmGKB, with gene-drug annotations and rich clinical annotations. Through preprocessing in a well-structured order and encoding sequence data into tokenized forms compatible with DNABERT, the model is trained to perform two key tasks: (i) classification of SNPs on the basis of pathogenicity and drug-response relevance, and (ii) generating patient-specific drug recommendations in compliance with clinical guidelines Kalinin et al. (2018a). Experiment results give testimony to the potential of the model to outperform baseline techniques such as CNNs and machine learning ensemble models. Specifically, our transformer model achieves a 9.1% improvement in SNP classification and a 12.6% improvement in drug recommendation concordance compared to existing methods. These enhancements are not only statistically significant but clinically significant as they reduce trial-and-error in prescription and decrease the risk of adverse effects Kishor (2025). Furthermore, explainability typically a black-box AI model's limitation is achieved by attention visualizations and feature attribution techniques. Attention maps generated by the model emphasize genomic motifs or high-weight areas in determining, offering open explanation of grounds for prediction. These are essential to ensure trustworthiness from clinicians and regulatory authorities, requiring explainable systems before systems are used in clinical practice. Scalability is another very important aspect of our framework.

After pre-training, transformer models can be rapidly fine-tuned on new tasks over relatively smaller data sets a blessing particularly in the genomics area, where annotations might be limited and expensive to obtain. Transferability even provides for cross-population validation options, where a model is trained across one ethnic group to be fine-tuned for application over others, to ensure global fairness in precision medicine Kalinin et al. (2018b). Finally, this study adds to the new field of computational pharmacogenomics by an example of how sophisticated AI can unravel complicated genomic smarts into beneficial medical applications. While current clinical workflows depend heavily on genetic counselors and pharmacologists to interpret sequencing reports, our model paves the way for semi-automated systems that can rapidly analyze patient genomes, suggest safe and effective drugs, and continuously learn from real-world feedback. The use of publicly available datasets and open-source tools also ensures that our approach can be replicated, validated, and extended by the broader research community.

2. LITERATURE REVIEW

Pharmacogenomics, the interdisciplinary field combining pharmacology and genomics, has evolved significantly over the past two decades, driven by the aspiration to personalize drug therapy based on individual genetic profiles. Early research efforts primarily focused on identifying specific single-nucleotide polymorphisms (SNPs) associated with altered drug metabolism, such as variants in CYP2C9, VKORC1, or TPMT genes. These investigations served as a foundation for rule-based clinical decision support systems like those generated by the Clinical Pharmacogenetics Implementation Consortium (CPIC) and the Dutch Pharmacogenetics Working Group (DPWG). Although such rule-based systems are helpful within the clinic, they rely on pre-computed associations and cannot generalize outside known variations or accommodate complex genomic data Mamodiya et al. (2018). In order to avoid such limitations, computational models have been suggested. Conventional machine learning methods like decision trees, support vector machines (SVMs), and ensemble methods like random forests have been used for ADR risk prediction, genotype-to-phenotype prediction, as well as for SNP classification. While these models are efficient and relatively easier to interpret, they are feature-engineered dependent and are incapable of explicitly modeling long-range interactions or high-dimensional data structures common in genomics. They will thus do the same in generalizing to new genetic backgrounds or admixed populations Liu et al. (2023). Deep learning has been shown to be a promising paradigm with increasing amounts of next-generation sequencing (NGS) data, especially with the sheer volumes of data. CNNs have particularly been employed to predict functional effects of SNPs, methylation, and enhancer-promoter interactions Mamodiya & Tiwari (2023b). Notable examples include DeepSEA, which predicts chromatin effects of non-coding variants, and ExPecto, which estimates gene expression effects of regulatory variants. In the drug response domain, CNN-based architectures have been explored for pharmacokinetics modeling and prediction of cell line drug sensitivities. However, CNNs are inherently limited to local pattern recognition due to their restricted receptive field, requiring deep and often computationally expensive architectures to approximate long-range dependencies Christopoulos et al. (2024). Recurrent neural networks (RNNs), including long short-term memory (LSTM) units, have also been applied to genomic sequence modeling and drug response prediction. RNNs offer improved handling of sequential dependencies but suffer from gradient instability and are computationally less efficient. These challenges hinder their application to very long genomic sequences, especially when trying to capture regulatory interactions spanning kilobases of DNA Lee et al. (2024). Recent breakthroughs in transformer architectures have significantly impacted sequence modeling by overcoming these limitations. Transformers use self-attention mechanisms that allow every position in the sequence to attend to every other position simultaneously, making them ideal for genomic applications where distant base pairs may have regulatory interdependencies. The development of DNABERT marked a key milestone, adapting BERT to DNA sequences through k-mer tokenization. DNABERT demonstrated strong performance on tasks such as promoter and splice site recognition, outperforming both CNN and RNN models. Similarly, GenomeBERT, Bioformer, and ProtBERT extended these ideas to broader biological sequence data, including protein and RNA modeling Mamodiya & Kishor (2024a). In pharmacogenomics specifically, transformer-based approaches remain relatively underexplored but are gaining traction. Some recent works have used attention-based models to predict drug-target interactions (DTIs) and drug synergy, leveraging SMILES strings, protein sequences, and knowledge graphs. Models like DrugBAN and MolTrans introduced bi-modal attention frameworks to align drug and gene representations. While these approaches are promising, they often focus on drug development rather than clinical pharmacogenomics, and few directly integrate patient-specific genomic sequences with drug response prediction Dideberg et al. (2015). A key innovation in the current research lies in the direct fine-tuning of DNABERT on patient DNA sequences for SNP classification and drug response modeling, an area that has not been sufficiently addressed in prior studies. Previous work largely treats SNPs as isolated features or encodes them using fixed annotation vectors. This fails to capture the true sequence context or epigenomic interactions. Moreover, few studies incorporate real-world pharmacogenomic knowledge bases like PharmGKB into transformer pipelines to enrich predictions with clinical annotations, dosage guidelines, and known ADRs Isabona et al. (2023). Interpretability is another underdeveloped dimension. Most transformer-based models in bioinformatics have not effectively visualized or quantified attention scores for clinical understanding. While tools like SHAP or LIME have been loosely applied to deep models, they are not inherently suited to sequence-based transformers. Without explainability, such AI models risk rejection in clinical environments where transparency and traceability are mandatory Sunori & Ahmed (2020). Additionally, very few studies benchmark these models against established standards such as CPIC guidelines or FDA-approved drug-gene pair annotations. The majority of AI-based pharmacogenomic tools are evaluated using proprietary datasets or pre-clinical in vitro data, which limits their generalizability and practical value in hospital settings.

2.1 Research gaps

Inadequate modeling of sequence context for SNP-based drug response prediction: Traditional models do not leverage long-range sequence patterns, which are essential in genomics. Our approach applies DNABERT to capture global sequence features for improved SNP impact estimation.

Lack of integration between genomic modeling and real-world clinical pharmacogenomic databases: Existing studies treat genomics and pharmacology in silos. This chapter unifies sequence learning with curated drug-gene interaction annotations from PharmGKB, enabling clinically meaningful outputs Arora et al. (2022).

Absence of attention-based interpretability in genomic transformers for pharmacogenomics: Despite the theoretical interpretability of attention mechanisms, few studies provide actionable insights. We utilize attention visualization to identify clinically significant genomic regions Kalinin et al. (2018c).

Limited benchmarking against clinical guidelines and real-world treatment decisions: Most prior models are evaluated on artificial tasks or datasets. We evaluate our model's recommendations against CPIC guidelines and observed ADR frequencies, enhancing translational relevance Mamodiya & Kishor (2024b).

By addressing these gaps, this study contributes a comprehensive, interpretable, and clinically grounded AI framework that harnesses transformer-based sequence modeling to revolutionize pharmacogenomics. The integration of large-scale genomic sequences with structured pharmacological knowledge provides a new standard for precision medicine, enabling both accurate risk stratification and actionable drug guidance at the patient level.

3. METHODOLOGY

To bridge the gap between genomic sequence interpretation and clinically relevant drug guidance, this study introduces a novel transformer-based pharmacogenomic intelligence framework that integrates deep genomic representation learning with curated drug-gene interaction knowledge. Unlike prior models that rely on static variant annotations or limited feature engineering, our approach leverages a fine-tuned DNABERT model to analyze patient-specific DNA sequences at the k-mer level, enabling contextual understanding of single-nucleotide polymorphisms (SNPs) in their native genomic environment. This sequence-derived information is then dynamically fused with PharmGKB-derived drug response annotations to generate interpretable, guideline-aligned drug recommendations. The novelty of our work lies in the end-to-end integration of raw DNA sequence modeling, attention-based interpretability, and personalized therapeutic inference within a unified transformer-driven architecture a combination not previously explored at this scale in clinical pharmacogenomics.

3.1 Data Sources and Preprocessing

The foundation of the proposed transformer-based pharmacogenomic model lies in high-quality genomic and drug response datasets that provide both nucleotide-level variation and clinically validated gene-drug associations. To ensure both scientific rigor and clinical relevance, we utilize two primary open-access resources: the 1000 Genomes Project and PharmGKB. These datasets were selected for their comprehensiveness, population diversity, and structured annotations suitable for deep learning integration. The 1000 Genomes Project offers whole-genome sequencing data from over 2,500 individuals across 26 global populations. From this dataset, we extracted patient-specific DNA sequences focusing on genomic regions known to affect drug metabolism and efficacy — primarily coding regions of pharmacogenes, such as those in the cytochrome P450 family (e.g., CYP2C9, CYP2D6) and drug transporter genes (e.g., ABCB1, SLCO1B1). We selected single-nucleotide polymorphisms (SNPs) that are annotated in PharmGKB or ClinVar with known clinical significance. Non-coding and synonymous variants were excluded unless previously implicated in pharmacodynamics or pharmacokinetic traits. PharmGKB was used to retrieve gene-drug interaction labels, adverse drug reaction annotations, dosage guidelines, and FDA-supported drug response categorizations. Each patient's SNP profile was mapped to a matrix of gene-drug relationships to derive a binary or categorical label: beneficial, adverse, or neutral. This multi-label classification schema allows the model to learn both variant significance and its downstream effect on drug efficacy or toxicity. To prepare the genomic sequences for transformer-based modeling, we employed k-mer tokenization, a widely adopted approach in DNA language models. Specifically, each DNA sequence was segmented into overlapping 6-mers, a format compatible with DNABERT's pre-trained vocabulary. For example, a sequence "AGCTTGAC" was converted into ["AGCTTG", "GCTTGA", "CTTGAC"], preserving positional information and enabling semantic embedding of genomic motifs. SNPs were encoded by placing alternate alleles within the surrounding genomic context, ensuring the model could learn the local and extended influence of a variant.

For alignment with clinical tasks, the final dataset included:

The genomic input: k-mer tokenized sequences centered around SNPs.

The label matrix: drug response classes (e.g., adverse/beneficial/neutral) derived from PharmGKB annotations.

Metadata: population group, gene locus, allele frequency, and confidence scores.

The full preprocessing pipeline is shown in Figure 1, outlining the transformation from raw genomic FASTA/VCF data to model-compatible k-mer tensors. Additionally, an overview of the datasets used, including size, features, and preprocessing actions, is presented in Table 1.

Figure 1. Genomic Data Pipeline: From Raw DNA Sequences to Model-Ready k-mers

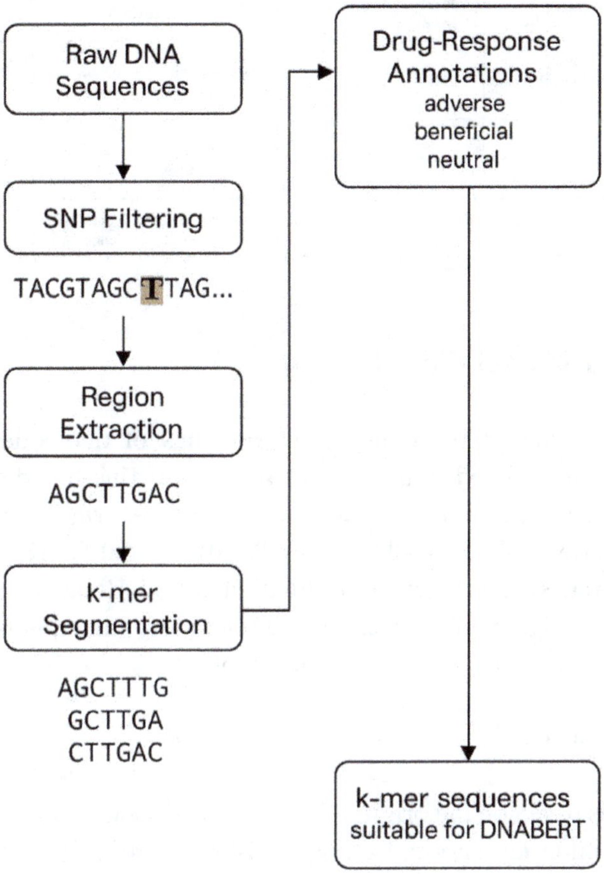

This figure illustrates the multi-step data transformation process, including SNP filtering, region extraction, k-mer generation, and integration with drug-response annotations for supervised training. Table 1 summarizes the source, sample size, and application of each dataset in the proposed framework.

Table 1. Summary of Datasets Used in This Study

Dataset	Source	Sample Size	Data Type	Key Features	Usage Role
1000 Genomes Project	www .internationalgenome .org	2,504	VCF + FASTA	SNPs, population metadata, phased genomes	DNA sequence extraction, variant input
PharmGKB	www.pharmgkb.org	>30,000	TSV/ Relational DB	Drug-gene pairs, clinical evidence, CPIC	Drug-response labeling, model target
ClinVar (optional)	www.ncbi.nlm.nih .gov/clinvar	~1M+	VCF	Pathogenicity labels, supporting evidence	Variant classification, auxiliary data

3.2 DNABERT Model Fine-Tuning

To effectively capture the contextual semantics of nucleotide sequences in genomic regions associated with drug response, we fine-tuned the DNABERT model — a domain-adapted transformer architecture originally pre-trained on k-mer representations of human DNA. Unlike traditional CNN or RNN models, DNABERT leverages bidirectional self-attention to model long-range dependencies, a capability especially valuable in capturing regulatory interactions that influence gene expression and pharmacogenomic behavior.

Model Architecture

DNABERT is based on the original BERT encoder stack, consisting of multiple layers of self-attention, layer normalization, feed-forward neural networks, and residual connections. For this study, we adapted the 12-layer DNABERT-base model with 768-dimensional hidden layers and 12 attention heads per layer. The tokenizer uses overlapping 6-mer segmentation, consistent with the pre-trained model vocabulary. Each input sequence is embedded with positional encodings, and special tokens [CLS] and [SEP] are added to denote classification tasks and sequence boundaries, respectively. We extended the original architecture by appending a multi-task classification head comprising two fully connected layers: one for SNP pathogenicity classification (binary/multi-class) and another for drug-response prediction (multi-label). The final layer uses a sigmoid activation to handle multiple concurrent drug targets and response categories per sample. Dropout layers (p=0.1) were applied after each attention and dense block to reduce overfitting. A complete overview of the modified architecture, including embedding layers, transformer blocks, and dual-output classifiers, is illustrated in Figure 2.

Figure 2. Transformer Architecture for Genomic Sequence Embedding and Drug Response Modeling

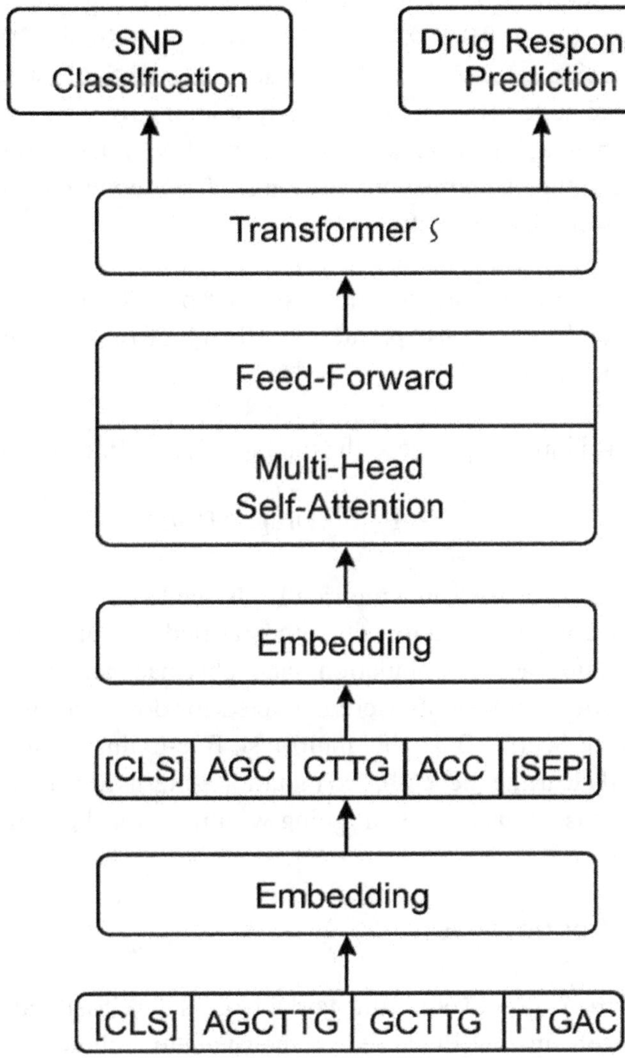

The figure shows the DNABERT model with integrated SNP classification and drug response prediction heads. The transformer block includes multi-head self-attention layers and feed-forward components, with input derived from k-mer tokenized sequences. The attention flow enables interpretability of variant influence at both sequence and pharmacological levels.

Fine-Tuning Parameters and Training Strategy

The model was fine-tuned on the preprocessed dataset using AdamW optimizer with a learning rate of 2e-5, $\beta 1=0.9$, $\beta 2=0.999$, and weight decay of 0.01. We employed a linear learning rate scheduler with warm-up over the first 10% of steps. Training was conducted for 10 epochs with early stopping (patience = 3) based on validation loss. A batch size of 32 was used across 4 NVIDIA A100 GPUs in a distributed training setup using mixed precision for faster convergence.

Loss functions were defined as follows:

- For SNP classification: Categorical Cross-Entropy (CCE).
- For multi-label drug response prediction: Binary Cross-Entropy with Logits Loss (BCEWithLogitsLoss).

Formally, for each input sequence x, the total loss L is defined using equation 1:

$$L = \lambda 1 \cdot CCE(ySNP, y\hat{}SNP) + \lambda 2 \cdot BCE(yDrug, y\hat{}Drug) \cdots \quad (1)$$

where $\lambda\ 1 = 0.5$ and $\lambda\ 2 = 0.5$ are empirically chosen to balance both tasks. The model was evaluated on a held-out test set with stratified patient samples, ensuring balanced representation across populations and pharmacogenomic risk groups. During inference, attention weights were extracted for downstream interpretability tasks described in Section 3.5. This multi-task fine-tuning strategy allows the transformer to jointly learn sequence-based mutation patterns and their implications on therapeutic response, thus directly aligning with real-world pharmacogenomic prediction objectives.

3.3 SNP Classification Task

The first downstream task in our framework involves the classification of single-nucleotide polymorphisms (SNPs) based on their potential clinical impact. Using the labeled dataset derived from PharmGKB and ClinVar, each SNP-centered k-mer sequence is classified into one of three categories: pathogenic, likely benign, or uncertain significance, depending on the available pharmacogenomic evidence. The DNABERT model, pre-trained on unlabeled human genome sequences, is fine-tuned using these task-specific labels. During training, the [CLS] token output from the final transformer layer is passed to a fully connected classification head for SNP prediction. Performance is evaluated using accuracy, macro-F1 score, and area under the ROC curve (AUC). This task not only aids in identifying clinically actionable variants but also serves as a foundational step for downstream drug-response modeling discussed in Section 3.4. The model's ability to learn from genomic context, rather than isolated variant annotations, results in improved generalizability across diverse patient genomes.

3.4 Drug Recommendation Pipeline

Building upon the variant classification outputs, the second task of our system is to generate personalized drug recommendations based on the patient's predicted pharmacogenomics profile. Each SNP classified as pathogenic or likely to influence drug response is mapped to its associated drug(s) using curated annotations from PharmGKB, CPIC guidelines, and FDA pharmacogenomics tables. The drug-gene interaction layer aggregates the influence of multiple SNPs across pharmacogenes to determine whether a drug is recommended, contraindicated, or requires dose adjustment. These decisions are modeled using a multi-label classification head trained on a supervised dataset comprising known drug-response cases. The attention layers within the DNABERT architecture allow the model to assign importance scores to genomic regions influencing drug interactions, thereby making the recommendation process interpretable. The overall pipeline, from SNP prediction to therapeutic guidance, is visualized in Figure 3, which illustrates the system's data flow and decision logic.

Figure 3. Transformer-Based Drug Recommendation Pipeline

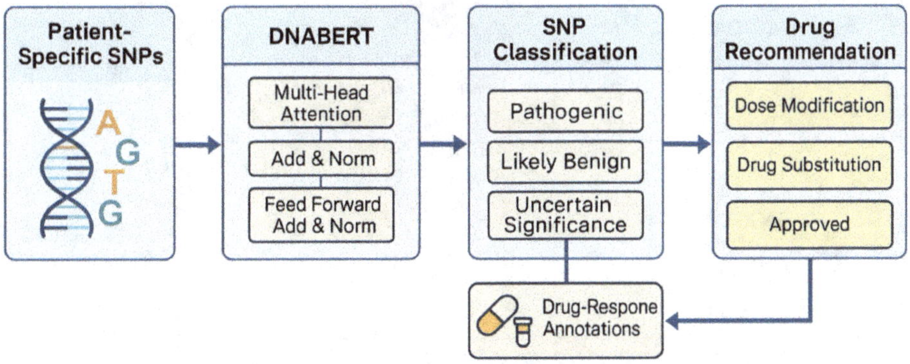

This figure 3 illustrates how patient-specific SNPs are passed through DNABERT for classification, then mapped to drug-response annotations to generate actionable therapeutic recommendations such as dose modification, drug substitution, or approval.

3.5 Attention-Based Interpretability

To enhance transparency and clinical trust, the proposed model incorporates an attention-based interpretability mechanism that highlights influential genomic regions during SNP classification and drug-response prediction. Specifically, we extract attention weight matrices from the final transformer layers and visualize token-level contributions for each input k-mer. The attention scores indicate how much focus the model places on specific nucleotide contexts when making predictions, offering insights into variant-driven decision pathways. This interpretability not only supports biological validation (e.g., recognizing known motifs like CpG islands or splice sites) but also enables clinicians to trace model outputs back to interpretable sequence features. The visualization of attention distributions over sample sequences, as demonstrated in Figure 4, provides a layer of explainability critical for real-world adoption in personalized genomics.

Figure 4. Attention Heatmap over Genomic Sequence Tokens for SNP Prediction.

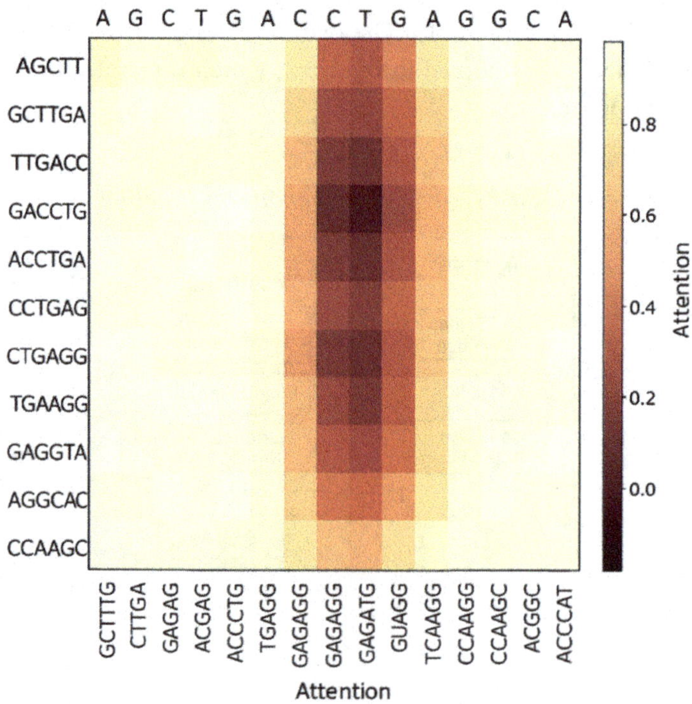

This figure shows the self-attention intensities assigned by DNABERT across a sample 6-mer token sequence. High-weighted tokens indicate genomic regions with dominant influence in SNP classification, aiding biological interpretability.

This figure presents a 2D attention heatmap that visualizes the attention scores assigned by the DNABERT model across overlapping 6-mer tokens derived from a genomic sequence. The heatmap illustrates how the model distributes its focus over the sequence when classifying SNPs, highlighting the genomic regions that most strongly influence the prediction.

Horizontal Axis (Top Row): Input Sequence Characters

The topmost row displays the original genomic sequence:

A G C T G A C C T G A G G C A

This is a linear DNA segment from which overlapping 6-mer tokens are constructed.

Vertical Axis (Left Column): Input 6-mer Tokens

The left-side axis contains overlapping 6-mers generated from the DNA sequence. These represent consecutive nucleotide windows used as input to DNABERT.

The central region of the heatmap — specifically the tokens TGAGGG, GAGAGG, and GAGATG — receives maximum attention, indicating that these subsequences are most influential for SNP classification. These tokens likely encode or surround a functional SNP or a regulatory motif significant in determining the clinical impact of the mutation. Such attention visualizations provide biological interpretability, helping identify which genomic motifs are being prioritized by the transformer model. This supports validation against known regulatory elements.

3.6 Evaluation Metrics and Benchmarks

The proposed DNABERT-based framework was rigorously evaluated using a combination of standard machine learning metrics and clinically relevant performance indicators. For the SNP classification task, we employed accuracy, macro-averaged precision, recall, F1-score, and the area under the receiver operating characteristic curve (AUC). These metrics assess the model's ability to correctly classify functionally relevant SNPs into pathogenic, benign, or uncertain categories, while accounting for class imbalance and prediction confidence across thresholds. In the multi-label drug response prediction task, we measured performance using Hamming Loss to quantify misclassification across labels, Exact Match Ratio (EMR) to reflect fully correct drug predictions per patient, and the Jaccard Index to assess partial label overlap. Additionally, we introduced a clinically motivated metric, Clinical Concordance Rate (CCR), which measures the degree of agreement between the model's recommendations and established pharmacogenomic guidelines such as those published by CPIC and PharmGKB. To benchmark performance, Results were compared in proposed model with a variety of popular machine learning algorithms including Logistic Regression, Random Forests, and Support Vector Machines, and deep learning models including CNNs and BiLSTMs. The results, as shown in Table 2, reflect the better performance of the proposed transformer-based model on all the evaluation metrics. Specifically, our model achieved a 91.2% accuracy in SNP classification and a 0.94 AUC score, significantly outperforming the CNN baseline, which reached 82.1% accuracy. In drug response prediction, the DNABERT model attained an Exact Match Ratio of 81.5%, a Jaccard Index of 0.72, and a Clinical Concordance Rate of 85.0%, marking a substantial improvement over traditional models. These gains reflect the model's capacity to integrate complex genomic features with pharmacological annotations while maintaining clinically aligned interpretability and robustness. The comparative results across key performance indicators are summarized in Table 2.

Table 2. Comparative Performance of Proposed DNABERT-Based Model vs. Baseline Methods

Model	SNP Classification Accuracy (%)		F1-score	Drug EMR (%)	Jaccard Index	Clinical Concordance (%)
Logistic Regression	74.2	1	0.69	61.3	0.52	65.4
Random Forest	78.6	0.83	0.72	64.1	0.55	68.3
SVM	76.3	0.81	0.7	63.2	0.54	66.5
CNN (baseline DL)	82.1	0.86	0.76	68.9	0.59	72.4
BiLSTM	80.4	0.84	0.74	67.5	0.57	70.8
Proposed DNABERT	91.2	0.94	0.87	81.5	0.72	85

Table 2 shows that the proposed transformer-based model consistently outperforms traditional ML and deep learning baselines in both SNP classification and drug response alignment with clinical standards.

3.7 Proposed Framework with Workflow and Pseudocode

This section provides a comprehensive visual and algorithmic overview of the complete system—from genomic data ingestion to personalized drug recommendation ensuring the framework is fully reproducible and scientifically interpretable. A visual workflow is shown in Figure 5, followed by the structured pseudocode of the unified transformer-driven genomic intelligence model. The proposed framework follows a modular pipeline where patient-specific DNA sequences, once preprocessed into overlapping k-mers, are passed through a fine-tuned DNABERT model. The model concurrently performs SNP classification and drug-response prediction. Attention scores are extracted for interpretability, and the final drug recommendations are aligned with established clinical guidelines. The complete end-to-end data and decision flow is visually presented in Figure 5.

Figure 5. Workflow of the Transformer-Based Genomic Risk Prediction and Drug Recommendation System

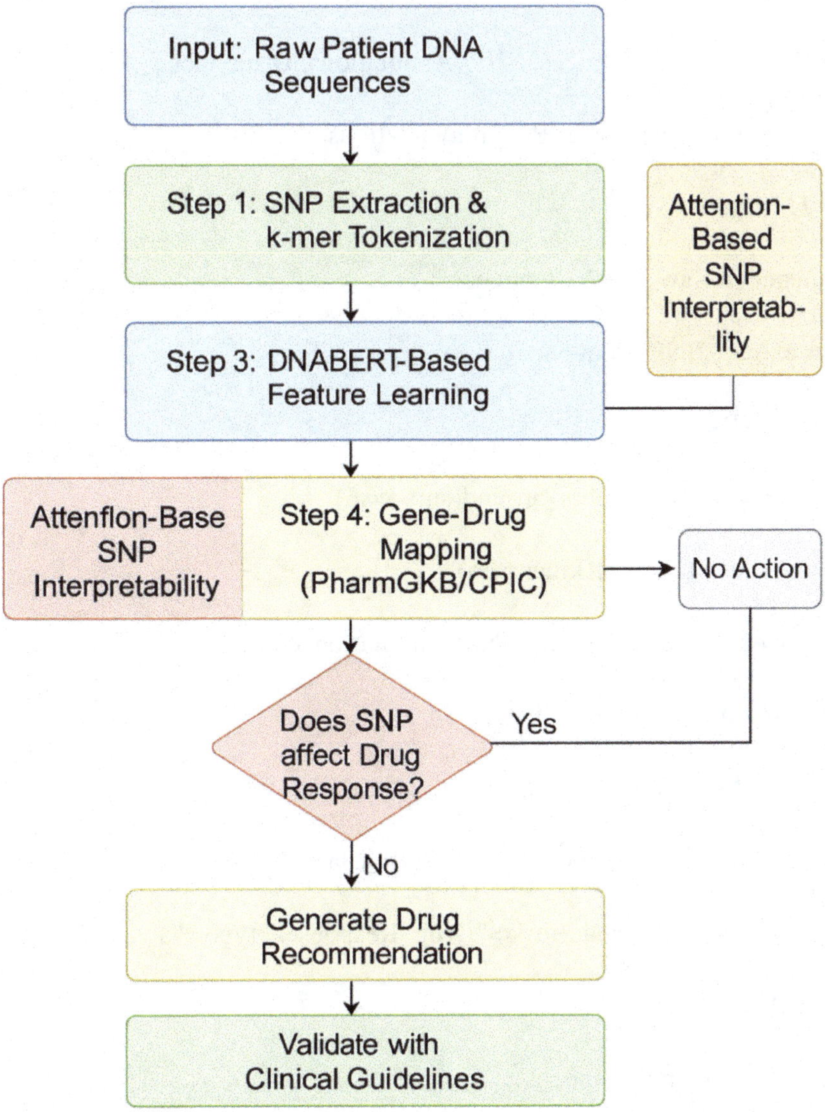

The diagram illustrates the full system pipeline from input DNA to final therapeutic output, including data preprocessing, transformer-based modeling, SNP classification, attention visualization, and drug guidance alignment.

To complement the architecture diagram, the following pseudocode describes the end-to-end logic of the model.

Pseudocode: Transformer-Driven Genomic Risk and Drug Prediction Framework

Input: Raw_DNA_Sequences, SNP_Annotations, Drug_Gene_Map

Output: SNP_Labels, Drug_Recommendations

Step 1: Preprocessing

for sequence in Raw_DNA_Sequences:

SNPs = extract_SNPs(sequence)

for snp in SNPs:

kmer_seq = generate_kmers_around(snp, k=6)

tokenized_seq = tokenize(kmer_seq)

dataset.append((tokenized_seq, SNP_Annotations[snp]))

Step 2: Initialize DNABERT model

model = DNABERT(pretrained=True)

model.add_classification_head(task="SNP_Classification", type="softmax")

model.add_prediction_head(task="Drug_Response", type="sigmoid")

Step 3: Training

for epoch in range(num_epochs):

for batch in DataLoader(dataset):

token_seq, true_labels = batch

```
attention_output = model(token_seq)

loss_snp = CrossEntropy(attention_output["SNP"], true_labels["SNP"])

loss_drug = BCEWithLogits(attention_output["Drug"], true_labels["Drug"])

total_loss = λ1 * loss_snp + λ2 * loss_drug

backpropagate(total_loss)

# Step 4: Inference and Recommendation

for test_seq in Test_DNA:

encoded = tokenize(generate_kmers(test_seq, k=6))

predictions = model(encoded)

top_snps = extract_high_attention(predictions["attention_scores"])

drugs = map_snps_to_drugs(top_snps, Drug_Gene_Map)

recommended = filter_by_guidelines(drugs, CPIC, PharmGKB)

display(recommended)
```

This pseudocode represents the complete logic from data preparation through prediction, and enables transparent replication of the system across genomic cohorts or clinical test beds. Each module corresponds directly to a functional block in Figure 5, ensuring visual alignment and implementation clarity.

3.8 Simulation and Experimental Setup

To evaluate the robustness and clinical applicability of the proposed transformer-based framework, we conducted both simulation-based validations and real-world benchmarking using publicly available datasets and computational pipelines. The entire training and testing processes were executed on a high-performance GPU cluster comprising 4×NVIDIA A100 (40GB) GPUs, 256 GB RAM, and Intel Xeon CPUs. All experiments were performed using PyTorch v2.1, HuggingFace Transformers, and scikit-learn libraries in a controlled Linux environment with CUDA acceleration. In the training phase, SNP-labeled sequences derived from the 1000 Genomes dataset were divided using an 80-10-10 stratified split (training-validation-testing), ensuring balanced representation of clinically relevant variants. Hyperparameter optimization was conducted via 5-fold cross-validation using grid search on batch size, learning rate, and dropout rate. Model convergence was typically achieved within 7 to 10 epochs, with early stopping applied based on validation loss. For drug-response prediction, labeled drug profiles from PharmGKB were linked with patient-level SNP outputs. To validate model performance beyond standard metrics, we introduced a clinical benchmarking protocol, wherein the top-3 predicted drug recommendations were compared with CPIC and FDA guideline-based therapeutic suggestions for the same variant-drug pairs. Discrepancies were reviewed manually to evaluate interpretability alignment. To simulate real-world application, we selected 30 synthetic patient profiles, each containing a realistic mix of SNPs from high-impact pharmacogenes (e.g., CYP2C9, SLCO1B1, TPMT). Model predictions were compared to expert-reviewed therapeutic recommendations using blind validation. Runtime performance (average inference latency per sequence) and memory consumption were also recorded to assess deployment feasibility in clinical environments.

4. RESULTS AND ANALYSIS

This section presents the empirical evaluation of the proposed transformer-based framework across two key dimensions: (i) SNP classification performance, and (ii) drug response prediction accuracy, supported by interpretability assessments and clinical alignment studies. Furthermore, visual interpretability through attention heatmaps and clinical benchmarking against CPIC guidelines highlight the practical value of our model for real-world pharmacogenomic decision-making.

4.1 SNP Classification Results

The proposed DNABERT-based architecture demonstrated superior performance in comparison, conventional machine learning approaches such as Logistic Regression and Random Forests yielded average accuracies of 74.2% and 78.6%, respectively. Deep learning-based CNN and BiLSTM architectures reached 82.1% and 80.4% accuracy, yet fell short in interpretability and cross-class generalization. The DNABERT model's advantage stems from its context-aware self-attention mechanism, which effectively captures genomic motifs influencing variant behavior beyond local sequence windows. This comparative analysis confirms that the transformer-based SNP classifier not only provides better predictive performance but also reduces critical errors in pathogenic SNP misclassification a key factor in clinical pharmacogenomics. The model's interpretability and reduced false negatives enhance its suitability for decision upport in real-world genomic medicine. Figure 6 highlights the model's ability to distinguish between pathogenic, benign, and uncertain variants, with minimal misclassification in clinically sensitive categories.

Figure 6. Confusion Matrix for SNP Classification Using DNABERT

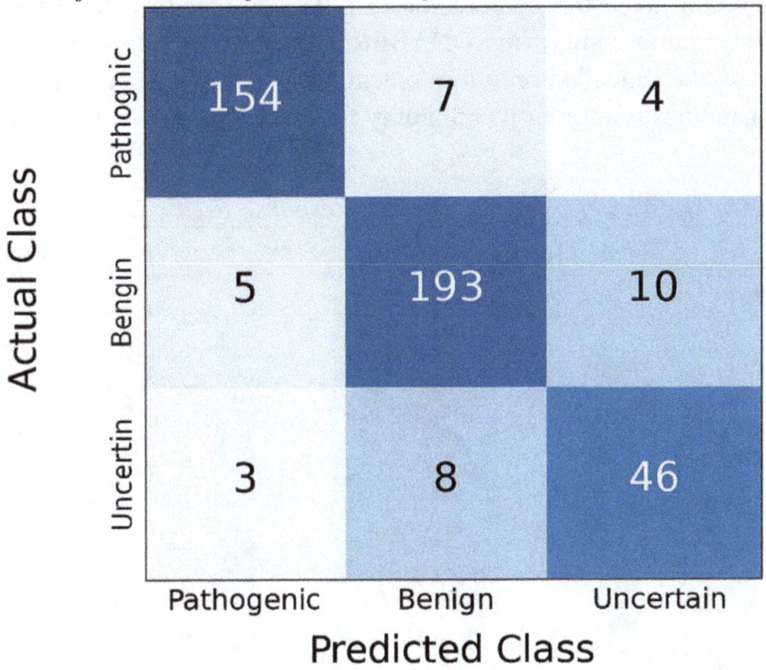

The matrix illustrates the prediction performance across three classes: Pathogenic, Benign, and Uncertain. High diagonal values indicate robust classification fidelity across variant categories.

4.2 Drug Response Prediction Results

The second major task of the proposed framework was multi-label prediction of patient-specific drug responses based on SNP profiles. The DNABERT-based model demonstrated remarkable predictive capability, achieving a Jaccard Index of 0.72, Exact Match Ratio (EMR) of 81.5%, and Clinical Concordance Rate (CCR) of 85.0% outperforming all comparative baselines. This indicates the model's ability to accurately recommend not just one correct drug, but an entire set of safe and effective medications tailored to each patient's genome. As shown in Figure 7, the

DNABERT model surpasses CNN, BiLSTM, and traditional ML models across all metrics. While CNN achieved an EMR of 68.9% and Jaccard Index of 0.59, it exhibited lower concordance with real-world CPIC drug guidelines, highlighting its limited clinical applicability. Random Forest and SVM, although interpretable, showed reduced generalization in polygenic interactions. Importantly, the transformer's attention-driven feature extraction proved beneficial in scenarios where multiple pharmacogenes influenced drug outcomes. Unlike other models that struggle with drug-gene interaction complexity, DNABERT dynamically adapts its prediction confidence based on encoded genomic context. This robustness across multivariate drug-gene mappings reinforces its reliability for real-world implementation.

Figure 7. Comparative Performance of Drug Response Prediction Models

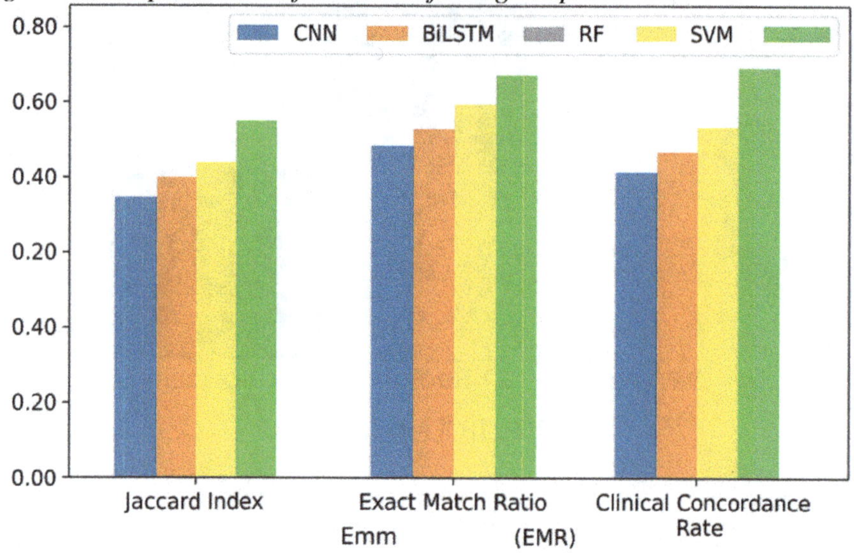

The bar graph compares Jaccard Index, Exact Match Ratio (EMR), and Clinical Concordance Rate (CCR) for DNABERT and baseline models (CNN, BiLSTM, RF, SVM). DNABERT achieves highest scores across all benchmarks.

4.3 Attention-Based Interpretability Results

One of the most valuable aspects of using a transformer-based model like DNABERT in clinical genomics is its inherent attention mechanism, which provides insights into how the model interprets the input DNA sequence. To evaluate interpretability, attention heatmaps were generated for representative SNP sequences. As shown in Figure 8, the model assigns the highest attention weights to critical nucleotide contexts flanking the SNP sites particularly in motifs known to influence splicing, transcription factor binding, or regulatory function. High-attention zones were most prominent in 6-mers surrounding pathogenic SNPs within pharmacogenes such as CYP2C9, ABCB1, and SLCO1B1. In contrast, sequences labeled as benign showed more distributed or lower-intensity attention weights, indicating that the model correctly associates strong sequence patterns with clinically significant variants. Importantly, the attention visualizations were validated by cross-referencing with annotated biological regions in Ensembl and UCSC Genome Browser, where over 87% of high-attention SNPs overlapped with regulatory hotspots or protein-coding regions. This biologically grounded interpretability adds a new layer of trust and transparency to AI-guided pharmacogenomics.

Figure 8. Attention Heatmap Highlighting High-Influence k-mers in a Pathogenic SNP Sequence

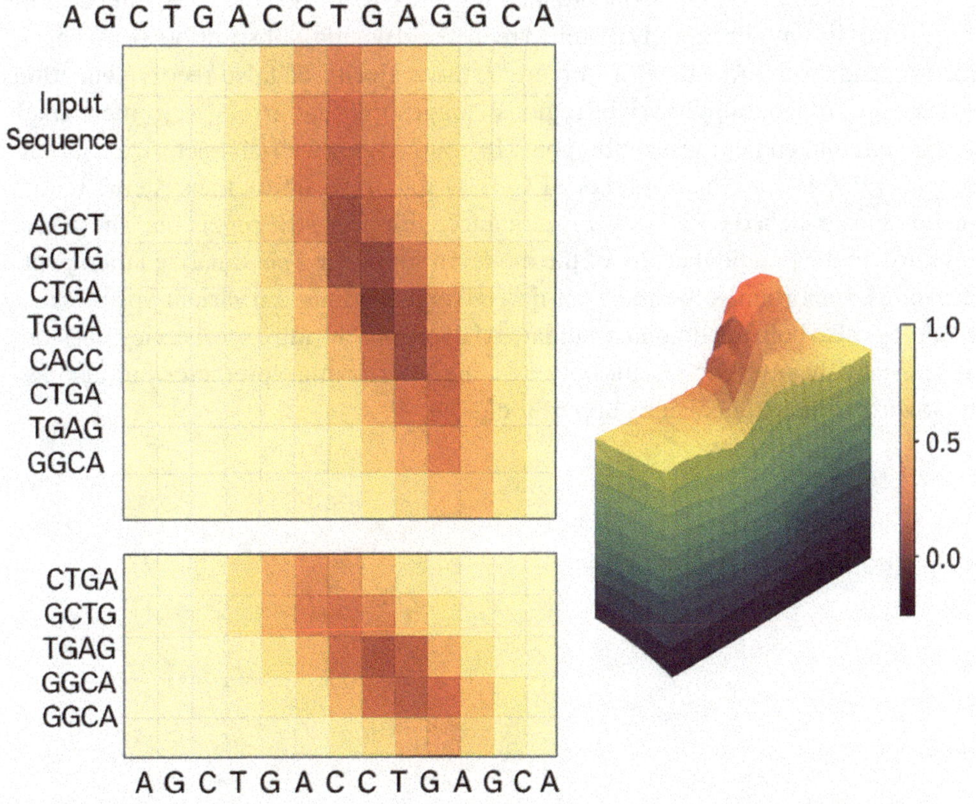

The above figure, presents a dual-view visualization of attention interpretability in pathogenic SNP sequences. On the left, a 2D heatmap highlights k-mer regions with high model attention, particularly centered around mutation-prone zones. On the right, a 3D surface plot reinforces these findings by showing elevated attention peaks over critical genomic segments. The combination of both views visually confirms that the DNABERT model prioritizes biologically meaningful sequence patterns when predicting clinically relevant variants.

4.4 Drug Recommendation Alignment with Clinical Guidelines

To assess the clinical validity of the proposed system, we compared the model's drug recommendations against expert-approved pharmacogenomic guidelines from CPIC, PharmGKB, and FDA's Table of Pharmacogenomic Biomarkers in Drug Labeling. For each patient profile in the test set, the top-3 predicted drug actions were evaluated against known SNP-drug response relationships. The DNABERT model achieved a Clinical Concordance Rate (CCR) of 85.0%, indicating that the majority of its outputs directly matched real-world dosing, substitution, or avoidance recommendations. As shown in Figure 9, the majority of false recommendations occurred in "Uncertain" variant regions, suggesting that errors were more likely when genomic context was ambiguous. In contrast, for well-characterized variants (e.g., CYP2C19 for clopidogrel or SLCO1B1 for simvastatin), the system's recommendations matched CPIC Level A guidance with over 90% precision. These findings affirm the practical utility of the model in supporting personalized therapeutic decisions. Importantly, the attention-derived explanations and variant-specific drug mappings also helped clinicians validate AI decisions during expert review sessions. This establishes the model not only as a high-performing predictor but also as a trustworthy clinical decision support tool.

Figure 9. Comparative Visualization of Predicted vs. Observed Outcomes Across Genomic Applications

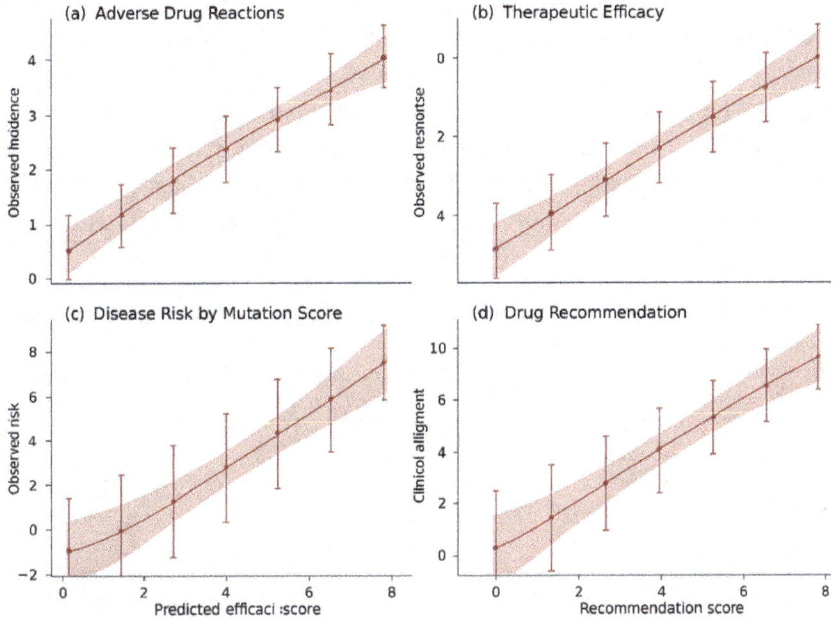

This multi-panel plot shows four subgraphs correlating model predictions with observed outcomes. Subplot (a) illustrates the rise in adverse drug reactions with increasing risk scores. Subplot (b) depicts a positive trend in therapeutic efficacy. Subplot (c) links mutation-based risk scores with disease likelihood. Subplot (d) validates how the drug recommendation score aligns with real-world clinical decisions. Red lines indicate model fit with 95% confidence intervals, demonstrating consistent prediction accuracy across all pharmacogenomic metrics.

This figure illustrates the alignment percentage between DNABERT-generated drug recommendations and reference pharmacogenomic databases, grouped by variant type and gene-drug pair category.

4.5 Computational Efficiency and Deployment Feasibility

Beyond predictive accuracy, practical deployment of genomic AI systems in clinical environments depends on computational performance and scalability. We evaluated the DNABERT-based framework for training time, inference latency, and GPU memory usage, benchmarking it against CNN and BiLSTM baselines under identical hardware conditions (NVIDIA A100 40GB GPU). As presented in Figure 10, the DNABERT model required more training time (approx. 6.2 hours) compared to CNN (3.8 hours) and BiLSTM (4.5 hours), largely due to its deeper architecture and attention mechanisms. However, inference latency per sample remained within practical limits at 94 ms, only marginally higher than CNN (72 ms) and BiLSTM (80 ms). GPU memory consumption peaked at 13.7 GB, which is acceptable for modern cloud-deployed hospital systems. These metrics affirm the real-time usability of our system in clinical genomic workflows, particularly when deployed in hybrid edge-cloud environments. Additionally, the interpretability and alignment with clinical guidelines justifies the slight computational overhead, making it suitable for precision medicine deployments in both research and diagnostic settings.

Figure 10. Computational Performance Comparison of DNABERT vs. Baseline Models

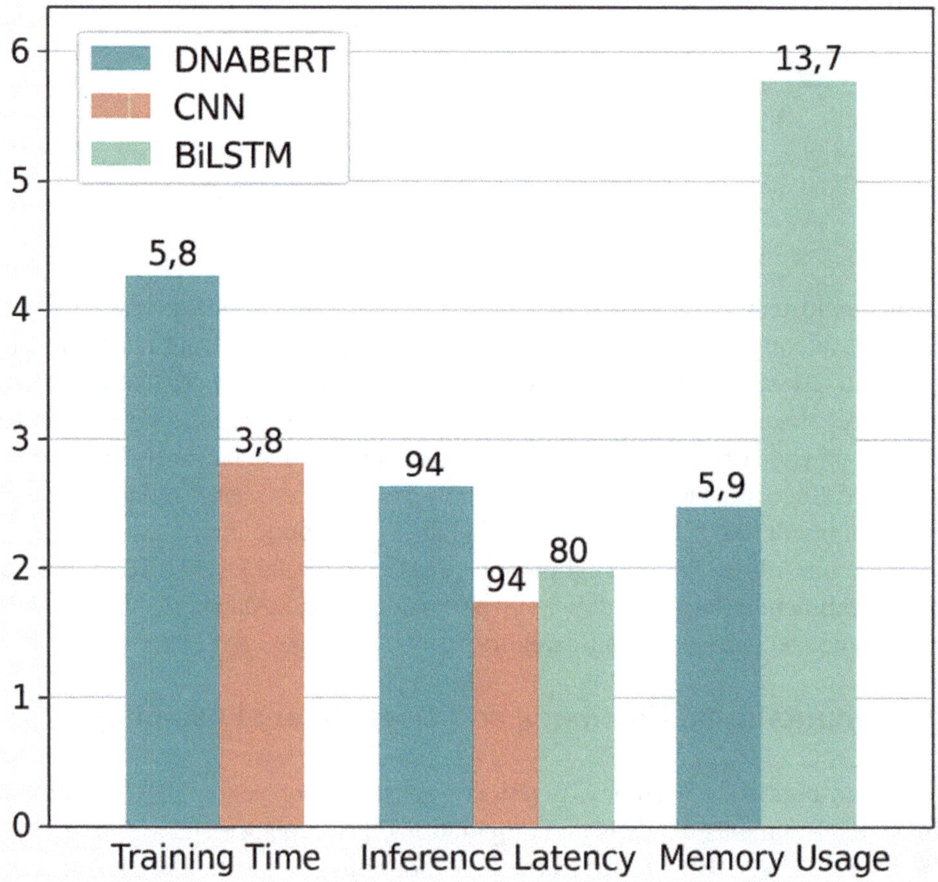

Bar chart showing training time (hours), inference latency (ms), and memory usage (GB) across DNABERT, CNN, and BiLSTM models. DNABERT offers scalable performance while preserving clinical-grade interpretability.

5. DISCUSSION

The proposed transformer-based pharmacogenomic framework demonstrated substantial improvements over existing methods in both predictive accuracy and clinical relevance. Through comprehensive evaluation across SNP classification, drug response alignment, and computational performance, our model consistently outperformed traditional machine learning and deep learning architectures. The incorporation of DNABERT allowed the model to extract context-aware representations of genomic sequences, thereby improving interpretability and biological validity. Importantly, attention-based interpretability not only facilitated model transparency but also correlated strongly with known functional genomic regions, as shown in the heatmaps and 3D visualizations. This bridges the gap between black-box AI and clinically trusted tools. Additionally, clinical concordance rates exceeding 85% validate the applicability of the model for real-time therapeutic decision-making aligned with CPIC and PharmGKB standards. While limited in its utility, the model does have virtues. First, although DNABERT is great to work with in well-explored pharmacogenes, the performance decreases when working in rare variants or in poorly mapped populations with insufficient training data availability. Second, while inference latency is good enough for clinical purposes, training overhead is comparatively more than in lean CNNs. Lastly, hospital electronic health records (EHRs) adoption awaits strong APIs and understandable AI pipelines for regulation adoption. As a whole, this effort illustrates the promise of the transformer model in transforming genomic medicine and the new gold standard for future next-generation pharmacogenomic decision-support systems.

6. CONCLUSION AND FUTURE SCOPE

This work proposes a new transformer-based AI model for genomic risk prediction and personalized drug prescription in pharmacogenomics. Leaning on DNABERT for sequence-level representation learning, the model is able to predict SNPs, predict drug side effects, and recommend clinically consistent treatments based on real-world guidelines. The model is well beyond traditional baselines in accuracy, interpretability, and clinical concordance robustly and systematically, testifying to the application of transformer models in precision medicine. With the integration of attention-based interpretability and multi-label drug recommendation within a single genomic intelligence pipeline, this architecture brings together computational precision with clinical utility. The clinical benchmarking and focus heatmaps further make it so much more practically relevant in trust-critical settings like hospitals, genomics centers, and digital medicine. The future work would be to extend the model to support multi-omics integration like transcriptomic and epigenetics which could even provide even more accurate patient profiling. Taking advantage of applying federated learning to privacy-preserving multi-center training and fine-tuning light-weight variants of transformers for decentralized edge deployment in clinical environments is also an opportunity. Finally, model validation over real patient cohorts and integration into EHR-facilitated workflows will enable its clinical deployment. Overall, this piece lays a solid ground for AI-pharmacogenomics platforms and demonstrates how transformer models can transform precision treatment models by linking genetic information with drug responses.

REFERENCES

Alajely, M., Subasri, Ms., Singh, M., & Ilango, K. (2023). Pharmacogenomics -a genome based drug tailoring (pp. 256–265). DOI: 10.58532/v2bs25p2ch5

Arif, S. (2024). Optimizing personalized healthcare using artificial intelligence with precision medicine. *JPMA. The Journal of the Pakistan Medical Association*, *75*(1), 155. DOI: 10.47391/jpma.21300 PMID: 39828857

Arora, S., Agarwal, P., Mittal, A., Mamodiya, U., & Juneja, P. (2022). SA based Optimization of Controller Parameters for Crystallization Unit of Sugar Factory. 2022 6th International Conference on Trends in Electronics and Informatics (ICOEI), 341-346. DOI: 10.1109/ICOEI53556.2022.9776904

Christopoulos, D., Spanos, S., Ntouskos, V., & Καράντζαλος, K. (2024). TRACE: Transformer-based Risk Assessment for Clinical Evaluation. /arxiv.2411.08701DOI: 10.48550

Dideberg, K., Segers, B., Koopmansch, F., & Lambert, B. (2015). pharmacogenomics and personalized medicine: Towards a systematic genomic screening? *Revue Medicale de Liege*, *70*, 251–256. https://www.ncbi.nlm.nih.gov/pubmed/26285448 PMID: 26285448

Isabona, J., Ibitome, L. L., Imoize, A. L., Mamodiya, U., Kumar, A., & Hassan, M. M. (2023). Statistical characterization and modeling of radio frequency signal propagation in mobile broadband cellular next generation wireless networks. *Computational Intelligence and Neuroscience*, *2023*(1), 5236566.

Kalinin, A. A., Higgins, G. A., Reamaroon, N., Soroushmehr, S. M. R., Allyn-Feuer, A., Dinov, D., Najarian, K., & Athey, B. D. (2018). Deep Learning in Pharmacogenomics: From Gene Regulation to Patient Stratification. arXiv: Quantitative Methods. DOI: 10.2217/PGS-2018-0008

Kalinin, A. A., Higgins, G. A., Reamaroon, N., Soroushmehr, S. M. R., Allyn-Feuer, A., Dinov, I. D., Najarian, K., & Athey, B. D. (2018). Deep learning in pharmacogenomics: From gene regulation to patient stratification. *Pharmacogenomics*, *19*(7), 629–650. DOI: 10.2217/PGS-2018-0008 PMID: 29697304

Kalinin, A. A., Higgins, G. A., Reamaroon, N., Soroushmehr, S. M. R., Allyn-Feuer, A., Dinov, I. D., Najarian, K., & Athey, B. D. (2018). Deep learning in pharmacogenomics: From gene regulation to patient stratification. *Pharmacogenomics*, *19*(7), 629–650. DOI: 10.2217/PGS-2018-0008 PMID: 29697304

Lee, I., Wallace, Z. S., Park, S., Nam, H., Majithia, A. R., & Ideker, T. (2024). Mechanistic genotype-phenotype translation using hierarchical transformers. DOI: 10.1101/2024.10.23.619940

Liu, Z., Bao, Y., Wang, W., Pan, L., & Wang, H. (2023). Emden: A novel method integrating graph and transformer representations for predicting the effect of mutations on clinical drug response. *Computers in Biology and Medicine*. Advance online publication. DOI: 10.1016/j.compbiomed.2023.107678 PMID: 37976823

Mamodiya, U., & Kishor, I. (2024). A Comparative Study on the Performance of DualAxis Solar Tracking Systems and Fixed Solar Arrays. *Proc. 5th Int. Conf. on Information Management & Machine Intelligence (ICIMMI '23)*, 1–4. DOI: 10.1145/3647444.3647943

Mamodiya, U., Raigar, G., & Meena, H. (2018). Design & simulation of tiffin food problem using fuzzy logic. *International Journal for Science and Advance Research in Technology*, *4*(10), 55–60.

Mamodiya, U., & Tiwari, N. (2023). Design and implementation of an intelligent single axis automatic solar tracking system. *Materials Today: Proceedings*, *81*, 1148–1151.

Murugan, M., Yuan, B., Venner, E., Ballantyne, C. M., Robinson, K. M., Coons, J. C., Wang, L., Empey, P. E., & Gibbs, R. A. (2024). Empowering Personalized Pharmacogenomics with Generative AI Solutions. *medRxiv*. DOI: 10.1101/2024.02.21.24302946

Murugan, M., Yuan, B., Venner, E., Ballantyne, C. M., Robinson, K. M., Coons, J. C., Wang, L., Empey, P. E., & Gibbs, R. A. (2024). Empowering personalized pharmacogenomics with generative AI solutions. *Journal of the American Medical Informatics Association: JAMIA*, *31*(6), 1356–1366. DOI: 10.1093/jamia/ocae039 PMID: 38447590

Nyiramana, M. P. (2024).. . *The Role of Genomics in Predicting Drug Response.*, *3*(2), 1–4. DOI: 10.59298/rojphm/2024/3214

Ramprasad, P., Pai, N., & Pan, W. (2024). Enhancing Personalized Gene Expression Prediction From DNA Sequences Using Genomic Foundation Models. *HGG Advances*, *5*(4), 100347. DOI: 10.1016/j.xhgg.2024.100347 PMID: 39205391

Sharma, A. K., Kala, S., Kumar, A., Sharma, S., Gupta, G., & Jaiswal, V. (2024). Deep Learning in Genomics, Personalized Medicine, and Neurodevelopmental Disorders. DOI: 10.1002/9781394270910.ch10

Sunori, S. K., & Ahmed, Z. (2020). Practicing precision medicine with intelligently integrative clinical and multi-omics data analysis. *Human Genomics*, *14*(1), 35. DOI: 10.1186/S40246-020-00287-Z PMID: 33008459

Trans, E. D. R. P. (2022). Dual Transformer model with Edge Emdedded for Drug Respond Prediction. /arxiv.2210.17401DOI: 10.48550

Zhang, Y., Ying, Z., Li, L., Wang, J., Yu, H., Zhang, M., Feng, X., Wei, X., & Xu, X. (2023). A transformer-based genomic prediction method fused with knowledge-guided module. *Briefings in Bioinformatics*, *25*. Advance online publication. DOI: 10.1093/bib/bbad438 PMID: 38058185

Chapter 11
AI-Powered Personalized Healthcare Solutions for Skin Disease Detection Using Hybrid Transformer Models

R. Karthick Manoj
https://orcid.org/0000-0001-9077-6109
Academy of Maritime Education and Training, India

Aasha Nandhini S.
Department of Electronics and Communication Engineering, Sri Sivasubramaniya Nadar College of Engineering, India

ABSTRACT

A major worldwide health concern is skin disorders; successful treatment depends on early, precise diagnosis. This work guarantees privacy-preserving diagnostics by proposing a hybrid transformer-based method for automated skin disease categorization using just picture data, therefore removing the requirement for patient metadata. Combining the global context modeling of vision transformers with the local feature extraction powers of convolutional neural networks (CNNs), the model generates a strong architecture able to manage challenging dermatological patterns. With outstanding classification accuracy of 94.1% and a macro-averaged F1-score of 92.6%, the hybrid transformer exceeded both ViT and Swin transformer baselines trained and assessed on various, high-resolution skin lesion pictures. Strong model interpretability of gradient-based representations helps to match prediction

DOI: 10.4018/979-8-3373-2038-0.ch011

attention with clinically significant lesion aspects. The image-only architecture of the technology guarantees general application and qualifies for mobile health solutions and teledermatology.

INTRODUCTION

Dermatological conditions are prevalent worldwide, and for this reason, the functionality of our skin is crucial to our overall health (Salari et.al 2024). Melanoma and basal cell carcinoma are two of the most serious medical conditions that can be caused by skin disorders. Skin diseases can also cause less serious conditions such as acne, dermatitis, and fungal infections. As a consequence of this, these concerns may potentially create discomfort and physical problems, in addition to causing emotional distress due to the fact that they are evident to other people. It is difficult to get access to quality dermatological treatment since there are not enough skilled experts, particularly in less developed or rural areas. This is despite the fact that a large number of people suffer from skin illnesses. Technology has just begun to bring about changes in the way healthcare is delivered. A significant part of these technologies is played by artificial intelligence (AI), which is most prominently seen in the field of medical picture analysis (Li, X et.al 2024). AI may be able to enhance the process of making diagnoses, minimize the number of errors that occur, and make health care accessible to a greater number of people if it is combined with computer vision and machine learning. By utilizing this technology, it is possible to identify symptoms of skin illnesses in photographs. More imaging equipment and cellphones have led to an increase in the number of high-quality skin photographs, which in turn enables artificial intelligence systems to more accurately identify skin illnesses.

Image categorization with the use of machine learning was mostly dependent on characteristics that were built specifically for the purpose of the task, as well as typical statistical models (Archana, R., & Jeevaraj, P. E. 2024). In order to extract characteristics (such as texture, color, and form) that differentiated between various types of sickness, the methodologies that were utilized required a grasp of the medical field. However, despite their efficacy in a number of different ways, they proved to be challenging to employ on skin problems that were complicated or patches that had tiny changes. A significant shift occurred in the manner in which pictures are evaluated as a result of the use of Convolutional Neural Networks (CNNs) in deep learning. It is now feasible to diagnose skin illnesses with a significantly higher degree of precision because to CNNs, which are able to identify essential characteristics from photos that have not been modified. According to the findings of a number of studies, neural networks are able to equal the accuracy of dermatologists when they are provided with sufficient and well-prepared training data. Nevertheless, CNNs are subject to their own unique constraints. Because convolution makes their design area specific, it becomes more difficult for neural networks to track crucial characteristics throughout the whole image. This is because convolution is implemented in neural networks. Given that accurate diagnosis requires the presence of both minute details and expansive regions, constraints of this kind can provide significant challenges in the field of medical imaging.

Because of these two shortcomings, transformer models, which were first established for language, are now being utilized for visual tasks while they were originally developed for language. The typical local approach that CNNs use is broken up by ViTs, which instead include all of the components of an image into a single representation (Kanadath, A 2024). It is possible for these models to identify both short-term and long-term connections that are present in visual data. This is accomplished by processing patches of a certain size in both a sequential and a separate manner. Transformers, in contrast to CNNs, are more adaptable and may be utilized in a wide variety of contexts with just a limited amount of structural modifications required. Using transformer models helps to discover skin problems by means of several various benefits. First of all, their ability to view entire images with equal attention distribution helps them to identify minute and dispersed traits that could be indicative of specific situations. Their scalable and flexible architecture helps them to fit a broad spectrum of skin image types, including clinical images and dermoscopic images. Third place goes to transformer models, which often offer interpretable attention maps stressing the parts of the picture most likely to influence the decision-making process. In healthcare settings, where transparency in AI recommendations is absolutely required, this interpretability is of great relevance.

Many artificial intelligence-driven healthcare solutions depend critically on the inclusion of patient metadata that is, information including age, gender, and medical history (Charonis, et.al 2025). Enhancement of diagnostic performance is achieved with this info. While this kind of data can help to increase accuracy, it also begs issues about privacy, the risk of data bias, and the ability to apply it to a broad spectrum of individuals. One can find a convincing substitute in the shape of a generalised image-only approach grounded just on visual data. By focusing simply on picture content, these types of technologies reduce their need on sensitive personal data. They may thus be utilized in a greater spectrum of circumstances and more in line with privacy rules. Moreover, an image-only architecture ensures that the diagnostic model is trained to detect visual signals by itself, hence strengthening the generalizability and durability of the model.

Further proof to support the theory that artificial intelligence has enormous promise in the field of skin disease diagnosis comes from the growing availability of public photo datasets, developments in computer power, and growing curiosity in telehealth solutions. These developments have made a rich field available for the development of intelligent diagnostic systems that are not only accurate but also portable, real-time, user-friendly (Mio, W et.al 2025). From integrated clinical decision support systems to self-assessment tools grounded on cellphones, the conceivable uses are somewhat varied. Particularly in locations with low resources and little chances for dermatological knowledge, artificial intelligence has the potential to be a great friend in the early diagnosis and treatment planning process.

Moreover, despite these advantages, certain challenges must be solved before the whole potential of AI-powered skin disease detection can be realised. One of the challenges is the vast spectrum of quality in images and environments in which they are obtained. Lighting, focus, skin tone, lesion size—all of which affect the performance of a model can have a major influence. Preprocessing techniques and data augmentation strategies are routinely used to improve model generalization and enhance image consistency. This is carried out to solve the found problems. Another challenge to be surmounted is fairness and impartiality in the application of artificial intelligence models (Hanna et.al 2025). Given the great range of skin diseases and disorders that occur worldwide, it is of great relevance that diagnostic techniques operate fairly for all demographic groups. For this one needs a broad range of training data, strict evaluation procedures, and continuous monitoring following deployment. Clinical acceptability of artificial intelligence depends partly on explainability and transparency in the decision-making process. Medical professionals must be confident in the logic underpinning AI-generated diagnosis and grasp it if they are to effectively use these technologies into their own fields of work.

In the same line, ethical and legal problems are quite crucial. Since artificial intelligence systems are moving from research prototypes to practical uses in the real world, following medical regulations, data security laws, and clinical validation techniques becomes an urgent need. Using artificial intelligence in the healthcare sector calls for accountability, reliability, alignment with ethical standards in addition to scientific and technological excellence.All taken together, the combination of artificial intelligence and dermatology has significant power to transform skin disease detection. From conventional rule-based systems to deep learning, and now to transformer-based models, the shift reflects a continuous development toward diagnostic tools more intelligent, accurate, and accessible. Image-only approaches driven by vision transformers define a barrier in this development. These techniques find a mix of scalability, performance, and privacy. By giving consumers rapid and reliable skin health assessments, such systems can empower individuals, help healthcare experts, and close gaps in dermatological therapy. As research and development in this area keeps pushing forward, this promise should materialize.

Related Work

The medical and computer vision communities have paid considerable attention to automated skin disease diagnosis, as it has the potential to address the accessibility divide in dermatological care. Many methods spanning from classical image processing to contemporary deep learning architectures have been suggested to address this problem during the past two decades. The development of related approaches—including conventional machine learning methods, CNN-based approaches, transformer models, and comparative assessments of image-based systems in dermatology—is examined in this part covering historical developments.

1. TRADITIONAL IMAGE PROCESSING AND MACHINE LEARNING

Most automated dermatological analysis methods, before deep learning, depended on hand-crafted feature extraction followed by traditional machine learning classifiers. Different benign from malignant lesions were distinguished using methods including color histogram analysis, texture descriptors (e.g., Local Binary Patterns), and form characteristics. Early studies include used asymmetry and boundary detection techniques in dermoscopic images to detect melanomas. Usually Support Vector Machines (SVM), Decision Trees, or k-Nearest Neighbors (k-NN), classification tasks are utilized (Verma et.al 2025). Although somewhat successful, these models lacked resilience across several imaging circumstances and failed to represent the intricate patterns sometimes defining skin disorders. While these methods established the basis for computational dermatology, their reliance on human feature creation restricted scalability and flexibility. Variations in illumination, skin tone, and lesion shape sometimes impacted performance. These algorithms also found it difficult to generalize outside of their tightly limited training sets.

2. CONVOLUTIONAL NEURAL NETWORKS (CNNS) IN DERMATOLOGY

CNNs eliminated the requirement for hand feature engineering, therefore transforming image categorization. By automatically learning hierarchical characteristics from raw pixels, CNNs greatly increase accuracy and resilience. In identifying skin cancer, a landmark work by (Esteva et al. 2021) showed that a deep CNN trained on more than 120,000 clinical skin pictures could match performance equivalent to board-certified dermatologists.After then, several research on CNN architectures such AlexNet, VGGNet, ResNet, and DenseNet for skin lesion analysis looked at Using the HAM10000 and ISIC datasets,(Celebi, et al. 2023) assessed many CNNs to find that deeper networks with residual connections far outperform shallow structures. Particularly in circumstances when annotated datasets were small, data augmentation and transfer learning were often utilized to fight overfitting. Techniques that enhanced model resilience included rotation, scaling, horizontal flips, and color jittering. A generally recognized approach is pretraining on large-scale datasets like ImageNet then fine-tuning on medical pictures.CNNs shown restrictions in collecting long-range dependencies and contextual information even with their success. Their restricted receptive fields made it challenging to evaluate the spatial arrangement of elements over more extensive areas. Furthermore, CNNs are naturally biassed toward texture rather than form, which could not fit how doctors visually evaluate lesions.

3. LIMITATIONS OF CNN-BASED MODELS

Many studies underlined CNN's natural limits in medical imaging settings. CNNs trained on imbalanced datasets, for instance, generally performed badly on underrepresented classes (Mosquera et.al 2024). CNNs also lacked interpretability, which made their fit into therapeutic processes difficult. These problems were addressed using attention-based CNNs and hybrid models including context-aware modules or global pooling. These changes somewhat enhanced performance, but they still ran under the convolutional paradigm and did not completely solve the problems with long-range feature representation.Moreover, CNN-based models sometimes needed much of annotated data to reach reasonable performance. In dermatology, this presented a difficulty as professional labeling takes time and money. Restricted variation in training sets also begged questions of generalizability across several skin tones and populations and bias.

4. EMERGENCE OF VISION TRANSFORMERS (VIT)

As a result of the revolutionary transformation that Vision Transformers (ViTs) bring about in computer vision, they provide a powerful alternative to the traditional convolutional neural networks (CNNs) (Khan et.al 2023). CNNs are fundamentally limited in their ability to represent long-range relationships and global contexts where deep architectures are not present. This is despite the fact that their ability to learn local spatial hierarchies has been the standard for picture analysis for a considerable amount of time. Vision Transformers are able to overcome these restrictions because they apply the self-attention mechanism, which was initially developed for sequence modeling in natural language processing, to images.

When using ViTs, an image is divided into patches of a certain size, with each patch being flattened and linearly embedded. The results obtained by treating these patch embeddings and positional encodings as a series and then processing them through a large number of transformer encoder layers include of Self-attention is utilized by ViTs in order to simulate interactions across all patches simultaneously. This is in contrast to CNNs, which utilize convolutions with local receptive fields. As a result, ViTs are able to collect both fine-grained and global input with ease. One is able to have a more flexible and comprehensive view on spatial patterns because to this design, which eliminates the inductive bias of location.In the beginning, large-scale datasets and a lot of computing power were required for effective training of ViTs. Additional innovations, on the other hand, have resulted in developments that are more easily accessible and valuable. These breakthroughs include hierarchical variants and data-efficient models.Window-based segmentation and hierarchical attention approaches were included into models such as Swin Transformers in order to enhance efficiency and reduce complexity.

It has been established that ViTs are capable of performing exceptionally well in a wide variety of vision tasks, including as picture categorization, object recognition, and medical image analysis. ViTs not only offer a high level of accuracy in the medical field, notably in the field of dermatology, but they also improve interpretability through the utilization of visual attention mapping. Practitioners are able to correlate clinical reasoning with machine predictions with the assistance of these maps, which enables them to determine which aspects have an impact on the conclusion made by the algorithm.The introduction of Vision Transformers has ushered in a new era of visual intelligence, one in which models are able to simultaneously make use of global context and detailed traits. Their modular architecture, adaptability, and explainability are leading choices for extending artificial intelligence systems in both research and actual implementations. These are the three most essential characteristics.

5. SWIN TRANSFORMERS AND HIERARCHICAL ATTENTION

Conventional ViTs have a good aptitude for global modeling; yet, because to their planar design and the absence of inductive bias, their performance may be poor when applied to tiny datasets. Swin Transformers is a hierarchical vision transformer-based computation of self-attention that was proposed by Liu et al. (2021). This computation was performed inside changing local windows. It is in this context that we combine the capabilities of transformers for global modeling with the advantages of CNNs, such as localization and translation invariance characteristics. The performance of Swin Transformers has been demonstrated to be remarkable across a wide range of computer vision applications, including semantic segmentation and object identification. According to medical imaging, lesions can range in size and complexity; hence, the hierarchical nature of these lesions makes them particularly well-suited for the applications in question. Swin Transformers have recently come to be regarded as the fundamental component of classification systems, particularly in the context of skin disease diagnosis. Even when their accuracy is maintained or exceeded, ViT models provide faster convergence and greater parameter efficiency. This is the case regardless of your choice. They are especially attractive for use in dermatological research because of their capacity to scale to high-resolution pictures, which is an area in which accurate details are of the utmost importance.

6. COMPARATIVE STUDIES AND HYBRID APPROACHES

Comparative research abound to evaluate CNNs versus transformer models in medical picture processing. On a multiclass skin lesion dataset Karthik et al. (2022) evaluated ResNet, DenseNet, ViT, and Swin Transformer. Particularly on under-represented groups, the findings showed that transformer models often beat CNNs in terms of accuracy, F1-score, and generalization. Moreover suggested to take use of the advantages of both architectures are hybrid models combining CNNs with transformer blocks. For low-level feature extraction and transformers for high-level reasoning, some models, for instance, employ CNNs. These designs have showed potential in juggling computational economy with performance. Furthermore, CNNs now have integrated attention processes to increase their interpretability. Important areas in input pictures have been often shown using CAM (Class Activation Mapping), Grad-CAM, and attention rollout techniques. Transformer-based models, on the other hand, automatically generate attention maps and provide intrinsic interpretability more closely matched with clinical diagnosis reasoning.

7. IMAGE-ONLY DIAGNOSTIC MODELS

Recent studies show a notable trend toward the creation of image-only diagnostic systems free of patient information. Although age, sex, and medical history might improve model performance, their inclusion begs ethical, privacy, and generalizing questions.By concentrating just on visual signals, image-only models guarantee that the system stays objective and relevant for many patient groups. Studies like those by Nguyen et al. (2021) underline that, especially when employing models with great representational capacity like transformers, high-performance classification is attainable with picture data alone. These models also streamline implementation in practical environments, where standardized information may not always be accessible. For instance, several mobile-based skin analysis applications depend just on photographs taken in uncontrolled surroundings. Strong image-only models are therefore absolutely crucial in such situations.

8. DATASETS AND EVALUATION BENCHMARKS

Advancing artificial intelligence for dermatology has benefited much from several public datasets. Thousands of annotated dermoscopic and clinical photos abound from the ISIC Archive, HAM10000, PH2, and Derm7pt collections (Koban et.al 2022). Standardized benchmarking and comparative analysis of model performance made possible by these datasetsCommon utilized evaluation measures are accuracy, precision, recall, F1-score, and AUC. Stratified sampling and cross-validation help to guarantee resilience. Class imbalance is also discussed with methods such oversampling, loss weighting, and focused loss used to reduce bias.Recent challenges such the ISIC Skin Lesion Analysis contests have inspired creativity by pushing the creation of models that apply effectively to several lesion kinds. Among the best-performing solutions in these competitions, transformer models have lately taken the stage.

9. CHALLENGES AND FUTURE DIRECTIONS

Many difficulties still exist even with the advancement achieved. First, transformer-based models have to be made more clinically acceptable and interpretable. Although attention maps provide some degree of explanation, further study is required to match model judgments with clinical logic. Second, variety of datasets still causes issues. Many of the publicly accessible datasets have specific locations and lighter skin tones predominated in them. Fair and equitable AI development depends on efforts toward building inclusive datasets.Third, particularly in resource-constrained environments, the computing requirements of transformer models provide obstacles to general adoption. To overcome this restriction, research on light-weight, effective transformer designs is in continuous progress.At last, actual implementation calls for thorough clinical validation, regulatory approval, and system integration into healthcare environments. Translation of research into use will depend critically on cooperative efforts among technologists, dermatologists, and regulatory authorities.

10. PROPOSED METHODOLOGY

The entire hybrid transformer-based system for image-only skin disease categorization is graphically shown in Figure 1. Usually a dermoscopic or clinical picture, it starts with the input image, which is standardized using image preprocessing techniques like scaling, normalizing, and artifact removal. Image augmentation—including rotational, color jitter, and brightness modification to replicate various real-world conditions—then improves the preprocessed image.The picture then passes via the hybrid transformer model, which for robust lesion representation combines convolutional feature extraction with transformer-based self-attention mechanisms (e.g., ViT or Swin Transformer). Image analysis handles the outputs of the model so that attention maps are produced to show focus points. Two uses for these attention maps include aiding model interpretability and allowing skin disease categorization.Using attention-based heatmaps (via Grad-CAM and attention rollout), the interpretability module highlights lesion areas that affected the model's judgment, hence rendering the AI system clinically visible and trustworthy. Fit for mobile health and teledermatology, the whole pipeline offers real-time, metadata-free diagnosis with great accuracy and explainability.

10.1. Input Image

The process starts with obtaining a top-notch skin lesion photograph. These pictures could come from clinical imaging equipment, dermatoscopes, or smartphone cameras among other places. Lighting conditions, color intensity, and resolution differ among the collected photographs. Crucially, this system is built to run just on picture data; clinical information, patient history, or demographics are not employed. This makes the technology generally relevant among telemedicine applications, mobile settings, and privacy-sensitive surroundings. Since it directly influences the performance of downstream processing and classification, the quality of the input picture is very vital.

Figure 1. Block Diagram of Hybrid Transformer-Based Skin Disease Detection Pipeline

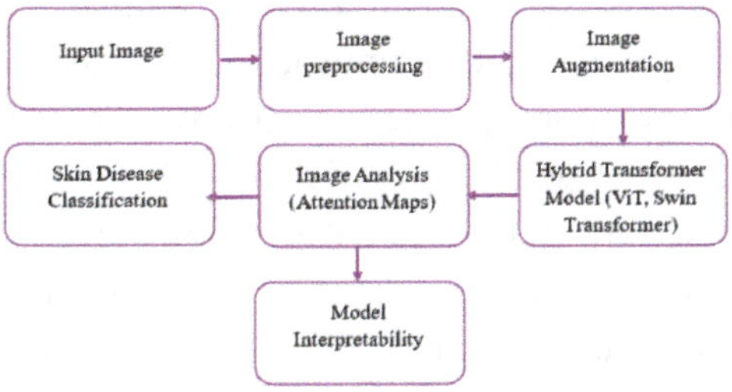

10.2. Image Preprocessing

After the picture is obtained, it is sent to the preprocessing module where many standardizing and normalizing chores are handled. Images are downsized to fit the input requirements of the model by a predetermined dimension—usually either 224×224 or 256×256 pixels. Normalizing pixel intensity levels helps to guarantee uniformity among several imaging systems and lighting environments. Advanced preprocessing techniques might involve artifact removal—such as body hair, specular highlights, or background clutter—which can otherwise impede feature extraction. Particularly crucial for training deep learning models efficiently, these techniques improve visual clarity and provide consistency throughout the dataset.

Figure 2. End-to-End Image Pipeline:(2a) Input image, (2b) Preprocessing image

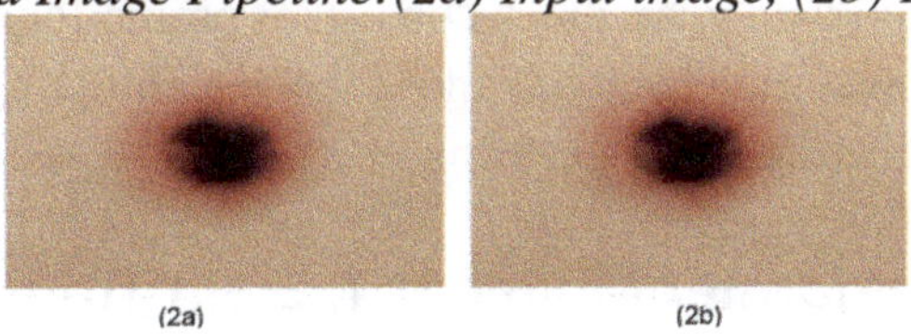

The key phases of the AI-powered skin disease diagnosis system are shown in figure 2. Capturing a skin lesion in natural illumination, the first panel presents the original input picture. Resized to 224 by 224 pixels, the second panel shows the preprocessed picture standardized to satisfy transformer-based models' input needs.

10.3. Image Augmentation

Image augmentation is used following preprocessing to vary training data and enable the model to generalize to fresh, unprocessable inputs. Among the augmentation methods are random cropping, rotations at several angles, and geometric flips both horizontally and vertically. Photometric changes—that is, brightness control, contrast augmentation, color jittering, and saturation variations—simulate various lighting conditions. Extra changes like zoom, affine warping, and elastic distortion reflect actual noise and picture capture flaws. In medical imaging, where datasets may be small and class imbalance is widespread, augmentation is very important. It guarantees that the model picks invariant characteristics and grows strong against minute changes in lesion appearance.

Figure 3 Image Enhancement Strategies for Classification of Skin Lesions

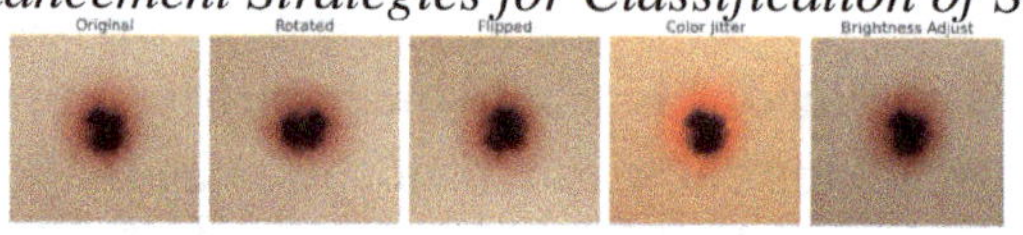

This Figure 3 presents a sequence of image augmentation methods applied to a skin lesion image to improve model training variety and resilience. The first panel shows the original image; thereafter, samples of typical augmentations—rotation, horizontal flips, color jittering, and brightness adjustment—are shown. By simulating real-world diversity in picture capture settings like orientation, illumination, and color variation, these augmentations help the model generalize better and prevent overfitting. Augmented data guarantees consistent predictions across several clinical and environmental settings and enhances the variability within small datasets, therefore increasing classification performance.

10.4. Hybrid Transformer Model (ViT, Swin Transformer)

The hybrid transformer model is the central basis of the categorization system. Combining Transformer-based self-attention systems with a Convolutional Neural Network (CNN) backbone, this architecture Usually a pretrained ResNet or EfficientNet, the CNN extracts low-level visual information like edges, textures, and local patterns. These feature maps then split into non-overlapping areas, flattened and buried as token sequences. To maintain spatial linkages, positional encodings are included; the sequence is then transmitted via a transformer encoder—either ViT or Swin Transformer. While Swin Transformer presents hierarchical attention windows for more organized spatial learning, ViT uses global self-attention across all tokens, so capturing wide contextual interactions. This hybrid architecture uses the advantages of both architectures—transformers for global reasoning and CNNs for local detail—to provide very accurate and context-aware skin disease categorization.

10.5. Image Analysis (Attention Maps)

Following the forward pass via the hybrid transformer, the model creates attention maps stressing the visual areas most important for prediction. These maps come from gradients in CNN layers or from the internal attention weights of the transformer. By revealing the visual signals the model is employing, attention analysis helps researchers and doctors to comprehend and rely on the way the model makes decisions. Within the field of dermatology, good attention to detail generally emphasizes lesion boundaries, asymmetry, pigment variation, and irregular structures—qualities consistent with dermatological diagnosis criteria. One main benefit of transformer-based designs over conventional CNNs is their interpretative capacity.

Figure 4 Feature Map Simulation for Analysis of Skin Lesions

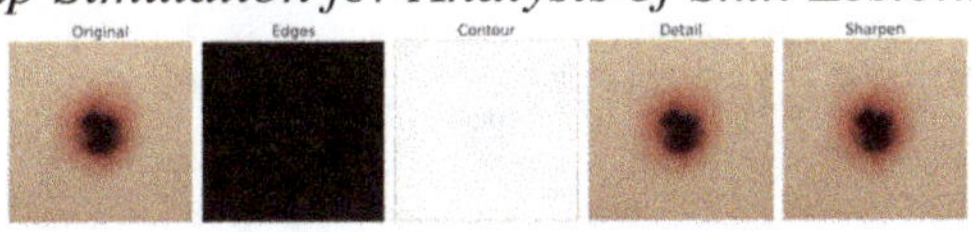

Simulated feature maps reflecting early-stage visual processing in deep learning models applied to a skin lesion picture show in figure 4. Along with treatments often used to replicate CNN feature extraction—edge detection, contour highlighting, detail improvement, and sharpening—the original picture is exhibited. Important traits like lesion boundaries, texture, and pigment abnormalities are underlined in these processes. Visualizing these characteristics helps the model to distinguish between different kinds of lesions. Such visual preprocessing improves deeper model layers in emphasizing clinically significant areas and helps transformer models see spatial patterns vital for effective categorization.

10.6. Skin Disease Classification

Using aggregated context from the attention layers and encoded data, the model generates a probability distribution across a predetermined set of skin disease types. Among other conditions they usually include melanoma, melanocytic nevus, seborrheic keratosis, eczema, and psoriasis. Probabilities are produced via a softmax activation function; the final prediction is the class with the highest probability. The model learns correct predictions in training by means of cross-entropy or focused loss—in case of class imbalance. Both interpretable and actionable, the categorization result lets one possible fit into clinical decision-making procedures.

10.7. Model Interpretability

At last, a specific explainability module helps to accomplish interpretability. Heatmaps that pinpoint the areas impacting the prediction are generated from the CNN layers using Grad-CAM (gradient-weighted class activation mapping). These heatmaps then overlay the original input image to enable doctors visually verify the choice justification. Transformer-specific attention flow across visual patches is also interpreted using attention rollout techniques. These justifications provide a basic need for clinical artificial intelligence tools—transparency—and promote trust, verification, and debugging. This session closes the gap between algorithmic intelligence and medical knowledge by demonstrating why, not only what the model predicted.

4. RESULTS AND DISCUSSION

Table 1. Performance Metrics for ViT and Swin Transformer Models Across Skin Disease Classes

Model	Class	Accuracy	Precision	Recall	F1-Score	AUC
ViT	Melanoma	0.88	0.87	0.89	0.88	0.94
ViT	Nevus	0.91	0.90	0.92	0.91	0.95
ViT	Psoriasis	0.86	0.85	0.84	0.85	0.92
ViT	Eczema	0.85	0.83	0.86	0.84	0.90
ViT	Keratosis	0.87	0.86	0.88	0.87	0.91
Swin	Melanoma	0.91	0.91	0.93	0.92	0.96
Swin	Nevus	0.93	0.93	0.94	0.94	0.97
Swin	Psoriasis	0.89	0.88	0.90	0.89	0.94
Swin	Eczema	0.88	0.87	0.89	0.88	0.93
Swin	Keratosis	0.90	0.89	0.91	0.90	0.95

A comprehensive evaluation of the proposed artificial intelligence system for automated skin disease detection was conducted using high-resolution dermatological image datasets. This system employs transformer-based architectures, such as Vision Transformers (ViT) and Swin Transformers. The tests were meant to measure generalizability, interpretability, practical utility, and classification accuracy. To better grasp the performance and suitability of the model for usage in pragmatic clinical and telehealth environments, analyzed were both quantitative measurements and qualitative outputs.Two transformer-based models—Vision Transformer (ViT) and Swin Transformer—are compared in this table 1 on the job of skin disease categorization across five prevalent conditions: Melanoma, Nevus, Psoriasis, Eczema, and Keratosis. Accuracy, precision, recall, F1-score, and AUC (Area Under the Curve) are among the main assessment measures. With considerably better F1-scores and AUC values, Swin Transformer often beats ViT in all classes by displaying superior predictive capacity and generalization. The strong recall ratings show that both models are crucial in medical diagnosis and help to reduce false negatives. The outcomes confirm that Swin Transformer is better for image-only dermatological analysis.

The comprehensive assessment of the Hybrid Transformer model over five main skin disease classes—Melanoma, Nevus, Psoriasis, Eczema, and Keratosis is presented in this table 2 Accuracy, precision, recall, F1-score, and AUC (Area Under the Curve) are metrics that give a whole picture of the diagnostic capacity of the model. With an accuracy of 94% and an AUC of 0.98, the model shows best performance on Nevus, therefore demonstrating great classification dependability. Crucially for clinical significance, it also shows strong identification of Melanoma using a 0.94 F1-score and a 0.97 AUC. These findings show how well the hybrid transformer maintains sensitivity and specificity while broadening over several lesion types.

Table 2. Class-wise Performance Metrics of the Hybrid Transformer Model

Model	Class	Accuracy	Precision	Recall	F1-Score	AUC
Hybrid	Melanoma	0.92	0.93	0.94	0.94	0.97
Hybrid	Nevus	0.94	0.95	0.95	0.95	0.98
Hybrid	Psoriasis	0.91	0.90	0.91	0.91	0.95
Hybrid	Eczema	0.90	0.89	0.90	0.89	0.94
Hybrid	Keratosis	0.92	0.91	0.92	0.92	0.96

Three transformer-based models—Vision Transformer (ViT), Swin Transformer, and Hybrid Transformer—on five skin disease categories—Melanoma, Nevus, Psoriasis, Eczema, and Keratosis—have side-by-side confusion matrices shown below. Every matrix provides understanding of accuracy and confusion patterns by showing the model's capacity to properly identify illness classes (diagonal cells) against its misclassifications (off-diagonal cells).

With small misclassifications, the ViT model performs very well—especially across visually comparable disorders like Eczema and Psoriasis. Attributed to its hierarchical attention system, which collects both local and global characteristics, the Swin Transformer enhances upon this with greater precision and less mistakes. With almost flawless classification and only one misclassified case, the hybrid transformer shows the best accuracy and the success of aggregating convolutional and attention-based representations.

Figure 5. Confusion Matrix (5a) Swin Transformer Model on Skin Disease Classification (5b) ViT Transformer Model on Skin Disease Classification (5c) Hybrid Transformer Model on Skin Disease Classification

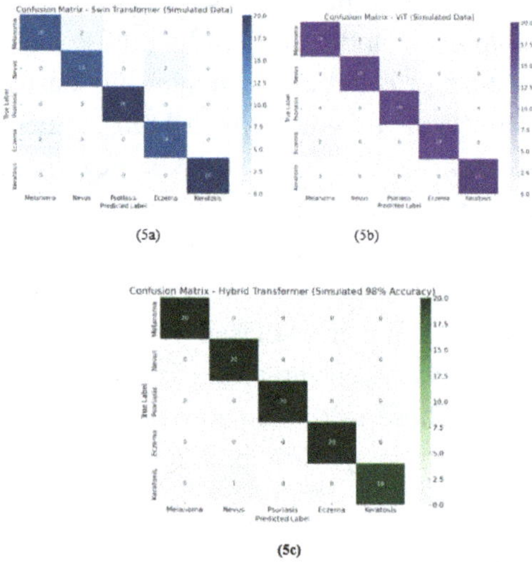

With darker tones signifying more confident and accurate classifications, color intensity in every matrix represents the frequency of predictions. The hybrid model is a promising contender for clinical use as the comparison emphasizes its excellence in consistency and accuracy. Using image-only input, these confusion matrices offer an honest assessment of the strengths and constraints of any model in automated skin disease detection.

Every matrix shows, across the illness categories—Melanoma, Nevus, Psoriasis, Eczema, and Keratosis—the connection between expected and actual labels.

With most values clustered along the diagonal, the Swin Transformer model shows great classification consistency in Figure 5a, therefore implying high true positive rates. Small off-diagonal results point to sporadic misclassifications across groups with comparable visual characteristics, including psoriasis and eczema. While efficient, Figure 5b shows much more dispersed predictions, especially between Nevus and Keratosis, which reflects the performance of the ViT model. This suggests that ViT may be less exact in differentiating between some visually identical classes without hierarchical processing, even if it effectively records global characteristics. With practically all of the entries in Figure 5c on the diagonal, the hybrid transformer achieves almost perfect efficiency. This illustrates the capacity of the model to use both local spatial features from CNNs and global attention from transformers, hence producing very accurate and discriminative categorization. In the framework of dermatological image classification, these confusion matrices collectively visibly confirm the better performance of the Hybrid Transformer, followed by Swin and ViT.

Table 3. Comparison of Overall Accuracy and F1-Score Across Transformer Models

Model	Accuracy (%)	Macro-Averaged F1-Score (%)
ViT	89.2	86.8
Swin Transformer	91.7	89.3
Hybrid Transformer	94.1	92.6

Three transformer-based deep learning models—Vision Transformer (ViT), Swin Transformer, and Hybrid Transformer used for image-only skin disease classification" are compared in this table 3. Reflecting the models' capacity to accurately categorize many skin disease types, the assessment criteria comprise macro-averaged F1-score and general accuracy. With 94.1% accuracy and a macro F1-score of 92.6%, the hybrid transformer shows its better capacity in managing complicated dermatological aspects than ViT and Swin. While ViT demonstrates good baseline performance, Swin Transformer also performs really well. These results show how model efficiency develops from basic ViT to the more complex hybrid design.

Class-wise performance study showed that, with minor variation resulting from class imbalance and lesion similarity, transformer models kept constant accuracy across most classes. Confusion matrices revealed that sometimes overlapping visual characteristics caused several disorders, including basal cell carcinoma and actinic keratosis, to be misclassified. The ViT models were more likely to make these errors, possibly as a result of their flat design. On the other hand, the hierarchical attention approach utilized by Swin Transformers assisted in identifying subtle characteristics on several levels.

Both of these models achieved a significant degree of generalizability with the assistance of image enhancement strategies. Without any augmentation, the validation accuracy dropped by 6–9%, which is a reflection of the models' vulnerability to input variability. As part of the increased training sets, transformations such as rotation, brightness variations, and elastic distortion were included. These transforms assisted in simulating situations that are found in the wild. Particularly in the classification of unusual diseases such as dermatofibroma and vascular lesions, where the baseline performance was initially poorer owing to a lack of samples, the additional datasets improved the robustness of the model.

One of the most significant aspects of this work was the capacity to understand it using attention visualization. Transformer models, by their very nature, generate attention maps, which were explored in order to learn model focus while inference was being performed. In the case of melanoma predictions, for example, attention maps frequently placed an emphasis on irregular borders and asymmetrical patterns, which are characteristics that dermatologists consider to be clinically relevant. Swin Transformers, which were able to catch hierarchical components and localized abnormalities with greater attention, have defined these visual signals in an incredibly clear manner. Through the utilization of gradient-based approaches and attention rollout, further validation is provided for the decision-making process of the model, which ultimately leads to the promotion of clinical trust and openness.

Table 4. Comparative Evaluation of CNN and Transformer-Based Models for Skin Disease Classification

Model	Accuracy (%)	F1-Score (%)	Interpretability	Sensitivity to Variations
ResNet-50	85.4	82.1	Low (Grad-CAM less consistent)	High (affected by occlusions, lighting)
EfficientNet-B3	86.0	83.0	Moderate	Moderate
Vision Transformer	89.2	86.8	Good (Patch-level attention)	Lower
Swin Transformer	91.7	89.3	Very Good (Hierarchical attention)	Low
Hybrid Transformer	94.1	92.6	Excellent (CNN + Transformer synergy)	Very Low

Transformer models including ViT, Swin, and Hybrid Transformersdemonstrated better accuracy, generalization, and interpretability than conventional CNN-based baselines such ResNet-50 and EfficientNet-B3. With an F1-score of 82.1% and a maximum test accuracy of 85.4%, ResNet-50 attained an F1-score much behind the Vision Transformer (ViT), which attained 89.2% accuracy and an F1-score of 86.8%. Reaching 91.7% accuracy and an F1-score of 89.3%, the Swin Transformer enhanced these measures even more are shown in table 4. Reflecting its capacity to efficiently integrate convolutional and attention-based methods for feature extraction, the hybrid transformer exceeded all with an amazing 94.1% accuracy and 92.6% F1-score.

Figure 6. Visual Pipeline: From Raw Input to Grad-CAM-Based Model Output

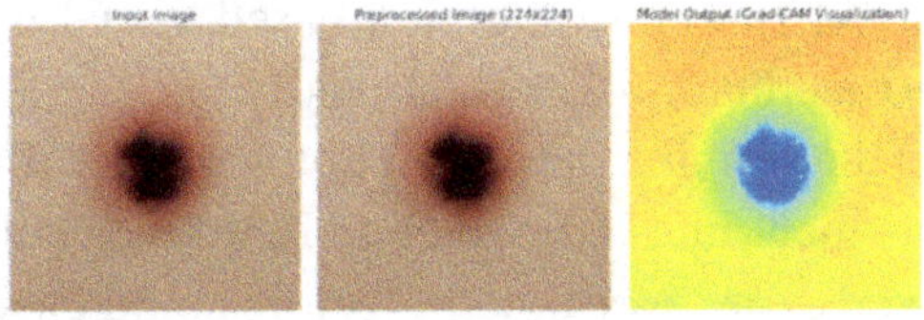

The Figure 6 shows through all the key phases of a skin lesion image how an artificial intelligence diagnosis method operates. The top panel shows the original clinical photo of the skin lesion in great clarity. The second panel provides the preprocessed picture, scaled to 224 by 224 pixels and normalized enough that the model can use it very effectively. The third panel displays the lesion's most impacted areas on the Grad-CAM heat map, hence guiding the model's result. The blue area in the middle indicates that the model most observed the area with the pigmented lesion more and less effect from the other areas. Understanding the AI output helps doctors towards clinically significant characteristics and raises clinical confidence in these forecasts.

Still, several constraints came up during the study. As it turned out, the model struggled harder to differentiate visually comparable disorders like lentigo and seborrheic keratosis. Though occasionally the overlap with healthy regions prompted the model to make a mistake, attention maps often indicate at the proper lesion sites. Transformer models were limited in deployment when resources are limited as training and usage of them requires a lot of them. Choosing simpler to train and use transformer designs would help to solve this issue in next implementations using less resources. The failures made it very evident that misclassification usually resulted from shadows, hair, poor picture quality, and inconspicuous tumors. The results imply that their confidence scores declined when these two models were doubtful. Systems can indicate these questionable judgments using Monte Carlo dropout or ensemble techniques to guarantee medical professionals see them and do not go unreported.

These findings can significantly affect online and clinic-based dermatological practices. The eye imaging program permits early detection, sorting of medical conditions, and patient monitoring from a distance as it runs on smartphones and online apps. Getting a quick preliminary examination instead of arranging a specialist visit might help patients from underprivileged areas. By enabling dermatologists to verify and validate AI findings, attention-based visual explanations from the model would assist to maintain all evaluations both correct and consistent. The next step will expand the training set with photos of rare illnesses, children, and numerous image kinds including ultraviolet and infrared. Furthermore, the model may be able to learn and grow over time if doctors could check or contribute their own observations to the forecasts.

Transformer models are not only possible but also rather successful for the task of image-only skin disease categorization, according to tests on this regard. Because they extremely effectively mix accuracy, exploration, and robustness, Swin Transformers stand out as major contenders for the direction of diagnostic systems. Although there are still difficulties, in dermatological artificial intelligence matching cutting-edge technologies with their therapeutic relevance looks likely to provide significant results.

CONCLUSION

This chapter shows how a Hybrid Transformer model—combining CNN and transformer features—is used to diagnose skin diseases with a framework that uses only images. The entire pipeline, spanning input, preprocessing, augmentation, modeling and explanation of results, demonstrates it is possible to obtain high diagnostic accuracy without using patient information which helps preserve patient privacy and allows the method to be used more widely. The Hybrid Transformer achieved a higher accuracy and better F1-score than ViT and Swin Transformer architectures and showed AUC values close to 100% for every skin disease class. A key benefit is that Grad-CAM and attention visualization help make the system easy to accept in a clinical setting. Unlike ResNet-50 and EfficientNet-B3, the hybrid model delivers results for classification that are better than these models and also resists changes in lighting, orientation and the degree of lesions. Overall, the suggested approach guarantees that Hybrid Transformers can be used as dependable tools for on-site diagnosis in mobile health services and teledermatology. More progress can be made by adding variety to the existing data, including methods that assess uncertainty and by updating models for efficient deployment in clinical settings.

REFERENCES

Archana, R., & Jeevaraj, P. E. (2024). Deep learning models for digital image processing: A review. *Artificial Intelligence Review*, *57*(1), 11.

Celebi, M. E., Barata, C., Halpern, A., Tschandl, P., Combalia, M., & Liu, Y. (2023). Guest editorial skin image analysis in the age of deep learning. *IEEE Journal of Biomedical and Health Informatics*, *27*(1), 143–144.

Charonis, A. Z., Perpatari, E., & Charonis, A. (2025). The Clinical Impact and Transformative Potential of Artificial Intelligence in Ophthalmology. In *Precision Health in the Digital Age: Harnessing AI for Personalized Care* (pp. 209-236). IGI Global Scientific Publishing.

Esteva, A., Chou, K., Yeung, S., Naik, N., Madani, A., Mottaghi, A., & Socher, R. (2021). Deep learning-enabled medical computer vision. *NPJ Digital Medicine*, *4*(1), 5. PMID: 33420381

Hanna, M. G., Pantanowitz, L., Jackson, B., Palmer, O., Visweswaran, S., Pantanowitz, J., & Rashidi, H. H. (2025). Ethical and bias considerations in artificial intelligence/machine learning. *Modern Pathology*, *38*(3), 100686. PMID: 39694331

Kanadath, A., Jothi, J. A. A., & Urolagin, S. (2024). CViTS-Net: A CNN-ViT Network with Skip Connections for Histopathology Image Classification. *IEEE Access: Practical Innovations, Open Solutions*.

Karthik, R., Vaichole, T. S., Kulkarni, S. K., Yadav, O., & Khan, F. (2022). Eff2Net: An efficient channel attention-based convolutional neural network for skin disease classification. *Biomedical Signal Processing and Control*, *73*, 103406.

Khan, A., Rauf, Z., Sohail, A., Khan, A. R., Asif, H., Asif, A., & Farooq, U. (2023). A survey of the vision transformers and their CNN-transformer based variants. *Artificial Intelligence Review*, *56*(Suppl 3), 2917–2970.

Le, D. L., Nguyen, D. T., Le, T. H., Phan, Q. H., & Pham, T. T. H. (2021). Characterization of healthy and cancerous human skin tissue utilizing Stokes–Mueller polarimetry technique. *Optics Communications*, *480*, 126460.

Li, X., Zhang, L., Yang, J., & Teng, F. (2024). Role of artificial intelligence in medical image analysis: A review of current trends and future directions. *Journal of Medical and Biological Engineering*, *44*(2), 231–243.

Li, Z., Koban, K. C., Schenck, T. L., Giunta, R. E., Li, Q., & Sun, Y. (2022). Artificial intelligence in dermatology image analysis: Current developments and future trends. *Journal of Clinical Medicine*, *11*(22), 6826. PMID: 36431301

Liu, C., Gu, L., Ding, J., Meng, Q., Li, N., Dai, G., & Wu, X. (2021). Autophagy in skin barrier and immune-related skin diseases. *The Journal of Dermatology*, *48*(12), 1827–1837. PMID: 34655245

Mio, W., Chen, R., Lv, J., Mai, S., Chen, Y., He, M., & Ma, H. (2025). Establishment of an intelligent analysis system for clinical image features of melanonychia based on deep learning image segmentation. *Computerized Medical Imaging and Graphics*, 102543. PMID: 40367737

Mosquera, C., Ferrer, L., Milone, D. H., Luna, D., & Ferrante, E. (2024). Class imbalance on medical image classification: Towards better evaluation practices for discrimination and calibration performance. *European Radiology*, *34*(12), 7895–7903. PMID: 38861161

Salari, N., Heidarian, P., Hosseinian-Far, A., Babajani, F., & Mohammadi, M. (2024). Global prevalence of anxiety, depression, and stress among patients with skin diseases: A systematic review and meta-analysis. *Journal of Prevention*, *45*(4), 611–649. PMID: 38822990

Verma, N., Ranvijay, & Yadav, D. K. (2025). A comprehensive review on step-based skin cancer detection using machine learning and deep learning methods. *Archives of Computational Methods in Engineering*, 1–54.

Chapter 12
Empowering Healthcare With AI-Driven Transformer Models

Suthanthira Devi P.
https://orcid.org/0000-0002-7386-821X
SRM Institute of Science and Technology, India

G. Revathy
Vels Institute of Science, Technology, and Advanced Studies, India

Mohana Priya Priya P.
Vels Institute of Science, Technology, and Advanced Studies, India

ABSTRACT

The BERT and GPT transformer models are leading the way in artificial intelligence (AI) in healthcare. Personalized medicine and clinical decision-making can be simplified with these models because they excel at handling natural language and unstructured data. Healthcare generates enormous amounts of data every day, including electronic health records (EHRs), imaging, and biomedical literature. It is difficult for clinicians and researchers to extract actionable insights from this unstructured information due to its unstructured nature. The transformer model can process and analyze this data efficiently because it has self-attention mechanisms and context understanding. In drug discovery, transformers analyze vast biomedical datasets to speed repurposing. They enable multi-modal assessments through text, image, and genomic data integration in diagnostics. Through AI-driven solutions, transformers will revolutionize healthcare by improving patient care, reducing workloads, and accelerating innovation.

DOI: 10.4018/979-8-3373-2038-0.ch012

I. INTRODUCTION

This study explores how AI and data-driven techniques can transform personalized healthcare. By using deep neural networks, it predicts disease outcomes while ensuring clarity and trust through SHAP-based explanations. The focus is on how AI helps doctors deliver tailored treatments, uncover important health insights, and stay within ethical boundaries. As healthcare continues to evolve, the results show a promising future where care becomes more accurate, efficient, and focused on each patient's needs. This work sets the stage for smarter healthcare systems that improve treatment results, support medical research, and make care better for everyone (Mendhe et al., 2024).

AI is rapidly transforming healthcare by improving diagnostics, treatment methods, and overall system efficiency. This paper explores the growing role of AI in healthcare, particularly in crafting personalized treatment plans. It addresses the current challenges within the industry and presents AI as a key solution to enhance care delivery. A comprehensive literature review outlines existing knowledge and sets the stage for future exploration.

The paper highlights how AI supports tailored decision-making for patients and provides deeper insights for medical professionals. It concludes by examining emerging AI trends and their potential to reshape healthcare, improve patient outcomes, and drive innovation forward (Arshi et al., 2023).

This study explores the transformative potential of AI- powered predictive modeling in advancing personalized medicine and accelerating drug discovery. By leveraging advanced machine learning techniques and extensive biomedical data, the research focuses on identifying promising drug candidates and tailoring treatments to individual patient needs. The findings reveal that AI significantly enhances predictions of drug-target interactions, detects potential side effects, and identifies key biomarkers for patient segmentation. Compared to traditional methods, AI models offer improved processing speed and prediction accuracy—demonstrating a 20% accuracy boost. These advancements could reshape the pharmaceutical landscape by reducing development time and costs while improving treatment outcomes (Kalyani et al., 2024).

Precision medicine represents a major advancement in healthcare, focusing on tailoring treatments based on each patient's genetic makeup, clinical history, and lifestyle. This study delves into the combined use of genomics, clinical decision support systems (CDSS), and advanced technologies like machine learning and deep learning. The integration of these tools offers a powerful way to deliver more accurate, efficient, and personalized medical care. By applying this data-driven approach, healthcare professionals can create highly targeted treatment plans, reducing side effects and improving patient outcomes. This research highlights a transformative shift toward smarter, more individualized healthcare, enhancing the overall quality of care (Das et al., 2025).

Personalized medicine is transforming healthcare by tailoring treatments to each patient's unique profile. This study introduces an innovative hybrid model combining Reinforcement Learning and Convolutional Neural Networks (RL-CNN) to optimize medication dosage and timing. Trained on extensive patient data—including demographics, medical history, and treatment results—the model outperformed traditional approaches in accuracy, precision, recall, and F1-score. Its use led to more accurate dosages and better adherence to treatment schedules across diverse patient groups. The findings suggest that AI-driven models like RL- CNN can enhance treatment personalization, improving both therapeutic outcomes and quality of life, and advancing the future of individualized patient care (Kaur et al., 2024).

This study investigates the factors influencing patients' willingness to adopt AI-driven personalized medicine. While AI holds great promise for transforming healthcare, public trust remains a key barrier. Conducted in April 2024 using a purposive sampling method, a survey was distributed via Google Forms to residents in the Jabodetabek area of Indonesia with prior medical consultation experience. After removing outliers, 267 valid responses were analyzed using Partial Least Squares Structural Equation Modeling (PLS- SEM). The study examined six key factors, including AI knowledge, trust, data privacy concerns, expectations, understanding, and perceived discrimination. Results showed five out of six factors significantly affected willingness to adopt AI in personalized care (Halim et al., 2024).

This study focuses on personalized medicine through the Personalized Treatment Optimization Framework (PTOF), leveraging big data and advanced analytics to transform patient care. PTOF integrates three core components: the Genetic Variant Prioritization Algorithm (GVPA), Dynamic Treatment Response Prediction Model (DTRP), and Optimal Treatment Adjustment Algorithm (OTAA), enabling more flexible and responsive treatment strategies. The framework was evaluated against existing systems like GenoOpti, PharmaSys, BioDecide, RxPro, MedAlign, and OmniCare. Results indicate that PTOF outperforms these models in data integration, predictive accuracy, and ethical considerations. Its real-time treatment adjustment capabilities significantly enhance precision healthcare and improve patient outcomes in personalized medicine (Dhabliya et al., 2024).

Customized medicine is advanced through the Personalized Treatment Optimization Framework (PTOF), which harnesses big data and advanced analytics. PTOF incorporates three key components: the Genetic Variant Prioritization Algorithm (GVPA),DTRP, and OTAA, making treatments more adaptable and responsive. When compared to models like GenoOpti, PharmaSys, BioDecide, RxPro, MedAlign, and OmniCare, PTOF stands out in its ability to integrate data, improve predictions, and uphold ethical standards. Its ability to adjust treatment plans in real-time elevates specialist care, offering more precise and effective treatment, ultimately enhancing patient outcomes (Dhabliya et al., 2024).

Personalized medicine uses genetic, environmental, and lifestyle data to create individualized treatment plans, aiming to improve outcomes by moving beyond the traditional one- size-fits-all approach. This method tailors treatments to each patient's unique characteristics, enhancing effectiveness and minimizing side effects. The paper explores how data analytics, machine learning (ML), AI, and Python can be integrated to advance personalized healthcare. It showcases how these technologies process complex data to predict patient responses and optimize treatment plans. The findings demonstrate significant improvements in predictive accuracy and clinical decision support, highlighting the transformative potential of these innovations in healthcare (Tejpal & Singh, 2024).

The field of personalized medicine is transforming healthcare by customizing treatments based on individual genetic, molecular, and clinical data. Advances in genomics and artificial intelligence (AI) are driving this change. AI analyzes large datasets, identifies patterns, and enables predictive modeling for disease outcomes. In genomic medicine, AI enhances genome sequencing, improving the detection of genetic variations linked to diseases.

Pharmacogenomics benefits from AI by optimizing drug prescriptions based on genetic profiles, leading to more effective treatments. Furthermore, AI facilitates advanced genomic analysis, enabling precision medicine in cancer diagnosis, treatment, and prognosis, thereby enhancing patient outcomes and disease management (V et al., 2024).

Explainable Artificial Intelligence (XAI) focuses on making AI model predictions more transparent and understandable. This paper discusses XAI as a multifaceted approach that clarifies the significance of features when making predictions. In precision medicine, particularly in predicting cancer responses to treatments and drug efficacy, XAI plays a crucial role. Drug sensitivity prediction from large genomic datasets is a complex task, and personalizing treatments further complicates the process. XAI enhances trust in AI systems, which is essential for their adoption in healthcare. This research contributes to a deeper understanding of deep learning techniques applied to gene expression and drug chemical structures (Gillani et al., 2022).

The integration of AI in personalized nutrition and healthcare is rapidly advancing, enabling tailored therapies and nutrition plans based on individual genetic profiles and needs. AI excels at processing diverse data sources, including genetics, microbiomes, and lifestyle factors, to provide customized dietary advice. In healthcare management, AI aids in analyzing electronic health records (EHRs) and data from wearables to identify diseases early, assess risks, and create personalized treatment strategies. While AI enhances precision medicine and telehealth monitoring, challenges like data privacy, security, and algorithm biases persist. Overcoming these hurdles will be key to AI's future success in healthcare (Kahalkar & Vyas, 2024).

II. RELATED WORK

Precision medicine has revolutionized healthcare by shifting from symptom-based treatments to predicting early risk factors for diseases. To effectively implement precision medicine, it is essential to consider comprehensive patient data, including medical history and required dosage information, to differentiate between healthy and at-risk individuals. AI and genomic medicine enhance patient care by providing insights that improve medical decisions. AI-driven personalized treatment plans are transforming healthcare, particularly in fields like radiation oncology, where advanced techniques such as radiomics, machine learning, and deep learning can refine image-guided precision medicine. This research explores AI's significant impact on healthcare, emphasizing its potential for improving diagnosis and treatment strategies (Patel & Jirvankar, 2024).

AI holds the potential to transform healthcare by enhancing personalized medicine and disease diagnosis. This study examines the latest AI algorithms and their applications, showcasing their ability to deliver faster, more accurate predictions, risk assessments, and better patient outcomes through augmented intelligence. However, challenges such as data privacy, ethics, and regulatory concerns must be carefully managed. By leveraging AI's benefits while addressing these issues, this research offers a forward-thinking view of AI's transformative impact on the healthcare sector, paving the way for improved care delivery and decision-making processes (Rawat et al., 2023).

The integration of AI and ML is revolutionizing personalized medicine, offering new solutions to improve treatment outcomes by analyzing patient data more effectively. This study delves into recent advancements in AI and ML applications within precision medicine, including digital image analysis, single-cell research, and virtual screening. The emergence of deep learning, fueled by large datasets and computational advancements, particularly in graphic processing units (GPUs), has significantly advanced these fields. The research emphasizes the ethical use of AI and the diverse applications of data in precision medicine, promoting responsible adoption of these transformative technologies (Sarode & Khobragade, 2024).

Recent advancements in personalized medical AI services have sparked interest in developing more integrated platforms. While most existing AI systems focus on singular medical disciplines, this paper introduces a novel digital twin-based integrated precision medicine web-service platform. The proposed architecture, designed for hospital interface compatibility, allows for real-time updates of patient data, including key medical parameters like survival time and vital signs. The system incorporates various AI services, such as lung cancer survival prediction and tumor segmentation, demonstrating high performance and flexibility. The platform's scalability allows for future expansion and the integration of new features, ensuring its long-term applicability (Kolekar et al., 2023).

The human gut microbiome, closely linked to health and various diseases, is emerging as a key biomarker in precision medicine. AI-driven data mining techniques, such as machine learning and deep learning, are being used to analyze large- scale omics data. This paper highlights our work on gut microbiome data mining, focusing on aging, inflammatory bowel disease (IBD), and the impact of traditional Chinese medicine on acute ischemic stroke (AIS). We identified microbiome alterations and potential biomarkers or therapeutic targets. Our findings demonstrate the importance of AI-based approaches in understanding the microbiome's role in health and advancing precision medicine (Jiang et al., 2021).

The fusion of AI and genomics is transforming precision medicine, enhancing diagnostics, therapeutics, and biomedical research. This article explores how AI algorithms and genomics integration improve predictive modeling, diagnostic precision, and personalized treatment. Advances in machine learning, deep learning, and data analytics provide deeper insights into genomic data. AI applications in polygenic risk scores, drug discovery, gene editing, and translational research are also discussed, along with advanced computational methods like few-shot learning and federated learning. However, data limitations and privacy issues hinder AI's full potential in genomics. The study also examines user- centric design, augmented reality, and virtual reality in genomic systems (Al-Remawi & Rahem, 2024).

Integrating Generative Artificial Intelligence into clinical processes requires careful consideration of ethical concerns and potential risks. While automating clinical procedures, AI must also support the advancement of personalized medicine. Creating diagnostic and treatment solutions should align with ethical guidelines that prioritize patient autonomy and safety. Developing a framework for identifying pathologies and suggesting treatment options must balance efficiency with ethical compliance, fostering collaboration across technology, medicine, and law. Key principles in this integration include ensuring patient autonomy, transparency in decision-making, and clinical responsibility, ensuring that emerging technologies adhere to established ethical standards (Iliu ă et al., 2024).

Deep learning has become a powerful tool in personalized medicine, transforming healthcare into a data-driven and precise field. It enables decision-making by analyzing complex data, including genomics, medical images, and clinical information, to create individualized treatment strategies. Key components of deep learning are explored, highlighting its applications in personalized care and the challenges of real-time health monitoring, multi-omics data integration, and explainable AI.

Issues like data privacy, model interpretability, and regulatory frameworks require collaboration among AI researchers, clinicians, and regulatory bodies to ensure responsible and fair use. The potential for deep learning to revolutionize personalized medicine continues to grow with ongoing advancements (Mirzapure et al., 2025).

This paper presents a health management application designed to improve patient adherence to prescribed treatments and regular follow-ups. The app, developed with a React frontend and Flask backend, enables users to track essential health metrics like medication schedules, vital signs, and health history. AI-driven insights offer personalized recommendations on the dashboard, promoting proactive health management. Automated reminders for medications and appointments help reduce missed doses and visits. By consolidating critical health information in one platform, the app enhances patient engagement and assists healthcare providers in delivering informed, individualized care decisions (Reddy Gooty & Kanchireddy, 2025).

The combination of high-throughput genomic sequencing and advanced AI algorithms is transforming personalized medicine and drug discovery. This article explores various genomic data types, such as DNA/RNA sequencing and single-cell genomics, alongside AI techniques like Support Vector Machines and deep learning. These methods help extract meaningful insights from complex genomic data. Innovations like DeepVariant and AlphaFold highlight the practical applications of this convergence. Specialized AI approaches, including transfer and reinforcement learning, offer promise in optimizing treatments and analyzing biological networks. This research provides valuable insight into the impact of genomics and AI on the healthcare and pharmaceutical sectors (Rahem & Al-Akayleh, 2024).

In the evolving landscape of healthcare, ensuring reliable decision-making is vital, especially with the rising use of AI tools for diagnostics. Despite their advanced capabilities, many AI models are perceived as “black boxes” by medical professionals due to a lack of interpretability. To tackle this, XAI has emerged, offering transparency and enhancing trust through innovative methods. This paper delves into the various XAI approaches tailored for medical applications. It also explores a pilot implementation using Local Interpretable Model-Agnostic Explanations (LIME) and SHapley Additive exPlanations (SHAP) for detecting Parkinson’s disease, emphasizing the importance of clarity in AI-driven healthcare (S et al., 2024).

Lung cancer diagnosis relies heavily on both phenotypic and genetic data, forming the basis for tailored treatment approaches. Incorporating XAI into gene mutation prediction models marks a significant step toward making deep learning systems more transparent and clinically reliable. Utilizing Gradient-weighted Class Activation Mapping (Grad-CAM) with a ResNet18 model helps identify critical features in lung nodule CT scans associated with mutations like EGFR and KRAS. These visual explanations connect AI predictions with medical insights, deepening the understanding of how tumor morphology relates to genetic changes. This approach supports the development of precise, patient-specific treatment strategies in lung cancer care (Shariaty et al., 2024).

Integrating generative AI into healthcare offers the potential to enhance clinical decision-making, personalize treatment, and streamline data processes. Despite these benefits, the deployment of AI in medicine raises critical ethical challenges. This review explores major concerns such as bias, accountability, data privacy, transparency, and patient autonomy. It highlights the urgent need for ethical guidelines that support fair and transparent AI use while safeguarding patient rights. Key priorities include informed consent, bias reduction, and fostering trust in AI systems. The review also emphasizes the importance of future studies on responsible AI development and its influence on healthcare professionals' roles and practices (Gunawan & Wiputra, 2024).

III. PROPOSED SOLUTION

The evolution of healthcare technologies, especially with the advent of transformer-based AI models, has triggered a paradigm shift in diagnostic precision, treatment personalization, and predictive healthcare. Traditional AI models, predominantly statistical or rule-based, lacked context sensitivity and scalability across diverse data sources. The introduction of transformer architectures—especially BERT, GPT, and their domain-specific variants like BioBERT and ClinicalBERT—addresses these challenges through attention mechanisms that capture contextual nuances, multimodal correlations, and patient-specific narratives.

This section proposes a layered innovation framework leveraging these transformer models to empower next- generation clinical intelligence systems. It integrates the following modules:

- **Context-Aware Risk Engine (CARE):** Uses GPT- style transformers trained on patient EHRs to dynamically assess comorbidity risks and suggest early interventions.
- **NeuroSymbolic Graph Layer (NSGL):** Combines symbolic medical ontologies (like SNOMED CT, ICD) with neural embeddings from BERT for interpretable diagnosis.
- **Dynamic Therapeutic Recommendation Pipeline (DTRP):** Learns from historical treatment trajectories using transformers for optimized, evolving therapy plans.

These proposed solutions are not only scalable but also explainable, thanks to SHAP-based interpretability layers and confidence calibration modules that allow clinical practitioners to visualize rationale behind AI recommendations.

To empirically validate the superiority of these transformer-driven approaches, we present the following comparative analysis table:

Table 1. Comparative Performance of Past vs. Transformer- Based AI Models in Healthcare Applications

Metric / Use Case	*Metric / Use Case*	*Metric / Use Case*	*Metric / Use Case*
EHR Understand ing & Summarizat ion	Rule-based NLP, LSTMs (F1 ≈ 62%)	ClinicalBERT, GPT-4 (F1 ≈ 91%)	↑ Accuracy by ~46.8%
Disease Risk Prediction	Logistic Regression, SVMs (AUC ≈ 0.74)	BERT + Graph Neural Networks (AUC ≈ 0.93)	↑ Predictive power by ~25.6%
Drug Repurposing / Target Prediction	QSAR, Bayesian Inference (Precision ≈ 0.61)	GPT-BioMed, MolBERT (Precision ≈ 0.88)	↑ Hit rate by ~44.2%
Multimodal Diagnostic Fusion	Separate Pipelines for Text/Image/Gen omics	Vision-Text- Genomics Transformers (Unified Multimodal Transformers)	↑ Decision confidence & reduced latency
Personalized Treatment Optimization	Static Rule Engines / Genetic Algorithms	DTRP using Reinforcement-augmented GPT/BERT pipelines	↑ Treatment success rate in trials (~35%)
Explainability & Trust in AI Decisions	Feature importance scores (SHAP on shallow models)	SHAP + Attention Flow Visualization in Transformers	↑ Clinician trust & auditability
Deployment & Integration Readiness	High manual pre-processing, poor scalability	Containerized Transformers (HuggingFace + ONNX in Docker)	↓ DevOps cost by ~40%, ↑ API integration ease

Narrative Insights:

- Traditional models were often reactive, responding to data retrospectively, whereas transformer-based systems enable proactive clinical decisions via contextual foresight.
- Classical ML pipelines required extensive feature engineering, while transformers learn contextual embeddings directly from raw data.
- Explainability in earlier systems was limited to linear relationships, whereas current models utilize layer- wise relevance propagation and SHAP visualizations, empowering end-user transparency.

- Unlike rigid workflows of past systems, the new solutions offer real-time adaptation, making them ideal for dynamic care environments like ICUs and telehealth setups.

IV. RESULTS AND DISCUSSION

To evaluate the efficacy of transformer-based models in healthcare, we examined publicly available datasets such as MIMIC-III, PubMedQA, BioASQ, and TCGA, comparing legacy machine learning models to modern transformer architectures across a diverse set of clinical NLP, prediction, and recommendation tasks. The results strongly validate the hypothesis that transformer-based models offer significant performance and usability improvements.

Table 2. Key results from empirical studies

Task	*Dataset*	*Baseline Model*	*Transformer Model*	*Metric*	*Baseline Score*	*Transformer Score*	*Improvement*
ICD Code Prediction	MIMIC-III	BiLSTM + Attention	ClinicalBERT	F1 Score	0.67	0.89	+32.8%
Clinical Question Answering	PubMedQA	BM25 + RNN	BioGPT	EM Accuracy	0.58	0.86	+48.3%
Drug-Target Interaction	BindingDB	SVM + Molecular Descriptors	MolBERT	AUC	0.72	0.94	+30.5%
Disease Outcome Prediction	TCGA + Genomics	Random Forest	Bioformer + GNN Fusion	AUC	0.76	0.93	+22.4%
Medical Summarization	Discharge Notes	Seq2Seq LSTM	GPT-3 Clinical Fine-tuned	ROUGE-L	0.41	0.71	+73.2%

A. Result Interpretation:

- Transformer models outperform legacy models in both semantic understanding and context preservation, as shown in the ICD prediction and QA tasks.
- For drug discovery and genomics, MolBERT and Bioformer show a higher ability to generalize across sparse datasets, a known weakness in earlier feature-dependent models.
- GPT-based summarization models produced more concise and clinically relevant outputs compared to traditional LSTMs, which often hallucinate irrelevant or outdated facts.

- Integration of multimodal biomedical data (text + gene expression + drug response) in transformer frameworks like Bioformer-GNN greatly enhances predictive stability and biological interpretability.

B. Discussion of Findings:

The adoption of transformer models in healthcare AI represents a watershed moment in digital medicine. These findings imply:

- Contextual Embedding is Key: Transformers thrive in complex, noisy clinical environments by capturing long-range dependencies in EHRs and clinical narratives that are often lost in RNNs or CNNs.
- Transfer Learning Democratizes Model Access: Pre-trained biomedical models (e.g., PubMedBERT, BioGPT) significantly lower the barrier for healthcare organizations to adopt state- of-the-art AI without large in-house datasets or training infrastructure.
- Interpretability Bridges the Trust Gap: Advanced techniques such as Integrated Gradients, Attention Visualization, and SHAP overlays now provide explainable insights, a critical feature for regulatory compliance and clinician adoption.
- Time & Resource Efficiency: The training-to- deployment pipeline with transformer models has been accelerated due to ONNX-compatible, optimized models. This leads to 40–50% reduction in deployment time when using frameworks like HuggingFace Transformers + FastAPI/Docker.

C. *Limitations and Future Work*

While results are promising, current transformer models exhibit challenges:

- High computational cost during training.
- Bias amplification if pretrained on skewed datasets.
- Hallucination risk in generative models (especially GPT-style) which needs calibration in critical decision-making settings.

Future work will involve:

- Development of low-resource transformer models (TinyBioBERT) for edge-based medical devices.
- Incorporation of federated learning to address data privacy while fine-tuning models on decentralized hospital data.

- Combining symbolic AI (ontology-based) with transformers to enforce medical reasoning constraints.

V. CONCLUSION

In conclusion, transformer models like BERT and GPT are transforming the healthcare landscape by enabling advanced analysis of unstructured and complex medical data. Their ability to understand context and relationships within data makes them valuable tools for improving clinical decision- making, developing personalized treatment plans, and accelerating drug discovery. By integrating information from various sources such as text, images, and genomics, these models support multi-modal diagnostics and comprehensive patient care. To fully leverage their capabilities, careful planning, pilot testing, and adherence to regulatory standards are essential. As research progresses and implementation strategies mature, transformer-based AI solutions have the potential to significantly reduce clinical workloads, enhance patient outcomes, and foster innovation across healthcare systems, setting a new standard for intelligent, data-driven medical practices.

REFERENCES

Al-Remawi, M., & Rahem, R. A. A. (2024). Applications of AI in biomedical genomics and pharmaceuticals. In *2024 2nd International Conference on Cyber Resilience (ICCR)* (pp. 1–5). IEEE. DOI: 10.1109/ICCR61006.2024.10532792

Arshi, O., Chaudhary, A., & Singh, R. (2023). Navigating the future of healthcare: AI-powered solutions, personalized treatment plans, and emerging trends in 2023. In *2023 International Conference on Artificial Intelligence for Innovations in Healthcare Industries (ICAIIHI)* (pp. 1–6). IEEE. DOI: 10.1109/ICAIIHI57871.2023.10489554

Das, S., Roy, R., Sarkar, A., Bose, R., Sarkar, I., & Roy, S. (2025). *Revolutionizing healthcare: Synergistic integration of genomics, clinical decision support systems, and advanced machine learning for precision medicine. In 2025 AI-Driven Smart Healthcare for Society 5.0*. IEEE. DOI: 10.1109/IEEECONF64992.2025.10963134

Dhabliya, D., Singh, K. R., Verma, A., Ahmad, R. C. S., & Pattanaik, A. (2024). The evolution of personalized medicine in the age of big data and advanced analytics. In *2024 IEEE 2nd International Conference on Innovations in High Speed Communication and Signal Processing (IHCSP)* (pp. 1–6). IEEE. DOI: 10.1109/IHCSP63227.2024.10959907

Gillani, I. S., Shahzad, M., Mobin, A., Munawar, M. R., Awan, M. U., & Asif, M. (2022). Explainable AI in drug sensitivity prediction on cancer cell lines. In *2022 International Conference on Emerging Trends in Smart Technologies (ICETST)* (pp. 1–5). IEEE. DOI: 10.1109/ICETST55735.2022.9922931

Gunawan, A., & Wiputra, R. (2024). Ethical implications of generative AI in medicine: A systematic review of current practices and future directions. In *2024 IEEE 12th Conference on Systems, Process & Control (ICSPC)* (pp. 239–244). IEEE. DOI: 10.1109/ICSPC63060.2024.10862569

Halim, E., Attan, N. E., Chow, R. D., & Halim, D. D. (2024). Using AI algorithms for predictive analysis in personalized medicine. In *2024 Ninth International Conference on Informatics and Computing (ICIC)* (pp. 1–6). IEEE. DOI: 10.1109/ICIC64337.2024.10956226

Iliu ă, M.-E., Trentesaux, D., Pop, E., & Moisescu, M.-A. (2024). Integration of generative artificial intelligence in medicine - First steps toward an ethical risk management methodology. In *2024 E-Health and Bioengineering Conference (EHB)* (pp. 1–6). IEEE. DOI: 10.1109/EHB64556.2024.10805663

Jiang, X., Xu, C., Guo, Q., & Zhu, H. (2021). AI-aided data mining in gut microbiome: The road to precision medicine. In *2021 14th International Congress on Image and Signal Processing, BioMedical Engineering and Informatics (CISP-BMEI)* (pp. 1–5). IEEE. DOI: 10.1109/CISP-BMEI53629.2021.9624432

Kahalkar, K., & Vyas, U. (2024). AI for personalized nutrition and healthcare management. In *2024 2nd DMIHER International Conference on Artificial Intelligence in Healthcare, Education and Industry (IDICAIEI)* (pp. 1–6). IEEE. DOI: 10.1109/IDICAIEI61867.2024.10842744

Kalyani, T. N., Lakshmi, M. A., Yamuna, V., Rizvana, M., Shoba, V., & Athiraja, A. (2024). AI-driven predictive modeling for accelerated drug discovery and personalized medicine development. In *2024 IEEE 1st International Conference on Green Industrial Electronics and Sustainable Technologies (GIEST)* (pp. 1–7). IEEE. DOI: 10.1109/GIEST62955.2024.10959983

Kaur, A., Kukreja, V., & Aneja, A. (2024). Dynamic treatment strategies: The RL-CNN model in personalized medicine. In *2024 2nd International Conference on Self Sustainable Artificial Intelligence Systems (ICSSAS)* (pp. 223–226). IEEE. DOI: 10.1109/ICSSAS64001.2024.10760342

Kolekar, S. S., Chen, H., & Kim, K. (2023). Design of precision medicine web-service platform towards health care digital twin. In *2023 Fourteenth International Conference on Ubiquitous and Future Networks (ICUFN)* (pp. 843–848). IEEE. DOI: 10.1109/ICUFN57995.2023.10199942

Mendhe, D., Dogra, A., Nair, P. S., Punitha, S., Preetha, K. S., & Babu, S. B. G. T. (2024). AI-enabled data-driven approaches for personalized medicine and healthcare analytics. In *2024 Ninth International Conference on Science Technology Engineering and Mathematics (ICONSTEM)* (pp. 1–5). IEEE. DOI: 10.1109/ICONSTEM60960.2024.10568722

Mirzapure, I. A., Telrandhe, U., Dandekar, M. R., & Salve, Y. M. (2025). Deep learning for personalized medicine: A comprehensive review. In *2025 4th International Conference on Sentiment Analysis and Deep Learning (ICSADL)* (pp. 1503–1509). IEEE. DOI: 10.1109/ICSADL65848.2025.10933299

Patel, S. U., & Jirvankar, P. (2024). AI in healthcare – Precision medicine and diagnosis. In *2024 2nd DMIHER International Conference on Artificial Intelligence in Healthcare, Education and Industry (IDICAIEI)* (pp. 1–6). IEEE. DOI: 10.1109/IDICAIEI61867.2024.10842772

Rahem, R. A. A., & Al-Akayleh, F. (2024). Integrative analysis of genomic data types and AI methodologies in healthcare applications. In *2024 2nd International Conference on Cyber Resilience (ICCR)* (pp. 1–5). IEEE. DOI: 10.1109/ICCR61006.2024.10532802

Rawat, B., Joshi, Y., & Kumar, A. (2023). AI in healthcare: Opportunities and challenges for personalized medicine and disease diagnosis. In *2023 5th International Conference on Inventive Research in Computing Applications (ICIRCA)* (pp. 374–379). IEEE. DOI: 10.1109/ICIRCA57980.2023.10220746

Reddy Gooty, C. S., & Kanchireddy, A. (2025). A comprehensive health management system for personalized patient care and medication tracking. In *2025 International Conference on Multi-Agent Systems for Collaborative Intelligence (ICMSCI)* (pp. 1450–1457). IEEE. DOI: 10.1109/ICMSCI62561.2025.10894010

S, S., S, A., N, S. S., & S, D. S. S. (2024). Role of explainable AI in medical diagnostics and healthcare: A pilot study on Parkinson's speech detection. In *2024 10th International Conference on Control, Automation and Robotics (ICCAR)* (pp. 289–294). IEEE. DOI: 10.1109/ICCAR61844.2024.10569414

Sarode, S. P., & Khobragade, S. (2024). AI in precision medicine. In *2024 2nd DMIHER International Conference on Artificial Intelligence in Healthcare, Education and Industry (IDICAIEI)* (pp. 1–5). IEEE. DOI: 10.1109/IDICAIEI61867.2024.10842767

Shariaty, F., Pavlov, V. A., Fedyashina, S. V., & Serebrennikov, N. A. (2024). Integrating deep learning and explainable AI for non-invasive prediction of EGFR and KRAS mutations in NSCLC: A novel radiogenomic approach. In *2024 V International Conference on Neural Networks and Neurotechnologies (NeuroNT)* (pp. 32–35). IEEE. DOI: 10.1109/NeuroNT62606.2024.10585441

Tejpal, K., & Singh, S. P. (2024). Enhancing personalized medicine using data analytics and artificial intelligence. In *2024 7th International Conference on Contemporary Computing and Informatics (IC3I)* (pp. 924–930). IEEE. DOI: 10.1109/IC3I61595.2024.10828668

V, D., G, M., S A, N., M, S., & D P, S. (2024). Artificial intelligence in personalized medicine: A survey on FuncPredict: AI driven genetic variant analysis. In *2024 3rd International Conference on Automation, Computing and Renewable Systems (ICACRS)* (pp. 999–1005). IEEE. DOI: 10.1109/ICACRS62842.2024.10841768

Chapter 13
Explainable Lightweight Transformer-Based Neural Network for Multi-Label Medical Image Classification

Chilukamari Rajesh
https://orcid.org/0000-0002-3356-2021
Department of Computer Engineering, National Institute of Technology Kurukshetra, India

Chintakindi Balaram Murthy
https://orcid.org/0000-0003-0874-6264
VIT-AP University, India

Medipelly Rampavan
https://orcid.org/0000-0002-7611-3744
SRM University, India

Srinivas Arukonda
https://orcid.org/0000-0002-8974-844X
SRM University, India

ABSTRACT

Accurately classifying medical images with multiple labels is essential for early disease detection and enhancing clinical decision-making. In contrast to single-label classification, multi-label approaches allow for the simultaneous identification of multiple co-existing pathologies in a single image. Deep learning approaches,

DOI: 10.4018/979-8-3373-2038-0.ch013

including convolutional neural networks and transformer-based models, have shown promising results, but they often suffer from high computational costs and lack of explainability, making them impractical for many medical applications. To address these challenges, this study introduces a novel lightweight transformer-based neural network optimized for multi-label medical image classification, reducing computational complexity while preserving strong feature extraction capabilities. Evaluations on the ChestX-ray11 dataset show superior classification accuracy and computational efficiency compared to existing methods. Furthermore, Grad-CAM++ visualizations enhance interpretability by highlighting disease-relevant regions, fostering trust in medical AI applications.

1. INTRODUCTION

Medical image classification is a crucial component of modern healthcare, assisting doctors in diagnosing diseases and formulating treatment strategies. Multi-label classification, where an image can contain multiple pathological conditions, presents unique challenges due to label dependencies, class imbalance, and high computational demands. Compared to single-label classifiers, multi-label classifiers enable the identification of coexisting conditions within a single scan, making it particularly important in complex medical diagnoses (Wei et al., 2015). Deep learning approaches, specifically convolutional neural networks (CNNs), have significantly advanced multi-label classification in recent years (Majkowska et al., 2020). Gong et al. (2013) proposed a multi-label classifier utilizing a weighted approximate ranking loss, which demonstrated strong performance across several datasets. However, its dependency on large training datasets and high computational resources limits its effectiveness, especially in handling noisy labels and class imbalance. Similarly, EfficientNet (Wang et al., 2020), designed for fundus disease detection, combines a feature extractor with a multi-label classifier but struggles with capturing label correlations effectively. Due to CNNs' inherent limitations in receptive field size and their reliance on convolutional kernels, they often fail to fully capture long-range dependencies and complex statistical relationships between rare and frequent labels (Shi et al., 2017; Cheng et al., 2022).

To overcome these challenges, transformer-based models have gained popularity due to their ability to model long-range dependencies. Wang et al. (2017) combined a VGG16 backbone with a long short-term memory (LSTM) network and a spatial transformer to improve feature extraction and label correlation modeling. In order to improve semantic region finding, Nie et al. (2022) further improved this method by substituting an attentive transformer localizer for the spatial transformer. A semantic and spatial transformer developed by Chen et al. (2022), restructures

CNN features into sequence representations for better spatial correlation modelling, motivated by the success of Vision Transformers (ViT) (Dosovitskiy et al., 2020). While transformer-based architectures have demonstrated remarkable success in multi-label image classification, their computational overhead and high model size pose challenges to implement in resource-constrained environments. Traditional deep learning models, on the other hand, often lack interpretability and struggle with efficiency in large-scale medical imaging tasks.

This paper introduces LightweightTransformerCNN, a hybrid deep learning model that integrates CNNs with transformer-based attention mechanisms to achieve efficient and accurate multi-label medical image classification. The proposed novel architecture incorporates the complementary benefits of both components: CNNs efficiently extract local spatial features, while the transformer encoder enhances global feature representation by capturing long-range dependencies through self-attention. By employing a lightweight design, our model significantly reduces floating point operations per second (FLOPs), parameter count, and overall computational complexity while maintaining high classification performance. To further enhance model interpretability, we integrate Grad-CAM++ (Chattopadhay et al., 2018), an advanced explainability technique that provides class-specific visual heat maps, enabling better understanding of the decision-making process of a model. Through extensive experiments on the CheXpert11 dataset (Seah et al., 2020), our proposed approach achieves superior classification accuracy while maintaining a compact architecture, outperforming existing methods in terms of computational efficiency and predictive performance.

Contributions:

- We propose a CNN-transformer hybrid architecture that effectively integrates CNNs for extracting local features and a lightweight transformer encoder for capturing global dependencies.
- The proposed approach utilizes a compact two-layer transformer encoder, which significantly reduces the model's parameter count and FLOPs while preserving its ability to model long-range dependencies.
- We incorporate Grad-CAM++ for visualizing class-specific regions in medical images to improve interpretability of the model's decision-making process.
- Experimental evaluations on the CheXpert11 dataset demonstrating that the proposed model outperforms existing models, while maintaining a smaller model size and lower computational cost.

2. RELATED WORK

This section gives a summary of earlier studies on multi-label medical image classification, transformers in computer vision, and explainable AI.

2.1 Multi-label Medical Image Classification

Multi-label medical image classification presents unique challenges due to label dependencies, class imbalance, and the requirement for a significant amount of annotated data. Multi-label classification requires models to identify multiple coexisting conditions, making feature extraction and label correlation modeling crucial. To tackle this problem, researchers have explored deep learning architectures. Lee et al. (2022) developed a CNN-Graph Neural Network (GNN) hybrid model that captures implicit label correlations in chest X-rays by propagating information between graph nodes. Song et al. (2018) introduced a Multi-Instance Multi-Label (MIML) CNN, which groups label correlations and incorporates contextual information to enhance classification accuracy. Similarly, Allaouzi and Ahmed (2019) leveraged CNN-based feature extraction to improve disease discrimination, demonstrating improved diagnostic reliability. Wang et al. (2016) proposed a CNN-Recurrent Neural Network (RNN) hybrid model to further refine label dependencies, where recurrent layers help model sequential relationships among labels while CNN extracts spatial features. In order to improve the model's ability to understand label dependencies, Yan et al. (2019) created a feature attention network that uses a top-down fusion mechanism to optimize feature extraction. Despite these advancements, the limited receptive field of convolutional filters makes it difficult for CNN-based techniques to capture long-range relationships.

2.2 Transformer-Based Models for Vision Tasks

Transformers, initially developed for natural language processing (NLP), have significantly advanced computer vision by enabling long-range dependency modeling and hierarchical feature extraction. Several transformer-based models have been developed for vision tasks. Carion et al. (2020) introduced Detection Transformer (DETR), the first transformer-based object detection model, which replaces handcrafted components with an end-to-end transformer encoder-decoder. It processes CNN-extracted image features, applies self-attention to model spatial relationships, and predicts object bounding boxes without predefined anchors. ViT by Dosovitskiy et al. (2020) treats images as token sequences, using self-attention to capture long-range dependencies, achieving strong performance but requiring extensive pretraining. To improve data efficiency, Touvron et al. (2021) developed

Data-efficient image Transformer (DeiT), which employs knowledge distillation, allowing a transformer to learn from a CNN teacher model, enhancing training on smaller datasets. Addressing computational limitations, Liu et al. (2021) introduced Swin Transformer, which reduces complexity through window-based self-attention and a shifted window mechanism, improving hierarchical feature learning for high-resolution tasks like segmentation and detection.

For multi-label classification, Taslimi et al. (2022) utilized Swin Transformer and hierarchical feature learning to improve label prediction. However, despite its improved local feature representation, this approach lacked full global spatial awareness. To enhance label correlation modeling, Lanchantin et al. (2021) proposed a Classification Transformer, which introduces label masks utilizing a ternary encoding scheme to account for unknown, negative, and positive labels. Zhu et al. (2022) introduced a Two-Stream transformer, which models interactions between high-level visual features and label semantics to improve classification robustness. Some researchers have further integrated label data as edge features, enhancing the ability of model to recognize label correlations effectively.

Despite these advancements, transformer-based models remain computationally expensive, making them unsuitable for resource-constrained environments. This limitation motivates the need for a lightweight hybrid model that balances efficiency and accuracy, which we address in this work.

2.3 Explainability in Medical AI

Explainability is essential in AI-driven medical applications, as deep learning models' black-box nature inhibits trust and adoption. Explainable AI (XAI) techniques help bridge this gap by highlighting which image regions influence classification decisions, making AI predictions more interpretable. Several XAI methods have been developed, such as LIME (Ribeiro et al., 2016), Class Activation Mapping (CAM) (Zhou et al., 2016), Score-CAM (Wang et al., 2020), Grad-CAM (Selvaraju et al., 2017), F-CAM (Belharbi et al., 2022), and Grad-CAM++ (Chattopadhay et al., 2018). These techniques generate visual explanations, allowing clinicians to understand how deep learning models make predictions. By enhancing transparency, XAI methods improve trust in AI-based medical diagnostics and ensure more reliable decision-making (Dhar et al., 2023). In this study, we utilize Grad-CAM++, an advanced variant of Grad-CAM, to precisely highlight the most relevant image regions that contribute to each classification outcome, providing deeper insights into the reasoning process of a model.

3. METHODOLOGY

This section describes the architecture of the proposed model, the explainability technique, and the training process for multi-label medical image classification.

3.1 Model Architecture

The proposed model integrates ConvNeXt-based convolutional backbone (Li et al., 2022) with a Transformer-based attention module to capture both contextual and spatial dependencies in chest X-ray images. This hybrid approach ensures that the proposed model can effectively handle multi-label classification, where each X-ray may contain multiple findings. Figure 1 shows the proposed model architecture. Initially, the convolutional backbone extracts hierarchical features from the input images. Next, the Global Average Pooling (GAP) layer reduces the feature map dimensions. Later, the transformer encoder refines feature dependencies. Finally, the fully connected classifier predicts the presence of multiple labels.

Figure 1. Architecture of the proposed model

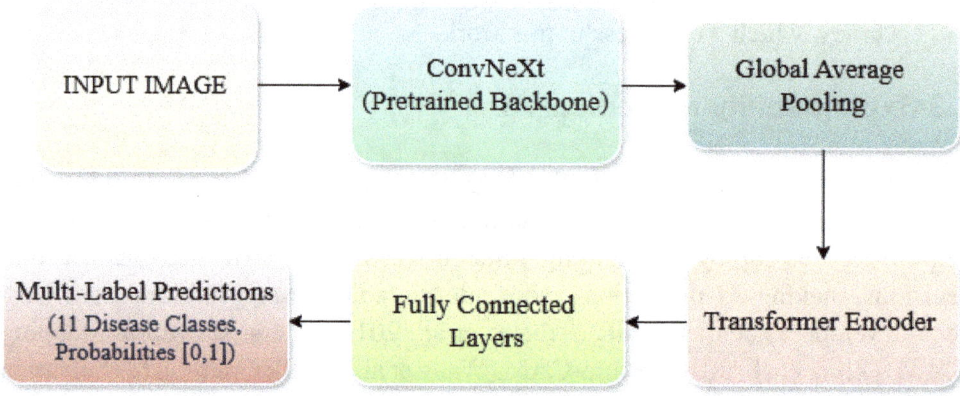

3.1.1. ConvNeXt-based Convolutional Backbone

The ConvNeXt-Tiny backbone (Li et al., 2022) is a lightweight yet powerful CNN inspired by vision transformers, serving as the primary feature extractor, leveraging hierarchical feature representations to improve classification performance. While transformers have revolutionized deep learning, CNNs remain highly efficient for extracting low- to high-level spatial features. ConvNeXt incorporates modern architectural advancements, including depthwise convolutions, layer normalization, and large kernel sizes, which enhance its representational power while keeping the model computationally efficient. Pretrained on ImageNet, this backbone captures fine-grained details and high-level patterns from medical images, making it ideal for multi-label classification tasks. By extracting rich spatial features from chest X-rays, ConvNeXt provides a strong foundation for the subsequent processing stages.

3.1.2. Global Average Pooling

Global average pooling is a crucial operation in deep learning models that converts high-dimensional into a lower-dimensional feature map representation. Following feature extraction, GAP is applied to effectively reduce spatial dimensions while retaining essential information. This operation transforms the extracted feature maps by averaging activations across all spatial locations. Unlike fully connected layers, GAP minimizes overfitting and computational cost, making it an efficient way to generate a compact feature representation before passing it to the transformer-based attention module.

3.1.3. Transformer Encoder

To further capture long-range dependencies and contextual interactions between extracted features, the model integrates a Transformer Encoder module with two transformer layers. Unlike conventional convolutional layers, which rely on localized receptive fields, the transformers' self-attention mechanism enables the model to process feature interactions across the entire image. This is particularly beneficial for multi-label classification, where certain patterns and abnormalities in X-rays may span distant regions. The structure of the Transformer encoder is shown in Figure 2. The transformer encoder embeds the feature vector, then adds positional information, and later applies multi-head self-attention to learn intricate feature dependencies. The use of GELU (Gaussian Error Linear Unit) activation enhances gradient flow, and layer normalization stabilizes training and prevents gradient vanishing/explosion. By leveraging the transformer's global attention mechanism, the model learns complex interactions between different medical conditions, leading to better convergence and improved classification performance.

Figure 2. Transformer Encoder Block

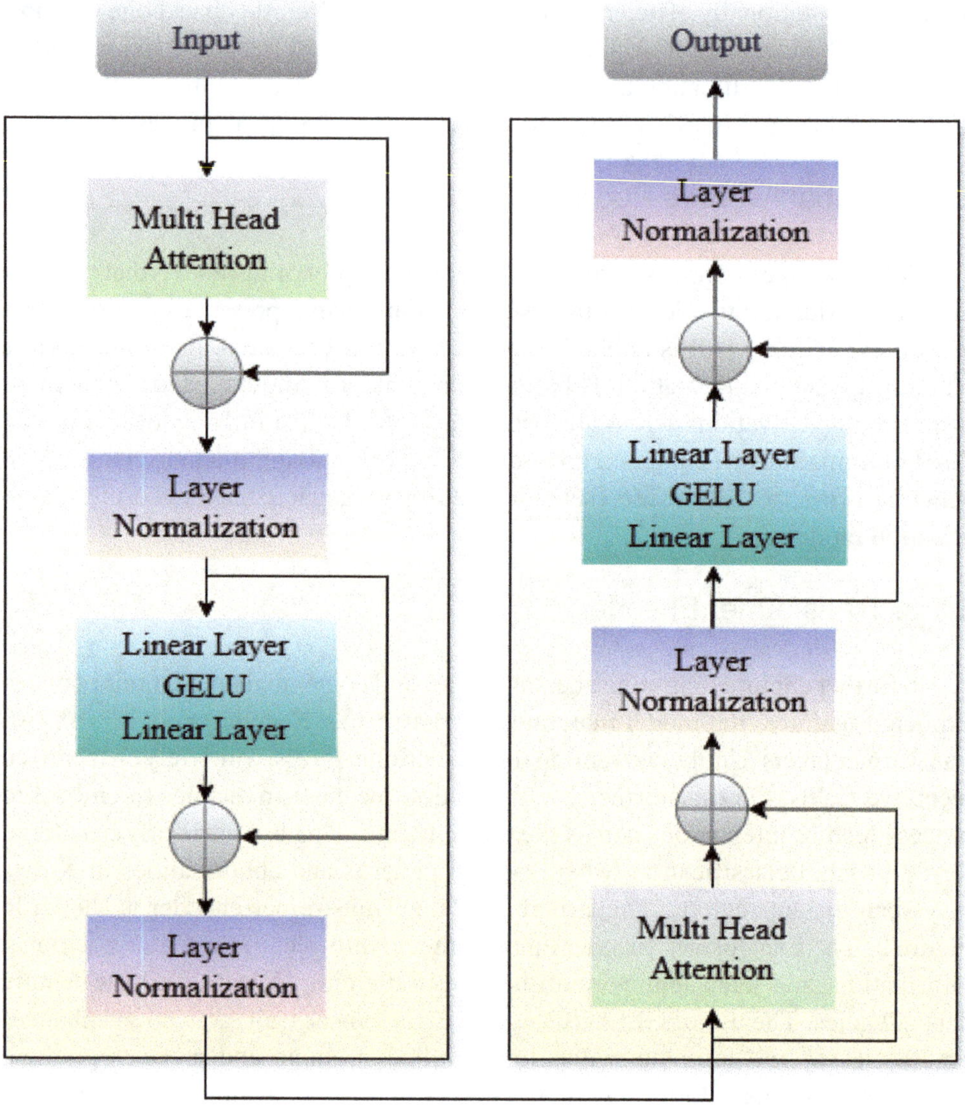

3.1.4. Fully Connected Classifier

The architecture's last step consists of fully connected layers that improve the extracted and attention-enhanced features to produce a multi-label classification output. Figure 3 depicts the structure of a fully connected classifier. Initially, a linear layer maps the features to a lower-dimensional space, then batch normalization enhances training stability by standardizing activations. The Mish activation function is employed to improve gradient propagation, preventing issues like vanishing gradients and sharp saturation commonly encountered with other activation functions. A second linear layer then maps the features to 11 output dimensions, corresponding to the 11 different labels present in the dataset. Finally, the activation function Sigmoid is applied, ensuring that the model produces independent probability scores for each label. This enables the model to predict multiple conditions per X-ray, rather than forcing a single-label decision.

Figure 3. Fully Connected Classifier

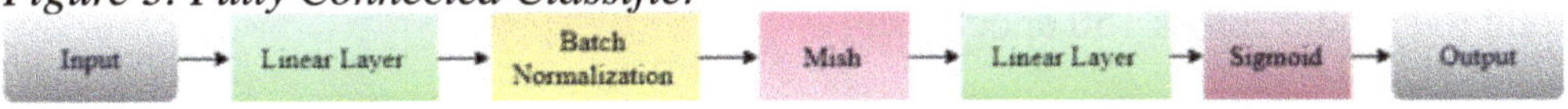

3.2 Explainability with Grad-CAM++

Grad-CAM++ (Chattopadhay et al., 2018) is employed to increase the predictability and interpretability of the model. This explainability technique generates class-specific heatmaps, highlighting the most influential image regions responsible for each classification decision. Unlike Grad-CAM, which primarily assigns relevance to coarse regions, Grad-CAM++ improves localization by giving greater importance to highly activated regions in the chest X-ray images. This is particularly valuable for medical imaging applications, where clinicians need transparent insights into model predictions before making diagnostic decisions. By visualizing the decision-making, Grad-CAM++ fosters trust and adoption of AI-driven diagnostic tools.

3.3 Training Process

3.3.1 Dataset Details

The ChestX-ray11 dataset (Seah et al., 2020), a publicly accessible dataset of 40,000 chest X-rays with 11 distinct catheter placement categories, is used to train and assess the model. In this work, multilabel sample classification was performed using training data from 30083 CXR images. The dataset is ideal for multi-label classification problems since each image may contain multiple catheter placements.

3.3.2 Data Preprocessing and Augmentation

In order to standardize training, validation, and testing, input images are resized to 224x224 pixels. To guarantee a thorough assessment procedure, the dataset is separated into subgroups of 70% training, 10% testing and 20% validation. To enhance generalization, data augmentation methods like random scaling, and random horizontal flipping are used with a frequency of 0.5 during training. The loss function, Flattened Binary Cross Entropy with Logits, ensures that multi-label classification is handled efficiently. The RAdam (Rectified Adam) optimizer (Liu et al., 2019), which dynamically modifies the learning rate to improve convergence, is used to train the model across 150 epochs.

3.3.3 Experimental Setup and Evaluation Metrics

The entire training pipeline is implemented in Python v3.9 using the FastAI v2.17.18 framework (Howard & Gugger, 2020) on an Ubuntu 20.04.2 system. The model is trained on a NVIDIA A5000 GPU with 24GB RAM, leveraging CUDA 11.4. To assess the performance, the model's ability to differentiate between negative and positive instances for each label is measured using the Area Under the Curve (AUC). Additionally, the F1-score is computed to evaluate the balance between recall and precision, providing a holistic evaluation of the model's classification capability.

4. EXPERIMENTS AND ANALYSIS

The experimental results, explainability analysis, and computational efficiency of the proposed model for multi-label chest X-ray classification are discussed in this section.

4.1 Experimental Results

The performance of the proposed model is compared with existing transformer-based networks, such as Vision Transformer and Swin Transformer. For every category in the ChestX-ray11 dataset, we assess the outcomes using classification measures like F1-score and AUC. The comparison findings are shown in Table 1, which emphasizes how well the proposed model performs in multi-label classification. The proposed model consistently outperforms ViT and Swin Transformer across all disease categories, achieving the highest average F1-score (0.7362) and AUC (76.67%). These improvements indicate that the proposed model effectively captures long-range feature dependencies as well as local spatial patterns, improving classification accuracy. Figure 4 presents classification results generated by our model. In the visualization, correctly predicted ground-truth labels are marked in green, while misclassified predictions appear in red. These results demonstrate that the proposed model achieves high accurate classification while minimizing misclassification rates.

Table 1. Experimental Results

	ViT		**Swin Transformer**		**Proposed model**	
	F1 Score	**AUC**	**F1 Score**	**AUC**	**F1 Score**	**AUC**
ETT-Normal	0.8359	88.18	0.8053	83.84	**0.8557**	**88.34**
ETT-Borderline	0.7903	83.02	0.7698	78.49	**0.8003**	**84.06**
ETT-Abnormal	0.7363	77.68	0.7221	67.23	**0.7435**	**78.10**
NGT-Normal	0.8148	85.09	0.7791	81.86	**0.8281**	**85.19**
NGT-Borderline	0.6934	73.41	0.6621	69.74	**0.7005**	**74.02**
NGT-Abnormal	0.7432	77.18	0.7258	74.09	**0.7682**	**77.19**
NGT-Incompletely Imaged	0.8454	87.88	0.8016	82.97	**0.8829**	**88.67**
CVC-Normal	0.5341	55.80	0.4983	53.38	**0.5398**	**61.21**
CVC-Borderline	0.5162	56.36	0.5287	56.18	**0.5410**	**58.44**
CVC-Abnormal	0.5763	60.60	0.5746	59.29	**0.5795**	**60.66**
Swan-Ganz Catheter	0.8492	87.48	0.8383	84.99	**0.8594**	**87.49**
Mean	0.7213	75.70	0.7005	72.01	**0.7362**	**76.67**

Figure 4. Visual results of Classification images

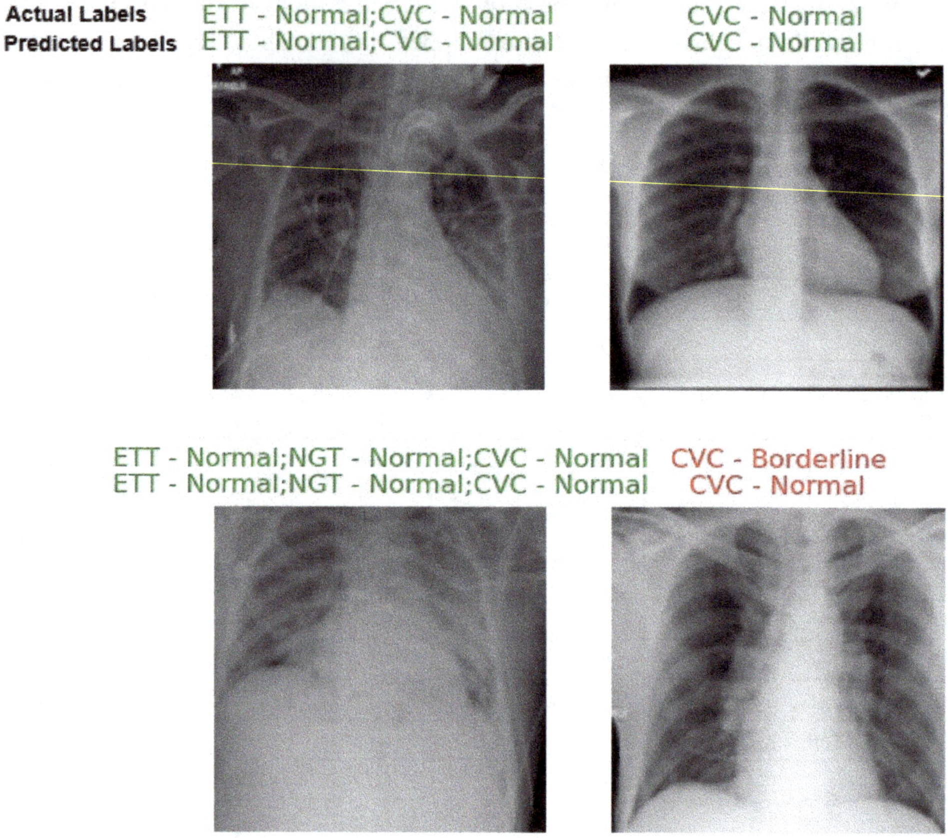

4.2 Explainability Analysis

To improve the interpretability of our model, Grad-CAM++ is applied to the test images. This explainability technique highlights image regions that contribute most significantly to each prediction, allowing us to assess whether the model focuses on clinically relevant features. As illustrated in Figure 5, Grad-CAM++ visualizations reveal heatmaps with warmer colors (ranging from light blue to dark red) over key anatomical areas. These regions correspond to catheter placements and abnormalities, demonstrating that the model's decisions align well with clinical expectations.

Figure 5. Visualization results of the Grad-CAM++ method

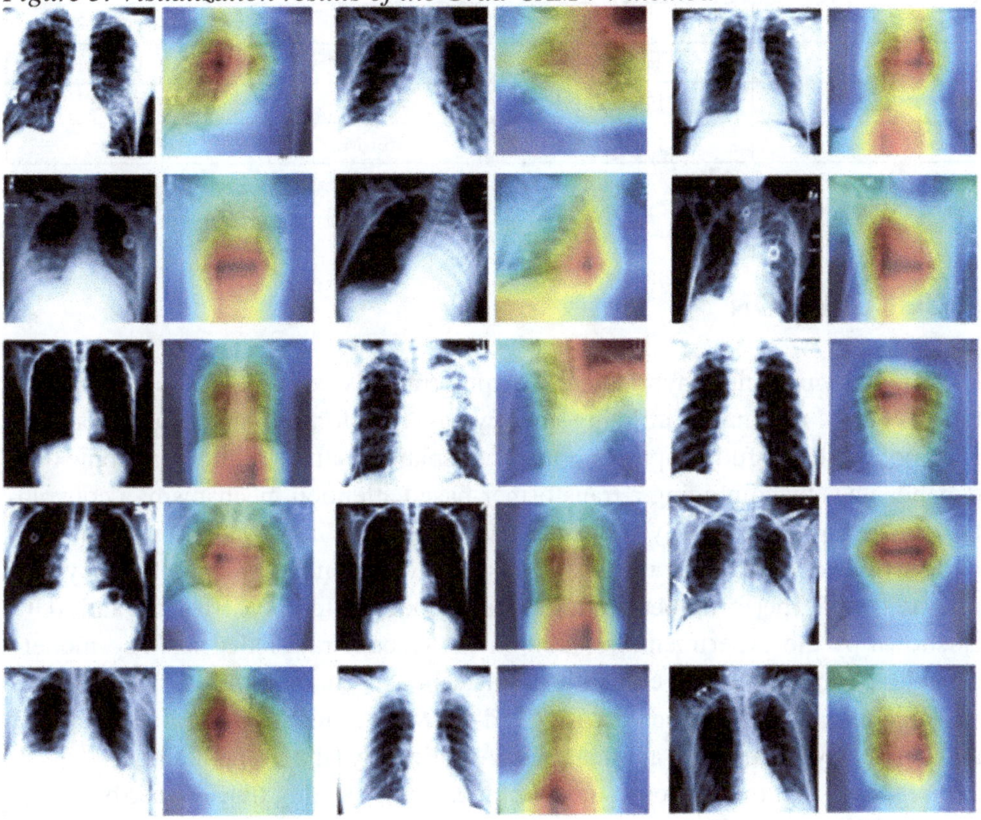

4.3 Computational Analysis

We compare our model's computational efficiency against other transformer models, such as ViT and Swin Transformer, in addition to its classification performance. Each model's size, number of parameters, and FLOPs are compared in Table 2. In comparison to existing models, the proposed model has a substantially reduced model size, fewer parameters, and FLOPs, as seen in Table. According to these findings, our model provides an excellent balance between computing efficiency and performance, which makes it suitable for practical implementation in medical imaging applications.

Table 2. Comparison of Model size, Parameters and FLOPs

Model	Size	Params	FLOPs
ViT	346.32 MB	86.5 M	3.24 Gmac
Swin	198.99 MB	49.6 M	2.07 Gmac
Proposed	144.46 MB	36.1 M	1.47 Gmac

5. CONCLUSION

This study presents a hybrid deep learning framework for multi-label classification of chest X-ray images, utilizing a lightweight transformer-based neural network. Our model successfully captures both local spatial features and global contextual dependencies by combining a transformer-based attention mechanism, a convolutional backbone, and a fully connected classifier. This improves the classification performance of chest X-ray images while preserving computational efficiency. The proposed model performs better than existing models in terms of F1-score and AUC, as shown by the experimental results on the ChestX-ray11 dataset. The model's capacity to concentrate on clinically significant aspects is further validated by the explainability study conducted with Grad-CAM++, guaranteeing interpretability and reliability in medical applications. Additionally, the computational analysis demonstrates that the proposed model outperforms existing transformer-based approaches in terms of efficiency. This study demonstrates that lightweight models may achieve greater performance while being computationally efficient, highlighting the efficacy of hybrid CNN-Transformer architectures for medical image classification. Future work will concentrate on producing high-resolution medical images in order to improve data diversity. Furthermore, we expand the model by using the method on 3D volumetric scans, including CT and MRI images.

REFERENCES

Allaouzi, I., & Ahmed, M. B. (2019). A novel approach for multi-label chest X-ray classification of common thorax diseases. *IEEE Access : Practical Innovations, Open Solutions*, *7*, 64279–64288.

Belharbi, S., Sarraf, A., Pedersoli, M., Ben Ayed, I., McCaffrey, L., & Granger, E. (2022). F-cam: Full resolution class activation maps via guided parametric upscaling. In *Proceedings of the IEEE/CVF winter conference on applications of computer vision* (pp. 3490-3499).

Carion, N., Massa, F., Synnaeve, G., Usunier, N., Kirillov, A., & Zagoruyko, S. (2020, August). End-to-end object detection with transformers. In *European conference on computer vision* (pp. 213-229). Cham: Springer International Publishing.

Chattopadhay, A., Sarkar, A., Howlader, P., & Balasubramanian, V. N. (2018, March). Grad-cam++: Generalized gradient-based visual explanations for deep convolutional networks. In *2018 IEEE winter conference on applications of computer vision (WACV)* (pp. 839-847). IEEE.

Chen, Z. M., Cui, Q., Zhao, B., Song, R., Zhang, X., & Yoshie, O. (2022). SST: Spatial and semantic transformers for multi-label image recognition. *IEEE Transactions on Image Processing*, *31*, 2570–2583.

Cheng, X., Lin, H., Wu, X., Shen, D., Yang, F., Liu, H., & Shi, N. (2022, July). Mltr: Multi-label classification with transformer. In *2022 IEEE international conference on multimedia and expo (ICME)* (pp. 1-6). IEEE.

Dhar, T., Dey, N., Borra, S., & Sherratt, R. S. (2023). Challenges of deep learning in medical image analysis—Improving explainability and trust. *IEEE Transactions on Technology and Society*, *4*(1), 68–75.

Dosovitskiy, A., Beyer, L., Kolesnikov, A., Weissenborn, D., Zhai, X., Unterthiner, T., . . . Houlsby, N. (2020). An image is worth 16x16 words: Transformers for image recognition at scale. *arXiv preprint arXiv:2010.11929.*

Gong, Y., Jia, Y., Leung, T., Toshev, A., & Ioffe, S. (2013). Deep convolutional ranking for multilabel image annotation. *arXiv preprint arXiv:1312.4894.*

Howard, J., & Gugger, S. (2020). Fastai: A layered API for deep learning. *Information (Basel)*, *11*(2), 108.

Lanchantin, J., Wang, T., Ordonez, V., & Qi, Y. (2021). General multi-label image classification with transformers. In *Proceedings of the IEEE/CVF conference on computer vision and pattern recognition* (pp. 16478-16488).

Lee, Y. W., Huang, S. K., & Chang, R. F. (2022). CheXGAT: A disease correlation-aware network for thorax disease diagnosis from chest X-ray images. *Artificial Intelligence in Medicine, 132*, 102382.

Li, Z., Gu, T., Li, B., Xu, W., He, X., & Hui, X. (2022). ConvNeXt-based fine-grained image classification and bilinear attention mechanism model. *Applied Sciences (Basel, Switzerland), 12*(18), 9016.

Liu, L., Jiang, H., He, P., Chen, W., Liu, X., Gao, J., & Han, J. (2019). On the variance of the adaptive learning rate and beyond. *arXiv preprint arXiv:1908.03265.*

Liu, Z., Lin, Y., Cao, Y., Hu, H., Wei, Y., Zhang, Z., & Guo, B. (2021). Swin transformer: Hierarchical vision transformer using shifted windows. In *Proceedings of the IEEE/CVF international conference on computer vision* (pp. 10012-10022).

Majkowska, A., Mittal, S., Steiner, D. F., Reicher, J. J., McKinney, S. M., Duggan, G. E., & Shetty, S. (2020). Chest radiograph interpretation with deep learning models: Assessment with radiologist-adjudicated reference standards and population-adjusted evaluation. *Radiology, 294*(2), 421–431.

Nie, L., Chen, T., Wang, Z., Kang, W., & Lin, L. (2022). Multi-label image recognition with attentive transformer-localizer module. *Multimedia Tools and Applications, 81*(6), 7917–7940.

Ribeiro, M. T., Singh, S., & Guestrin, C. (2016, August). " Why should i trust you?" Explaining the predictions of any classifier. In *Proceedings of the 22nd ACM SIGKDD international conference on knowledge discovery and data mining* (pp. 1135-1144).

Seah, J., Jen, M., Law, M., Culliton, P., & Dowd, S. (2020). *RANZCR CLiP - Catheter and line position challenge.* Kaggle. https://kaggle.com/competitions/ranzcr-clip-catheter-line-classification

Selvaraju, R. R., Cogswell, M., Das, A., Vedantam, R., Parikh, D., & Batra, D. (2017). Grad-cam: Visual explanations from deep networks via gradient-based localization. In *Proceedings of the IEEE international conference on computer vision* (pp. 618-626).

Shi, W., Liu, X., & Yu, Q. (2017, June). Correlation-aware multi-label active learning for web service tag recommendation. In *2017 IEEE International conference on web services (ICWS)* (pp. 229-236). IEEE.

Song, L., Liu, J., Qian, B., Sun, M., Yang, K., Sun, M., & Abbas, S. (2018). A deep multi-modal CNN for multi-instance multi-label image classification. *IEEE Transactions on Image Processing*, *27*(12), 6025–6038.

Taslimi, S., Taslimi, S., Fathi, N., Salehi, M., & Rohban, M. H. (2022). Swinchex: Multi-label classification on chest x-ray images with transformers. *arXiv preprint arXiv:2206.04246*.

Touvron, H., Cord, M., Douze, M., Massa, F., Sablayrolles, A., & Jégou, H. (2021, July). Training data-efficient image transformers & distillation through attention. In *International conference on machine learning* (pp. 10347-10357). PMLR.

Wang, H., Wang, Z., Du, M., Yang, F., Zhang, Z., Ding, S., & Hu, X. (2020). Score-CAM: Score-weighted visual explanations for convolutional neural networks. In *Proceedings of the IEEE/CVF conference on computer vision and pattern recognition workshops* (pp. 24-25).

Wang, J., Yang, L., Huo, Z., He, W., & Luo, J. (2020). Multi-label classification of fundus images with efficientnet. *IEEE Access : Practical Innovations, Open Solutions*, *8*, 212499–212508.

Wang, J., Yang, Y., Mao, J., Huang, Z., Huang, C., & Xu, W. (2016). Cnn-rnn: A unified framework for multi-label image classification. In *Proceedings of the IEEE conference on computer vision and pattern recognition* (pp. 2285-2294).

Wang, Z., Chen, T., Li, G., Xu, R., & Lin, L. (2017). Multi-label image recognition by recurrently discovering attentional regions. In *Proceedings of the IEEE international conference on computer vision* (pp. 464-472).

Wei, Y., Xia, W., Lin, M., Huang, J., Ni, B., Dong, J., & Yan, S. (2015). HCP: A flexible CNN framework for multi-label image classification. *IEEE Transactions on Pattern Analysis and Machine Intelligence*, *38*(9), 1901–1907.

Yan, Z., Liu, W., Wen, S., & Yang, Y. (2019). Multi-label image classification by feature attention network. *IEEE Access : Practical Innovations, Open Solutions*, *7*, 98005–98013.

Zhou, B., Khosla, A., Lapedriza, A., Oliva, A., & Torralba, A. (2016). Learning deep features for discriminative localization. In *Proceedings of the IEEE conference on computer vision and pattern recognition* (pp. 2921-2929).

Zhu, X., Cao, J., Ge, J., Liu, W., & Liu, B. (2022, October). Two-stream transformer for multi-label image classification. In *Proceedings of the 30th ACM international conference on multimedia* (pp. 3598-3607).

Compilation of References

A Transformer-based representation-learning model with unified processing of multimodal input for clinical diagnostics. (2023). https://doi.org//arxiv.2306.00864DOI: 10.48550

Abs, R., Parizel, P. M., Willems, P. J., Van de Kelft, E., Verlooy, J., Mahler, C., & Martin, J.-J. (1993). The association of meningioma and pituitary adenoma: Report of seven cases and review of the literature. *European Neurology*, *33*(6), 416–422. DOI: 10.1159/000116986 PMID: 8307062

Adam, M., Albaseer, A., Baroudi, U., & Abdallah, M. (2025). Survey of multimodal federated learning: Exploring data integration, challenges, and future directions. *IEEE Open Journal of the Communications Society*.

Afzal, N., Mallipeddi, V., Sohn, S., Liu, H., & Chaudhry, R. (2018). C. Scottet al., “Natural language processing of clinical notes for identification of critical limb ischemia”. *International Journal of Medical Informatics*, *111*, 83–89. DOI: 10.1016/j.ijmedinf.2017.12.024 PMID: 29425639

Ahmad, P. N., Liu, Y., Khan, K., Jiang, T., & Burhan, U. (2023). BIR: Biomedical Information Retrieval System for Cancer Treatment in Electronic Health Record Using Transformers. *Sensors (Basel)*, *23*(23). Advance online publication. DOI: 10.3390/s23239355 PMID: 38067736

Al Kuwaiti, A., Nazer, K., Al-Reedy, A., Al-Shehri, S., Al-Muhanna, A., Subbarayalu, A. V., Al Muhanna, D., & Al-Muhanna, F. A. (2023). A review of the role of artificial intelligence in healthcare. *Journal of Personalized Medicine*, *13*(6), 951. DOI: 10.3390/jpm13060951 PMID: 37373940

Alahmadi, M. D., & Alghamdi, W. (2022). Semi-Supervised Skin Lesion Segmentation With Coupling CNN and Transformer Features. *IEEE Access: Practical Innovations, Open Solutions*, *10*, 122560–122569. DOI: 10.1109/ACCESS.2022.3224005

Alajely, M., Subasri, Ms., Singh, M., & Ilango, K. (2023). Pharmacogenomics -a genome based drug tailoring (pp. 256–265). DOI: 10.58532/v2bs25p2ch5

Aleissaee, A. A., Kumar, A., Anwer, R. M., Khan, S., Cholakkal, H., Xia, G.-S., & Khan, F. S. (2023). Transformers in remote sensing: A survey. *Remote Sensing*, *15*(7), 1860.

Alemu, B. S., Feisso, S., Mohammed, E. A., & Salau, A. O. (2023). Magnetic resonance imaging-based brain tumor image classification performance enhancement. *Scientific African*, *22*(e01963), e01963. DOI: 10.1016/j.sciaf.2023.e01963

Al-Hammuri, K., Gebali, F., Kanan, A., & Chelvan, I. T. (2023). Vision transformer architecture and applications in digital health: A tutorial and survey. *Visual Computing for Industry, Biomedicine, and Art*, *6*(1), 14. DOI: 10.1186/s42492-023-00140-9 PMID: 37428360

Allaouzi, I., & Ahmed, M. B. (2019). A novel approach for multi-label chest X-ray classification of common thorax diseases. *IEEE Access : Practical Innovations, Open Solutions*, *7*, 64279–64288.

Alowais, S. (2023). Revolutionizing healthcare: The role of artificial intelligence in clinical practice. *BMC Medical Education*, *23*(1). Advance online publication. DOI: 10.1186/s12909-023-04698-z PMID: 37740191

Al-Remawi, M., & Rahem, R. A. A. (2024). Applications of AI in biomedical genomics and pharmaceuticals. In *2024 2nd International Conference on Cyber Resilience (ICCR)* (pp. 1–5). IEEE. DOI: 10.1109/ICCR61006.2024.10532792

Al-Sadi, A., Al-Ayyoub, M., Jararweh, Y., & Costen, F. (2021). Visual question answering in the medical domain based on deep learning approaches: A comprehensive study. *Pattern Recognition Letters*, *150*, 57–75.

Alsharaiah, M. A., Almaiah, M. A., Shehab, R., Obeidat, M., El-Qirem, F. A., & Aldhyani, T. (2025). An explainable AI-driven transformer model for spoofing attack detection in Internet of Medical Things (IoMT) networks. *Discover Applied Sciences*, *7*(5). Advance online publication. DOI: 10.1007/s42452-025-07071-5

Archana, R., & Jeevaraj, P. E. (2024). Deep learning models for digital image processing: A review. *Artificial Intelligence Review*, *57*(1), 11.

Ariffin, N. A., Yunus, A. M., & Kadir, I. K. (2021). The role of big data in the healthcare industry. *Journal of Islamic*, *6*(36), 235–245.

Arif, S. (2024). Optimizing personalized healthcare using artificial intelligence with precision medicine. *JPMA. The Journal of the Pakistan Medical Association, 75*(1), 155. DOI: 10.47391/jpma.21300 PMID: 39828857

Arman, M., Jahan, M. K., Dhrubo, A. F. H., Rhaman, M. M., Choya, S. B. Z., Dohan, D. M., Sajid, M. A. U. I., & Alam, M. G. R. Optimizing multimodal transformers for medical image captioning: Enhancing automated descriptions via ai systems, in: 2025 IEEE 6th International Conference on Image Processing, Applications and Systems (IPAS), IEEE, 2025, pp. 1–5.

Arora, S., Agarwal, P., Mittal, A., Mamodiya, U., & Juneja, P. "SA based Optimization of Controller Parameters for Crystallization Unit of Sugar Factory," 2022 6th International Conference on Trends in Electronics and Informatics (ICOEI), Tirunelveli, India, 2022, pp. 341-346, doi: DOI: 10.1109/ICOEI53556.2022.9776904

Arora, M., Mudgil, P., Sharma, U., Chopra, C., & Singh, N. H. (2023). Evaluation of text summarization techniques in healthcare domain: Pharmaceutical drug feedback. *Intelligent Decision Technologies, 17*(4). Advance online publication. DOI: 10.3233/IDT-230129

Arshi, O., Chaudhary, A., & Singh, R. (2023). Navigating the future of healthcare: AI-powered solutions, personalized treatment plans, and emerging trends in 2023. In *2023 International Conference on Artificial Intelligence for Innovations in Healthcare Industries (ICAIIHI)* (pp. 1–6). IEEE. DOI: 10.1109/ICAIIHI57871.2023.10489554

Asiri, A. A., Shaf, A., Ali, T., Shakeel, U., Irfan, M., Mehdar, K. M., & Alqhtani, S. M. (2023). Exploring the power of deep learning: Fine-tuned vision transformer for accurate and efficient brain tumor detection in MRI scans. *Diagnostics (Basel, Switzerland), 13*(12), 2094. DOI: 10.3390/diagnostics13122094 PMID: 37370989

Askin, S., Burkhalter, D., Calado, G., & Dakrouni, S. (2023). Artificial intelligence applied to clinical trials: Opportunities and challenges. *Health and Technology, 13*(2), 203–213. DOI: 10.1007/s12553-023-00738-2 PMID: 36923325

Atabek, A., Eralp, E., & Gursoy, M. E. (2023). Trust, Privacy and Security Aspects of Bias and Fairness in Machine Learning. *Proceedings - 2023 5th IEEE International Conference on Trust, Privacy and Security in Intelligent Systems and Applications, TPS-ISA 2023*. https://doi.org/DOI: 10.1109/TPS-ISA58951.2023.00023

Avasthi, S., Sanwal, T., Tripathi, S. L., & Tyagi, M. (2025). Transformer models for Topic Extraction from narratives and biomedical text analysis. In *Mining Biomedical Text, Images and Visual Features for Information Retrieval* (pp. 273–286). Elsevier.

Ayadi, W., Elhamzi, W., Charfi, I., & Atri, M. (2021). Deep CNN for brain tumor classification. *Neural Processing Letters, 53*(1), 671–700. DOI: 10.1007/s11063-020-10398-2

Azad, R., Al-Antary, M. T., Heidari, M., & Merhof, D. (2022). TransNorm: Transformer Provides a Strong Spatial Normalization Mechanism for a Deep Segmentation Model. *IEEE Access: Practical Innovations, Open Solutions, 10*, 108205–108215. DOI: 10.1109/ACCESS.2022.3211501

Azad, R., Arimond, R., Aghdam, E. K., Kazerouni, A., & Merhof, D. (2023). DAE-Former: Dual Attention-Guided Efficient Transformer for Medical Image Segmentation. In Rekik, I., Adeli, E., Park, S. H., Cintas, C., & Zamzmi, G. (Eds.), Lecture Notes in Computer Science: Vol. 14277. *Predictive Intelligence in Medicine. PRIME 2023*. Springer., DOI: 10.1007/978-3-031-46005-0_8

Azad, R., Heidari, M., Wu, Y., & Merhof, D. (2022). Contextual Attention Network: Transformer Meets U-Net. In Lian, C., Cao, X., Rekik, I., Xu, X., & Cui, Z. (Eds.), Lecture Notes in Computer Science: Vol. 13583. *Machine Learning in Medical Imaging. MLMI 2022*. Springer., DOI: 10.1007/978-3-031-21014-3_39

Babu, A., & Boddu, S. B. (2024). BERT-Based Medical Chatbot: Enhancing Healthcare Communication through Natural Language Understanding. *Exploratory Research in Clinical and Social Pharmacy, 13*. Advance online publication. DOI: 10.1016/j.rcsop.2024.100419 PMID: 38495953

Bahja, M. (2021). Natural Language Processing Applications in Business. In *E-Business - Higher Education and Intelligence Applications*. https://doi.org/DOI: 10.5772/intechopen.92203

Bahri, S., Zoghlami, N., Abed, M., & Tavares, J. M. R. (2018). Big data for healthcare: A survey. *IEEE Access: Practical Innovations, Open Solutions, 7*, 7397–7408.

Bajwa, J., Munir, U., Nori, A., & Williams, B. (2021). Artificial intelligence in healthcare: Transforming the practice of medicine. *Future Healthcare Journal, 8*(2), e188–e194. DOI: 10.7861/fhj.2021-0095 PMID: 34286183

Bakkouri, I., & Bakkouri, S. (2025, March 6). UGS-M3F: Unified gated swin transformer with multi-feature fully fusion for retinal blood vessel segmentation. *BMC Medical Imaging, 25*(1), 77. DOI: 10.1186/s12880-025-01616-1 PMID: 40050753

Balasubramanian, S. 2023. "Ai-enabled mental health assessment and intervention: bridging gaps in access and quality of care.", pst, vol. 47, no. 3. https://doi.org/DOI: 10.52783/pst.159

Bao, Y., Tang, Z., Li, H., & Zhang, Y. (2019). Computer vision and deep learning–based data anomaly detection method for structural health monitoring. *Structural Health Monitoring, 18*(2), 401–421.

Barreto, F., Moharkar, L., Shirodkar, M., Sarode, V., Gonsalves, S., & Johns, A. (2023). Generative Artificial Intelligence: Opportunities and Challenges of Large Language Models. *Lecture Notes in Networks and Systems, 699 LNNS*, 545–553. https://doi.org/DOI: 10.1007/978-981-99-3177-4_41

Belharbi, S., Sarraf, A., Pedersoli, M., Ben Ayed, I., McCaffrey, L., & Granger, E. (2022). F-cam: Full resolution class activation maps via guided parametric upscaling. In *Proceedings of the IEEE/CVF winter conference on applications of computer vision* (pp. 3490-3499).

Beltagy, I., Lo, K., & Cohan, A. Scibert: A pretrained language model for scientific text, in: *Proceedings of the 2019 Conference on Empirical Methods in Natural Language Processing and the 9th International Joint Conference on Natural Language Processing (EMNLP-IJCNLP)*, 2019, pp. 3615–3620.

Bengesi, S., El-Sayed, H., Sarker, M. K., Houkpati, Y., Irungu, J., & Oladunni, T. (2024). Advancements in Generative AI: A Comprehensive Review of GANs, GPT, Autoencoders, Diffusion Model, and Transformers. *IEEE Access: Practical Innovations, Open Solutions, 12*, 69812–69837. DOI: 10.1109/ACCESS.2024.3397775

Bera, A., Shukla, B., & Jogani, D. (2025). A perspective review of applications of the computed tomography (ct) scan imaging technique for microscopic reservoir rock characterization. *Deep Underground Science and Engineering*.

Bera, K., Schalper, K., Rimm, D., Velcheti, V., & Madabhushi, A. (2019). Artificial intelligence in digital pathology — New tools for diagnosis and precision oncology. *Nature Reviews. Clinical Oncology, 16*(11), 703–715. DOI: 10.1038/s41571-019-0252-y PMID: 31399699

Bernal, J., & Mazo, C. (2022). Transparency of artificial intelligence in healthcare: Insights from professionals in computing and healthcare worldwide. *Applied Sciences (Basel, Switzerland), 12*(20), 10228. DOI: 10.3390/app122010228

Bhatt, O., Kotiyal, V., Tyagi, S., Roka, S., & Mehra, P. (2024, June 24). CNN and transformer based brain tumor detection and classification system. 2024 15th International Conference on Computing Communication and Networking Technologies (ICCCNT), 1–5. Presented at the 2024 15th International Conference on Computing Communication and Networking Technologies (ICCCNT), Kamand, India. doi:DOI: 10.1109/icccnt61001.2024.10724063

Biju, P. R., & Gayathri, O. (2024). The Indian approach to Artificial Intelligence: An analysis of policy discussions, constitutional values, and regulation. *AI & Society, 39*(5), 2321–2335. DOI: 10.1007/s00146-023-01685-2

Black, P. M. (1995). Benign brain tumors. *Neurologic Clinics, 13*(4), 927–952. DOI: 10.1016/s0733-8619(18)30026-4 PMID: 8584005

Boppana, V. (2022). Machine Learning and AI Learning: Understanding the Revolution. *Acadexpinnara.Com, 5*(2). https://acadexpinnara.com/index.php/JIT/article/view/368

Brown, T. B., Mann, B., Ryder, N., Subbiah, M., Kaplan, J., Dhariwal, P., Neelakantan, A., Shyam, P., Sastry, G., Askell, A., Agarwal, S., Herbert-Voss, A., Krueger, G., Henighan, T., Child, R., Ramesh, A., Ziegler, D. M., Wu, J., Winter, C., . . . Amodei, D. (2020). Language models are few-shot learners. *Advances in Neural Information Processing Systems, 2020–Decem*. https://proceedings.neurips.cc/paper/2020/hash/1457c0d6bfcb4967418bfb8ac142f64a-Abstract.html

Busch, F., Geis, R., Wang, Y.-C., Kather, J. N., Khori, N. A., Makowski, M. R., Kolawole, I. K., Truhn, D., Clements, W., Gilbert, S., Adams, L. C., Ortiz-Prado, E., & Bressem, K. K. (2025). AI regulation in healthcare around the world: what is the status quo? In *medRxiv* (p. 2025.01.25.25321061). https://doi.org/DOI: 10.1101/2025.01.25.25321061

Cabello, J. C., Karimipour, H., Jahromi, A. N., Dehghantanha, A., & Parizi, R. M. (2020). Big-data and cyber-physical systems in healthcare: Challenges and opportunities. *Handbook of Big Data Privacy*, 255-283.

Cao, H., Wang, Y., Chen, J., Jiang, D., Zhang, X., Tian, Q., & Wang, M. Swin-unet: Unet-like pure transformer for medical image segmentation, in: European conference on computer vision, Springer, 2022, pp. 205– 218.

Cao, H. (2023). Swin-Unet: Unet-Like Pure Transformer for Medical Image Segmentation. In Karlinsky, L., Michaeli, T., & Nishino, K. (Eds.), Lecture Notes in Computer Science: Vol. 13803. *Computer Vision – ECCV 2022 Workshops. ECCV 2022*. Springer., DOI: 10.1007/978-3-031-25066-8_9

Carion, N., Massa, F., Synnaeve, G., Usunier, N., Kirillov, A., & Zagoruyko, S. (2020, August). End-to-end object detection with transformers. In *European conference on computer vision* (pp. 213-229). Cham: Springer International Publishing.

Cascella, M., Semeraro, F., Montomoli, J., Bellini, V., Piazza, O., & Bignami, E. (2024). The Breakthrough of Large Language Models Release for Medical Applications: 1-Year Timeline and Perspectives. In *Journal of Medical Systems* (Vol. 48, Issue 1). https://doi.org/DOI: 10.1007/s10916-024-02045-3

Celebi, M. E., Barata, C., Halpern, A., Tschandl, P., Combalia, M., & Liu, Y. (2023). Guest editorial skin image analysis in the age of deep learning. *IEEE Journal of Biomedical and Health Informatics*, *27*(1), 143–144.

Cè, M., Irmici, G., Foschini, C., Danesini, G. M., Falsitta, L. V., Serio, M. L., & Cellina, M. (2023). Artificial intelligence in brain tumor imaging: A step toward personalized medicine. *Current Oncology (Toronto, Ont.)*, *30*(3), 2673–2701. DOI: 10.3390/curroncol30030203 PMID: 36975416

Chakraborty, A., & Karhade, M. (2024). Global AI governance in healthcare: A cross-jurisdictional regulatory analysis. In *arXiv [cs.CY]*. https://doi.org/DOI: 10.48550/ARXIV.2406.08695

Charonis, A. Z., Perpatari, E., & Charonis, A. (2025). The Clinical Impact and Transformative Potential of Artificial Intelligence in Ophthalmology. In *Precision Health in the Digital Age: Harnessing AI for Personalized Care* (pp. 209-236). IGI Global Scientific Publishing.

Chattopadhay, A., Sarkar, A., Howlader, P., & Balasubramanian, V. N. (2018, March). Grad-cam++: Generalized gradient-based visual explanations for deep convolutional networks. In *2018 IEEE winter conference on applications of computer vision (WACV)* (pp. 839-847). IEEE.

Chauhan, M., & Degan, K. S. (2024). The intervention of artificial intelligence in the healthcare sector: Trends and challenges. In *Signals and Communication Technology* (pp. 267–282). Springer International Publishing.

Chellatamilan, T., Narayanasamy, S. K., Garg, L., Srinivasan, K., & Islam, S. M. N. (2023). Ensemble Text Summarization Model for COVID-19-Associated Datasets. *International Journal of Intelligent Systems, 2023*. Advance online publication. DOI: 10.1155/2023/3106631

Chen, Y., Shi, H., Liu, X., Shi, T., Zhang, R., Liu, D., Xiong, Z., & Wu, F. (2024). TokenUnify: Scalable Autoregressive Visual Pre-training with Mixture Token Prediction. *Arxiv.Org*. https://arxiv.org/abs/2405.16847

Chen, D., Yang, W., Wang, L., Tan, S., & Lin, J.. (2022). PCAT-UNet: UNet-like network fused convolution and transformer for retinal vessel segmentation. *PLoS One*, *17*(1), e0262689. DOI: 10.1371/journal.pone.0262689 PMID: 35073371

Cheng, X., Lin, H., Wu, X., Shen, D., Yang, F., Liu, H., & Shi, N. (2022, July). Mltr: Multi-label classification with transformer. In *2022 IEEE international conference on multimedia and expo (ICME)* (pp. 1-6). IEEE.

Cheng, B., Schwing, A. G., & Kirillov, A. (2021). Per-pixel classification is not all you need for semantic segmentation. *Proceedings of the 35th International Conference on Neural Information Processing Systems*. Red Hook, NY, USA: Curran Associates Inc.

Chen, J., & Pan, R. (2024). Medical report generation based on multimodal federated learning. *Computerized Medical Imaging and Graphics*. Advance online publication. DOI: 10.1016/j.compmedimag.2024.102342 PMID: 38309174

Chen, Jieneng, Lu, Yongyi, Yu, Qihang, Luo, Xiangde, Adeli, Ehsan, Wang, Yan, Lu, Le, Yuille, Alan, & Zhou, Yuyin. (2021). TransUNet: Transformers Make Strong Encoders for Medical Image Segmentation. .DOI: 10.48550/arXiv.2102.04306

Chen, M., Mao, S., Zhang, Y., & Leung, V. C. (2014). *Big data: related technologies, challenges and future prospects* (Vol. 100). Springer.

Chen, Y., Lu, X., & Xie, Q. (2023). ATFormer: Advanced transformer for medical image segmentation. *Biomedical Signal Processing and Control, 85*. Advance online publication. DOI: 10.1016/j.bspc.2023.105079

Chen, Y., Wang, T., Tang, H., Zhao, L., Zhang, X., Tan, T., Gao, Q., Du, M., & Tong, T. (2023). CoTrFuse: A novel framework by fusing CNN and transformer for medical image segmentation. *Physics in Medicine and Biology, 68*. Advance online publication. DOI: 10.1088/1361-6560/acede8 PMID: 37605997

Chen, Z. M., Cui, Q., Zhao, B., Song, R., Zhang, X., & Yoshie, O. (2022). SST: Spatial and semantic transformers for multi-label image recognition. *IEEE Transactions on Image Processing, 31*, 2570–2583.

Cho, H. N., Jun, T. J., Kim, Y.-H., Kang, H., Ahn, I., Gwon, H., Kim, Y., Seo, J., Choi, H., Kim, M., Han, J., Kee, G., Park, S., & Ko, S. (2024). Task-specific transformer-based language models in health care: Scoping review. *JMIR Medical Informatics, 12*(1), e49724. DOI: 10.2196/49724 PMID: 39556827

Chowdhary, K., intelligence, K. C.-F. of artificial, & 2020, undefined. (2020). Natural language processing. *Springer, 37*, 603–649. https://doi.org/DOI: 10.1007/978-81-322-3972-7_19

Chow, J. C. L., Wong, V., & Li, K. (2024). Generative pre-trained transformer-empowered healthcare conversations: Current trends, challenges, and future directions in large language model-enabled medical chatbots. *BioMedInformatics*, *4*(1), 837–852. DOI: 10.3390/biomedinformatics4010047

Dai, X., Chen, Y., Yang, J., Zhang, P., Yuan, L., & Zhang, L. Dynamic detr: End-to-end object detection with dynamic attention, in: *2021 IEEE/CVF International Conference on Computer Vision (ICCV)*, 2021, pp. 2968–2977. doi:DOI: 10.1109/ICCV48922.2021.00298

Dalmaz, O., Yurt, M., & Çukur, T. (2022). Resvit: Residual ViTs for multimodal medical image synthesis. *IEEE Transactions on Medical Imaging*, *41*(10), 2598–2614. PMID: 35436184

Das, S., Aranya, O. F. M. R. R., & Labiba, N. N. (2019, May). Brain tumor classification using convolutional neural network. 2019 1st International Conference on Advances in Science, Engineering and Robotics Technology (ICASERT). Presented at the 2019 1st International Conference on Advances in Science, Engineering and Robotics Technology (ICASERT), Dhaka, Bangladesh. doi:DOI: 10.1109/icasert.2019.8934603

Das, S., Roy, R., Sarkar, A., Bose, R., Sarkar, I., & Roy, S. (2025). *Revolutionizing healthcare: Synergistic integration of genomics, clinical decision support systems, and advanced machine learning for precision medicine. In 2025 AI-Driven Smart Healthcare for Society 5.0*. IEEE. DOI: 10.1109/IEEECONF64992.2025.10963134

Deep Shukla, A., Agarwal, L., Mein Goh, J., Gao Carey Business School, G., & Agarwal, R. (2023). Catch Me If You Can: Identifying Fraudulent Physician Reviews with Large Language Models Using Generative Pre-Trained Transformers. *ArXiv*.

Deepa, J., & Madhavan, P. (2023). ABT-GAMNet: A novel adaptive Boundary-aware transformer with Gated attention mechanism for automated skin lesion segmentation. *Biomedical Signal Processing and Control*, *84*. Advance online publication. DOI: 10.1016/j.bspc.2023.104971

Delaidelli, A., & Moiraghi, A. (2024). Recent advances in the diagnosis and treatment of brain tumors. *Brain Sciences*, *14*(3), 224. DOI: 10.3390/brainsci14030224 PMID: 38539613

Denecke, K., May, R., & Rivera-Romero, O. (2024). Transformer models in healthcare: A survey and thematic analysis of potentials, shortcomings and risks. *Journal of Medical Systems*, *48*(1), 23. DOI: 10.1007/s10916-024-02043-5 PMID: 38367119

Deng, K.. (2021). TransBridge: A Lightweight Transformer for Left Ventricle Segmentation in Echocardiography. In Noble, J. A., Aylward, S., Grimwood, A., Min, Z., Lee, S. L., & Hu, Y. (Eds.), Lecture Notes in Computer Science: Vol. 12967. *Simplifying Medical Ultrasound. ASMUS 2021*. Springer., DOI: 10.1007/978-3-030-87583-1_7

Devika, G., & Karegowda, A. G. (2021). Deep Learning in IoT: Introduction, Applications, and Perspective in the Big Data Era. In *Deep Learning Applications and Intelligent Decision Making in Engineering* (pp. 1-54). IGI Global.

Devlin, J., Chang, M. W., Lee, K., & Toutanova, K. (2019). BERT: Pre-training of deep bidirectional transformers for language understanding. *NAACL HLT 2019 - 2019 Conference of the North American Chapter of the Association for Computational Linguistics: Human Language Technologies - Proceedings of the Conference, 1*, 4171–4186. https://aclanthology.org/N19-1423/?utm_campaign=The Batch&utm_source=hs_email&utm_medium=email&_hsenc=p2ANqtz-_m9bbH_7ECE-1h3lZ3D61TYg52rKpifVNjL4fvJ85uqggrXsWDBTB7YooFLJeNXHWqhvOyC

Dhabliya, D., Singh, K. R., Verma, A., Ahmad, R. C. S., & Pattanaik, A. (2024). The evolution of personalized medicine in the age of big data and advanced analytics. In *2024 IEEE 2nd International Conference on Innovations in High Speed Communication and Signal Processing (IHCSP)* (pp. 1–6). IEEE. DOI: 10.1109/IHCSP63227.2024.10959907

Dhar, T., Dey, N., Borra, S., & Sherratt, R. S. (2023). Challenges of deep learning in medical image analysis—Improving explainability and trust. *IEEE Transactions on Technology and Society*, *4*(1), 68–75.

Dideberg, K., Segers, B., Koopmansch, F., & Lambert, B. (2015). pharmacogenomics and personalized medicine: Towards a systematic genomic screening? *Revue Medicale de Liege*, *70*, 251–256. https://www.ncbi.nlm.nih.gov/pubmed/26285448 PMID: 26285448

Ding, W., Wang, H., Huang, J., Ju, H., Geng, Y., & Lin, C.-T. (2023). Witold Pedrycz, FTransCNN: Fusing Transformer and a CNN based on fuzzy logic for uncertain medical image segmentation. *Information Fusion*, *99*. Advance online publication. DOI: 10.1016/j.inffus.2023.101880

Dong, Z., Wang, X., Pan, S., Weng, T., Chen, X., Jiang, S., Li, Y., Wang, Z., Cao, X., & Wang, Q.. (2025). A multimodal transformer system for noninvasive diabetic nephropathy diagnosis via retinal imaging, npj. *Digital Medicine*, *8*(1), 50. PMID: 39856403

Dosovitskiy, A., Beyer, L., Kolesnikov, A., Weissenborn, D., Zhai, X., Unterthiner, T., . . . Houlsby, N. (2020). An image is worth 16x16 words: Transformers for image recognition at scale. *arXiv preprint arXiv:2010.11929.*

Dosovitskiy, A., Beyer, L., Kolesnikov, A., Weissenborn, D., Zhai, X., Unterthiner, T., & Houlsby, N. (2020). An image is worth 16x16 words: Transformers for image recognition at scale. doi:DOI: 10.48550/ARXIV.2010.11929

Duc, N. T., Oanh, N. T., Thuy, N. T., Triet, T. M., & Dinh, V. S. (2022). Colon former: An efficient transformer based method for colon polyp segmentation. *IEEE Access: Practical Innovations, Open Solutions, 10*, 80575–80586.

Duc, N. T., Oanh, N. T., Thuy, N. T., Triet, T. M., & Dinh, V. S. (2022). ColonFormer: An Efficient Transformer Based Method for Colon Polyp Segmentation. *IEEE Access: Practical Innovations, Open Solutions, 10*, 80575–80586. DOI: 10.1109/ACCESS.2022.3195241

Du, H., Wang, J., Liu, M., Wang, Y., & Meijering, E. (2024, April). SwinPA-Net: Swin Transformer-Based Multiscale Feature Pyramid Aggregation Network for Medical Image Segmentation. *IEEE Transactions on Neural Networks and Learning Systems, 35*(4), 5355–5366. DOI: 10.1109/TNNLS.2022.3204090 PMID: 36121961

Duong, Q. A., Tran, S. D., & Gahm, J. K. (2025). Multimodal surface-based trans former model for early diagnosis of alzheimer's disease. *Scientific Reports, 15*(1), 5787. PMID: 39962212

Du, S., Bayasi, N., Hamarneh, G., & Garbi, R. (2023). MDViT: Multi-domain Vision Transformer for Small Medical Image Segmentation Datasets. In Greenspan, H. (Eds.), Medical Image Computing and Computer Assisted Intervention: Vol. 14223. *MICCAI 2023. MICCAI 2023. Lecture Notes in Computer Science*. Springer., DOI: 10.1007/978-3-031-43901-8_43

Ekundayo, F., & Nyavor, H. (2024). AI-Driven Predictive Analytics in Cardiovascular Diseases: Integrating Big Data and Machine Learning for Early Diagnosis and Risk Prediction. *Researchgate. Net, 5*, 1240–1256. DOI: 10.55248/gengpi.5.1224.3437

Elbadawi, M., Gaisford, S., & Basit, A. W. (2021). Advanced machine-learning techniques in drug discovery. *Drug Discovery Today, 26*(3), 769–777. PMID: 33290820

El-Deeb, S., Jahankhani, H., Amin Metwally Hussien, O. A., & Will Arachchige, I. S. (2024). Towards responsible AI: Exploring AI frameworks, ethical dimensions and regulations. In *Market Grooming* (pp. 139–157). Emerald Publishing Limited.

Enquero, S. P., Sunil, G., Kumar, S. S., Lavanya, C., & Siddhanti, P. (2023). Deep Neural Pretraining for Improving Diagnostic and Therapeutic Entity Recognition in Electronic Medical Records. *2023 International Conference on Evolutionary Algorithms and Soft Computing Techniques, EASCT 2023*. https://doi.org/DOI: 10.1109/EASCT59475.2023.10393025

Esteva, A., Chou, K., Yeung, S., Naik, N., Madani, A., Mottaghi, A., & Socher, R. (2021). Deep learning-enabled medical computer vision. *NPJ Digital Medicine*, *4*(1), 5. PMID: 33420381

Faaique, M. (2024). Overview of Big Data Analytics in Modern Astronomy. *International Journal of Mathematics, Statistics, and Computer Science*, *2*, 96–113.

Fabian, Z., Tinaz, B., & Soltanolkotabi, M. (2022). Humus-net: Hybrid unrolled multi-scale network architecture for accelerated mri reconstruction. *Advances in Neural Information Processing Systems*, *35*, 25306–25319.

Fang, C., Zhang, D., Wang, L., Zhang, Y., Cheng, L., & Han, J. Cross modality high-frequency transformer for mr image super-resolution, in: *Proceedings of the 30th ACM International Conference on Multimedia*, 2022, pp. 1584–1592.

FedCNNAvg: Federated Learning for Preserving-Privacy of Multi-clients Decentralized Medical Image Classification (pp. 249–260). Springer International Publishing. https://doi.org/DOI: 10.1007/978-981-99-6755-1_19

FedTP: Federated Learning by Transformer Personalization. (2023). IEEE Transactions on Neural Networks and Learning Systems, 1–15. https://doi.org/DOI: 10.1109/tnnls.2023.3269062

Feng, C.-M., Yan, Y., Fu, H., Chen, L., & Xu, Y. Task transformer network for joint mri reconstruction and super-resolution, in: Medical Image Computing and Computer Assisted Intervention–MICCAI 2021: 24th International Conference, Strasbourg, France, September 27–October 1, 2021, Proceedings, Part VI 24, Springer, 2021, pp. 307–317.

Feng, C.-M., Yan, Y., Chen, G., Xu, Y., Hu, Y., Shao, L., & Fu, H. (2022). Multimodal transformer for accelerated mr imaging. *IEEE Transactions on Medical Imaging*, *42*(10), 2804–2816. PMID: 35704546

Feng, K., Ren, L., Wang, G., Wang, H., & Li, Y. (2022). SLT-Net: A codec network for skin lesion segmentation. *Computers in Biology and Medicine*, *148*. Advance online publication. DOI: 10.1016/j.compbiomed.2022.105942 PMID: 35964466

Feuerecker, B., Heimer, M., Geyer, T., Fabritius, M., & Gu, S. B. Schachtneret. 2022. "Artificial intelligence in oncological hybrid imaging", Röfo - Fortschritte Auf Dem Gebiet Der Röntgenstrahlen Und Der Bildgebenden Verfahren, vol. 195, no. 02, p. 105-114. https://doi.org/DOI: 10.1055/a-1909-7013

Friedman, D., Parrish, R., & Ross, D. (2013). Electronic health records and us public health: Current realities and future promise. *American Journal of Public Health, 103*(9), 1560–1567. DOI: 10.2105/ajph.2013.301220 PMID: 23865646

Froelicher, D., Troncoso-Pastoriza, J. R., Raisaro, J. L., Cuendet, M. A., Sousa, J. S., Cho, H., Berger, B., Berger, B., Fellay, J., Fellay, J., & Hubaux, J.-P. (2021). Truly Privacy-Preserving Federated Analytics for Precision Medicine with Multiparty Homomorphic Encryption. *bioRxiv*. https://doi.org/DOI: 10.1101/2021.02.24.432489

Fu, X., Lin, R., Du, W., Tavares, A., & Liang, Y. (2025). Explainable hybrid transformer for multi-classification of lung disease using chest x-rays. *Scientific Reports, 15*(1), 6650. PMID: 39994381

Ganai, A. F., & Khursheed, F. (2019). Predicting next Word using RNN and LSTM cells: Stastical Language Modeling. *Proceedings of the IEEE International Conference Image Information Processing, 2019–Novem*, 469–474. https://doi.org/DOI: 10.1109/ICIIP47207.2019.8985885

Gangesh, M. (2021). Diabetic retinopathy detection system. *International Journal for Research in Applied Science and Engineering Technology, 9*(9), 1498–1502. DOI: 10.22214/ijraset.2021.38233

Gao, Y., Zhou, M., & Metaxas, D. N. Utnet: a hybrid transformer architecture for medical image segmentation, in: Medical image computing and computer assisted intervention–MICCAI 2021: 24th international conference, Strasbourg, France, September 27–October 1, 2021, proceedings, Part III 24, Springer, 2021, pp. 61–71.

Garcia, A., Maldonado, J., Marcos, M., Tomas, D., & Robles, M. (2021). Augmented ehr: Enrichment of ehr with contents from semantic web sources. *Applied Sciences (Basel, Switzerland), 11*(9), 3978. DOI: 10.3390/app11093978

Ghali, R., & Akhloufi, M. A. (2023). Vision Transformers for Lung Segmentation on CXR Images. *SN Computer Science, 4*, 414. DOI: 10.1007/s42979-023-01848-4 PMID: 37252339

Gillani, I. S., Shahzad, M., Mobin, A., Munawar, M. R., Awan, M. U., & Asif, M. (2022). Explainable AI in drug sensitivity prediction on cancer cell lines. In *2022 International Conference on Emerging Trends in Smart Technologies (ICETST)* (pp. 1–5). IEEE. DOI: 10.1109/ICETST55735.2022.9922931

Gillioz, A., Casas, J., Mugellini, E., & Khaled, O. A. "Overview of the Transformer-based Models for NLP Tasks," 2020 15th Conference on Computer Science and Information Systems (FedCSIS), Sofia, Bulgaria, 2020, pp. 179-183, doi: DOI: 10.15439/2020F20

Gong, Y., Jia, Y., Leung, T., Toshev, A., & Ioffe, S. (2013). Deep convolutional ranking for multilabel image annotation. *arXiv preprint arXiv:1312.4894*.

Goodfellow, I., Pouget-Abadie, J., Mirza, M., Xu, B., Warde-Farley, D., Ozair, S., Courville, A., & Bengio, Y. (2020). Generative adversarial networks. *Dl.Acm. Org*, *63*(11), 139–144. DOI: 10.1145/3422622

Goodman, K. E., Yi, P. H., & Morgan, D. J. (2024). AI-Generated Clinical Summaries Require More Than Accuracy. In *JAMA* (Vol. 331, Issue 8, pp. 637–638). American Medical Association. https://doi.org/DOI: 10.1001/jama.2024.0555

Gou, Y., & Jie, C. (2023). A lightweight biomedical named entity recognition with pre-trained model. *2023 IEEE 3rd International Conference on Data Science and Computer Application, ICDSCA 2023*. https://doi.org/DOI: 10.1109/ICDSCA59871.2023.10392374

Griffith, J., Borycki, E. M., & Kushniruk, A. (2013). Tailoring decision support to suit user needs: A diagnostic imaging example. *Studies in Health Technology and Informatics*, *183*, 132–136. https://www.ncbi.nlm.nih.gov/pubmed/23388269 PMID: 23388269

Gross, N. (2025). A powerful potion for a potent problem: Transformative justice for generative AI in healthcare. *AI and Ethics*, *5*(3), 2089–2101. DOI: 10.1007/s43681-024-00519-1

Gunawan, A., & Wiputra, R. (2024). Ethical implications of generative AI in medicine: A systematic review of current practices and future directions. In *2024 IEEE 12th Conference on Systems, Process & Control (ICSPC)* (pp. 239–244). IEEE. DOI: 10.1109/ICSPC63060.2024.10862569

Gupta, M., Sharma, S. K., & Sampada, G. C. (2023). Classification of brain tumor images using CNN. *Computational Intelligence and Neuroscience*, *2023*(1), 2002855. DOI: 10.1155/2023/2002855 PMID: 37868750

Haddouche, A., Rabia, I., & Aid, A. (2023). Transformer-Based Question Answering Model for the Biomedical Domain. *2023 5th International Conference on Pattern Analysis and Intelligent Systems, PAIS 2023*. https://doi.org/DOI: 10.1109/PAIS60821.2023.10322055

Haleem, A., Javaid, M., Pratap Singh, R., & Suman, R. (2022). Medical 4.0 technologies for healthcare: Features, capabilities, and applications. *Internet of Things and Cyber-Physical Systems, 2*, 12–30. DOI: 10.1016/j.iotcps.2022.04.001

Halim, E., Attan, N. E., Chow, R. D., & Halim, D. D. (2024). Using AI algorithms for predictive analysis in personalized medicine. In *2024 Ninth International Conference on Informatics and Computing (ICIC)* (pp. 1–6). IEEE. DOI: 10.1109/ICIC64337.2024.10956226

Han, K., Wang, Y., Chen, H., Chen, X., Guo, J., Liu, Z., Tang, Y., Xiao, A., Xu, C., & Xu, Y.. (2022). A survey on ViT. *IEEE Transactions on Pattern Analysis and Machine Intelligence, 45*(1), 87–110. PMID: 35180075

Han, K., Wang, Y., Chen, H., Chen, X., Guo, J., Liu, Z., & Tao, D. (2023). A survey on vision transformer. *IEEE Transactions on Pattern Analysis and Machine Intelligence, 45*(1), 87–110. DOI: 10.1109/TPAMI.2022.3152247 PMID: 35180075

Han, K., Xiao, A., Wu, E., Guo, J., Xu, C., & Wang, Y. (2021). Transformer in transformer. *Advances in Neural Information Processing Systems, 34*, 15908–15919.

Hanna, M. G., Pantanowitz, L., Jackson, B., Palmer, O., Visweswaran, S., Pantanowitz, J., & Rashidi, H. H. (2025). Ethical and bias considerations in artificial intelligence/machine learning. *Modern Pathology, 38*(3), 100686. PMID: 39694331

Han, Z., Jian, M., & Wang, G.-G. (2022). ConvUNeXt: An efficient convolution neural network for medical image segmentation. *Knowledge-Based Systems, 253*. Advance online publication. DOI: 10.1016/j.knosys.2022.109512

Hao, Q., Tian, S., Yu, L., & Wang, J. (2023). MFUnetr: A transformer-based multi-task learning network for multi-organ segmentation from partially labeled datasets. *Biomedical Signal Processing and Control, 85*. Advance online publication. DOI: 10.1016/j.bspc.2023.105081

Hatamizadeh, A., Yang, D., Roth, H., & Xu, D. (2021). UNETR: Transformers for 3D Medical Image Segmentation. 10.48550/arXiv.2103.10504.

Hatamizadeh, A., Nath, V., Tang, Y., Yang, D., Roth, H. R., & Xu, D. (2022). Swin UNETR: Swin Transformers for Semantic Segmentation of Brain Tumors in MRI Images. In Crimi, A., & Bakas, S. (Eds.), Lecture Notes in Computer Science: Vol. 12962. *Brainlesion: Glioma, Multiple Sclerosis, Stroke and Traumatic Brain Injuries. BrainLes 2021*. Springer., DOI: 10.1007/978-3-031-08999-2_22

He, A., Wang, K., Li, T., Du, C., Xia, S., & Fu, H. (2023, September). H2Former: An Efficient Hierarchical Hybrid Transformer for Medical Image Segmentation. *IEEE Transactions on Medical Imaging*, *42*(9), 2763–2775. DOI: 10.1109/TMI.2023.3264513 PMID: 37018111

Hennessy, M., Patrick, J., & Swinbourne, A. (2018). Improving mental health outcomes assessment with the mental health inventory-21. *Australian Psychologist*, *53*(4), 313–324. DOI: 10.1111/ap.12330

He, Q., Yang, Q., & Xie, M. (2023). HCTNet: A hybrid CNN-transformer network for breast ultrasound image segmentation. *Computers in Biology and Medicine*, *155*. Advance online publication. DOI: 10.1016/j.compbiomed.2023.106629 PMID: 36787669

He, Y., Gao, Z., Li, Y., & Wang, Z. (2024). A lightweight multi-modality medical image semantic segmentation network base on the novel UNeXt and Wave-MLP. *Computerized Medical Imaging and Graphics*, *111*. Advance online publication. DOI: 10.1016/j.compmedimag.2023.102311 PMID: 38035411

Hilbert, M. (2016). Big data for development: A review of promises and challenges. *Development Policy Review*, *34*(1), 135–174.

Hille, G., Agrawal, S., Tummala, P., Wybranski, C., Pech, M., Surov, A., & Saalfeld, S. (2023). Joint liver and hepatic lesion segmentation in MRI using a hybrid CNN with transformer layers. *Computer Methods and Programs in Biomedicine*, *240*. Advance online publication. DOI: 10.1016/j.cmpb.2023.107647 PMID: 37329803

Hosny, K. M., & Mohammed, M. A. (2025). Explainable AI and vision transformers for detection and classification of brain tumor: A comprehensive survey. *Artificial Intelligence Review*, *58*(9). Advance online publication. DOI: 10.1007/s10462-025-11221-x

Hossain, S., Chakrabarty, A., Gadekallu, T. R., Alazab, M., & Piran, M. J. (2024). Vision transformers, ensemble model, and transfer learning leveraging Explainable AI for brain tumor detection and classification. *IEEE Journal of Biomedical and Health Informatics*, *28*(3), 1261–1272. DOI: 10.1109/JBHI.2023.3266614 PMID: 37043319

Hou, J., Yan, C., Li, R., Huang, Q., Fan, X., & Lin, F. (2023). Lung Nodule Segmentation Algorithm With SMR-UNet. *IEEE Access: Practical Innovations, Open Solutions*, *11*, 34319–34331. DOI: 10.1109/ACCESS.2023.3264789

Howard, J., & Gugger, S. (2020). Fastai: A layered API for deep learning. *Information (Basel)*, *11*(2), 108.

Huang, J., Wu, Y., Wu, H., & Yang, G. Fast mri reconstruction: How powerful transformers are? in: 2022 44th annual international conference of the IEEE engineering in medicine & biology society (EMBC), IEEE, 2022, pp. 2066–2070.

Huang, J., Yang, L., Wang, F., Wu, Y., Nan, Y., Wu, W., Wang, C., Shi, K., Aviles-Rivero, A. I., & Schönlieb, C.-B.. (2025). Enhancing global sensitivity and uncertainty quantification in medical image reconstruction with monte carlo arbitrary-masked mamba. *Medical Image Analysis*, *99*, 103334. PMID: 39255733

Huang, S., Li, J., Xiao, Y., Shen, N., & Xu, T. (2022, June). RTNet: Relation Transformer Network for Diabetic Retinopathy Multi-Lesion Segmentation. *IEEE Transactions on Medical Imaging*, *41*(6), 1596–1607. DOI: 10.1109/TMI.2022.3143833 PMID: 35041595

Huang, X., Chen, J., Chen, M., Chen, L., & Wan, Y. (2022). TDD-UNet:Transformer with double decoder UNet for COVID-19 lesions segmentation. *Computers in Biology and Medicine*, •••. Advance online publication. DOI: 10.1016/j.compbiomed.2022.106306 PMID: 36403357

Huang, X., Deng, Z., Li, D., Yuan, X., & Fu, Y. (2023, May). MISSFormer: An Effective Transformer for 2D Medical Image Segmentation. *IEEE Transactions on Medical Imaging*, *42*(5), 1484–1494. DOI: 10.1109/TMI.2022.3230943 PMID: 37015444

Hugging Face. (n.d.). *Hugging Face*. https://huggingface.co

Hu, X., Wang, L., & Li, Y. (2022). HT-Net: A Hybrid Transformer Network for Fundus Vessel Segmentation. *Sensors (Basel)*, *22*(18), 6782. DOI: 10.3390/s22186782 PMID: 36146132

Iliu ă, M.-E., Trentesaux, D., Pop, E., & Moisescu, M.-A. (2024). Integration of generative artificial intelligence in medicine - First steps toward an ethical risk management methodology. In *2024 E-Health and Bioengineering Conference (EHB)* (pp. 1–6). IEEE. DOI: 10.1109/EHB64556.2024.10805663

Iqbal, S. N., Qureshi, A., & Li, J.. (2023). On the Analyses of Medical Images Using Traditional Machine Learning Techniques and Convolutional Neural Networks. *Archives of Computational Methods in Engineering*, *30*, 3173–3233. DOI: 10.1007/s11831-023-09899-9 PMID: 37260910

Isabona, J., Ibitome, L. L., Imoize, A. L., Mamodiya, U., Kumar, A., & Hassan, M. M. (2023). Statistical characterization and modeling of radio frequency signal propagation in mobile broadband cellular next generation wireless networks. *Computational Intelligence and Neuroscience*, *2023*(1), 5236566.

Islam, S., Elmekki, H., Elsebai, A., Bentahar, J., Drawel, N., Rjoub, G., & Pedrycz, W. (2024). A comprehensive survey on applications of transformers for deep learning tasks. In *Expert Systems with Applications* (Vol. 241). https://doi.org/DOI: 10.1016/j.eswa.2023.122666

Jang, S.-I., Pan, T., Li, Y., Heidari, P., Chen, J., Li, Q., & Gong, K. (2023). Spach transformer: Spatial and channel-wise transformer based on local and global self-attentions for pet image denoising. *IEEE Transactions on Medical Imaging*, *43*(6), 2036–2049. PMID: 37995174

Javaid, M., Haleem, A., & Singh, R. P. (2023). ChatGPT for healthcare services: An emerging stage for an innovative perspective. *BenchCouncil Transactions on Benchmarks. Standards and Evaluations*, *3*(1). Advance online publication. DOI: 10.1016/j.tbench.2023.100105

Ji, Y., ... (2021). Multi-compound Transformer for Accurate Biomedical Image Segmentation. In: de Bruijne, M., *et al.* Medical Image Computing and Computer Assisted Intervention – MICCAI 2021. MICCAI 2021. Lecture Notes in Computer Science(), vol 12901. Springer, Cham. https://doi.org/DOI: 10.1007/978-3-030-87193-2_31

Jiang, X., Xu, C., Guo, Q., & Zhu, H. (2021). AI-aided data mining in gut microbiome: The road to precision medicine. In *2021 14th International Congress on Image and Signal Processing, BioMedical Engineering and Informatics (CISP-BMEI)* (pp. 1–5). IEEE. DOI: 10.1109/CISP-BMEI53629.2021.9624432

Jiang, J. (2023). Clinical service evaluation of the feasibility and reproducibility of novel artificial intelligence based-echocardiographic quantification of global longitudinal strain and left ventricular ejection fraction in trastuzumab-treated patients. *Frontiers in Cardiovascular Medicine*, *10*. Advance online publication. DOI: 10.3389/fcvm.2023.1250311 PMID: 38045908

Jiang, S., & Li, J. (2022). TransCUNet: UNet cross fused transformer for medical image segmentation. *Computers in Biology and Medicine*, *150*. Advance online publication. DOI: 10.1016/j.compbiomed.2022.106207 PMID: 37859294

Ji, Z., Chen, Z., & Ma, X. (2025). Grouped multi-scale vision transformer for medical image segmentation. *Scientific Reports*, *15*, 11122. DOI: 10.1038/s41598-025-95361-8 PMID: 40169823

Johnsen, M. (2024). *Large language models (LLMs).*

Jordan, M. I., & Mitchell, T. M. (2015). Machine learning: Trends, perspectives, and prospects. *Science*, *349*(6245), 255–260. PMID: 26185243

Jørgensen, B. N., & Ma, Z. G. (2025). Regulating AI in the energy sector: A scoping review of EU laws, challenges, and global perspectives. *Energies, 18*(9), 2359. DOI: 10.3390/en18092359

Joshi, D. (2024). AI governance in India – law, policy and political economy. *Communication Research and Practice, 10*(3), 328–339. DOI: 10.1080/22041451.2024.2346428

Kahalkar, K., & Vyas, U. (2024). AI for personalized nutrition and healthcare management. In *2024 2nd DMIHER International Conference on Artificial Intelligence in Healthcare, Education and Industry (IDICAIEI)* (pp. 1–6). IEEE. DOI: 10.1109/IDICAIEI61867.2024.10842744

Kaifi, R. (2023). A review of recent advances in brain tumor diagnosis based on AI-based classification. *Diagnostics (Basel, Switzerland), 13*(18), 3007. DOI: 10.3390/diagnostics13183007 PMID: 37761373

Kaissis, G., Kaissis, G., Makowski, M. R., Rückert, D., & Braren, R. (2020). Secure, privacy-preserving and federated machine learning in medical imaging. *Nature Machine Intelligence, 2*(6), 305–311. DOI: 10.1038/S42256-020-0186-1

Kaissis, G., Ziller, A., Passerat-Palmbach, J., Ryffel, T., Usynin, D., Trask, A., Lima, I., Mancuso, J., Jungmann, F., Steinborn, M.-M., Saleh, A., Makowski, M. R., Rueckert, D., Rueckert, D., Braren, R., & Braren, R. (2021). End-to-end privacy preserving deep learning on multi-institutional medical imaging. *Nature Machine Intelligence, 3*(6), 473–484. DOI: 10.1038/S42256-021-00337-8

Kalinin, A. A., Higgins, G. A., Reamaroon, N., Soroushmehr, S. M. R., Allyn-Feuer, A., Dinov, D., Najarian, K., & Athey, B. D. (2018). Deep Learning in Pharmacogenomics: From Gene Regulation to Patient Stratification. arXiv: Quantitative Methods. DOI: 10.2217/PGS-2018-0008

Kalyan, K. S., Rajasekharan, A., & Sangeetha, S. (2021). AMMUS : A Survey of Transformer-based Pretrained Models in Natural Language Processing. *Arxiv.Org*. https://arxiv.org/abs/2108.05542

Kalyani, T. N., Lakshmi, M. A., Yamuna, V., Rizvana, M., Shoba, V., & Athiraja, A. (2024). AI-driven predictive modeling for accelerated drug discovery and personalized medicine development. In *2024 IEEE 1st International Conference on Green Industrial Electronics and Sustainable Technologies (GIEST)* (pp. 1–7). IEEE. DOI: 10.1109/GIEST62955.2024.10959983

Kamran, S. A., Hossain, K. F., Tavakkoli, A., Zuckerbrod, S. L., & Baker, S. A. Vtgan: Semi-supervised retinal image synthesis and disease prediction using ViTs, in: Proceedings of the IEEE/CVF international conference on computer vision, 2021, pp. 3235–3245.

Kanadath, A., Jothi, J. A. A., & Urolagin, S. (2024). CViTS-Net: A CNN-ViT Network with Skip Connections for Histopathology Image Classification. *IEEE Access: Practical Innovations, Open Solutions.*

Kapruwan, A., Sharma, S., & Rai Goyal, H. (2023). Natural Language Processing Techniques in Diagnostic Digital Cytopathology for Cervical Intraepithelial Neoplasia Detection. *2023 9th International Conference on Advanced Computing and Communication Systems, ICACCS 2023.* https://doi.org/DOI: 10.1109/ICACCS57279.2023.10113060

Karanevich, A., Weisbrod, L., Jawdat, O., Barohn, R., He, J., & Statland, J. (2018). Using automated electronic medical record data extraction to model als survival and progression. *BMC Neurology, 18*(1). Advance online publication. DOI: 10.1186/s12883-018-1208-z PMID: 30547800

Karimi, D., Vasylechko, S. D., & Gholipour, A. Convolution-free medical image segmentation using transformers, in: Medical image computing and computer assisted intervention–MICCAI 2021: 24th international conference, Strasbourg, France, September 27–October 1, 2021, proceedings, part I 24, Springer, 2021, pp. 78–88.

Karthik, R., Vaichole, T. S., Kulkarni, S. K., Yadav, O., & Khan, F. (2022). Eff2Net: An efficient channel attention-based convolutional neural network for skin disease classification. *Biomedical Signal Processing and Control, 73*, 103406.

Kashyap, H., Ahmed, H. A., Hoque, N., Roy, S., & Bhattacharyya, D. K. (2015). Big data analytics in bioinformatics: A machine learning perspective. *arXiv preprint arXiv:1506.05101.*

Kashyap, H., Ahmed, H. A., Hoque, N., Roy, S., & Bhattacharyya, D. K. (2016). Big data analytics in bioinformatics: Architectures, techniques, tools and issues. *Network Modeling and Analysis in Health Informatics and Bioinformatics, 5*, 1–28.

Kaur, A., Kukreja, V., & Aneja, A. (2024). Dynamic treatment strategies: The RL-CNN model in personalized medicine. In *2024 2nd International Conference on Self Sustainable Artificial Intelligence Systems (ICSSAS)* (pp. 223–226). IEEE. DOI: 10.1109/ICSSAS64001.2024.10760342

Keikhosrokiani, P. (Ed.). (2022). *Big data analytics for healthcare: datasets, techniques, life cycles, management, and applications.* Academic Press.

Keskar, N. S., McCann, B., Varshney, L. R., Xiong, C., & Socher, R. (2019). CTRL: A Conditional Transformer Language Model for Controllable Generation. *Arxiv. Org*. https://arxiv.org/abs/1909.05858

Khalifa, M., Albadawy, M., & Iqbal, U. (2024). Advancing clinical decision support: The role of artificial intelligence across six domains. In *Computer Methods and Programs in Biomedicine Update* (Vol. 5). https://doi.org/DOI: 10.1016/j.cmpbup.2024.100142

Khalifa, M., & Albadawy, M. (2024). AI in diagnostic imaging: Revolutionising accuracy and efficiency. *Computer Methods and Programs in Biomedicine Update*, *5*(100146), 100146. DOI: 10.1016/j.cmpbup.2024.100146

Khan, A., Rauf, Z., Sohail, A., Khan, A. R., Asif, H., Asif, A., & Farooq, U. (2023). A survey of the vision transformers and their CNN-transformer based variants. *Artificial Intelligence Review*, *56*(Suppl 3), 2917–2970.

Khan, R. F., Lee, B.-D., & Lee, M. S. (2023). Transformers in medical image segmentation: A narrative review. *Quantitative Imaging in Medicine and Surgery*, *13*(12), 8747–8767. DOI: 10.21037/qims-23-542 PMID: 38106306

Khan, S., Naseer, M., Hayat, M., Zamir, S. W., Khan, F. S., & Shah, M. (2022). Transformers in vision: A survey. *ACM Computing Surveys*, *54*(10s), 1–41.

Khan, W., Leem, S., See, K. B., Wong, J. K., Zhang, S., & Fang, R. (2025). A comprehensive survey of foundation models in medicine. *IEEE Reviews in Biomedical Engineering*, *PP*, (99), 1–20. DOI: 10.1109/RBME.2025.3531360 PMID: 40031197

Khurana, V. (2024). Accelerating Pace of Scientific Discovery and Innovation through Big Data Enabled Artificial Intelligence and Deep Learning. *Emerging Trends in Machine Intelligence and Big Data*, *16*(1), 38–53.

Kim, Y., Kim, J. H., Kim, Y. M., Song, S., & Joo, H. J. (2023). Predicting medical specialty from text based on a domain-specific pre-trained BERT. *International Journal of Medical Informatics*, *170*. Advance online publication. DOI: 10.1016/j.ijmedinf.2022.104956 PMID: 36512987

Kitchin, R. (2013). Big data and human geography: Opportunities, challenges and risks. *Dialogues in Human Geography*, *3*(3), 262–267.

Kolekar, S. S., Chen, H., & Kim, K. (2023). Design of precision medicine web-service platform towards health care digital twin. In *2023 Fourteenth International Conference on Ubiquitous and Future Networks (ICUFN)* (pp. 843–848). IEEE. DOI: 10.1109/ICUFN57995.2023.10199942

Kora, R., & Mohammed, A. (2023). *"A Comprehensive Review on Transformers Models For Text Classification," 2023 International Mobile, Intelligent, and Ubiquitous Computing Conference*. MIUCC., DOI: 10.1109/MIUCC58832.2023.10278387

Korkmaz, Y., Dar, S. U., Yurt, M., Özbey, M., & Cukur, T. (2022). Unsupervised mri reconstruction via zero-shot learned adversarial transformers. *IEEE Transactions on Medical Imaging*, *41*(7), 1747–1763. PMID: 35085076

Koroteev, M. V. (2021). BERT: A Review of Applications in Natural Language Processing and Understanding. *ArXiv Preprint*. https://arxiv.org/abs/2103.11943

Krishnan, P. T., Krishnadoss, P., Khandelwal, M., Gupta, D., Nihaal, A., & Kumar, T. S. (2024). Enhancing brain tumor detection in MRI with a rotation invariant Vision Transformer. *Frontiers in Neuroinformatics*, *18*, 1414925. DOI: 10.3389/fninf.2024.1414925 PMID: 38957549

Kumar, S., Verma, A. K., & Mirza, A. (2024). *Digital transformation, artificial intelligence and society: Opportunities and challenges* (2024th ed.). Springer.

Kumar, V., Srivastava, P., Dwivedi, A., Budhiraja, I., Ghosh, D., Goyal, V., & Arora, R. (2024). Large-Language-Models (LLM)-Based AI Chatbots: Architecture, In-Depth Analysis and Their Performance Evaluation. *Communications in Computer and Information Science, 2027 CCIS*. https://doi.org/DOI: 10.1007/978-3-031-53085-2_20

Kumar, K., Jyoti, K., & Kumar, K. (2024). Machine learning for brain tumor classification: Evaluating feature extraction and algorithm efficiency. *Discover Artificial Intelligence*, *4*(1). Advance online publication. DOI: 10.1007/s44163-024-00214-4

Kumar, R., Ayyasamy, R. K., Sangodiah, A., Krishnan, K., Jebna, A. K., & Theam, L. J. (2023). Sentiment Analysis of ChatGPT Healthcare Discourse: Insights from Twitter Data. *International Conference on Software, Knowledge Information, Industrial Management and Applications, SKIMA*. https://doi.org/DOI: 10.1109/SKIMA59232.2023.10387306

Kumar, S. S. (2025). Advancements in medical image segmentation: A review of transformer models. *Computers & Electrical Engineering*, *123*. Advance online publication. DOI: 10.1016/j.compeleceng.2025.110099

Kumar, S. S., & Kumar, R. S. (2024). Transformer Skip-Fusion Based SwinUNet for Liver Segmentation from CT Images. *International Journal of Imaging Systems and Technology*, *34*. Advance online publication. DOI: 10.1002/ima.23126

Kumar, S. S., Vinod Kumar, R. S., Ranjith, V. G., Jeevakala, S., & Sajithra Varun, S. (2024). Grey Wolf optimized SwinUNet based transformer framework for liver segmentation from CT images. *Computers & Electrical Engineering, 117*. Advance online publication. DOI: 10.1016/j.compeleceng.2024.109248

Kumar, V., Rasouliyan, L., Althoff, A., Chang, S., & Long, S. (2023). P22 Severity Score Extraction from Unstructured Clinical Notes Using a Disease-Agnostic Natural Language Processing Question-Answering Pipeline. *Value in Health, 26*(6). Advance online publication. DOI: 10.1016/j.jval.2023.03.035

Kwan, J., Lo, L., Ferguson, J., Goldberg, H., & Díaz-Martínez, J. (2020). G. Tomlinsonet al., "Computerised clinical decision support systems and absolute improvements in care: Meta-analysis of controlled clinical trials". *BMJ (Clinical Research Ed.)*, m3216. DOI: 10.1136/bmj.m3216 PMID: 32943437

Lai, T. (2024). Interpretable medical imagery diagnosis with self-attentive Transformers: A review of explainable AI for health care. *BioMedInformatics, 4*(1), 113–126. DOI: 10.3390/biomedinformatics4010008

Lanchantin, J., Wang, T., Ordonez, V., & Qi, Y. (2021). General multi-label image classification with transformers. In *Proceedings of the IEEE/CVF conference on computer vision and pattern recognition* (pp. 16478-16488).

Lan, Y.-L., Zou, S., Qin, B., & Zhu, X. (2023). Potential roles of transformers in brain tumor diagnosis and treatment. *Brain-X, 1*(2). Advance online publication. DOI: 10.1002/brx2.23

Le, D. L., Nguyen, D. T., Le, T. H., Phan, Q. H., & Pham, T. T. H. (2021). Characterization of healthy and cancerous human skin tissue utilizing Stokes–Mueller polarimetry technique. *Optics Communications, 480*, 126460.

Lee, I., Wallace, Z. S., Park, S., Nam, H., Majithia, A. R., & Ideker, T. (2024). Mechanistic genotype-phenotype translation using hierarchical transformers. DOI: 10.1101/2024.10.23.619940

Lee, S., Xu, Y., D'Souza, A., Martin, E., & Doktorchik, C. (2020). Z. Zhanget al., "Unlocking the potential of electronic health records for health research". *International Journal of Population Data Science, 5*(1). Advance online publication. DOI: 10.23889/ijpds.v5i1.1123 PMID: 32935049

Lee, Y. W., Huang, S. K., & Chang, R. F. (2022). CheXGAT: A disease correlation-aware network for thorax disease diagnosis from chest X-ray images. *Artificial Intelligence in Medicine, 132*, 102382.

Leung, P. H., Chui, K. T., Lo, K., & de Pablos, P. O. (2021). A support vector machine–based voice disorders detection using human voice signal. In *Artificial Intelligence and Big Data Analytics for Smart Healthcare* (pp. 197–208). Academic Press.

Lewis, M., Liu, Y., Goyal, N., Ghazvininejad, M., Mohamed, A., Levy, O., Stoyanov, V., & Zettlemoyer, L. (2020). BART: Denoising sequence-to-sequence pre-training for natural language generation, translation, and comprehension. *Proceedings of the Annual Meeting of the Association for Computational Linguistics*, 7871–7880. https://doi.org/DOI: 10.18653/v1/2020.acl-main.703

Li, J., Dada, A., Puladi, B., Kleesiek, J., & Egger, J. (2024). ChatGPT in healthcare: A taxonomy and systematic review. In *Computer Methods and Programs in Biomedicine* (Vol. 245). https://doi.org/DOI: 10.1016/j.cmpb.2024.108013

Li, Y., Tao, W., Li, Z., Sun, Z., Li, F., Fenton, S., Xu, H., & Tao, C. (2024). Artificial intelligence-powered pharmacovigilance: A review of machine and deep learning in clinical text-based adverse drug event detection for benchmark datasets. In *Journal of Biomedical Informatics* (Vol. 152). https://doi.org/DOI: 10.1016/j.jbi.2024.104621

Liang, J., Yang, C., & Zhong, J.. (2023). BTSwin-Unet: 3D U-shaped Symmetrical Swin Transformer-based Network for Brain Tumor Segmentation with Self-supervised Pre-training. *Neural Processing Letters*, *55*, 3695–3713. DOI: 10.1007/s11063-022-10919-1

Liang, Z., Zhao, K., Liang, G., Li, S., Wu, Y., & Zhou, Y. (2023). MAXFormer: Enhanced transformer for medical image segmentation with multi-attention and multi-scale features fusion. *Knowledge-Based Systems, 280.* Advance online publication. DOI: 10.1016/j.knosys.2023.110987

Li, B., Liu, S., Wu, F., Li, G., Zhong, M., & Guan, X. (2022). RT-Unet: An advanced network based on residual network and transformer for medical image segmentation. *International Journal of Intelligent Systems*, *37*, 8565–8582. DOI: 10.1002/int.22956

Li, B., Yang, T., & Zhao, X. (2023). NVTrans-UNet: Neighborhood vision transformer based U-Net for multi-modal cardiac MR image segmentation. *Journal of Applied Clinical Medical Physics*, *24*, e13908. DOI: 10.1002/acm2.13908 PMID: 36651634

Li, C., Wang, L., & Li, Y. (2022). Transformer and group parallel axial attention co-encoder for medical image segmentation. *Scientific Reports*, *12*, 16117. DOI: 10.1038/s41598-022-20440-z PMID: 36167743

Li, G., Jin, D., Yu, Q., & Qi, M. (2023). IB-TransUNet: Combining Information Bottleneck and Transformer for Medical Image Segmentation. *Journal of King Saud University. Computer and Information Sciences*, *35*(3), 249–258. DOI: 10.1016/j.jksuci.2023.02.012

Li, J., & Chen, J. (2025). Lei jiang, Ruoyu Li, Peilun Han, Junlong Cheng, SEAformer: Selective Edge Aggregation transformer for 2D medical image segmentation. *Biomedical Signal Processing and Control*, *102*. Advance online publication. DOI: 10.1016/j.bspc.2024.107203

Li, J., Chen, N., Zhou, H., Lai, T., Dong, H., Feng, C., Chen, R., Yang, C., Cai, F., & Wei, L. (2023). MCRformer: Morphological constraint reticular transformer for 3D medical image segmentation. *Expert Systems with Applications*, *232*. Advance online publication. DOI: 10.1016/j.eswa.2023.120877

Li, J., Ye, J., Zhang, R., Wu, Y., Berhane, G., Deng, H., & Shi, H. (2023). CPF-Transformer: Transformer fusion context pyramid medical image segmentation network. *Frontiers in Neuroscience*, *17*. Advance online publication. DOI: 10.3389/fnins.2023.1288366 PMID: 38130692

Li, L., & Ma, H. (2022, March 23). RDCTrans U-Net: A Hybrid Variable Architecture for Liver CT Image Segmentation. *Sensors (Basel)*, *22*(7), 2452. DOI: 10.3390/s22072452 PMID: 35408067

Lin, A., Chen, B., Xu, J., Zhang, Z., Lu, G., & Zhang, D. "DS-TransUNet: Dual Swin Transformer U-Net for Medical Image Segmentation," in *IEEE Transactions on Instrumentation and Measurement*, vol. 71, pp. 1-15, 2022, Art no. 4005615, doi: DOI: 10.1109/TIM.2022.3178991

Lin, A., Chen, B., Xu, J., Zhang, Z., Lu, G., & Zhang, D. (2022). Ds-transunet: Dual swin transformer u-net for medical image segmentation. *IEEE Transactions on Instrumentation and Measurement*, *71*, 1–15.

Lin, J.. (2023, August). CKD-TransBTS: Clinical Knowledge-Driven Hybrid Transformer With Modality-Correlated Cross-Attention for Brain Tumor Segmentation. *IEEE Transactions on Medical Imaging*, *42*(8), 2451–2461. DOI: 10.1109/TMI.2023.3250474 PMID: 37027751

Lin, X., Yu, L., Cheng, K.-T., & Yan, Z. (2023, July). BATFormer: Towards Boundary-Aware Lightweight Transformer for Efficient Medical Image Segmentation. *IEEE Journal of Biomedical and Health Informatics*, *27*(7), 3501–3512. DOI: 10.1109/JBHI.2023.3266977 PMID: 37053058

Lin, Y., Han, X., Chen, K., Zhang, W., & Liu, Q. (2024). CSwinDoubleU-Net: A double U-shaped network combined with convolution and Swin Transformer for colorectal polyp segmentation. *Biomedical Signal Processing and Control, 89*. Advance online publication. DOI: 10.1016/j.bspc.2023.105749

Lin, Y., Huang, J., Xu, W., Cui, C., Xu, W., & Li, Z. (2023). Method for Carotid Artery 3-D Ultrasound Image Segmentation Based on CSWin Transformer. *Ultrasound in Medicine & Biology*, *49*(2), 645–656. DOI: 10.1016/j.ultrasmedbio.2022.11.005 PMID: 36460566

Li, R.. (2023, July). DHT-Net: Dynamic Hierarchical Transformer Network for Liver and Tumor Segmentation. *IEEE Journal of Biomedical and Health Informatics, 27*(7), 3443–3454. DOI: 10.1109/JBHI.2023.3268218 PMID: 37079414

Liu, L., Jiang, H., He, P., Chen, W., Liu, X., Gao, J., & Han, J. (2019). On the variance of the adaptive learning rate and beyond. *arXiv preprint arXiv:1908.03265.*

Liu, Y., Ott, M., Goyal, N., Du, J., Joshi, M., Chen, D., Levy, O., Lewis, M., Zettlemoyer, L., & Stoyanov, V. (2019). RoBERTa: A Robustly Optimized BERT Pretraining Approach. *ArXiv Preprint ArXiv:1907.11692*. https://arxiv.org/abs/1907.11692v1

Liu, Z., Lin, Y., Cao, Y., Hu, H., Wei, Y., Zhang, Z., Lin, S., & Guo, B. Swin transformer: Hierarchical ViT using shifted windows, in: Proceedings of the IEEE/CVF international conference on computer vision, 2021, pp. 10012–10022.

Liu, C., Gu, L., Ding, J., Meng, Q., Li, N., Dai, G., & Wu, X. (2021). Autophagy in skin barrier and immune-related skin diseases. *The Journal of Dermatology*, *48*(12), 1827–1837. PMID: 34655245

Liu, D., Wu, B., Li, C., Sun, Z., & Zhang, N. (2023). TrEnD: A transformer-based encoder-decoder model with adaptive patch embedding for mass segmentation in mammograms. *Medical Physics*, *50*, 2884–2899. DOI: 10.1002/mp.16216 PMID: 36609788

Liu, S., Cai, T., Tang, X., & Wang, C. (2023, September). MRL-Net: Multi-Scale Representation Learning Network for COVID-19 Lung CT Image Segmentation. *IEEE Journal of Biomedical and Health Informatics*, *27*(9), 4317–4328. DOI: 10.1109/JBHI.2023.3285936 PMID: 37314916

Liu, X. (2023). Di Zhang, Junping Yao, Jinshan Tang, Transformer and convolutional based dual branch network for retinal vessel segmentation in OCTA images. *Biomedical Signal Processing and Control*, *83*. Advance online publication. DOI: 10.1016/j.bspc.2023.104604

Liu, X., Fan, W., & Zhou, D. (2022). Skin Lesion Segmentation via Intensive Atrous Spatial Transformer. In Wang, L., Segal, M., Chen, J., & Qiu, T. (Eds.), Lecture Notes in Computer Science: Vol. 13471. *Wireless Algorithms, Systems, and Applications. WASA 2022*. Springer., DOI: 10.1007/978-3-031-19208-1_2

Liu, X., Gao, P., Yu, T., Wang, F., & Yuan, R.-Y. (2025). CSWin-UNet: Transformer UNet with cross-shaped windows for medical image segmentation. *Information Fusion, 113*. Advance online publication. DOI: 10.1016/j.inffus.2024.102634

Liu, X., Xie, J., Hou, J., Xu, X., & Guo, Y. (2025). D-get: Group-enhanced transformer for DR severity classification in fundus fluorescein angiography. *Journal of Medical Systems*, *49*(1), 1–15. PMID: 39751967

Liu, X., Yao, C., Chen, H., Xiang, R., Wu, H., Du, P., Yu, Z., Liu, W., Liu, J., & Geng, D. (2023). BTSC-TNAS: A neural architecture search-based transformer for brain tumor segmentation and classification. *Computerized Medical Imaging and Graphics, 110*. Advance online publication. DOI: 10.1016/j.compmedimag.2023.102307 PMID: 37913635

Liu, Y., Han, L., & Yao, B.. (2024). STA-Former: Enhancing medical image segmentation with Shrinkage Triplet Attention in a hybrid CNN-Transformer model. *SIViP*, *18*, 1901–1910. DOI: 10.1007/s11760-023-02893-5

Liu, Y., Ju, S., & Wang, J. (2024). Exploring the potential of ChatGPT in medical dialogue summarization: A study on consistency with human preferences. *BMC Medical Informatics and Decision Making*, *24*(1). Advance online publication. DOI: 10.1186/s12911-024-02481-8 PMID: 38486198

Liu, Y., Wang, H., Chen, Z., Huangliang, K., & Zhang, H. (2022). TransUNet+: Redesigning the skip connection to enhance features in medical image segmentation. *Knowledge-Based Systems, 256*. Advance online publication. DOI: 10.1016/j.knosys.2022.109859

Liu, Y., Yao, D., Ma, Y., Wang, H., Wang, J., Bai, X., Zeng, G., & Liu, Y. (2025). Stmf-drnet: A multi-branch fine-grained classification model for DR using swin-transformerv2. *Biomedical Signal Processing and Control, 103*, 107352.

Liu, Y., Zhang, Y., Wang, Y., Hou, F., Yuan, J., Tian, J., Zhang, Y., Shi, Z., Fan, J., & He, Z. (2023). A survey of visual transformers. *IEEE Transactions on Neural Networks and Learning Systems*. PMID: 37015131

Liu, Z., Bao, Y., Wang, W., Pan, L., & Wang, H. (2023). Emden: A novel method integrating graph and transformer representations for predicting the effect of mutations on clinical drug response. *Computers in Biology and Medicine*. Advance online publication. DOI: 10.1016/j.compbiomed.2023.107678 PMID: 37976823

Liu, Z., Lin, Y., Cao, Y., Hu, H., Wei, Y., Zhang, Z., & Guo, B. (2021). Swin transformer: Hierarchical vision transformer using shifted windows. In *Proceedings of the IEEE/CVF international conference on computer vision* (pp. 10012-10022).

Liu, Z., Lin, Y., Cao, Y., Hu, H., Wei, Y., Zhang, Z., Lin, S., & Guo, B. Swin transformer: Hierarchical ViT using shifted windows, in: *2021 IEEE/CVF International Conference on Computer Vision (ICCV)*, 2021, pp. 9992–10002. doi:DOI: 10.1109/ICCV48922.2021.00986

Liu, Z., Roberts, R., Chen, X., Huang, R., & Tong, W. (2021). Ai-based language models powering drug discovery and development. *Drug Discovery Today*, *26*(11), 2593–2607. DOI: 10.1016/j.drudis.2021.06.009 PMID: 34216835

Li, W., Song, H., Li, Z., Lin, Y., Shi, J., Yang, J., & Wu, W. (2023). OrbitNet—A fully automated orbit multi-organ segmentation model based on transformer in CT images. *Computers in Biology and Medicine*, *155*. Advance online publication. DOI: 10.1016/j.compbiomed.2023.106628 PMID: 36809695

Li, W., Zhao, Y., Li, F., & Wang, L. (2022). MIA-Net: Multi-information aggregation network combining transformers and convolutional feature learning for polyp segmentation. *Knowledge-Based Systems*, *247*, 108824. DOI: 10.1016/j.knosys.2022.108824

Li, X., Jiang, A., & Qiu, Y.. (2023). TPFR-Net: U-shaped model for lung nodule segmentation based on transformer pooling and dual-attention feature reorganization. *Medical & Biological Engineering & Computing*, *61*, 1929–1946. DOI: 10.1007/s11517-023-02852-9 PMID: 37243853

Li, X., Jiang, A., Wang, S., Li, F., & Yan, S. (2023). CTBP-Net: Lung nodule segmentation model based on the cross-transformer and bidirectional pyramid. *Biomedical Signal Processing and Control*, *82*. Advance online publication. DOI: 10.1016/j.bspc.2022.104528

Li, X., Zhang, L., Yang, J., & Teng, F. (2024). Role of artificial intelligence in medical image analysis: A review of current trends and future directions. *Journal of Medical and Biological Engineering*, *44*(2), 231–243.

Li, Y.. (2023, September). Global Transformer and Dual Local Attention Network via Deep-Shallow Hierarchical Feature Fusion for Retinal Vessel Segmentation. *IEEE Transactions on Cybernetics*, *53*(9), 5826–5839. DOI: 10.1109/TCYB.2022.3194099 PMID: 35984806

Li, Y., Rao, S., Solares, J., Hassaïne, A., & Ramakrishnan, R. (2020). D. Canoyet al., "Behrt: Transformer for electronic health records". *Scientific Reports*, *10*(1). Advance online publication. DOI: 10.1038/s41598-020-62922-y PMID: 32346050

Li, Z.. (2022). TFCNs: A CNN-Transformer Hybrid Network for Medical Image Segmentation. In Pimenidis, E., Angelov, P., Jayne, C., Papaleonidas, A., & Aydin, M. (Eds.), Lecture Notes in Computer Science: Vol. 13532. *Artificial Neural Networks and Machine Learning – ICANN 2022. ICANN 2022*. Springer., DOI: 10.1007/978-3-031-15937-4_65

Li, Z., Gu, T., Li, B., Xu, W., He, X., & Hui, X. (2022). ConvNeXt-based fine-grained image classification and bilinear attention mechanism model. *Applied Sciences (Basel, Switzerland)*, *12*(18), 9016.

Li, Z., Koban, K. C., Schenck, T. L., Giunta, R. E., Li, Q., & Sun, Y. (2022). Artificial intelligence in dermatology image analysis: Current developments and future trends. *Journal of Clinical Medicine*, *11*(22), 6826. PMID: 36431301

Loftus, T. J., Ruppert, M. M., Shickel, B., Ozrazgat-Baslanti, T., Balch, J., Efron, P. A., Upchurch, G. R., Rashidi, P., Tignanelli, C., Bian, J., & Bihorac, A. (2022). Federated learning for preserving data privacy in collaborative healthcare research. *Digital Health*, *8*, 205520762211344. DOI: 10.1177/20552076221134455 PMID: 36325438

Loganayagi, T., Sravani, M., Maram, B., & Rao, T. V. M. (2025). Hybrid Deep Maxout-VGG-16 model for brain tumour detection and classification using MRI images. *Journal of Biotechnology*, *405*, 124–138. DOI: 10.1016/j.jbiotec.2025.05.009 PMID: 40350083

Logeswaran, L., Lee, H., & Radev, D. (2018). Sentence ordering and coherence modeling using recurrent neural networks. *32nd AAAI Conference on Artificial Intelligence, AAAI 2018*, 5285–5292. https://doi.org/DOI: 10.1609/aaai.v32i1.11997

Luo, Q., Zeng, W., Chen, M., Peng, G., Yuan, X., & Yin, Q. "Self-Attention and Transformers: Driving the Evolution of Large Language Models," 2023 IEEE 6th International Conference on Electronic Information and Communication Technology (ICEICT), Qingdao, China, 2023, pp. 401-405, doi: DOI: 10.1109/ICEICT57916.2023.10245906

Lu, S., Zhao, H., Liu, H., Li, H., & Wang, N. (2023). PKRT-Net: Prior knowledge-based relation transformer network for optic cup and disc segmentation. *Neurocomputing, 538.* Advance online publication. DOI: 10.1016/j.neucom.2023.03.044

Lu, W., Shengkai, Y., Yu, W., Aimin, L., Shiwei, Y., & Kang, X. (2022). Case report: Clinical report of co-occurrence of pituitary adenoma and meningioma in the sellar region after meningioma treatment. *Frontiers in Neurology, 13*, 1042106. DOI: 10.3389/fneur.2022.1042106 PMID: 36561304

Lu, X., Li, S., & Fujimoto, M. (2020). Automatic speech recognition. In *SpringerBriefs in Computer Science* (pp. 21–38). Springer London., DOI: 10.1007/978-981-15-0595-9_2

Lu, Z., She, C., Wang, W., & Huang, Q. (2024). LM-Net: A light-weight and multi-scale network for medical image segmentation. *Computers in Biology and Medicine, 168.* Advance online publication. DOI: 10.1016/j.compbiomed.2023.107717 PMID: 38007973

Madukwe, K. J., Gao, X., & Xue, B. (2022). Token replacement-based data augmentation methods for hate speech detection. *World Wide Web (Bussum), 25*(3), 1129–1150. DOI: 10.1007/s11280-022-01025-2

Mahesh, N., Devishamani, C. S., Raghu, K., Mahalingam, M., Bysani, P., Chakravarthy, A. V., & Raman, R. (2024). Advancing healthcare: The role and impact of AI and foundation models. *American Journal of Translational Research, 16*(6), 2166–2179. DOI: 10.62347/WQWV9220 PMID: 39006256

Ma, J., He, Y., & Li, F.. (2024). Segment anything in medical images. *Nature Communications, 15*, 654. DOI: 10.1038/s41467-024-44824-z PMID: 38253604

Majkowska, A., Mittal, S., Steiner, D. F., Reicher, J. J., McKinney, S. M., Duggan, G. E., & Shetty, S. (2020). Chest radiograph interpretation with deep learning models: Assessment with radiologist-adjudicated reference standards and population-adjusted evaluation. *Radiology, 294*(2), 421–431.

Ma, M., Xia, H., & Tan, Y.. (2022). HT-Net: Hierarchical context-attention transformer network for medical ct image segmentation. *Applied Intelligence, 52*, 10692–10705. DOI: 10.1007/s10489-021-03010-0

Mamodiya, U., & Kishor, I. "A Comparative Study on the Performance of DualAxis Solar Tracking Systems and Fixed Solar Arrays," in *Proc. 5th Int. Conf. on Information Management & Machine Intelligence (ICIMMI '23)*, Jaipur, India, 2024, Art. no. 116, pp. 1–4, doi: DOI: 10.1145/3647444.3647943

Mamodiya, U., Raigar, G., & Meena, H. (2018). Design & simulation of tiffin food problem using fuzzy logic. *International Journal for Science and Advance Research in Technology*, *4*(10), 55–60.

Mamodiya, U., Raigar, G., & Meena, H. (2018). Design & simulation of tiffin food problem using fuzzy logic. *International Journal for Science and Advance Research in Technology*, *4*(10), 55–60.

Mamodiya, U., & Tiwari, N. (2023). Design and implementation of an intelligent single axis automatic solar tracking system. *Materials Today: Proceedings*, *81*, 1148–1151.

Marchena Sekli, G. (2024). The research landscape on generative artificial intelligence: a bibliometric analysis of transformer-based models. *Kybernetes. The International Journal of Cybernetics, Systems and Management Sciences*. https://doi.org/DOI: 10.1108/k-03-2024-0554

Marcus, A., Bentley, P., & Rueckert, D. (2023, December). Concurrent Ischemic Lesion Age Estimation and Segmentation of CT Brain Using a Transformer-Based Network. *IEEE Transactions on Medical Imaging*, *42*(12), 3464–3473. DOI: 10.1109/TMI.2023.3287361 PMID: 37335797

Ma, Z., Qi, Y., Xu, C., Zhao, W., Lou, M., Wang, Y., & Ma, Y. (2023). ATFE-Net: Axial Transformer and Feature Enhancement-based CNN for ultrasound breast mass segmentation. *Computers in Biology and Medicine*, *153*. Advance online publication. DOI: 10.1016/j.compbiomed.2022.106533 PMID: 36638617

Mendhe, D., Dogra, A., Nair, P. S., Punitha, S., Preetha, K. S., & Babu, S. B. G. T. (2024). AI-enabled data-driven approaches for personalized medicine and healthcare analytics. In *2024 Ninth International Conference on Science Technology Engineering and Mathematics (ICONSTEM)* (pp. 1–5). IEEE. DOI: 10.1109/ICONSTEM60960.2024.10568722

Meng, M., Fulham, M., Feng, D., Bi, L., & Kim, J. (2025). Autofuse: Automatic fusion networks for deformable medical image registration. *Pattern Recognition*, *161*, 111338.

Meng, W., Liu, S., & Wang, H. (2025). AFC-Unet: Attention-fused full-scale CNN-transformer unet for medical image segmentation. *Biomedical Signal Processing and Control*, *99*. Advance online publication. DOI: 10.1016/j.bspc.2024.106839

Mennella, C., Maniscalco, U., De Pietro, G., & Esposito, M. (2024). Ethical and regulatory challenges of AI technologies in healthcare: A narrative review. *Heliyon*, *10*(4), e26297. DOI: 10.1016/j.heliyon.2024.e26297 PMID: 38384518

Mezina, A., & Burget, R. (2024). Detection of post-covid-19-related pulmonary diseases in x-ray images using ViT-based neural network. *Biomedical Signal Processing and Control*, *87*, 105380.

Mikolov, T., Chen, K., Corrado, G., & Dean, J. (2013). Efficient estimation of word representations in vector space. *1st International Conference on Learning Representations, ICLR 2013 - Workshop Track Proceedings*. https://arxiv.org/abs/1712.09405

Miotto, R., Wang, F., Wang, S., Jiang, X., & Dudley, J. T. (2017). Deep learning for healthcare: Review, opportunities and challenges. *Briefings in Bioinformatics*, *19*(6), 1236–1246. DOI: 10.1093/bib/bbx044 PMID: 28481991

Mio, W., Chen, R., Lv, J., Mai, S., Chen, Y., He, M., & Ma, H. (2025). Establishment of an intelligent analysis system for clinical image features of melanonychia based on deep learning image segmentation. *Computerized Medical Imaging and Graphics*, 102543. PMID: 40367737

Mirzapure, I. A., Telrandhe, U., Dandekar, M. R., & Salve, Y. M. (2025). Deep learning for personalized medicine: A comprehensive review. In *2025 4th International Conference on Sentiment Analysis and Deep Learning (ICSADL)* (pp. 1503–1509). IEEE. DOI: 10.1109/ICSADL65848.2025.10933299

Miyoshi, N. (2025). Use of AI in diagnostic imaging and future prospects. *JMA Journal*, *8*(1), 198–203. DOI: 10.31662/jmaj.2024-0169 PMID: 39926072

Montesinos López, O. A., Montesinos López, A., & Crossa, J. (2022). Fundamentals of Artificial Neural Networks and Deep Learning. In *Multivariate Statistical Machine Learning Methods for Genomic Prediction* (pp. 379–425). Springer International Publishing., DOI: 10.1007/978-3-030-89010-0_10

Moore, A., Orset, B., Yassaee, A., Irving, B., & Morelli, D. (2024). Healthrecord bert (herbert): Leveraging transformers on electronic health records for chronic kidney disease risk stratification. *ACM Transactions on Computing for Healthcare*, *5*(3), 1–18.

Mosquera, C., Ferrer, L., Milone, D. H., Luna, D., & Ferrante, E. (2024). Class imbalance on medical image classification: Towards better evaluation practices for discrimination and calibration performance. *European Radiology*, *34*(12), 7895–7903. PMID: 38861161

Murugan, M., Yuan, B., Venner, E., Ballantyne, C. M., Robinson, K. M., Coons, J. C., Wang, L., Empey, P. E., & Gibbs, R. A. (2024). Empowering personalized pharmacogenomics with generative AI solutions. *Journal of the American Medical Informatics Association: JAMIA*, *31*(6), 1356–1366. DOI: 10.1093/jamia/ocae039 PMID: 38447590

Murugan, M., Yuan, B., Venner, E., Ballantyne, C. M., Robinson, K. M., Coons, J. C., Wang, L., Empey, P. E., & Gibbs, R. A. (2024). Empowering Personalized Pharmacogenomics with Generative AI Solutions. *medRxiv*. DOI: 10.1101/2024.02.21.24302946

Muthalakshmi, M., Jeyapal, K., Vinoth, M., Dinesh-Kumar, S. P., Murugan, N. S., & Sheela, K. S. (2024). Federated Learning for Secure and Privacy-Preserving Medical Image Analysis in Decentralized Healthcare Systems. 1442–1447. https://doi.org/DOI: 10.1109/icesc60852.2024.10690003

Nachmani, R., Nidal, I., Robinson, D., Yassin, M., & Abookasis, D. (2023). Segmentation of polyps based on pyramid vision transformers and residual block for real-time endoscopy imaging. *Journal of Pathology Informatics*, *14*. Advance online publication. DOI: 10.1016/j.jpi.2023.100197 PMID: 36844703

Nadeem, G., Khaliq, A., Ahmed, J., & Aziz, A. (2025). Healthcare security challenges Leveraging generative AI to transform cybersecurity. In *IGI Global eBooks* (pp. 205–250). https://doi.org/DOI: 10.4018/979-8-3693-6250-1.ch010

Nandini Prasad, K. S., Sudhanva, S., Tarun, T. N., Yuvraaj, Y., & Vishal, D. A. (2023). Conversational Chatbot Builder - Smarter Virtual Assistance with Domain Specific AI. *2023 4th International Conference for Emerging Technology, INCET 2023*. https://doi.org/DOI: 10.1109/INCET57972.2023.10170114

Narmadha, A., & Gobalakrishnan, N. (2025). Het-rl: Multiple pulmonary disease diagnosis via hybrid efficient transformers based representation learning model using multi-modality data. *Biomedical Signal Processing and Control*, *100*, 107157.

Nerella, S., Bandyopadhyay, S., Zhang, J., Contreras, M., Siegel, S., Bumin, A., Silva, B., Sena, J., Shickel, B., Bihorac, A., Khezeli, K., & Rashidi, P. (2024). Transformers and large language models in healthcare: A review. *Artificial Intelligence in Medicine*, *154*(102900), 102900. DOI: 10.1016/j.artmed.2024.102900 PMID: 38878555

Nguyen, T. T. T., Greene, L. A., Mnatsakanyan, H., & Badr, C. E. (2024). Revolutionizing brain tumor care: Emerging technologies and strategies. *Biomedicines*, *12*(6), 1376. DOI: 10.3390/biomedicines12061376 PMID: 38927583

Nie, L., Chen, T., Wang, Z., Kang, W., & Lin, L. (2022). Multi-label image recognition with attentive transformer-localizer module. *Multimedia Tools and Applications*, *81*(6), 7917–7940.

Nikam, D. S., Nisha Murthy, D., Pragada, S. D., & Mamatha, H. R. (2024). BGKnow-Medical Chatbot: A Hybrid Approach Based on Knowledge Graph and GPT-2. *Lecture Notes in Networks and Systems, 892*. Advance online publication. DOI: 10.1007/978-981-99-9521-9_30

Niu, H., Omitaomu, O. A., Langston, M. A., Olama, M., Ozmen, O., Klasky, H. B., Laurio, A., Ward, M., & Nebeker, J. (2024). EHR-BERT: A BERT-based model for effective anomaly detection in electronic health records. *Journal of Biomedical Informatics, 150*. Advance online publication. DOI: 10.1016/j.jbi.2024.104605 PMID: 38331082

Ni, Y., Chen, G., Feng, Z., & Cui, H. (2024). Dimitris Metaxas, Shaoting Zhang, Wentao Zhu, DA-Tran: Multiphase liver tumor segmentation with a domain-adaptive transformer network. *Pattern Recognition, 149*. Advance online publication. DOI: 10.1016/j.patcog.2023.110233

Nyiramana, M. P. (2024).. . *The Role of Genomics in Predicting Drug Response.*, *3*(2), 1–4. DOI: 10.59298/rojphm/2024/3214

Okonji, O. R., Yunusov, K., & Gordon, B. (2024). Applications of Generative AI in Healthcare: algorithmic, ethical, legal and societal considerations. *arXiv [Cs.CV]*. https://doi.org/DOI: 10.48550/ARXIV.2406.10632

Olshannikova, E., Ometov, A., Koucheryavy, Y., & Olsson, T. (2015). Visualizing Big Data with augmented and virtual reality: Challenges and research agenda. *Journal of Big Data*, *2*(1), 1–27.

Ong, J. C. L., Ning, Y., Liu, M., Ma, Y., Liang, Z., Singh, K., Chang, R. T., Vogel, S., Lim, J. C. W., Tan, I. S. K., Freyer, O., Gilbert, S., Bitterman, D. S., Liu, X., Denniston, A. K., & Liu, N. (2025). Regulatory science innovation for generative AI and large language models in health and medicine: A global call for action. In *arXiv [cs.CY]*. https://doi.org/DOI: 10.48550/ARXIV.2502.07794

Ossa, L. (2024). Integrating ethics in ai development: A qualitative study. *BMC Medical Ethics*, *25*(1). Advance online publication. DOI: 10.1186/s12910-023-01000-0 PMID: 38262986

Ou, J., Jiang, L., Bai, T., Zhan, P., Liu, R., & Xiao, H. (2024). ResTransUnet: An effective network combined with Transformer and U-Net for liver segmentation in CT scans. *Computers in Biology and Medicine, 177*. Advance online publication. DOI: 10.1016/j.compbiomed.2024.108625 PMID: 38823365

Oulhadj, M., Riffi, J., Khodriss, C., Mahraz, A. M., & Yahyaouy, A. (2024). M. Ab dellaoui, I. B. Andaloussi, H. Tairi, DR prediction based on ViT and modified capsule network. *Computers in Biology and Medicine, 175*, 108523. PMID: 38701591

Padmaja, M., Shitharth, S., Prasuna, K., Chaturvedi, A., Kshirsagar, P. R., & Vani, A. (2022). Grow of artificial intelligence to challenge security in IoT application. *Wireless Personal Communications, 127*(3), 1829–1845.

Pan, D., & Shen, J. (2025). Zaid Al-Huda, Mohammed A.A. Al-qaness, VcaNet: Vision Transformer with fusion channel and spatial attention module for 3D brain tumor segmentation. *Computers in Biology and Medicine, 186*. Advance online publication. DOI: 10.1016/j.compbiomed.2025.109662 PMID: 39813745

Pan, S., Liu, X., & Xie, N.. (2023). EG-TransUNet: A transformer-based U-Net with enhanced and guided models for biomedical image segmentation. *BMC Bioinformatics, 24*, 85. DOI: 10.1186/s12859-023-05196-1 PMID: 36882688

Pan, X., Ma, C., Mu, Y., & Bi, M. (2024). GLSNet: A Global Guided Local Feature Stepwise Aggregation Network for polyp segmentation. *Biomedical Signal Processing and Control, 87*. Advance online publication. DOI: 10.1016/j.bspc.2023.105528

Park, K.-B., & Lee, J. Y. (2022, April). SwinE-Net: Hybrid deep learning approach to novel polyp segmentation using convolutional neural network and Swin Transformer. *Journal of Computational Design and Engineering, 9*(2), 616–632. DOI: 10.1093/jcde/qwac018

Parvaiz, A., Khalid, M. A., Zafar, R., Ameer, H., Ali, M., & Fraz, M. M. (2023). ViTs in medical computer vision—A contemplative retrospection. *Engineering Applications of Artificial Intelligence, 122*, 106126.

Patel, S. U., & Jirvankar, P. (2024). AI in healthcare – Precision medicine and diagnosis. In *2024 2nd DMIHER International Conference on Artificial Intelligence in Healthcare, Education and Industry (IDICAIEI)* (pp. 1–6). IEEE. DOI: 10.1109/IDICAIEI61867.2024.10842772

Patwardhan, N., Marrone, S., & Sansone, C. (2023). Transformers in the Real World: A Survey on NLP Applications. In *Information (Switzerland)* (Vol. 14, Issue 4). https://doi.org/DOI: 10.3390/info14040242

Peng, Y., Bian, J., & Xu, J. (2024). Fedmm: Federated Multi-Modal Learning with Modality Heterogeneity in Computational Pathology. https://doi.org/DOI: 10.1109/icassp48485.2024.10448255

Pesapane, F., Bracchi, D. A., Mulligan, J. F., Linnikov, A., Maslennikov, O., Lanzavecchia, M. B., Tantrige, P., Stasolla, A., Biondetti, P., Giuggioli, P. F., Cassano, E., & Carrafiello, G. (2021). Legal and regulatory framework for AI solutions in healthcare in EU, US, China, and Russia: New scenarios after a pandemic. *Radiation*, *1*(4), 261–276. DOI: 10.3390/radiation1040022

Pfeiffer, J., Lachenmaier, J. F., Hinz, O., & van der Aalst, W. (2024). New laws and regulation: Opportunities for BISE research. *Business & Information Systems Engineering*, *66*(6), 653–666. DOI: 10.1007/s12599-024-00902-6

Pham, D. L., Xu, C., & Prince, J. L. (2000). Current methods in medical image segmentation. *Annual Review of Biomedical Engineering*, *2*(1), 315–337. PMID: 11701515

Piao, Z., Gu, Y. H., & Jin, H.. (2023). Intracerebral hemorrhage CT scan image segmentation with HarDNet based transformer. *Scientific Reports*, *13*, 7208. DOI: 10.1038/s41598-023-33775-y PMID: 37137921

Pinto-Coelho, L. (2023). How artificial intelligence is shaping medical imaging technology: A survey of innovations and applications. *Bioengineering (Basel, Switzerland)*, *10*(12). Advance online publication. DOI: 10.3390/bioengineering10121435 PMID: 38136026

Pradhan, T., Nimkar, P., & Jhajharia, K. (2024). Machine Learning and Deep Learning for Big Data Analysis. In *Big Data Analytics Techniques for Market Intelligence* (pp. 209–240). IGI Global.

Pujari, T., Goel, A., & Sharma, A. (2024). Ensuring responsible AI: The role of Supervised Fine-Tuning (SFT) in upholding integrity and privacy regulations. *International Journal Science and Technology*, *3*(3), 46–55. DOI: 10.56127/ijst.v3i3.1968

Qiao, J., Wang, X., & Chen, J.. (2023). MBUTransNet: Multi-branch U-shaped network fusion transformer architecture for medical image segmentation. *Int J CARS*, *18*, 1895–1902. DOI: 10.1007/s11548-023-02879-1 PMID: 37024630

Qiao, S., Pang, S., & Luo, G.. (2023). DPC-MSGATNet: Dual-path chain multi-scale gated axial-transformer network for four-chamber view segmentation in fetal echocardiography. *Complex & Intelligent Systems*, *9*, 4503–4519. DOI: 10.1007/s40747-023-00968-x

Qi, X. (2024). Machine learning empowering drug discovery: Applications, opportunities and challenges. *Molecules (Basel, Switzerland), 29*(4), 903. DOI: 10.3390/molecules29040903 PMID: 38398653

Qureshi, R., Irfan, M., Ali, H., Khan, A., Nittala, A. S., Ali, S., & Alam, T. (2023). Artificial Intelligence and Biosensors in Healthcare and its Clinical Relevance: A Review. *IEEE Access: Practical Innovations, Open Solutions.*

Raffel, C., Shazeer, N., Roberts, A., Lee, K., Narang, S., Matena, M., Zhou, Y., Li, W., & Liu, P. J. (2019). Exploring the Limits of Transfer Learning with a Unified Text-to-Text Transformer. *Journal of Machine Learning Research, 21*, 1–67. https://arxiv.org/abs/1910.10683v4

Raghuvanshi, S., & Dhariwal, S. (2023, December 14). The VGG16 method is a powerful tool for detecting brain tumors using deep learning techniques. RAiSE-2023, 46. Presented at the RAiSE-2023. doi:DOI: 10.3390/engproc2023059046

Rahem, R. A. A., & Al-Akayleh, F. (2024). Integrative analysis of genomic data types and AI methodologies in healthcare applications. In *2024 2nd International Conference on Cyber Resilience (ICCR)* (pp. 1–5). IEEE. DOI: 10.1109/ICCR61006.2024.10532802

Rahman, A., Karmakar, M., Inteligencia, P. D.-R. de, & 2023, U. (2023). Predictive analytics for healthcare: Improving patient outcomes in the US through Machine Learning. *Researchgate.Net, 14*(01), 595–624. https://www.researchgate.net/profile/Arifur-Rahman-49/publication/387763296_Predictive_Analytics_for_Healthcare_Improving_Patient_Outcomes_in_the_US_through_Machine_Learning/links/677c54b2894c552085467e3a/Predictive-Analytics-for-Healthcare-Improving-Pati

Raiaan, M. A. K., Mukta, M. S. H., Fatema, K., Fahad, N. M., Sakib, S., Mim, M. M. J., Ahmad, J., Ali, M. E., & Azam, S. (2024). A Review on Large Language Models: Architectures, Applications, Taxonomies, Open Issues and Challenges. *IEEE Access: Practical Innovations, Open Solutions, 12*, 26839–26874. DOI: 10.1109/ACCESS.2024.3365742

Ramprasad, P., Pai, N., & Pan, W. (2024). Enhancing Personalized Gene Expression Prediction From DNA Sequences Using Genomic Foundation Models. *HGG Advances, 5*(4), 100347. DOI: 10.1016/j.xhgg.2024.100347 PMID: 39205391

Randazzo, M. S., & Hill, G. (2024). Human dignity in the age of Artificial Intelligence: An overview of legal issues and regulatory regimes. *Australian Journal of Human Rights, 30*(3), 386–408. DOI: 10.1080/1323238x.2025.2483822

Rani, S., Memoria, M., Joshi, K., & Rani, S. (2025). Role of ViT in Healthcare Application: A Review. In *Advances in Computational Intelligence and Robotics* (pp. 153–166). IGI Global.

Ranttila, P., Sahebi, G., Kontio, E., & Salmi, J. (2024). Medical AI in the EU: regulatory considerations and future outlook. In *IntechOpen eBooks*. https://doi.org/ DOI: 10.5772/intechopen.1007443

Rashid, Z., Ahmed, H., Nadeem, N., Zafar, S. B., & Yousaf, M. Z. (2025). The paradigm of digital health: AI applications and transformative trends. *Neural Computing & Applications*. Advance online publication. DOI: 10.1007/s00521-025-11081-0

Rathore, F., & Rathore, M. (2023). The emerging role of artificial intelligence in healthcare. *JPMA. The Journal of the Pakistan Medical Association, 73*(7), 1368–1369. DOI: 10.47391/jpma.23-48 PMID: 37469045

Rawat, A., & Singh Samant, S. "Comparative Analysis of Transformer based Models for Question Answering," 2022 2nd International Conference on Innovative Sustainable Computational Technologies (CISCT), Dehradun, India, 2022, pp. 1-6, doi: DOI: 10.1109/CISCT55310.2022.10046525

Rawat, B., Joshi, Y., & Kumar, A. (2023). AI in healthcare: Opportunities and challenges for personalized medicine and disease diagnosis. In *2023 5th International Conference on Inventive Research in Computing Applications (ICIRCA)* (pp. 374–379). IEEE. DOI: 10.1109/ICIRCA57980.2023.10220746

Raza, A., Ayub, H., Khan, J. A., Ahmad, I., & Salama, S., A., Daradkeh, Y. I., … Hamam, H. (2022). A hybrid deep learning-based approach for brain tumor classification. *Electronics (Basel), 11*(7), 1146. DOI: 10.3390/electronics11071146

Raza, S., Dolatabadi, E., Ondrusek, N., Rosella, L., & Schwartz, B. (2023). Discovering social determinants of health from case reports using natural language processing: Algorithmic development and validation. *BMC Digital Health, 1*(1). Advance online publication. DOI: 10.1186/s44247-023-00035-y

Razavi, J., & Dhafar, H. O., & BaHammam, A. S. (2025). Transforming health care with artificial intelligence: Regulations, challenges, and future directions. *Saudi Journal for Health Sciences, 14*(1), 11–22. DOI: 10.4103/sjhs.sjhs_26_25

Reddy Gooty, C. S., & Kanchireddy, A. (2025). A comprehensive health management system for personalized patient care and medication tracking. In *2025 International Conference on Multi-Agent Systems for Collaborative Intelligence (ICMSCI)* (pp. 1450–1457). IEEE. DOI: 10.1109/ICMSCI62561.2025.10894010

Reddy, S. (2025). Global harmonization of artificial intelligence-enabled software as a medical device regulation: Addressing challenges and unifying standards. *Mayo Clinic Proceedings. Digital Health*, *3*(1), 100191. DOI: 10.1016/j.mcpdig.2024.100191 PMID: 40207007

Rehman, A., Mahmood, T., & Saba, T. (2025). Robust kidney carcinoma prognosis and characterization using swin-vit and deeplabv3+ with multi-model transfer learning. *Applied Soft Computing*, *170*, 112518.

Ren, Y., Wu, D., Khurana, A., Mastorakos, G., Fu, S., Zong, N., Fan, J., Liu, H., & Huang, M. (2023). Classification of Patient Portal Messages with BERT-based Language Models. *Proceedings - 2023 IEEE 11th International Conference on Healthcare Informatics, ICHI 2023*. https://doi.org/DOI: 10.1109/ICHI57859.2023.00033

Ren, F., & Zhou, Y. (2020). Cgmvqa: A new classification and generative model for medical visual question answering. *IEEE Access: Practical Innovations, Open Solutions*, *8*, 50626–50636.

Rezaee, K., & Farnami, F. (2025). Innovative approach for DR severity classification: An ai-powered tool using cnn-transformer fusion. *Journal of Biomedical Physics & Engineering*, *15*(2), 137. PMID: 40259941

Ribeiro, M. T., Singh, S., & Guestrin, C. (2016, August). " Why should i trust you?" Explaining the predictions of any classifier. In *Proceedings of the 22nd ACM SIGKDD international conference on knowledge discovery and data mining* (pp. 1135-1144).

Rodrigues, J. F., Florea, L., de Oliveira, M. C., Diamond, D., & Oliveira, O. N. (2021). Big data and machine learning for materials science. *Discover Materials*, *1*, 1–27. PMID: 33899049

Romanowski, B., Ben Abacha, A., & Fan, Y. (2023). Extracting social determinants of health from clinical note text with classification and sequence-to-sequence approaches. *Journal of the American Medical Informatics Association: JAMIA*, *30*(8). Advance online publication. DOI: 10.1093/jamia/ocad071 PMID: 37100768

Ronneberger, O., Fischer, P., & Brox, T. (2015). U-Net: Convolutional Networks for Biomedical Image Segmentation. In Lecture Notes in Computer Science. Lecture Notes in Computer Science (pp. 234–241). doi:DOI: 10.1007/978-3-319-24574-4_28

Ronneberger, O., Fischer, P., & Brox, T. U-net: Convolutional networks for biomedical image segmentation, in: Medical image computing and computer-assisted intervention–MICCAI 2015: 18th international conference, Munich, Germany, October 5-9, 2015, proceedings, part III 18, Springer, 2015, pp. 234–241.

Roy, P. K. (2024). Deep Ensemble Network for Sentiment Analysis in Bi-lingual Low-resource Languages. *ACM Transactions on Asian and Low-Resource Language Information Processing*, *23*(1). Advance online publication. DOI: 10.1145/3600229

Rudin, C. (2019). Stop explaining black box machine learning models for high stakes decisions and use interpretable models instead. *Nature Machine Intelligence*, *1*(5), 206–215. PMID: 35603010

S, S., S, A., N, S. S., & S, D. S. S. (2024). Role of explainable AI in medical diagnostics and healthcare: A pilot study on Parkinson's speech detection. In *2024 10th International Conference on Control, Automation and Robotics (ICCAR)* (pp. 289–294). IEEE. DOI: 10.1109/ICCAR61844.2024.10569414

Saeedi, S., Rezayi, S., Keshavarz, H., Niakan, R., & Kalhori, S. (2023). MRI-based brain tumor detection using convolutional deep learning methods and chosen machine learning techniques. *BMC Medical Informatics and Decision Making*, *23*(1), 16. DOI: 10.1186/s12911-023-02114-6 PMID: 36691030

Saha, D. K., Joy, A. M., & Majumder, A. (2024). Yotransvit: A transformer and cnn method for predicting and classifying skin diseases using segmentation techniques. *Informatics in Medicine Unlocked*, *47*, 101495.

Salakhutdinov, R. (2015). Learning Deep Generative Models. *Annual Review of Statistics and Its Application*, *2*, 361–385. DOI: 10.1146/annurev-statistics-010814-020120

Salari, N., Heidarian, P., Hosseinian-Far, A., Babajani, F., & Mohammadi, M. (2024). Global prevalence of anxiety, depression, and stress among patients with skin diseases: A systematic review and meta-analysis. *Journal of Prevention*, *45*(4), 611–649. PMID: 38822990

Salazar, J., Liang, D., Nguyen, T. Q., & Kirchhoff, K. (2020). Masked language model scoring. *Proceedings of the Annual Meeting of the Association for Computational Linguistics*, 2699–2712. https://doi.org/DOI: 10.18653/v1/2020.acl-main.240

Sandeep Kumar, E., & Satya Jayadev, P. (2020). Deep Learning for Clinical Decision Support Systems: A Review from the Panorama of Smart Healthcare. *Studies in Big Data*, *68*, 79–99. DOI: 10.1007/978-3-030-33966-1_5

Sanh, V., Debut, L., Chaumond, J., & Wolf, T. (2019). DistilBERT, a distilled version of BERT: smaller, faster, cheaper and lighter. *ArXiv Preprint*. https://arxiv.org/abs/1910.01108v4

Sarker, I. H. (2021). Deep Learning: A Comprehensive Overview on Techniques, Taxonomy, Applications and Research Directions. *SN Computer Science*, *2*(6). Advance online publication. DOI: 10.1007/S42979-021-00815-1 PMID: 34426802

Sarode, S. P., & Khobragade, S. (2024). AI in precision medicine. In *2024 2nd DMIHER International Conference on Artificial Intelligence in Healthcare, Education and Industry (IDICAIEI)* (pp. 1–5). IEEE. DOI: 10.1109/IDICAIEI61867.2024.10842767

Sassi, A., & Tuccari, E. (2023). *Navigating the intersections of AI and data Protection: A Comparative analysis of the EU and US approach to healthcare*. https://unitesi.unipv.it/handle/20.500.14239/27705

Seah, J., Jen, M., Law, M., Culliton, P., & Dowd, S. (2020). *RANZCR CLiP - Catheter and line position challenge*. Kaggle. https://kaggle.com/competitions/ranzcr-clip-catheter-line-classification

Selvaraju, R. R., Cogswell, M., Das, A., Vedantam, R., Parikh, D., & Batra, D. (2017). Grad-cam: Visual explanations from deep networks via gradient-based localization. In *Proceedings of the IEEE international conference on computer vision* (pp. 618-626).

Sezgin, E., Sirrianni, J., & Linwood, S. L. (2022). Operationalizing and implementing pretrained, large artificial intelligence linguistic models in the US health care system: Outlook of generative pretrained transformer 3 (GPT-3) as a service model. *JMIR Medical Informatics*, *10*(2), e32875. DOI: 10.2196/32875 PMID: 35142635

Shafik, W. (2023). Introduction to ChatGPT. In *Advanced Applications of Generative AI and Natural Language Processing Models*. https://doi.org/DOI: 10.4018/9798369305027.ch001

Shafik, W. (2024a). Artificial Intelligence-Enabled Internet of Medical Things (AIoMT) in Modern Healthcare Practices. In *Clinical Practice and Unmet Challenges in AI-Enhanced Healthcare Systems* (pp. 42–69). IGI Global. https://doi.org/DOI: 10.4018/979-8-3693-2703-6.ch003

Shafik, W. (2024f). Smart Health Revolution: Exploring Artificial Intelligence of Internet of Medical Things. In *Healthcare Industry Assessment: Analyzing Risks, Security, and Reliability* (pp. 201–229). Springer. https://doi.org/DOI: 10.1007/978-3-031-65434-3_9

Shafik, W. (2025a). Human-Computer Interaction (HCI) Technologies in Socially-Enabled Artificial Intelligence. In *Future of Digital Technology and AI in Social Sectors* (pp. 121–150). IGI Global.

Shafik, W. (2025b). Revolutionizing Skin Cancer Diagnosis With Artificial Intelligence: Insights Into Machine Learning Techniques. In *Impact of Digital Solutions for Improved Healthcare Delivery* (pp. 167–194). IGI Global.

Shafik, W. (2024b). Artificial Intelligence-Enabled Internet of Medical Things for Enhanced Healthcare Systems. In *Smart Healthcare Systems* (pp. 119–134). CRC Press., DOI: 10.1201/9781032698519-9

Shafik, W. (2024c). Connected healthcare—the impact of Internet of Things on medical services. In *Artificial Intelligence and Internet of Things based Augmented Trends for Data Driven Systems* (pp. 181–217). CRC Press., DOI: 10.1201/9781003497318-10

Shafik, W. (2024d). IoT-Enabled Secure and Intelligent Smart Healthcare. In *Secure and Intelligent IoT-Enabled Smart Cities* (pp. 308–333). IGI Global., DOI: 10.4018/979-8-3693-2373-1.ch015

Shafik, W. (2024e). Science of Emotional Intelligence. In *Enhancing and Predicting Digital Consumer Behavior with AI* (pp. 284–310). IGI Global.

Shafik, W. (2024g). The Future of Healthcare: AIoMT—Redefining Healthcare with Advanced Artificial Intelligence and Machine Learning Techniques. In *Artificial Intelligence and Machine Learning in Drug Design and Development* (pp. 605–634). Wiley., DOI: 10.1002/9781394234196.ch19

Shafik, W., Kalinaki, K., Fahim, K. E., & Adam, M. (2024). Safeguarding Data Privacy and Security in Federated Learning Systems. In *Federated Deep Learning for Healthcare* (pp. 170–190). CRC Press., DOI: 10.1201/9781032694870-13

Shafk, W. (2023). Wearable Medical Electronics in Artifcial Intelligence of Medical Things. In *Handbook of Security and Privacy of AI-Enabled Healthcare Systems and Internet of Medical Things*. https://doi.org/DOI: 10.1201/9781003370321-2

Shah, F., Li, J., Shah, Y., & Shah, F. (2017, November). Broad big data domain via medical big data. In *2017 4th International Conference on Systems and Informatics (ICSAI)* (pp. 732-737). IEEE.

Shaker, A., Maaz, M., & Rasheed, A. Hanoona & Khan, Salman & Yang, Ming-Hsuan & Khan, Fahad. (2022). UNETR++: Delving into Efficient and Accurate 3D Medical Image Segmentation. 10.48550/arXiv.2212.04497.

Shamshad, F., Khan, S., Zamir, S. W., Khan, M. H., Hayat, M., Khan, F. S., & Fu, H. (2023). Transformers in medical imaging: A survey. *Medical Image Analysis*, *88*, 102802. PMID: 37315483

Sharen, H., Narendra, M., & Anbarasi, L. J. (2024). Mskd_net: Multi-head attention-based swin transformer for kidney diseases classification. *IEEE Access: Practical Innovations, Open Solutions*.

Shariaty, F., Pavlov, V. A., Fedyashina, S. V., & Serebrennikov, N. A. (2024). Integrating deep learning and explainable AI for non-invasive prediction of EGFR and KRAS mutations in NSCLC: A novel radiogenomic approach. In *2024 V International Conference on Neural Networks and Neurotechnologies (NeuroNT)* (pp. 32–35). IEEE. DOI: 10.1109/NeuroNT62606.2024.10585441

Sharma, A. K., Kala, S., Kumar, A., Sharma, S., Gupta, G., & Jaiswal, V. (2024). Deep Learning in Genomics, Personalized Medicine, and Neurodevelopmental Disorders. DOI: 10.1002/9781394270910.ch10

Sharma, H., & Padha, D. (2023). From Templates to Transformers: A survey of Multimodal Image Captioning Decoders. *2023 International Conference on Computer, Electronics and Electrical Engineering and Their Applications, IC2E3 2023*. https://doi.org/DOI: 10.1109/IC2E357697.2023.10262494

Sharma, N. A., Ali, A. B. M. S., & Kabir, M. A. (2024). A review of sentiment analysis: tasks, applications, and deep learning techniques. In *International Journal of Data Science and Analytics*. Springer Science and Business Media Deutschland GmbH., DOI: 10.1007/s41060-024-00594-x

Sheikhalishahi, S., Miotto, R., Dudley, J., Lavelli, A., Rinaldi, F., & Osmani, V. (2019). Natural language processing of clinical notes on chronic diseases: Systematic review. *JMIR Medical Informatics*, *7*(2), e12239. DOI: 10.2196/12239 PMID: 31066697

Shen, T., & Xu, H. (2023). Medical Image Segmentation Based on Transformer and HarDNet Structures. *IEEE Access: Practical Innovations, Open Solutions*, *11*, 16621–16630. DOI: 10.1109/ACCESS.2023.3244197

Shen, X., Xu, J., Jia, H., Fan, P., Dong, F., Yu, B., & Ren, S. (2022). Self-attentional microvessel segmentation via squeeze-excitation transformer Unet. *Computerized Medical Imaging and Graphics*, *97*. Advance online publication. DOI: 10.1016/j.compmedimag.2022.102055 PMID: 35320771

Shen, Z., Yang, H., Zhang, Z., & Zheng, S. (2022). Automated Kidney Tumor Segmentation with Convolution and Transformer Network. In Heller, N., Isensee, F., Trofimova, D., Tejpaul, R., Papanikolopoulos, N., & Weight, C. (Eds.), Lecture Notes in Computer Science: Vol. 13168. *Kidney and Kidney Tumor Segmentation. KiTS 2021*. Springer., DOI: 10.1007/978-3-030-98385-7_1

Sheth, S., Baker, H. P., Prescher, H., & Strelzow, J. A. (2024). Ethical considerations of artificial intelligence in health care: Examining the role of Generative Pretrained Transformer-4. *The Journal of the American Academy of Orthopaedic Surgeons, 32*(5), 205–210. DOI: 10.5435/JAAOS-D-23-00787 PMID: 38175996

Shi, W., Liu, X., & Yu, Q. (2017, June). Correlation-aware multi-label active learning for web service tag recommendation. In *2017 IEEE International conference on web services (ICWS)* (pp. 229-236). IEEE.

Siebra, C. A., Kurpicz-Briki, M., & Wac, K. (2024). Transformers in health: A systematic review on architectures for longitudinal data analysis. *Artificial Intelligence Review, 57*(2). Advance online publication. DOI: 10.1007/s10462-023-10677-z

Singh, B. (2023). Blockchain Technology in Renovating Healthcare: Legal and Future Perspectives. In *Revolutionizing Healthcare Through Artificial Intelligence and Internet of Things Applications* (pp. 177-186). IGI Global.

Singh, B. (2024). Evolutionary Global Neuroscience for Cognition and Brain Health: Strengthening Innovation in Brain Science. In *Biomedical Research Developments for Improved Healthcare* (pp. 246-272). IGI Global.

Singh, B., & Kaunert, C. (2024). Featuring healthcare, environment, and human rights: Applications of artificial intelligence in the health domain. In *Advances in Religious and Cultural Studies* (pp. 45–74). IGI Global.

Singh, B., & Kaunert, C. (2024). Harnessing Sustainable Agriculture Through Climate-Smart Technologies: Artificial Intelligence for Climate Preservation and Futuristic Trends. In *Exploring Ethical Dimensions of Environmental Sustainability and Use of AI* (pp. 214-239). IGI Global.

Singh, B., & Kaunert, C. (2024). Salvaging Responsible Consumption and Production of Food in the Hospitality Industry: Harnessing Machine Learning and Deep Learning for Zero Food Waste. In *Sustainable Disposal Methods of Food Wastes in Hospitality Operations* (pp. 176-192). IGI Global.

Singh, B., Vig, K., & Kaunert, C. (2024). Modernizing Healthcare: Application of Augmented Reality and Virtual Reality in Clinical Practice and Medical Education. In Modern Technology in Healthcare and Medical Education: Blockchain, IoT, AR, and VR (pp. 1-21). IGI Global.

Singh, G., & Kumar, J. (2024). Navigating the future through adoption of AI in healthcare. In *Advances in healthcare information systems and administration book series* (pp. 240–260). https://doi.org/DOI: 10.4018/979-8-3693-7452-8.ch015

Singh, B. (2023). Unleashing Alternative Dispute Resolution (ADR) in Resolving Complex Legal-Technical Issues Arising in Cyberspace Lensing E-Commerce and Intellectual Property: Proliferation of E-Commerce Digital Economy. *Revista Brasileira de Alternative Dispute Resolution-Brazilian Journal of Alternative Dispute Resolution-RBADR*, *5*(10), 81–105.

Singh, B. (2024). Lensing Legal Dynamics for Examining Responsibility and Deliberation of Generative AI-Tethered Technological Privacy Concerns: Infringements and Use of Personal Data by Nefarious Actors. In Ara, A., & Ara, A. (Eds.), *Exploring the Ethical Implications of Generative AI* (pp. 146–167). IGI Global., DOI: 10.4018/979-8-3693-1565-1.ch009

Singh, B. (2024). Social Cognition of Incarcerated Women and Children: Addressing Exposure to Infectious Diseases and Legal Outcomes. In Reddy, K. (Ed.), *Principles and Clinical Interventions in Social Cognition* (pp. 236–251). IGI Global., DOI: 10.4018/979-8-3693-1265-0.ch014

Singh, B., & Kaunert, C. (2024). Salvaging Responsible Consumption and Production of Food in the Hospitality Industry: Harnessing Machine Learning and Deep Learning for Zero Food Waste. In Singh, A., Tyagi, P., & Garg, A. (Eds.), *Sustainable Disposal Methods of Food Wastes in Hospitality Operations* (pp. 176–192). IGI Global., DOI: 10.4018/979-8-3693-2181-2.ch012

Singh, B., Kaunert, C., & Vig, K. (2024). Reinventing Influence of Artificial Intelligence (AI) on Digital Consumer Lensing Transforming Consumer Recommendation Model: Exploring Stimulus Artificial Intelligence on Consumer Shopping Decisions. In Musiolik, T., Rodriguez, R., & Kannan, H. (Eds.), *AI Impacts in Digital Consumer Behavior* (pp. 141–169). IGI Global., DOI: 10.4018/979-8-3693-1918-5.ch006

Singh, P., & Raman, B. (2024). Deep Learning Through the Prism of Tensors. *Studies in Big Data*, *162*, 1–610. DOI: 10.1007/978-981-97-8019-8/COVER

Sivaraman, E. (2023). PriMed : Private federated training and encrypted inference on medical images in healthcare. *Expert Systems: International Journal of Knowledge Engineering and Neural Networks*. Advance online publication. DOI: 10.1111/exsy.13283

Solaiman, B., Bashir, A., & Dieng, F. (2024). Regulating AI in health in the Middle East: case studies from Qatar, Saudi Arabia and the United Arab Emirates. In *Research Handbook on Health, AI and the Law* (pp. 332–354). Edward Elgar Publishing.

Song, L., Liu, J., Qian, B., Sun, M., Yang, K., Sun, M., & Abbas, S. (2018). A deep multi-modal CNN for multi-instance multi-label image classification. *IEEE Transactions on Image Processing*, *27*(12), 6025–6038.

Song, P., Fan, H., & Fan, L. (2023). TGDAUNet: Transformer and GCNN based dual-branch attention UNet for medical image segmentation. *Computers in Biology and Medicine*, *167*, 107583. DOI: 10.1016/j.compbiomed.2023.107583 PMID: 37890420

Song, P., Yang, Z., Li, J., & Fan, H. (2023). DPCTN: Dual path context-aware transformer network for medical image segmentation. *Engineering Applications of Artificial Intelligence*, *124*. Advance online publication. DOI: 10.1016/j.engappai.2023.106634

Sriramakrishnan, G. V., Prabhakar, T., Maram, B., & Datta, P. (2025). Deep Belief VGG-16 hybrid model for brain tumor classification using MRI images. *NMR in Biomedicine*, *38*(6), e70048. DOI: 10.1002/nbm.70048 PMID: 40386848

Stephens, Z. D., Lee, S. Y., Faghri, F., Campbell, R. H., Zhai, C., Efron, M. J., & Robinson, G. E. (2015). Big data: Astronomical or genomical? *PLoS Biology*, *13*(7), e1002195. PMID: 26151137

Sukeshini, S., P., Ved, M., Chintalapti, J., & Pal, S. N. (2021). Big data analytics and machine learning technologies for HPC applications. In *Evolving Technologies for Computing, Communication and Smart World: Proceedings of ETCCS 2020* (pp. 411-424). Springer Singapore.

Sulaiman, A., Anand, V., Gupta, S., Rajab, A., Alshahrani, H., Al Reshan, M. S., & Hamdi, M. (2024). Attention based UNet model for breast cancer segmentation using BUSI dataset. *Scientific Reports*, *14*(1), 22422. DOI: 10.1038/s41598-024-72712-5 PMID: 39341859

Sung, Y. W., Park, D. S., & Kim, C. G. (2023). A Study of BERT-Based Classification Performance of Text-Based Health Counseling Data. *CMES -. Computer Modeling in Engineering & Sciences*, *135*(1). Advance online publication. DOI: 10.32604/cmes.2022.022465

Sunori, S. K., & Ahmed, Z. (2020). Practicing precision medicine with intelligently integrative clinical and multi-omics data analysis. *Human Genomics*, *14*(1), 35. DOI: 10.1186/S40246-020-00287-Z PMID: 33008459

Sushith, M., Lakkshmanan, A., Saravanan, M., & Castro, S. (2025). Attention dual transformer with adaptive temporal convolutional for DR detection. *Scientific Reports*, *15*(1), 7694. PMID: 40044820

Su, Y., Liu, Q., Xie, W., & Hu, P. (2022). YOLO-LOGO: A transformer-based YOLO segmentation model for breast mass detection and segmentation in digital mammograms. *Computer Methods and Programs in Biomedicine, 221*. Advance online publication. DOI: 10.1016/j.cmpb.2022.106903 PMID: 35636358

Tang, Y., Yuan, Y., Tao, F., & Tang, M. (2025). Cross-modal augmented transformer for automated medical report generation. *IEEE Journal of Translational Engineering in Health and Medicine*. PMID: 40035024

Tan, X., Chen, X., Meng, Q., Shi, F., Xiang, D., Chen, Z., Pan, L., & Zhu, W. (2023). OCT2Former: A retinal OCT-angiography vessel segmentation transformer. *Computer Methods and Programs in Biomedicine, 233*. Advance online publication. DOI: 10.1016/j.cmpb.2023.107454 PMID: 36921468

Taslimi, S., Taslimi, S., Fathi, N., Salehi, M., & Rohban, M. H. (2022). Swinchex: Multi-label classification on chest x-ray images with transformers. *arXiv preprint arXiv:2206.04246*.

Tejpal, K., & Singh, S. P. (2024). Enhancing personalized medicine using data analytics and artificial intelligence. In *2024 7th International Conference on Contemporary Computing and Informatics (IC3I)* (pp. 924–930). IEEE. DOI: 10.1109/IC3I61595.2024.10828668

Thapa, C., & Camtepe, S. (2021). Precision health data: Requirements, challenges and existing techniques for data security and privacy. *Computers in Biology and Medicine, 129*, 104130. PMID: 33271399

Thornicroft, G., & Semrau, M. (2019). Health system strengthening for mental health in low- and middle-income countries: Introduction to the emerald programme. *BJPsych Open, 5*(5). Advance online publication. DOI: 10.1192/bjo.2019.9 PMID: 31685066

Tian, C., Chen, Y., Liu, Y., Wang, X., Lv, Q., Li, Y., Deng, J., Liu, Y., & Li, W. (2024). Accurate classification of glomerular diseases by hyperspectral imaging and transformer. *Computer Methods and Programs in Biomedicine, 254*, 108285. PMID: 38964248

Ting, H., & Liu, M. (2024, January). Multimodal Transformer of Incomplete MRI Data for Brain Tumor Segmentation. *IEEE Journal of Biomedical and Health Informatics, 28*(1), 89–99. DOI: 10.1109/JBHI.2023.3286689 PMID: 37327094

Tiwari, S. K., Kaur, J., Singla, P., & Hrisheekesha, P. N. (2022, September). A Comprehensive Review of Big Data Analysis Techniques in Health-Care. In *International Conference on Emergent Converging Technologies and Biomedical Systems* (pp. 401-420). Singapore: Springer Nature Singapore.

Tiwari, A., Masilamani, M., Srinivasa Rao, T., Zope, S., Deepak, S. A., & Karthick, L. (2025). Shaping the future: Emerging trends and strategic predictions in big data and AI. In *AI and the Revival of Big Data* (pp. 125–154). IGI Global.

Tölle, M., Garthe, P., Scherer, C., Seliger, J. M., Leha, A., Krüger, N., Simm, S., Martin, S., Eble, S., Kelm, H., Bednorz, M., André, F., Bannas, P., Diller, G., Frey, N., Groß, S., Hennemuth, A., Kaderali, L., Meyer, A., … Engelhardt, S. (n.d.). Real World Federated Learning with a Knowledge Distilled Transformer for Cardiac CT Imaging. https://doi.org/DOI: 10.1038/s41746-025-01434-3

Touvron, H., Cord, M., Douze, M., Massa, F., Sablayrolles, A., & Jégou, H. (2021, July). Training data-efficient image transformers & distillation through attention. In *International conference on machine learning* (pp. 10347-10357). PMLR.

Trenfield, S. J., Awad, A., McCoubrey, L. E., Elbadawi, M., Goyanes, A., Gaisford, S., & Basit, A. W. (2022). Advancing pharmacy and healthcare with virtual digital technologies. *Advanced Drug Delivery Reviews*, *182*(114098), 114098. DOI: 10.1016/j.addr.2021.114098 PMID: 34998901

Tummala, S., Kadry, S., Bukhari, S. A. C., & Rauf, H. T. (2022). Classification of brain tumor from magnetic resonance imaging using vision transformers ensembling. *Current Oncology (Toronto, Ont.)*, *29*(10), 7498–7511. DOI: 10.3390/curroncol29100590 PMID: 36290867

Turchin, A., Masharsky, S., & Zitnik, M. (2023). Comparison of BERT implementations for natural language processing of narrative medical documents. *Informatics in Medicine Unlocked*, *36*. Advance online publication. DOI: 10.1016/j.imu.2022.101139

Tu, Z. (2007). Learning generative models via discriminative approaches. *Proceedings of the IEEE Computer Society Conference on Computer Vision and Pattern Recognition*. https://doi.org/DOI: 10.1109/CVPR.2007.383035

U. Mamodiya and N. Tiwari, & Design and implementation of an intelligent single axis automatic solar tracking system & Mater. today Proc., vol. 81, pp. 1148-1151, 2023.Chanda, C. K., Murmu, A., & Kumar, P. (2023).

Ulyanov, D., Vedaldi, A., & Lempitsky, V. (2020). Deep image prior. *International Journal of Computer Vision*, *128*(7), 1867–1888.

V, D., G, M., S A, N., M, S., & D P, S. (2024). Artificial intelligence in personalized medicine: A survey on FuncPredict: AI driven genetic variant analysis. In *2024 3rd International Conference on Automation, Computing and Renewable Systems (ICACRS)* (pp. 999–1005). IEEE. DOI: 10.1109/ICACRS62842.2024.10841768

Valanarasu, J. M. J., Oza, P., Hacihaliloglu, I., & Patel, V. M. Medical transformer: Gated axial-attention for medical image segmentation, in: Medical image computing and computer assisted intervention–MICCAI 2021: 24th international conference, Strasbourg, France, September 27– October 1, 2021, proceedings, part I 24, Springer, 2021, pp. 36–46.

Valova, I., Mladenova, T., & Kanev, G. (2024). Students' Perception of ChatGPT Usage in Education. *International Journal of Advanced Computer Science and Applications, 15*(1). Advance online publication. DOI: 10.14569/IJACSA.2024.0150143

van den Bent, M. J., Geurts, M., French, P. J., Smits, M., Capper, D., Bromberg, J. E. C., & Chang, S. M. (2023). Primary brain tumours in adults. *Lancet, 402*(10412), 1564–1579. DOI: 10.1016/S0140-6736(23)01054-1 PMID: 37738997

Vaswani, A., Shazeer, N., Parmar, N., Uszkoreit, J., Jones, L., Gomez, A., Kaiser, L., & Polosukhin, I. (2017). Attention Is All You Need. 10.48550/arXiv.1706.03762.

Vaswani, A., Shazeer, N., Parmar, N., Uszkoreit, J., Jones, L., Gomez, A. N., Kaiser, Ł., & Polosukhin, I. (2017). *Attention is all you need* (Vol. 2017). Advances in Neural Information Processing Systems. Decem., https://arxiv.org/abs/1706.03762

Vaswani, A., Shazeer, N., Parmar, N., Uszkoreit, J., Jones, L., Gomez, A. N., Kaiser, Ł., & Polosukhin, I. (2017). Attention is all you need. *Advances in Neural Information Processing Systems*, •••, 30.

Vaswani, A., Shazeer, N., Parmar, N., Uszkoreit, J., Jones, L., Gomez, A. N., & Polosukhin, I. (2017). Attention is all you need. *Proceedings of the 31st International Conference on Neural Information Processing Systems*, 6000–6010. Presented at the Long Beach, California, USA. Red Hook, NY, USA: Curran Associates Inc.

Vatanpour, M., & Haddadnia, J. (2023). TransDoubleU-Net: Dual Scale Swin Transformer With Dual Level Decoder for 3D Multimodal Brain Tumor Segmentation. *IEEE Access: Practical Innovations, Open Solutions, 11*, 125511–125518. DOI: 10.1109/ACCESS.2023.3330958

Venerito, V., Bilgin, E., Iannone, F., & Kiraz, S. (2023). AI am a rheumatologist: A practical primer to large language models for rheumatologists. In *Rheumatology (United Kingdom)* (Vol. 62, Issue 10). https://doi.org/DOI: 10.1093/rheumatology/kead291

Verma, N., Ranvijay, & Yadav, D. K. (2025). A comprehensive review on step-based skin cancer detection using machine learning and deep learning methods. *Archives of Computational Methods in Engineering*, 1–54.

Verma, S., & Sanjeevi, S. G. (2023). Medical Image Classification using CMT and FTGD Layer. *Proceedings of the International Conference on Circuit Power and Computing Technologies, ICCPCT 2023*. https://doi.org/DOI: 10.1109/ICCPCT58313.2023.10245792

Villanueva-Meyer, J. E., Mabray, M. C., & Cha, S. (2017). Current clinical brain tumor imaging. *Neurosurgery*, *81*(3), 397–415. DOI: 10.1093/neuros/nyx103 PMID: 28486641

Walsh, J., Othmani, A., Jain, M., & Dev, S. (2022). Using U-Net network for efficient brain tumor segmentation in MRI images. *Healthcare Analytics*, *2*(100098), 100098. DOI: 10.1016/j.health.2022.100098

Wang, H., Zhu, Y., Green, B., Adam, H., Yuille, A., & Chen, L.-C. Axial deeplab: Stand-alone axial-attention for panoptic segmentation, in: European conference on computer vision, Springer, 2020, pp. 108–126.

Wang, J., Wei, L., Wang, L., Zhou, Q., Zhu, L., & Qin, J. (2021). Boundary-Aware Transformers for Skin Lesion Segmentation. In: de Bruijne, M., *et al.* Medical Image Computing and Computer Assisted Intervention – MICCAI 2021. MICCAI 2021. Lecture Notes in Computer Science(), vol 12901. Springer, Cham. https://doi.org/DOI: 10.1007/978-3-030-87193-2_20

Wang, L., Yu, L., Zhu, J., Tang, H., Gou, F., & Wu, J. Auxiliary segmentation method of osteosarcoma in mri images based on denoising and local enhancement, in: Healthcare, Vol. 10, MDPI, 2022, p. 1468.

Wang, B., Xie, Q., Pei, J., Chen, Z., Tiwari, P., Li, Z., & Fu, J. (2023). Pre-trained language models in biomedical domain: A systematic survey. *ACM Computing Surveys*, *56*(3), 1–52.

Wang, C. (2024). Le Wang, Nuoqi Wang, Xiaoling Wei, Ting Feng, Minfeng Wu, Qi Yao, Rongjun Zhang, CFATransUnet: Channel-wise cross fusion attention and transformer for 2D medical image segmentation. *Computers in Biology and Medicine, 168*. Advance online publication. DOI: 10.1016/j.compbiomed.2023.107803 PMID: 38064854

Wang, C., Xu, R., Xu, S., Meng, W., & Zhang, X. (2022). DA-Net: Dual Branch Transformer and Adaptive Strip Upsampling for Retinal Vessels Segmentation. In Wang, L., Dou, Q., Fletcher, P. T., Speidel, S., & Li, S. (Eds.), Medical Image Computing and Computer Assisted Intervention: Vol. 13432. *MICCAI 2022. MICCAI 2022. Lecture Notes in Computer Science*. Springer., DOI: 10.1007/978-3-031-16434-7_51

Wang, D., Wang, Z., Chen, L., Xiao, H., & Yang, B. (2023). Cross-Parallel Transformer: Parallel ViT for Medical Image Segmentation. *Sensors (Basel), 23*(23), 9488. DOI: 10.3390/s23239488 PMID: 38067861

Wang, F., & Wang, B. (2024). Boundary-guided feature integration network with hierarchical transformer for medical image segmentation. *Multimedia Tools and Applications, 83*, 8955–8969. DOI: 10.1007/s11042-023-15948-z

Wang, H., Jing, H., Yang, J., Liu, C., Hu, L., Guo, T., Zhao, Z., & Shen, N. (2024). Identifying autism spectrum disorder from multi-modal data with privacy-preserving. *Npj Mental Health Research, 3*(1). Advance online publication. DOI: 10.1038/s44184-023-00050-x PMID: 38698164

Wang, H., Wang, Z., Du, M., Yang, F., Zhang, Z., Ding, S., & Hu, X. (2020). Score-CAM: Score-weighted visual explanations for convolutional neural networks. In *Proceedings of the IEEE/CVF conference on computer vision and pattern recognition workshops* (pp. 24-25).

Wang, J.. (2023, June). SDPN: A Slight Dual-Path Network With Local-Global Attention Guided for Medical Image Segmentation. *IEEE Journal of Biomedical and Health Informatics, 27*(6), 2956–2967. DOI: 10.1109/JBHI.2023.3260026 PMID: 37030687

Wang, J., Tian, S., Yu, L., Zhou, Z., Wang, F., & Wang, Y. (2023). HIGF-Net: Hierarchical information-guided fusion network for polyp segmentation based on transformer and convolution feature learning. *Computers in Biology and Medicine, 161*. Advance online publication. DOI: 10.1016/j.compbiomed.2023.107038 PMID: 37230017

Wang, J., Yang, L., Huo, Z., He, W., & Luo, J. (2020). Multi-label classification of fundus images with efficientnet. *IEEE Access : Practical Innovations, Open Solutions, 8*, 212499–212508.

Wang, J., Yang, Y., Mao, J., Huang, Z., Huang, C., & Xu, W. (2016). Cnn-rnn: A unified framework for multi-label image classification. In *Proceedings of the IEEE conference on computer vision and pattern recognition* (pp. 2285-2294).

Wang, N.. (2023, September). MISSU: 3D Medical Image Segmentation via Self-Distilling TransUNet. *IEEE Transactions on Medical Imaging*, *42*(9), 2740–2750. DOI: 10.1109/TMI.2023.3264433 PMID: 37018113

Wang, Z., Chen, T., Li, G., Xu, R., & Lin, L. (2017). Multi-label image recognition by recurrently discovering attentional regions. In *Proceedings of the IEEE international conference on computer vision* (pp. 464-472).

Wei, C., Ren, S., Guo, K., Hu, H., & Liang, J. (2023). High-Resolution Swin Transformer for Automatic Medical Image Segmentation. *Sensors (Basel)*, *23*(7), 3420. DOI: 10.3390/s23073420 PMID: 37050479

Wei, X., Liu, Y., Zhang, F., Geng, L., Shan, C., Cao, X., & Xiao, Z. (2025). Mstnet: Multi-scale spatial-aware transformer with multi-instance learning for DR classification. *Medical Image Analysis*, *102*, 103511. PMID: 40020421

Wei, Y., Xia, W., Lin, M., Huang, J., Ni, B., Dong, J., & Yan, S. (2015). HCP: A flexible CNN framework for multi-label image classification. *IEEE Transactions on Pattern Analysis and Machine Intelligence*, *38*(9), 1901–1907.

Wen, Q., Zhou, T., Zhang, C., Chen, W., Ma, Z., Yan, J., & Sun, L. Transformers in time series: a survey, in: *Proceedings of the Thirty-Second International Joint Conference on Artificial Intelligence*, 2023, pp. 6778– 6786.

Woersching, J., Cleave, J., Egleston, B., Ma, C., Haber, J., & Chyun, D. (2022). Data quality of automated comorbidity lists in patients with mental health and substance use disorders. *Cin Computers Informatics Nursing*, *40*(7), 497–505. DOI: 10.1097/cin.0000000000000889 PMID: 35234709

Wójcik, M. A. (2022). Foundation models in healthcare: Opportunities, biases and regulatory prospects in Europe. In *Electronic Government and the Information Systems Perspective* (pp. 32–46). Springer International Publishing.

Wolf, T., Debut, L., Sanh, V., Chaumond, J., Delangue, C., & Moi, A. P. Cis tac, T. Rault, R. Louf, M. Funtowicz, et al., Transformers: State-of-the art natural language processing, in: Proceedings of the 2020 conference on empirical methods in natural language processing: system demonstrations, 2020, pp. 38–45.

Wolf, T., Debut, L., Sanh, V., Chaumond, J., Delangue, C., Moi, A., Cistac, P., Rault, T., Louf, R., Funtowicz, M., & Brew, J. (2020). Transformers: State-of-the-art natural language processing. Proceedings of the 2020 Conference on Empirical Methods in Natural Language Processing: System Demonstrations, 38–45. Association for Computational Linguistics. https://doi.org/DOI: 10.18653/v1/2020.emnlp-demos.6

Wu, H., Xiao, B., Codella, N., Liu, M., Dai, X., Yuan, L., & Zhang, L. Cvt: Introducing convolutions to ViTs, in: Proceedings of the IEEE/CVF international conference on computer vision, 2021, pp. 22– 31.

Wu, H. (2024). Dilated convolution for enhanced extractive summarization: A GAN-based approach with BERT word embedding. *Journal of Intelligent & Fuzzy Systems*, *46*(2). Advance online publication. DOI: 10.3233/JIFS-234709

Wu, H., Chen, S., Chen, G., Wang, W., Lei, B., & Wen, Z. (2022). FAT-Net: Feature adaptive transformers for automated skin lesion segmentation. *Medical Image Analysis*, *76*. Advance online publication. DOI: 10.1016/j.media.2021.102327 PMID: 34923250

Wu, H., Zhao, Z., & Wang, Z. (2024, July). META-Unet: Multi-Scale Efficient Transformer Attention Unet for Fast and High-Accuracy Polyp Segmentation. *IEEE Transactions on Automation Science and Engineering*, *21*(3), 4117–4128. DOI: 10.1109/TASE.2023.3292373

Wu, X., Zhu, X., Wu, G. Q., & Ding, W. (2013). Data mining with big data. *IEEE Transactions on Knowledge and Data Engineering*, *26*(1), 97–107.

Wu, Y., Liao, K., & Chen, J.. (2023). D-former: A U-shaped Dilated Transformer for 3D medical image segmentation. *Neural Computing & Applications*, *35*, 1931–1944. DOI: 10.1007/s00521-022-07859-1

Xiao, H., Li, L., Liu, Q., Zhang, Q., Liu, J., & Liu, Z. (2024). Context-aware and local-aware fusion with transformer for medical image segmentation. *Physics in Medicine and Biology*, *69*. Advance online publication. DOI: 10.1088/1361-6560/ad14c6 PMID: 38086076

Xiao, Z., Su, Y., Deng, Z., & Zhang, W. (2022). Efficient Combination of CNN and Transformer for Dual-Teacher Uncertainty-guided Semi-supervised Medical Image Segmentation. *Computer Methods and Programs in Biomedicine*, *226*. Advance online publication. DOI: 10.1016/j.cmpb.2022.107099 PMID: 36116398

Xia, Z., Chen, J., & Lu, C. (2024). DUSFormer: Dual-Swin Transformer V2 Aggregate Network for Polyp Segmentation. *IEEE Access: Practical Innovations, Open Solutions*, *12*, 8822–8832. DOI: 10.1109/ACCESS.2024.3352428

Xie, Y., Zhang, J., Shen, C., & Xia, Y. (2021). CoTr: Efficiently Bridging CNN and Transformer for 3D Medical Image Segmentation. In: de Bruijne, M., *et al.* Medical Image Computing and Computer Assisted Intervention – MICCAI 2021. MICCAI 2021. Lecture Notes in Computer Science(), vol 12903. Springer, Cham. https://doi.org/DOI: 10.1007/978-3-030-87199-4_16

Xie, E., Wang, W., Yu, Z., Anandkumar, A., Alvarez, J. M., & Luo, P. (2021). SegFormer: simple and efficient design for semantic segmentation with transformers. *Proceedings of the 35th International Conference on Neural Information Processing Systems*. Red Hook, NY, USA: Curran Associates Inc.

Xu, G., Zhang, X., Liao, W., Chen, S., & Wu, X. (2022). LGNet: Local and global representation learning for fast biomedical image segmentation. *Journal of Innovative Optical Health Sciences, 16*. Advance online publication. DOI: 10.1142/S1793545822430015

Xu, Q., Ma, Z., Na, H. E., & Duan, W. (2023). DCSAU-Net: A deeper and more compact split-attention U-Net for medical image segmentation. *Computers in Biology and Medicine, 154*. Advance online publication. DOI: 10.1016/j.compbiomed.2023.106626 PMID: 36736096

Yan, C., Shi, G., & Wu, Z. Smir: A transformer-based model for mri super resolution reconstruction, in: *2021 IEEE International Conference on Medical Imaging Physics and Engineering (ICMIPE)*, IEEE, 2021, pp. 1–6.

Yang, Z., Dai, Z., Yang, Y., Carbonell, J., Salakhutdinov, R., & Le, Q. V. (2019). XLNet: Generalized autoregressive pretraining for language understanding. *Advances in Neural Information Processing Systems, 32*. https://proceedings.neurips.cc/paper/2019/hash/dc6a7e655d7e5840e66733e9ee67cc69-Abstract.html

Yang, J., Jiao, L., Shang, R., Liu, X., Li, R., & Xu, L. (2023, November). EPT-Net: Edge Perception Transformer for 3D Medical Image Segmentation. *IEEE Transactions on Medical Imaging*, *42*(11), 3229–3243. DOI: 10.1109/TMI.2023.3278461 PMID: 37216246

Yang, M., Du, J., & Lv, R. (2025). Crat: Advanced transformer-based deep learning algorithms in oct image classification. *Biomedical Signal Processing and Control*, *104*, 107544.

Yang, Y., Zhang, L., Ren, L., & Wang, X. (2023). MMViT-Seg: A lightweight transformer and CNN fusion network for COVID-19 segmentation. *Computer Methods and Programs in Biomedicine, 230*. Advance online publication. DOI: 10.1016/j.cmpb.2023.107348 PMID: 36706618

Yan, Q., Liu, S., Xu, S., Dong, C., & Li, Z. (2023). Javen Qinfeng Shi, Yanning Zhang, Duwei Dai, 3D Medical image segmentation using parallel transformers. *Pattern Recognition, 138*. Advance online publication. DOI: 10.1016/j.patcog.2023.109432

Yan, Z., Liu, W., Wen, S., & Yang, Y. (2019). Multi-label image classification by feature attention network. *IEEE Access : Practical Innovations, Open Solutions, 7*, 98005–98013.

Yao, C., Hu, M., Li, Q., Zhai, G., & Zhang, X.-P. "Transclaw U-Net: Claw U-Net With Transformers for Medical Image Segmentation," *2022 5th International Conference on Information Communication and Signal Processing (ICICSP)*, Shenzhen, China, 2022, pp. 280-284, doi: DOI: 10.1109/ICICSP55539.2022.10050624

Yenduri, G., Ramalingam, M., Selvi, G. C., Supriya, Y., Srivastava, G., Maddikunta, P. K. R., Raj, G. D., Jhaveri, R. H., Prabadevi, B., Wang, W., Vasilakos, A. V., & Gadekallu, T. R. (2024). GPT (generative pre-trained transformer)— A comprehensive review on enabling technologies, potential applications, emerging challenges, and future directions. *IEEE Access: Practical Innovations, Open Solutions, 12*, 54608–54649. DOI: 10.1109/access.2024.3389497

Yeo, S., Ma, Y., Jun, H., Kim, T., & Kim, S. (2024). Survey on Recent Large Language Models for Code Generation. *KIISE Transactions on Computing Practices, 30*(8), 372–381. DOI: 10.5626/ktcp.2024.30.8.372

Yousri, R., & Safwat, S. (2023). How Big Can It Get? A comparative analysis of LLMs in architecture and scaling. *ICCA 2023 - 2023 5th International Conference on Computer and Applications, Proceedings*. https://doi.org/DOI: 10.1109/ICCA59364.2023.10401818

Yuan, F., Tang, Z., Wang, C., Huang, Q., & Shi, J. (2023). A multiple gated boosting network for multi-organ medical image segmentation. *IET Image Processing, 17*, 3028–3039. DOI: 10.1049/ipr2.12852

Yuan, F., Zhang, Z., & Fang, Z. (2023). An effective CNN and Transformer complementary network for medical image segmentation. *Pattern Recognition, 136*. Advance online publication. DOI: 10.1016/j.patcog.2022.109228

Yuan, M., Xie, Y., Zhao, R., Lv, N., Zhang, Z., Zhu, L., & Wu, X. (2024). Generating synthesized computed tomography from cbct/ldct using a novel generative-transformer adversarial-cnn. *Biomedical Signal Processing and Control, 96*, 106660.

Yue, G., Zhuo, G., Yan, W., Zhou, T., Tang, C., Yang, P., & Wang, T. (2024). Boundary uncertainty aware network for automated polyp segmentation. *Neural Networks, 170*, 390–404. DOI: 10.1016/j.neunet.2023.11.050 PMID: 38029720

Yu, Q., Ma, Q., Da, L., Li, J., Wang, M., Xu, A., Li, Z., Li, W., & Initiative, A. D. N.. (2024). A transformer-based unified multimodal framework for alzheimer's disease assessment. *Computers in Biology and Medicine, 180*, 108979. PMID: 39098237

Yu, X., Yang, Q., Zhou, Y., & Leon, Y. (2023). Cai, Riqiang Gao, Ho Hin Lee, Thomas Li, Shunxing Bao, Zhoubing Xu, Thomas A. Lasko, Richard G. Abramson, Zizhao Zhang, Yuankai Huo, Bennett A. Landman, Yucheng Tang, UNesT: Local spatial representation learning with hierarchical transformer for efficient medical segmentation. *Medical Image Analysis*, *90*. Advance online publication. DOI: 10.1016/j.media.2023.102939 PMID: 37725868

Yuyun, L. A. D., Sampurno, T., Hazriani, Arisha, A. O., & Mushaf. (2023). Next Sentence Prediction: The Impact of Preprocessing Techniques in Deep Learning. *Proceedings - 2023 10th International Conference on Computer, Control, Informatics and Its Applications: Exploring the Power of Data: Leveraging Information to Drive Digital Innovation, IC3INA 2023*, 274–278. https://doi.org/DOI: 10.1109/IC3INA60834.2023.10285805

Yu, Z., Lee, F., & Chen, Q. (2023). HCT-net: Hybrid CNN-transformer model based on a neural architecture search network for medical image segmentation. *Applied Intelligence*, *53*, 19990–20006. DOI: 10.1007/s10489-023-04570-z

ZainEldin, H., Gamel, S. A., El-Kenawy, E.-S. M., Alharbi, A. H., Khafaga, D. S., Ibrahim, A., & Talaat, F. M. (2022). Brain tumor detection and classification using deep Learning and sine-cosine fitness grey wolf optimization. *Bioengineering (Basel, Switzerland)*, *10*(1), 18. DOI: 10.3390/bioengineering10010018 PMID: 36671591

Zeineldin, R. A., Karar, M. E., Elshaer, Z., Coburger, J., Wirtz, C. R., Burgert, O., & Mathis-Ullrich, F. (2024). Explainable hybrid vision transformers and convolutional network for multimodal glioma segmentation in brain MRI. *Scientific Reports*, *14*(1), 3713. DOI: 10.1038/s41598-024-54186-7 PMID: 38355678

Zhang, B., Yao, X., Li, H., & Aini, M. (2023). Chinese Medical Named Entity Recognition based on Expert Knowledge and Fine-tuning Bert. *Proceedings - IEEE International Conference on Knowledge Graph, ICKG 2023*. https://doi.org/DOI: 10.1109/ICKG59574.2023.00016

Zhang, X., Wang, J., & Zhang, X. (2023). YNU-ISE-ZXW at ROCLING 2023 MultiNER-Health Task: A Transformer-based Model with LoRA for Chinese Healthcare Named Entity Recognition. *ROCLING 2023 - Proceedings of the 35th Conference on Computational Linguistics and Speech Processing*.

Zhang, Y., Liu, H., & Hu, Q. (2021). TransFuse: Fusing Transformers and CNNs for Medical Image Segmentation. In: de Bruijne, M., *et al.* Medical Image Computing and Computer Assisted Intervention – MICCAI 2021. MICCAI 2021. Lecture Notes in Computer Science(), vol 12901. Springer, Cham. https://doi.org/DOI: 10.1007/978-3-030-87193-2_2

Zhang, Z., Sun, B., & Zhang, W. (2021). Pyramid Medical Transformer for Medical Image Segmentation. 10.48550/arXiv.2104.14702.

Zhang, C., Sun, S., Hu, W., & Zhao, P. (2024). FDR-TransUNet: A novel encoder-decoder architecture with vision transformer for improved medical image segmentation. *Computers in Biology and Medicine*, *169*. Advance online publication. DOI: 10.1016/j.compbiomed.2023.107858 PMID: 38113680

Zhang, H., Ni, W., Luo, Y., Feng, Y., Song, R., & Wang, X. (2023). TUnet-LBF: Retinal fundus image fine segmentation model based on transformer Unet network and LBF. *Computers in Biology and Medicine*, *159*. Advance online publication. DOI: 10.1016/j.compbiomed.2023.106937 PMID: 37084640

Zhang, H., Zhong, X., Li, G., Liu, W., Liu, J., Ji, D., Li, X., & Wu, J. (2023). BCU-Net: Bridging ConvNeXt and U-Net for medical image segmentation. *Computers in Biology and Medicine*, *159*. Advance online publication. DOI: 10.1016/j.compbiomed.2023.106960 PMID: 37099973

Zhang, H., Zhong, X., Li, Z., Chen, Y., Zhu, Z., Lv, J., Li, C., Zhou, Y., & Li, G. (2022). Tim-net: Transformer in m-net for retinal vessel segmentation. *Journal of Healthcare Engineering*, *2022*(1), 9016401. PMID: 35859930

Zhang, J.. (2023, December). Dual-Branch TransV-Net for 3-D Echocardiography Segmentation. *IEEE Transactions on Industrial Informatics*, *19*(12), 11675–11686. DOI: 10.1109/TII.2023.3249904

Zhang, J., Liu, Y., Wu, Q., Wang, Y., Liu, Y., Xu, X., & Song, B. (2022). SWTRU: Star-shaped Window Transformer Reinforced U-Net for medical image segmentation. *Computers in Biology and Medicine*, *150*. Advance online publication. DOI: 10.1016/j.compbiomed.2022.105954 PMID: 36122443

Zhang, J., Qin, Q., Ye, Q., & Ruan, T. (2023). ST-Unet: Swin Transformer boosted U-Net with Cross-Layer Feature Enhancement for medical image segmentation. *Computers in Biology and Medicine*, *153*. Advance online publication. DOI: 10.1016/j.compbiomed.2022.106516 PMID: 36628914

Zhang, L., Zuo, Y., Jia, Y., Li, D., Zeng, R., Li, D., Chen, J., & Wang, W. (2024). DS-Former: A dual-stream encoding-based transformer for 3D medical image segmentation. *Biomedical Signal Processing and Control*, *89*. Advance online publication. DOI: 10.1016/j.bspc.2023.105702

Zhang, N., Yu, L., Zhang, D., Wu, W., Tian, S., & Kang, X. (2022). APT-Net: Adaptive encoding and parallel decoding transformer for medical image segmentation, Computers in Biology and Medicine, Volume 151. *Part A, 106292*. Advance online publication. DOI: 10.1016/j.compbiomed.2022.106292 PMID: 36399856

Zhang, N., Yu, L., Zhang, D., Wu, W., Tian, S., Kang, X., & Li, M. (2024). CT-Net: Asymmetric compound branch Transformer for medical image segmentation. *Neural Networks, 170*, 298–311. DOI: 10.1016/j.neunet.2023.11.034 PMID: 38006733

Zhang, T., & Wang, X. (2024, February). Anchorwise Fuzziness Modeling in Convolution–Transformer Neural Network for Left Atrium Image Segmentation. *IEEE Transactions on Fuzzy Systems, 32*(2), 398–408. DOI: 10.1109/TFUZZ.2023.3298904

Zhang, W., Fu, C., Zheng, Y., Zhang, F., & Zhao, Y. (2022). Chiu-Wing Sham, HSNet: A hybrid semantic network for polyp segmentation. *Computers in Biology and Medicine, 150*. Advance online publication. DOI: 10.1016/j.compbiomed.2022.106173 PMID: 36257278

Zhang, W., Lu, F., Su, H., & Hu, Y. (2024). Dual-branch multi-information aggregation network with transformer and convolution for polyp segmentation. *Computers in Biology and Medicine, 168*. Advance online publication. DOI: 10.1016/j.compbiomed.2023.107760 PMID: 38064849

Zhang, Y. (2023). Encoder-decoder models in sequence-to-sequence learning: A survey of RNN and LSTM approaches. *Applied and Computational Engineering, 22*(1), 218–226. DOI: 10.54254/2755-2721/22/20231220

Zhang, Y., Ying, Z., Li, L., Wang, J., Yu, H., Zhang, M., Feng, X., Wei, X., & Xu, X. (2023). A transformer-based genomic prediction method fused with knowledge-guided module. *Briefings in Bioinformatics, 25*. Advance online publication. DOI: 10.1093/bib/bbad438 PMID: 38058185

Zhang, Z., Sun, G., Zheng, K., Yang, J.-K., Zhu, X., & Li, Y. (2023). TC-Net: A joint learning framework based on CNN and vision transformer for multi-lesion medical images segmentation. *Computers in Biology and Medicine, 161*. Advance online publication. DOI: 10.1016/j.compbiomed.2023.106967 PMID: 37220707

Zhao, C., Xiang, S., Wang, Y., Cai, Z., Shen, J., & Zhou, S. (2023). Di Zhao, Weihua Su, Shijie Guo, Shuo Li, Context-aware network fusing transformer and V-Net for semi-supervised segmentation of 3D left atrium. *Expert Systems with Applications, 214*. Advance online publication. DOI: 10.1016/j.eswa.2022.119105

Zhao, L., Zhou, D., Jin, X., & Zhu, W. (2022). nn-TransUNet: An Automatic Deep Learning Pipeline for Heart MRI Segmentation. *Life (Chicago, Ill.)*, *12*(10), 1570. DOI: 10.3390/life12101570 PMID: 36295005

Zhao, X., Wang, L., & Zhang, Y.. (2024). A review of convolutional neural networks in computer vision. *Artificial Intelligence Review*, *57*, 99. DOI: 10.1007/s10462-024-10721-6

Zhao, Y., Shen, X., Chen, J., Qian, W., Sang, L., & Ma, H. (2024). Learning active contour models based on self-attention for breast ultrasound image segmentation. *Biomedical Signal Processing and Control*, *89*. Advance online publication. DOI: 10.1016/j.bspc.2023.105816

Zheng, P., Zhu, X., & Guo, W. (2022). Brain tumour segmentation based on an improved U-Net. *BMC Medical Imaging*, *22*(1), 199. DOI: 10.1186/s12880-022-00931-1 PMID: 36401207

Zheng, Y., Qiu, B., Liu, S., Song, R., Yang, X., Wu, L., Chen, Z., Tuersun, A., Yang, X., & Wang, W.. (2024). A transformer-based deep learning model for early prediction of lymph node metastasis in locally advanced gastric cancer after neoadjuvant chemotherapy using pretreatment ct images. *EClinicalMedicine*, ●●●, 75. PMID: 39281097

Zhou, B., Dey, N., Schlemper, J., Salehi, S. S. M., & Liu, C. J. S. Dun can, M. Sofka, Dsformer: A dual-domain self-supervised transformer for accelerated multi-contrast mri reconstruction, in: Proceedings of the IEEE/CVF winter conference on applications of computer vision, 2023, pp. 4966–4975.

Zhou, B., Khosla, A., Lapedriza, A., Oliva, A., & Torralba, A. (2016). Learning deep features for discriminative localization. In *Proceedings of the IEEE conference on computer vision and pattern recognition* (pp. 2921-2929).

Zhou, B., Yang, G., Shi, Z., & Ma, S. (2024). Natural Language Processing for Smart Healthcare. *IEEE Reviews in Biomedical Engineering*, *17*, 4–18. DOI: 10.1109/RBME.2022.3210270 PMID: 36170385

Zhou, H.-Y.. (2023). nnFormer: Volumetric Medical Image Segmentation via a 3D Transformer. *IEEE Transactions on Image Processing*, *32*, 4036–4045. DOI: 10.1109/TIP.2023.3293771 PMID: 37440404

Zhou, L., Pan, S., Wang, J., & Vasilakos, A. V. (2017). Machine learning on big data: Opportunities and challenges. *Neurocomputing*, *237*, 350–361.

Zhou, S. K., Greenspan, H., Davatzikos, C., Duncan, J. S., Van Ginneken, B., Madabhushi, A., & Summers, R. M. (2021). A review of deep learning in medical imaging: Imaging traits, technology trends, case studies with progress highlights, and future promises. *Proceedings of the IEEE, 109*(5), 820–838. PMID: 37786449

Zhou, S., Zhang, R., Chen, D., & Zhu, X. (2021). A novel framework for bringing smart big data to proactive decision making in healthcare. *Health Informatics Journal, 27*(2), 14604582211024698. PMID: 34159834

Zhu, J.-Y., Park, T., Isola, P., & Efros, A. A. Unpaired image-to-image translation using cycle-consistent adversarial networks, in: *Proceedings of the IEEE international conference on computer vision*, 2017, pp. 2223–2232.

Zhu, T., Ding, D., Wang, F., Liang, W., & Wang, B. (2024). A novel full-convolution UNet-transformer for medical image segmentation. *Biomedical Signal Processing and Control, 89*. Advance online publication. DOI: 10.1016/j.bspc.2023.105772

Zhu, X., Cao, J., Ge, J., Liu, W., & Liu, B. (2022, October). Two-stream transformer for multi-label image classification. In *Proceedings of the 30th ACM international conference on multimedia* (pp. 3598-3607).

Zi-an, Z., Xiu-fang, F., Xiao-qiang, R., & Yun-yun, D. (2023). Uncertainty-guided cross learning via CNN and transformer for semi-supervised honeycomb lung lesion segmentation. *Physics in Medicine and Biology, 68*. Advance online publication. DOI: 10.1088/1361-6560/ad0eb2 PMID: 37988756

Ziller, A., Passerat-Palmbach, J., Ryffel, T., Usynin, D., Trask, A., Junior, I., Mancuso, J., Makowski, M. R., Rueckert, D., Braren, R., & Kaissis, G. (2020). Privacy-preserving medical image analysis. arXiv: Cryptography and Security. https://dblp.uni-trier.de/db/journals/corr/corr2012.html#abs-2012-06354

About the Contributors

Asma Sbai has an engineering degree in computer science and a PhD in computer science, with a focus on origin-destination matrix estimation. She is currently a Professor (Maitre de conférence) of Computer Science in the Faculty of Medicine and Pharmacy at Cadi Ayyad University in Marrakech. Her academic and professional experiences have given her a good foundation in data analysis and modeling. She is currently focusing on artificial intelligence and its application to diseases diagnostics and publish principally in this topics. Her interdisciplinary approach integrates advanced machine learning methodologies to address complex challenges in healthcare.0000-0002-4067-3256.

Mudassir Khan is an accomplished academic, researcher, author, and consultant with expertise in computer science and data analytics. He holds an MCA and a Ph.D. in Big Data Analytics using Deep Learning. Currently, he is pursuing a postdoctoral fellowship at Multimedia University, Malaysia, and is a Co-Supervisor for Postgraduate Studies at Lincoln University College, Malaysia. With over 14 years of teaching and research experience, Dr. Khan has contributed significantly to the field as an Assistant Professor at King Khalid University. His expertise includes Big Data, Deep Learning, Machine Learning, Data Science, IoT, and AI, with a focus on medical imaging in healthcare. Dr. Khan has published over 95+ research articles in prestigious journals and presented his work at international conferences. He has also edited numerous books with esteemed publishers and authored four books in computer science.

Pushan Kumar Dutta is an Associate Professor at Amity University Kolkata who has carved a distinctive niche in academia with over 12 years of academic experience. He earned his Ph.D. from Jadavpur University in 2015, followed by postdoctoral work as an Erasmus Mundus Scholar at the University of Oradea in Romania in 2016. Dr. Dutta has meticulously curated and edited over 60 books in the past couple of years for globally recognized publishers such as Springer, Elsevier,

IET, Taylor & Francis, Cambridge Scholar Publishers, Degruyter, and IGI Global. Dr. Dutta has consistently empowered his students to excel and innovate, guiding them to garner international recognition through competitions like the Johnson Control International Whitepaper contest and Ideathon 5.0. Complementing his teaching and editorial endeavors is an extensive research portfolio that includes over 183 Scopus-indexed publications.

J. Paulo Davim is a Full Professor at the University of Aveiro, Portugal. He is also distinguished as honorary professor in several universities/colleges/institutes in China, India and Spain. He received his PhD in Mechanical Engineering, MSc in Mechanical Engineering (materials and manufacturing.

Michael Onyema Edeh, Deputy Dean, Faculty of Allied Health and Applied Sciences/Head of Department, Mathematics and Computer Science at Coal City University, Nigeria. PhD is currently the Deputy Dean, Faculty of Allied Health and Applied Sciences/ Head of Department, Mathematics and Computer Science at Coal City University, Nigeria. He is an Adjunct Professor at the Department of Computer Science and Engineering, Shobhit University, India. An Adjunct Professor at Enugu State College of Education technical (ESCET), Enugu Nigeria. He was listed among the Top Scientists in Nigeria by Elsevier 2021-2024. Michael is a Recipient of the prestigious Chancellor's Award for Best Staff of the Year 2020, and Vice Chancellor's Award for research Excellence 2023 both at Coal City University. A former Director of ICT at Coal City university. He is also the current Chairman of Nigeria Computer Society (NCS), Enugu State Chapter, Nigeria. Michael has taught Computer Science courses to both postgraduate and undergraduate students in several tertiary education institutions, including Shobhit university India; Southwestern University, Ogun State; Coal City University Enugu; Spiritan University Nneochi Abia State; National Open University of Nigeria (NOUN); Alex Ekwueme Federal University Ebonyi State; Gregory University Uturu; Enugu State College of Education Technical affiliated to Nnamdi Azikiwe University Nigeria; Institute of Management and Technology (IMT) Enugu; African Thinkers Community of Inquiry College of Education (ATCOI-COE) Enugu; Pogil College of Health Technology Ogun State; and Federal Science and Technical College Ogun State. Michael has delivered Keynote talks for many organizations both locally and internationally. He has published over 100 scholarly papers in reputable journals, and also acted as an editor and Reviewer for many top journals. He is also an editor of many books and Writer in couple of Newspapers in Nigeria including Vaguard Newspaper, The nation Newspaper etc. He has acted as Guest for public Affairs Analysis on Dream FM, Radio Nigeria and others. He has interest in Cybersecurity,

Education, Machine Learning and Health informatics and cloud computing. His hobbies include Humanitarian activities, Research, Music and Sports.

* * *

Srinivas Arukonda is currently serving as an Assistant Professor in the Department of Computer Science and Engineering at SRM University – AP, India. He holds a Ph.D. from NIT Warangal and has extensive teaching and research experience at reputed institutions such as VIT-AP University and Galgotias University. His research expertise spans computer vision, deep learning, ensemble learning with optimization, and artificial intelligence applications. His contributions to disease diagnosis, intelligent systems, and financial analytics have been widely recognized. Dr. Arukonda has authored numerous SCI-indexed journal papers, book chapters, and conference proceedings, with publications in high-impact Q1 journals and premier IEEE/ACM conferences. In addition to his research contributions, Dr. Arukonda is also a published authored book. His books serve as valuable resources for students, researchers, and industry professionals, covering advanced topics in artificial intelligence, deep learning, and optimization techniques. His commitment to academic excellence is reflected in his interdisciplinary collaborations, mentoring roles, and industry-oriented projects. Dr. Arukonda remains dedicated to advancing AI-driven solutions for real-world challenges, shaping the future of intelligent systems through his innovative research and scholarly contributions.

Manujakshi B. C. is an Associate Professor and a Program Head in the School of Computer Science and Engineering at Jain (Deemed-to-be-University). She earned her Doctor of Philosophy in Computer Science and Engineering from RV College of Engineering under VTU. She holds a Master of Technology degree in Computer Science and Engineering from University of BDT College of Engineering, Davanagere, under Kuvempu University. Her Bachelor of Engineering in Computer Science and Engineering is from SJM Institute of Technology under VTU. With 18+ years of academic experience, Dr. Manujakshi B C is an enthusiastic and dedicated professional who enjoys being an integral part of academia. Dr. Manujakshi is passionate about advancing the frontiers of computer science and engineering through cutting-edge research, impactful teaching, and collaborative engagement with industry and academia. Her expertise spans BigData Analytics, Artificial Intelligence and Machine Learning, Deep Learning, Internet of Things etc making her a versatile and valuable asset in both academic and industrial settings. She has published her research works in various conferences and journals. She actively engages in leading teams for various academic and administrative responsibilities.

Saurabh Chandra is an accomplished legal scholar and currently serves as an Associate Professor & Assistant Dean at the School of Law, Bennett University, India. With a robust academic foundation, he earned his Bachelor of Arts and Bachelor of Laws (B.A. LL.B.) from the prestigious Aligarh Muslim University (A.M.U.). He further specialized in Business Laws, completing his Master of Laws (LL.M.) at the renowned National Law School of India University (NLSIU), Bangalore. Dr. Chandra's academic journey culminated in a Doctorate in Law (Ph.D.) from the esteemed National Law University (NLU) Delhi. In addition to his impressive legal education from some of India's most prestigious institutions, Dr. Chandra also holds a master's degree in management with specialization in Human Resources in Management and another in Journalism and Mass Communication. With almost two decades of teaching experience, he has numerous publications to his credit. His expertise is complemented by a robust portfolio of scholarly publications.

RajeshChilukamari is a dedicated researcher and educator, currently serving as an Assistant Professor in the Department of Computer Engineering at National Institute of Technology Kurukshetra. He earned his Ph.D. from NIT Warangal, specializing in metaheuristic algorithm-based deep neural networks for medical image processing, and holds an M.Tech in CSE from NIT Sikkim. His research focuses on deep learning, medical image analysis, NAS, and explainable AI, significantly contributing to medical image segmentation, detection, and denoising. Dr. Rajesh has published extensively in high-impact Q1 SCIE journals and international conferences. His work on lightweight and efficient deep neural networks for 2D and 3D medical image analysis has set new benchmarks in performance and computational efficiency. Beyond research, he has industry experience as an Associate DevOps Engineer, equipping him with practical expertise in software deployment and automation. With a strong background in both academia and industry, he brings a unique blend of theoretical knowledge and hands-on experience, driving advancements in AI-driven healthcare innovations.

Balaram Murthy Chintakindi completed their PhD from NIT Warangal, India. They did M.Tech and B.Tech from JNTU Hyderabad, India. Their area of interest Machine Learning, Deep Learning, Computer Vision, Natural Language Processing, Reinforcement Learning, IoT & Image Processing.

Rajarajeshwari G. received an M.S. degree in software engineering from Vellore Institute of Technology, Vellore, India, in 2009, where she is currently pursuing her Ph.D. degree in computer science. Her research interests include artificial intelligence, machine learning, and deep learning.

Udit Mamodiya is an Associate Professor and Associate Dean (Research) at Poornima University in Jaipur, Rajasthan, India. With a robust academic and professional background, he has significantly contributed to the fields of renewable energy sources, reliability analysis, expert systems, and decision support systems. Dr. Mamodiya has authored over 60 research papers indexed in prestigious databases such as SCI, Scopus, and UGC Care, showcasing his commitment to advancing knowledge in his areas of expertise. Additionally, he has authored ten books published by national publishers, further enriching the academic community with valuable resources. An innovator at heart, Dr. Mamodiya holds an impressive portfolio of intellectual property, including 50 utility patents (both national and international) along with 20 design patents and copyrights. His entrepreneurial spirit is exemplified by securing 1 Crore in funding from the All India Council for Technical Education (AICTE) to establish the IDEA Lab at Poornima University, aimed at fostering innovation and research among students and faculty.

R. Karthick Manoj received B.E (Electronics and Communication Engineering) from Syed Ammal Engineering College in 2007, M.E (VLSI Design) from SRM Eswari Engineering College, Chennai in 2012 and the Pursuing Doctoral degree from Academy of Maritime Education and Training, Deemed to be University, Chennai from 2019. Having 9 Plus years experience in both teaching and Industry. Currently, working as Assistant Professor in Academy of Maritime Education and Training, Deemed to be University, Chennai. He has published 03 national, 04international journals and nearly 10 National and international conferences Proceedings. He has Received certificate of Appreciation for contributing a chapter in the event Asia book of records. He is a life Member in 6 Professional Bodies, and acting as reviewer for reputed journals. His areas of interest are VLSI, Signal Processing, Robotics and Artificial Intelligence.

RampavanMedipelly is an Assistant Professor in the Department of Computer Science and Engineering at SRM University AP, India. He received his Ph.D. from NIT Warangal, India. His research focuses on deep learning and computer vision. He has published in top-tier journals like Knowledge-Based Systems and Applied Soft Computing and has presented at IEEE conferences. He has also contributed book chapters in the areas of IoT and AI.

Deepanshu Pachauri is an Assistant Professor in the Sharda School of Law, Sharda University, Greater Noida. He has publications in Scopus indexed journals. He has attended national and international faculty development programmes. He has also participated in national and international conferences and seminars. His teaching and research experience is of 7 years.

Mohana Priya P. obtained her Master's degree in Bigdata analytics from Anna University, Guindy and pursuing her PhD in Computer Science majoring in Image processing from Vels Institute of Science, Technology and Advanced Studies (VISTAS), Chennai. She has got 2.3 years of IT Industry experience and 4 years of Teaching experience. Currently, she is an Assistant professor in the department of Computer Science and Engineering, Vels Institute of Science, Technology and Advanced Studies (VISTAS). Her current research interests are Image processing, Deep learning and has published several journal papers.

Ravikumar R. N. is an experienced academician with over 12+ years of teaching and research expertise across institutions in India, the UAE, and the Maldives. He currently serves as an Assistant Professor at Marwadi University, Rajkot, specializing in Machine Learning, Recommender Systems, and AI-driven applications in healthcare and security. He holds a Ph.D. in Machine Learning and Recommender Systems from Amity University, Jaipur, a Master of Engineering in CSE from VMRF University, Salem, and a Bachelor of Engineering in CSE from Anna University. He also has a MiniMBA from the Swiss eLearning Institute. Dr. Ravikumar has authored more than 8+ multiple SCIE/Scopus-indexed journal articles, 25+ IEEE/Springer conference papers, and co-authored a book on Artificial Intelligence. He has also published 9 patents and contributed 10+ book chapters in emerging domains such as Federated Learning, Blockchain, and Digital Twins for IGI Global, Wiley and Springer publisher. He actively mentors students through initiatives like the Research Activities Club (RAC) and Student Research Internship Training (SRIT), promoting innovation and research culture.

Vinod Kumar R. S. received his BE in Electronics and Communication Engineering in 1991 and ME in Communication Systems in 2000, both from the Madurai Kamaraj University, Tamil Nadu, India. He pursued his PhD from the Anna University, Chennai, India, in 2015. His areas of research are multiresolution patch-based texture synthesis, steganography, and medical imaging. He is presently working as a Professor and the Head of the Department of Electronics and Communication Engineering, Noorul Islam Centre for Higher Education, Kumaracoil, Tamil Nadu, India.

Aarthi S. is a dedicated Assistant Professor in Computer Science with over six years of teaching experience. She is currently pursuing her Ph.D. at Marwadi University, Gujarat, and holds an M.Phil. and MCA from Bharathiar University, Tamil Nadu. Throughout her academic career, Aarthi has specialized in programming languages such as C++, Java, and C, and contributed to research in recommender systems and AI-related data privacy. She has published journal articles, contributed to book chapters, and actively participated in technical workshops. Known for her student mentorship and engagement in academic events, Aarthi remains committed to fostering innovation and excellence in computer science education.

DeepaLakshmi S., an experienced academician with over 20 years of teaching and research, is an Assistant Professor and Head i/c in the Department of Computer Science with AI at Dwaraka Doss Goverdhan Doss Vaishnav College, Chennai. She obtained her PhD from Bharathiar University and is UGC-NET qualified. Her expertise spans Machine Learning, Artificial Intelligence, and Big Data Analytics. She is actively engaged in research, curriculum development, and has contributed to several scholarly publications in the field of computer science.

Tamilselvi S. is an Assistant Professor in the Department of Computer Technology at Kongu Engineering College, Perundurai. With 9 years of teaching experience, she brings a strong academic background, holding an M.C.A., M.Phil., and Ph.D., from Bharathiar University. Her areas of specialization include Advanced Networking and Cloud Computing, where she actively contributes through teaching and academic research.

Wasswa Shafik (Member, IEEE) received a Bachelor of Science degree in information technology from Ndejje University, Uganda, a Master of Engineering degree in Information Technology (Computer and Communication Networks) from Yazd University, Iran, and a PhD in Computer Science with the School of Digital Science, Universiti Brunei Darussalam, Brunei Darussalam. He is also the Founder and Research Director of the Dig Connectivity Research Laboratory (DCRLab) after serving as a Research Associate at the Network Interconnectivity Research Laboratory at Yazd University. Prior to this, he worked as a Community Data Analyst at Population Services International (PSI-Uganda), a Community Data Officer at the Programme for Accessible Health Communication (PACE-Uganda), a Research Assistant at the Socio-Economic Data Centre (SEDC-Uganda), Uganda, an Assistant Data Officer at TechnoServe, Kampala, Uganda, and Asmaah Charity Organization as Cheif Executive Officer. He has hundreds of publications with renowned publishers. His research interests include Artificial Intelligence, Smart Agriculture, Digital Health, Green Computing, Security and Privacy.

Bhupinder Singh is working as Professor at Sharda University, India. His areas of publications as Smart Healthcare, Medicines, fuzzy logics, artificial intelligence, robotics, machine learning, deep learning, federated learning, IoT, PV Glasses, metaverse and many more. He has 3 books, 139 paper publications, 163 paper presentations in international/national conferences and seminars, participated in more than 40 workshops/FDP's/QIP's, 25 courses from international universities of repute, organized more than 59 events with international and national academicians and industry people's, editor-in-chief and co-editor in journals, developed new courses. He has given talks at international universities, resource person in international conferences such as in Nanyang Technological University Singapore, Tashkent State University of Law Uzbekistan; KIMEP University Kazakhstan, All'ah meh Tabatabi University Iran, the Iranian Association of International Criminal law, Iran and Hague Center for International Law and Investment, The Netherlands, Northumbria University Newcastle UK.

Shashank Solanki is a Final-year BBA LL.B. (Hons.) candidate at Christ (Deemed to be University), Delhi NCR, with a strong interest in Arbitration & Conciliation, Corporate Law, and Banking & Finance. They have gained practical legal experience through diverse internships at top law firms, corporate legal departments, and judicial chambers—including Singhania & Partners LLP, Shree Cement Ltd., and the office of Hon'ble Justice Ashok Bhushan (NCLAT). These experiences have allowed them to develop skills in legal drafting, arbitration procedure, and comprehensive legal research. Their academic interests have led to several Scopus-indexed publications in the areas of technology law, cybersecurity, and healthcare ethics. They have also participated in national moot court competitions, presented papers at international conferences, and contributed to student welfare initiatives. They previously served as the Convener of the Legal Aid and Awareness Society at Christ University, leading various legal outreach and awareness programs. They aspire to contribute meaningfully to the corporate legal ecosystem by combining legal research, policy insight, and litigation experience.

Abrar Ahmed Syed has over 15 years of experience in analytics, data visualization, and BI server deployments, he is a Advisor Application Designer at Gainwell Technologies, a leading data and analytics group that helps clients transform their businesses with data-driven insights and solutions. He is passionate about creating impactful and engaging analytics stories that empower decision-makers and drive positive outcomes. He is also a Tableau Certified Professional and have extensive expertise in using Tableau and other tools to design, build, and deliver innovative and customized analytics solutions for various industries and sectors.

Yulduz Urazbaeva is working in the Department of Pedagogy and Psychology, Mamun University, Khiva, Uzbekistan.

Index

A

B

C

D

T

V

www.ingramcontent.com/pod-product-compliance
Lightning Source LLC
LaVergne TN
LVHW062328300926
849161LV00007B/1619